Chicago Tribune

Sunday Crossword Omnibus

Chicago Tribune
Sunday Crossword Omnibus

Edited by

Wayne Robert Williams

**Random House
Puzzles & Games**

NEW YORK   TORONTO   LONDON   SYDNEY   AUCKLAND

Visit the Random House Web site: www.randomhouse.com.

First Edition

Printed in the United States of America

20 19 18

ISBN: 978-0-375-72209-7

Introduction

Everyone who loves crossword puzzles can recognize a good one after the last square is filled in. The fair challenge was there, the enjoyment was there, and the satisfaction of completing a job well done was there. An editor's first task is to make sure that the puzzles presented to the audience are the best ones to be found. He needs to be able to recognize a good one long before the first square is filled in.

Making puzzles fair, challenging, enjoyable, and satisfying is the heart of the editor's job. Weeding out the errors and inaccuracies, while not adding any new ones of our own, is of foremost importance. When mistakes make it into print, they are sure to be spotted by at least one, more likely hundreds, and often thousands of puzzle solvers all across the land. The *Chicago Tribune* Crossword Puzzles are syndicated by Tribune Media Services to hundreds of newspapers. When trying to make puzzles fair and challenging, ensuring accuracy is of prime importance. We take that part of our job very seriously.

Making puzzles enjoyable is the fun part of the job. You need to start with a group of puzzle creators, such as those whose works you will discover in this volume, with that sense of humor unique to crossword puzzles. They believe it is humorous when, say, they discover people whose first and last names, presented in reverse order, can be defined in a whole new way. You see the clues: "Feline of the forest?"; "Surcharge for a sleeper?"; "Cheap gem?"; and "Loaded chum?" Crossword creators hope you will laugh out loud when you fill in the answers: Woods Tiger; Pullman Bill; Buck Pearl; and Rich Buddy.

An editor ensures fairness with accuracy. He adds to the challenge of the puzzles with some harder, but fair, clues. He adds to the enjoyment of puzzle solving with wordplay in the clues intending to make you laugh. He hopes that putting all of these elements together will add to your satisfaction after you have filled in that last square.

All the best,
Wayne Robert Williams, Editor

PUZZLES

WHY I NEVER MARRIED

by Frances Hansen

ACROSS

1 Spanish moss victims
5 Simple organism
10 Crop of a bird
14 "Over There" composer
19 End of a demo?
20 Actress Massey
21 Healthy
22 Old-womanish
23 Why I didn't marry the carpenter?
26 View twice
27 California wind
28 Plant with tubular yellow blooms
29 Used talons
30 "QB VII" author
31 Victor, the comic pianist
32 Bread or dough
33 Pen pal, e.g.
36 Mrs. Mertz's portrayer
37 Persistently tormented
40 Olympic runner Johnson
41 Why I didn't marry the mason?
43 Fauna starter?
44 Fruit drinks
45 Sen. Claiborne __
46 Served perfectly
47 The East
48 Up to, briefly
49 Why I didn't marry the ditch-digger?
53 Tidy up
54 Tight spot
56 Plane fronts
57 Principal ore of lead
58 Bill attachment
59 Ankara populace
60 Had a bite
61 Mountaineer
63 Basketball game
64 Identical words with different meanings
67 Sheep sheds
68 Why I didn't marry the tailor?
70 Cup rim
71 Drained of color
72 Like a cube
73 Incite
74 Ms. Lollobrigida
75 Hwy. sign
76 Why I didn't marry the baker?
80 Morley of "60 Minutes"
81 Released from liability
83 Woody Woodpecker's creator
84 Aristo patriarchs
85 Natalie and Paula
86 Muslims who have been to Mecca
87 Stir up
88 Brief Bikini blasts
90 Boat lift
91 Ecclesiastic income
95 "The Man Who Fell to Earth" star
96 Why I didn't marry the charming millionaire?

98 Gage book
99 Israeli airline
100 Artist Dufy
101 Clytemnestra's mother
102 Tempted into trouble
103 Soccer org., once
104 Act fraction
105 Consider

DOWN

1 Folk singer Phil
2 Vicinity
3 Actress Madeline
4 Established laws
5 During flight
6 Ken and Lena
7 Mrs. Nick Charles
8 Social insect
9 __ Beach, Florida
10 Alterations
11 Elevate
12 One on one's side
13 Bridge-party pairings
14 Full Ford
15 "Paper Moon" pair
16 Why I didn't marry the gardener?
17 On the sheltered side
18 Requirement

24 Chicken caller
25 DEA employees
29 Like a baked apple
31 Wails lustily
32 "Luncheon on the Grass" painter
33 "Star Trek II: The __ of Khan"
34 Communication device
35 Why I didn't marry the dairy farmer?
36 Of the soft palate
37 Slip a Mickey
38 Water maker
39 Ross or Rigg
41 Lumberjack, e.g.
42 Noxious weeds
45 Firth or Finch
47 Marcus or Irwin
49 Greek underworld
50 Habituate
51 Scandinavian
52 Invited
53 Tippy transportation
55 Aviator Post
57 "__ Shelter"
59 Orlando and Dorsett
60 Hazardous
61 Base of a mesa

62 __ Rica
63 Series of six
64 Frequency unit
65 Collier
66 Stout poles
68 Sally Ann __
69 Overwhelming cravings
72 Seinfeld, Costanza, Kramer and __
74 Expandable magazine page
76 Henry VIII's court painter
77 Author of "Shogun"
78 One of the Gandhis
79 Those who make two one
80 Starchy meal from tubers
82 Masquerade mask
84 Flour of the southwest
86 Mandlikova and others
87 Second showing
88 Genesis character
89 Tree stump
90 Walter __ Mare
91 Fraternal grp.
92 Ah, yes
93 Surrender formally
94 Mild, yellow cheese
96 Biddy
97 AAA, in the U.K.

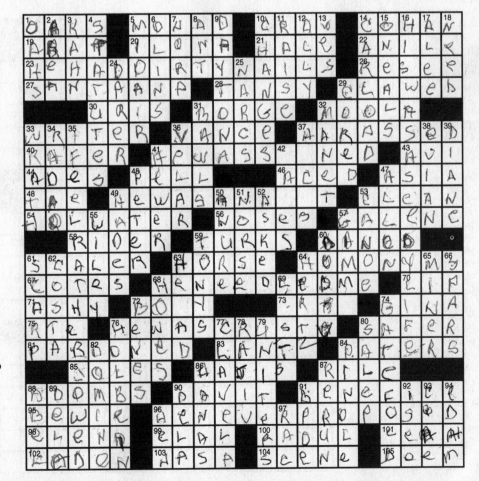

by Gayle Waters Dean

ACROSS

1 Mort, the comic
5 Dining out experiences
10 Actresses Tilly and Ryan
14 Old Irish alphabet
19 On the briny
20 Where van Gogh painted like mad
21 Former draft classification
22 One of the seven deadly sins
23 Single thing
24 See it through
27 Brothers of Marlins
29 Israel's national airline
30 Cartwright or Down
31 Okefenokee resident
32 Jacob and Esau's father
34 Supporting pieces
35 See it through
40 Make laugh
41 Pretty twins?
42 "48 __"
43 Transport
47 Solemn agreement
48 Four-time Indy winner
50 Neighborhood
52 Completely lacking sense
53 Suffix used in chemistry
54 Unwrap fruit
55 Asks intrusive questions
56 San Francisco gridder, for short
57 See it through
61 Relaxing
64 Liquefy
65 Say one's piece
66 See it through
71 Writer Zola
72 Yothers and Louise
73 Contends
74 Mel, the legendary Giant
77 Hefti and others
78 Young 'uns
79 Young 'un
81 Herman Melville novel
82 Actress Merrill
83 Iniquitous locale
84 Showing strain
85 Give-and-take transaction
86 See it through
91 Out of sight, out of mind?
95 Creates an airtight closure
96 Module
97 Wholly
98 Wide-mouthed water pitcher
99 City on the Isere River
103 See it through
107 Julia of "Kiss of the Spider Woman"
108 Railroad's road
109 Old-time TV actor Andrews
110 Bay window
111 Egyptian goddess of fertility
112 The frosh of last year
113 Lump of loose earth
114 Cheryl and Alan
115 Pile Pelion on __

DOWN

1 Chimed in
2 Regarding
3 Dishonorable man
4 Streetlight support
5 Slander
6 Heretofore
7 Woe is me
8 "My Name is Asher __"
9 Wind dir.
10 Simoleons
11 Tie together
12 Subj. of rocks
13 __ Paulo, Brazil
14 Reveal oneself
15 Maddux and Norman
16 Earl "Fatha" __
17 Confuse
18 Tablelands
25 __-foot oil
26 Indira's wardrobe
28 Gordie of the NHL
32 Way to Rome
33 "(__) Leaving Home"
34 Toss and turn
35 Stand open
36 Arabian sultanate
37 Italian chief
38 Calvino or Balbo
39 Piece of paper
43 Squealer
44 Capital of Vietnam
45 All thumbs
46 Intrinsically
48 Donnybrook
49 Jellied delicacy
50 Specter of Pennsylvania
51 Irritated
52 Pictures in pictures
54 Las Vegas draws
55 Legal aides, casually
57 Spanish rice dish
58 Overturn
59 Albacore and bluefin
60 Dropped the ball
61 Rectify
62 "My Cousin Vinny" Oscar winner
63 French water-bottler
67 Go to
68 Article of food
69 Title role for Madonna
70 Feel poorly
74 Tentmaker of note
75 Pitcher Stottlemyre
76 Tootsies
79 Icahn or Sagan
80 Nexus
81 Sacred story set to music
83 Neon Sanders
84 Inclined to weep
85 Castor or Pollux
86 Colorful Asian fabrics
87 New York river
88 Went off course
89 Turned
90 Prepares to pray
91 Wet sprays
92 Emcee's lead-in
93 Guitar holder
94 Family of fish
98 Bad to the bone
99 Crisscross framework
100 Operatic voice
101 Director Bunuel
102 "Lohengrin" lady
104 And so forth: abbr.
105 Lon __ of Cambodia
106 Stretch of time

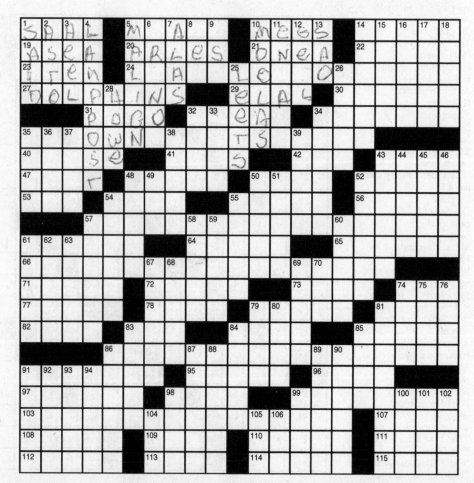

ADVICE TO HUSBANDS

by Robert H. Wolfe

ACROSS

1 Call back
5 Henry VIII's family name
10 Split prefix
15 Wild party
19 Fellow
20 Wed without warning
21 Task
22 __ Ata, Kazakhstan
23 Part 1 of a verse
27 Sailors' milieu
28 Copland and Spelling
29 Flaky, layered rock
30 Cubic meter
31 Chinese-American architect
32 Coquettes
33 Ezra Pound's state
36 River rising in the Krkonose Mountains
37 Flair
38 Part 2 of the verse
47 Resting on
48 Harvest bundlers
49 Chan portrayer
50 Miscue
51 Moon vehicle, for short
52 Sandwich shops
53 Acknowledge
54 Avant-garde composer
55 "The Clock Symphony" composer
56 Promised land
58 Equilibrium situations
60 Once more
63 Inspiration for the verse
67 Mimics
68 Botches (up)
70 Grow less
71 Attacks with repeated blows
73 "Sixteen __"
74 Sahara mount
77 Columbus' port
78 Pharmaceutical watchdog grp.
81 Ship back?
82 Computer language
83 "Rambo" co-star
85 Written part
86 Part 3 of the verse
90 Shoshones
91 Donations to the poor
92 At full speed, old-style
93 Church of England priest
96 Fancy lily
98 Auk's kin
101 Toggle switch
102 Use bleach
103 Constrictor snake
107 Last part of the verse
110 Piano-violin piece
111 Input data
112 State of an anchor
113 "__ brillig..."
114 Caesar and Luckman
115 Gang hangers-on?

116 Christmas songs
117 Normandy town

DOWN

1 External: pref.
2 Short, downward blow
3 Atlantic food fish
4 Union-friendly workplace
5 Plains shelter
6 Of an arm bone
7 Throw water on
8 Antithesis, briefly
9 Redo alterations
10 Beat a retreat from Carnaby Street
11 "__ in the Afternoon," 1972 Rohmer film
12 Mubarak of Egypt
13 Vexes
14 Branch of Buddhism
15 Applying water
16 Temple table
17 Silvery fish
18 Abode of the dead
24 Bar, legally
25 Prosodic foot
26 Leyte or Lanai
32 Source for sparks

33 Slanted ltrs.
34 Overplay the TLC
35 Molecule element
36 Gives the once-over
37 Writer Hunter
39 Follow directions
40 Giant of British golf
41 Throw aside
42 Singer Luft
43 Pay attachment?
44 Cut it out
45 Inciter
46 Try hard to persuade
52 Polonius or Ophelia, e.g.
53 Beyond recovery
54 Pitchers' toppers
55 Sibilant sound
56 Diligent devotion
57 B & B
59 Casual farewell
60 Mongolian range
61 Explode
62 Familiar family member
64 Resided
65 Exhausted
66 Hair coloring
69 Olympic official
72 Demand for service

75 Burrows and Vigoda
76 Extinct flightless bird
77 Solidifies
78 Greek salad requirement
79 Twice CCLVI
80 Ltr. directive
82 Relay-man's action
83 One of two on the phone
84 Man from Bucharest: var.
85 Sports breaks
87 Ensembles
88 Wavers
89 Military music
93 Public works projects
94 Boredom
95 Encrypted
96 Inclined channel
97 Ventilator
98 Olympic skiing brothers
99 From now to then
100 Coarse files
102 Absolutely refuses
104 Product package info.
105 Twofold
106 Lhasa __
108 Sure enough
109 Pontiac of the past, in brief

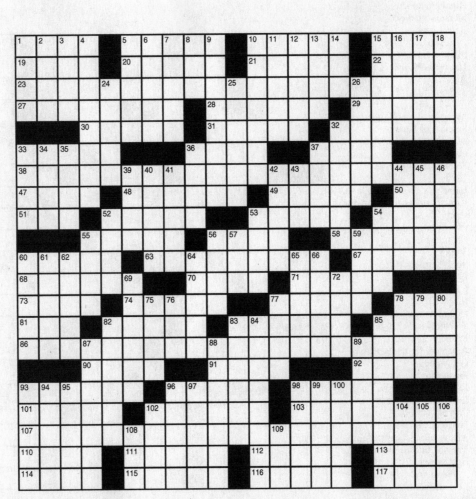

(A Puzzle to) DO TWICE

by Annabel Michaels

ACROSS

1 Fell back
8 Current unit
14 Dig
20 Ape
21 Colorful perch
22 Words of wisdom
23 Awkward situation
25 Conversation
26 T-shirt size
27 Manhattan sch.
28 Pen points
29 Nero's tutor
30 Bombeck and others
33 Arab cloak
36 Courtship
38 Gain a lap
39 Long gone
43 Roger Miller hit of 1965
47 Theatrical lament
48 Flexibility
50 Renter
51 Holiday prelude
54 Molecule component
56 Tropical tree
58 Gaucho's cattle-catcher
59 Scale
63 Half of B.S.
66 One of the Pointer Sisters
67 Highland honey
68 Memory method
69 Before long
70 Perfect places
71 Silent greeting
72 Does something
73 Andes animal
74 Signoret film, "Madame __"
75 Kemo __ (Lone Ranger)
76 Satellite of Saturn
77 Man on a quest
78 Came down with
79 Peter Frampton hit of 1976
82 Entre __
83 Para-aminobenzoic acid, for short
84 Pique performance
85 Chemical giant
86 Stupor
90 Verdi heroine
92 Eye in Aix
94 Cadillac models
96 Rules
101 "Stand by Me" actor Wheaton
102 Beanery sign
104 Adjective for the Beatles
105 Ger. warship
106 Frosh cap
110 Linguist Chomsky
112 Last letter of words?
115 Fish eggs
116 Pot roast ingredient
117 African district capital
122 Enzyme that curdles milk
123 Horse disease
124 Authenticity
125 Contravene
126 Belgian seaport
127 Takes off

DOWN

1 Ransacked
2 Political refugee
3 Movies
4 Nice summer
5 Morse symbol
6 English boys' school
7 Freshly moist
8 Excitement
9 Has permission
10 Pt. of speech
11 Needle cases
12 Decorative tree
13 Wearing away
14 Pops
15 Singer Brickell
16 Writer Hunter
17 Makes a heap
18 Environmental disaster
19 Denier
24 Couple
31 Vladimir Nabokov book
32 Island in the Saronic Gulf
34 Marshland
35 Fatty
37 Quarter
40 The "Velvet Gentleman"
41 From
42 Cricket pitches
44 Battery's negative electrode
45 Neighbor of N.Mex.
46 Niger-Congo language
49 Dining area
51 Two-time Wimbledon winner
52 Black magic
53 Country and Western singer Tubb
55 Capital of Equatorial Guinea
57 Wavy hairdo
60 Sicilian resort town
61 Amass money
62 Bottom lines
63 Thoroughly wet
64 Blackhead
65 Lined up
69 Offed, once
71 Area along the road
72 Before
73 Ocean motion with the wind
75 "Semper Fidelis" composer
76 Bridge action
77 Hit the slopes
79 Access indication
80 Air-travel watchdog grp.
81 Part of
82 Sgt. or Cpl., e.g.
86 Incubator occupant
87 Property recipient
88 Author of "Knots"
89 Kin of a son of a gun
91 Botanist Gray
93 Reply to a smash
95 Oliver Goldsmith's "She __ to Conquer"
97 Help on a heist
98 Norse goddesses of destiny
99 Follower of a Chinese philosophy
100 Cooks in vapors
103 Former Egyptian president
107 Nine: pref.
108 Laverne's L, e.g.
109 Medieval slave
111 Chess act
113 Deep-orange chalcedony
114 Dunfermline dagger
118 Hr. fraction
119 In addition
120 Laser strike
121 Auburn U's state

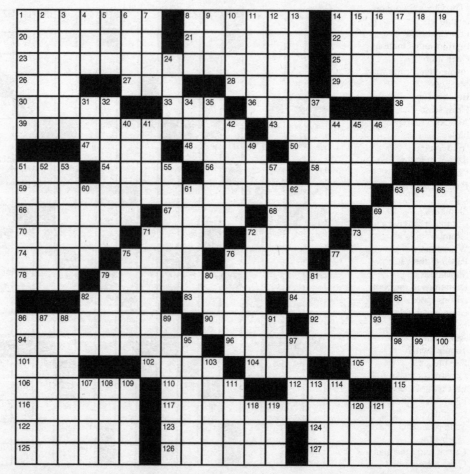

RE DOUBLE

by Susan Delgado

ACROSS

1 Neighbors of knights
8 Progressed laboriously
15 Tabernacle table
20 Elaine, the "Lily Maid of __"
21 Public spectacle
22 "Chinatown" screenwriter
23 Get ready for a shock
25 Conrad and Barbara
26 Riverside
27 European white-tailed eagle
28 Eliot's Marner
29 Is unable
30 Why not?
31 Notes of the scale
32 D-Day transportation
33 Came down with
34 Classic Pontiac letters
35 "Do Ya" rock grp.
36 African fox
37 Love and hate, e.g.
40 Musician's organ
41 Kitchen occupant of song
43 Eg.-Syr., once
45 Recipient of largesse
46 Take in
47 Clubs in Fred's bag
51 Surmise
52 Church leaders
55 Location
56 Stood very tall
58 Buddha
60 US weather grp.
62 Porcine comment
63 Poetry from Pindar
66 Melville's "Typee" sequel
67 Mothers' helpers
70 Channel marker
71 Heavy-hearted
72 Spanish port on the Atlantic
73 The Pres., militarily
74 Make inoperative
76 Keep out
79 Director Bunuel
81 Blew in strong blasts
82 Chairmaker
84 Minute fractions
87 Historic stretches
88 Hot medicated compress
89 Took off
90 Bobby of the Chicago Seven
94 Mule of song
95 Captivated
98 Depend
100 __ Romana
101 __ Simbel (Ramses temple)
102 Moving vehicle
103 6 on the phone
104 Mauna __
105 Pain in the neck
106 Jump over again
108 One of Harpo's brothers
110 Pause fillers
111 Word in an ultimatum
112 Spanish hero
113 Alert and listening stretch
116 Coeur d'__, ID
117 "The New Colossus" poet
118 Inflicted
119 Nostrils
120 Vain
121 Old-time inn employees

DOWN

1 Ran off at the mouth
2 Tel Aviv citizen
3 "Repo Man" star, Harry Dean __
4 Horse ankles
5 Grand __ Opry
6 Check writers
7 Accumulates
8 Life-saving meth.
9 Fight, country-style
10 Generation-based bias
11 Prosperous
12 Future rocks
13 Chemical suffixes
14 Drunk-tank letters
15 Plate appearances
16 Bank deal
17 Slight lack of confidence
18 Supply commentary
19 Antique shop employee
24 Breaks open shrink-wrap
29 David, the pitcher
33 Loses all inhibitions
36 Now in Guadalajara
38 Horn honk
39 Homebound
42 Vinegary: pref.
44 Queen of Spain
46 Compass dir.
48 Postal service
49 Follower of Zeno
50 With little energy left
51 Nettle
52 Inspirations of individualists
53 Tibetan monk
54 Intestinal disorder
57 Navy flag
59 Of the first Roman emperor
61 "__ Dei"
64 Welfare in Wolverhampton
65 Ogled
68 Lecturer's platform
69 Slicker
70 __-Terre
72 TV adjunct
75 Full of lather
77 Makes a cross
78 Montreal ballplayer, once
80 Bright red
82 Surgical birth method
83 Richard Strauss opera
85 Concluding
86 Less than three
88 Lose one's cool
91 Monkeyish
92 Cowboy, at times
93 Draws out
95 Gets around
96 Curtain call
97 Clumsy clod
99 Light beams
105 Element of a flower
107 Mozart's "__ kleine Nachtmusik"
108 Figures experts: abbr.
109 Brume
113 Sch. in Canton, NY
114 Ninnyhammer
115 Bottom line

THREE IN A ROW

by Frances Burton

ACROSS

1 Resting atop
5 Urbane
10 No frills
15 Creates an instant lawn
19 Ripped
20 Ore analysis
21 City on the Mohawk
22 Inland sea of Asia
23 Actor Guinness
24 Extra-strong cotton thread
25 Stenographer
26 Notoriety
27 __ and sinker
29 __ and delivered
32 Strong flavors
33 Empty space
34 At any time, in poetry
35 Dwell
38 List of candidates
40 Down-to-earth types
45 Suffered soreness
46 Thingamajig
47 Feed-bag morsels
48 Bottom-line figure
49 Lingerie purchases
50 Create a totem pole
51 Fills the space
52 Sound of a sarcastic laugh
53 Guillemot's cousin
54 Move upward
55 Fiery gem
57 Mature
58 African flies that carry sleeping sickness
60 Capital of Vietnam
62 Punished with an arbitrary fine
64 Remove soap
65 In plain view
66 Errand boy
67 Ski lodges
69 Last inning
70 Middle of the road
73 Grade-B western
74 Sondheim play, "Sweeney __"
75 Fence-clearing shot
77 Motor vehicle
78 Sound mental faculties
79 Clairvoyant
81 Portuguese ladies
82 Thin coating
83 Dining area
84 Reasons
85 Embankment sides
87 Prison rooms
88 Keeps on reverberating
90 Board
91 Most unrefined
92 Peggy or Spike
93 Earth
94 Picture in the mind
96 __ and tomato
101 __ and serial number
105 Disagreeable responsibility

106 Localities
107 States with confidence
109 __ vera
110 Pot starter
111 Beg
112 Border
113 Departed
114 Back talk
115 Curvy letters
116 Go-aheads
117 English boys' school

DOWN

1 Bryce Canyon's state
2 Italian traveler to China
3 Sandwich cookie
4 Cravats
5 Salt spring
6 Calling into play
7 Tax evaluators
8 Actor Kilmer
9 Visor
10 Mishandled
11 Make amends
12 Location
13 Chilled
14 Vehicle perches for tots
15 Overland expedition
16 By mouth
17 Title for a knight's lady
18 Luge
28 Alan or Diane
30 Small amount
31 Cave-dwelling fish
35 Capital of Morocco
36 Beige shades
37 __ and roll
39 __ and obey
40 Vex
41 Swallow
42 __ and pop
43 Sound of snickering laughter
44 Endure
46 Speakers' platforms
50 Wave top
51 __ and charity
52 Employer
54 Ed who played Lou Grant
55 Upright
56 Harbor
57 Attribute
59 Pieces of mosaics
61 Ardent
62 Old World lizards
63 Changes one's address
67 Cringe in fear
68 Ethiopia's Selassie

71 Devers and Parent
72 German Dadaist painter
74 Thomas Hardy novel, "__ of the d'Urbervilles"
76 Jokes like Rodney Dangerfield's
79 Wingtip adjunct
80 Ogle
81 Author of "The Ginger Man"
82 Waste
84 At what time
85 Mates
86 Non-cleric
87 Animal confinement
89 Shuts
91 Father of the Egyptian pharaoh Seti
93 Actors' platform
95 Bart Simpson's mom
96 Feather scarves
97 Freud's daughter
98 Removes from the squad
99 Memorable periods
100 Turner and Danson
102 Oodles
103 Childhood taboo
104 Enthusiastic
108 Sign of victory

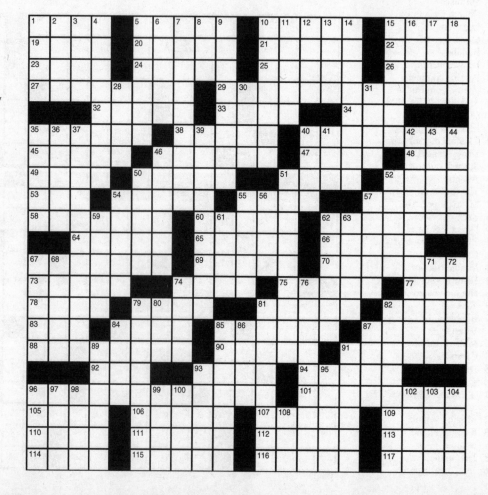

ACROSS

1 Roof's overhang
6 Product pitch
15 Baked desserts
20 Reeked
21 Animated film of 1997
22 Get out of bed
23 American waterfowl
25 Segment of a flower
26 Mohammad's son-in-law
27 Smash on Broadway
28 Word ignored by alphabetizers
29 Writing implement
30 Ardent love
33 Merchant's goal
36 Former duchess of York
37 Under control
38 Companions of chips
41 Youngest son of Adam
44 Goblet elements
45 Old-fashioned euphemistic oaths
46 Overact
48 Gun lobby, briefly
49 Frenzied
50 Old West lawman Wyatt
51 Double-edged sword
52 Big __, CA
53 Canadian part of Niagara
57 Equal: pref.
58 Author of "A Perfect Spy"
61 Changes
62 Abbr. in airport names
63 Skirt styles
64 Neptune's spear
66 Strangled
68 Greek letter
69 Polishes
70 Tops to go with skirts
71 "The Joy Luck Club" author Tan
72 Outdoor urban staircases
76 Ump's cohort
77 Wood sorrel
78 "American Gothic" painter
79 Bit of butter
82 Numero __
83 The Velvet Fog
84 Shrimp in Soho
86 Biblical queen
88 Small ornamental button
90 Eye's output
92 Empty spots
93 Low point
95 Crimson and scarlet
96 Dock workers, at times
97 Sir __ Hardwicke
99 Salary
101 Open hostilities
102 Uganda's infamous Amin
103 Where the Magic played
104 Harborside haunts of sailors
110 Sea nymph
111 Begged
112 Shooting at clay targets
113 Unit of magnetic flux density
114 Nervousness
115 Birds resembling gulls

DOWN

1 Daydreaming, e.g.
2 Mythological female runner
3 Disappeared
4 Letter carrier: abbr.
5 Jamaican music
6 Polio vaccine developer
7 Art school subj.
8 French lake
9 Inuit: abbr.
10 Universal meas.
11 Draw tight
12 Writer Sholem
13 Similar to
14 Egyptian souls
15 Frolic
16 Sports venues
17 Where dishes are done
18 Morales of "Bad Boys"
19 Move merchandise
24 Like horse's hooves
29 Delicate hue
31 Detective Spade
32 Election winners
33 Ginger cookies
34 Assistance
35 __ Alamos, NM
36 Ruins
38 Hideous creature
39 Overwhelm with noise
40 Bestow
42 Board member
43 Lloyd and Arlen
45 Facility
47 Pause fillers
50 Does wrong
51 Check results
53 Mandlikova of tennis
54 Lodestone or pyrite
55 __ City, Florida
56 Bygone
58 Statue of Liberty poet
59 Naturally suitable environment
60 First residents
62 Paper bets
64 "__ & Louise"
65 More covered with frost
66 Lummox
67 Bound
69 Trapper
70 Blessing
72 Small child
73 Excitingly strange
74 Exchanges
75 Drags behind
79 One who misleads
80 North Sea port
81 Members of rhythm sections
84 Cursor starter?
85 Fishing pole
86 Healthy spot
87 Possessed
89 Rye grass
91 Laundry machines
92 Alphabetize
94 Ross or Rigg
96 Touches down
97 Toll
98 One of HOMES
99 Sheet of glass
100 Bus. letter abbr.
101 Sorrows
104 Dampen
105 Arikara people
106 Bleacher bum
107 Hwy. sign
108 Summer hrs.
109 Eisenhower, casually

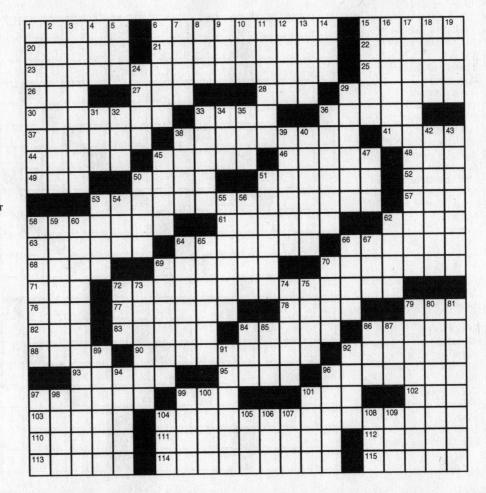

ALL UPSET

by Arthur S. Verdesca

ACROSS

1 Theatrical sketch
5 Brownish yellow color
10 Follow
15 First man
19 Scuttlebutt
20 Hazy purple
21 Classic TV Western
22 1993 Nobel Prize winner Morrison
23 Upset
25 Upset
27 Incentive
28 Free-for-all
30 Most docile
31 Teen follower?
32 Calls to the phone
33 Outmoded sound system
34 Counterbalance
37 Quips
38 Skunks
42 Fly like a butterfly
43 Racing boats for rowers
45 Emerald mineral
46 Prune
47 Butterball
49 Upset
51 Conference site of 1945
53 Superlative ending
54 Tiny
56 Desirable reviews
58 Scandinavian nation: abbr.
59 Zimbabwe, previously
61 Subdivision of a people
63 On land
65 Founder of modern chemistry
66 Yucatan people
67 Prickly rosebush
68 Black Sea port
70 Annoyed
71 Birthday suit of a walrus
74 Location on the Web
75 Augusta's state
77 City near Offut AFB
78 Memorable time
79 Fresh and firm
81 Upset
84 Faceted
86 Number of a birthday
87 Deserves
89 Put in a box
91 Academy Award winner of 1936
92 Coupon presenter
94 Have scruples
95 Door knocker
97 To a distance
98 Hereditary units
99 Moore of "G.I. Jane"
100 Idolized
103 Deuce toppers
104 FSU team member
108 Upset
110 Upset
112 Complete hastily, with "off"
113 Function

114 Disney World attraction
115 Ireland
116 Bowl over
117 Twilled, worsted cloth
118 Put into words
119 Ollie's partner in comedy

DOWN

1 Moral misjudgments
2 Tie tie
3 Former Spanish toehold in Africa
4 Sailing ships' high spots
5 Necklace charms
6 "Rhoda" co-star Richard
7 Quick kiss
8 Holiday prelude
9 Ornamental tree
10 Oar holders
11 Reprobates
12 First of the pot
13 Altar sentence
14 Haughtily
15 Like nuclear energy
16 First two notes
17 Ubiquitous bugs
18 Highland haze
24 Olympic sled

26 With due care
29 Excrete
32 __-walsy
33 Tribe on the move
34 Part of a negotiation
35 Brief bright light
36 Upset
37 Coup group
38 Nettle
39 Upset
40 Carrier
41 Digging tool
44 Adorable one
45 Spills the beans
48 Follows orders
50 Trinity
52 Grate collection
55 Shiite's belief
57 Former duchess of York
60 Medicinal quantities
61 Government's due
62 Cereal grass
64 Eliot's Marner
66 Restaurant handouts
67 Necklace units
68 Academy Award
69 Funereal piece
70 Even more despicable

71 Slander
72 Dancing Castle
73 Low point
76 Subsequently
77 Roman Hades
80 Give priority
82 Minuscule
83 Catches in a net
85 Trespasses
88 Shaffer's Mozart play
90 Religious recluse
93 Hearty and natural
94 Clinton press secretary Myers
96 Infamous Idi
98 Pitman's shorthand competition
99 Train station
100 Annexes
101 Clock face
102 Mountain in Thessaly
103 Former Russian ruler
104 Pet protection grp.
105 Leave out
106 "Doctor Zhivago" heroine
107 Earthly paradise
109 Opp. of NNW
111 Make a choice

ONE FOR THE BIRDS

by Susan Delgado

ACROSS

1 Thick, creamy soups
8 Strawberry tree
15 Couric of CBS News
20 Throwback characteristic
21 ASAP
22 Clasp in an embrace
23 Architect of St. Paul's Cathedral
25 French lace
26 Comparative ending
27 City near Leipzig
28 Gas: pref.
29 Pitcher, sometimes
30 Go ga-ga
32 A/C measure
33 Ben and Bobby
35 Hesitating
36 Of the small intestine
38 Get lost!
41 Maiden name lead-in
42 City NE of Seville
45 Public prosecutors, for short
46 Put back pictures
48 Long John Silver feature
50 Noon and midnight, e.g.
52 Customary extras, briefly
55 Carrier bag
59 Fear response
61 Early-stage seed
62 Russian ruler
63 Wildebeest
64 Tabula __
65 Meadowsweet
66 Absconded
68 Stored supply
70 Cat on the prowl
71 Joy-bringer
72 History Muse
73 Long scarf
74 __ majesty
75 Eagle's nest
76 Beat a hasty retreat
79 Ogled
80 BLT topping
81 Storage buildings
82 Past and present
84 Between-molts stage
86 Surprised exclamations
87 Angels' home
92 Males
94 Chinese gooseberries
98 Blackmore's "__ Doone"
99 Hungering for news
101 Secular
102 Helping hand
105 German river
106 Brains
107 Brit. flyboys
108 Queen __ lace
110 CD's competition
111 Burn the ends of
112 Dey, Bonaduce, Cassidy et al., on TV
116 Zeal

117 Tapering tower
118 More mannerly
119 Ship's poles
120 Kiddies' bears
121 Balances on the brink

DOWN

1 One-third of the world
2 Moor of Venice
3 Sojourner
4 Fauna starter?
5 Lillian or Dorothy
6 Cornerstone abbr.
7 Young salmon
8 U.S. tennis stadium
9 Lobster eggs
10 One-fifth of NYC
11 Off guard
12 Mother __ of Calcutta
13 Addict
14 RR stop
15 Hawaiian volcano
16 Blue-dye plants
17 Speaking frankly
18 Mandrell sister
19 Materialize
24 Stopper
29 Photographic solutions

31 Tablet
33 Old enough
34 "Kidnapped" author's inits.
35 Boardwalk extensions
37 Flatfoot
39 Poetic pieces
40 Drummer Gene
43 Mendicant
44 Intense emotion
47 Chamberlain, the British PM
49 Reed or Rawls
50 Red Scare grp.
51 City on the Irtysh
53 "Fawlty Towers" star
54 Scorched
55 Distress call
56 Flowering shrub
57 Tenerife, Las Palmas, etc.
58 WWII soldier's meal
60 Streamlet
61 WWII ration-book grp.
65 New York island
67 Like a little Scotsman
68 Lost it on ice
69 Muscle spasms
70 The March King

72 French dear
73 __ voyage!
76 Tobacco mouthfuls
77 Set of principles
78 Viper collective
81 Mixes
83 Mule of song
85 Boitano and Button, e.g.
86 Assent, in Aix
88 Vertical's opp.
89 Well-read
90 Breathing device
91 Suffering saints
92 Painter Childe __
93 New York city
95 Burst into flames
96 Traveled like Huck
97 Warbled
100 Grain rot
103 Bungling
104 Author of "Moll Flanders"
107 Deserve
108 Fruity quaffs
109 Mall event
112 L.A. clock setting
113 Upstate NY school
114 __-de-France
115 Cambridge sch.

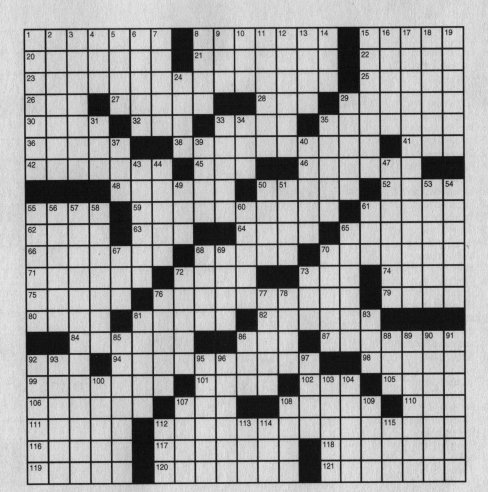

by Annabel Michaels

ACROSS

1 Taps horn
6 Layered pavement
13 Map collections
20 Rubber capital of the world
21 Walkway of the Southwest
22 Leak stopper
23 Secondary locations
25 Out of the ordinary
26 Yin's counterpart
27 Scottish Gaelic
28 Penultimate Greek letter
30 First name of 98D
31 Iniquity
32 One: pref.
33 More frequently
37 Exchange
38 Negatively charged atoms
40 Genealogical chart
43 "__ Gotta Be Me"
44 Prepare to drive a golf ball
45 Nebula
46 Opened, as sneakers
48 Samson's undoer
50 Accuse a public official
52 Roadside purchase
55 Perplexing problem
58 Fifer's drum
61 Gulf of the Ionian Sea
63 36D on "Star Trek: Deep Space Nine"
64 Fairy-tale monsters
65 French school
66 Add muscle
68 Homemade brick
70 Court proceedings
71 Broadcasting
72 Joyce Carol __
74 Team cheer
76 Piece of Puccini
77 Titles
78 Naval vacations
82 Susan of "L.A. Law"
83 Snobbery
85 Cooperative agreement
87 Erle Stanley __
89 More chipper
91 Strongman of myth
95 Gradually slower, in music: abbr.
96 "Flipper" star
99 Mysterious
100 Does wrong
102 American botanist
103 Writer Tan
104 AFL-__
105 Touches against
107 __ tai cocktail
108 Pre-school lesson
110 Chauffeur-driven wheels
111 Riviera resort
114 Spent a restful night
118 Inuits
119 Fell as ice
120 Pooh's creator

121 Consider beneath contempt
122 Maui and Manhattan
123 __ on (victimizes)

DOWN

1 Tended tots
2 Kiev's country
3 Mom's mom
4 Extended
5 Bus. letter abbr.
6 New Zealand native
7 Landon et al.
8 Coffee shop
9 Friend in France
10 Mo. winter begins
11 With skill
12 "Abe Lincoln in Illinois" star
13 Silly billy
14 Asian holiday
15 Zhivago's love
16 Shepard and King
17 Picketer's placards
18 Inscribe
19 Soaked
24 Female fowl
29 $ from a bank
32 Dismantle mortise joints

33 Nebraska city
34 Repair
35 Becomes violently active
36 Actor Auberjonois
39 African lute
40 Three-time Masters winner
41 Jai __
42 One who brings joy
45 Encircle with a belt
47 Gum arabic tree
49 Part of a bow
50 Concerning
51 Leader of 94D
52 Libreville's country
53 Sports venue
54 Liner luggage
56 Hangman's knot
57 CIA of Russia
59 Kukla's friend
60 Repeat oneself
62 Away from home
67 Bearlike
68 Small particle
69 German article
70 Next
72 Egyptian god
73 Contented sighs

74 Gave a score
75 State categorically
79 Director Mervyn
80 War goddess
81 Actor Keach
84 Brain tissue
86 And so forth: abbr.
87 Lubricated
88 Military landing field
89 Utters piercing cries
90 New Deal agcy.
92 Ball of comedy
93 Payment to an ex
94 Comic threesome
97 Gridlock
98 1992 Wimbledon winner
99 City on the Irtysh
101 Landing area
103 Corrosive substances
106 Partial prefix
108 Business letter abbr.
109 Used leeches
110 Den
112 Jan. and Dec.
113 Full of: suff.
115 Conger
116 Green veggie
117 Sovereign: abbr.

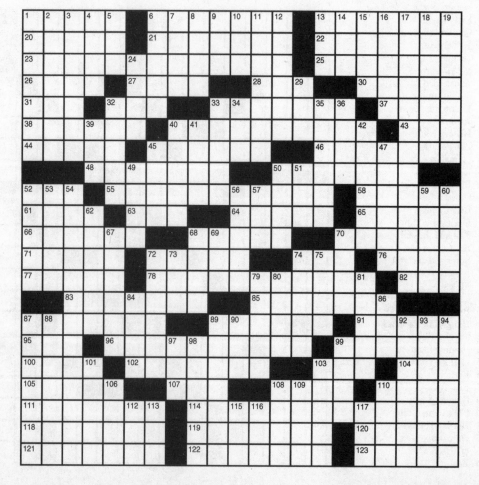

1997 HEADLINES

by Stanley B. Whitten

ACROSS

1 Sour
5 Start again from scratch
12 Small amount
15 Deeply absorbed
19 Toward shelter
20 Justice Sandra Day __
21 Goof
22 Lotion ingredient, often
23 1997 sports headline
27 Writer Loos
28 French born
29 Vigor
30 Inspects
31 Send again
33 Nancy the detective
36 Toiled
38 Black or White
40 Destitute
42 3, to Cato
43 Cursor starter?
46 1997 sports headline
54 "Fargo" director Coen
55 Coop resident
56 Mineral spring
57 Serengeti predators
58 Light gas
59 Priestly robes
60 Gabor sister
62 Two under par
63 Flop
64 Neighbor of Ga.
65 Stooped
67 Hodges of baseball
68 1997 science headline
76 "__ Miserables"
77 Prepared
78 Label
79 Set on fire
80 Plant louse
83 Prohibit
84 Classify
86 Flute
87 Hole enlarger
89 Archaeological site
91 Fuss
92 Sacred book
93 1997 science/sports headline
98 President after FDR
99 Phi-psi separator
100 Emcee
101 Collector's old French coin
102 Fabric folds
105 Accomplishment
107 Inflame with love
112 Birthplace of St. Francis
115 Also
117 Another name for romaine
119 Split to get hitched
120 1997 medical headline
125 Legal starter?
126 Hamilton bill
127 Honors formally
128 Cattle collective
129 Stone and Stallone
130 Mayday letters
131 Large, strong-willed women
132 Martial or liberal follower

DOWN

1 Crimean resident
2 Skirt type
3 Philbin of TV
4 Grin exposure
5 Drive a dinghy
6 $ subject
7 Voiced disapproval
8 Supports below
9 Elected ones
10 Base
11 Faucet problem
12 Plunder
13 Provide weapons
14 Salty
15 Gave a score
16 Baldwin brother
17 __ barrel
18 Hardy heroine
24 Dried grape
25 Unused
26 Female
32 Ballpoint, e.g.
34 Long time
35 Astounds
37 Shed
39 Masonry block
41 Suspended cable
43 __-pong
44 Actual
45 Being: Lat.
46 Repairs
47 Enjoyed avidly
48 Valerie Harper sitcom
49 Computer syst.
50 Internet
51 Poe's bird
52 Observing
53 Kingdom
59 Swiss mountains
61 Supplement
64 Tributary stream
65 Down on the market?
66 Ancient
67 USNA mascot
69 Ascend
70 Sphere
71 Necklace units
72 Timing signal
73 Excuse
74 Long gun
75 Cattle
80 Monumental entrance
81 Little legumes
82 Mary or Moss
84 California island
85 Strange
86 Conifer
88 Tax-time documentation
90 Blunder
92 South China Sea sultanate
94 Unmasker's cry
95 Baby cats
96 Employ
97 Serve perfectly
102 Pocket breads
103 Fighting Tigers of the NCAA
104 Boozer
106 Lone Ranger's sidekick
108 Hawaiian ciao
109 Lawn leveler
110 '60s creative movement
111 Splits apart
112 Venomous vipers
113 Emblem
114 Chipper
116 Greek peak
118 British gun
121 Zodiac sign
122 Wham __
123 Pay attachment?
124 CIA predecessor

ACROSS

1 Makes pink blue, e.g.
5 Dads
10 Right on maps
14 Ratchet latches
19 Oriental nursemaid
20 Country hit song by Tom T. Hall
21 Reveal the inner man?
22 Not cool
23 BARK
26 Military foul-up
27 __ for (had a craving)
28 Tantalize
29 More bleached
30 Jug handles
31 Memphis song, "__ Street Blues"
32 Quickly to the point
33 Safe
36 Old-time entertainer Lenya
37 Blight on the landscape
40 Abrupt transitions
41 LIGHTER
44 Defensive reply to a smash
45 Coffee servers
46 Fiddlesticks!
47 Will, the actor
48 Amorphous mass
49 Actress Scala
50 SHELL
54 Old hag
55 More than two
57 Ventilated
58 Braked
59 Walks off the stage
60 Musical conclusions
61 Green years
62 Allowance provider
64 Dyed using indigo
65 Cochise's clan
68 Participate in charades
69 GONDOLA
72 Ref's relative
73 Hole-making tools
74 Meaney of "Star Trek: The Next Generation"
75 Elaborate inlay
76 Hoops grp.
77 Hep character
78 SMACK
82 Stir from sleep
83 Removal mark
85 Oxygen compound
86 Woodland minor deities
87 Buddy-boy
88 Pickling agent
89 Diminutive ending
90 Handles the ship's helm
92 Planet
93 500 B.C. Greek poet
97 Part of Stein's line
98 YAWL
100 Peachy keen
101 On the sheltered side

102 Surpass
103 Suffer heartbreak
104 Seats for several
105 That woman's
106 Farm equipment manufacturer
107 Mumford or Busby

DOWN

1 Short race
2 Athletic org.
3 Merit
4 Drastic reorganizations
5 Coyote State's capital
6 Fugard play, "A Lesson from __"
7 Tadpole's milieu
8 "__ Maria"
9 Sonnet stanzas
10 Breathes out
11 Crop up
12 In one's right mind
13 Hardin and Cobb
14 More forward
15 Potts and Lennox
16 DORY
17 Unending sentence?
18 Side track
24 Boscs and Bartletts
25 Pacific pact: abbr.
29 More ironic
31 South Africa's first prime minister
32 Neuwirth and Daniels
33 Punches
34 Ghostly
35 LAUNCH
36 Downtown Chicago
38 Arledge of TV
39 Flowed back
41 Christmas carols
42 S-shaped moldings
43 Nevada lake
46 Brooklyn art institute
48 Bucking horse
50 Fabric pattern
51 "Eating __," 1982 black comedy
52 Soft down
53 Madrid museum
54 Jump, as a fence
56 CEOs, VPs, etc.
58 Calyx part
60 Scale the heights
61 Dashboard gauges, briefly
62 War's end

63 Sadat of Egypt
64 Indonesian island
66 Burning coal
67 Bridges
69 Roundup finale
70 Tolerate
71 Bernhardt's rival Eleonora __
74 __ and whey
76 Semiaquatic rodent
78 Hepburn and Meadows
79 British trucks
80 Self-imposed absence
81 Ignited
82 Keep an eye on
84 Nap in Nogales
86 Rice to Chinese
88 Sparring dog?
89 Jump-rope turner
90 __ serif type
91 Small combo
92 Artifice
93 Allow ending?
94 For one
95 Workplace injury grp.
96 Requirement
98 Morse symbol
99 Felling tool

ANIMAL TALK

by Edgar Fontaine

ACROSS

1 Brazilian soccer great
5 Parody
10 Despised
15 Once more
19 Trebek of "Jeopardy!"
20 Of ocean motion
21 Of use
22 Vague amount
23 Dubious buy
25 Tux
27 Jewish holiday
28 Disfigures
30 Applies color
31 Hammered on a slant
32 Female red deer
33 Marshes
34 Fasten tightly again
37 __ Domingo
38 Shabbiest
42 Greek goddess of peace
43 Striped semi-precious gemstone
45 Zodiac sign for most of August
46 __ one's heels
47 Occupant of a marina
49 Suckered
50 William, the Quaker
51 State official: abbr.
52 Indoor television antenna
56 Gap in time
57 Lifts
59 Lean and lanky
60 Pester
61 Dilapidated
62 Everly Brothers hit of 1957, "Wake up Little __"
63 Persona non __
64 Shades of black and brown
66 " __ of Fortune"
67 Thin coverings, say of silver
70 Church singing group
71 Guffaw
73 Skater Babilonia
74 __ in the sand
75 Eastern bigwig
77 Well-practiced skills
78 Sooty matter
79 Ruin
80 Hoax
84 Enact
85 Misfits
88 Job stations
89 Listed to one side
90 Al Capone's nemesis
91 Moves at a quick pace
92 Wild pig
93 Debates
96 Polish
97 Storage structure
101 Dow slump
103 Greatest part of anything
105 __ noire (bugbear)
106 Lift
107 Expansive
108 Terrible name?
109 __ out a living (scraped by)
110 Affirmatives
111 Spooky Belgian artist
112 Mosquito, e.g.

DOWN

1 "Hair" producer Joseph __
2 Lamb's pen name
3 Table support
4 Alive
5 __ off (repelled)
6 Like church organs
7 Stench
8 __ Ridge Boys
9 Bond creator
10 Cigar container
11 Components of everything
12 Metal containers
13 Moose
14 Became more intense
15 St. Francis of __
16 Person, place or thing
17 Send out
18 Dampens
24 Nary a soul
26 Yin and __
29 Poker pot starter
32 Part of Hispaniola
33 Actress Dunaway
34 Long, narrow crest
35 Swashbuckling Flynn
36 Building material for walls
37 Uses a stiletto
38 Sloppy
39 Hopkins-Hurt film (with "The")
40 Intuit
41 Copier fluid
44 Sudden onrush
47 Stuffing materials
48 Follow orders
50 Singer Page or LaBelle
52 Estimator
53 More authentic
54 __ along (ambles)
55 Old-womanish
56 Reluctant
58 Bona fide
60 Quotes one's own autobiography?
62 Seaside
63 Satiate
64 Likeable loser
65 In front
66 Rotation sounds
67 Splits hair
68 Speedometer, e.g.
69 Located
72 Goes on and on
75 Special messenger
76 West and others
78 The "Enterprise," e.g.
81 Elves
82 High time?
83 Getty of "The Golden Girls"
84 Makes airtight
86 Accustomed
87 Abound (with)
89 More relaxed
91 "We hold __ truths to be..."
92 Drum
93 Singer Lane
94 Smell strongly (of)
95 Entryway
96 Aspen mode of travel?
97 High crags
98 Own
99 Periods of time
100 Concavity
102 "Norma __"
104 Charleson or McKellen

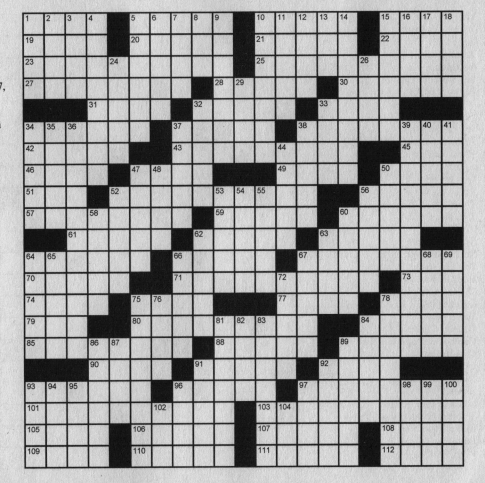

QUESTIONNAIRE

by Harvey L. Chew

ACROSS

1 Velvety plant
5 Amazing woman of song?
10 Sovereign
15 Indigo dye
19 Dog in "The Thin Man"
20 Enticed
21 French school
22 Half of a golf course
23 Bugs' question
25 Goren's question
27 Cattlemen
28 Coeur d'__, ID
30 Send back to the labs
31 Rescuer
32 Tibetans and Thais
33 Swiss river
34 Single
37 Inclement winter weather
38 Loose and illegible signatures
42 Sci-fi author of "Narabedla"
43 Diarist Nin
45 Nursery-rhyme Jack and spouse
48 In what way?
49 Paid players
50 "__ in the Attic"
51 Attila's crowd
52 Manufactured
53 Twisting turn
54 Danza's question
58 Fully full
59 Align again
61 Occurrence
62 Pilgrim's destination
63 Backs of necks
64 When to eat apples?
65 Private schs.
66 French tower
68 Former hostess Mesta
69 Borrower's opposite number
72 Less humid
73 Daly's question
75 Think better afterward
76 Teri, the actress
77 Acquire
78 Seine tributary
79 Stroke on the green
80 Printer's spaces
81 Hood and others
83 Old Germanic letters
84 Gillette blade
85 Tot tenders
87 Dancing Castle
89 One not mentioned
90 Over the hill
91 Increasing
93 Painter Chagall
95 Shrewd
98 Lewis Carroll heroine
99 Terrier type
103 Butler's question
105 Bartender's question
107 River rising in the Czech Republic

108 Of a people: pref.
109 Host
110 Oklahoma city
111 Parakeet staple
112 Senior member
113 Cabinet feature
114 Fishing gear

DOWN

1 Bryn __ College
2 Workplace watchdog grp.
3 Comic Laurel
4 Tote bags
5 Paste-up artist
6 Publishable copy
7 Annexes
8 Dove's cry
9 Contains in a box
10 Uses a microwave
11 Sch. in Storrs, CT
12 Edmund and Rob
13 Trains on trestles
14 Eats one's words
15 "Peer Gynt" dancer
16 Considerate
17 Writing fluids
18 "__ we forget..."
24 Lean-to

26 Brings up
29 Commit perjury
32 Social category
34 Higher one of two
35 Scandinavian
36 Costello's question
37 Speak, biblically
38 Without: Fr.
39 Pilate's question
40 Waterproof wool
41 Edberg or Borg
43 Following close behind
44 High times
46 Counterfeit
47 Iron oxide
52 __ Gras
54 Windshield cleaner
55 Valentine shape
56 Bad deeds
57 Brazilian port
58 Cast a shadow
60 Johnson, the Olympic runner
62 Act parts
64 Country singer Carter
65 Get up
66 Outer reaches
67 Tehran resident

68 Collins or Donahue
69 "Crazy" singer
70 Highly unconventional
71 Patch roads
73 Violent conflicts
74 Not of age
77 Worked in the yard
79 More sparsely distributed
81 Silt formation
82 Club for a par 3, maybe
83 Continued a subscription
86 Traveled from place to place
88 Ocasek of the Cars
89 Hurler Hershiser
91 Wishy-__
92 Skirt shape
93 Corner joint
94 City on the Rhone
95 Nautical assents
96 One-and-only
97 London subway
99 Baylor U. city
100 Chemical element #
101 Latin "ditto"
102 Beatty film
104 Classic Pontiac
106 Med. care plan

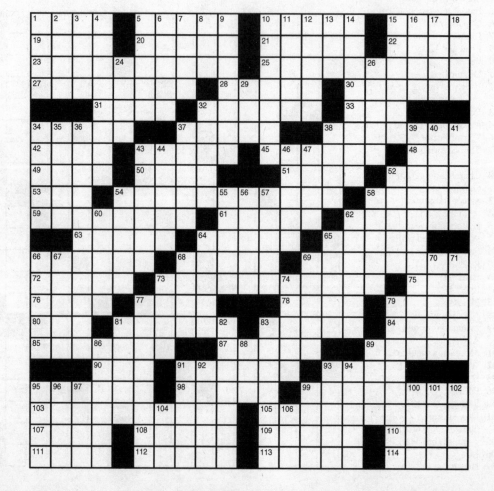

by Susan Delgado

ACROSS

1 Promissory notes
5 Zig's partner?
8 Gee whiz!
13 __ borealis
19 Phnom __, Cambodia
20 People of Nigeria
21 Cocoons
22 Andes animals
23 Facet
24 Baseball moment of truth
27 Zeno of __
28 Knock off a mount
29 Tehran resident
30 Civil liberties: abbr.
32 "__ That a Shame"
33 Tapered tucks
35 Singer Damone
38 When the cavalry arrives
43 Hubbub
44 Stick together
45 Upstate rival of Las Vegas
46 Of nerves
48 Resembling: suff.
49 Martino and Pacino
51 Roman autocrat
53 Tubb or Truex
54 State of Australia: abbr.
55 Barely avoiding catastrophe
58 Requirement for a UFO: abbr.
59 Vidal of hair-care products
60 Publishers
64 Painful
66 Gorby's nation
67 MDs
70 Scheme
71 Eagle-eyed fisherman
74 New York resort lake
77 Language ending
78 Reprieved in the ring
82 Batman portrayer Kilmer
83 Experience a flashback
86 Southern phrase
87 Stephen of "The Crying Game"
88 Pic blowup
89 Makes amends
90 First governor of Alaska
91 "The Real McCoys" co-star Richard
93 Vocalized, like a melody
94 Moment of truth
99 Sty occupant
100 Came up
102 Promised land
103 Acad.
104 Fence-clearing shot
106 Poem divisions
109 Resistance units
112 NFL crunch time
116 Chess piece
117 Create aquarium bubbles
118 Tall pile
119 Permit
120 Ballerina's skirt
121 Hill and Goodman
122 Trousers
123 Time meas.
124 Mlle. from Madrid

DOWN

1 __ dixit
2 Eye in Aix
3 Just before the finish
4 Encase a sword
5 Domesticated ox
6 God, in Hebrew text
7 Medieval
8 Portuguese port
9 Bee buzzes, e.g.
10 Fraternal org.
11 Clumsy clod
12 Up until now
13 Warning signal
14 Arm bones
15 Precipitation
16 One who eats all
17 Fink
18 Last of a log
25 Honky-__
26 Employ
31 Glacial pinnacles
33 Shore of songs
34 "That's __"
36 Lupino and Tarbell
37 Stable youngster
38 Frigidity
39 Without interruption
40 "Gianni Schicchi" soprano
41 Refrigerant
42 Sample a sample
43 Car maintenance check
46 Beatty and Buntline
47 Work units
50 That certain
51 Corp. honchos
52 Noun-forming suffix
56 Draft letters
57 Former Disney honcho Michael __
61 Critical moment
62 Cash's singing daughter
63 Concerning constellations
65 Palliating
67 Willie Wonka's writer
68 Hurler Hershiser
69 Taxi
72 Speak out wildly
73 Holiday preludes
74 Reeked
75 Guinness and Baldwin
76 Bow and Barton
79 Color changers
80 One over par
81 Chinese currency
83 Speak roughly
84 Pin box
85 Bull of Texas
92 Debs' dates
94 Irish king, Brian __
95 Arkansas range
96 Helsinki native
97 Sleepily
98 Even sillier
100 Friendship
101 Descartes and Russo
105 Arabian sultanate
106 Graceful fowl
107 Diplomacy
108 Some NCOs
110 Feminist Lucretia Coffin __
111 Predatory bird
112 File marker
113 Like a little Scotsman
114 Recipe meas.
115 Sked letters

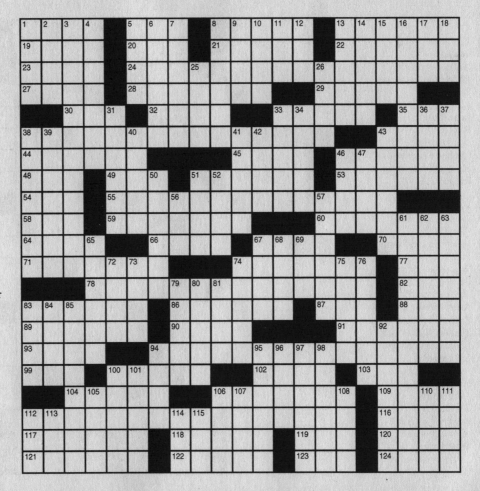

INTUITIVE SUSPICION

by Edgar Fontaine

ACROSS

1 Period of distraction
6 Endure
10 Vamoose!
14 French clerics
19 Bay window
20 __ vera
21 Ill-smelling
22 Minimum
23 Bumpkin
24 Speeder catcher
26 Mockery
27 Part of USA
28 Central American nation
29 Start of a quotation by 25D
31 Highland miss
33 Forerunners of CDs
35 Finished first
36 Rural stopover
37 Blunders
42 Divides into three
44 Part 2 of the quotation
49 Bring joy
50 Having the look of love
51 Ingenuity
52 Gobi Desert's continent
56 U.S. tennis stadium
57 Pitch symbol
58 Worship
60 Software buyers
61 Mile High Center architect, I.M. __
62 ZZZ letters
63 Garbles
64 Nikes, casually
65 Philosophy associated with 25D
70 East
72 In profusion
73 Period
74 __ of the blue
77 Cook with dry heat
78 Shoot at from cover
79 Rescue
81 Faultless
82 M. Descartes
83 Nothing in tennis
84 Florida city
86 Mountain subdivision
87 Part 3 of the quotation
91 Withholds approval
94 Bedroom pieces
95 Toronto's prov.
96 Army officer: abbr.
97 Predecessor of the CIA
98 Slanting type
103 End of the quotation
106 Excursion
111 Actress Sorvino
112 Hang in loose folds
113 Sweetheart
115 Sub tracker
116 Pariah
117 Actor Jannings
118 Trajectories
119 Long, narrow ridge
120 Curvy letters
121 Nevada destination
122 NBA team from 84A
123 Surrendered formally

DOWN

1 Faithful
2 Bouquet
3 __ Peak
4 Oracles
5 Open-plan dining area
6 Zhivago's love
7 Shepard or Greenspan
8 Soft drink
9 Sports group
10 Mil. rank
11 Golfers' vehicles
12 Oriental nursemaid
13 Printed mechanically
14 First king of Portugal
15 Boyfriend
16 Poetic
17 Opal or irid ending?
18 Backs of boats
25 American poet/philosopher
28 Quick kiss
30 Meat cuts
32 __ of Man
34 Greek letter
38 Domains
39 Transition point
40 Womanizer
41 E.T.'s vehicle
42 Need for liquid
43 Rubs out
44 Jalopy
45 Different
46 Papeete resident
47 Had a bite
48 Bound by an oath
53 Marine peak
54 Vex
55 Blockhead
57 Penny
59 Piano-violin piece
60 Module
62 Declaim violently
63 Clipped-off piece
64 __ gin fizz
66 Changes the timer
67 Boxing surface
68 Iroquois tribe
69 Word to the wise
70 Hockey great
71 Agile deer
75 Exhort
76 Prepared to drive
78 Paperback
79 Old adages
80 City in Iowa
81 Scathing review
83 In a slow tempo, musically
85 Wrath
86 Iron oxide
88 Assistants
89 6-pointers
90 Genesis: abbr.
91 Scribble
92 Habituates
93 Sandal ties
97 Country singer K.T. __
99 Love Italian-style
100 Formed a row
101 Enraged
102 Showed concern
104 "Pursuit of the Graf __"
105 Dub
107 Western state
108 Road roller
109 Andes autocrat
110 Home in a hemlock
114 "Telephone Line" rock grp.
115 U.S. defense grp.

INTERVIEW WITH A SHEPHERD

by Frances Hansen

ACROSS

1 Twin Cities suburb
6 Beer barrels
10 Queen's address
14 Buckets
19 Stinger's poison
20 Euphemistic oath
21 State on Lake Erie
22 "A Passage to __"
23 For the birds?
24 "Star Wars" princess
25 Hand: Sp.
26 Girder substance
27 Do male sheep behave well?
31 Dispatched
32 Tenth of DXX
33 Political coalition
34 Coming up
38 Act out
39 Top off a room
40 Explosive sound
43 31-syllable Japanese poem
44 Top-drawer
45 Where Anna met the king
46 Coadjutant
47 Why do young sheep never disobey?
52 Pause fillers
53 Ostrich kin
54 Violent conflicts
55 Video-game company
56 Swed. transportation company
57 Greek cross
58 Moving air
59 Yow, it's cold!
60 Why aren't sheep intelligent?
69 Caviar
70 Make dirty
71 Unnaturally pale
72 Motorists' org.
73 Kafka novel, with "The"
76 Smallest amount
77 Boitano or Boru
80 Chicago hrs.
81 Is it tiring to clip sheep?
86 Bar in a car
87 Anthem starter
88 First of the pot
89 Spooky
90 Comic Louis
91 German industrial region
92 Performer's engagements
93 "Out of Africa" author
95 Cut corners
96 City east of Moscow
97 "Lisa" of the Louvre
98 What is a shepherd's chief complaint?
108 Blanche's first name?
109 Italian automaker
110 Sicilian resort
111 One of the archangels
112 Leaves the stage
113 Greek bone
114 Tallow base
115 Of the kidneys

116 Finger or toe
117 Bring up
118 Highland Gaelic
119 Barcelata tune, "Maria __"

DOWN

1 "Mrs. Bridge" novelist Connell
2 "Whip It" group
3 1st letter
4 Genesis character
5 Man with no past?
6 "Constant Craving" singer
7 Standing
8 Way of walking
9 Iridescent birds
10 "__ Dearest"
11 Queequeg's captain
12 Japanese aboriginal
13 Night rays?
14 Six-shooter
15 Playful prank
16 Graphic starter?
17 In __ of
18 Mineo and Maglie
28 Hankering
29 Evangelist __ Semple McPherson
30 Ascend

34 Bear witness
35 Gung-ho
36 In actuality: Lat.
37 Wild blue yonder
38 Italian fashion
39 "I Met a Man" poet
40 Pocket bread
41 __-Neisse line
42 Start of cure?
44 Beer choice
45 Casual coinages
46 "The Jetsons" dog
48 Spout one's views
49 Inelegant denial
50 Castor to Pollux
51 Hammerin' Hank
57 Fairy-tale villain
58 Wheaton of "Stand by Me"
59 Bob Hope movie, "Call Me __"
61 In high dudgeon
62 Beatty-Hoffman bomb of 1987
63 Clamorous
64 DIY buys
65 Did the crawl
66 Shoe tiers
67 Highland miss

68 China's Sun __
73 Govt. agent
74 Bryan Ferry's group, __ Music
75 Land in the drink?
76 Hoped to have
77 Some Indians
78 Unpopular rodents
79 Wrath
82 "__ So Vain"
83 Seaport of Israel
84 Adulterate
85 French born
91 Most uncommon
92 Street edge
93 Offer free
94 Gerundial ending
95 __ Palace of Florence
97 Underground excavations
98 On the rocks
99 Ankle-length skirt
100 Math subj.
101 Seine tributary
102 __ morgana (mirage)
103 Bump on a log
104 Hurler Hershiser
105 "__ kleine Nachtmusik"
106 Break a habit
107 First lady of scat

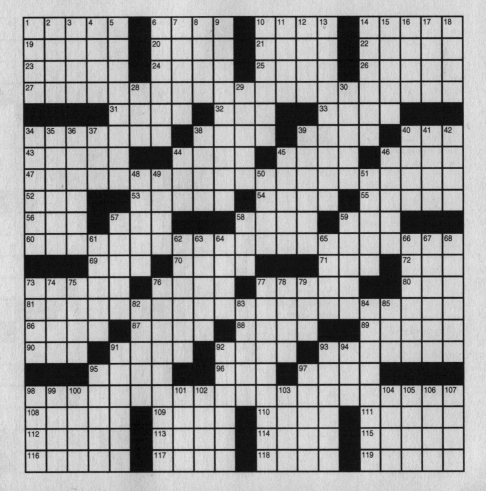

by Josiah Breward

ACROSS

1 Enlighten
6 Lambaste
10 Rise up
15 Dudley Do-Right's grp.
19 Taylor of "The Nanny"
20 Sacred
21 Type of orange
22 Greek philosopher, Zeno of __
23 PIERCE
26 Burst into flames
27 Completely rational
28 Crushable hats
29 Unit of magnetic flux density
30 Compass dir.
31 Khartoum's river
33 Actress Ruby
34 As cold as it gets?
35 GRANT
40 Chemical suffix
41 Shade of purple
44 Organized record
45 "NYPD Blue" co-star Jimmy
46 Southern hemisphere nat.
47 Doing the same old same old
49 Sked elements
52 Blind drunk
54 Pose questions
55 Wind organ
58 Anesthetic
60 Processes flour
63 Inhabitant of: suff.
64 Moises and Felipe of baseball
66 Cylindrical
69 U.S. tennis stadium
70 __ Rafael, CA
71 FORD
74 Broadway smash
75 Power current: abbr.
77 "The Merchant of Venice" lady
78 Spanish diacritical mark
79 Q-U connection
80 Palm-face encounters
82 African-American equality grp.
84 Bomb type
85 Shoshone
86 Whitewater
89 Elevator man?
91 Deft
93 Printer's measures
95 Selling feature
97 Finchley floozy
100 Sniffers
101 Comprehend
102 CLEVELAND
106 Minute amounts
108 Teachers' org.
109 Turn on a pivot
110 Droop
113 Gam and Moreno
114 Heritage
117 Mythological female runner
120 Business letter abbr.
121 LINCOLN
123 Remove from text
124 Shakespearean sprite
125 St. Paul's architect
126 Highest country
127 Fruity quaffs
128 Heavens to __!
129 Covers
130 TV's Cagney

DOWN

1 Bombeck and others
2 Bargains
3 Braided linen tape
4 Supporting pieces
5 Slangy okay
6 County cop
7 Marilyn's "blonde" part?
8 Presidential candidate Landon
9 Advice-column initialism
10 Lion, at times
11 Values highly
12 Enticement
13 Inspirations of individualists
14 Thriller writer Deighton
15 Medieval stringed instrument
16 BUSH
17 Pigeon hawks
18 Cure-all
24 Quaker William
25 Make over
29 Secret meetings
32 Mystery writer, __ Stanley Gardner
34 Palo __, CA
35 Sedan or SUV, e.g.
36 Eyelike
37 Outdoor gala
38 Food of the gods
39 __ Abner
41 Acts as the go-between
42 Put on the hard drive
43 WASHINGTON
48 Dutch flower
50 Magnetize
51 Skedaddle!
53 Spanish aunt
56 Porto-__, Benin
57 One of the Channel Isles
59 In the past, in the past
61 Bloom on a brae
62 Small sofas
65 Mlle. from Madrid
67 Delta deposit
68 Not sideways
72 Ferrara farewell
73 Zodiac sign
76 Tax adviser: abbr.
81 Empty spots
83 Pocketed bread?
87 Egyptian fertility goddess
88 Spring fwd. system
90 Department store on Fifth Avenue
92 Leader of the Three Stooges
93 Erik of "CHiPs"
94 Deserved
96 Languages
98 Associated
99 Germans
103 Just about
104 Like delicate fabric
105 Paper quantity
107 Stems of bamboo
110 Shoot from hiding
111 World supporter?
112 Highlanders
114 Attract
115 Egress
116 Ketch's sister
118 Yearn
119 Son of Adam
121 Practical sci. class
122 Mentalist Geller

by Ed Voile

ACROSS

1 Pope who negotiated with Attila
6 Facing
14 Twin city
20 Arum family plant
21 Laundry detergent additive
22 Baby's berth
23 Feature of a Chinese jacket
25 Put in new padding
26 Like an epee
27 Breach of secrecy
28 Sling more mud
29 Actor Curry
30 Japanese electronics giant
31 Hive builder
32 Yours and mine
33 Mantle's teammate
36 Platform in a theater
38 Programming language
40 "Roll Over Beethoven" singer
42 Actress Ryan
43 __ City, Florida
47 Trucker's perch
48 Neighbor of Israel
49 Tropical plant with brilliant flowers
51 Sailor's call
52 Ham radio operator
54 Human seat
55 Make by putting parts together
57 "Born Free" lioness
58 Mai __ cocktail
60 Artistic conservative
62 2nd smallest state
63 180 degrees longitude, roughly
69 Above, poetically
70 Bricklayers
71 Have lunch
72 Small combo
74 In an unkempt manner
75 Our sun
77 Avant-garde art movement
81 Keep from happening
83 Girder substance
84 Soup servings
86 Actor Brynner
87 "Calendar Girl" singer
89 "Another 48 __"
90 Do some yard maintenance
92 Snacks
94 Thwarts
95 Rene of "Get Shorty"
96 Pedantic person
99 Bro's sib
100 Father
101 Charged particle
102 Failed to carry out a promise
104 Wind blast
105 Some desks
110 Codger
111 Experiencing fame
113 As if this __ enough...

114 Infrequency
115 Chilling
116 Wasp wounds
117 Shatner show
118 Frock

DOWN

1 Identical
2 Abbr. on folk music lyrics
3 Extensive
4 Like very clear memories
5 Harem members
6 Medical suffix
7 Soprano Lily __
8 New G.I.
9 Medical study of the ear
10 Greek goddess of the moon
11 Dental filling
12 Tropical wood
13 Slip up
14 Sound of locked brakes
15 Very French
16 Soap choice
17 Nice goodbye?
18 Of an arm bone
19 Lascivious looks
24 Dreamer's letters
28 Occupant: abbr.

30 Poet Teasdale
31 Author of "National Velvet"
33 Roman 1300
34 Melville's captain
35 Midway mark?
36 Medical fluids
37 Stumble
38 Correspondents
39 Letters on cars
41 Writers' credits
42 Of the breasts
44 Nita, the old-time actress
45 Ruhr Valley city
46 Hackneyed
49 Ivy League school
50 Largest land mass
53 66 or A1A, e.g.
55 Body lice
56 Actress Getty
59 Javelin's path
60 Successful searchers
61 Pekoe or oolong
63 Minute amounts
64 Pluck
65 Tested or tasted
66 Iowa college town
67 Grows choppers
68 Inc. in Britain

73 Protestant Irish
75 Spirit
76 Has the title
78 Nautical assents
79 Club fees
80 Besides
82 Ring decision: abbr.
84 French cheese
85 Moseyed
88 Concurs
90 Omen
91 Even more puny
93 Covered up
94 "Star Wars" star
96 Ship fronts
97 Find a new tenant
98 Madagascar primate
100 Kama __
101 French island
103 Band of hoods
104 No-see-um
105 Upslope
106 City on the Irtysh
107 Hideous creature
108 Greek letters
109 Marie and Therese, e.g.
111 Tax grp.
112 Celtic Neptune

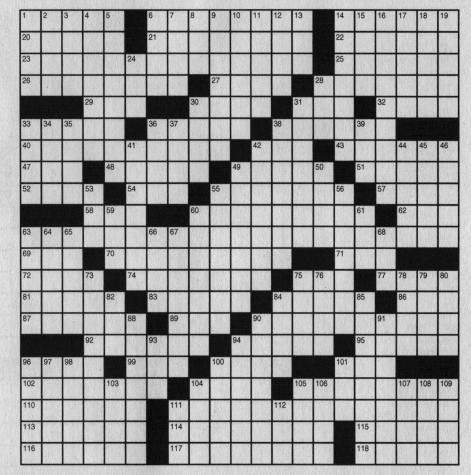

by Alan P. Olschwang

ACROSS

1 Lump of dirt
5 Another time
10 Assns.
14 Irene and Meg
19 Wedding shower?
20 Nero's successor
21 Seldom seen
22 Macabre
23 "Funny Girl" co-star Sharif
24 Mr. T's outfit
25 Grace ending
26 Particular bias
27 Movie industry
30 Getty and Winwood
32 Step
33 Single guy
34 Peachy keen
35 Slammin' Sammy
39 Proficiently
41 Used to be
45 False leads
49 That ship
50 Daisylike flower
51 The Greatest
52 Waits on
53 Greek crosses
54 Knocks for a loop
55 Tooted
57 Normandy town
58 Ships' tillers
59 Hackneyed
60 Second Hebrew letter
61 Capital of Phoenicia
62 Metrical foot
63 Adversary
64 Guts
66 Genesis craft
67 Esters of boric acid
71 Wee bit
72 Starting place
74 Former Russian ruler
76 Aga __ III
77 Cooked in a wok
80 __ Island, NY
81 Right on maps
82 Desert lily
83 Survived
84 Off one's rocker
85 French port
87 Part of Canada's Y.T.
88 European peninsula
89 Earth: pref.
90 Combat decoration
92 Sheet of glass
93 Track tout
95 Bewildered
96 "Common Sense" writer
98 Dynamic starter?
100 Create a gorge
104 Turner of "Body Heat"
107 Leopard without spots
111 Trojan War story
112 Environmental science: abbr.

114 Australian actor Sam
115 Mandlikova of tennis
116 Prima __
117 Take the bus
118 Card for readers
119 Goddess of strife
120 Does ushering
121 Luge
122 Cut pieces
123 Tom, Dick or Harry, e.g.

DOWN

1 Span
2 Demarcate
3 City in central Florida
4 Whirling __
5 Seaweed product
6 Hoods' heaters
7 Actor Guinness
8 Girder pieces
9 Kin of ID cards
10 Sun's color, at times
11 Hit head-on
12 Gardener's appendage
13 Lacking meaning
14 Video-game button
15 Cowardly characteristics
16 Inland sea of Asia

17 Baseball team
18 Hardens
28 Sea eagles
29 St. Louis bridge
31 Perth's river
36 Put up
37 Displays
38 Pearl gatherer
40 Sacred hymn
42 Needle case
43 Tenant's expense
44 Highland tongue
45 Jewish teacher
46 DeGeneres series
47 Weight-loss plans
48 Hawaiian goose
50 "The Maltese Falcon" co-star
53 Yellowish-brown wood
56 Something of dubious value
58 Employs
63 Mid-life decade
65 __ longlegs
66 Sale-tag disclaimer
67 Dense volcanic rock
68 Eighth Greek letter

69 More than ready
70 Contemptuous sound
72 Edit
73 Choir section
74 Glum drop?
75 Simple marine organism
77 Go ga-ga
78 Comic Rudner
79 Infamous tsar
80 Railroad employees
85 Alternative to raisins
86 Luster
90 Outer banana
91 Made of baked clay
93 Cravat
94 Set aside for later
97 Robert and Alan
99 Saltwater expanse
101 Scarlett's last name
102 Jeans fabric
103 Delete
104 Youngsters
105 Spiny African plant
106 Turner of tunes
108 Soprano __ Te Kanawa
109 Drop heavily
110 Contingencies: abbr.
113 Lofty work

by Bill Swain

ACROSS

1 Lay eyes on
5 Infamous Soviet dictator
11 Consciousness
20 Hoarfrost
21 Desert Inn or Mirage, e.g.
22 Interior designer
23 Start of a comment by Theodore Roosevelt
26 Aerial combat mission
27 Sports officials, for short
28 Menu plan
29 Kin through marriage
32 Difficult undertaking
34 Slobbers
39 Part 2 of the comment
44 Eyelashes
45 Adolescent
46 Sis's sib
47 Oozes
50 First name in crooners
51 19th-century botanist Gray
52 Erie Canal mule
54 Gun-owners' lobby, briefly
57 Clumsy fellow
58 Went by horse
59 Passing fancy
60 Red's Kadiddlehopper
62 Donkey
64 Drum beat
66 Part 3 of the comment
71 Gaucho's address
72 Pronounced indistinctly
73 Bonheur and Parks
77 Part 4 of the comment
82 Accumulated
85 Qty.
86 French city on the Riviera
87 Freq. units
88 Tapered tuck
89 Finished growing
92 987-65-4321 grp.
94 Simple bed
95 Cipher code
96 Nobel Prize winner, __ Wiesel
97 Entity
99 Light touch
101 Bell tone
102 Tissue: suff.
104 Part 5 of the comment
109 Having a will
112 Bridge coup
113 Hang down
114 "Legends of the Fall" star Brad
116 Work gang
118 Bind with bandages
122 End of Theodore Roosevelt's comment
129 State a parallel example
130 Intercede
131 Melody
132 Grew more gravelly
133 Polishing machine
134 Ollie's funny partner

DOWN

1 Mardi __
2 Celeb's ride
3 __ the tentmaker
4 Refer to
5 Actor Maximilian
6 The way, in China
7 Gray shade
8 Perjurer
9 Pix in pix
10 Dieting adjective
11 Pt. of speech
12 Garden invader
13 Bitterly pungent
14 CBer's "message received"
15 Amatory
16 Bobbsey twin
17 Tours summer
18 Drunkard
19 Sell-out letters
24 Drunkard
25 Zigzag turns
30 Casual walker
31 Military science
33 Film critic Pauline
35 Tremulous pitch changes
36 T.S. __
37 Singer Ronstadt
38 Home-video show host
39 Shepherds' crooks
40 One Borgia
41 Frontal
42 Hither's partner
43 Lion's name
48 Run smoothly
49 Piercing pain
52 Eats voraciously
53 Candidate Landon
55 Sicilian city
56 Gurus' compounds
61 Netting
63 Pompous gaits
65 Gunner's spot
67 Damp to the max
68 Stevedores' grp.
69 100 yrs.
70 Tennis situation
74 Himalayan state
75 Parthenon honoree
76 Sun-moon-Earth configuration
78 Seasoning
79 Actress McClurg
80 Conquering hero
81 Environmental pref.
82 Skillful
83 "My Dinner with Andre" director
84 Opera songs
90 Pizza order
91 Concludes
93 Appropriate
98 Arroyo
100 Assistance
101 Takes off
103 Syrup sources
105 Christmas songs
106 Feminist Bloomer
107 More likely to pry
108 Wolf's wail
110 Book name
111 Actor Hawke
115 Head of France
117 Break a habit
119 Brazen solicitor
120 Mandlikova of tennis
121 Idyllic garden
122 Learning inst.
123 Excessively
124 Memorable time
125 Timetable abbr.
126 Make one
127 Make free
128 Enzyme: suff.

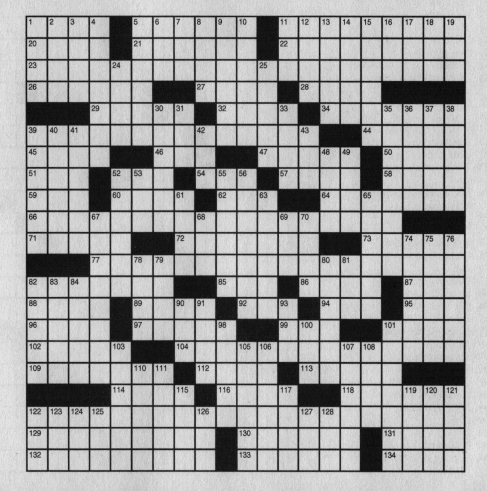

ANIMAL CRACKERS

by Edgar Fontaine

ACROSS

1 Chuckle
5 Bouquet
10 Embarrass
15 First husband?
19 Got an A
20 Coffeehouses
21 Calgary Stampede, e.g.
22 Withered
23 FOX
26 Gush forth
27 Liner stops
28 Baldwin and Guinness
29 Textbook forward pass
31 Oodles
32 Horse do
33 Distant ones
34 Encloses snugly: var.
37 Entertainment venue
39 Fires upon
42 Parts
43 MONKEY
45 Filthy place
46 God of love
47 Climb a rope
49 West and Murray
50 Be up and about
51 This moment
52 WOLF
56 Exuberant cry
57 Wholeness
59 Of sheep
60 Groups of 13 witches
61 Parts of parkas
62 Tolerate
63 Site of 1692 witchcraft trials
64 Garbo and others
66 Sierra __
67 Structure of a plane
70 Mountain ash
71 BUFFALO
73 Word with session or sheet
74 Exclamations of surprise and pleasure
75 "__ Lisa"
76 Firepower
77 Inner Hebrides island
78 Cycle or pod starter?
79 APE
83 Wide receiver Don
84 In the same breath
86 Dialogue of a drama
87 Jalopies
88 Sacred Hebrew scripture
89 Pops
90 Soft, thick lump
91 Southern beauties
93 Of primary importance
94 Lieutenants' commands
98 Logical beginning?
99 DOG
102 Erelong
103 Betel palm
104 Equality group est. in 1910
105 Civil rights leader Parks
106 Carried a tune
107 Transparent wrap
108 Ocean-current vortexes
109 Residue

DOWN

1 Headgear
2 Pain in the neck, e.g.
3 Vindictive Greek goddess
4 Emigrants from orphanages
5 Next century oaks
6 Inflatable boats
7 Switch positions
8 Ran into
9 Feeling inadequate
10 Stock of weapons
11 Italian bowling game
12 Summer thirst quenchers
13 DC bigwig
14 Self-assured succeeders
15 Help
16 BEAR
17 Length times width
18 Whimper
24 Tiger's long clubs
25 African antelope
30 Fiddlesticks!
33 Second-story man
34 Dancing Castle
35 Imbecile
36 RAT
37 Friendship
38 Nevada destination
39 Marshy lowland
40 Noun-forming suffix
41 Amateurs
44 Make scholarly corrections
47 Luges
48 Crude shelters
50 Rescuer
52 React to a bad pun
53 Off
54 Dame Edith __
55 Muscular power
56 "The Right Stuff" writer
58 Scintillas
60 Reiner and Jung
62 Crevasse pinnacle
63 Indication
64 Persona non __
65 Lion's plaints
66 Anderson and others
67 Shivering fits
68 Perchance
69 Some rapiers
71 Romanian round dance: var.
72 Fairy-tale monster
75 Site of the Battle of Bull Run
77 Land on a coast
79 Center
80 Nome resident
81 Of ocean motion
82 Take off, as a backpack
83 Stock
85 Oriental tea
87 Metal fasteners
89 Capital of Bangladesh
90 Candied
91 Prejudice
92 Best of fiction
93 Coffin platform
94 Bosc or anjou
95 Smell
96 Rocket cap
97 Stolen money
100 La-la lead-in
101 Jay follower

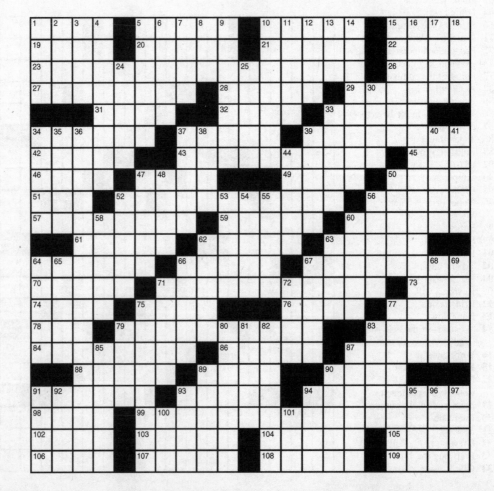

POETIC JUSTICE

by Robert H. Wolfe

ACROSS
1 __ Carta
6 End-table item
10 Outline
14 Brainy
19 Sign on: var.
20 Nobel Prize winner Wiesel
21 Italian currency, once
22 Edible root
23 Not the least bit
24 Bad habit
25 Irish Rose lover
26 Stood
27 First line of a verse
31 Skinny twins?
32 Poetic valley
33 Cave-dwelling fish
34 Doctrines
35 Sets sights
36 Thwack
38 Surrender formally
39 Burn the midnight oil
42 Cries of discovery
43 Folkways
45 Docs' grp.
48 Second line of the verse
53 Touched down
54 Colossus
55 Another time
56 Guam capital
57 Chilean currency
58 To be, in Toulouse
59 Practice one's uppercut
60 Posts on a bulletin board
61 Attracted
63 Exclamations of comprehension
64 Rich kid in "Nancy"
66 Poems with pastoral themes
69 With skill
71 Weather grp.
72 Sitarist Shankar
76 Geneva's lake
77 Woodwind instrument
78 Beer stimulant
79 In the center of
80 Third line of the verse
84 __ Yoelson, a.k.a. Al Jolson
85 "Planet of the __"
86 Rhythmic cadence
87 Sartre novel
88 Old sailors
90 Obstacles
91 Knights' titles
92 On land
95 Reach for a pianist
97 Flatten
98 Aging gravitation
101 Last line of the verse
106 "The Lost Galleon" poet
107 Telephoned
108 Standard image of a business
109 Weasellike mammal
110 City near Bremen, Germany
111 In the direction of shelter
112 __ vincit omnia
113 McClurg and Brickell

114 Burpee order
115 Nebbish
116 Selfsame
117 Dispatches

DOWN
1 Gettysburg winner
2 Writer Chekhov
3 Neutral shades
4 __ contendere
5 Delta sediment
6 Tiers
7 Carroll's girl
8 Isinglass
9 Outer banana
10 Saturn or Mercury, e.g.
11 Calumny's kin
12 Opera songs
13 __-do-well
14 Spoke
15 Of rodents
16 Overhead
17 Change an alarm
18 Lock or shock
28 Frenzied rioters
29 Chow chow controller
30 Dutch genre painter
35 __ Khomeini

36 Polish
37 Steam engine inventor
38 Work gang
39 Exchange
40 Narrative
41 Sale-tag disclaimer
42 Conferrable
43 Fugard play, "Boesman and __"
44 Burn the beef
45 Gardner and others
46 Server's handout
47 Pronto!
49 Nickelodeon's Nick at __
50 Gullible dupes
51 Pitiful cry
52 Know-nothing
59 Timid
60 Coat with a valuable metal
62 Arm bone
63 Designer Cassini
65 Drying kiln
66 Ingrid in "Casablanca"
67 __ ex machina
68 Family activities org.
70 "__ on the Side" (Goldberg film)

71 Simon and Young
73 Amo, __, amat...
74 Depraved
75 Inspiration
77 Sorry 'bout that
78 Norse giant
81 Removed skin
82 "The George and __ Show"
83 Tender touches
88 Solicited orders
89 Harold and Michael
90 Slammed
91 Appetizing
92 Grate collection
93 Ignominy
94 Tribe on the move
95 Bobby of the Chicago Seven
96 One who yearns
97 Strictness
98 Polio vaccine developer
99 Suffered sickness
100 TV's Cagney
102 Husk of grain
103 Eastern European
104 Weighty volume
105 Green shade

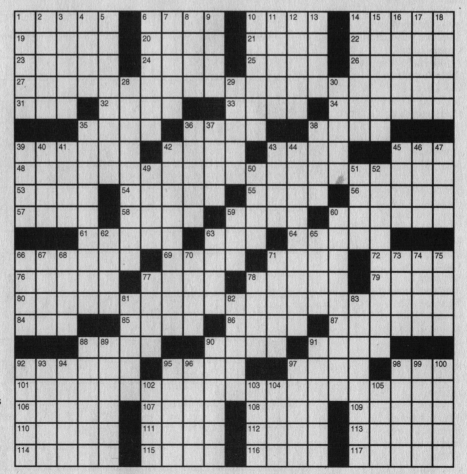

BOWLERAMA

by Alan P. Olschwang

ACROSS

1 Off to one side
6 "The Purple People Eater" singer Wooley
10 Rembrandt, the painter
15 Mil. rank
19 Recipient
20 Mandlikova of tennis
21 Monte, of the Negro Leagues
22 Bull of the Pampas
23 Temple table
24 Adam's grandson
25 One of the Judds
26 Destroy
27 X marks the spot?
30 "__ It a Pity?"
31 Feather stickum?
32 Mapped
33 Gilbert and Sullivan opera, with "The"
35 Concerning
38 __ Khan IV
40 Goof
41 Peel
42 Items in trunks
46 So that's it
48 Residence
52 Short jaunt
53 Journey segment
54 Gather in
56 News carrier, of a sort
58 Corrected manuscript
60 Gossip channel?
62 "__ kleine Nachtmusik"
63 Second viewing
64 Breed of cat
65 Makes more current
67 Chair-maker's material
69 Captured back
71 Brief investigation
74 Simoleons
78 Jerry Stiller's Anne
82 Fit
83 Recipe quantities
85 "Gidget" co-star James
86 Molecular chains
88 O.T. book
89 Onassis to pals
90 Response time
91 Great __ Lake
92 Sports stn.
94 Rhythmic hoofers
97 Suckered
99 Inventor Whitney
101 Detroit workers' grp.
102 Helper: abbr.
103 Bitter fruit
106 Tigers of the ACC
109 Addams Family cousin
111 Landed
112 Jekyll and Hyde, e.g.
118 African fetish
119 Elite social category
120 High: pref.
121 Cranny
122 Fragrance

123 On edge
124 Christmas carol
125 Nordic toast
126 M. Descartes
127 One-hit wonders of '69, __ & Evans
128 Chipper
129 Streisand film

DOWN

1 Jewish month
2 Actress Negri of silent movies
3 Against: pref.
4 Property merchant
5 __ incognita
6 Mets' stadium
7 Human-powered vehicle
8 Methuselah's father
9 Port of Iraq
10 Yankee uniforms
11 Pencil ends
12 Duck and dodge
13 Paint a word picture
14 Conundrum
15 Union buster
16 Composer John Philip __
17 Pulverize

18 Kemo Sabe's pal
28 Spoke from a soapbox
29 Mine vein
34 "Dies __" (day of wrath)
35 "My Name Is __ Lev"
36 China from Stoke-on-Trent
37 Animal with a fleshy proboscis
39 Entertainer's engagement
41 Carter's harvest
43 Verdugo and Bonner
44 Short trips
45 Connection line
47 Center starter?
49 Final notice, briefly
50 Over with
51 Gives a once-over
55 Mimic
57 Pumpkin or squash
59 Red-headed buzzard
60 Actress Scala
61 Gallery porch
64 Handled the helm
66 Bailiwick
68 Head of France
70 Pause fillers
71 Track circuits
72 Ancient Greek coin

73 __ podrida
75 Published epistle
76 Bagel topper
77 Pickings
79 City on the Rhone
80 Brings up
81 Feeling of anxiety
84 Donkey
85 Retract
87 Tableland
89 Nabokov book
93 Loose cloak
95 Words wit
96 Quiet and stealthy
98 Bogus
100 Little devil
103 Paramount
104 Escape detection
105 French mustard
106 Resist separation
107 Penn and Connery
108 Lowest deck
110 Fragrant yellow flower
113 Not guilty, e.g.
114 Unctuous
115 Image of a god
116 One singled out
117 Cry for attention

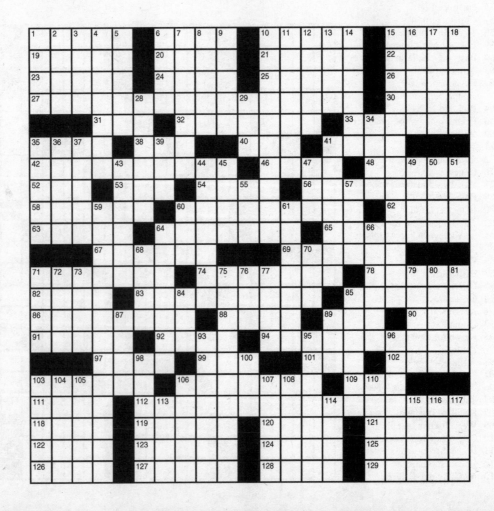

BY THE NUMBERS

by Edgar Fontaine

ACROSS

1 Flaccid
5 Outfit
10 Corday's victim
15 Nora's pooch
19 Gobi's continent
20 Astrologer Sydney
21 Ballplayer Jerry
22 Glum drop?
23 "79 __" (Robbins novel)
25 "__ 451" (Bradbury novel)
27 Glorifiers
28 Disfigures
30 Tasteful
31 Nimble
32 Director Forman
33 "The Man" of baseball
34 Eavesdrop
37 Luxury car model
38 Tangible
42 Nile dam
43 Naughty
44 "60 __" (TV news show)
46 Union letters in Mich.
47 Lament loudly
48 Sages
49 Galena and cuprite
50 End of cigar?
51 Afore
52 "3 __" (B.B. King song)
56 Evaluator
57 Unanticipated delays
59 Goddess of peace
60 Dissuades
61 "Bad, Bad __ Brown"
62 Police blotter entry
63 Iron clothes?
64 Yankee lefty Ford
66 People with upturned noses?
67 Quantity of medicine
70 Despised
71 "77 __" ('60s TV drama)
73 Eisenhower
74 Meal scraps
75 Land of llamas
76 __ back (relaxed)
77 Jump
78 Choice: abbr.
79 "16 __" (hit by the Crests)
82 Popeye's Olive
83 Rhythmic throb
84 Green beryls
86 George Bernard and Robert
88 Baby sitter
89 Mimics
90 Uses a stiletto
91 Polynesian dance
92 Band for identification
95 Military dress hat
96 Despot
100 "21 __" (TV police drama)
102 "101 __" (Disney film)
104 Yiddish writer Sholem __

105 Spooky
106 __ John and Bernie Taupin
107 Sicilian volcano
108 Warren Beatty film
109 Wets thoroughly
110 Active pastime
111 Clairvoyant

DOWN

1 Reindeer herdsman
2 Munich's river
3 Actress Sorvino
4 Neighbor of Iran
5 Keep under control
6 Coarse variety of corundum
7 Brown shades
8 S. Amer. nation
9 Blend beforehand
10 Italian gangsters
11 Second president
12 Arena cheers
13 Jordan's nickname
14 Bridge supports
15 Goddess of wisdom
16 Appear
17 Shadow
18 Bohemian

24 Quaking tree
26 Lowest levels of high tide
29 College grad, casually
32 Field doc
33 Fills completely
34 Bodies of water
35 Val d'__ , France
36 "__ 16" (Jerry Lee Lewis tune)
37 Largest city of Nigeria
38 Use a blender
39 "__ 8" (Liz Taylor film)
40 Some time after
41 Pitchers
43 Contrary
45 Parts of speech
48 The real __
50 Cyrus, the financier
52 Equipped with paddles
53 Metric weights
54 Illegal contribution
55 Minimum
56 Swab twice
58 French beasts
60 Artoo Detoo, e.g.
62 Invalidate
63 Month in Paris?
64 "__ Life Is It, Anyway?"

65 Sheik's women
66 Irrational numbers
67 Sticks it out
68 Proclamation of the czar
69 Pariah
71 Transmits
72 Brakes
75 Color ranges of artists
77 Wildly foolish acts
79 Fear and Cod
80 Landed properties
81 Bard of Avon: abbr.
83 Flyer
85 Nader and others
87 Homes
88 "Teenage __ Ninja Turtles"
90 Valentino role
91 Wit
92 Partly open
93 Subterfuge
94 C times XXIV
95 Inoculators
96 Palo __, CA
97 Evaluate
98 __ of Cleves
99 Former Russian ruler
101 Old-time motorcar
103 High mountain

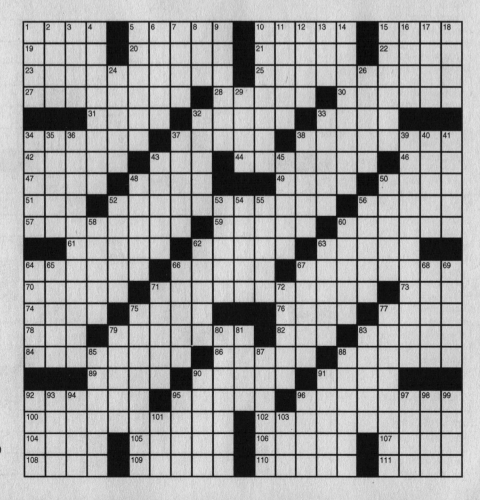

by Josiah Breward

ACROSS

1 Hollow tube
5 Dispatch
9 Hunter and Ward
16 Hoodwinked
19 Les Etats-__
20 Optimistic
21 Select a jury
22 Bonzo or Clyde of the movies
23 John le Carre novel
26 San Francisco hill
27 Curses
28 Lines for notes
29 Kisser
30 U.S. Federal Agcy.
31 Moving swiftly
32 Heavy volume
33 One woodwind
35 Mach+ jets
36 __ wheel
38 Betty Grable, e.g.
41 Adjective-forming suffix
42 Moped
44 Game played on horseback
45 Used push-buttons
46 Australian state: abbr.
49 Third grade
50 Vision starter?
51 Granny
53 Hebrew letter
55 Descendant
58 Preventer
61 Raccoonlike carnivore
62 1965 Disney movie
65 Otto I's realm
66 Caribbean capital
68 Thurman of "Pulp Fiction"
69 Wish undone
70 Piloted a glider
72 Any person
73 Shell games
77 Danish physicist Bohr
78 Belgrade populace
80 Maui's neighbor
81 Backspace
82 Brazilian dance
83 "__ Dick"
85 Want __
87 Narcs' grp.
88 Earth pigment
90 Architect Saarinen
91 Paid a visit
94 Change unit
95 In the bag
98 Breaks out
102 Impatient interjections
103 Highland miss
104 Historic stretches
106 Saltwater expanse
107 N. Mandela's party
108 Watch kids
109 Larry of "F Troop"
111 Half a Washington river
112 Ultimate degree
113 Hard-to-find item
117 Wide shoe width
118 Trap
119 Nudnik
120 1958 Pulitzer winner
121 '60s campus activist group
122 Contents of wills
123 Tongue-clicking sounds
124 Beatty and Buntline

DOWN

1 Postpone
2 Collect a lungful
3 Flemish painter, __ Brueghel
4 Rolle and Williams
5 __ Lanka
6 Composer of "The Planets"
7 Form of a chemical element
8 Lake near Tahoe
9 Abundantly prevalent
10 Current units, for short
11 Auditor's letters
12 Solo of "Star Wars"
13 Captivate
14 __ Gulliver
15 Smeltery residue
16 Is touch and go
17 Disciple
18 Humiliated
24 Anticipatory action
25 Hot box
33 Leer at
34 Brief life?
35 Tuscany city
37 Observe
39 Make vertical
40 __ Pot
43 Wagon train direction
45 Look sullen
46 Tijuana nosh
47 "Citizen Kane" co-star Everett
48 Sheet bends
50 Bottom line
51 Peacock network
52 Gardner et al.
54 Education-minded grp.
56 Pals
57 Metrical foot
58 Lake in northwest Russia
59 Ultimatum phrase
60 Exodus division?
63 Panoply
64 Destroy
67 Queequeg's captain
71 Atmosphere
74 One-million connection
75 Nudge
76 Thailand, formerly
79 Shelters for livestock
83 Recruit's dinner
84 Mine vein
86 Barely passing grade
88 Gas grades
89 Had value
90 U.S. Open golf champion of 1994
91 Bush fruit
92 Cochise and Geronimo
93 Mexican peninsula
95 UFO crew
96 Right up-to-date
97 Inert gas
99 Mammal's coat
100 Powdered
101 Moves sinuously
105 Greg Norman's nickname
108 Dundee dagger
109 Withered
110 Equal scores
114 Recombinant letters
115 Long.'s counterpart
116 Gridiron meas.

JUNIOR ACHIEVEMENT

by Robert H. Wolfe

ACROSS

1 Shadowy
6 Feature of a fedora
10 Wine stopper
14 Disconcert
19 Remove knots
20 Mother of Apollo and Artemis
21 Bologna hello or goodbye
22 Mythological half-woman monster
23 Chelsea apartments
24 Young cowboy's song?
27 Closed hand
28 Blue ceramic pigments
29 Rubber bands
30 Forsyth novel for youngsters?
34 Trawling device
35 One of the Bobbsey Twins
36 IBM units, once
37 Enduring
40 Banished people
44 Stick it out
45 F in music?
49 Semi-eternity?
50 Say more
51 Cheers for matadors
52 Old
53 Calls it quits
55 Descriptive name
57 Cousteau invention
58 Actor Wynn
59 Envelop
60 Flatfoot
62 Eleventh letters
63 Timeless
65 Go back over
68 Bit of derring-do
71 Touch lightly
72 Unadulterated
73 Took spoils
77 Pond scum
79 Giving more lip
82 Guy Fawkes Day blaze
83 Xylophone's cousin
85 Prepared to hit a driver
86 Operated
87 Indigo dye
88 Actor Estevez
89 Lah-de-dah ways
90 Suffers in reputation
92 Drool
94 Cereal grain
95 Mediocre grade
96 Part of AT&T
99 Children's song?
104 Fliers
107 Small crowns
108 Utensil
110 Makes childishly angry?
113 Former name for an English county
114 Square
115 European sea eagle
116 Teardrop-shaped fruit
117 Evita or Juan of Argentina
118 Ancient Greek colonnades
119 Extremely short time: abbr.
120 River of Caen, France
121 __ we all?

DOWN

1 What you sit on
2 In the dark
3 Secret supply
4 Child's whip?
5 Sure thing!
6 Nonrigid airship
7 Changed charts
8 Slanted type
9 Markham et al.
10 Quarter M
11 Resembling: suff.
12 Horse track
13 Eucalyptus eaters
14 Landon et al.
15 Thai cash
16 At full speed: archaic
17 Inasmuch as
18 Old verb form
25 CIA's predecessor
26 World Series perfect-game pitcher
28 Browned
31 Golf score
32 Group of eight
33 Split second
38 Adherents: suff.
39 Similar children?
40 Nighttime
41 Bigfoot's shoe size
42 Dissimulation
43 McBain and McMahon
44 Lose footing
46 Marine color
47 July birthstone
48 Little legumes
51 Translucent gem
52 Doer: suff.
54 Hood's heater
55 Historic period
56 __ homo (Behold the man!)
59 Hoops grp.
61 Collar types
64 Tabula __
65 Felt regret
66 Blow it
67 Male heir
68 Notoriety
69 Biblical land
70 Soil: pref.
72 Fruit desserts
74 Actress Yothers
75 __ the Red
76 Remove text
78 First Oscar-winning actor Jannings
80 Ex-Blue Jay pitcher Dave
81 Missionary Junipero __
82 __-relief
84 Child's injury
86 Member of a service club
89 Degraders
90 California basketball player
91 Choice: abbr.
93 Drinks makers
94 San Luis __, CA
96 Iberian river
97 Meet segment
98 Stone: pref.
100 Had lunch
101 Personnel subgroup
102 Watered silk
103 Semimetallic element
105 Large land mass
106 Recipe abbr.
109 Easter season
111 First grade
112 Required: abbr.
113 Health haven

by Ed Voile

ACROSS

1 Squid's defense
4 Wander
8 Frederick Loewe musical, "__ Your Wagon"
13 Doctrines
19 Bossy bellow
20 Musical medley
21 Impertinent gazer
22 Nation of Roma
23 Political favors
27 Brainstorms
28 John Smith, perhaps
29 Soup dispensers
30 Rub out
31 Verdi opera
33 Traditional knowledge
34 Land mass: abbr.
37 Farm layer
38 Making a chancy purchase
42 Tapestry in "Hamlet"
43 Yo!
44 Kidney enzyme
45 Eared seal
48 In front
51 Gets by with less
53 Like Cheerios
54 "Waiting for Lefty" dramatist
55 Sri Lanka language
56 Support one's family
60 Mom-&-pop store grp.
63 Model Macpherson
64 Airline to Jerusalem
65 Humdinger
66 Females
67 Soak flax
68 Amateur broadcasters
73 Roman tyrant and others
74 Flinch
75 __ blanche (unconditional authority)
76 Lassos
79 Enticements
80 Word used to describe Snow White
82 __ we all?
83 Campus org.
84 Lacked
85 Enjoy the lap of luxury
91 Golf score
94 Lemon or orange ending
95 French city near Le Havre
96 Plants of the arum family
97 Spout nonsense
98 Put back in the granary
101 Hunter of the stars
102 Walks worriedly
103 Waste
108 John and Maureen
109 Loom bar
110 Bruins of coll. sports
111 Enjoyable
112 Innate ability
113 Chestnut-and-white horses
114 Preserving substance
115 Still

DOWN

1 Like a little devil
2 Brain box
3 Chosen one?
4 Reiner and Lowe
5 End of pay?
6 Broadcast
7 Rick of "Ghostbusters"
8 Propelling a raft
9 One of the three Graces
10 French islands
11 Reverse pic
12 Group of three
13 7-time U.S. tennis champion
14 Latin and others: abbr.
15 Cager Archibald
16 Pronunciation skips
17 Yucatan uncle
18 __ Diego
24 Jay follower
25 Spirited vigor
26 Indian garb
31 Continental prefix
32 Meg or Irene
33 Invented facts
35 Stopping wedge
36 Jay, the comic
38 Take along
39 Look of the moon
40 "Catch-22" star
41 Outer banana
42 Coeur d'__, Idaho
45 Temperate
46 Gen. __ G. Wheeler
47 Listing to one side
48 Ms. Rogers St. Johns
49 __ up (angry)
50 Fractional ending
51 Twinned crystal
52 Love on the Loire
54 Sharif and Epps
55 Neutral shade
57 Valentine shape
58 "Miami Vice" co-star
59 Political coalitions
60 Beach
61 Lahr and Lance
62 Plus feature
66 Get the ball rolling
68 Former British PM
69 Miniature
70 Sundial three
71 Can. province
72 Getting the top grade
73 Half a golf course
76 Refrain syllables
77 Saharan
78 "__ of Fortune"
79 Blessing
80 Saudi leader
81 Fusses
83 More inclined
84 Grossly wicked
86 Most slippery
87 Festive occasion
88 German chemical cartel, I.G. __
89 Attempters
90 Ungulate's foot
91 Conciliate
92 Line of inquiry
93 Act offended
97 Uncooked
99 Tours to be
100 Hand's breadth
101 Greek peak
102 H.S. junior's exam
103 Foldaway bed
104 Gotcha!
105 Thai's neighbor
106 Electronics co.
107 Corner pipe

by C.L. Flowers

ACROSS

1 Greek fabulist of yore
6 Whip stroke
10 Armenian composer Khachaturian
14 Commerce
19 City on the Ganges
20 Durante's theme song, "__ Dinka Doo"
21 Program choices
22 Healthier
23 Spoiled kids
24 Iwo Jima flag
27 Do 360s
29 Stupor
30 Mesabi Range output
31 Hasty marriage
34 Heritages
36 Sports off.
37 Medicinal herbs
39 Blue jeans
40 School in Dallas, TX
43 Protuberance
45 Tidy up
47 Saint of It.
48 Poor grades
49 Public storehouse
51 Find secondary corrections
53 Engenders
56 Coming to the rescue
58 Indonesian currency
60 Library patron
61 French flag
64 Image on a red-and-white flag
66 Say more
67 Pigmented part of the eye
69 "Stride la vampa" or "Vissi d'arte," e.g.
70 Tight spot
73 United Kingdom flag
78 See 24A
81 B-complex vitamin
84 Applied by pats
86 Sets of steps over fences
87 Twist together
89 Vivid purplish red
92 Success in spades
93 "Rhoda" co-star David
94 Assn.
96 Fiscal deficit
98 "Jane __"
99 Get the point
100 Light beams
103 Precipitate
105 Karel Capek sci-fi play
106 Light plays
108 Study of rocks
110 Before
113 Conn of "Grease"
115 "Illness as Metaphor" writer
116 Symbols on a red flag
119 Proficient
122 Earth visitor
123 Composed
124 Poet's Ireland
125 __ incognita
126 Cotton capsules
127 Summers on the Somme
128 Kin of CHiPs
129 Ford failure

DOWN

1 Cop call
2 Musical gift
3 Double triangle on a flag
4 Victorious
5 Makes adhere
6 Eavesdropper
7 Sensory organs
8 Reggae's cousin
9 Rigorous
10 Astounded
11 Bridge blunders
12 Furthermore
13 Session player
14 Condition of agonizing struggle
15 Water falls
16 Rival rival
17 Woods ruminant
18 Highland tongue
25 Actor Mineo
26 In good shape
28 So be it!
31 One of "The Snoop Sisters"
32 Workout wear
33 Spud
35 Offbeat main character
38 Orpine plant
40 Future plant
41 Earlier Persian
42 Gorby's nation
44 Monumental
46 Malay thatch
48 Not listening
50 Roxy Music member, once
52 Betting advice
54 Coats with crumbs
55 Stephen of "The Crying Game"
57 Applying epoxy
59 After the style of
62 Egg: pref.
63 Depicted
65 __ Abner
68 Steely Dan album
70 Black-and-white flags
71 Small carpet
72 Puzzling crime
73 Beehive State
74 Anais the diarist
75 Easy as __
76 Pers. with a handle?
77 Pueblo tribe
79 Phone co.
80 Human parasites
81 Grovels
82 Concerning
83 Sioux tribe: var.
85 Buttoned
88 Suffer a reputation setback
90 Skid on an angle
91 Like cars in a traffic jam
95 Cooking surface
97 "Smoke Gets in Your Eyes" guy
100 Woolen fabrics
101 __ vincit omnia
102 Earthquakes
104 Write music
106 Desert ride
107 Star Wars: abbr.
109 Took on cargo
110 Queequeg's boss
111 Ring of saints
112 Oscar-winning actor Jannings
114 Reykjavik's isl.
117 __ "King" Cole
118 Malay isthmus
120 Prefix's prefix
121 Russian chess master

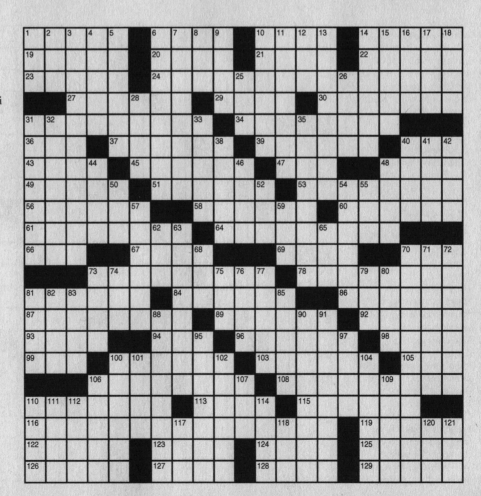

by Edgar Fontaine

ACROSS

1 Splinter group
5 Musical staff sign
10 Compulsions
15 Loser to the tortoise
19 Heart problem?
20 Playwright Pirandello
21 Stability
22 Periods of time
23 Father Brown's creator
25 Father Christmas
27 Programs
28 Tended grasslands
30 Football miscue
31 Barely perceptible
32 Looks aghast
33 Glut
34 French Louisiana people
37 Rajah's wife
38 Elastic
42 Unburned brick
43 Our Father
45 Tiller's tool
46 Strike an attitude
47 Flop
48 Assert positively
49 Kilauea flow
50 Afore
51 "The Father of Medicine"
55 Proofreading symbol
56 Collapses
58 Irritated
59 Ices
60 Merchant's figures
61 One who gives his heart?
62 Writer __ Boothe Luce
63 Tea-party host
65 Tell me the explanation
66 Kiddie spoilers?
69 Indian nursemaids
70 "The Father of Radio"
72 Santa __ winds
73 Disgusting
74 Hit's counterpart
75 Parks oneself
76 __ on (incites)
77 Sailors' grp.
78 Father of Flavius Julius Crispus
82 Tibia and femur
83 Honor recipient
85 Showed concern
86 Edible green stalk
87 Told a whopper
88 Gossip
89 Memento __ (reminder of mortality)
90 Dundee of boxing
93 Broad-winged hawk
94 Combustible building
98 Father of science fiction
100 Deucalion's father
102 Entrance of a mine
103 WWW communications
104 Swiss mathematician
105 Signs, Hollywood-style
106 Confederate soldiers, casually
107 Inclined to flow
108 Foxx and others
109 Amount paid

DOWN

1 Pouchlike parts
2 Parrot
3 Child's profession
4 Laboratory vial
5 Washes
6 Spicy sauce
7 Less caloric
8 Hot dog's problem
9 Helsinki's country
10 Off-the-neck hairdo
11 Chestnut-and-white horses
12 Cotton separators
13 Approx.
14 Sailor
15 Motorcyclist's protection
16 Part of U.A.E.
17 Actor Julia
18 In __ (existing): Lat.
24 Coil about
26 More adorable
29 "Planet of the __"
32 "Camille" star
33 Eyelid maladies
34 Like Batman and Robin
35 Revere
36 Svetlana Alliluyeva's father
37 Frolics
38 Squirreled away
39 Louis I's father
40 Rundown dwelling
41 Abbey Theatre founder
43 Runs at a steady gait
44 Movie evaluator
47 Mosquito or flea
49 Nixon's Secretary of Defense
51 Alan and Nathan
52 Audience
53 Washer cycle
54 High and mighty
55 Singsong mode of speaking
57 Machine-shop machine
59 Social stratum
61 "When thou __ thine alms"
62 Greek island
63 Widespread confusion
64 __ acids
65 "Siddhartha" author
66 __ to a halt
67 Ire
68 Jaunty
70 Tablet choice
71 Basketry willow
74 Besides
76 Earliest period of human culture
78 Covers a room
79 Sharply
80 Monicker
81 State police officer
82 Tours topper
84 Armadas
86 Kitchen tools
88 Altercation
89 Played charades
90 Open slightly
91 Unclothed
92 Silver-tongued
93 Cereal choice
94 Flock of sheep
95 Gambling mecca
96 Diving sea birds
97 Attention-getting sound
99 Ostrich kin
101 Have regrets

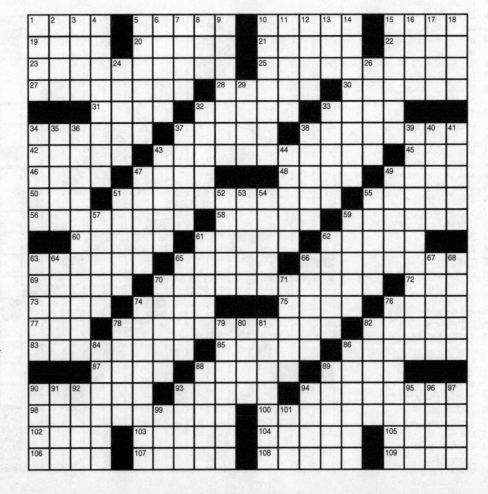

by Bernice Gordon

ACROSS

1 Gone by
5 Zigzag turns
10 Sophia Loren's Carlo
15 Floating jail?
19 "Typee" sequel
20 Alexander of "60 Minutes," once
21 NYC theater awards
22 Architect Saarinen
23 Sultan Qabus bin Said's capital
25 Edo, today
27 Acquires with special effort
28 Wild Asian dog
30 Woolly
31 Hebrew month
32 Components of everything
33 Wee woolly one
34 Scheduled
37 Parallel bands
38 Pathetic
42 Site of Morro Castle
44 Largest city in Africa
46 Only thing I have for you?
47 Harvests
49 Back part
50 Self-esteem
51 Neighbor of Syr.
52 Journal
54 Loud, raucous cry
56 Lazy lady?
58 State gambling scheme
60 Capital near the Red Sea
63 San __, CA
64 Proprietor
65 Of words
69 Qin Dynasty capital
71 Banished
72 Survives
75 Bullets, briefly
76 Fetters
78 Excavated
79 Grand __ Opry
80 MX divided by V
82 Stupor: pref.
84 Marketing starter?
85 Burial site of William the Conqueror
89 View from the Elburz Mountains
92 Marching for inspection
93 Pocket breads
95 Filmed, slangily
96 Confederate soldiers, casually
97 Get on
98 Vamoose!
99 Mortgage condition, often
102 Food from heaven
103 Head shrinkers
107 Location of "The Last Supper"
109 City northwest of Gibraltar
111 1st letter
112 Town known for its witches
113 Silent-films actress Bara
114 Sea eagle
115 Easy gait
116 Bagnold and others
117 More rational
118 Ramona, by another name

DOWN

1 Magnificence
2 Manchurian border river
3 No great shakes
4 Keyboard compositions
5 Erik of "CHiPs"
6 Smithy, at times
7 Huff and Jaffe
8 Alfonso's queen
9 Bunker
10 View from Mount Vernon
11 Ancient coins
12 Reebok rival
13 Writer Josephine
14 Quarantine imposer
15 Shapeless chair
16 Stanton movie, "__ Man"
17 Remsen and Levin
18 Left
24 Poet W.H. __
26 __ Lee Curtis
29 __ polloi
32 Up a tree
33 Old Italian bread?
34 "The Last of __"
35 Applies to a surface
36 Wards off
37 Litigant
38 Reverence
39 Automatic advances in a tournament
40 Org. of Pepper
41 English school
43 Wax stick
45 Boisterously
48 Irish river
52 Cold-cut palaces
53 "My Friend __"
55 Draft classification
56 Male and female
57 DOS rival
59 Written part
60 Travel in water
61 Donahue of "Father Knows Best"
62 Repair
64 Of a resistance unit
66 Apple juices
67 Ends of wings
68 Popularized myth
70 Star of "Alfie"
72 Wacko
73 Mr. Greenspan
74 Ooze
76 Sandwich holder
77 Folk singer Phil
80 Sideways
81 Blackguards
83 Draws towards
84 Old photographs
86 Supply a running commentary
87 Refrigerant
88 Names turned into words
90 Palace in Seville
91 Actress Patricia et al.
94 Actor McKellen
97 Tied in bundles
98 Maliciously derogatory
99 Actor Jannings
100 Chinese: pref.
101 Swindle
102 Bamako's country
103 Arabian gulf
104 Actress Gilbert
105 Metallic sound
106 Dundee dagger
108 Brown in the sun
110 Unmasker's cry

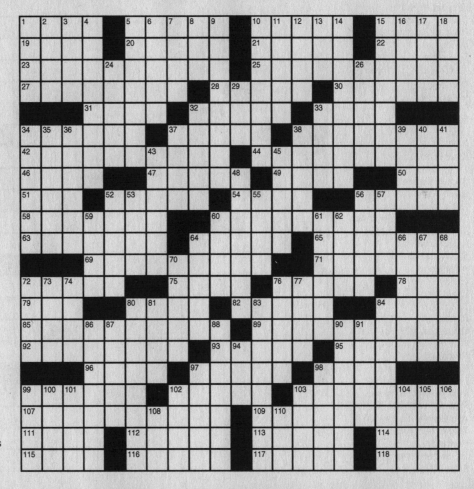

TIME AFTER TIME

by Josiah Breward

ACROSS

1 Designate
8 Church books
16 Switch positions
20 View from Mount Pisgah
21 Of an embryo's sac
22 Black sheep
23 1998 John Irving novel
25 Italian actress Eleonora
26 First name of a canine star
27 Pope who negotiated with Attila
28 Drooled
30 Robert Fulton's power
33 Boat holder
37 "Frankenstein, or the Modern Prometheus" author Shelley
38 Time magazine honor, formerly
43 Requirements
46 Desertlike
49 Russian president Boris
51 Art of the absurd
52 Flightless bird from down under
53 Stravinsky and Sikorsky
56 Bar legally
58 Operated
59 A month of Sundays
64 Diminutive ending
65 Dancer Charisse
66 Pakistani language
67 Indian tea
68 Shipworm
70 "Hello, Dolly!" producer
74 Secret agents
76 Drive back
79 Of Icelandic tales
81 Small land mass
83 Whip
84 Blue
86 River in Tuscany
87 1/1 to 12/31
91 Back of station?
92 Family car
94 Cubic meter
95 College seniors' test: abbr.
96 Sch. on the Rio Grande
98 Large purse
102 Most packed with evergreens
104 Get into one's head
106 Rapid growth scheme
109 Telephoned
111 Pay back
112 Often fatal African fever
116 "Unforgiven" man
120 Narrates
123 Goddess of the dawn
124 Former Rep. Gingrich
125 Marilyn Monroe movie
131 Spoken
132 Airplane pilot's concern
133 Take by surprise
134 Painful
135 Unleavened cornmeal bread
136 Small sofas

DOWN

1 Hebrew months
2 Lapwing
3 "Common Sense" writer
4 Quaint
5 Late starter?
6 Daily report
7 __-Hartley Labor Act
8 Allowance provider
9 Kissy?
10 East Coast cape
11 Abandon truth
12 Plaything
13 French summers
14 Money of Iran
15 Beat it!
16 Requested
17 School classification
18 Melt together
19 Potential plant
24 Norwegian king
29 Moving vehicle
31 Docs' grp.
32 Madame Curie
34 "__ Haw"
35 Popeye's Olive
36 Network of nerves
39 Hungarian leader, Imre __
40 Yoko's family
41 Selling feature
42 Thelma or Tex
44 6/6/44
45 Smooth wood
46 Orpine plant
47 "That's __"
48 1337–1453 conflict
50 __ Dame
54 Scandinavian rug
55 Hr. with a shrink
57 Barest sound
60 Resident of northern Iraq
61 Meat jelly
62 Gorbachev's wife
63 Get a noseful
69 Raoul, the painter
71 Lupino and Tarbell
72 Insertion symbol
73 Quasi
75 Spots
77 Glides high
78 Long-plumed bird
80 Raccoon's kin
82 Blow-up letters?
84 Man from Tarsus
85 Comic Johnson
88 Star of "Edward Scissorhands"
89 Seed coat
90 Of the kidneys
93 St. Petersburg's river
97 Chatter
99 Sills, casually
100 Shipmate's reply
101 Elegantly stylish
103 Balin or Claire
105 Opposite of SSE
107 Order of the day
108 Depend
110 Attained
113 Seven of Rome
114 Foundation piece
115 Cigar droppings
116 Son of Seth
117 Space starter?
118 Buckeye state
119 Earl __ Biggers
121 Fewer
122 Surfeit
126 Fast jet: abbr.
127 Starting center?
128 Or: Lat.
129 Squealer
130 NYC subway line

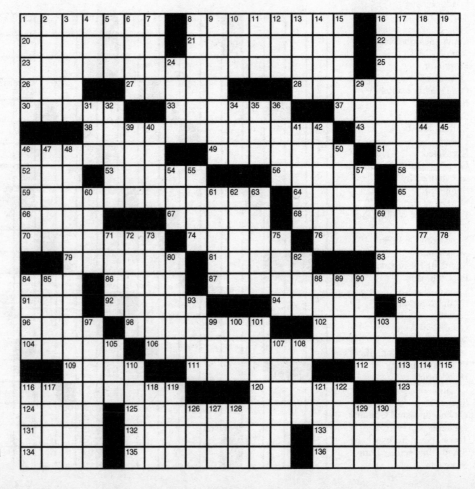

ACROSS

1 Pass
4 Of the cheekbone
9 Parcel out
14 Regions
19 Felling tool
20 Colorful ornamental stone
21 Hamlet, to Horatio
22 Book datum
23 __ Paese cheese
24 Two under par
25 Biller's partner?
26 Contain
27 Sprite
28 Save buried treasure?
31 Disney movie, "__ Dragon"
33 Exclamations
34 Charles Camille Saint-__
35 Fewer and farther between
37 French opera composer
39 Eliminate
40 Black-and-white Antarctic whale
43 Treasure in Pandora's box?
49 Letter abbr.
50 Leisure
51 Olive __
52 Opera solo
53 Entreaties
54 Became a gully
56 Brink
57 Process for sorting the injured
58 Sicilian wine
60 Bided one's time
62 Ransacker
63 4-wheel drive transport
64 Small child
65 White heron
66 Cylindrical hat
67 Food scrap
68 Red table wine
70 Way up or down
71 Changes precinct classification
73 Scorers
74 In __ (in actual being)
75 Happen to
76 Zodiac sign
77 Shank
78 January in Juarez
80 Egyptian fertility goddess
83 Self images
84 Treasured singers?
87 Bigwig in DC
88 "The Raven" poet
89 Fruity quaffs
90 Separates out
91 Field movie, "__ Rae"
93 Jurist Fortas
94 Taiwan Strait island
96 Here for a share of treasure?
102 Protest vote
105 Stand by
106 Redden
107 Bar legally
108 Expected
109 Poetry
110 Revere
111 Solo
112 Time period
113 Organic compound
114 Outcast
115 Customs
116 Collegiate cheer

DOWN

1 Comic Kaplan
2 Figure-skater's jump
3 Instinct to save treasure?
4 Eminent conductor
5 Open-mouthed
6 Nigeria's capital
7 Legendary Norse king
8 Scottish dance
9 Part of ATF
10 Silverdome team
11 August-born, mostly
12 Curved moldings
13 Lizard containers
14 Imminent
15 Mob melees
16 Needle case
17 Besides
18 Spotted
29 Soft drinks
30 Netting of the bride
32 Conger catchers
35 Hwy. abbr.
36 Spotter's cry
37 Cargo
38 Mil. installation
40 Get another's treasure first?
41 Curio shelves
42 Puts between
44 Stock units of fewer than 100 shares
45 Medicate
46 Soup dispenser
47 Plant fungi
48 Room's asset
49 First Arabic letter
53 Nicholson film's man of "honor"
55 Grade-B westerns
56 Eagle's nest: var.
57 Christmas star's place
58 Gordon and Sheila
59 On the loose
60 Eases
61 1992 Wimbledon winner
66 French brother
69 "Cheers" actor Roger
70 Withered
72 Hateful
75 Grovels
77 Word with analysis or compound
78 Mormon leader
79 Stirling negative
81 Badly
82 His: French
84 Breach of contract, for example
85 Workman
86 Reproductions
88 Baggage handler
91 Dissonance
92 Positively charged electrode
93 Ere
94 Word with oil or pool
95 Make amends
96 Enthusiastic opinion
97 She sheep
98 Separate
99 Gooey substance
100 Smile broadly
101 Scandinavian capital
103 Ambiance
104 Slangy affirmative

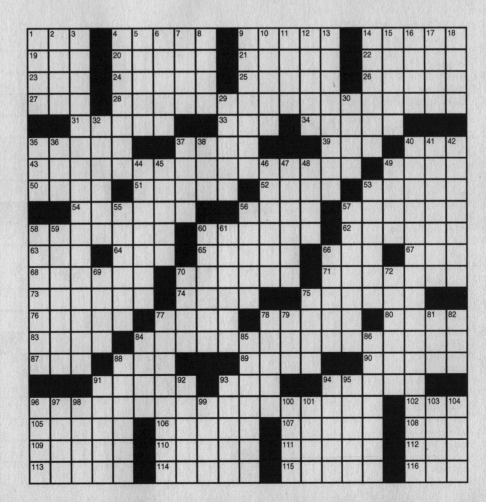

ASHORE

by Edgar Fontaine

ACROSS

1 Wife of a rajah
5 Chew noisily
10 Accumulate
15 Storage structure
19 Tennis situation, for short
20 "Taxi" dispatcher
21 Shade of purple
22 Goddess of the moon
23 Temporary structure?
25 Recreational vehicle
27 Rolling grasslands
28 Small songbirds
30 Commands
31 Nice legs: slang
32 Dresses in
33 Smelting residue
34 Quaking trees
37 Fine-grained silica
38 Keyboard element
42 Reek
43 Take after
44 Valentine shape
45 Grow old
46 Ancient people of northern Britain
47 Winglike
48 "Trees" and "The Raven," e.g.
49 Wild shot
50 One of T. Turner's channels
51 Shore transportation?
54 Raj's title
55 Worked up
58 Covers with fat
59 Lynx or tiger
60 Showed sympathetic concern
61 __-Terre, Guadeloupe
62 "Biloxi Blues" playwright
63 Packing material
65 Hackneyed
66 Falling in
69 Reprobates
70 Protection, of a sort
72 Jamaican music
73 Sheridan and Miller
74 Slacken
76 Witches
77 McCarthyism letters
78 Muscle spasm
79 Worship
80 Golfer Stewart
82 Elevate
83 Plotters
85 Granges
86 Stroked lightly
87 Solitary
88 Between then and now
89 Expeditious
90 Female graduate
93 Nativity
94 Solar system models
98 Swimmers' protection
100 New-swimmer's devices
102 Fragrance
103 Glorify

104 Dispatch boat
105 Demo ending?
106 Coin flip
107 Lacoste and Russo
108 Pleasure cruiser
109 Youngsters

DOWN

1 Abrasive tool
2 Hebrew month
3 Pinta's sister ship
4 Impoverished
5 Insurance cases
6 Firefighter's equipment
7 Inning enders
8 1,000,000: slang
9 Runts
10 Einstein or Gore
11 Bearings
12 Lamenter's cry
13 US defense grp.
14 Students
15 Oozy sediment
16 Colossal
17 Art print: abbr.
18 Periods of light
24 Turn a handle
26 Leaflike plant part

29 Seldom seen
32 Pier
33 Canned-pork product
34 Pet watchdog org.
35 Smarting pain
36 Shore fare, often
37 Beet with thick stalks
38 Kernels
39 Trunks, e.g.
40 Once more
41 Hasidic teacher
43 Supplied hints
44 Tribe on the move
47 Fall flower
48 Unit of astronomical length
49 Beauty parlor
52 Actress Vivian
53 Tobacco kilns
54 Partial: pref.
56 Fireside yarns
57 God of war
59 Some Scandinavians
61 Entirely physical
62 Blockade
63 College groups, briefly
64 Type of column
65 Former Russian rulers

66 Tilts
67 Russian proclamation
68 Walked worriedly
71 Greeting-card message, typically
74 Former German leader
75 Make a hole
77 Three consecutive goals
79 In the company of
80 Breathe heavily
81 Castle entrance
82 Repair a hem
84 Fudd and Gantry
85 Initial ones
86 Imitate without comprehension
88 Edge along
89 New
90 Oodles
91 Italian beach
92 Space saucers, briefly
93 Grain coat
94 Auricular
95 Cross inscription
96 Mild oath
97 Fast planes, for short
99 Issue a pink slip
101 Gardner of "The Killers"

by Bill Swain

ACROSS

1 French subway
6 Fix up furniture
14 Hawklike?
20 River's end, often
21 Texas city
22 Overnight flight
23 Amy Tan novel about golf?
25 Slurs over
26 Tiny bit
27 Otherwise
28 "Les Miserables" writer
29 Metallic sound
30 Churchill's gesture
31 Farm enclosure
32 __ Ice Shelf, Antarctica
33 Feline
34 Squirmy catch
37 Misprint
39 Hackneyed
41 Black goo
42 Vague amount
43 Pilots' perches
46 Father
47 Andes resident
48 Transmitted
51 Selassie of Ethiopia
52 To come
53 Easily imposed upon
54 Hot diamonds
55 Pass time on a practice green?
57 Clamps
58 Rainbow shape
59 Individuals
60 Soggy, unappetizing food
61 Part to play
62 Arctic boots
64 Bamboo stems
66 Passes gossip
69 Trigger's lunch
70 Merchant's goal
71 Kevin Kline film
72 Cost to participate
73 Frizzell or Grove
75 Golfer's drink?
78 Business abbr.
79 Solemn vow
80 Stirling citizens
81 More infrequent
82 Mini-army?
83 U.S. tennis stadium honoree
84 Masculine
85 Part of a bench
87 Woodland ruminant
88 Word in partnerships
89 Calls to the phone
90 Minimum
94 Opposite of NNE
95 Well-honed skill
96 Weldon and Wray
97 Give recompense
99 Actor Scheider
100 Leave out
102 Authoritative prohibition
103 Takes off
105 Inland sea of Asia
106 Actress Shields
108 Golfer's various business interests?
111 Lots and lots
112 Position of superiority
113 Two-time tennis grand-slam winner
114 Away
115 Maladies
116 Savage and Friendly

DOWN

1 Cause
2 Parrot
3 Wobble
4 Hindu ruler
5 Lennon's widow
6 Come from behind
7 Flightless fowl
8 Turn toward
9 Irritate
10 "The Graduate" director
11 Treat badly
12 Punches
13 Vagabond
14 Ready
15 Used used candles
16 Norse Zeus
17 Squeeze into a golf cart?
18 Gob's agreement
19 Scale notes
24 Still
31 Sell-out letters
32 Movie star-giver
33 Jewel weight
35 Host
36 Plumbing problems
38 One meaning of 10
39 Roasting sticks
40 Mosaic piece
41 Traffic jam
42 Comparative construction
44 Substantial pieces
45 Millett and Nelligan
46 Frightens away
48 Thailand, once
49 Beige
50 Copse on a golf course?
52 Having the skill
55 Sulky
56 Nixon V.P.
57 Citizen with a voice
61 Revolutionary rider
63 Shaving foam
64 __ blanche
65 Pub fare
66 Vocal enthusiast
67 Period after Mardi Gras
68 Brief times: abbr.
70 Reprimand
71 Daggers
73 Burdens
74 Soothes
75 Meager
76 Pulls behind
77 Speed along
80 Superlatively wise
82 Consumed
85 City in France or New Jersey
86 Stallone, to friends
89 Regional dialect
91 Show up
92 Piloted a glider
93 Family of the 10th President
95 Conrad, the poet
96 Physicist Enrico
97 Rose and Rozelle
98 Gray shade
101 Sleeper spy
102 Contended
103 Cotton separators
104 In the past
105 From a distance
106 Scarf like a snake?
107 Stick up
109 Red or Yellow, e.g.
110 Pixie

BREAKFAST FARE

by Stanley B. Whitten

ACROSS

1 Giacomo Puccini opera
6 Stage whispers
12 Jamaican citrus fruit
16 Pinch
19 "Middlemarch" author
20 Like a busybody
21 Light gas
22 "We __ the World"
23 Breakfast menu item
25 Breakfast menu items
27 Philippines metropolis
28 Change the wall covering
30 Penny
31 Willingly, old-style
34 Mature
35 Lion groups
37 Play divisions
41 Molecule element
43 High-level D.C. grp.
44 State of mind
45 Breakfast menu item
48 Breakfast menu items
52 Islamic text
53 Soft-toy substance
54 Use a whetstone
55 Part of a bow
56 Activities
58 Individuality
61 Kitchen appliance
62 Marry
63 Otherwise
65 "The Thin Man" co-star Myrna
66 Artisan's tool
68 Breakfast menu item
72 Ultimate
75 Flight from the law
76 Shaped like a wing
77 Altar vow
80 Squared up
81 Worldwide in scope
85 Lumberjack
87 Peak in northern Greece
88 Tacks on
89 "Diana" singer
91 Writer Cather
92 Breakfast menu items
94 Breakfast menu item
97 Roseanne, once
98 Dickens novel, "Dombey and __"
99 Smack
100 Defeat
101 Shakespeare's "The __ of Errors"
104 Supporting framework
106 Dance movement
108 Environs
109 Rat catcher
111 Wanderer
116 Breakfast menu item
119 Breakfast menu item
122 Part of the U.K.
123 Butcher's cut
124 Puts up
125 Mortise insert
126 Caviar base
127 Departed
128 Transmitter
129 Go-ahead

DOWN

1 Abound (with)
2 Russian saint
3 Indication
4 "__ fan tutte"
5 Not the least bit
6 In addition
7 Shed tears
8 Munich's river
9 Craps shooter
10 Marrying in haste
11 Nerve junction
12 Loose cattle
13 Toothed device
14 Actor Chaney
15 Business abbr.
16 Nude
17 Castle or Dunne
18 Bothersome ones
24 River nymph
26 Acetify
29 Round vegetable
32 English school
33 Know beforehand
35 Dissimulation
36 Mythical bird
37 Awry
38 Garlic section
39 Exhausted
40 Examine quickly
42 Stable female
44 Attentive
46 Went in
47 Org. of Green Bay
48 Surprising word
49 Charged particles
50 Forum attire
51 Pour out
54 Axton or Wilhelm
57 Bridge coup
59 Chute for logs
60 __ polloi
61 Enthrone again
64 Dangerous driver
67 Iranian currency
68 Canadian lake
69 Contagious maladies, for short
70 Butt
71 Doglike mammals
72 Cease
73 Celestial bear
74 Cat in boots
77 Snow abode
78 Small valleys
79 Face-to-face exams
82 Today's LPs
83 Fabray, familiarly
84 Rustic hotels
86 Pink baby?
88 Ethereal
90 Amo, amas, __...
93 Way cool!
94 Pairs
95 Stimulate to creativity
96 La Scala offering
98 Spanish Mrs.
101 Prank
102 Maine town
103 Unite
104 City on the Adige
105 __ deadly sins
107 Sulks
109 Wage-slave's refrain
110 Mailroom stamp abbr.
112 On the briny
113 Numerous
114 Inspirations of individualists
115 Nevada destination
117 Not up to snuff
118 Female deer
120 Hwy. abbr.
121 Russia or Latvia, once: abbr.

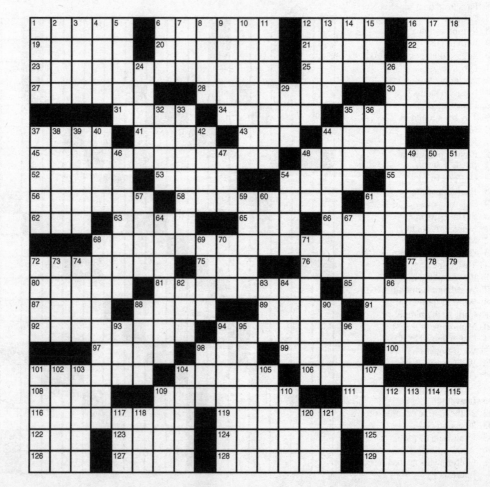

SEEING DOUBLE

by Alan P. Olschwang

ACROSS

1 Elite social category
6 Former Russian ruler
10 See 22A
14 Spiral pin
19 More prudent
20 Zenith
21 North Carolina college
22 With 10A, silent-screen star
23 Domesticated guanaco
24 Capacity
25 Naval: pref.
26 Surprise attacks
27 Extend a series?
30 Acquiescing
32 Throw in the towel
33 Tutor
35 Attractive object?
36 Build up
40 Colonist
42 Inhabitant of: suff.
43 Israeli nationalist
45 Fervor
47 Brilliance
51 Law practice?
53 Sacrifice play
55 Ring around the moon
56 White-tailed European eagle
57 List-ending abbr.
58 Play producer
60 Seed coat
61 Whitney Houston's singing mom
64 Dumbfound
66 Existing naturally
68 Bard
70 Beat it!
71 Keenly eager
72 Principal ore of lead
75 Onetime Argentine president
79 Profundity
83 Ancient Greek coin
84 Waits on
86 One of the DiMaggio brothers
87 Stretch of time
88 Saved by the __
89 Zeno of __
90 Ultimate test?
94 Reduce drastically
96 Of the forehead
99 Penthouse porch
100 Red or Yellow, e.g.
102 Actress Fabray
104 Antenna
105 One of the wise men
108 Extensive
109 Foster film "Little Man __"
111 Olympic discus legend
113 Trifling snub?
119 Shopping centers
120 Sugar source
122 Fourth little piggie's fare
123 Where lovers walk?
124 "__ Gay"
125 Nota __ (mark my words)

126 Spanish cubist painter
127 In flames
128 Impudent
129 Lose one's self-control
130 Splinter group
131 Recipient

DOWN

1 Hole-making tools
2 Rhythmic cadence
3 Munich's river
4 Partial: pref.
5 Serene
6 Ankle bones
7 Sir Walter and Randolph
8 __ vincit omnia
9 Remission
10 Cincinnati team
11 Pie __ mode
12 Bad place for Couples to be?
13 Opposed
14 Grooved like muscle
15 Get five nickels for a quarter?
16 Hold the throne
17 Jockey Arcaro
18 "The Man Who __ There"
28 Invitee

29 New Jersey five
31 Citadel's rival: abbr.
34 Silk-cotton trees
36 Nahuatl speaker
37 High clouds
38 Mints
39 Genetic letters
41 Solar-lunar calendar differential
44 Provide care
46 Opposite of SSW
48 Zhivago's beloved
49 Landed
50 Lacquerware
52 "__ Not Unusual"
54 Math subj.
58 States of agitation
59 Brazilian monkey
62 Survives an easy round in the bee?
63 Hither's partner
65 Eye covetously
67 Silent assent
69 Relaxation
71 Set sights
72 Large quantity
73 Eve's son
74 1970 hit by the Kinks

75 Healthy putting surface?
76 Incarnation of Vishnu
77 Proclamation
78 Director Howard
80 Of punishment
81 Vestige
82 More robust
85 Shade tree
90 Tailor's tasks
91 Lane-crossing turns
92 Sponge
93 Wrath
95 Inadmissible evidence
97 Simplest of procedures
98 Chime
101 __ Deco
103 Racial
105 Some pastimes
106 Model Stewart
107 Performs alone
110 Bomb blast, in headlines
112 Recedes
114 Tipper's last name
115 Scuttlebutt
116 Increase
117 Employ
118 Family chart
121 Alfonso's queen

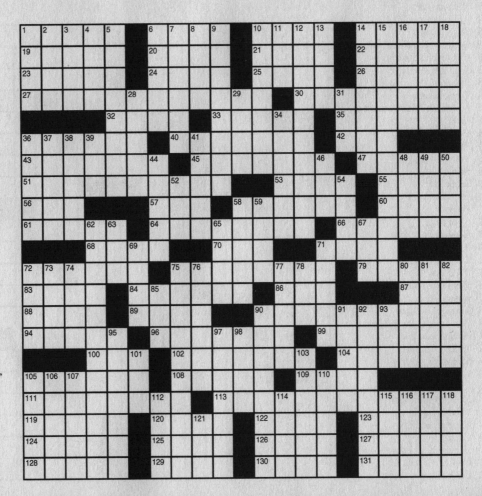

FAMILY AFFAIR

by Edgar Fontaine

ACROSS

1 Taxis
5 Typefaces
10 Metric units
15 Rescue
19 Baldwin brother
20 "Murder in the Cathedral" dramatist
21 Make alterations
22 Part of QED
23 Docking place
24 Co-star of "Rebel Without a Cause"
25 Opening bars
26 Bygone
27 Garth Brooks hit
30 Opie's guardian
32 Be dull
33 Passing with flying colors
35 Draw
36 Neighbor of Zimbabwe
39 Storage film, briefly
41 Constructors
46 Ancient Greek silver coins
47 Nursery rhyme character
49 Baby's seat?
50 Network of vessels
51 Painter Chagall
52 Mine entrance
53 Icelandic saga
54 Collegiate cheer
55 Stern adviser
59 On the up-and-up
60 Egg dish, British style
62 Window elements
63 Fisher of "Star Wars"
64 Track events
65 __-Martin (vintage racing car)
66 Golan Heights claimant
67 Avoids duty
69 Vote in
70 Sapped
73 Suspends
74 Overprotective persons
76 Patriotic grp.
77 __ of Man
78 Country bumpkin
80 Assists
81 Transition point
82 RR depot
83 Vicki Lawrence sitcom
87 Australian marsupial
88 Resident of Maui
90 Comment to the audience
91 Having less hair
92 Twice DLXXV
93 Miniature race cars
95 Indonesian island
96 Kidder movie
100 Main/Kilbride film
106 Needy
107 Having paddles
109 Get up
110 Gardener, at times
111 Dancer Pavlova
112 Entertainment venue

113 Manufacturer
114 Hostelries
115 Chore
116 "__ Long Legs"
117 Coarse variety of corundum
118 Relinquish

DOWN

1 Li'l Abner's creator
2 Inter __ (among other things)
3 Answering-machine signal
4 Board game with tiles
5 Thighbones
6 Martini garnish
7 Half a golf course
8 Hammered on a slant
9 Belly
10 Covered with more soot
11 French historian
12 Rear of the space shuttle
13 Actress Sorvino
14 Most stalwart
15 Group of seven
16 Part of U.A.E.
17 Urn
18 Back end of a kitchen?
28 Lane of the Daily Planet

29 Suffer heartbreak
31 French Riviera resort
34 Crystal-filled rocks
36 "The Mark of __"
37 Nautical position
38 '60s hit by Ernie K-Doe
39 Coerce
40 Hankering
42 King of France
43 Bourbon brand
44 Wheel spokes
45 Sudden flow
47 Dillon and McCoy
48 Greek physician
51 Muffles
53 Spooky
55 Sets of cards
56 Underdog's win
57 Slangy of course
58 $100 bill
59 Escapades
61 Expansive
63 Greenish blues
65 African succulents
66 Squalid
67 __ kebab
68 "__ la vista, baby!"
69 Build a levee

70 In the meantime
71 Two under par
72 Dismal in poetry
75 Sudden attack
78 Brook no delay
79 Actress Thurman
81 Postulated earliest period of human culture
83 "Of __ and Men"
84 Electromagnetic induction man
85 Nick and Nora's pooch
86 Identify incorrectly
87 Hardy cabbage
89 U.S. train system
91 Pastry palace
94 Remedy
95 More dishonorable
96 Tiff
97 One of the Inner Hebrides
98 Chips off the old block
99 Poet Teasdale
101 1/16 ounce
102 Freshwater fish
103 Color variation
104 Allow to use
105 Scottish Gaelic
108 Burned by the sun

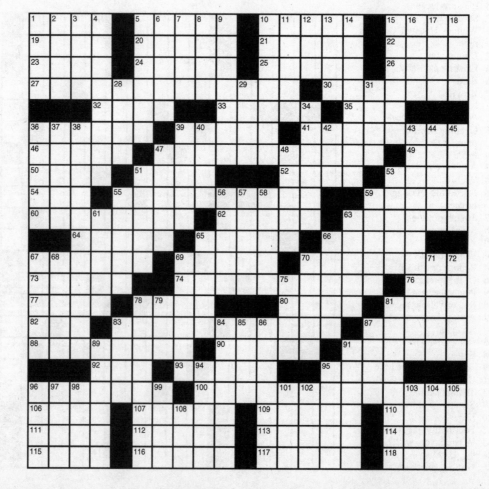

CAPITAL IDEA

by Josiah Breward

ACROSS

1 Flap gums
4 Capture again
10 Witty remark
14 Biscuitlike pastry
19 Period
20 Star in a French sky
21 Cupid
22 Metal mixture
23 "The Iron Chancellor"
26 Island in the Philippines
27 Refuse heaps
28 "Fargo" director Joel
29 Choose a side
30 "Dies __" (Day of Wrath)
31 President born in Virginia
37 "The Fall of the House of Usher" writer
38 Substantial
40 Electra's brother
41 Election winners
42 Necessitate
45 Blanched
46 Rope fiber
47 '79 and '81 U.S. Open tennis champion
52 Profit figure
53 Past prime
54 Picture puzzle
55 Indulgent
57 Obscures
60 Concerning
61 Light musical production
63 Copse
64 Lamb's lament
65 War god
66 Mil. address
67 Island group off Donegal
68 Literary collection
69 Emily Dickinson's life-long home
71 More penurious
73 Actor Tamiroff
74 Simple shed
75 Exceptional
76 Watered silk
77 One of the Stooges
78 Orbiting part of Russia?
79 One of "Charlie's Angels"
82 __ never fly
84 Florida team
86 Orange oil
87 Med. scan
88 Parts of eyes
90 Long-hitting clubs
95 Bell that's "Big"
96 "Stand by Me" co-star
99 Privy to
100 Ethnic
102 Island in the Netherlands Antilles
103 Sicilian volcano: var.
104 Sch. in Storrs
105 "From Here to Eternity" co-star
111 Songwriter Greenwich
112 Vicinity
113 Medicated liquid
114 Bub
115 Fender flaws
116 Adolescent
117 As a precaution
118 African nat.

DOWN

1 Of crystal-filled stones
2 Mr. Toscanini
3 Val Kilmer role
4 Guns it in neutral
5 WWII arena
6 Weighty weight
7 Chest bone
8 Writer Walker
9 Monterrey money
10 Founder of Dada
11 Slip up
12 Org.
13 Tongue click
14 Beauty parlors
15 Red's Kadiddlehopper
16 "Moonstruck" Oscar winner
17 Conceptions
18 Sight exam
24 Fuel cartel, briefly
25 Office note
29 For both sexes
31 Napoleon victory site
32 Aleutian island
33 Rubeola
34 Actress Durbin
35 Ait
36 Leave text as is
39 Alejandro and Fernando
43 Latin way
44 Striped
46 Political coalition
47 Of clan groups
48 Change a file
49 16th president
50 Pool stick
51 Quibble
53 Ken or Lena
56 English schoolboy
57 Scorch
58 "Raging Bull" Oscar winner
59 Pollen organ
61 Approximately
62 Classroom favorite
63 Three: It.
65 Comic Johnson
67 Wing flap
70 Tautomeric compound
71 More nimble
72 City entrance
73 In working order
75 Actress Hasso
76 DLI doubled
78 Sportscaster Albert
80 Singer Mitchell
81 Trebek or Karras
82 Saturated
83 British molasses
84 Work hard
85 Tape recorder element
88 Stretches one's neck
89 Uneven hairstyle
91 Cambodian monetary unit
92 Punctual
93 Dieting adjective
94 Grasp suddenly
97 Greek coins
98 De Valera of Ireland
101 Laverne's L, e.g.
103 Complexion damage
105 Floor cushion
106 Mine vein
107 Born in Bordeaux
108 And so forth: abbr.
109 Long, narrow inlet
110 Attention-getting calls

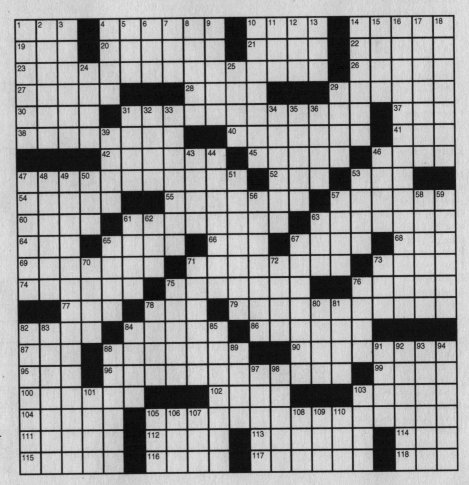

PARTICIPLES ON PARADE

by Bernice Gordon

ACROSS

1 Embarrass
6 Wanes
10 Cause anxiety
15 Manipulated
19 Gospels' source material
20 Walloping wind
21 "The Hobbit" character
22 Celestial explosion
23 Blue
25 Accepting humiliating defeat
27 Interstice
28 Eminent conductor
30 Obtained
31 Neighbor of Syr.
33 Moves at a quick pace
34 Memento __ (reminder of mortality)
35 Lacks
40 Mimic
41 Barbecues
45 Cooperating
47 Prettifying
49 Units of work
50 Parent, for example
52 Shelterward
53 College seniors' test: abbr.
54 Give a face-lift
56 Gardner of "Mogambo"
57 Brief death notices
59 Gaze
61 "A Visit from St. Nicholas" poet
63 Knitting stitches
64 Pointed a finger at
65 High-fiber ingredient
68 Fireside yarns
69 Chinese religionists
70 Fairy-tale villains
71 Kind of sandwich
72 Soviet collective
73 Domesticated
74 W. Hemisphere protection syst.
75 One: It.
76 Vowed
80 Creative skill
81 Relative of an anapest
82 Exam compositions
85 Branding tool
86 Standing by
90 Indicating
92 Lawyer
93 Night flyer
95 Bad 'uns
96 Actor Julia
97 Mr. T's outfit
99 Rent-sign abbr.
100 Jewish mystic of old
103 Hillary or Chelsea
105 Disney Studios head, once
110 Forming couples
112 Not taking seriously
114 Comparative phrase
115 Tractor manufacturer

116 Power current: abbr.
117 From now on
118 Guevara and others
119 Sequence
120 Score
121 Play pranks

DOWN

1 __-Romeo (Italian car)
2 Afrikaner
3 "A Death in the Family" author
4 Missile shelter
5 Saluting
6 Coop item
7 Aromatic unguent
8 Become inflated
9 Sanitation system
10 Aided in crime
11 Truth twisters
12 Palo __, CA
13 Slugger's stat
14 Snake-killing mammal
15 Anointment
16 Alphabetize
17 Bacchanalian cry
18 Daily start
24 Winston Cup circuit

26 Russian writer
29 Saturate
32 Study anew
34 Hebrew lawgiver
35 Teen follower?
36 Be dull
37 Indication
38 Coordinated outfit
39 Dry, white wine
41 B.C. Europeans
42 Singer Leslie
43 Corner tower
44 Proceeds quickly
46 Gun-owners' lobby
48 Train tracks
51 Drum roll
55 Planet
58 British gun
59 Blackthorn berries
60 Plane pusher?
62 New World grp.
63 Sunscreen ingredient
64 Night flyer
65 City on the Rideau Canal
66 Noah's peak
67 Small bird
68 Prop or charger starter
69 Pie in Cooperstown

71 Cozy
72 Diarist Nin
74 Actor Conrad
75 G.I. entertainment unit
77 Assns.
78 Newspaper section, once
79 Adam's grandson
81 Subtle implication
83 Splash of liquid
84 Pollen-bearing organ
87 Matadors
88 Tehran resident
89 Minute aquatic organism
91 Intuition
94 Sebaceous cyst
97 Actress Woodard
98 Smackers
100 Grand saga
101 Window element
102 Web location?
103 For both sexes
104 No, in Russia
106 Popeye's Pea
107 Pinta's sister ship
108 Customary extras, briefly
109 Syngman of South Korea
111 European nat.
113 Saloon rocks?

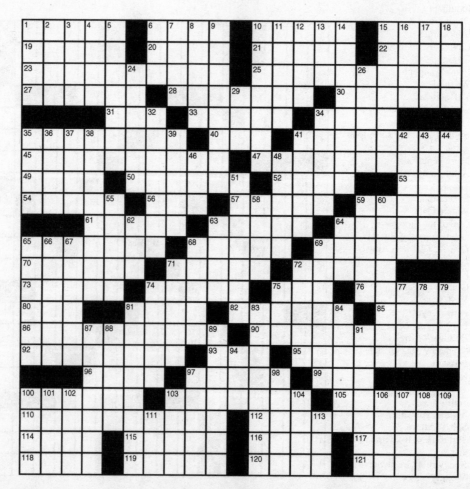

by Ed Voile

ACROSS

1 Common garden pest
6 Largest part of the former Yugoslavia
12 Fifth of MXXX
16 Cotillion attendee, for short
19 Simoleons
20 Babies, at times
21 Ancient Greek philosopher, Zeno of __
22 Suffix in linguistics
23 Part 1 of a quotation, with "The"
26 "__ the season to be..."
27 Gambler's risk
28 Day's end
29 Field of moles?
31 Onassis to pals
32 Mine vein
33 Legendary founder of Carthage
35 Square measure
36 Part 2 of the quotation
44 Got an A
46 Underground growth
47 Strong dislike
48 Intentional
52 Superlatively acrid
56 Part 3 of the quotation
57 Extremely severe
59 Noun-forming suffix
60 Lively pace
61 "Lawrence of __"
63 "The Phantom of the Opera" writer Leroux
65 Madagascar's neighbor: abbr.
68 Speaker of the quotation
71 RR stop
72 Satisfy
74 Counsel
75 Sea eagles
77 Cloth connection
78 Pack animals
79 Part 4 of the quotation
83 Abrade
86 Spicy topping
88 Pen of old
89 Common infant malady
91 Close-fitting
92 Part 5 of the quotation
99 Medical school subj.
100 Approximately
101 Color of the Italian sky
102 Sharp turn
105 Prim and proper to the max
109 Cornerstone tablets
112 Gardener's implement
113 Play on words
114 End of the quotation
118 DDE's predecessor
119 Poker stake
120 Cold pack
121 Shire of "Rocky"
122 Surprised exclamations
123 Bridge support
124 Scuffle
125 Wet impact

DOWN

1 One-celled organism
2 Model, at times
3 With aggressive intent
4 Island: Fr.
5 "Cheers" star
6 Act parts
7 Aphrodite's child
8 Abundant
9 Encircling route
10 Fury
11 Comparison phrase
12 Morality enforcer
13 Cut short
14 I came: Latin
15 Othello's nemesis
16 Separations
17 Political refugee
18 Be appropriate for
24 Remedy
25 Make over
30 Characters
33 Period
34 Contingencies
37 Ninny
38 Persia, now
39 Drunkard
40 Lower digit
41 Ancient European
42 NYC summer hrs.
43 Even score
44 Want __
45 Bus. honcho
49 Small towns
50 French school
51 Cost per unit
52 Comic Fanny
53 Writer Dinesen
54 Glaswegian
55 Neighbor of Ark.
57 Mecca pilgrims
58 Down with "le roi"
61 Muddle
62 Spout nonsense
63 Writer Maxim
64 Queen __ lace
65 Church projection
66 Display muscle
67 Refamiliarizes
69 Naval: pref.
70 Tight closure
73 Quantities
76 Secret supply
78 African nation
79 Neighbor of Wisc.
80 Member of the Bowery Boys
81 Old French coin
82 Actress Ryan
84 Eliminate
85 Not up to snuff
86 Actor Gulager
87 Strike
89 Young and others
90 Tic-tac-toe win
92 Greek lyric poet
93 Forward flow
94 Ritually pure, in Judaism
95 Art Deco designer
96 Make grateful
97 __ Bator
98 Visitors
103 Ancient region in Asia Minor
104 Reach
106 Cleansing agent
107 Former Spanish toehold in Africa
108 Back of the kitchen?
109 Females
110 Bar bills
111 & others: Lat.
115 Cambridge sch.
116 Fort Worth sch.
117 Keg feature

by Marian Baran

ACROSS

1 Puccini opera
6 Ready to swing
11 Teensy
15 Peter or Ivan, e.g.
19 Nymph of mythology
20 "Casablanca" co-star Peter
21 Actor Rob
22 Verdi opera
23 Breakfast in Paris?
25 Belfast repast?
27 Govt. farm group
28 Actress Gaynor
29 Legendary Giant
30 Functional
31 Two performers
33 Burned slightly
35 Conference
37 Another time
40 Distance runners
41 Highland group
42 Plumbers and mechanics
44 Old Testament bk.
46 Airport buildings
50 Contaminated
51 Branch of the mil.
53 Play part
55 Permit
56 Language of Lebanon
57 Gas additive letters
58 Blanched
59 Actress Lollobrigida
60 Gardner of "On the Beach"
61 Atoms of different masses
63 Clark Kent's foster father on TV in the '50s
64 Thanksgiving dessert
68 __ de plume
69 Sacristies
72 Butter's bro?
73 Hot rod competition
76 Multiply-curved wheel
77 Duck feathers
78 Judy of "Laugh-In"
79 "Le Coq __," Rimsky-Korsakov opera
80 Parasitic pest
84 Compass point
85 Babism offshoot
86 Part of AT&T
87 Consisting of three parts
88 Singer Al
90 Pasture in poetry
92 Architect's aide
94 Ringlike earring
95 Classified
97 Gap in time
98 Italian astronomer
101 Endow with spirit
102 Manhattan sch.
103 Magic showplace, once
104 Roof piece
106 Pipe root
108 Put to sea
112 Peruvian legumes?
114 Sitka dessert?

116 Moore of "Ghost"
117 Portico of ancient Greece
118 French student
119 Curved moldings
120 Winged
121 Millennia
122 Senior member
123 Leavening agent

DOWN

1 Bean curd
2 Ben and Bobby
3 Potential plant
4 B.C. breakfast item?
5 Military asst.
6 High: pref.
7 Hoffman movie
8 Bar fare in Rio?
9 Garlicky poisonous gas
10 Asian New Year
11 Homeric epic
12 British Conservative
13 Geneva sandwich filler
14 Affirmative
15 Sampling
16 Non-violent protest
17 Ms. Rogers St. Johns
18 More untested

24 Contemporary med. coverage
26 Merciful
29 Military meal
32 Serving to make one
34 Show teeth
36 Large antelope
37 Ionian Sea gulf
38 Equipment
39 Capital of Western Samoa
40 2,500 in letters
43 Hit the high points
45 Quickly, for short
47 Excuse
48 Taylor of "The Nanny"
49 Laurel and Musial
52 Freeload
54 Dexterous
57 __ Leone
58 Hair ointment
59 Frankfurt frankfurter?
62 Rocky crag
64 Computer communicator
65 Actress Massey
66 Dated later
67 Boise fry?
70 Neck warmer
71 Without speaking

74 Indigo dye
75 Ankara leftovers?
78 Tippy craft
81 Access road
82 Pension funds: abbr.
83 Unit of force
85 Research facility
86 N.M. art colony
87 Little bit
89 "Into __," Everest chronicle
91 Medieval slave
93 Palliate
96 Atlantic fish
98 Israel's Meir
99 Character in "The Tempest"
100 Glossary term
101 "__ Dream," Wagner aria
102 Shooters' grp.
105 Aware of
107 Arabian seaport
109 On the briny
110 Turner and Clanton
111 Endure
113 Language suffix
114 __ of roses
115 "The Thin Man" star

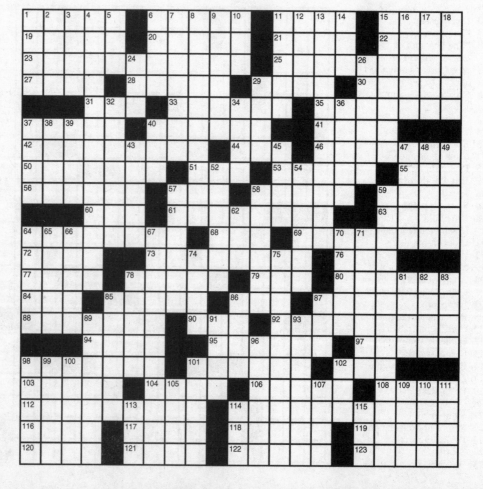

PUN AND GAMES

by Robert H. Wolfe

ACROSS

1. Pinta's sister ship
5. "R.U.R." dramatist
10. Seaweed product
14. Exhausted
19. Wedding vows
20. United
21. Childhood taboo
22. Willful destruction
23. Young lice
24. Medicinal ointment
25. Machu Picchu resident
26. Tiny
27. Philanthropist with six pockets?
30. Cigar droppings
31. Not accented
32. Hall-of-Famer Phil
33. Ship's personnel
34. Afternoon in Acapulco
36. Stephen of "The Crying Game"
37. Custody
41. Easy as __
44. Smithy's furnace
46. Diarist Samuel
47. Nest-egg $$
48. Cowardly Lion's portrayer
50. Siamese sounds
52. Fills completely
53. Former Russian ruler
54. Enjoyed avidly
56. Beget
57. Well-honed skill
58. More hackneyed
60. Say the same thing again
62. Hot chamber
64. Old Testament prophet
66. Docs
67. Teed-off Frenchman?
70. Musical gift
73. Copper crust
75. Stand on hind legs
76. Riding
78. Few and far between
80. POW, possibly
82. End-table item
84. Playwright Neil
85. Whimper
86. Type of pneumonia
88. Indifferent person
90. First name of 48A
91. Branch
92. Actor Alain
93. Unique things: slang
95. Inhabitant: abbr.
96. Split into splinters
98. Belief: suff.
101. Govt. funds group
103. Overly curious
104. Remove from a box
106. Greek markets
110. Singer LaBelle
112. Court troublemaker?
115. Speak scornfully
116. "Dancing Queen" singers
117. Drudge
118. Touch against
119. Eagle's home
120. Unruly child
121. Conger catcher
122. Yugoslavian dictator
123. Coil about
124. Painful point
125. Humanlike toys
126. Arabian seaport

DOWN

1. Japanese mercenary
2. Senseless person
3. Untrue!
4. Nod of the head
5. Farm income producer
6. Memo acronym
7. Actress on horseback?
8. Poem postscript
9. Dancer Ruby
10. "Peer Gynt" dancer
11. Bizarre
12. Allow ending?
13. Bellow
14. Knights' tunics
15. Egyptian birds
16. Doctor of cards?
17. Ferrara family of art patrons
18. Former Tunisian rulers
28. Old-time singer Edith
29. Alibi guy
33. Glass objects
35. Of a Syrian religious sect
37. Patricia of "thirtysomething"
38. Uncouth clod
39. "Dies __"
40. Henry VIII's last Catherine
41. Cause anxiety
42. Moderated
43. Knighted 1994 Oscar nominee?
45. Flynn of films
46. Golf score
49. Routine
51. More than two
52. Open footwear
53. Aunt in Alicante
55. International agreements
59. Breaks in friendly relations
61. Larceny
63. Compass pt.
65. More lathery
68. Exemplar of stiffness
69. Muse of lyric poetry
71. Love deeply
72. Tears
74. "We __ the World"
77. Chest bone
78. Health resorts
79. Sound of rippling water
81. Bond's Fleming
83. Game-show gambler?
87. __-de-France
89. Tea set pitchers
92. Brando film
94. Wise person
97. Elect
98. Existing naturally
99. H.S. subj.
100. Gathered together
102. Musical composition
104. Open a castle door
105. Pope who dealt with Attila
107. Fanatical
108. Keenly perceptive
109. Attack
110. H.S. junior's exam
111. Afresh
112. Slot fillers
113. Spanish river
114. Daredevil Knievel

by Harvey L. Chew

ACROSS

1 Wanamaker and Houston
5 Buckets
10 Larceny
15 Columnist Bombeck
19 Austen novel
20 Director of "The Pawnbroker"
21 "A Man and a Woman" star Anouk
22 Destine to tragedy
23 Dessert for Peter?
25 White's dessert?
27 Multiple births
28 More fit
30 Vaughan and Bernhardt
31 Dame Myra __
32 Avaricious
33 "__ Be Seeing You"
34 Hobgoblin
37 Promontory
38 "Citizen Kane" sled
42 Abu Dhabi ruler
43 Bound by an oath
45 Tejano superstar
48 Noshed
49 Deadly poison
50 5,280 feet
51 Ships' records
52 Thin coating
53 Assn.
54 Dessert for Chiquita?
58 Hardy wheat
59 One who makes ready
61 Greek colonnades
62 Lyric poems
63 Break times
64 Day in the movies
65 Courtyards
66 Paintbrush choices
68 Last
69 "Iliad" hero
72 Jurgens and Gowdy
73 Jerry's dessert?
75 Docs' group
76 Thirst quenchers
77 Chromosome unit
78 Ray or Moro
79 H.S. junior's exam
80 Long, narrow inlet
81 Procreates
83 Try hard to persuade
84 Dust-bowl migrant
85 Government division
87 More free from adulterants
89 Makes airtight
90 Guys
91 Sports venues
93 Breezy talk
95 One-name comic
98 Cloth from flax
99 Document restrictions
103 Weakling's desserts?
105 Photographer's dessert?
107 Actor Sharif
108 Nimble
109 Cosmetician Lauder
110 Taj Mahal site
111 Lecture
112 Nearly perpendicular
113 Staircase
114 Low-fat

DOWN

1 Calendar 9
2 Manchurian border river
3 Start of the 4th millennium
4 Deep blue gem
5 Ballet movements
6 Bee and Em, e.g.
7 Little devils
8 Fragrant neckwear
9 Solid fat
10 Writer's blocks?
11 Employed
12 Atlanta university
13 Weak in numbers
14 Stresses
15 English Channel swimmer Gertrude
16 Church court
17 Fluttery flyer
18 Tan and Irving
24 Swiss artist Paul
26 Wood for models
29 Blue or Cross
32 Bridge guru
34 Jazz style
35 Syndicated astrologer
36 Ms. Rogers' dessert?
37 Like the Arctic
38 Mil. division
39 Dessert after the Iditarod?
40 Of service
41 Fender flaws
43 Brains
44 Port and claret
46 Raines and Fitzgerald
47 Superman's Lane
52 Ruin
54 Military installations
55 In unison
56 Guitar holder
57 French soldier of WWI
58 Twig with leaves
60 Bombards
62 Cultural group
64 Chopped into small cubes
65 Corrosive substances
66 Head wrap
67 Hero turned actor Murphy
68 Cash penalty
69 Contemporary of Freud
70 Computer messages
71 Fills completely
73 Lively dance
74 Challenges
77 Pops' poppas
79 Fancifully depicted
81 Silvery fish
82 Writer of "The Faerie Queene"
83 Struts
86 Board a vessel
88 French one
89 Rescue
91 Michael Caine film
92 Long gun
93 Slink
94 Fire truck equipment
95 Dundee fellow
96 "__ la Douce"
97 "Hud" star Patricia
99 Sampras of tennis
100 Wise guy
101 Gumbo ingredient
102 Actor Connery
104 Inarticulate grunt
106 FDR follower

by Willy A. Wiseman

ACROSS

1 Volcanic crater
8 Pilgrimage to Mecca
12 Baby food
15 Dinner
19 Pilot
20 Moises or Felipe of baseball
21 Japanese sash
22 Comic Johnson
23 Regional farm organization?
27 Scottish dagger
28 RN's thoughtfulness
29 Indeed
30 Neighbor of Martinique
31 "Little Brown Jug" refrain
34 4-wheel drive transport
36 Comparative suffix
37 Fortress-dwelling monarch's clemency?
46 City in S.E. Mexico
47 Biblical twin
48 Golfer "Champagne Tony"
49 Unmasker's cry
50 Silently ill-humored
51 Site of the Palazzo Ducale
54 Culture medium
55 Religious poet of the commonwealth?
63 Get the picture
64 Nostalgic fashion
65 H. Hughes' airline
66 Is
67 "Black Magic Woman" group
69 Board member
72 Commits theft
75 Call-day connection
77 Nightmarish Belgian artist
78 Sun Devils sch.
81 Royal locks?
86 Inactive
87 Church speaker's platforms
88 Smoke deposit
89 Lamb's lament: var.
90 Last of a teen?
92 Abbr. in airport names
95 "A Night to Remember" star
97 Growth in a mossy stream?
102 Orinoco tributary
103 Bud's Costello
104 Native American language of the Northwest
105 Heroic accomplishment
109 Mach+ jet
111 They: Fr.
112 Heart problem?
116 Buddy's religious servant?
121 Supporters
122 Alias letters
123 Comfort
124 Enmity
125 Meth. of operation
126 Psychedelic drug, for short
127 Faded in the stretch
128 In __ (eventually)

DOWN

1 Metal containers
2 Severn tributary
3 Bologna money, once
4 See regularly
5 African nat.
6 Drive a dinghy
7 Singer Franklin
8 Hinged rear doors
9 Bass or ginger
10 Actor Victor
11 Alaska's capital
12 Luau fare
13 Rudiments
14 Sanctimony
15 Fertilizer
16 __ the Red
17 To you: Fr.
18 Musical Horne
24 Donahue movie, "Susan __"
25 Evaluate
26 Muslim scholars
31 __ jacet (here lies)
32 Alma-__, Kazakhstan
33 Texas shrine
35 Soft palate
37 Fusses
38 Non-Polynesian Hawaiian
39 Ooze out
40 Corker
41 Miniskirt Mary
42 Tidal term
43 Hindu melodies
44 Visual aid
45 Gridiron lines
52 Package info.
53 Ripper
54 Irish Rose lover
56 In-person exams
57 High-IQ group
58 Addams Family member
59 Shooters' grp.
60 Isotope of thorium
61 Admit
62 Bring to bear
67 Wise person
68 Gillette blade
70 Numero __
71 Opposite of NNE
72 Clears the surface
73 Of ocean motion
74 China's Zhou __
76 Playful prank
78 Ere
79 Rock
80 You in the Yucatan
82 Over, in Germany
83 Emerald mineral
84 Riversides
85 Computer owner
90 Cook's coverage
91 Of a hypothetical Earth surface
93 Followed
94 Soprano Lehmann
95 DDE's opponent
96 Queen's letters
98 Least colorful
99 Bonheur or Parks
100 Ejected
101 Covered with a sticky coating
105 Studio apts.
106 Medical picture
107 Bowler's targets
108 Clicking sounds
110 Siamese
112 Chem. chart figure
113 Tenth of MDXX
114 Ship's tiller
115 Mystery writer __ Stanley Gardner
117 Scoundrel
118 Chemical suffix
119 Italian sky's color
120 Glob ending?

SCALE NOTES

by Edgar Fontaine

ACROSS

1 Practical sci. classes
5 Isolated state of India
10 Islamic pilgrim's destination
15 Tours summers
19 Melville's sequel to "Typee"
20 Sister's daughter
21 Off to one side
22 "Love Songs" poet Teasdale
23 Bassoon or oboe
25 Beatles song of 1968
27 Appreciated
28 Climbing plants
30 Type of computer
31 Louis XIV and others
32 Taskbar images
33 Tizzy
34 Greenish film
37 Winged
38 Interrupted
42 Air views
43 Pioneer of cool jazz
45 Pay attachment?
46 Wedding token
47 Buffalo of the Celebes
49 Memorable times
50 Colonial black cuckoos
51 Light knock
52 Like audited courses
56 Woman in the kitchen?
57 Getting tangled
60 CEOs, VPs and others
61 Hair ointment
62 Hangman's knot
63 Do-re-mi-fa-sol-la-ti-do
64 Spouses
65 __ longue
67 Loop of land
68 Ballet men
71 Word before Kitchen or Angels
72 Sea devils
74 Do a greenskeeping task
75 Building add-ons
76 Type of shark?
78 Singer Anita
79 Bullets, for short
80 Grow old
81 Weighty singer?
85 Look scornfully
86 Installments
88 Grannies
89 Dragster
90 Roman Catholic calendar
91 Feudal lord's peons
92 Indonesian island
93 King David's poetry
96 Wind: pref.
97 Male voice
101 Hit by the Shirelles
103 Bob Dylan hit
105 Surfeit
106 Mother-of-pearl

107 Mollycoddles
108 Pocket bread
109 Walked (on)
110 Gave medicine
111 Snow-day rides
112 Slaughter in Cooperstown

DOWN

1 Ore source
2 Biblical prophet
3 Boxing match
4 Serious
5 Lack of vigor
6 Fathers
7 Ranked player
8 High card
9 Insurance coverage
10 Leathernecks
11 Dueling swords
12 Ohio team, to fans
13 __-Magnon
14 Legendary island
15 Landed property
16 Follow
17 Last of a switch?
18 Carried a tune
24 Sierra __

26 Modular parts
29 Ballot
32 Of a pelvic bone
33 Fiji Islands capital
34 Sailors' stopovers
35 Of bees
36 Music way?
37 In the company of
38 Simpson and Maverick
39 "Last Dance" singer
40 Homeric epic
41 English anti-Puritan satirist
44 Clear the windshield
47 Plant with sweet seeds
48 Zilch
50 Actress Anouk
53 Surveillance, briefly
54 Praise
55 Perry Mason's Ms. Street
56 Periods
58 Stirs up liquid
59 Defeat
61 Flower with velvety petals
63 Endure
64 Yucatan Indians
65 Low-cost
66 Hagar the Horrible's lady
67 Pile up

68 Carpenter's grooves: var.
69 Juliet's beau
70 Excalibur, e.g.
73 Jaffe and Barrett
76 L.L. Bean rival
77 Mr. Preminger
79 Contrasting kind
81 Physicist Enrico
82 Like some jacks
83 Address for a lady in Westerns
84 Bends inward
85 Unbroken
87 Shaped
89 Torment persistently
91 REM sound?
92 Tied in bundles
93 Sibilant sound
94 Fly high
95 Palo __, CA
96 Rudiments
97 Eight bits
98 Ken or Lena
99 Western alliance, briefly
100 Unfledged bird
102 Indian P.M. after Rajiv Gandhi
104 Internet provider: abbr.

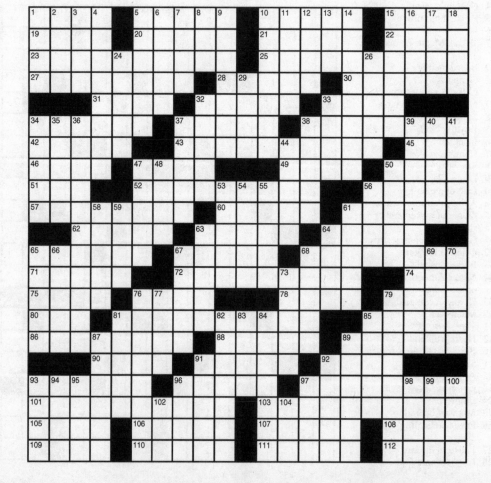

PERSONAL SONGS

by Robert H. Wolfe

ACROSS

1 Literary snippets
4 Craps shooter
9 Speech problem
13 Huns' leader
19 Buddy
20 Cognizant
21 Opposed to: pref.
22 Defroster
23 Crude shelter
24 Green beans
25 H.S. junior's exam
26 Son of William the Conqueror
27 Church song?
31 Actress Lupino
32 Jumps the tracks
33 Inventor Whitney
34 Like leftovers
36 Can. province
37 Page number
40 Barry and Nelson
43 Writing tools
44 Writer Asch
46 Audible breaths
47 Drunkard
48 __ Lanka
51 Barcelata tune, "Maria __"
52 Sioux tribe
53 Prickled
56 "__: United States Marshal"
58 Auction action
60 Clan
62 Gabor sister
63 Fruity quaffs
64 Starts
67 Holiday seasons
68 Polite address
69 Actor Neeson
70 Mournful cries
71 Jane Wyman film
72 Stones hit, "Honky __ Women"
73 Golf 3, 4 or 5
74 Red pepper pod
75 Timid: var.
76 Formerly
77 End of a flight, maybe: abbr.
78 French city known for textiles
79 Police call letters
80 Atmosphere element
82 Shut forcefully again
84 Infamous tsar
86 Glass vial
89 Draft letters
90 M-m-m-m good!
91 Appears
92 Peter Pan's creator
94 First word, often
96 Egyptian corn
97 Jazz style
98 Pet protection grp.
102 Attributer
104 Pod starter?
106 Final remarks
108 O.T. book

109 Glasses-wearer's song?
114 Philippine seaport
116 August in Paris
117 Of part of the eye: pref.
118 Civil War side: abbr.
119 Chopping device
120 Indian gown
121 North Dakota city
122 Neighbor of Leb.
123 Dorothy of mysteries
124 Church projection
125 Hammer heads
126 Moon car

DOWN

1 Garden pests
2 Upset stomach
3 Tabernacle tables
4 __ Lama
5 Bounty hunter's song?
6 Short negligee
7 Quod __ demonstrandum
8 Those not listed
9 Element of a jacket
10 Animate
11 Arcturus or Alpha Centauri, e.g.
12 Pocketed bread?
13 University of Georgia's city
14 Over yonder
15 Cure hide
16 Ditty Rodgers sang to Hammerstein?
17 City in the Netherlands
18 Parliament add-ons?
28 Chatters
29 Name for a lion
30 A few laughs
35 End of time, briefly
38 Sportscaster Berman
39 Billy Graham song?
41 Mrs. Ruth's song?
42 Small angels
45 Norse goddess
46 Creates a new lawn
47 French religious figures: abbr.
48 Illegal ticket reseller
49 Emerge in waves
50 Song by Zubin Mehta?
53 Tune Nixon sang to Ford?
54 Manifests
55 Adds shadows
57 Ending for a belief
59 "__ a Most Unusual Day"
61 Nastase of tennis

65 Toe tip
66 Zanier
71 Saturate
72 Trifle
74 Cherrystone or littleneck, e.g.
75 Takes up stations
81 Letters for 41
83 Hawaiian feast
85 Dabblers
87 Queen of the fairies
88 Old-time dental anesthetic
91 Chapter of the Koran
93 Catch sight of
94 Half notes
95 Lost aviator Earhart
96 Furnishings
97 Pen manufacturer
99 Writing implement
100 La __, WI
101 Teeming
103 Flooring maker
105 Get back to even
107 Scenarios
110 Shuttle grp.
111 Cleansing substance
112 Hanging loosely
113 __-Lackawanna Railroad
115 Arctic surface

LOST SHIPS

by Josiah Breward

ACROSS

1 Pours the wine
8 Novelist Le Guin and others
15 Pointed
20 Lost aviator Amelia
21 James Bond portrayer
22 Ancient region in Asia Minor
23 Subduer
24 Find palatable
26 The Greatest
27 Form starter?
28 Guitar adjunct
29 Commemorative monuments
30 Attention-getting calls
31 DLIII doubled
33 Addictive drug
37 Balin or Claire
38 Nickname for Mr. Scrooge
40 Gardener's implement
44 Reverse pic
45 Beautiful Bo
47 Toxin or surgeon starter
48 Olympic runner Devers
49 Father of France
50 Half a fortnight
52 Sandwich meat
54 Winglike
56 Had a bite
58 Football play
61 Movement to unite Cyprus and Greece
65 Cartilage in meat
67 Greek colonnades
69 Desert bloom
70 Mil. division
71 Preface
75 Medical condition: suff.
77 Children's writer Silverstein
78 Anesthetic
80 Cuban cohort of Che
82 Full speed
84 Contents of one's will
86 Record jacket information
90 Harvest goddess
91 Netting
93 Undertaker
94 "The Man" of baseball
96 Big pigs
99 Greater omentum
101 Scheduled next
103 Guinness and Baldwin
106 Gardner of "The Killers"
107 Neglect to knock
110 End of a buck?
111 Fam. member
112 Stand against
113 Sked figures
115 The: It.
116 Mandarin or navel
118 Festive occasion
122 Nabokov novel
123 Celtic Neptune
124 Postal worker
128 Like a feather
130 Oxeye __
131 Ease of movement

132 Pretentious performer?
133 Wild guesses
134 Tunes in
135 African flies

DOWN

1 Rotten
2 Place for a ring
3 Boxing category
4 Contented sounds
5 Old Testament book
6 Deep furrow
7 Endeavored
8 West Coast sch.
9 Capital of Italia
10 Ginger cookie
11 Not hip at all
12 Prairie chicken's display area
13 Orinoco tributary
14 Equivalent wd.
15 Lady of the cloth
16 Target on a green
17 Benzene derivative
18 Maturing agent
19 Way by
25 Getty of "The Golden Girls"
32 That is (to say): Latin
34 Crude ingots

35 Dict. pronunciation letters: abbr.
36 Capital of Samoa
39 Born in France
41 Forage legume
42 __ Stanley Gardner
43 Paint layers
46 Maintained
49 "Remembrance of Things Past" author
51 Nancy of "The Beverly Hillbillies"
53 Silent
55 Even one
56 Think alike
57 Waste allowances
59 Soft-toy substance
60 __ "King" Cole
62 Beer vessel
63 Freeze
64 Epsom __
66 Cooks in vapors
68 Process flour
72 Black gold
73 Food stuffs
74 Program choices
76 Pub beers
79 Hwy. sign abbr.
81 "Slave Ship" writer __ Jones

83 Cinema canine
85 Fleer
87 Call on the phone
88 European nat.
89 Speak one's mind
92 Angel's instrument
95 Miss. neighbor
96 Lloyd and Arlen
97 Pig out
98 Ancient region in Asia Minor
100 Actor Tognazzi
102 Series of quick, light steps
104 Author of "Gigi"
105 Evening affairs
107 Hobgoblins
108 Mourn
109 Lowest points
114 A votre __! (French toast)
117 Plane-crash investigation grp.
119 Helper
120 Ponce de __
121 Weapons
125 Org. of Argonauts
126 Onassis to pals
127 Scale notes
129 Something to pick?

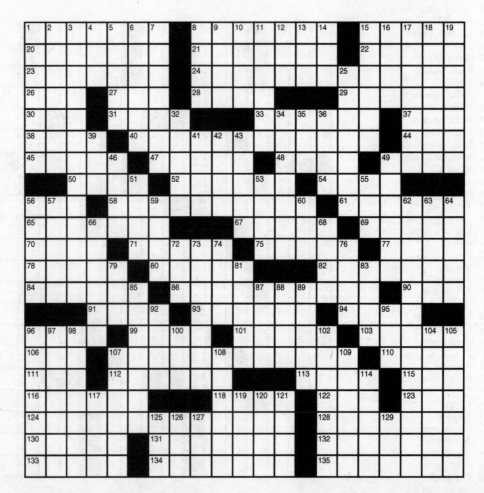

STEPHEN KINK?

by Willy A. Wiseman

ACROSS

1 Flock females
5 Adam's grandson
9 Bony
15 19th-century actress Menken
19 Donated
20 Reclined
21 Hall of "Our House"
22 Fuji flow
23 Last stretch of an S.K. marathon?
25 S.K.'s tribute to runway models?
27 Mid-ocean
29 Kipling book
30 Besmirches
31 Bush or Boxer
34 Of the nose
37 Wetlands
38 S-shaped molding
39 Sportscaster Bob
42 Passover meal
44 S.K.'s philosophical tome?
48 S.K.'s Krazy cartoon?
52 Legendary golfer Byron
53 Is able
54 Undue speed
56 __ Aviv
57 Took on cargo
59 Hand-tied fly
61 Ring within the iris
63 Harebrained
67 Coercion
69 Wading bird
70 Child's construction toy
71 S.K.'s simian travelogue?
74 Toward shelter
75 Oriental nursemaids
77 Sports venues
78 Kitchen appliances
80 Close a purse
82 Grace ending
83 Threadlike structure: Brit.
84 Twisting turn
85 Hand grip
87 Last of pay?
88 1998 winner of two golf majors
93 S.K.'s learned treatise?
95 S.K.'s creepy western?
99 Egyptian weight
101 Stop
102 By __ of (using effort)
103 Author of "The Trial"
106 Texas-Louisiana border river
108 Baltic nation
111 For each
113 Negative conjunction
114 More with it
117 S.K.'s zombie horror?
120 S.K.'s watery play?
124 Bunker or Nob, e.g.
125 Navy builder
126 Old codger
127 Continental prefix
128 Water whirl
129 Full of turns
130 Defeat
131 "Wild at Heart" star Laura

DOWN

1 Easter item
2 Open hostilities
3 Holiday lead-in
4 Garden
5 "__ Gantry"
6 Writer V.S. __
7 Lubricates
8 Dundee dagger
9 G.I. wear
10 Inspiration for "Robinson Crusoe"
11 Related product
12 Swellings
13 Genesis craft
14 Ayres and Wallace
15 Ready to listen
16 Capital of Senegal
17 States forcefully
18 Grating
24 New Zealand bird
26 Instruments for measuring current
28 "Catch-22" star
31 Beethoven's birthplace
32 Film critic James
33 Virginia dance
35 Coop layer
36 Birds' display areas
40 Extras
41 African nation
43 Computer input
45 People
46 Not likely
47 Scolding woman
49 French star
50 Disney classic "Old __"
51 Brings joy
55 German shepherds
58 Qatar's capital
59 Chinese cuisine
60 Work units
62 State: Fr.
63 Wine choice
64 Interlock anew
65 1992 Wimbledon winner
66 Marc or Mindy
67 Accomplished
68 Mess maker
72 Trim and tidy
73 John Paul II, __ Wojtyla
76 Picnic contest
79 18-wheeler
81 Stated one's case
83 Chimney passage
86 God of war
87 Made-up monsters
89 Approved
90 Related by blood
91 Kidneys: pref.
92 Ionian Sea gulf
94 Vulnerably
96 Snood
97 Sea eagle
98 Music systems
100 Japanese battle cry
103 German artist Kollwitz
104 Plant louse
105 Ballpark
107 Ninnies
109 Editorial directives
110 Shatner novel "__ Power"
112 Right on maps
115 1250 in letters
116 End of a buck?
118 Dawn lawn layer
119 Code base
121 Coloration
122 Hockey great
123 Took first

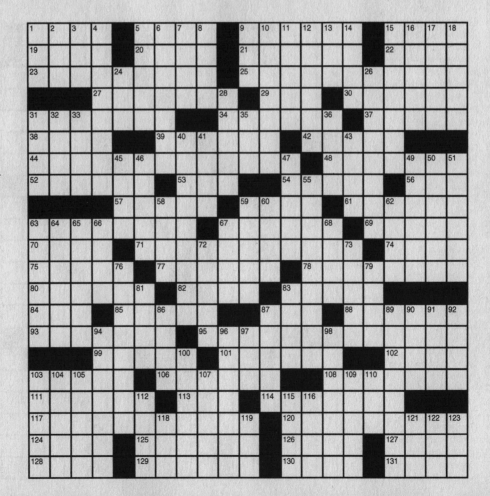

by Bill Swain

ACROSS

1 H.S. subj.
4 Quarters
9 "Two Women" star Sophia
14 Chagall and Connelly
19 Assn.
20 Susann's "Valley of the __"
21 Sign of spring?
22 Shaq or Tatum
23 Lower slopes
25 Boondocks
27 Shamir and Rabin
28 Surf sound
29 Garden gnome, e.g.
30 Makes certain
31 Nothing but
32 Vilnius lang.
34 CIA's predecessor
35 Newsman Koppel
36 Blue and Cross
37 Procession of matadors
38 Ready or __
39 Invited
42 Take out
43 Isolated
45 Deviate
46 Stream sources
48 Shaded area
52 Chemical suffix
53 Mom's sisters
54 Land of Los Angeles?
55 Author of "The End of the Affair"
56 Grp. of Sampras, Agassi et al.
57 Home runs, e.g.
58 Commit a gaffe
59 Positions properly
60 Betting guide
61 Wharton School deg.
62 Grace closings
63 11 on calendars
64 Word ignored by alphabetizers
65 Streaking
67 Swine
68 Sewer segment
69 Drench
70 Brazilian port
71 Roseanne, once
72 Smithy, at times
73 Horse morsel
74 Sacked out
75 Isthmus
77 Seethe
78 Sword cases
80 Highland miss
81 Nucleus of personnel
82 Spanish couple?
85 Privileged few
86 Sugar quantity
87 Heavy imbiber
88 One: pref.
89 Highly spiced stew
90 Spherical bodies
91 Dispose of by deception
95 Jason's objective
97 James Merritt or Charles Edward
98 Trump namer
99 Seneca, Cayuga et al.
102 Part of Texas
103 Nine: pref.
104 Warning signal
105 Digestive disorder
106 Evanston's transp.
107 Memorize
108 Comes out on top
109 Red vegetables
110 Team cheer

DOWN

1 Capital of Bulgaria
2 Span
3 Stravinsky and Sikorsky
4 Stuck
5 Vexed
6 __ Island, NY
7 "__ Well That Ends Well"
8 Draft letters
9 Tasks
10 Speak bombastically
11 Houston school
12 Comic scream
13 Grp. of D.C. advisers
14 Delta
15 Paquin of "The Piano"
16 Olympian gymnast Mary Lou
17 Baez song about a singer
18 Crafty to the max
24 Tighter
26 Start of a path?
28 Make over
31 Card-game displays
32 Classic Preminger movie
33 Suffix for adherents
36 Pulsations
37 "Mission: Impossible" character
39 Post and Earhart
40 Guard
41 Stay with the pack
42 Repudiation
43 Laundry problems
44 Let loose
46 Space telescope
47 Pace of music
49 Type of rocker
50 Broadcasting
51 Repopulate
53 Marine extension?
55 Felt one's way
58 Self-satisfied smiles
59 Pot roast ingredient
62 Southwest tribesman
66 Tears
68 Temporary pattern of behavior
71 Siamese fighting fish
72 Weighty pieces
75 Toe tip
76 Misplays
77 The Caped Crusader
79 Carl of the gridiron
81 Peter Pan and Eton
82 Army bag
83 Surfing the web
84 Brown shade
86 Whitecaps
87 Sweet-smelling sack
90 Out in the open
91 Pieces of a pound
92 Sequence
93 Guy
94 New
96 Elbe tributary
97 Turner and Clanton
98 Valley
100 Research room
101 Pale or ginger
102 Tavern by a tube station

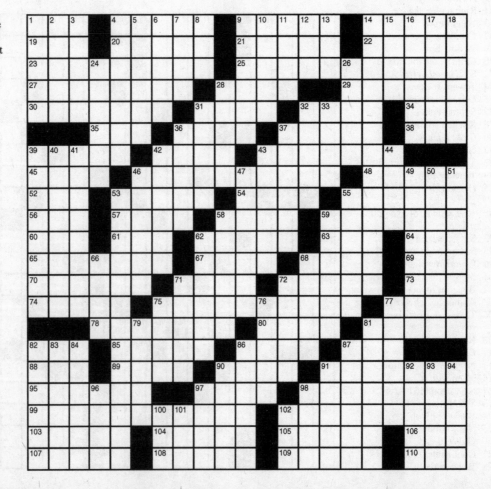

SHIP AHOY!

by Arthur S. Verdesca

ACROSS

1 Wedge for stopping
5 Lucine of the New York Metropolitan Opera
10 Mell Lazarus comic strip
15 Breathe heavily
19 Emerald Isle
20 Chan's portrayer in films
21 Lake Geneva spa
22 Herman Melville's "Typee" sequel
23 STEAMER
25 SCHOONER
27 Lip curlers
28 Chicago airport
30 Erects
31 Goose on Oahu
32 Author of "Historia Naturalis"
33 Clumsy clod
34 Vents ill will
37 French Open winner of 1993
38 Eau de __ (cologne)
42 Loathed
43 Small, low islet
44 Protects
46 Auto gear: abbr.
47 Got a perfect grade
48 Body of a ship
49 Residents of: suff.
50 Walking stick
51 Dreamer's letters
52 TENDER
56 More timid
57 Desecrates
59 Shelters a fugitive, e.g.
60 Evasive
61 Destined
62 Fine-grained corundum
63 Baby grand, e.g.
64 Mental health
66 Milk top, once
67 Eastern Hemisphere
70 Long-time pal
71 LINER
73 Pipe buildup
74 Touch against
75 Lorre in eight movies
76 Top-notch
77 Eight bits
78 __ Alamos
79 Word with bridge or wagon
82 New Zealand parrot
83 Fear and May, e.g.
84 One who makes ready
86 Actress Phoebe
88 Light beams
89 Sea east of the Caspian
90 Shroud of __
91 God of war
92 Rocks
95 Comic-actress Pflug
96 Russian despot, Ivan the __
100 BARK
102 CLIPPER
104 Wood trimmer

105 Poetic Muse
106 Eradicate
107 Watch over
108 State of mind
109 Gaucho's address
110 Also-ran
111 Influence

DOWN

1 Min. parts
2 Baking chamber
3 Wrath of Caesar
4 Insane
5 University of Georgia's city
6 Sculptor Henry
7 Muhammad and others
8 Game room, for short
9 Space between leaf veins
10 Hodgepodge
11 Egg-producing organ
12 Stick in the mud
13 Periodical, briefly
14 Some barometers
15 Civil
16 Amo, __, amat...
17 Rocket cap
18 Fling
24 Confession of faith
26 Franks' predecessors

29 Posterior
32 Biology kingdom divisions
33 Hermit
34 Clearly detailed
35 Expectant dad, e.g.
36 JUNK
37 Soothes
38 Heads of France
39 GALLEY
40 Doctrine
41 __ now and again
43 Made well
45 Grant's bill?
48 Bee product
50 Coarse, twilled cotton fabric
52 Comic Arbuckle
53 Hobbled
54 West Indian religious belief
55 Physicist Enrico
56 Shoulder warmer
58 Dim
60 Edge along
62 Blooper
63 First choice of schemes
64 Head skin
65 Shaded area
66 Supply the food

67 Some woodwinds
68 Some time after
69 Apparel
71 Run-down dwelling
72 Already claimed
75 Swamps
77 Members of rhythm sections
79 Showed concern
80 Quito's land
81 Mild oath
83 Keep in stock
85 Reviewed harshly
87 December decoration
88 Pantry
90 Lone Ranger's pal
91 Former Attorney General Edwin
92 Junk e-mail
93 Fuss
94 Aniseed-flavored liqueur
95 San __, Puerto Rico
96 Assam and pekoe
97 Tooted
98 Singer Horne
99 Whirlpool
101 Bauxite or galena
103 In favor of

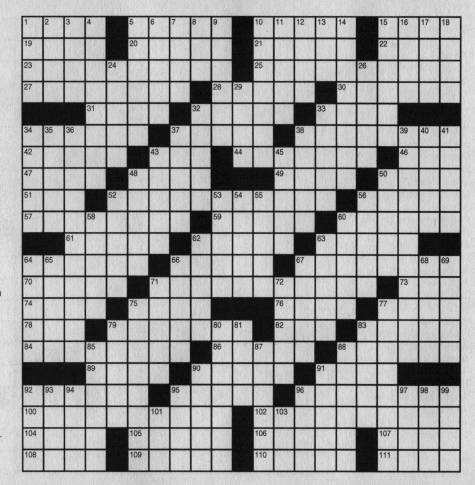

TWO-TIMERS

by Robert H. Wolfe

ACROSS

1 Complain
7 Goldblum of "The Fly"
11 Insect snares
15 Blighted trees
19 Titania's man
20 General Bradley
21 Japanese golfer Aoki
22 Genesis character
23 Two types of jackets?
26 Melody
27 Carried
28 Buy the farm
29 Mormon leader
30 Natural hair coloring
31 "Night Moves" singer
33 Ice on the move
34 More time-consuming
35 Stupid
39 Lady's address
40 Barry of the Detroit Lions
41 Nine-days' devotion
42 And others, in brief
44 More aloof
45 Rocky outcrop
46 Twofold?
53 Early lab burner
54 Stringed instruments
55 Spoils
56 Squirmy
57 Learned papers
59 Common maladies
60 Low hisser
61 Women
64 Oral statement
66 Loathing
67 __ and kicking
68 Game akin to bingo
70 Give one's consent
73 Take lunch
74 Southern constellation
75 Cacophonously
76 Astronaut's negative
80 Two measures?
83 Surrealist painter Salvador
84 People conquered by the Iroquois
85 Work station
86 Outpouring of gossip
88 Sudden digression
91 Grace ending
93 Transfixes
94 Relaxing
95 At any time
96 "The Planets" composer
98 Sports pages' figs.
99 Be real
100 Arctic surface
101 Disney and Whitman
106 South American monkey
107 Two images?
110 Alt.
111 Enthusiastic
112 __ avis
113 Ascended
114 Challenge

115 Pipe bends
116 School on the Thames
117 Michelle Kwan's footwear

DOWN

1 Senator from Virginia, once
2 River of Spain
3 Equal
4 Persian Gulf country
5 Pries
6 Way in: abbr.
7 Foster of "The Silence of the Lambs"
8 Burning coal
9 Much removed
10 Skydiver's thrill
11 Common sense
12 Cosmetician Lauder
13 Heavyweight champ of 1934
14 Greensward
15 Two meanings?
16 Waiting room
17 Behavior
18 Does barbering
24 Advantage
25 __ breve

30 Sharpener
32 Makes possible
34 Haunts
35 Allow ending?
36 Classify
37 Infamous tsar
38 Two grammatical errors?
39 West and Murray
40 Reads quickly
42 Russian-born illustrator
43 Infringement
44 In the same place: Lat.
47 Group of GIs
48 Switch tail?
49 Dolts
50 Father of Regan, Cordelia and Goneril
51 Actress Sommer
52 Soaked in anil
58 "__ Haw"
59 __-Magnon
60 Downcast
61 Fellas
62 Touched down
63 Actress Merrill
65 Medical school subj.
66 Cowboys, at times
68 French topper

69 Terminates
71 Checked garment?
72 Train unit
74 Ship to remember
75 Unknown auth.
77 Clumsy lummoxes
78 Surfeit
79 Lubricates
81 Accoutrement
82 Slit
87 Gallery display
88 Sampled
89 5th-century leader
90 More organized
91 French airplanes
92 Recruit's dinner
93 Trebek of "Jeopardy!"
95 Send packing
96 Sacred: pref.
97 Watery expanse
99 Cager Nick Van __
102 Large land mass
103 __ for life
104 Elder or alder
105 D.C. VIPs
107 Scrimp
108 Fink
109 __ de deux

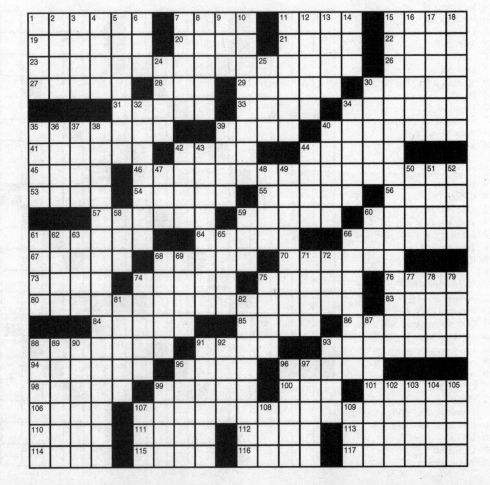

by Josiah Breward

ACROSS

1 Single-masted sailing vessels
7 Cheap cigar
13 Way off the mark
20 Stinging wasp
21 Greetings
22 Two-syllable foot
23 Ethnic issue
25 Temporary cars
26 Too quickly
27 No longer in use
29 Fig. of speech
30 __ Simon Theater
31 College figs.
34 European nat.
35 Hereditary factor
36 Hall of Leno's show, once
37 Thai or Korean, e.g.
39 Former Russian rulers
42 Open area of a blood vessel
43 Worldwide revolutionary communists
45 Chapter of the Koran
46 Melonlike fruit
49 Finnish baths
50 Country on Lake Tanganyika
53 Menu option
55 Mothers
56 Delight
57 "Star Wars" pilot Solo
58 Legal permission
59 Car panel
61 __ gratia artis
62 Act as a lookout, e.g.
63 Nabokov heroine
65 Kimono sash
66 Gudrun's victim
67 Greek letter or cross
68 Discordance
73 Fused (ores)
76 Naut. direction
77 Greek god of war
78 Ford or Dodge, e.g.
79 Island hopper
80 Holy
82 French actress Jeanne
84 Keaton and Ladd
85 Victory signs
86 Author of "The Moviegoer"
88 Composer Charles Camille Saint-__
90 Glass pieces
91 City on the Rhone
92 School trainees, in brief
95 Wear out
96 Sportscaster Scully
97 Jai __
98 Math subj.
99 Writer's writings, in brief
100 Sire
104 Make bigger
107 Lurie and Krauss
109 Utensil for serving hors d'oeuvres
112 Reveals
113 Temper
114 "Nausea" novelist
115 "2001: A Space __"
116 Lethal
117 Balanced conditions

DOWN

1 Pilgrim's destination
2 Gave temporarily
3 Pale purple
4 Cager Shaquille
5 Individual: abbr.
6 Leave text in
7 __ Na Na
8 Hanoi holiday
9 Medleys of songs
10 Soft, thick lump
11 Charged particles
12 Exxon, formerly
13 Agamemnon's father
14 Is vexed
15 First-class
16 GI
17 Bank of America competition
18 Add new padding
19 Sycophants
24 On the up-and-up
28 "I Remember Mama" character
32 Out of fashion
33 "Diana" singer
35 Spiritual adviser
37 Indo-Iranian
38 Travels by glider
39 Turner and Louise
40 Secret supply
41 '50s Democrat
42 Enticed
43 Silent, in music
44 Arizona city
45 Litigant
46 Gourmets' pride
47 "Open, sesame!" guy
48 School in New York City
50 M. Pascal
51 Roseanne's TV kid
52 Guts
54 Wept
56 Swabbie
59 June honoree
60 Singer George?
64 Opposite of: pref.
66 Set to rest
68 Fills completely
69 Very, on the Moselle
70 French school
71 Drug cops: var.
72 Canadian tribe
74 Spanish mother
75 Sweeping sagas
79 Toyota model
81 Hawaiian goose
82 Playing piece
83 Inland sea of Asia
86 Grow less
87 Eero Saarinen's father
88 Gulf off Brittany
89 Like theaters and churches
90 Messy quarters
92 Reading decks
93 Veep of the '90s
94 Act parts
96 Locale
97 Rainbow-shaped
98 "It's a Wonderful Life" director
100 Relatives of raspberries
101 Folk-song abbr.
102 Ditty
103 Sicilian resort
105 Capone's undoer
106 Coll. exam
108 Draft letters
110 Adjective-forming suffix
111 Old-time journalist Nellie

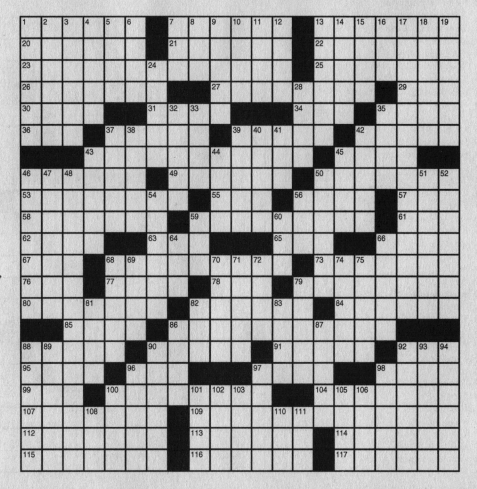

by Edgar Fontaine

ACROSS

1 Injure
5 Support crew
10 Coral colonies
15 Baby's word
19 Toward shelter
20 "As You Like It" role
21 "Borsalino" star Delon
22 Orbit-shaped
23 Gift from Santa
25 Gift from Santa
27 West Indies islands
28 Film snippets
30 More than enough
31 Stock-car racer Yarborough
32 Glorifies
33 Mineral springs
34 Hindu souls
37 Noisemaker
38 Pitcher's opponents
42 Greg Norman's sobriquet
43 "Abe Lincoln in Illinois" star Raymond
44 Vocal inflection
45 Outdo
46 Foster film, "Little Man __"
47 Squirrel away
48 Uneven hairstyle
49 Twice DLIII
50 Business letter abbr.
51 Gift from Santa
55 Writer/singer Leonard
56 Stiffen again
58 Perfume from petals
59 Wide stretches in rivers
60 Construct
61 Broadcasting
62 Repasts
63 Flashy or jaunty
65 Deep draft of liquor
66 Renounces
69 Second-largest state
70 Gift from Santa
72 Tarzan on TV
73 Contest of speed
74 Pokes fun
75 Geological time periods
76 Knock for a loop
77 After the style of
78 Young society women, briefly
79 Acmes
82 Right-hand page
83 Treachery
85 Urban distance units
86 Soaked oneself
87 Andes autocrat
88 Fugard play, "A Lesson from __"
89 Oodles
90 Seem
93 Braincase
94 Importunes
98 Gift from Santa
100 Gift from Santa
102 Granular seasoning
103 Shop

104 Slithering hisser
105 Different
106 Scatter Fitzgerald
107 Sits tight
108 Overstuffed
109 Unit of electricity

DOWN

1 Sarcastic chuckle
2 Shepard or Greenspan
3 Become a lessee
4 Social Security program
5 Racing boats
6 Conical shelter
7 Swiss range
8 Expression of distaste
9 Fund-raiser VIPs
10 Like a mad dog
11 Slip by
12 Listening devices
13 Lie a little
14 Barbering
15 Unassuming
16 Bard's river
17 Beer ingredient
18 Comrade in arms
24 Pirate's last walk, perhaps
26 Bring joy

29 Pear-shaped instrument
32 Star Wars weapon
33 Sandbank
34 Daisylike flower
35 Macbeth's title
36 Gift from Santa
37 Bird that can parrot
39 Gift from Santa
40 Roamed
41 Turns around
43 Wed
44 God of thunder
47 Lamentably
48 Lead actor
49 Dinero
51 Court orders
52 Terror
53 Balbo or Calvino
54 Yet
55 Crude
57 Distinctive atmospheres
59 Masses of ice
61 Has
62 Natural satellites
63 Lash
64 "The Power of Positive Thinking" author
65 Bro's bros

66 Ice on the move
67 Extract with a solvent
68 Church council
70 Egypt's neighbor
71 Narrow stretches
74 Humanitarian organization
76 Device to regulate spring tension
78 Shore or Washington
79 Enticements
80 Still part of a river
81 Like neat drinks
82 Relative degree
84 Religious holiday
85 Supermarket adjunct
86 Like a shot lock
89 Empirical philosopher
90 Church recess
91 Ring bells
92 Cast gloom over
93 Greek colonnade
94 Resting spot
95 Madonna hit, "La __ Bonita"
96 Trial by fire
97 Leave text in
99 Giant slugger?
101 Cellular letters

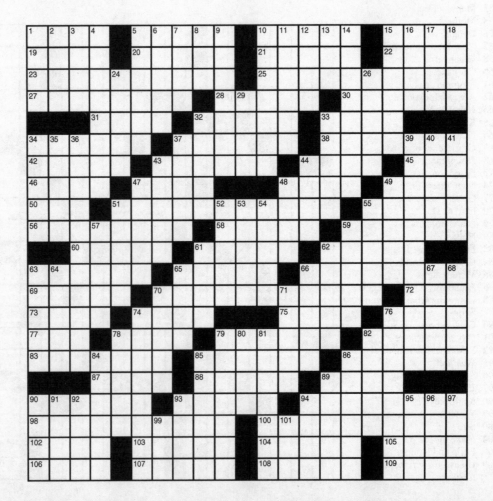

UNUSUAL POSSESSIONS

by Ed Voile

ACROSS
1 Legally recognized entity: abbr.
5 To err is __
10 Trajectories
14 Crush
19 Eye part
20 Habitual practice
21 Festive occasion
22 Expectant dad, e.g.
23 Supplication of an insect?
25 Chess piece
26 Harden
27 On cloud nine
28 Sass of a psychiatrist?
31 Lacking meaning
35 Lamprey
36 Fools
37 Produce from Georgia
39 Lady of "la casa"
41 Dance of hairstylists?
45 Roof of a tube train?
50 Emily Dickinson's town
51 New version
53 North American defense grp.
54 Talons
55 Handles the helm
56 Model-airplane builders
59 Chemical chart figure abbr.
60 Caribbean vacations
62 Former leader of Argentina
64 Rabbit of a big cat?
66 Relative of a ram?
70 Lead
71 Cornering in branches
74 Dwindle
75 Numbered musical compositions
78 Posterior
79 Prose romances
80 Distant
81 Evening receptions
83 Soothsayer
85 Bone of a buddy?
89 Sailors of films?
91 Stadium levels
92 Boone and Travanti
93 Bony
96 Carbohydrate: suff.
98 Cried in a strident voice
103 Characteristic of Washington?
107 In
108 Natural hair coloring
109 Old World blue dye
110 Vehicle of the Unification Church leader?
114 Rose essence
115 Russian-born American actress Nazimova
116 "A Delicate Balance" playwright
117 Oh yeah, right
118 Simoleons
119 Evaluation
120 River nymph
121 Potential plant

DOWN
1 Ice portions
2 Early-stage seed
3 Goneril's sister
4 Times gone by
5 Track jumpers
6 "Born in the __"
7 Has permission
8 Time period
9 Soft-toy stuff
10 Think alike
11 "Eating __"
12 Lummox
13 H.H. Munro
14 Washer cycle
15 Buttonlike flowers
16 Eye: pref.
17 Deserve
18 Makes ready, for short
24 Furtive viewers
29 Occupant: abbr.
30 Verdi opera
32 Bridge position
33 Acad.
34 Runt's nickname
38 Some rapiers
39 Post-grad deg.
40 Hole-making tool

41 Commonplace
42 Violin maker
43 Horned animal
44 Fits in
45 Gentlemen
46 Amer. ship letters
47 Half a fly?
48 Rower
49 IBM units
52 Churchill's gesture
55 Positive
56 Golfer Norman
57 Trim
58 In need of a broom
60 Greek letters
61 Way cool!
62 Comic Hartman
63 Bard's contraction
65 "A Boy Named __"
66 Annual cycles
67 Buckwheat groats
68 Bury
69 Hemlock homes
71 Infield cover, for short
72 Have regrets
73 Botanical swelling
75 Slightly askew
76 Average score
77 Magician Geller

78 Tenth of MXX
79 "Iron Eagle" star
81 Russia or Latvia, once: abbr.
82 Exclamations of comprehension
83 Docking place
84 Set free
86 Everlasting
87 River name that means "flood"
88 Cut text
90 Singer Damone
92 Roman gods
93 Old Irish alphabet
94 Take care of
95 Silverheels role
96 In-person exams
97 Anwar of Egypt
99 Rock or Schenkel
100 Contain
101 Host
102 Feinted
104 Thwack
105 Lacquered metalware
106 Government agt.
111 Pay attachment?
112 Kimono sash
113 Teachers' org.

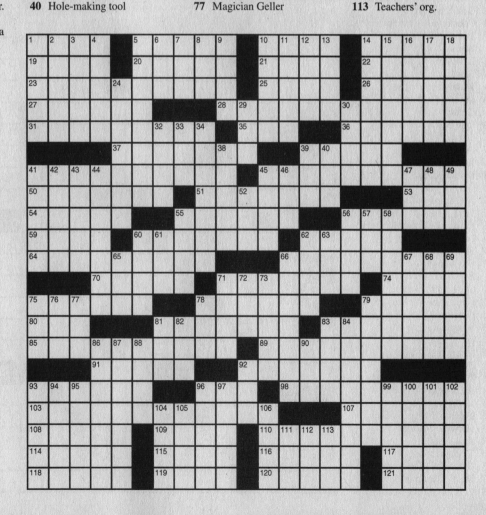

by Harvey Chew

ACROSS

1 Menu entree
5 Move in a sudden sweep
10 Dull pains
15 Twaddle
19 Jacob's brother
20 Prentiss or Abdul
21 Losing streak
22 Capital of Norway
23 Measure up
25 Nina, to Pinta
27 Rear gates
28 Kin of Brens
30 Hors d'oeuvre
31 Fast time
32 Power
33 X – VII
34 Aspect
37 Job duration
38 Deli offerings
42 German industrial region
43 Preliminary work
45 Stable units
48 Cool down
49 Pindar's output
50 Clothed
51 Creative work
52 Gobi's continent
53 Constantine's birthplace
54 Star of "The Silence of the Lambs"
58 Input data
59 Fated
61 Make fit
62 Gambler's pledges
63 Collier
64 Lytton Strachey's first name
65 Older companion?
66 Knee-ankle connections
68 Bottled spirit?
69 Getaway driver
72 Nathanael and Mae
73 White shade
75 Newcastle brown or ginger
76 Part of B.A.
77 Stronghold
78 Challenging
79 Eye amorously
80 Shemp's tormentor
81 Conical residences
83 Noggins
84 Stimulate
85 Encroachments
87 Mine cars
89 Donahue and Aikman
90 "__ Ventura: Pet Detective"
91 Adds protective layers
93 Christmas decoration
95 Helen of "City Slickers"
98 Shoulder warmer
99 Awe-inspiring
103 Vintage evaluator
105 Author of "The Virginian"
107 State categorically
108 Church congregation
109 Awaken
110 Latin & others: abbr.
111 Cathedral benches
112 Categorizes
113 Passover meal
114 Flatfish

DOWN

1 Star of "Edward Scissorhands"
2 Golfer Aoki
3 Lip
4 Silver-tongued liars
5 Reject disdainfully
6 "The Man Who __ There"
7 Inning sixths
8 Bullring cheer
9 White root food
10 States positively
11 Resist separation
12 Impudent girl
13 Ambulance worker: abbr.
14 TV one-shots
15 __-Herzegovina
16 Workplace injury grp.
17 Inadvertent error
18 Dream
24 Encounter
26 Pool-table sides
29 Downing Street address
32 Practice piece of music
34 Palm leaf
35 War hero turned actor Murphy
36 Karpov or Kasparov, e.g.
37 Serious
38 Pronounce indistinctly
39 Nearsighted character
40 Chillier
41 Chicago tower
43 Tea biscuits
44 Senior
46 Lugs
47 Mimic
52 Heavenly harpist
54 Sudden turns
55 Suddenly weak
56 Stan's partner
57 Guide
58 Stand for a portrait?
60 Color shades
62 Handles effectively
64 "The Last Remake of Beau __"
65 In what place
66 Hindu mystic
67 Shallow-water hunter
68 Circular ocean current
69 "__ Up, Doc?"
70 Put to rest
71 Requires
73 Sorry 'bout that
74 Transparent fakes
77 Union soldiers
79 Female monsters
81 Silent, in music
82 "The Bells of __"
83 Living rooms
86 Grade-B westerns
88 Drive a dinghy
89 Actress Garr
91 Out of bed
92 Scarlett's Butler
93 On edge
94 More untested
95 Exchange
96 Breathe
97 Freshly
99 Internecine conflict
100 Eight: It.
101 Repast
102 Perry's penner
104 Portuguese saint
106 Misfortune

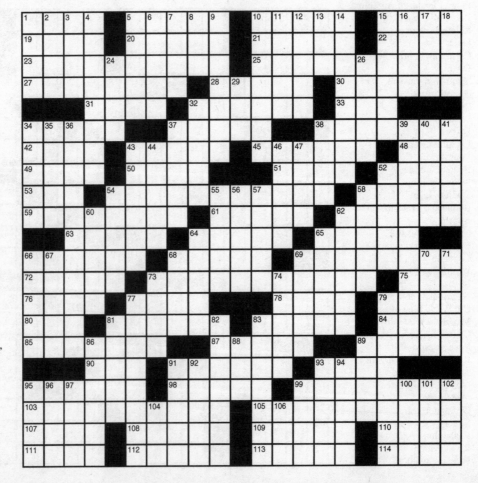

GET BEAT

by Xan Lattimore

ACROSS

1 Prison sentence
5 Model
10 Mischievous rascal
15 American military grp.
19 Julius Caesar's egg
20 Arledge of ABC
21 Two-time tennis grand slam champion
22 Amazon estuary
23 BEAT
25 BEAT
27 Like Las Vegas bandits?
28 Roof's overhang
30 __ Knight & the Pips
31 Tears
32 Miles of jazz
33 Ill-mannered child
34 Missile
37 City on the Rhone River delta
38 Absorbed
42 Merman and Waters
43 BEAT
45 __ Yoelson, a.k.a. Al Jolson
46 Everett and Lowe
47 Heaviness meas.
48 Corn serving
49 __ metabolism
51 Also-ran of the '50s
52 BEAT
56 Jughead's comic-strip buddy
57 Evangelist
60 Chuckle
61 Chevy model
62 German sub
63 French fathers
64 Norwegian composer
65 1935 Astaire film
67 Seed coats
68 Declared false
71 Specialized vocabularies
72 BEAT
74 Balin or Claire
75 Raises
76 Gender
77 __ de mer (seasickness)
78 Dunkable snack
80 Uncle __
81 BEAT
85 __-cafe (colorful drink)
86 Symbol
89 Current fashions
90 Epistle
91 Furtive glance
92 Drive off
93 1968-85 sports org.
94 Liver, heart, etc.
97 One hundred: pref.
98 Large cacti
102 BEAT
104 BEAT
106 Old Testament twin
107 Immerse
108 Occupation
109 Greek philosopher, Zeno of __
110 Appraise
111 Flowed back
112 Penultimate tennis round
113 Office piece

DOWN

1 Gray wolf
2 Terrible tsar
3 Feel vexation
4 Set sail
5 Reminds
6 Seeps
7 Marketed
8 Compass pt.
9 Gave another hand
10 Extremely servile
11 Has concern for
12 Urban thoroughfares: abbr.
13 __ culpa
14 12-step __
15 Newsflash
16 Saudi Arabian king, Ibn __
17 Bohemian
18 Weldon and Wray
24 Bay windows
26 Strong criticism
29 Affirm
32 Frock
33 Danish physicist Niels __
34 Brief summation
35 Additional
36 BEAT
37 Out of bed
38 Secret supply
39 BEAT
40 United rival, for short
41 Ancient: pref.
44 Safecrackers
47 Sharpen
49 Egghead
50 High points
52 Streisand movie, "__ Up, Doc?"
53 Fashion designer Calvin
54 Country singer Steve
55 Invitee
56 Pungent
58 Dislike intensely
59 Paint layers
63 Absentee ballot
64 Highlander
65 Ankle bones
66 Mountain nymph
67 At a right angle to the keel
68 Lawn
69 Currently occupied
70 Number stamper
73 Urge to action
76 Rebuff
78 Fastens
79 Prohibited
81 Act as chair
82 Evidenced a tendency
83 Deeply absorbed
84 Gray Panther targets
85 Injurious outbreaks
87 Without luster
88 Knee: Lat.
92 "Harlem Nights" co-star Della
93 Old-time actress Nita
94 Done
95 Tabula __
96 Insect pest
97 Tautog or whitefish
98 Thailand, once
99 Agitate
100 Singles
101 Nebr. neighbor
103 Shed tears
105 100 square meters

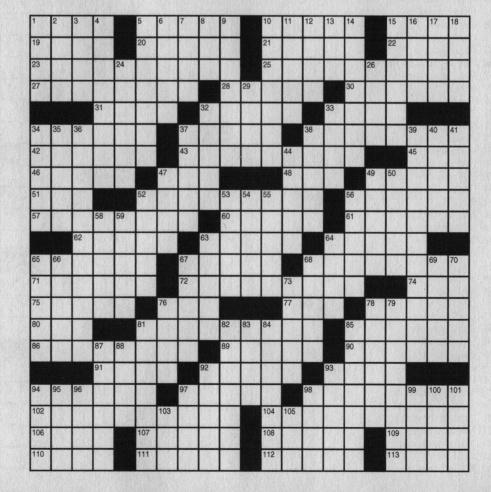

ACROSS

1 Temple University team
5 Bigotry
11 Type of pear
15 Rehan and Huxtable
19 Cure
20 Romanian violinist Georges
21 Inspiration
22 Citrus fruit
23 City southeast of Calgary
25 Apiarist's interest
26 Publishing #
27 Walks worriedly
28 "Of __ and Men"
30 Pastry-enclosed croquette
32 Sheds
35 Thread reels
37 Word with acid or oxide
38 Cheerful
39 Crafty press agent
41 Genetic letters
42 Small bills
43 Bric-a-__
45 Bristles
46 Beer barrels
47 Open hostilities
48 Female in the cult of Dionysus
50 Big house
53 Noah's peak
55 End of a post?
58 Side views
61 Chummy
63 Functioning
66 Play-by-play announcer
67 Inter __ (among other things)
68 Cordial treatment
71 Easy pace
72 Slow-but-sure one
74 Opening bars
75 Poetic dawns
76 Like plain typefaces
78 Compass dir.
79 On the way to
82 Panacea
84 Biko or Bochco
86 Nightmare street?
89 Beef and moan
91 Artless
94 Part of U.A.E.
95 Malayan outrigger
96 John Lennon's Plastic __ Band
97 One of Superman's powers
100 Calm intervals
101 Highland miss
103 Earthquakes
104 Ladd and Miller
106 Howard and Caron
108 Per __ (for each day)
109 In front
110 Dextrous beginner?
111 No great shakes
113 Marine scavengers
118 Civil unrest
119 Biblical twin
120 Cargo cases
121 Villainous Uriah
122 Carpentry tools
123 Preserving substance
124 Friend of Winnie the Pooh
125 Electronics company

DOWN

1 Resistance unit
2 Like a little Scot
3 Young Scot
4 Mistakes
5 Psychoanalyst Wilhelm
6 Boleyn and Bancroft
7 Mediocre grades
8 Suffix for approximations
9 Garlic shrimp
10 Gestures
11 Miniature books
12 Poem of praise
13 Clairvoyant
14 Luxor or Mirage, e.g.
15 Elite category
16 Jerry Lewis movie, with "The"
17 Strolling
18 One of the Five Nations
24 Good at dodging questions
29 Secret system
31 Knight's address
32 Display
33 Actress Turner
34 Sophia Loren film
35 Pet protection grp.
36 Head skin
39 Christmas workers
40 Rip into
43 Cake of soap
44 Stephen of "The Crying Game"
46 Radio host Garrison
48 Has permission
49 Obligations
51 Half a 1987 Billy Idol hit
52 Designer's deg.
54 Studies
56 Dove and Rudner
57 Gets around
59 Sports channel
60 Fr. religious figs.
61 Atlas collection
62 __ breve
64 Lowest NCO
65 Inventor Whitney
68 Roll-call call
69 Journalist Fallaci
70 Practical trainee
73 German article
75 British isle
77 Whips
80 Caesar's eggs
81 __ of intrigue
83 Worked as a daily domestic
85 New Mexico city
87 Lounge about
88 Large group
89 Peter Pan and Eton
90 Blood deficiency: var.
92 Sundial 8
93 Intrinsic quality
95 Social seclusions
97 Noon on a sundial
98 Pee Wee and Della
99 Imprison
100 Jacob's first wife
102 Narrow openings
104 Mirth
105 "Demian" author
107 Slugger Sammy
109 Concerning
112 Actor Mineo
114 Sea skate
115 Old Olds
116 Writer Kesey
117 Secret agent

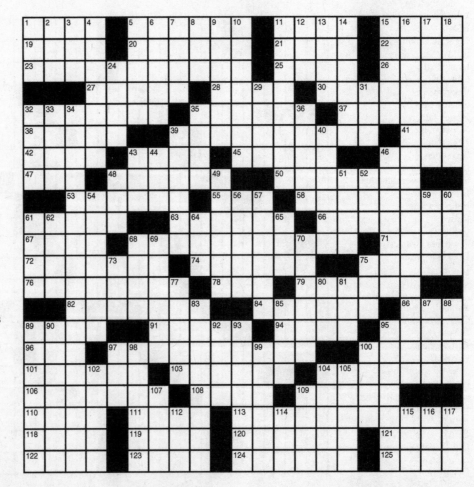

NFL CONTENDERS

by Alan P. Olschwang

ACROSS

1 Pacific island group
6 Swedish singers
10 Diversify
14 Trade association
19 Higher
20 Historic times
21 Shelterward
22 Pakistan's neighbor
23 "Rebel Without a Cause" co-star
24 Ans.
25 Turner of "Peyton Place"
26 Rectify
27 Topping containing shallots
30 Moves quietly
31 Helper: abbr.
32 __ Paese cheese
33 Pay close attention
35 Paddle
37 Separated
40 Longest or shortest day
44 NASA's __ Laboratory
49 Ruby of "Peyton Place"
50 Newsman Rather
51 Type of general
52 Give thumbs up
54 Pursuit
56 Assn.
57 Tooth: pref.
59 __ Lanka
60 Parish clergyman
61 "__ Dream," Lohengrin aria
64 Travels by glider
66 Sacker
68 Military trainee
70 Ordinal ending
72 "A Generation of Vipers" writer
73 Nationalistic
77 Second crop of hay in one season
79 Choir section
83 Delon and Prost
84 Table protector
86 House of __
88 Pindar poem
89 George of "Cheers"
90 "Butterfield 8" co-star Dina
92 Disinclination to act
95 Drag something heavy
96 Youth org.
98 Consequences
100 Prehistoric period
103 "Peer Gynt" playwright
104 __-10 Conf.
105 Arranged in rows
107 __ Paulo, Brazil
109 Cause to stop
113 Bring into harmony
116 1, 2, 3, etc.
120 __ Jean Baker
121 Traditional stories
122 Clinton Attorney General
123 Covered with a smoky residue
124 Look scornfully
125 Son of Aphrodite
126 Prayer closer
127 Kashmir river
128 Syrian leader
129 Lions' lairs
130 Painful
131 Proficient

DOWN

1 Brazilian dance in duple time
2 "__ Irish Rose"
3 Van Duyn and Washbourne
4 Outdoes
5 Semi-eternity?
6 Eagle's nest
7 City on the Oder
8 First, second or third, e.g.
9 Small vipers
10 Appraisers
11 Interjection of regret
12 Taylor and Adoree
13 Affirmative vote
14 Big redwood
15 Not proper
16 Cartoon light bulb
17 Connection
18 Fathers
28 Overseas
29 Anchor position
30 One-and-only
34 Focal point
36 Knack
38 Rio de la __
39 Seek
41 Just right
42 Social class
43 Join in
44 San __, CA
45 Chemical compound
46 Gumshoes
47 Lock in the dials
48 North of Paris?
53 Observer
55 One of the archangels
58 Wink of an eye
60 U.S. Army rank
62 Bitterly pungent
63 Swiss dog
65 Ocean passage: abbr.
67 Business agent
69 Spanish couple?
71 Stacy of the LPGA
73 Ratchet latches
74 Native Alaskan
75 "Last __ in Paris"
76 John Dickson or Vikki
78 "The Right Stuff" writer
80 Oz dog
81 Chief Norse god
82 Yellow and Black
85 Female Benedict Arnold
87 Like detachable parts
90 Sages
91 Fix firmly in: var.
93 Greek vowel
94 City on the James River
97 "Smooth Operator" singer
99 More irrational
101 Capital of New Caledonia
102 Curtain call
106 Home-run king
108 By oneself
110 Dwelling
111 Slacken
112 Lover's get-together
113 Latin handle
114 2,000-pound weights
115 Very French
117 Pension $$
118 "Nautilus" captain
119 VOA group
121 Went first

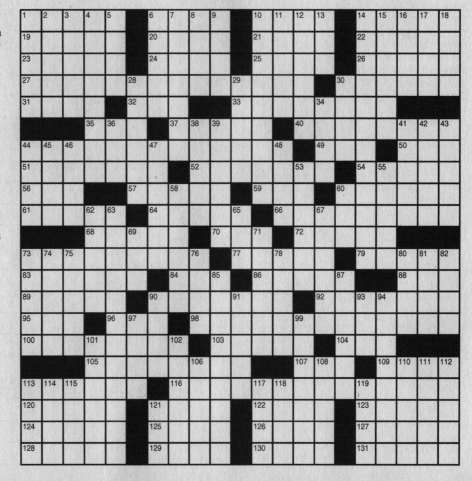

by Josiah Breward

ACROSS

1 Tent stake
4 Lady's address
9 Silly fowl
14 Subdue
19 Thurman of "The Truth About Cats and Dogs"
20 Loos or Baker
21 Wasted time
22 Chamber instrument
23 Luxuriously confined prisoner, familiarly?
27 Half a tape
28 Yashmaks
29 Org. for seniors
30 Sprint rival
31 AC/DC power
32 Manush of the Hall of Fame
34 Part of MIT
35 Scoundrel
36 Woodwinds member
38 Khaki shade
40 More rational
41 Getting low on money, familiarly?
48 Year in the Yucatan
49 Adversary
50 Biddy
51 Russian mountain range
52 Camera letters
53 Solar-system mobile
56 Tuber, casually
58 Ad __ committee
61 Pulpy refuse
63 Call from the cradle
65 Imitate
66 BYU location
68 Canadian waterway, familiarly?
72 Of the kidneys
73 Compass dir.
74 Worn out
75 SF gridders
76 '60s radical campus org.
77 Chum
79 Going cheap
81 Have regrets
82 In the know
84 Corn serving
86 __ Vegas
87 NYC hours
88 Candidates for colorization, familiarly?
95 Seaside golf course
96 Sea eagle
97 Lax to the max
98 "The Nazarene" writer Sholem
99 Gone by
102 Cooks' coverage
104 Gooey
108 High-ranking sailor
109 Knight's lady
110 Make off with
111 Setting
112 Advice from Greeley, familiarly?

117 Last Greek letter
118 Piece of bric-a-brac
119 "__ Frome"
120 Night before
121 Make lawn repairs
122 Sharif and Epps
123 Markets
124 Retreat

DOWN

1 Heartbeat
2 Computer post
3 Avant-__
4 Early Guatemalan
5 Colonial cuckoo
6 Noisy disturbance
7 Throwback characteristic
8 Vivid purplish red
9 Schick's competition
10 Chances
11 Bullring cheer
12 Car choice
13 Best and O'Brien
14 Cyrillic USSR
15 Old-time motorcar
16 Liv of "Persona"
17 Slow down
18 Legwear
24 Patrol, briefly

25 Sundial three
26 NYC subway line
32 One showing respect
33 "The __ Sanction"
34 Crosby film, "Holiday __"
35 College cheers
37 Like some glasses
39 "__ She Sweet"
40 Our sun
41 Rough talkers?
42 Hated
43 Lear and Mailer
44 Standard poem
45 Manufactures
46 Removed handcuffs
47 Jostle
54 Improved by editing
55 Spread like wildfire
57 Brother of Moses
58 Hummingbird, e.g.
59 Exploitation
60 Close-fitting undergarments
62 Docs' group
64 __ gratia artis
66 Catholic clerics
67 __ Tin Tin
69 Entomb
70 Woody spine

71 Intertwines
77 Lamb's lament
78 Birthdays' separation
80 Outsider
82 Egyptian symbol
83 Heaviness meas.
85 Yellow-dye trees
88 Loud racket
89 Easily bent
90 Revenues
91 Old hand, for short
92 Typical ski lodges
93 Like an elongated spheroid
94 New York city
99 "__ Joey"
100 Exxon rival
101 Medicinal fluid
103 Round legume
105 Surrendered formally
106 Unprincipled fellow
107 Neighbor of Saudi Arabia
109 Deceased
110 Recipe direction
111 "All My __"
113 In the past
114 Period
115 Org. of Flyers and Jets
116 Guy's date

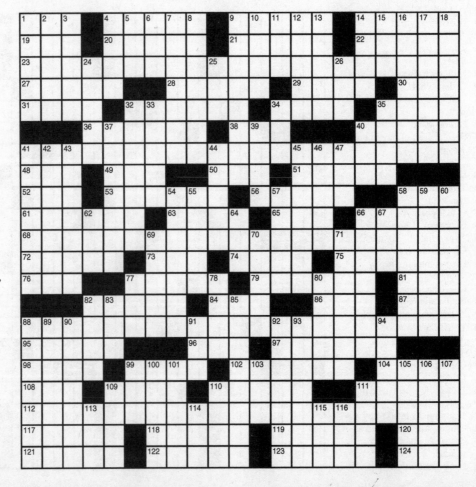

ACROSS

1 Tangy
5 Scruff
9 1997 20-game winner Denny
15 Manchurian border river
19 Washington bills
20 Greek philosopher, Zeno of __
21 Luzon Island battle site
22 Force unit
23 1960 Etta James hit
26 Arabian sultanate
27 H. Hughes' airline
28 Ornate style
29 Basswood
31 Flock female
32 Grade-B western
34 Gangster's gun
36 Legal code of the Franks
38 1975 Frankie Valli hit
44 Routine duty
45 Third-party contract
46 Persia, today
47 Made useless
48 Theological sch.
51 See ya!
52 __ Khayyam
53 Add up
54 "The Asphalt Jungle" star Sterling
56 1962 Duprees hit
60 Actor Davis
61 Burns with light
63 Millennia
64 Opposite of masc.
65 Cup brims
66 Bridge positions
67 Make adjustments
69 Superficially fluent
70 Grand __ Opry
71 Training rooms
72 Watered silk
73 Rock
74 1969 Stevie Wonder hit
78 Used a strainer
79 Ancient region in Asia Minor
80 Ship's post for securing ropes
81 Yellowish-brown wood
83 Begley and Wynn
84 River of British Columbia
86 Persian fairy
87 Method of voting
89 Conger catcher
90 1995 Paula Abdul hit
95 Lenin's first name
97 "Star Trek" extras
98 Composer of "The Nubians of Plutonia"
99 German article
100 Appetizer
103 Dramatist Ibsen
107 Uncooked
108 Laws, briefly
110 1959 Tommy Edwards hit

113 Continuously
114 Persistent harasser
115 Beech or birch
116 Mayberry kid
117 Sandwich shop
118 Waiting to bat
119 Droops
120 Play lead

DOWN

1 Small drum
2 Regardless
3 Estimate a new age
4 Half a fly?
5 Roman despot
6 Actor Baldwin
7 Mexican coin
8 Accept humiliation
9 Cagers' org.
10 Justice Warren
11 Gudrun's victim
12 Makes up ground
13 Martin of "Mission: Impossible"
14 Actress Georgia
15 Commotion
16 1974 Bobby Vinton hit
17 Oblivious
18 Restored
24 Patrol-car passenger
25 Portal
30 Kidman and Bobek
33 CBS logo
35 Satellite of Mars
37 Ice
39 Give a once-over
40 Well-honed skill
41 Morgue letters
42 Sketch
43 Tall tale
47 Brag about
48 Writer Aleichem
49 With no sweat
50 1968 Vogues hit
52 Law court opening word: var.
53 Figurative use of a word
55 Opposite of: pref.
56 CO clock setting
57 Glum drop?
58 Reticulated
59 Encloses snugly
61 Female vampire
62 African fox
66 Icelandic currency unit
67 August in Paris
68 N, E, W or S
69 Former phone co.
71 Prescription option

72 Cause
73 Helicopter inventor
75 Watered (a lawn)
76 Eve's son
77 Spanish painter
78 Pasolini movie
81 Univ. trainees
82 Mischievous fairy
84 Running a temperature
85 Palliate
86 Pharaoh's tomb
87 Cuts in half
88 Play about Capote
90 Minimum of ten Jews for worship
91 Of a people: pref.
92 Totally captivated
93 Persian Gulf peninsula
94 Attorney
96 Latin American dance
101 Sneaky guy?
102 Power current: abbr.
104 Racing org.
105 "Performance" director Nicolas
106 French islands
109 __ Lanka
111 Noah's vessel
112 Derek and Jackson

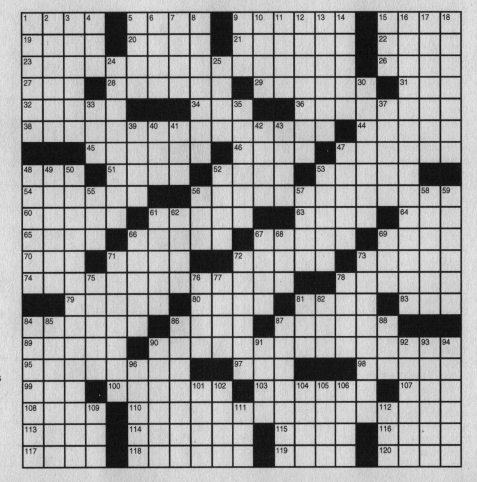

by Ed Voile

ACROSS

1 Roman Catholic cap
8 Formed into whirlpools
14 Slip with clippers
20 Coming up
21 Bribe money
22 Much the same
23 Think hard
25 Guys from the sea?
26 Burgundy summer
27 Teensy
28 Ancient Greek colony
30 Wicked
31 Answer
35 Comden-Green 1958 film, "__ Mame"
37 Lo-cal
38 Place to take a dive
41 More free from impurities
42 Six-line poem
45 Recent walkers
46 Pinkerton and Sherman
47 Money from a bank: abbr.
48 Duck down
51 Seek to enroll new members
54 Mrs. Archie Bunker
57 Aw, come on now!
60 Little devil
63 Disloyal individuals
65 African capital city near Masai Mara Park
66 Paddle
67 Leaf collectors
68 Arthur of "The Golden Girls"
69 Simple, attached shed
71 Word before nouveau or Deco
72 Cordon
76 Proof of purchase
79 High-ranking sailor
80 Show up on stage
82 Paddle holder
83 Impels
85 Impels
87 Half of CM
88 Hebrew toast
90 Land east of the Urals
92 Skier Hess and others
95 Entertainment venue
96 Burrowing animal
101 Umps' cohorts
102 Vijay Singh, for one
103 Traded without money
107 Society of physicians: abbr.
108 Titlark
109 Slant
111 Former union of Egypt and Syria: abbr.
112 Derisive mimic
114 East River span
120 Air shaft
121 A.A. Milne's "__ the Pooh"
122 Comes forth
123 Spring holiday

124 Opening part of a play
125 Calorie counters

DOWN

1 Less decorated
2 Very angry
3 Chops very fine
4 Inuit: abbr.
5 Spanish uncle
6 Former station from Tenn.
7 Anti-elderly bias
8 Wanes
9 Small boat
10 Morgue letters
11 Amin of Uganda
12 Pacific weather phenomenon
13 Spanish explorer
14 Mrs. Eisenhower
15 Ends of intestines
16 Letters on cameras
17 Security device
18 Like leftovers
19 Formal offers
24 Pipe part
29 Nothing
32 L.A. clock setting
33 Have debts
34 Nickelodeon's Nick at __
35 Artist's rep.
36 Boom times
37 "Darling __"
39 Particulars
40 "Cheers" barfly
41 Most uncertain
42 Like rugged mountains
43 Makes beloved
44 Be truthful
46 Fit for cultivation
49 Car starter: abbr.
50 Morse unit
51 Slugger's stat
52 Goof up
53 Bus. honcho
55 Italian three
56 Dried-plant collections
58 January in Juarez
59 Motorists' org.
61 "Waltzing __"
62 Pushes onward
64 Aromatic root
68 Spelling contest
70 Cigar dropping
73 B&O and others
74 Gradually slower, in music: abbr.
75 Med. feeders
76 Scrawny person

77 Summer mo.
78 Peggy or Spike
81 Night in Nevers
84 Painter Holbein
86 Very German
88 Wyoming city
89 Amati's hometown
90 Police file abbr.
91 DC VIP
93 Veteran's abbr.
94 Fury
96 Domino dot
97 Great Lakes tribe
98 __ acid (fruit flavoring)
99 Follow orders
100 Hocked
102 Pink-slip dispenser?
104 "Barnaby __"
105 More than ready
106 Apparel
108 Lapdog, briefly
109 Pelt
110 Swiss artist Paul
113 Krazy __
115 Toronto's prov.
116 Lennon's widow
117 Radio grp.
118 Female sandpiper
119 NYC subway line

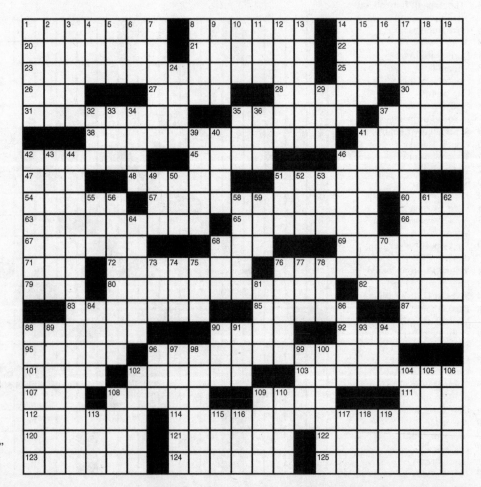

by Willy A. Wiseman

ACROSS

1 Modicums
8 Six feet of water
14 Proverbs
20 One-celled organisms
21 On land
22 Gilbert and Sullivan opera, with "The"
23 B
25 Prepare to cry
26 One more time
27 Frasier Crane's brother
28 God of war
30 Morse symbol
31 Weapons talks, briefly
32 The Caped Crusader
34 Poet Teasdale
35 Gilpin of "Frasier"
36 Q
39 Additional conjunctions
40 Puts in danger
43 Held first place
44 Chunk of the fairway
45 Witness
46 Group of shrinks
47 Soft drink
50 Mary Tyler or Henry
52 Senator Hatch of Utah
54 T
58 Needle-nosed fish
61 Set sights incorrectly
63 Boxer Spinks
64 Very strong winds
65 Ecological watchdog grp.
66 Chemical compound
67 Love of Luigi
69 "I __ the Songs"
70 Editorial directive
71 "Apollo 13" director Howard
72 Missouri tributary
73 Very French
74 African expanse
76 987-65-4321 grp.
77 C
80 Red figure
81 "Moonlight Gambler" singer Frankie
83 Sorry 'bout that!
84 Altar constellation
86 Pasture in poetry
87 McIntosh, e.g.
89 And so forth, briefly
91 Superlatively spurious
93 Decoy
94 Y
99 Some born in August
100 "Doctor Zhivago" heroine
101 Three-bagger
102 Melt together
106 Vessel with a spigot
107 Mrs. Copperfield
108 Full of suds
109 Soprano Callas
110 Semiconductors
112 I
116 Ducks and dodges

117 Muffle
118 Put on a revival
119 Lookout
120 Intuits
121 More bold

DOWN

1 Carvey and others
2 Last Greek letter
3 Nearby
4 Beatles movie
5 Town northwest of Glasgow
6 Golf norm
7 Module: abbr.
8 Mohammed's daughter
9 Stone worker's block
10 Dom DeLuise film
11 __ d'oeuvres
12 Valuable vein
13 Davy Jones' girlfriend?
14 U.S. rail system
15 Passes away
16 Alias letters
17 P
18 Scottish sculptor Paolozzi
19 Pre-Socratic philosopher
24 Those opposed

29 Slice of a circle
32 Radar image
33 God of Islam
34 Sault __ Marie
35 Couple
37 Shiraz resident
38 Serb or Croat, e.g.
40 Chemically similar substances
41 Spanish sheep
42 U
44 Accomplishes
47 Sound system
48 Orchestra member
49 Cave dwelling
50 Beer ingredient
51 S-shaped moldings
53 Adjective-forming suffix
55 Branch of science: suff.
56 White herons
57 Lift
59 Mimicries
60 Drum beat
62 Stone worker
68 Created
69 Swaddle
70 "__ Loves You"
72 Theatrical award

73 Couple
75 "A Bell for __"
78 Entertainer Nina
79 1986 Indy winner
82 Alternatives to lagers
85 Stood up
87 Makes an indirect reference
88 Immature
89 Short trips for tasks
90 H. Hughes' airline
91 Diarist Samuel
92 Pre-toddlers
94 Superficially stylish
95 Pole with a blade
96 In conflict
97 Killarney's neighbor
98 Matures
103 Dickens' Heep
104 Burn the ends of
105 Impatient
107 Woods ruminant
108 Connery or Penn
109 Tableland
111 Old insecticide
113 Wide shoe width
114 Spherical object
115 For each

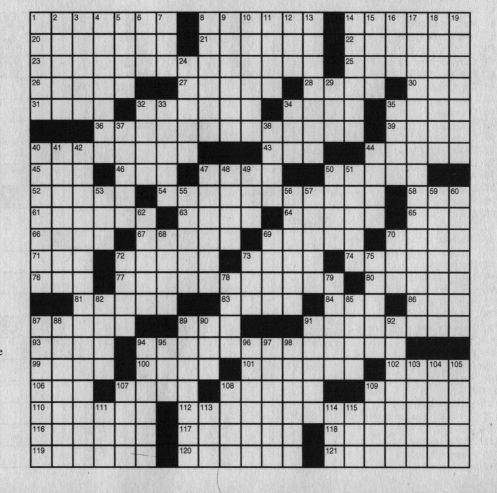

HOUSES

by Edgar Fontaine

ACROSS

1 Principal
5 Meal scraps
9 Old World lizard
14 Jacks and jokers
19 Hit by the Kinks
20 Writer Uris
21 Medieval violin
22 Au revoir!
23 Double
24 Absurdist art
25 Vanzetti's cohort in anarchy
26 Buy new weapons
27 Kenny Loggins hit, "House __"
30 Calculator key abbr.
32 Body toss
33 Leather wine container
34 Central American language group
36 Even score
37 Regard as true
40 Nutmeg spice
42 Home-repair series, "__ House"
44 Ducklike birds
45 Like sheltered horses
48 Let up
49 Shade trees
50 Le Carre novel, "__ House"
52 "The Raven" lady
56 Mediocre grade
57 Man's bathing suit
58 "__ Lang Syne"
60 Guaranteed to get
61 Hautboy players
63 Band for identification
65 Ornamental case
66 Sovereign
68 Contend
69 Made of baked clay
71 Part of QED
72 Sharper
75 Arbitrate
77 Pinnacles
79 Retarding force
80 Section of train track
81 Guided
84 Amateur
86 __ house (tenement)
88 Fishing rod
89 Inter __ (among other things)
91 Striking with a joint?
92 "Cheers" barmaid
93 __ house (eerie building)
96 Man or Capri
97 "On __ Pond"
98 Possess
99 Heir
101 Pimento
105 Huh?
107 Pollution patrol grp.
108 __ House (Congressional leader)
112 Zodiac scales
114 Fragrant rootstock
116 Inclination
117 Sailor's call
118 __ Island, NY
119 French river
120 Engrave
121 Cod or Fear
122 Has an opinion
123 Bordered
124 Poor grades
125 Rams' mates

DOWN

1 "Paper Lion" star
2 Landslide
3 Applaud
4 Chlorine and iodine
5 Behind the times
6 Respond
7 Hubbubs
8 "The Hunting of the __" (Carroll poem)
9 Arms depots
10 Equipment
11 2 on the phone
12 Mohammed's birthplace
13 Liturgical assistant
14 Train unit
15 Summer coolers
16 Bridge of Venice
17 Jump the tracks
18 Added
28 Sorry 'bout that!
29 Rain cloud
31 1986 Indy winner
34 Spirit world communicator
35 Child of Japanese immigrants
37 Smart guy?
38 Composer Porter
39 Clooney tune, "__ House"
41 A Borgia
43 Keystone Kops filmmaker
45 Sought silence
46 Camper's abode
47 Large boats
50 Treat's alternative
51 Entirely
53 House __ (place of worship)
54 Reprobate
55 Poet's Ireland
57 Rocky crag
59 Transferring (property) officially
62 Actor Jason or Justine
63 Jordan's nickname
64 Contaminate
66 Repast
67 Killer whale
68 Plants-only vegetarians
70 Tattered cloth
73 Epoch
74 Serviette
75 "La Boheme" girl
76 Idyllic garden
78 Food seasonings
80 "Remington __"
82 French fashion magazine
83 College VIP
85 Sister's daughter
87 Backslid
88 Hope movie, "Son of __"
90 Fatty
92 Chanel of fashion
93 Made wolf calls
94 Some time
95 Incompetent
97 Waistlines
100 Having paddles
102 Entwined
103 Emulate Nancy Kerrigan
104 Pieces of a pound
106 In good shape
108 Reciprocal of a cosecant
109 Annual melt
110 Have aspirations
111 "For Your __ Only"
113 Dunderhead
115 Oil-well device

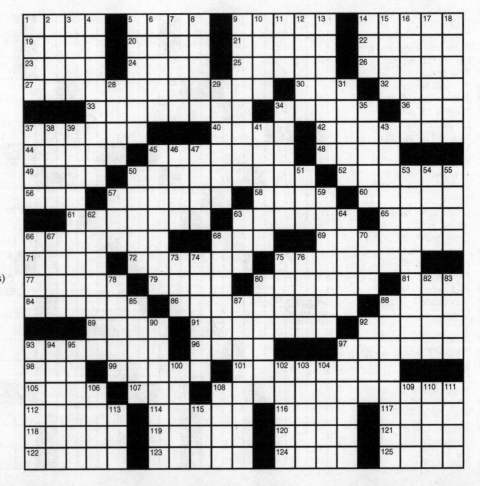

by Willy A. Wiseman

ACROSS

1 Set up for a drive
5 Surpass capacity
9 New York city
15 Horse of a different color
19 Capri or Wight, e.g.
20 Fourth book of "The Alexandria Quartet"
21 Ancient region in Asia Minor
22 Otherwise
23 Knife in prison
24 Vegetarian's condiment?
26 Leatherwood
27 Game-show host Pat
29 Neat and tidy
30 Abu Dhabi, Dubai et al.
31 Barry and Brubeck
32 Muse of astronomy
34 Vegetarian's treat?
38 Nearly leafless desert plant
40 Pasturage grass
41 Reinforcing rib used in Gothic vaulting
42 California wine county
44 Thrash
47 Vegetarian's dessert?
53 Defeated in a joust
59 Sulky
60 Connery or O'Casey
61 Yemen capital
63 Now __ talking!
64 Bushes
66 April 15 addressee
68 Method-acting teacher
70 Vegetarian's vegetable?
74 Soldier
77 Part of rpm
78 Ebb
82 Clean one's feathers
83 Ponselle or Bonheur
85 Cushions
88 Fragrant bed?
89 Car with a rumble seat
91 Vegetarian's flavorings?
94 Shrewd
96 Ratchet part
97 Type of pill
102 Hospital employee
105 Motivations
110 Vegetarian's fruit?
114 Vacuum-cleaner attachment
115 South American plain
116 Pub pint
117 Settlement
119 Exchange
120 Enticement
121 Vegetarian's dish?
125 Turquoise
126 First garden
127 Child's marbles
128 Major or Minor constellation
129 Green superhero
130 Checkers side
131 Winter apple
132 European river
133 Dates regularly

DOWN

1 Thin paper
2 F in music?
3 Biblical prophet
4 "McCabe and Mrs. Miller" co-star
5 Learning inst.
6 More than enough
7 __ cotta
8 Palliating
9 Dumbo's wing
10 Pastoral pasture
11 Designed with standardized units
12 Relating to a pelvic bone
13 Stairway segment
14 Fire flakes
15 Capture back
16 Director Stone
17 Away from the bow
18 Oder-__ Line
25 Abu Dhabi ruler
28 Vegetarian's vegetable?
31 Cato's 601
33 Saudi, e.g.
35 Manly
36 Build up
37 Richard Cowper sci-fi novel
39 Simians
43 Exist
45 Approach quickly
46 Render harmless
47 Docs
48 La-la lead-in
49 "__ Miss Brooks"
50 Snuffed (out)
51 John and Bonnie
52 Concerning
54 Vegetarian's vegetable?
55 Peter Weller movie
56 Bring to court
57 Drop the ball
58 U. acquisition
62 From the stars
65 TV
67 Sucker
69 Berne's river
71 Paying riders
72 Derisive noise
73 French cap
74 Life-saving meth.
75 Spanish gold
76 __ culpa
79 Language suffix
80 German article
81 Double curve
84 Misbehave
86 Roller-coaster thrill
87 Train to box
90 Casual farewell
92 Roll-call call
93 Rams' mates
95 Civil disturbances
97 Loftier
98 Hint at
99 Sounded stridently
100 Sheets, etc.
101 Creative drive
103 Actress Thompson
104 Ross Island volcano
106 Vaughan and Bernhardt
107 Without luster
108 Protuberance
109 Moves furtively
111 South Korean city
112 Earthenware crocks
113 Kibbutz resident, perhaps
118 Actress Kudrow
121 Military science
122 "__ Haw"
123 Q-U connection
124 Black goo

by Robert H. Wolfe

ACROSS

1 Mischievous rogue
6 Oklahoma city
10 Dismounted
14 Source of the family mutt: abbr.
19 Debate
20 Hamlet, e.g.
21 In __ veritas
22 Hits high
23 Trampling shorebirds?
26 Fear and May, e.g.
27 Daredevil Knievel
28 Dem. of the '50s
29 Likes and dislikes
30 Bomb blast, briefly
31 Sends back
33 S. Connery movie
34 Harvested
36 Clan members
37 Head cover
38 Spanish painter
39 Killer whale
42 Industrious insect
45 Talkative, shaggy oxen?
48 Batting order
50 Yogi of baseball
52 Stirling negatives
53 Coal mine
54 Air shaft
55 Arum plant
56 Hosp. sections
57 Cut-glass object
59 __ Republic (Cambodia, once)
60 Perplexing posers
62 North Carolina college
63 Standardization group's acronym
65 O.T. book
66 Drone in a contest?
69 Unless, in law
73 Tony Musante's TV series
75 Urban roads: abbr.
76 Weather-map delineations
78 After-market item
81 Ancient Welsh priest
83 Artist's rep.
84 Vinegary: pref.
85 Give priority to
87 Slip up
88 Russian autocrat
89 Himalayan country
90 Perplex
91 Mental image of Yogi?
94 Oolong or pekoe
95 Editor's directive
96 Hebrew month
98 1934 Nobel-winning chemist
99 Altar of stars
101 Alpine abode
103 Docking place
104 Sun
108 Carrier
110 Some Dutch genre paintings
112 Winter mo.
113 Cupbearer of the gods
114 Excuse
115 Walruses' kin with veto power?
118 Alternative beau
119 Old Gaelic
120 Glandular fever, for short
121 Novelist Jong
122 Frost and Dove, e.g.
123 Ferrara family
124 Part of QED
125 Bothersome

DOWN

1 Lumberjack, at times
2 Desire urgently
3 Lace end
4 Eskimo boot
5 Architect I.M. __
6 Outer reaches
7 Ancient temple
8 Lodging house
9 Demolishes
10 Dispatch boat
11 Rhythmic cadence
12 Hobbies and pastimes
13 Flipper
14 Tin Pan Alley letters
15 Ray in a risky position?
16 Vain hope
17 Average grades
18 Helper: abbr.
24 Granny
25 Actress Jessica
32 Capital of Saudi Arabia
33 Mollycoddles
35 Gudrun's victim
37 Transportation to a cemetery
38 Snow sport
40 Salad staple, briefly
41 Impersonator
42 Wane
43 Roman tyrant and others
44 Freshwater fish
46 Patella protector
47 Cooks' protectors
49 Writing fluids
51 Direct from a night flier?
57 Wielded
58 Eminent conductors
61 Ending for a belief
62 1967 Swedish film, "__ Madigan"
64 Modern: pref.
67 Hardy's partner
68 Criminal second marriage
70 Clumsy
71 Bristles
72 Island: It.
74 "The __ lama..."
77 Former Cowboys' coach
78 Police broadcast alerts: abbr.
79 Mild oath
80 Faulty
82 Those who refute
83 "Lou Grant" star
86 Scottish dance
88 Boring
92 Spoils
93 Integration grp.
97 Renter
100 Off the briny
102 Seed coverings
103 Caribbean peak
104 Bus station
105 Author of "The Man Who Fell to Earth"
106 Taken __ (surprised)
107 Pass along
108 Infield cover, for short
109 Spicy stew
111 Right on maps
112 Carvey or Andrews
116 In favor of
117 House member, briefly

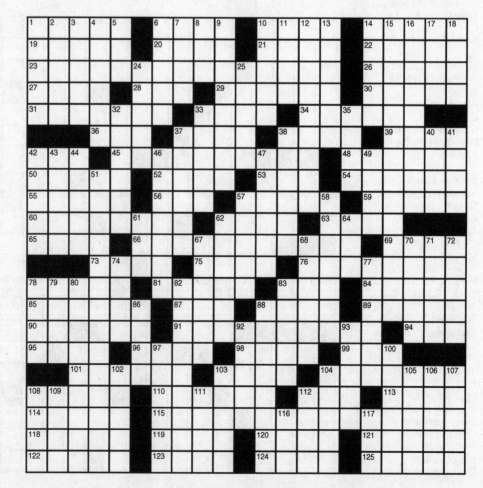

ACROSS

1 Compared with
8 Eccentrics
16 National poet
20 Lens maker
21 Handyman's space
22 Certain stiffness
23 Dessert choice
25 Eager
26 Being: Lat.
27 Jelling agent
28 Date of baptism
30 Finish line
32 Customary extras, briefly
35 Make free (of)
36 Dessert choice
42 Entertainer Falana
44 Insertion indicator
48 Actor Estevez
49 Fancy socks
51 Coeur d'__, ID
52 Let out
53 Department head
55 "__ brillig..."
57 Tacks on
58 Flower support
59 Greek letters
60 Kingsley or Martin
62 Endow with a spirit
64 St. Paul, once
65 12/24 and 12/31
66 Missouri tribe
67 Dessert choice
72 Long steps
73 Spheres
74 Estrada of "CHiPs"
75 Jong and others
76 Mexican moola
77 Farrow and Hamm
78 Mail letters?
82 Church area
83 __ off (angry)
85 Seed coats
87 Prohibit, legally
88 Elements in a procedure
90 Used an editorial
   instruction
92 "The Left Hand of
   Darkness" writer Le Guin
93 Enjoy avidly
94 Wharf
95 Dessert choice
98 European crow
100 H.S. math course
102 Chops
103 Parachute delivery
107 Homecoming guests
110 Actress Conn
114 Role of 56D
115 Dessert choice
120 "Death in Venice" author
121 Damage
122 Delights
123 Hidden obstacle
124 Made tight
125 Curvaceous

DOWN

1 Short-tailed rodent
2 Chills
3 Amounts
4 Lotion ingredient, often
5 Sportscaster Scully
6 Doctrine
7 Siberian plain
8 Of the ear
9 Presley hit of 1958
10 Stray calf
11 With too much frankness
12 "__ You Lonesome
   Tonight?"
13 Prune
14 Meat cut
15 Besmirch
16 Dessert choice
17 Served perfectly
18 Ostrich kin
19 Contradict
24 Virginia dance
29 Isinglass
30 Watery
31 I love: Latin
33 Frisky
34 Oodles
36 Church seats
37 Give off
38 Assistant
39 Red's Kadiddlehopper
40 Ovine utterances
41 Onassis, to pals
43 __ Yoelson, a.k.a. Al Jolson
45 City near Council Bluffs
46 Last
47 Unit of magnetic flux
   density
50 Elongated pitcher
53 Relatives of carps and
   minnows
54 Empty space
56 Marina of "Star Trek: The
   Next Generation"
59 Most unrefined
61 Disorder
63 Shallow notch
64 Thompson of "Family"
65 Goofs
66 Tapestry in "Hamlet"
67 Horizontal layers
68 Hot-platter platform
69 Dessert choice
70 Eurasian ruminant
71 Eye in Aix
72 Intuit
76 Little in Lille
77 South of France
78 Former superpower's letters
79 Ticket end
80 Magnet end
81 Quarrel
84 Sixth sense
86 Fam. member
87 Cupid
89 Box to train
91 That which can be tested
92 Employ
96 Scads
97 Lives
99 Most inferior
101 Collect bit by bit
103 $$ dispensers
104 One of Turkey's neighbors
105 Gossip columnist Barrett
106 Hemingway's sobriquet
108 Press
109 TV's talking horse
110 Plumbing problem
111 Adjective-forming suffix
112 Secluded valley
113 __-bitsy
116 Five centimes, once
117 Hole
118 LBJ's VP
119 Victorian or
   Edwardian, e.g.

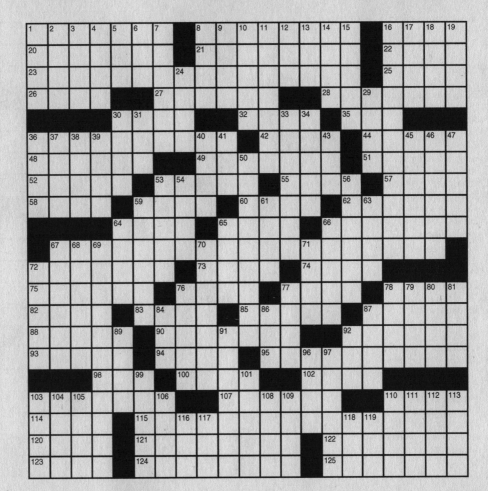

by Arthur S. Verdesca

ACROSS

1 Pastimes
6 Taj Mahal site
10 "__ of Athens"
15 H.S. math class
19 Eero Saarinen's father
20 "Cheers" actor Roger
21 Battery electrode
22 Latvian capital
23 Urgent need to shave?
26 Make eyes at
27 Coupon presenter
28 Black eye
29 Shucks!
30 Printer's measures
31 Swenson of "Benson"
33 Chowed down
34 Flurry
35 Not so exceptional?
40 __ Cruces, NM
41 Germanic invaders of Kent
44 Fill too much
45 Pleasure cruiser
46 Superlative suffix
47 Get to the present?
49 Scatters seed
52 Least
54 Fermented drink
55 "__ Lang Syne"
58 Rights org.
60 Sacred ceremonies
63 Nada
64 Supplied hints
66 Netlike caps
69 Breathing: abbr.
70 Itemized list of fees: abbr.
71 More than a little advice?
74 Indianapolis dome
75 Adolescent
77 Shop owner
78 Trap
79 Simple card game
80 Make sense
82 "Seascape" playwright
84 Subway station
85 Take one's pick
86 Diminishes
89 Ye __ Shoppe
91 Joel of "Sullivan's Travels"
93 __ the piper
95 Intuit
97 Periods
100 "The Age of Anxiety" poet
101 Emma's twins?
102 Very complex gambling game?
106 Dumbfounds
108 Kilmer of "The Doors"
109 "Rule, Britannia" composer
110 Spanish Mrs.
113 Formed an arc
114 Winding shape
117 Fills with life
120 "A Room of __ Own"
121 In even greater confusion?
123 Food fad
124 Blaze of light
125 Nimes night
126 Embankment
127 Asian oxen
128 Overbearing
129 Eve's grandson
130 Hank of hair

DOWN

1 Art category
2 Green-card holder
3 Objects to
4 Bigfoot's shoe size
5 Blackthorn
6 Dahl and Francis
7 East Coast state
8 Pastime: abbr.
9 Questions
10 One of the Society Islands
11 Senselessly
12 Fashion
13 Fragrance
14 Original
15 Flagrant
16 Really bad vulgarity?
17 Crazy Horse's tribe
18 Inflatable life jacket
24 CCXXVI quadrupled
25 Counterfeit
29 Football team member
32 Tiny army?
34 Physicist Niels
35 __-de-lance
36 Newton and Asimov
37 Ages and ages
38 Satirizes
39 Cool down
41 Hall of "Flower Drum Song"
42 Like typing paper
43 Longer version of a Beatles hit?
48 Hungarian sheepdogs
50 Profligate
51 Without: Fr.
53 Military address
56 De __ (sumptuously)
57 Of inferior status
59 Intimidates
61 One on the run
62 Austere
65 Secluded valley
67 Euphemistic oath
68 Senator Thurmond
72 Moses' mount
73 Cool dude
76 Crux
81 Went by
83 German river
87 Golf-shop buy
88 Ltr. holder
90 "The Ring of the Nibelung" character
92 Dramatic signal
93 Television award
94 Pungent gas
96 Green people?
98 One type of signal transmission
99 14-line verses
103 "Harry and Tonto" Oscar winner
104 "__, poor Yorick"
105 Simon or Diamond
107 Piquancies
110 Martin of "L.A. Story"
111 Descartes and Auberjonois
112 Saps
114 Normandy town
115 School orgs.
116 Bowling alley
118 Run in the heat
119 Affirm
121 Eglin or Lackland, e.g.
122 Church sister

by Annabel Michaels

ACROSS

1 Sadat and others
7 Flamenco accompaniment
14 Cow's third stomach
20 "Magic __ Ride"
21 Affluent
22 Dogtooth
23 1965 Simone Signoret movie
26 Subterfuge
27 Quarter
28 Gradually slower, in mus.
29 Grant of the White House
30 End hunger
31 6/6/44
32 Gibson of "Hamlet"
33 Mehemet and Muhammad
34 NJ inventor's inits.
35 Blues or Cardinals
37 Abu Dhabi, Dubai et al.
38 World Series precursor: abbr.
39 Blackguards
40 1993 Meg Ryan movie
44 Napoleon's marshal
45 Ballpoint
46 Grammatical witticisms
47 Make suitable
51 Loathe
54 Help out
55 God of war
56 Scornful looks
57 Conduct business
59 __ avis
60 Naughty
61 Scottish river
62 Duration
63 1946 Humphrey Bogart movie
66 Kitchen glove
67 PC maker
68 Opposite of SSW
69 Reprobate
70 Symbolic configurations
72 Say again and again
74 Singer Domino
75 One NCO
76 Type of daisy
77 Bonehead play
78 Seedy bar
79 Born in Brest
80 Medical pic.
81 1979 Dennis Christopher movie
88 __ mater
91 Angry states
92 Industrious insect
93 Alternative fuel
94 Oriental sauce
95 Folk singer Phil
96 Uno, due, __...
97 Taverns
98 Onassis, to pals
99 Ancient region in Asia Minor
101 Eg.-Syr., once
102 Gilpin of "Frasier"

103 "__ Gun for Hire"
104 1984 Johnny Depp movie
108 Gas up
109 Common plant with yellow flowers
110 Process for sorting the injured
111 Dismal
112 Reddens
113 Below standard

DOWN

1 Female lead, e.g.
2 Native Mexican people
3 Grapple
4 Church area
5 Theol. belief
6 Without respite
7 Gloomily sulky
8 Upolu Island city
9 Operate
10 "Let's Stay Together" singer
11 Beany's seasick sea serpent
12 Art school subj.
13 Orch. section
14 Eye doctor
15 Chapin Carpenter and Tyler Moore
16 Additional conjunctions
17 Nicaraguan nap
18 Like unopened e-mail
19 Untidy states
24 Expunge
25 Cash penalties
31 Deceivers
32 Primary
33 Dershowitz and Greenspan
36 Wife of Paris
37 Pre-owned
38 Of the spinal cord
39 Surrender formally
41 Malicious ill will
42 Widely scattered
43 Come down to earth
48 Roman games official
49 Attractive
50 African fly
51 Garb
52 Sop dispenser
53 "If I Had a __"
54 Painful throb
55 Fowles novel, with "The"
56 Devitalizes
58 Chem. chart figure
59 Mob member
60 Sugar source
64 Audience shouts

65 __ on (incited)
66 Nissan model
68 Auto-racing org.
71 Synagogue scrolls
73 Zany Imogene
74 High-pitched flutes
75 Ticket datum
78 Libyan currency
79 September's number
80 Prosodists
82 Legitimately
83 New York harbor entrance
84 Give new weapons
85 Randomly piled
86 Panamanian dictator
87 Lustrous reflection
88 Home of the Norse gods
89 Repair-shop car
90 Chekhov story
95 Alternate
96 South Korean metropolis
97 Encircling routes
100 Spanish water
101 Caspian feeder
102 Father of France
103 Chi-town paper
105 Bark in comics
106 Japanese drama
107 Play about Capote

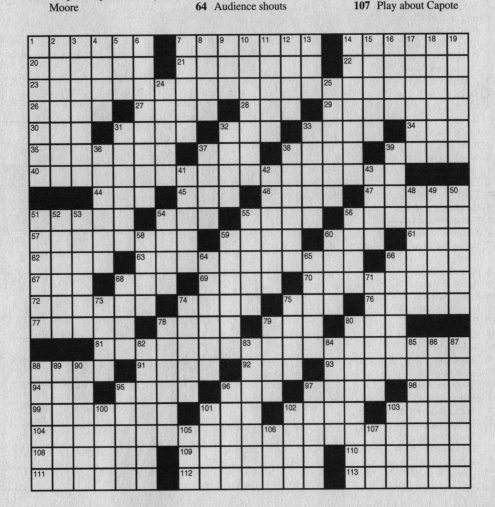

MANSIONS

by Edgar Fontaine

ACROSS

1 Pathogen
5 Fairy tale
10 Fairy-tale monsters
15 Victory signs
19 Jai __
20 Stew vegetable
21 Medieval note
22 Gardner of mysteries
23 Jefferson's mansion
25 Throat prob.
26 Hoarfrost
27 Type of cat or goat
28 Drawn tight
30 William Randolph Hearst's mansion
32 Oregon's capital
34 Flip Wilson persona
36 Composer Scarlatti
39 Make sound
40 Cuts corners
44 Periods
45 Former Seahawks QB
47 Subway stations
50 Ashcan School painter John
51 ATM maker
52 Virgil's hero
54 Act testy
56 End of a post?
57 Paintbrushes
59 "__ Framed Roger Rabbit"
61 Dwarflike creature
62 DC advisory grp.
63 __ Alamos, NM
64 Steps
67 Number one
69 Cast off
71 Cornelius Vanderbilt's mansion
73 Holiday lead-ins
74 Papeete resident
76 Spuds
77 Exist
78 Guadalajara gold
79 Great Mosque city
81 Susan of "L.A. Law"
82 Danny DeVito movie, "Get __"
85 S. Amer. nation
86 Heretofore
88 Trims, as meat
91 Part of USNA
92 Turkish official
94 Senator Thurmond
96 Be bold
97 First-class
98 Bed linen
100 Computer connection
102 Hockey venues
104 One who carries on
107 Cowboy, at times
108 Presley's mansion
111 Toy person
113 Journalist Bly
117 Actress Sorvino
118 Toy-truck sound effect
120 John Adams' mansion
122 Dismounted
123 Conger catcher
124 Window parts
125 Bogus
126 Beatty and Rorem
127 Pairs
128 Removes a cover
129 Word in comparisons

DOWN

1 Vasco da __
2 Carolina college
3 Pealed
4 Cell divisions
5 Concentrates
6 Sue __ Langdon
7 George Vanderbilt's mansion
8 "Whatever __ Wants"
9 Sufficient
10 Switch positions
11 Is on harmonious terms
12 Part of RFD
13 Revise
14 Poisoned state
15 Bright red
16 Buffalo's lake
17 Tickle Me __
18 Spotted
24 Modern Persia
29 Golf gadgets
31 Juli of the LPGA
33 J.K. Galbraith's field
35 Charlie Brown's exclamation
36 Bears' lairs
37 Killer whale
38 William K. Vanderbilt's mansion
41 Washington's mansion
42 Modern Zoroastrian
43 J.C. and Sammy
46 Indian potentate
48 Heavy breather
49 Animal trails
52 DDE's opponent
53 T follower?
55 Guitar adjuncts, briefly
58 City near Stockton
60 Mountain nymph
64 Allotments
65 Lodger
66 Gorged
68 Aircraft: pref.
69 Holy-water basins
70 Former Texas Rangers manager Toby
71 Stadium level
72 Used push-buttons
75 London stage
77 Expressions of delight
80 Used a sub's weapons
82 Precipitousness
83 Armored vehicle
84 Actor Montand
87 Forest product
89 Henry Ford's mansion
90 Exxon competitor
93 Cool dudes
95 Sitcom equine
97 1948-49 flights to Berlin
99 Figured out
101 Non __ (in moderation): mus.
103 Great Barrier __
105 Mariah of music
106 "__ Gay"
108 Fed
109 Agitate
110 Parched
112 "__ of Faith"
114 Jacob's first wife
115 Panelist Chase
116 Idyllic garden
119 "__ Miniver"
121 100 yrs.

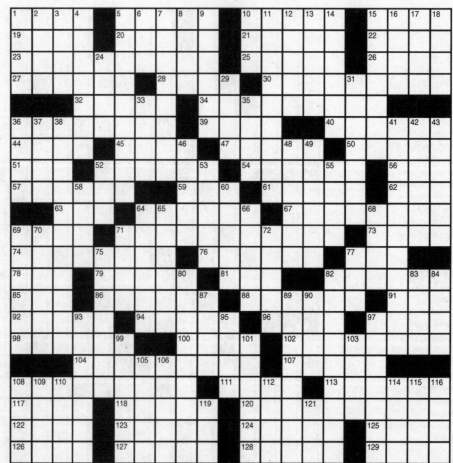

ACROSS

1 Warning
6 "Married...With Children" co-star Katey
11 State of mind
15 Make cuts
19 Computer display
20 1984 Oscar nominee for "Amadeus"
21 Ticklish Muppet
22 Slugger's stat
23 Muse of poetry
24 Palm cockatoo
25 Oblique: abbr.
26 Periods
27 1961 hit by the Edsels
30 Bowling alley
31 Ford fuel
32 Paradigms
33 Ousts
35 Center starter?
38 __ facto
41 66 or A1A, e.g.
42 __ ballerina
43 1956 hit by Gene Vincent
47 Roman games officials
49 Mil. honor
52 Pipe root
53 Cuckoopint and flamingo lily
55 Stand
57 Japanese menu entree
58 24 hours ago
61 Hautboy
62 Two-toed sloth
64 Greater omentum
65 Egyptian judge of the dead
67 Advanced deg.
70 1963 hit by Bob B. Soxx and the Blue Jeans
75 Expert
76 Enlarged (a hole)
78 Charlie Parker's nickname
79 Mineral veins
81 GM make
82 Agnes of "Citizen Kane"
86 Patch roads
90 Untied
93 Foundation piece
94 Brief coming attraction
95 Ike's arena
96 Seoul resident
99 1971 hit by Daddy Dewdrop
101 "Harlem Nights" co-star Della
103 Michael Stipe's group
105 Jacob's twin
106 Malay isthmus
107 Bombshell's color
109 Lofty
111 Computer abbr.
114 Litter's littlest
115 1981 hit by the Police
122 Land measure
123 Graven image
124 Madrid mister
125 Descendant
126 Christian of fashion
127 Designer Wang
128 Gage bestseller
129 Beat
130 Without: Fr.
131 Sea eagles
132 Family car
133 Actress Spacek

DOWN

1 Assert
2 Bologna currency, once
3 West or Sandler
4 Change prices
5 Dough
6 Deceptive appearance
7 Ambiance
8 Sword lily
9 Bitter
10 Horseshoes point
11 Interfered
12 Medleys of songs
13 Arabian sultanate
14 Crudely fashioned verse
15 Early round, briefly
16 1982 hit by the Steve Miller Band
17 Laughing
18 Curvy letters
28 Gobi's continent
29 Entryway
34 Shop grip
35 Recedes
36 Lima's country
37 Nile wading bird
39 Emphasize
40 Certain
42 Stratagem
44 Honolulu's island
45 Comic Freddie
46 Qty.
48 Italian novelist Calvino
50 Impassive
51 Former Attorney General Edwin
54 Leaves the Union
56 King of France
59 Way cool!
60 Twosome
63 Lend a hand
65 Sculling tool
66 Hillary's Everest guide
67 Worker
68 Athenian slave
69 1963 hit by the Crystals
71 Dwelling
72 "History of Rome" author Cassius
73 Misdo
74 Twelve: pref.
77 Writer's writings, in brief
80 Croat's neighbor
82 Slight
83 Ad __ committee
84 Arranged in troop formations
85 Mehemet and Mohammad
87 Captured
88 __ vincit omnia
89 Fellini film
91 Just managed
92 Sudden plunge
97 Spaces between leaf veins
98 Nudnik
100 Resident of northern Iraq
102 Penetrates
104 Pupil contractions
107 Thin wire nails
108 "Santa __"
109 Embellish
110 Dancer Astaire
112 Tobacco kilns
113 CCLXVII x VI
116 German river
117 Lady of Spain
118 Actress Moran
119 Affectations
120 Accomplishes
121 Gibb or Garcia

by Bernice Gordon

ACROSS

1 Longhaired sheepdog
5 Painter Rembrandt
10 Deadly
15 Long, narrow cut
19 Copycat
20 Astronaut Aldrin
21 Field of action
22 Leaning Tower city
23 Cindy Crawford, Christie Brinkley et al.
25 Donna Karan or Vera Wang
27 Colonial cuckoo
28 Repulsive
29 Steel girder type
31 Matador
32 Hook's underling
33 Social stratum
34 Intersects
35 Stood up to
38 Colette novel
39 Cast a shadow
40 Coll. Huskies
41 Meryl Streep or Julia Roberts
43 __ Na Na
46 1996 also-ran
47 Writer Morrison
48 Distinctive air
49 Burn slightly
50 Wapiti
51 Mary Cassatt or Annie Leibovitz
55 Divvy up
56 Activity periods
58 Fidelity
59 Losing streaks
60 Braided linen tape
61 Stable youngsters
62 Iridescent gems
63 Recipients
65 "Teachers" star
66 Maintaining full force
69 English composer
70 Margot Fonteyn, Gelsey Kirkland et al.
72 Stephen of "The Crying Game"
73 Ran like madras
74 "Aurora" fresco painter Guido
75 "Miss __ Regrets"
76 Lahr or Lance
77 Black goo
78 Myra Hess or Amy Marcy Cheney Beach
82 Count of jazz
83 __ New Guinea
84 Velocity detector
85 Became uptight
86 Anklebones
89 Childhood taboos
90 Tennis legend
91 Humiliator
92 Pole of Highland games
93 On a cruise
94 Period
97 Sophie Tucker sobriquet

99 Florence Nightingale, at times
102 Model Macpherson
103 Beginning
104 McClurg and Brickell
105 Melt together
106 Offspring
107 __ Dame
108 "Divine Poems" poet
109 Arabian sultanate

DOWN

1 Agouti's cousin
2 Resting atop
3 Jacob's third son
4 Wrath
5 Categorized
6 Roman official
7 In a twisted position
8 __ Abner
9 Stored, as fodder
10 Gradually becomes clearer
11 "Hamlet" tapestry
12 Abound (with)
13 Part of Q&A
14 1954 Fellini film
15 Meager
16 Preferences
17 Val d'__, France

18 Cocoyams
24 Cow's paunch
26 Temperamental
30 Adriatic seaport
32 Reciprocal of a cosecant
33 Department head
34 Visual aid
35 Weekend cowboys
36 School of Paris
37 Joan Baez or Mimi Farina
38 Pennies
39 Watery ice
41 Actor Greene
42 Ways of walking
43 Betsy Ross, e.g.
44 Angel's instrument
45 God of war
47 Worker's gear
49 Former Dolphins coach
51 Tightwad
52 Island loop
53 Very angry
54 For rent, in London
55 Substantial chunks
57 Slammin' Sammy
59 Ship's poles
61 Page number
62 During a broadcast
63 Obligation

64 Earthenware jar
65 Mama's mom
66 Absolute
67 Unearthly
68 Out-of-fashion
70 Boyfriends
71 Legumes with oily seeds
74 Singer Minnie
76 Cause of ruin
78 Bullring procession
79 Certification of a will
80 Superman's Lois
81 Decorated
82 Irish dramatist Brendan
83 Shoved
85 Sleeping sickness spreader
86 Common vetches
87 White poplar
88 Long-handled spoon
89 Dubber
90 Gray-faced
92 Play's players
93 Opposed to: slang
94 Conga or bongo
95 Greek peak
96 Twixt 12 and 20
98 6 on the phone
100 Wedding vow
101 E.T. craft

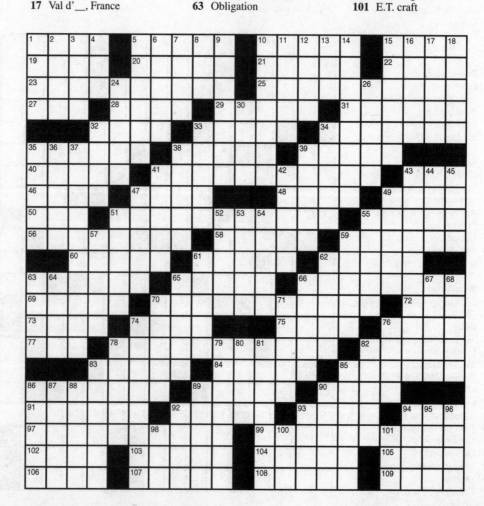

ACROSS

1. Young cod
6. __ Clayton Powell, Jr.
10. Rajas' wives
15. Heart of the matter
19. Nettle
20. Burt Reynolds' ex
21. "Love Story" author Segal
22. Woodwind instrument
23. Queen Elizabeth I's mother
25. Queen Juliana's mother
27. Places for keeping goods
28. Liqueur flavor
30. Suggest additional revisions
31. Quarry
32. Male honeybee
33. Cambodian monetary unit
34. Capture back
37. Mountain nymph
38. Cowboys' sleeping gear
42. Faulty
43. Solomon's mother
45. Supreme: abbr.
46. Pelvic projections
47. Well in France
49. Ireland, poetically
50. Cicatrix
51. Mont Blanc, e.g.
52. Lorna Luft's mother
56. Backbone
57. Relaxation times
59. Big name in farm equipment
60. Guy
61. "Philadelphia" star
62. Soft drinks
63. Of the Vatican
64. Dodger Reese
66. Evert of tennis
67. Remorseful one
70. Chilean range
71. Constantine the Great's mother
73. Fluffy scarf
74. Reynolds film, "The Longest __"
75. Daybreak
76. Depend
77. Beef and moan
78. Shoshone
79. Caesarion's mother
83. Edible red seaweed
84. Catholic sacraments
87. Cinders
88. Lounged about
89. Be a bookworm
90. Nicene, for one
91. Horn honk
92. Lacking values
95. Episcopal cleric
96. Dustin Hoffman film (with "The")
100. Jamie Lee Curtis's mother
102. Larry Hagman's mother
104. Perfect serves
105. Bones in forearms
106. Hertz rival
107. Went steady
108. Take five
109. "Wayne's World" star Mike
110. Period after Mardi Gras
111. Garbles

DOWN

1. Health resorts
2. Penny
3. Vegas rival
4. Highway crossing
5. Goes ashore
6. Backstreet
7. Performs
8. Whatever
9. Mosque tower
10. Resets a tape
11. Turn up
12. Sudan river
13. "__ bin ein Berliner": JFK
14. Union general
15. Shaddock
16. In the same place: Lat.
17. Novelist Morrison
18. Miami team
24. Curved molding
26. Lascivious look
29. Ark man
32. Sturm und __
33. Name the same suit
34. 1986 Indy winner
35. Sociologist Durkheim
36. Melanie Griffith's mother
37. Follows orders
38. Swiss capital
39. Desi Arnaz, Jr.'s mother
40. Argentine plain
41. Scatter
44. Gets wind of
47. Billie of "The Wizard of Oz"
48. March time
50. Wet impact
52. Allyson and Lockhart
53. Beautify
54. Ignited again
55. Chihuahua tether
56. Dark brown
58. Cut wood
60. John Cleland novel, "__ Hill"
62. Coarse, twilled cotton fabric
63. Banana wrapper?
64. Discharge a debt
65. Related on the mother's side
66. Has concern for
67. Supplications
68. Scandinavian
69. Recorded
71. Did some cobblers' work
72. Made a mistake
75. "The Man From U.N.C.L.E." co-star
77. Ethnic
80. Becomes very dry
81. On the waves
82. Rising current of warm air
83. Thingamabobs
85. Collar
86. Orderly
88. Fertile soil
90. Close, but no __
91. Rendezvous
92. Open slightly
93. Nutmeg spice
94. Washington bills
95. Climbing plant
96. Show teeth
97. Alaskan island
98. Stadium level
99. Remnants
101. Bridge expert Culbertson
103. "__ Maria"

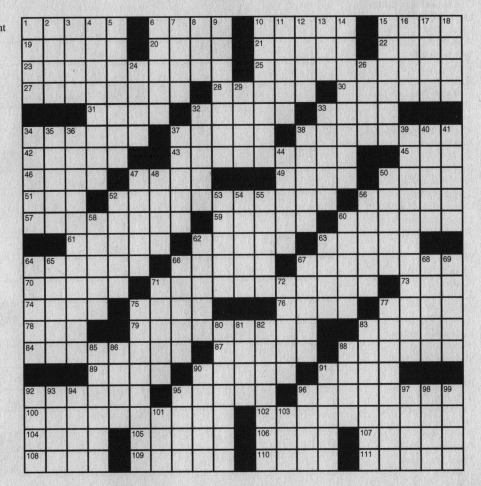

by Robert H. Wolfe

ACROSS

1 Cabbage salads
6 Cooking smell
11 Lyme-disease carrier
15 Celeste or Ian
19 Gemstone weight
20 Orange variety
21 Two-toed sloth
22 Hand-cream ingredient
23 Work of art
25 Communication route
27 Sirtis role on "Star Trek: The Next Generation"
28 Marion or Diana
29 Vital rules for Burr and Hamilton
30 Snare
31 Assam or pekoe
33 Nora's pooch
36 Sci. or math, e.g.
38 Come through under pressure
45 In good order
49 Language suffix
50 Regan's father
51 Self-evident truth
52 Tommy Lee's group, Motley __
53 Angler's bait
55 Is opposite to, in math
57 Legendary Chicago Blackhawk
59 "Get Shorty" author Leonard
62 Word of honor
63 Finds
64 Scan-line pattern
65 Source of poi
66 Most tranquil
67 Brunch concoctions
69 Windward Islands nation
71 Backtracked
74 Start of a day?
75 Had dinner
79 Religious recluse
80 Stinging wasp
82 Gyrocompass inventor
83 Established principles
84 Steven Spielberg film, "__ Park"
86 Father
87 Aleutian island
88 Nimble
89 Turndowns
92 Afr. nation
93 Part of USPS
96 Advances one's own interests
99 Main part of a bust
101 "__ we forget..."
102 Hodges of baseball
103 Boxing great
106 Egyptian judge of the dead
109 Top-drawer
112 French cleric
116 Legendary outlaw
118 Tip of Manhattan
121 Landed
122 Icelandic saga
123 "Waiting for Lefty" dramatist
124 Publish
125 Fellas
126 Sandra and Ruby
127 Taboo acts
128 Prepares to lay eggs

DOWN

1 Highlander
2 Hideaway
3 Singer Guthrie
4 Elk
5 RR depot
6 __ Domini
7 Squealers
8 Egg capsule
9 Fellows
10 Math subj.
11 Ballerina's skirt
12 Regarding
13 Birth sacs
14 Chinese range
15 Actor Holbrook
16 Lena of "Havana"
17 Sole
18 Get together
24 Fuming
26 Honshu port
29 Seeing regularly
32 Blowup of a pic
34 Roofers using stone
35 Formal attire
37 Impudent person
38 Tree feller
39 Island: It.
40 Periods in office
41 Is down with
42 Forced out violently
43 Encryption
44 "__ Pinafore"
46 Banal
47 Stringed instruments
48 Leavening agent
54 Constant talker
56 Utter without thinking
57 Soggy ground
58 Froze over
60 Tarry
61 Constructs
63 Actor Cariou
66 Provencal verse
68 Actor Marvin
69 Hoodlums with heaters
70 "Cheers" actor Roger
71 Hit the high points
72 Muse of poetry
73 Camp shelters
74 Irish seaport
76 __ ballerina
77 Flynn of "Captain Blood"
78 Color changers
80 Hefner or Grant
81 Bay windows
84 Yammer
85 Opposing position
90 Lawn-care tool
91 Star Wars letters
94 Long time period
95 Whipped
97 __ Island, NY
98 Slip by
100 Electron tube
103 Inland sea of Asia
104 Hit by the Kinks
105 In the same place: Lat.
107 Went by car
108 Lupino and Tarbell
110 Von Bismarck or Klemperer
111 Scottish loch
113 Deep singer
114 Very dry, as champagne
115 Just gets by
117 Possessive pronoun
118 __ appetit!
119 Commotion
120 Yang's partner

FIVE TIMES THREE

by Ed Voile

ACROSS

1 Cause to appear smaller
6 Long, feather scarves
10 George Eliot novel, "__ Marner"
15 Wicked
19 Muslim porter
20 Large musical group: abbr.
21 Banal
22 Make over
23 Of sheep
24 Honolulu's island
25 Wears
26 Pesky insect
27 Three sailors in a wooden shoe
31 Glaswegian
32 __ Aviv-Jaffa
33 Type of masochism?
34 Superlative suffix
37 Winter mo.
40 Long commute location
43 __ Perce
45 Actress Swit
47 Shepard and Greenspan
49 Ancient Irish king, Brian __
51 Born in Bordeaux
53 Former Portland Trailblazer Bill
54 Louise of "Gilligan's Island"
55 Three folk singers
58 Frozen eaves-dropper?
60 MX divided by V
61 Ave. crossers
62 __ of Galilee
63 Accidents
65 Staunch
67 Lubricated
71 Three swordsmen
77 Fashion
78 End of a spin?
79 Unmanly
80 Old English letter
83 Put two and two together
85 End of cigar?
87 Czar's edicts
88 Three comics
94 Attention-getting sound
95 Existing naturally
96 "Telephone Line" grp.
97 Continental currency
98 Computer clicker
99 Gullets
101 Ike's command
103 Last movement of a sonata
105 Classroom favorite
106 Cover crop
107 Tears
109 Dining area
111 Tobacco kiln
113 Three virtues
121 Off-base GI
123 Infamous Helmsley
124 Drudgery
125 Samos region, once
126 Apple discard
127 Dropped the ball
128 Window element
129 Doctor, at times
130 Turner and Danson
131 Soothsayers
132 Droops
133 Ship end

DOWN

1 Ship with a lateen sail
2 Undulating
3 Ugandan despot
4 Puts in order
5 Swindles
6 Idiot box
7 Spoken
8 Sore
9 Railroad switch
10 Napoleon's final place of exile
11 Modern Persia
12 Bonet and Kudrow
13 Lacking pitch
14 Dismiss from Oxford
15 Cogito __ sum
16 Feuds
17 Neighbor of Mont.
18 Fate
28 Primeval deity
29 Kesey or Follett
30 W. Hemisphere protection syst.
35 Shop
36 Singer Tucker
37 Mohammed's daughter
38 Bring out
39 Send packing
41 Campus military grp.
42 "The Threepenny Opera" dramatist
44 Olympus honcho
46 "A Nightmare on __ Street"
48 Mexican snack
50 Heep and others
52 Singer/pianist John
55 Lively
56 Held the helm
57 Comment to the audience
59 Endure
64 Power option
66 African fly
68 Drink like a cat
69 Composer Satie
70 From the beginning, in music
72 Change color again
73 Legendary king
74 Make a mistake
75 Being: Latin
76 Sonnet ending
80 Gives off
81 Hawaiian singer
82 Automotive pioneer
84 Broad valley
86 Architect Saarinen
89 Buddhist Thai
90 Video-game company
91 Gives a new name
92 Stationery buys
93 Single lenses
98 Tile creations
100 Domain
102 Spanish cheer
104 Lah-di-__
108 Lakeside
110 Lanterns
112 Brook fish
114 Beer picks
115 Lulu
116 U.S. weather grp.
117 Bell tone
118 Regarding
119 Wedding-cake layer
120 Tall tale
121 Take steps
122 Sadness

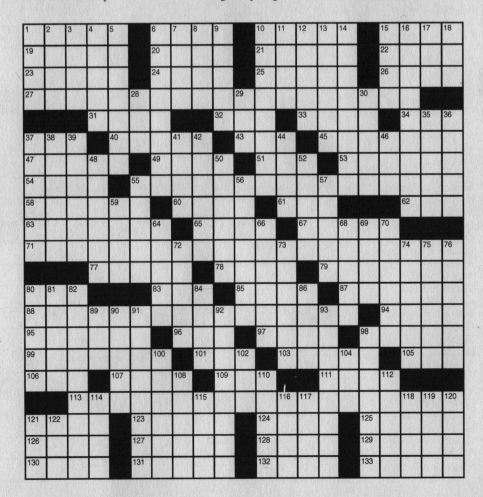

ALL IN THE FAMILY

by Annabel Michaels

ACROSS

1 Black shade
4 Teeter-totter
10 Venomous snake
15 Shortened wd.
19 Woodshed tool
20 Respiratory ailment
21 Sign of spring?
22 Kicker Yepremian
23 DiCaprio movie, with "The"
26 Kimono sashes
27 Shapeless form
28 Kept back
29 Perch
30 Fingerboard ridges
31 Landing area
33 "Kidnapped" author's initials
34 Fedora feature
35 Speaks too proudly
36 Disney dwarf
38 Inarticulate sounds
40 "M*A*S*H" clerk
42 __-de-France
43 Opposite of NNE
46 Chandler mystery
50 Learning org.
51 Acute infectious disease
53 Amazon estuary
54 Stupefy with drink
56 Colonists' desire
58 Ya dig?
61 Russian villas
64 McGregor of "Emma"
65 Tight closure
67 Misbehave
69 Grenoble's river
70 Hr. fraction
71 Matt Crowley play, with "The"
74 Misfortune
75 Benefactor Yale
77 Senator Thurmond
78 Brief note
79 Two squared
80 Generator
82 Oregon capital
84 Release
86 Actress Hedren
88 Art school subj.
90 Madonna's child
91 Japanese drama
93 Dave Foley's former troupe
97 Draft letters
98 Mine vein
99 Head bulge
100 Stevedores' org.
101 Earlike projection
103 Writer Gordimer
105 Bank security letters
108 Letter carrier: abbr.
110 Sword stroke
114 Dazes
115 Bea Arthur sitcom
116 Wage-slave's refrain
118 __ podrida

119 Chinese-American secret society
120 Zsa Zsa Gabor movie, with "The"
123 Sandwich cookie
124 Mature insect
125 Toiled
126 Tack on
127 Attention-getter
128 Plague
129 __ kick (football gamble)
130 Yo!

DOWN

1 Door columns
2 Glorify
3 Choir voice
4 __ Luis Obispo, CA
5 Old Testament book: abbr.
6 Knockout gas
7 Winters of Hollywood
8 Equidistant from bow and stern
9 Open hostilities
10 Landed estate
11 Ornate wardrobe
12 Like noxious air
13 Top of the heap
14 Invite
15 Spartan marketplace
16 Easy marks
17 Likely to crack
18 Antarctic body of water
24 Latin ditto
25 Sphere
30 Spoken of previously
32 Oarsman on a punt
35 __ beans
37 Tenor Enrico
39 Hidden obstacle
41 Small amount
43 Plotted
44 Ostentatiously
45 Teshigahara film
47 Two Chicago mayors
48 Therapy
49 Break out of one's shell?
52 "The Ipcress File" author Deighton
55 Mil. training course
57 Bridge positions
59 Gossip tidbit
60 London subways
62 Moves to action
63 Prescient woman
66 Turkish monetary unit
68 "__: or, Virtue Rewarded"
71 Yokels

72 Pitcher Ryan
73 Characteristic of freeways
76 Yokohama OK
79 In place of
81 Spout thoughts
83 Half a dolphin fish?
85 Humdingers
87 Infamous Amin
89 Fund-raising event
91 Unceasing
92 Eloquent public speakers
94 To the extent that
95 Pamper
96 Closet items
102 Lay eyes on
104 Bar of metal
106 Ninny
107 Five score: abbr.
109 "It Must Be Him" singer Carr
111 Muezzin's God
112 Playground ride
113 Readily available
115 Play charades
117 Friendly or Couples
120 Friction reduction device
121 Even prime number
122 Dutch commune

by Josiah Breward

ACROSS

1 Breaks off
7 Distress call
13 Prepared a bow
20 Red wine
21 Husky
22 "Hamlet" Oscar winner
23 Comic with a violin
25 Handcuff
26 Mineral deposits
27 Irrationality
29 "__ Gay"
30 Adam's grandson
31 Paquin and Moffo
32 Australian isl.
35 Long and lean
36 __ favor, senor
37 Followed a trajectory
38 Like Perrier and Pepsi, e.g.
41 Just get by
42 Took for granted
44 "Shotgun" singer of 1965
46 Bullock and Dee
47 Facet
48 Half of CXIV
49 Writer Fleming
50 Bit of butter
51 Highland hats
55 Madagascar primate
58 Completely
61 Move quickly
63 Workout wetness
64 Relinquish
65 Fur-covered
68 Singer O'Dowd, to fans
70 Obstacles
71 Boredom
72 "Casablanca" co-star
73 Charged particles
75 Vote against
76 Sierra __ Mountains
77 Otherwise
78 Comic's bit
79 Half a dance?
82 Noted drama school
84 First victim
86 African bombax trees
90 American Impressionist
95 Former Ethiopian ruler
96 Biddy
97 Spiritualistic gatherings
98 More of a wallflower
99 Red or White follower
100 Landon and others
102 Eastern ruler
103 Woman's netlike cap
104 Pain in the neck
105 Cabbage salads
107 Intoxicating beverage
110 Fly constellation
111 Forum honcho
114 Olympian turned golfer
116 Put one's nose in
117 Side-by-side ones?
118 Like a broken promise
119 Soil for future transplants
120 Dissuades
121 Prejudices

DOWN

1 Lugs laboriously
2 Actress Duse
3 Blonde bombshell Mamie
4 Sea eagles
5 Alejandro and Fernando
6 Pigpen
7 Avoided
8 "Nostromo" author
9 Violent tirades
10 Writer Bombeck
11 Gray and Candler
12 "The Consul" composer
13 CD-__
14 End of pay?
15 Trigonometric function
16 Lendl and Pavlov
17 Mrs. Tom Cruise, once
18 Squiggly and slippery
19 Visionary
24 Pound pieces
28 Western alliance, briefly
31 Assante or Hammer
33 Abbr. on many cameras
34 Whimper
37 Surrounding glow
38 Flower at first
39 Combo punch
40 Spade and Frost
43 R. Reagan's Star Wars
44 Crane's arm
45 Common shower gift
47 Woodland deities
50 Go gaga
52 Antenna
53 One of Satan's nations
54 British gun
56 Baltic capital
57 __-bitsy
58 Attention-getting sound
59 Actress Turner
60 Former coach of the Colts
62 Fit
63 Observe
66 Rustic
67 Says uncle
69 Animal fat
74 Climbed
78 Ritzy rock
80 Rime
81 Belly muscles, casually
83 Bigfoot's shoe size
85 __-relief
86 Surpassing
87 Evaluates
88 Early movie projector
89 Navigators' devices
90 Car frame
91 Greek
92 Scene stealer
93 Indigo dye
94 Wrote
95 Likely winners
98 Dodger Duke
101 Grassland
103 Singer Winwood
104 Genuine
106 Torn ticket
108 Bundled package
109 Incite
110 Brief skirt
112 Poetic piece
113 Roulette bet
115 Tight spot

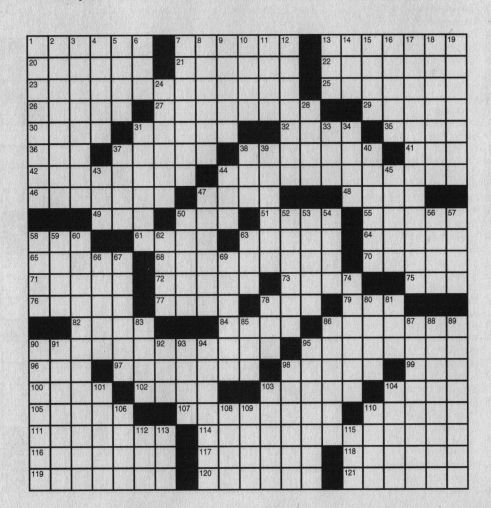

LEADING MEN

by Alan P. Olschwang

ACROSS

1 Sacred hymn
6 Birthday number
9 Rote and Petty
14 Was in accord
19 Scoundrel
20 Valuable stone
21 Believer in God
22 United
23 Frighten
24 Wildebeest
25 Simple weapon
26 W. Coast state
27 Man at the beginning of statistical study?
30 Viking poets
31 Villain's look
32 ER personnel
33 Principle of good conduct
35 Powerful sphere
38 Language of the Philippines
40 Rodeo cowboy Larry
41 Touch lightly
44 Man at the beginning improves?
46 Dormant
47 Mine vein
48 Moran and Gray
49 Spanish uncle
50 Transgression
51 Gazes at
53 Firepower
54 Semi-eternity?
55 Dispatch boat
57 Disney World attraction
58 Of Chilean mountains
60 Disregards
62 Malt beverages
63 Golfer Stadler
65 Cart track
66 "The Maltese Falcon" co-star
68 Approximately
71 Endurance race
74 Demands
78 Actress Pola
79 Swiftly
80 Graven image
82 Singer Amos
83 Tower of London?
85 Koppel or Turner
86 Like Abner
87 Missile garages?
88 Afore
89 Examples in context
91 Man at the beginning is blessed: Lat.
93 Half of the UAR
94 Some time after
95 Negotiate terms
96 Pen on the farm
97 More than ready
98 __ Paese cheese
99 White Sea bay
101 Tongue-lash
104 Man at the beginning of six-pocket furniture?
110 Expunge

111 Type of pneumonia
112 Pindar poem
113 Push upward
114 Anaheim player
115 Slur over
116 Saul's uncle
117 Tropical vine
118 Impoverished
119 Highway curves
120 Pause fillers
121 Mormon leader

DOWN

1 Chelsea carriage
2 Direction for a woman alone on stage
3 Culture medium
4 Lies in wait
5 Keepsakes
6 Total
7 Man at the beginning of father-son separation?
8 Cassowary's relatives
9 "Constant Craving" singer
10 Full calendars
11 "Mod Squad" character
12 Reversion of property to the state
13 Sault __ Marie, MI

14 Man at the beginning of child's toy?
15 Jacob's father
16 1972 Nobelist in literature
17 Oklahoma city
18 Dict. meanings
28 Sorrowful drop
29 God of love
30 Alan Ladd classic
34 Springsteen's epithet
35 Last Greek letter
36 Second showing
37 Unsighted
39 Sierra __
40 Frenzied
41 Fellini film, "La __ Vita"
42 Zeal
43 Outdoes
45 Lacking self-confidence
46 Exists, biblically
50 Greeted with respect
52 Like arias
54 Literary snippets
56 Man at the beginning of house rule?
59 Man at the beginning succinctly?
61 Slick and Kelly

64 Mosque prayer leader's office
67 __ Aviv-Jaffa
68 Chips in chips
69 Hollywood Noah
70 Lustful looker
72 Movie critic
73 Lubricator
75 Young horses
76 Freshwater fish
77 Actress Spacek
81 Rosebays
84 Missouri feeder
87 Fit for the choir
90 Rodent pets
91 Indonesian island
92 Middle management?
95 Ball favorites
97 Relaxed
98 Cutting edge
100 Seething
101 Noggin
102 Sea eagle
103 Burn out of control
105 Eye part
106 First-rate
107 Install software
108 Feudal serf
109 Lead actor
111 Victory sign

ACROSS

1 Proofreaders' symbols
7 Cheap hotel
14 Insurrection
20 "Peer Gynt" dancer
21 Travel faster
22 Estevez of "St. Elmo's Fire"
23 John Forsythe TV series
25 Hamilton and Darnell
26 City in Germany
27 Domesticate
29 French friends
30 Overthrowers
34 Gerald McRaney TV series
38 Enzyme: suff.
39 Runaway lovers
40 Spiritual adviser
41 Repudiated
43 Two-footed animal
44 Tennyson poem
47 Oklahoma city
48 Hamlet
49 The Lord's Prayer
52 The haves and have-__
55 Sports figure, for short
56 Contribution to the pot
57 Part of mph
58 "Under the Volcano" author
59 "Performance" director Nicolas
61 Computer input
65 "A Spy in the House of Love" writer
67 Farm enclosure
69 Crane fly
73 Half an African fly?
74 Powers of "Hart to Hart"
76 Against
77 Colorful marine fish
79 Legal phrase
80 Jamaican musical beat
82 Asian ox
85 Cotillion attendees, for short
88 Vault
89 1970 Carl Reiner movie
93 Part of QED
94 Smell
96 Spaces between leaf veins
97 United
98 Lives on easy street
102 Healthy in Spanish
103 Having a will
105 At the age of: Lat., abbr.
106 Percy Kilbride movie role
108 Drank like a dog
109 Ernest of country music
111 Weighty volume
112 The king of France
113 Hebrew prophet
115 Hit by Madonna
123 Journalist Bly
124 Erik of "CHiPs"
125 Disney Studios head, once
126 Felix and Polly
127 Arrives at
128 Arrives on stage

DOWN

1 Trucker's perch
2 Literary collection
3 Singer Ocasek
4 Afr. nation
5 Having hair
6 Preserver
7 Stream crossings
8 Singer Lorna
9 Greek vowel
10 Gallery display
11 Scornful cry
12 Vinegary: pref.
13 Actor Depardieu
14 Prison warden, at times
15 Radio static, in brief
16 Indian instrument
17 John Fogerty hit, with "The"
18 Intercede
19 Threw
24 Paddler
28 1501
30 Obligations
31 "The Waste Land" poet
32 Kin of Little League baseball
33 Willing to listen
34 "The Ghost and Mrs. __"
35 Island off Galway
36 Wife of Jupiter
37 Put on
40 Avaricious
42 Sots
45 Lawyer: abbr.
46 Egyptian cobra
49 Heathen
50 Blue shade
51 Sea eagle
53 Speaker of the Hall of Fame
54 "Auld Lang __"
58 Enunciation problem
60 Mild cheese
62 After a fashion?
63 Weighty weight
64 Syn.'s opposite
66 Athenian market
67 Greek letters
68 Sicilian peak
70 Culinary concoction
71 Astronaut Slayton
72 Gere title role
75 Nourishes
78 "__ Fideles"
81 Altar constellation
83 Copy
84 Parvenu
86 Language group of Swahili
87 Precipitous
89 Coils and curls
90 Formerly, formerly
91 Emblem
92 Corn concoction
95 Antithesis, briefly
97 Pain pill
98 Copper coat
99 Recycled
100 Major studio, once
101 __ fidelis
104 Epic poetry
107 Play pranks
108 Horne and Olin
110 Liver secretion
112 Bonanza
114 Ventilate
116 School grp.
117 Circle segment
118 Lah-di-__
119 Cornerstone abbr.
120 Organic suffix
121 Waxy: pref.
122 60-minute units

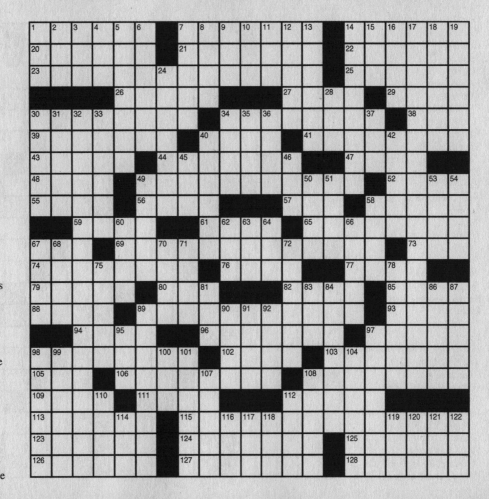

by Stanley B. Whitten

ACROSS

1 Height: pref.
5 Sound system
9 Chinese adders
14 Duchess of York
19 Quaker pronoun
20 Remove wrinkles
21 Humdingers
22 Jiffy
23 Spanish fool?
25 Italian bank employee?
27 Passes over
28 Incline
30 Wakame and kelp
31 Binges
33 Gazer
36 Rascals
37 Trudeau and Curie
39 Beaver State
41 French mathematician Blaise
45 Ad __ committee
46 Marine shockers
48 Old World lizards
50 __ Jean Baker (Marilyn Monroe)
51 Ways in: abbr.
53 Agronomist's concern
55 "Strange Interlude" playwright
57 Decisive defeat
58 Really stinks
60 Cupid
62 See 63D
64 Employ
65 Formed whirlpools
67 Adequate
70 "__ John, M.D."
72 "Gentlemen Prefer Blondes" novelist
74 Egyptian corn
75 Trigonometric function
76 Edible shellfish
79 East
81 And others: Lat.
85 Simian
86 Memorize
88 Finish line
90 __ we all?
91 Fissure
93 Porterhouse and T-bone
96 Fossil fuel
98 Persian poet of "Garden of Roses"
99 Adorable one
101 Lure
103 Sirtis role on "Star Trek: The Next Generation"
105 Church sister
106 Former name of Izmir, Turkey
108 Dark Chinese tea
110 Jack of "City Slickers"
112 Charity
114 Helicopter parts
116 "Cyrano de Bergerac" star
117 Droopy-eared dogs

121 Stage scenery
123 Jungian soul
124 French courier?
127 Italian hired killers?
129 Lethargic
130 Garbage
131 Verve
132 E-mailed
133 Watches over
134 Parking spot
135 Table supports
136 Mach+ jets

DOWN

1 Earth's envelope
2 Stood up for
3 Changed the course of
4 Olympic discus legend
5 Stashed away
6 "The Black Prince" novelist Murdoch
7 Deceives
8 Altogether
9 Second self
10 Prickly husk
11 Boxing great
12 Stage signals
13 Japanese immigrant
14 Saucepot kin
15 French landlord?
16 Provoke
17 Served perfectly
18 Word on a towel
24 Val d'__, France
26 Pack down tightly
29 Amazon estuary
32 Spots
34 Alaska's first governor
35 Italian auto repairman?
38 Blackthorn
40 Brad or spike
42 Larynx ailment
43 Titillate
44 Afterwards
47 Father
49 Louvers
52 Deftness
54 English contributor?
56 "Foreign Affairs" author
59 Site of the 1988 Olympics
61 Excessively acid
63 With 62A, man in a red suit
66 Medicinal quantities
68 William Tell's canton
69 Expanded
71 Bosc and Anjou
73 Glide on ice
76 Chagall and Connelly

77 Poppy product
78 Grove of baseball
80 Jog
82 "Blue" singer
83 Incentive
84 Wanderers
87 Vegas rival
89 Lawman Wyatt
92 Albanian dweeb?
94 Metric measure, briefly
95 Not subject to punishment
97 Bread buy
100 Joins the army
102 Organic compound
104 Of the intestines
107 Iowa college town
109 Mixture of pebbles
111 "Gunsmoke" star
113 Turns on an axis: var.
115 Inscribed stone marker
117 Fit of pique
118 Evergreen
119 Final word?
120 Break sharply
122 Hitch
125 U.S. government agcy.
126 And so forth: abbr.
128 Elected ones

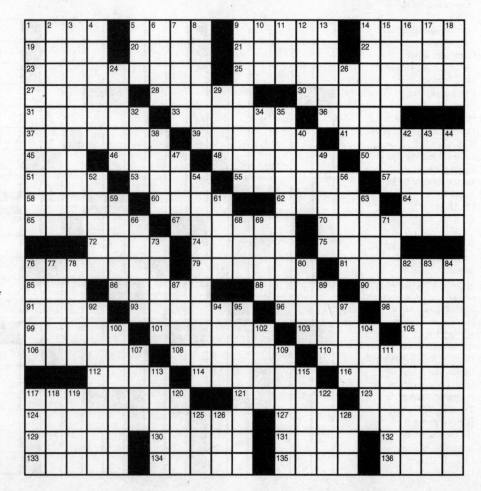

by Edgar Fontaine

ACROSS

1 Susan Dey series
6 1990-92 French Open champion
11 Fictional detective Spade
14 Agitate
19 Veracity
20 One hundred bucks
21 Reverence
22 Broaden
23 With 53A, colonial proclamation
25 Floor cover
27 Charlie Chan portrayer
28 Icy
29 CBS logo
30 Self-evident truth in 23A
37 Venezuelan currency
38 Shape using an ax
39 Wildebeest
40 Pontificate
41 Puppeteer Lewis
44 Partial prefix
47 Track-and-field rec. keepers
51 Charades participants
53 See 23A
56 Wall Street pessimist
57 Collapsible shelters
59 Part of QED
60 Make amends
61 Three satisfactory grades
62 Marketed
63 Mai __ cocktail
64 Portended
65 Author of 23A
70 Prohibited
73 Guided
74 Be inclined
75 '50s revival group, __ Na Na
78 Spirit of "The Tempest"
79 Burden
81 Make a watertight seal
83 Wine sediment
84 With 99A, unalienable rights in 23A
87 Entertainment venues
89 Foolish
90 Parts of a byte
91 Senior
93 Related on the mother's side
94 Mispickel or galena
96 Hit the slopes
97 Stone tools
99 See 84A
107 "A Few Good Men" director Reiner
108 Feinstein or Wiest
109 Fairy-tale monsters
110 Shunning
112 Last words of 23A
118 Percentages of a pound
119 Keg feature
120 Youngsters
121 Barcelata tune, "Maria __"
122 Having more cunning
123 Choose
124 Affirmatives
125 Loser to Truman

DOWN

1 Inc. in the U.K.
2 "We __ the World"
3 Jean-__ Godard
4 City in GA
5 Of any kind at all
6 Calibrated quantities
7 Penetrate
8 Roanne's river
9 Ike's arena
10 Dignitary in DC
11 Pelvic bones
12 Stand by
13 Come together
14 Sorenstam's land
15 Strike
16 Au revoir
17 Nairobi's nation
18 "The Mary Tyler Moore Show" co-star Georgia
24 Barrett of gossip
26 Hybrid language
28 Weak in numbers
30 Weapons of mass destruction
31 Australian parrots
32 Andes herd
33 Corner joint
34 Evert of tennis
35 Bridle strap
36 Calm down
42 Automaker
43 Toward the stern
44 Letter flourish
45 Org. concerned with air pollution
46 NYC opera house
48 Erelong
49 Skin problem
50 Nourish
52 Got up
54 Unhearing
55 Friend of Pythias
58 Nightmare street?
62 Casing
63 Newsman Koppel
64 Japanese city
65 Christmas star's place
66 Garbles
67 Joke
68 Dodge
69 Theol. belief
70 Smooth-headed
71 "Norma" melody
72 Guitar solo
75 Legislative body
76 Moors
77 Take stock of
79 __-Wan Kenobi
80 Profit
81 Part of UCLA
82 Also
83 Bolshevik leader
85 Portugal's peninsula
86 Lennon's Ono
88 Savored
92 Subjugate
95 Steering mechanism
96 Sault __ Marie
98 Opinion pg.
99 Ensnares
100 Run-down abode
101 "__ and Ivory"
102 __ Domingo
103 Remove the top
104 Clumsy
105 Pawns
106 Concur
111 Cool down
112 Pen on the farm
113 Positive vote
114 Toreador cheer
115 Fresh
116 Washington bill
117 Beam of light

by Ed Voile

ACROSS

1 Fashionable
5 Mourning period of Judaism
10 Leg bone
16 Possesses
19 Kilauea flow
20 Seagoing
21 Worshipper
22 10 of dates
23 Reasoning of Onassis?
26 Be penitent
27 Keeps on reverberating
28 Act subdivision
29 Feeble
30 Categorizes
31 Seek
33 "The Piano" co-star
35 Tarzan's kid
36 Recipients
37 Takes back
38 Phooey!
41 Alluring women
42 Leon lady
43 Sailor's hail
44 Golfer Calvin
45 Approves
46 Collar
49 Ebullient energy
50 Years when "Your Show of Shows" was on?
53 __ of Wight
54 Night before
55 Long in the tooth
56 Chips in chips
57 Golf course hazards
58 Leatherneck
60 Unspecified object
63 Rodeo ropes
64 Moran and Gray
65 Wedding VIP
66 Bo's number
67 Swelling retardant
68 Narrow stretch of land
69 Friendship with actress Dana?
73 Periphery
74 __ Aviv-Jaffa
75 Answering-machine signals
76 Bearings
77 Nota __ (note well)
78 Lessens
80 Lines for notes
82 Baseball-cap feature
83 Goaded
85 Folk singer Pete
86 Confirmed
87 Ben of golf and Paul of films
88 Clandestine
89 Choral and instrumental composition
93 Sore point
94 Target sighter
95 Ornate wardrobes
96 Balderdash
97 Math class in an Ohio town?
101 Indefinite pronoun

102 What we will?
103 Mourning Madonna artwork
104 Trigonometric function
105 Neither fish __ fowl
106 Actress Louise
107 Standish's messenger
108 Examination

DOWN

1 Santa __, CA
2 Rabbits' kin
3 Climbing vines
4 Maine inlet
5 Highfalutin
6 Loathes
7 James Merritt or Charles Edward
8 __ d'Isere, France
9 Actress MacGraw
10 Whims
11 Couch potatoes
12 "Have Gun Will Travel" star
13 Argue for
14 Luau souvenir
15 Trajectory
16 Greeley's parodies?
17 Perspicacity
18 Toughens up

24 Toss
25 Quaking tree
29 Perjurer
31 Principal artery
32 Villain's look
33 Mau Mau country
34 Prima donnas' problems
36 Conks out
37 Brings up
38 Walkway
39 Noisy mock serenade for newlyweds
40 Bart Simpson's dad's guffaws?
41 Parakeet staple
42 Shooting at clay targets
44 Washed-out
45 In the know
47 "Dog Day Afternoon" star
48 Metallurgist Sir Henry __
50 Cellmates, casually
51 Consumed
52 Dancer Miller
53 Pers. pension
57 Pitchfork prong
59 Press coverage
60 Envelops
61 Successful at-bats
62 Excitement

63 Guns it in neutral
65 Remove air from pipes
66 Heavy weights
69 Rose and Sampras
70 Mental picture
71 Musky cat
72 Lascivious gander
75 Farm building
77 Superlatively tiny
79 Slope by a loch
80 Confederate state, e.g.
81 __ Haute, IN
82 Poisonous secretion
83 Stone or Gless
84 Mount __, PA
85 Descendant of Shem
86 Upolu resident
88 Eliot's Marner
89 Greek island
90 Bandleader Shaw
91 Gull-like birds
92 So far
94 Does something
95 Matured
97 Squirmy catch
98 "Born in the __"
99 Grp. of mental-health workers
100 Nary a one

INTERNATIONAL LANGUAGE

by Ernest Lampert

ACROSS

1 Qatar's capital
5 Off-base GI
9 Pre-owned
13 Copper coat
19 God's reproduction
20 Roll-call call
21 Laugh heartily
22 Some binary compounds
23 Type of washing establishment
26 Come up with a new scheme
27 Textile-dyeing substance
28 Fay Wray movie, "King __"
29 Listing to one side
31 Fountain of Dixieland
32 Like a family flick
34 Strip between Pomerania and East Prussia
37 Stock-market abbr.
39 Anais the diarist
40 Jacob's twin
41 Supply for the fireplace
46 Mistake
49 Rhee of Korea
54 Honolulu's island
55 Evening in Bologna
57 Like
59 Old Norse character
60 Slink
62 Suicidal game
67 Botanist Gray
68 Engraved
70 Turned aside
71 More solemn
72 Composer Donizetti
73 Dark wine
76 Snake in the grass
77 Still
80 Sobriquet for Stallone
82 "The Medium" or "The Bat"
84 British Open winner Tony
85 Ancient Persian
86 Ship's personnel
88 Graceful bird
89 Green beryl
93 Black sheep
95 Ivan the Terrible's supporters
97 Picturesque panorama
99 RN's niceness
101 Corn or pod starter?
102 Alsatian
109 "Big D"
114 Vocal starter?
115 Tuscany city
116 Farrow and Hamm
118 Pope's triple crown
119 Genevan nationality
121 Water over the Chunnel
124 Hot-fudge creation
125 Hawaiian feast
126 Builder's map
127 "Citizen __"
128 Kuralt's replacement
129 Lift one's voice
130 Former Air France fliers, for short
131 Thailand, once

DOWN

1 Craps shooter
2 Biochemist who synthesized RNA
3 Device for lifting
4 "Tomorrow" show
5 Contented sighs
6 Half a fortnight
7 Lowest deck
8 Put the screws to
9 Coffee server
10 Fountain orders
11 Our planet
12 Solid carbon dioxide
13 Depict
14 Woodsman's tool
15 Actress Hedren
16 Loafed about
17 Peachy keen
18 "Lou Grant" star
24 Provide income
25 Jamaican fruits
30 Defeat
33 Classic Pontiacs
35 Like cloisonne
36 Stocking flaw
38 Duress
41 Zany Imogene
42 Paddles
43 Mother of Zeus
44 Expected
45 Celtic religion
47 O.T. book
48 Lofty Latin ode
50 Hellenic: pref.
51 Pound pup
52 Pot starter
53 Require
56 Opinion stater
58 City in the Bahamas
61 __ Palace of Florence
63 Speech on Sun.
64 Most frequent
65 __ Bator
66 Slowly, in music
69 Granny
71 Power option
72 Hairstyling product
73 Heap
74 Newspaper piece
75 Title
76 Miss Marple, e.g.
77 Poisonous evergreens
78 Part of Q.E.D.
79 Processes leather
81 Bother
83 Greek letter
87 Large hospital room
90 Gardner of "The Killers"
91 Flax product
92 Bandleader Arnaz
94 Resin for varnish
96 Pampas lasso
98 Steering devices
100 English potato chips
102 Coating for canvas
103 Shaffer play
104 Feeling regret
105 Accomplish incorrectly
106 Boredom
107 Irreligious
108 Arlene and Roald
110 Seaside golf course
111 Maui's neighbor
112 Type of stage
113 Oregon capital
117 Ella's singing style
120 Port. saint
122 Loutish fellow
123 Washington or Jackson in NYC

MARKS

by Xan Lattimore

ACROSS

1 Historic stretches of time
5 Of the ear
10 Borden's cow
15 Large, commodious boats
19 Lollapalooza
20 Josiah of bone china
21 Gwyn and Carter
22 Nevada tourist destination
23 MARK
25 MARK
27 Mystery pointers
28 Modern Persians
30 High-pitched flutes
31 Prehistoric murals
34 40th president of the United States
35 Shoshone
36 Narcotic
37 French aunt
38 Irons
42 Billiards shot
43 MARK
46 Tout's offering
47 Soft French cheese
48 Little legumes
49 Blunders
50 Large, bundled package
51 Gambling parlor: abbr.
52 MARK
56 Warning signal
57 City near Rawalpindi
59 Thread made from flax
60 Came to a complete stop
61 Noblewoman
63 Type of Dutch pottery
64 Saxophonist Coleman
65 Engrossed
66 Cavalryman's weapon
67 Merchant's inducement
68 Jewel weight
69 MARK
71 Gosh!
74 Amo, __, amat...
75 California beach
76 River to the Caspian Sea
77 Talon
78 Mythical bird
79 MARK
83 Stability
84 Elicited
86 Orange variety
87 Leather worker
88 "__ a Most Unusual Day"
89 Rouse
91 Dangling ornaments
92 Fly apart
95 United
96 Painted pony
97 MARK
99 MARK
104 Parasitic arachnid
105 Olympic skater Sonja
106 Country in the Himalayas
107 Call back
108 Hip ending?
109 Calculating snake?
110 Rib
111 See fit

DOWN

1 Wallach of "The Magnificent Seven"
2 Daiquiri need
3 High mount
4 Come to an end
5 Guarantee
6 Overturn
7 Fontainebleau residents
8 Fuss
9 Indulgent
10 Booker
11 Infamous Helmsley
12 Killed
13 Misfortunes
14 Superlative suffix
15 Military forces
16 Diver's milieu
17 Low-blow weapon
18 Barflies
24 Make joyful
26 Many times
29 Evaluate
31 Burger, fries and a drink, e.g.
32 Off to one side
33 MARK
34 Lift
35 "Exodus" author
37 Occupation
38 Cowboy's chum, for short
39 MARK
40 Actress Brennan
41 Exhausts
43 Dresses in
44 Fundamental principle
45 Architect of St. Paul's
48 Auto racer Alain
50 Silvers' TV role
52 Flemish capital
53 English church land
54 Suffered sickness
55 Structure starter?
56 Made logs
58 Quarters
60 Actress Veronica
61 "Enterprise" captain
62 Captivate
63 Capital of Senegal
64 Golfer Ben
66 Corn porridge
67 Christmas song
69 Mixed pooch
70 Ponderer
72 Tripod for art
73 Water pitchers
75 Olympus honcho
77 Allayed sorrow
79 __ voce (softly)
80 Cabal member
81 Actress Blanchett
82 Plain to see
83 Adhesive substance
85 Author of "The Virginian"
87 Snarl
89 Fair-haired
90 Songwriter Greenwich
91 Turner and Louise
92 Hobos
93 Module
94 Sacred ceremony
95 Mature
96 Pop
98 Government-insured loan: abbr.
100 Fork in the road
101 Frozen expanse
102 That woman
103 Mister turkey

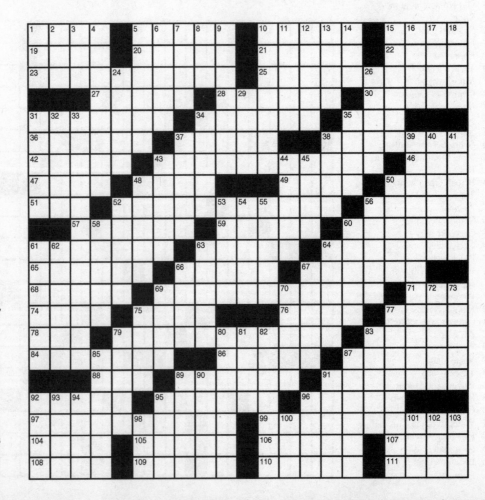

ACROSS

1 Indian tea
6 Usual practice
11 RBI or ERA, e.g.
15 Arab garments
19 Architect Jones
20 Red chalcedony
21 Dear: It.
22 Kedrova of "Zorba the Greek"
23 Husband-hunter's directory?
26 Holy smoke!
27 Freeload
28 O.T. book
29 Map book
30 Govt. source
31 Labored
33 "Silkwood" star
34 Job shift
35 1900
38 Yoko's family
39 TLC provider
41 Impartial
42 Altar of stars
43 Chromosome unit
44 Wallach and Lilly
45 Royal residences
48 King of France
49 "Topaz" author
50 Wheaton of "Stand by Me"
51 Love song
52 Current
54 Used a loom
55 List-ending abbr.
56 Murdered
57 Economize
58 Puppeteer Lewis
60 S-shaped moldings
62 Green-card org.
63 Soccer player Hamm
64 Salary dispenser
66 Slightly askew
68 Agent, briefly
70 Talons
72 Brush collection
73 Appearances
76 Paddles
78 __ Victor
79 Witticisms
80 Channel-swimmer Gertrude
81 Winners' prizes
83 Q-U connection
84 Branches of blood vessels
86 Long of "Made in America"
87 Green-eyed?
88 Ponselle or Parks
89 Edgeless sword
90 Rural stopover
91 Adam's grandson
92 Diarist Samuel
93 Earl __ Biggers
94 Loser of the '50s
95 Tracked to the end
97 Zany Imogene
98 Roman political subdivisions
100 Mr. Knievel
101 Poe's middle name
102 Bub

103 Some sports cars
107 Bus route
108 Film about calls from gals?
111 Tolkien's trees
112 Belgian composer Jacques
113 "The Jetsons" dog
114 For rent, in Kent
115 Scottish loch
116 Just gets by
117 The ones here
118 Mob endings?

DOWN

1 Establishes a target
2 Lose one's self-control
3 Missile shelter
4 Go-between
5 Manly Chinese dish?
6 Formerly possessed
7 Incomplete organ developments
8 Exposed
9 Hankering
10 Herbal drink
11 Lambastes
12 Loftier
13 Cacophonous
14 Labels
15 Alaskan island chain
16 West Coast town for he-men?
17 French actor Delon
18 Assassinated Egyptian president
24 Carl and Rob
25 Perceptible by touch
32 Anderson of "WKRP in Cincinnati"
34 Merchant's success
35 Shopping areas
36 Shepherd's staff
37 Better female servants?
39 Treat a puppy, perhaps
40 Brazen star of "Romeo and Juliet"?
41 Obvious pretense
45 __ out (dwindles)
46 Adam's garden
47 Stitches
51 "Night Moves" singer Bob
53 French friend
54 Methods
58 Cinnamon and nutmeg
59 Football coaching legend George
60 Singer Redding

61 Army of female relatives?
65 Christmas employees
67 Adversary
68 Memory method
69 Merit
71 Greek Christian theologian
74 Kevin of "Dave"
75 Penn and Connery
77 Cowardly
79 Barbecue fuel
80 Retired professors
82 Head cover
84 Dieters
85 Impersonator
88 Brings to mind
92 Subject of a canvass
95 Trojan beauty
96 Of sheep
97 Filer
98 __ blanche
99 Grain rot
101 French cleric
102 Pound to a pulp
104 Liver secretion
105 Lulu
106 Some NCOs
109 Used chairs
110 Fish eggs

by Ed Voile

ACROSS

1 Bryn __ College
5 Tax agcy.
8 Actress Louise
14 Clowns
19 Writer Seton
20 Instigate litigation
21 "The Condemned of __"
22 Wipe memory
23 Shore in Florida?
26 Collections of fluff
27 "Nashville" director
28 Go downhill
29 Sternutations
31 Strike count
32 Buddhist Thai
33 HST follower
35 Hawks' former arena
36 Software buyers
38 "Enigma Variations" composer
41 Lost traction
43 Ski tow
46 President's financial grp.
47 Wildlife exhibit in Michigan?
50 King topper
51 Layers
54 Maliciously derogatory
55 Welty and others
57 Sheepskin
59 Jose's houses
62 Ms. Streisand
63 Army post in Kentucky?
67 Talon
68 Buffalo hockey player
71 Scottish turndown
72 Onassis, to pals
73 Composer Grofe
74 Motley __
75 Harbor in Iowa?
80 Cowboy, at times
82 Moises, Jesus and Felipe
83 Hitting with heavy blows
87 Maine catch
89 Powdery volcanic rock
92 Sound system
93 Guido's highest note
94 Greensward in New York?
98 Spherical object
99 Breathe shallowly
101 Drop dramatically
102 Windmill blades
103 Wedding loops
105 Eland's cousin
107 Air-travel watchdog grp.
109 OSS, today
110 Printer's measures
111 Lacking chest bones
114 __ Island, NY
117 Lofty
120 "The Gods Themselves" author Asimov
121 Span in England?
124 Tropical plant with brilliant flowers
125 Take to the air
126 Tours season
127 Sea swallow
128 Noticeably contrived
129 Drink of the gods
130 Q-U connection
131 Gray and Candler

DOWN

1 Baby's word
2 Indigo dye
3 Old West marshal
4 Batterer
5 Publishing #
6 Wish undone
7 Shoreline barriers
8 Entertainer Bert
9 Priestly robes
10 Mighty mount
11 Such a one
12 Bus. letter abbr.
13 Cheers
14 Brazilian port
15 Set in position
16 Saloon in Tanzania?
17 Bone: pref.
18 Meeting: abbr.
24 McKellen and Woosnam
25 "The Kid" star Jackie
30 Certainly
32 80 yards of wool
34 "Evil Woman" grp.
36 Tritons' sch.
37 Successor of Ramses I
39 Italian boyfriend
40 Velocity detector
42 Verb-forming suffix
44 Mite or tick
45 Used-car buy
47 "__ Sutra"
48 Spiciness
49 Harem room
52 Nobel and Noyes
53 Barreled (along)
56 Saxophonist Coleman
58 "__ Karenina"
60 From a distance
61 Alphabetize
64 Polynesian drink
65 Sense
66 Rends
68 Lug laboriously
69 Iris ring
70 Savings & loan in California?
73 Glass base
75 Wrongly convicted French soldier of the 1890s
76 __ bene
77 Siamese sounds
78 Japanese city
79 City on the Irtysh
81 Numerical ending
84 Cromwell's nickname
85 Nebbish
86 Large quantities
88 Vitamin fig.
90 Seasoned
91 Author J.D. __
95 Pixie
96 Of a blood fluid
97 Pretoria's nation: abbr.
100 New Orleans university
103 Stout or bock
104 Ambrosia
106 Rot
108 Up, in baseball
111 Sumptuous
112 Golfer Aoki
113 Look over
115 Gulf of the Ionian Sea
116 Stadium level
117 Drive the getaway car, e.g.
118 India tourist stop
119 Telescope element
122 Hail to Horace
123 "Star Trek" extras

by Josiah Breward

ACROSS

1 Philippines city
7 Ultimatum words
13 Botanist Gray
16 Rapping Dr.
19 TNT
20 Antenna
21 Dreamer's letters
22 Capek play
23 Mo. starts star of "Take the Money and Run"
25 Mo. starts feverish
27 Ancient philosophy
28 Vegetarian cook Katzen
30 Like many European languages
31 City on the Missouri
33 Samos region, once
35 Phenomenon
36 Mo. starts soak in wine
40 Mo. starts ties to mother
42 Sitcom equine
43 __ oxide (anesthetic)
45 Signal for help
46 Eyelashes
48 Pinball goof
49 Writer Stoker
51 Meal scraps
55 Mo. starts municipal leadership position
58 Mo. starts teenage girl
60 "Pursuit of the Graf __"
61 The March King
63 Attacks
64 Sells direct to customers
68 Strong flavors
69 Gardeners, at times
70 Graduates
71 Bridge positions
72 Bog substance
73 Mo. starts Elizabethan headgear
75 Mo. starts increaser
80 Shelterward
81 Also
82 __ van der Rohe
84 Junipero __
85 Earth: pref.
86 Haciendas
89 Nathanael or Mae
90 Mo. starts isolation
96 Mo. starts groups of eight
98 "Foreign Affairs" author
99 Pays attention to
100 Gridlock
101 Homes
103 Edit
105 Restricted
110 Mo. starts small book
112 Mo. starts affirmatively
114 Golf gadget
115 Continental abbr.
116 Sea nymph
117 Skulls
118 Heavy-hearted
119 Affirmative
120 Tire patterns

121 Gunnar of "The Texas Chainsaw Massacre"

DOWN

1 "The Naked __"
2 Amo, amas, __...
3 One-billionth: pref.
4 News piece
5 Cosmetic liquid
6 Charity case
7 Sculling pole
8 Dry fruit
9 Switch tail?
10 Land in "Gulliver's Travels"
11 Mariners
12 Current off Ecuador
13 Comics bark
14 Discerns
15 Strollers
16 Forced forward
17 Judgment
18 Builds
24 Classic violin maker
26 Sitarist Shankar
29 German article
32 Henrietta's nickname
34 Very, in music
36 XXIX times C
37 Piece of Puccini
38 Depend
39 Personal prefix
40 Internet provider: abbr.
41 Type of X-ray
44 Grave letters
47 Poisonous gas
49 Quick kiss
50 Genetic letters
51 Augury
52 Stand
53 Russian sovereign
54 Mach+ planes
56 Soup choice
57 Males
58 Moonshine containers
59 Sales trails
61 Be mouthy
62 Can. province
64 Indian prince
65 Hebrew month
66 Bulrush
67 Nice friend?
68 Funeral bugle call
69 Game counter
71 Vichy water
72 Continue
74 Fabric
75 Former nuclear power agcy.
76 Eft
77 Transport-loss allowance
78 Old Gaelic
79 Ship deserters
82 Wanton slaughter
83 Elected ones
85 Journalist Horace
86 City near Calgary
87 Florida city
88 Actress Elaine
90 Biases
91 Greek island
92 Showed to be right
93 Assistant
94 Always, to Shelley
95 Doesn't have to
97 New York city
100 Reserved
102 Twist sideways
104 "The Alexandria Quartet" book
106 Infamous czar
107 Hamilton bills
108 Nobelist Wiesel
109 Actress Cannon
111 __ gratia artis
113 Hwys.

PEOPLE AND PLACES

by Annabel Michaels

ACROSS

1 Likable loser
6 Worsted cloth
11 Set sights
16 T. Turner channel
19 Zodiac sign
20 King Arthur's father
21 Madrid museum
22 Arikara
23 Actress Jodie's place?
25 Depiction
27 Latin handle
28 Uncorks
29 Hindu princess
30 Wet sprays
31 Bread choice
32 Fred's dancing sister
33 Stupid ones
35 Town in N. France
36 Diabetes treatment
38 Standard charge
40 Rand of writing
41 Novelist George's place?
44 Leafstalk angle
46 Letters openers?
49 Passions
50 Weights in a handicap horse race
53 Prop starter?
54 Italian city with two leaning towers
56 Dandy
57 Verbal skirmish
58 Requirement for a UFO
59 Wolves and foxes
60 Center
62 Sheik's garment
63 Ump's cohort
64 French students
65 Hors d'oeuvre
66 Drag something heavy
67 Worldwide $ group
68 Inventor Howe
69 New Jersey river
70 Tankard filler
71 Pick players
73 '60s campus org.
74 Terrorized
75 Wound reminder
76 Pyrenees country
78 Joan or John
79 Boardwalk extensions
80 Sot
81 Singer Billie's place?
84 Poetic piece
86 Short musical piece
88 Roy's horse
92 Shout
94 Dull finishes
95 Canadian territory
97 Otto I's realm
98 Beauty business
100 Swan genus
101 Samurai bandit
102 Hope-Crosby title word
103 Clan members

105 Tennis player Margaret's place?
107 A German
108 Slap on the __
109 In the dark
110 Back street
111 Std.
112 Renaissance poet
113 Mollusk's appendages
114 "Siddhartha" author

DOWN

1 Trip in the bush
2 Hume of "Cocoon"
3 Snake speech
4 Change: pref.
5 Carbohydrate: suff.
6 Postpone
7 Barrymore or Merman
8 Avignon's river
9 Jewels
10 Before, in poetry
11 Garments
12 Mesabi Range product
13 Yacht basin
14 Summer hours in St. Pete
15 U. building
16 Actor Billy's place?
17 In good order
18 Byron of golf
24 "The Thinker" sculptor
26 Greenish sloths
29 Daises
32 Winglike parts
33 Stonecutters
34 Actor Terence's place?
37 Government farm grp.
38 Emblems
39 Stop-skipping train, briefly
42 Oral moistures
43 Old hags
45 Island south of Naxos
46 Diamond hit
47 Jason or Justine
48 Singer Jimmy's place?
50 Use a cut medication
51 Organized as a list
52 Theater troupes
54 Actress Lucille's place?
55 Iroquois tribe
56 Overly particular
59 Mediocre grade
60 Shaken instrument
61 Half a score
65 North American country

69 Copal and amber
72 You to Yves
74 More stubborn
75 Lift up one's voice
77 ER workers
78 Develop a liking for
79 Nabokov novel
81 Lacking headwear
82 __ and Nevis
83 "Reversal of Fortune" star Jeremy
84 Word with bed or crackers
85 Sweet'ums
87 Judd and Campbell
89 Grave robbers
90 Deletes
91 Overnight flight
93 Seles shot
95 "__ Never Walk Alone"
96 Open roughly
99 "Eye of __..."
101 Novelist Jaffe
102 __ model
104 Spanish Mrs.
105 Yachting trophy
106 Exclamation of doubt

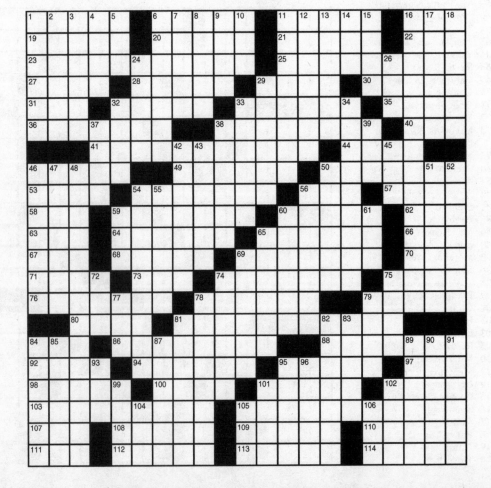

89   FILL-IN-THE-BLANKS FLIX

by Xan Lattimore

ACROSS

1 Pour profusely
5 Fills to overflowing
10 Daughter of Ops
15 Compare prices
19 High: pref.
20 Earth pigment
21 Divert
22 Labels
23 Michael J. Fox film, "__ to the __"
25 Richard Benjamin film, "The __ of __"
27 Kept private
28 Metro terminal?
30 Objective
31 Chopped
32 "Spanish Rhapsody" composer
33 Number of Muses
34 Refused
37 Detroit player
38 Evening starters
42 Seed coats
43 Melina Mercouri film, "__ on __"
45 King of France
46 Recycled garments
47 Language subtlety
48 Equal scores
49 Comic Sahl
50 Numerical ending
51 Howard Keel film, "The __ of the __"
55 Extent
56 Traffic circles
58 Pope's fanon
59 Door elements
60 Items in the fire?
61 Use a poker
62 Gospels' source material
63 Majestic
65 Play pranks
66 Tyrant
69 Fleshy fruits
70 Frank Sinatra film, "__ as a __"
72 6 on the phone
73 Claire and Balin
74 Scotch companion
75 Christmas carol
76 Cut short
77 Fabray, casually
78 Michael York film, "The __ of the __"
82 Paint layers
83 Breakfast mixes
85 Actress Roker
86 Irish city
87 German auto make
88 Oberon of "Wuthering Heights"
89 Cowboy's chum
90 Hot
93 Indiana player
94 Marketing agent, casually
98 Joan Collins film, "__ from the __"

100 Jack Lemmon film, "The __ of __"
102 Island guitars, briefly
103 "Guitar Town" singer Steve
104 Ex-quarterback Bart
105 Colonial black cuckoos
106 Grovels
107 Spirited horse
108 Uncanny
109 Appointment

DOWN

1 No-no
2 Gusto
3 Customary extras, briefly
4 Fokine and Baryshnikov
5 Made rancid
6 Played a part
7 Muffled sound
8 Mess up
9 Amount of ooze
10 Square-dance leaders
11 Computer messages
12 Moscow lang.
13 Superlative ending
14 Provencal verses
15 Hi-fi's successor
16 Gen. Alexander __
17 Leer
18 H.S. junior's exam
24 Electronic copies
26 Readily available
29 Done
32 Missouri or Ohio
33 Life-drawing subjects
34 Challenger
35 Muse of poetry
36 Richard Burton film, "The __ of the __"
37 Temporary abodes
38 Maliciously sarcastic
39 Sellers film, "The __ __ of the __"
40 Norway, to natives
41 Locations
43 "The Highwayman" poet
44 Functional
47 Contaminate
49 Frenzied
51 Metal scum
52 Scintillas
53 Chilly coating
54 Malingerer
55 Strictness
57 Cuckoopint and flamingo lily
59 Traveler's stop
61 Of bristles
62 Olympic sleds
63 Mimicry

64 Of an arm bone
65 Worrell and Zeile
66 Battery electrode
67 Writer Loos
68 __-turvy
70 Of a junction
71 Actress Potts
74 Gags
76 Winter spell
78 Uses a lasso
79 Put up
80 Painful point
81 "Sweet Child O' Mine" singer
82 Seven-time batting champ
84 At least as much as
86 In abundance
88 Syrup source
89 "Gloria __"
90 Ticket receipt
91 Seize
92 Designer Cassini
93 Bonfire pile
94 Headliner
95 Vegas rival
96 Goddess of discord
97 Attention-getting sound
99 Squealer
101 Shoshone

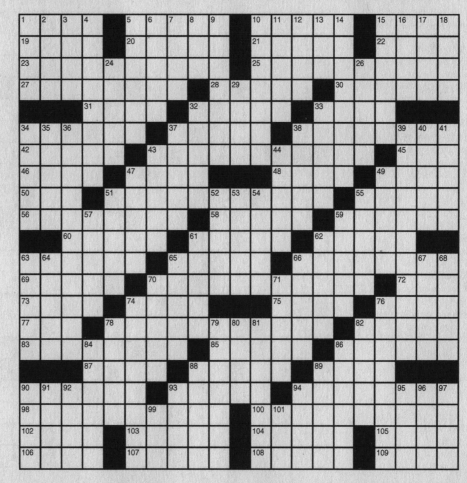

by Tom Pruce

ACROSS

1 Tumults
8 Falls short
13 Dodge model
20 Sore
21 Roman port
22 Maiden turned into a spider
23 1967 Shelley Winters movie
25 Camper's light
26 Negative adverbs
27 Trigger-happy
28 Engraved pillar
30 Karate schools
31 Pieces for two
33 Director Kazan
35 Secret store
37 Prefix for cop?
38 "Sophie's Choice" Oscar winner
40 Doctrines
42 God of France
44 Beatles song, "__ Blues"
45 Front attachment: abbr.
47 Ron Howard sitcom
50 Mormons: abbr.
51 French sculptor
54 Burden
56 New guy
57 Indian jacket style
59 Actress Ruby
60 Japanese horseradish
62 Go-aheads
64 Parrot again
67 One who does: suff.
69 Green shade
70 Move in a sudden sweep
72 Gardener, at times
73 Gandolfo resident
74 Dave Clark Five hit
77 Fifth of MMMDV
78 Road charges
80 Quality of taste
81 Baseball team
82 Vitreous residue
83 Ice falls
85 Current, for short
86 Like rhymes
88 Shoshone
89 Not the least bit
91 European river
93 Sushi fish
94 Cross or Affleck
95 Mongrel
97 Jimmie Walker sitcom
100 Fringe benefit
102 Opposite of WSW
103 TV award
104 Fire-sale phrase
106 Alleviation
110 Took off
112 Conforms
115 Successor of Ramses I
117 Conehead?
118 Supply
120 Vicinities
122 Soft drink
124 Shine brightly
125 More genial
127 Joan Fontaine movie
130 Intertwined
131 British naval base, __ Flow
132 Gasoline hydrocarbons
133 Champs __
134 Braxton and Morrison
135 Most cruel

DOWN

1 Overturns
2 Come to fruition
3 Thelma or Tex
4 Simplest of procedures
5 Part of R.S.A.
6 Hold sway
7 Troy Donahue movie, "Susan __"
8 Like an old codger
9 Blond shade
10 Suffix for diseases
11 Collections of fluff
12 Home-video show host
13 Society of St. Francis member
14 La-la lead-in
15 "Atlas Shrugged" author Ayn
16 Player
17 Amy Tan novel
18 Removed clothes
19 "Enterprise" detectors
24 Jamaican citrus fruit
29 "Shane" star
32 Sikkim antelope
34 Noted violin maker
36 Writer Georgette
39 Malaysian city
41 Secret agent
43 Show to seats
46 Flintlock muskets
48 Roam stealthily
49 John Lennon's widow
51 Upgrades
52 Upgrade machinery
53 Art Linkletter's TV show
55 Dar es __
58 Enjoys a mystery?
61 Certain canopy support
63 Part of USSR
65 Underworld goddess
66 Theologian from Alexandria
68 Find a new tenant for a flat
70 Camera letters
71 Choked back
75 Hanoi dress
76 Director of 23A
79 Part of a process
84 Sports replay, often
86 Squeeze
87 Showed concern
90 Actress Carole and others
92 Physicians' soc.
95 Actress Holm
96 Non-uniform
98 Color changer
99 Sonora snoozes
101 Jack of "Quincy, M.E."
105 Greek portico
107 Like some skates
108 French schools
109 Most infrequent
111 Light, metallic sounds
113 Beer stimulant
114 Vanzetti's cohort
116 Language nuance
119 Stack
121 "The Plough and the Stars" playwright O'Casey
123 Allow ending?
126 Shoe width
128 Troy, NY school
129 Saint of It.

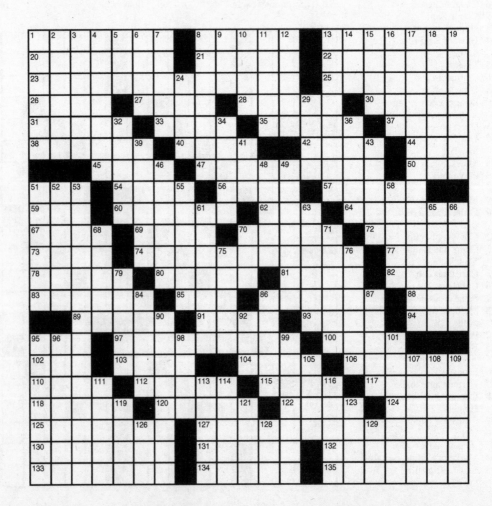

by **Willy A. Wiseman**

ACROSS

1 Selling point
6 Channel of politicos
11 Palm thatch
15 Burl on a tree
19 Hackneyed
20 Serviceable
21 Gershwin and Levin
22 Space starter?
23 Last name in Communism
24 Everly Brothers hit
26 Biblical pronoun
27 Gabor sister
28 Shed, as blood
30 Mil. rank
31 Evert of tennis
32 German article
33 Baseball's Charlie Hustle
36 Cause to become closed
38 Pitchers Martinez and Astacio
40 Marx Brothers movie
43 Mark sale items
45 Better
46 Medicine that induces vomiting
50 Stepped on it
52 Pitch a tent
55 Chemical suffix
57 __ contendere
58 Pekoe or oolong
59 1932 Bette Davis movie
65 Zilch
66 Confused
68 City on the Penobscot
69 Swindled
71 Pertains
73 Steve McQueen movie
76 Barkin and Burstyn
77 Benefactor
79 French students
81 Ottoman dynasty founder
82 Tempe sch.
83 Song from "Fiddler on the Roof"
87 Sch. group
88 Narrated
90 Former Dolphin Marino
91 New York nine
92 Part of a process
93 Penetrates
96 Actress Scacchi
100 Pope who negotiated with Attila
102 Anopheles protection
106 Sailor's jacket
109 Acupressure massage
112 Tegucigalpa's country
114 Actor Gulager
115 Tips off
116 Ireland
119 Neutral shades
120 W. Hemisphere grp.
121 Matured
122 In advance
125 Break out
127 Melody
128 Rustic hotels
129 Japanese gateway
130 Intrinsically
131 Ranked player
132 Medical suffix
133 Frank of CNN
134 Gorged

DOWN

1 Napping
2 Singer Wonder
3 California feature
4 Inventor Whitney
5 Sawbuck
6 Noah's ark measurement
7 Fashion maker
8 Poet Metastasio
9 Mass gown
10 Napoleon's marshal
11 Khartoum's river
12 Remove wrinkles
13 Man with salivating dogs
14 Gynt's mother
15 Actress Turner
16 Former Indian leader
17 Arum family plant
18 Awaken
25 Excrete
29 Passover
31 Cyrillic USSR
34 Tic-tac-toe win
35 Dallas sch.
37 Tenth of MXX
39 Skelton or Buttons
41 Dutch cheese
42 Novelist Jaffe
44 Outfit
47 Judge's charge
48 Estrange
49 Winter spell
50 1994 Kurt Russell movie
51 AFB in Colorado
53 Lion's fare
54 Phnom __
56 And so forth: abbr.
59 Small pies
60 Curved moldings
61 Lordly
62 Van Gogh location
63 Cohort of Fidel
64 Greek slave
67 Back of car?
70 Capp and Capone
72 Five centimes, once
74 Nero's egg
75 Nota __ (note well)
78 Circular: abbr.
80 Mach toppers
84 Italian sauce
85 Cross inscription
86 Lost dogie, e.g.
89 Brooked no refusal
92 Get the point
94 Decomposes
95 Draft letters
97 Former anesthetic
98 In addition
99 New England cape
101 Panama Canal engineer
103 Ashe Stadium location
104 Guest and Degas
105 Go to bed
107 Slip by
108 Oxidized
109 Swings of the bat
110 The __, the Netherlands
111 Goddess of peace
113 Wireless
117 Former Spanish toehold in Africa
118 Supreme Diana
122 Brief life
123 UFO pilots
124 Soil turner
126 Stephen of "The Crying Game"

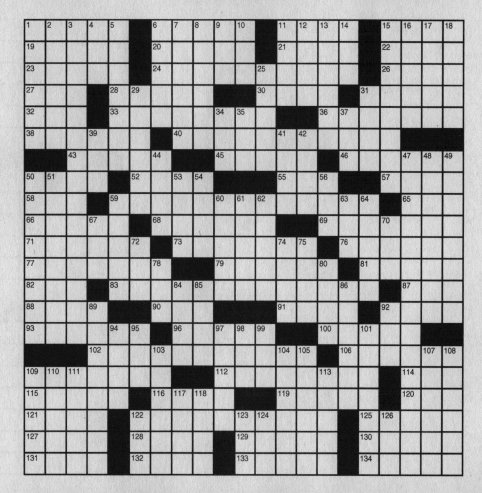

by Alan P. Olschwang

ACROSS
1 Cell body
5 Goddess of discord
9 Dunfermline dagger
13 __ longue
19 Tot's bed
20 Loaf about
21 Car tooter
22 Computer buff
23 Actor Arkin
24 Writer/director Kazan
25 Medical school subj.
26 Roast hosts
27 Alaskan city in system of names
30 Utopian
32 Taps
33 Winter fall
34 French city in topmost moldings
38 Duck and dodge
40 Responses
42 Money factory
43 Montana city in Confederate uniforms
47 Amin of Uganda
48 Chip dip
49 Pale
50 Doughboys?
53 Subtitle
55 Come to regret
56 Year in the Yucatan
59 Happen to
61 Tuck and his ilk
62 Manchester man
64 Arab robe
66 Trap bait
67 Taylor or Claiborne
68 English city in stretching
71 Pennsylvania city in zoo
76 Medical pic
77 Warning
81 Totality
82 Puts on
83 Evening repast
86 Soap opera
88 Western writer Buntline
90 Classified __
91 Side by side
93 "__ Doria"
95 Singer Fisher
97 Burgundy blacks
98 Sea eagle
100 French city in metaphor
103 Lady of Spain
104 Act as chair
107 Part of a pansy
108 Florida city in Revolutionary War precursor
110 Mardi __
112 One who transfers property
116 Avid
117 New York city in mariner's measure
119 ASAP
122 Tiny particle
124 College cries

125 Ancient Iranian
126 Raved wildly
127 "__ Mia"
128 Curved molding
129 Crack shots
130 Port on the Black Sea
131 Very French
132 Playwright Hart
133 Withered

DOWN
1 Reads quickly
2 Lowest deck
3 Home of the Heat
4 Renounce
5 Qualified voter
6 Accumulates quickly
7 Pelvis bones
8 Louvers
9 Tate or Stone
10 Nothing to report
11 End of an __
12 Lured
13 Danson sitcom
14 Old Testament Persian villain
15 Peruvian city in adapted
16 ETO commander

17 Comprehend
18 Hesitator's sounds
28 Nine-days' devotion
29 Not invited
31 Greek column type
35 Eyelashes
36 Belgian artist
37 Musial and Mikita
39 Localize the soundtrack
41 Common sense
43 Pointed remarks
44 Overthrow
45 Possessive pronoun
46 Bar bill
48 Small shoot
51 Somme summer
52 Singer Ocasek
54 Blazing
57 Lowest points
58 Sapporo sash
60 Ogles
63 Arizona city in dispositions
65 Literary collections
69 Vicinities
70 Collects bit by bit
72 Sister
73 Glory and Tobacco, e.g.
74 California desert town

75 German industrial city
78 Prince Valiant's son
79 Disencumber
80 Mime Marcel
83 "__ of Iwo Jima"
84 WWII menace
85 __ ballerina
87 Zodiac sign
89 Jump the tracks
92 Third canonical hour
94 Current unit, for short
96 Sticky situations
99 Take back
101 Georgia fruit
102 Map books
104 Buddhist tower
105 Look away
106 Theatrical works
109 Noggins
111 Senator Thurmond
113 Family member
114 Senior
115 "Touched by an Angel" star
118 Shakespearean villain
119 Paid athlete, briefly
120 Groovy, updated
121 Indefinite pronoun
123 Black goo

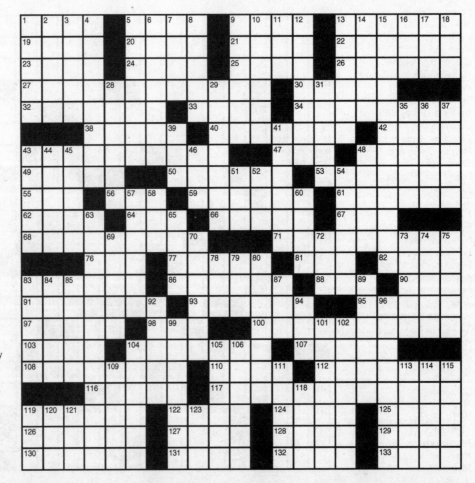

DEFINITIVE CONCLUSIONS

by Robert H. Wolfe

ACROSS

1 Given life
5 Causing death
10 Five-pointed figure
14 Machu Picchu builders
19 End of a switch?
20 Group of Islamic scholars
21 Comic Jay
22 Satchel of baseball
23 Touch against
24 I don't know what "apathy" means and I'm...
27 Conservatives
29 Mimics
30 Sunflower seed
31 Fat salt
32 Sulky
33 Roman autocrat
34 Brooch
35 Rascal
37 Command to Rover
38 Fatty
42 Clay, today
43 Winglike parts
45 Twinge
49 Gainsay
50 Flaw
52 Gods' images
53 Nobelist Wiesel
54 I don't know what "fearful" means but I'm...
59 Houston school
60 Mineral of antimony
61 Set in from the margin
62 Subsequently
63 Canadian prov.
64 Arum plant
65 United
66 Soft mass of chewed food
69 Short-lived Tejana superstar
71 Fiercely loyal
76 Way out
77 I don't know what "bewildered" means and I'm...
79 Cold-cut palace
80 Embellish
81 Afore
82 Gray wolf
83 Agitated state
84 Come up short
85 Half a bikini
87 Remains home
90 Edge
91 Baby grand or spinet
93 After a fashion?
94 Ranges
98 Meager
100 White-maned golden horse
105 Out-and-out
106 Zesty bite
107 Intercoastal region
108 I don't know what "curious" means but I'm...
111 Site of Hannibal's defeat
112 Drop in one's two cents
113 Der __ (Adenauer)
114 Small band
115 Israeli airline
116 Affirmatives
117 Marsh grass
118 Throat-clearing sounds
119 Symbols in Internet addresses

DOWN

1 Grizzlies
2 Solar circuit
3 Blusher
4 I don't know what "melancholy" means and I'm...
5 Suva populace
6 An absolute necessity
7 Likes and dislikes
8 Quantities: abbr.
9 Baton Rouge sch.
10 Mistake
11 Religious principle
12 Squirmy
13 Caviar
14 Medicine that induces vomiting
15 Critic Thomas
16 Uses a source
17 Rocket launcher
18 Jewish meal
25 Mother-in-law of Ruth
26 Closest to blue?
28 Small combo
32 Buddy
36 Icahn or Sagan
37 Port __ cheese
38 Rehan and others
39 Quick and skillful
40 Crucifixion inscription
41 Give off
43 Said further
44 Crazy bird?
45 I don't know what "astonished" means and I'm...
46 Touched down
47 Considerate
48 Will of "The Waltons"
51 Stout's cousin
52 Bombay resident
55 Hostelries
56 Morse unit
57 Shoot at
58 Turkish leader Ismet __
62 Actor Garcia
64 Actress Woodard
65 Sphere
66 Cots and cradles
67 Cart pullers
68 Movie "Darling"
69 __ and Gomorrah
70 Adam's grandson
71 "And I Love __"
72 Fruity quaffs
73 Exclamations of discovery
74 Physics Nobelist
75 English school
77 Flockhart of "Ally McBeal"
78 College bigwig
85 Target-spotter's interjection
86 Squealer
88 Abilities
89 In an orlop
90 Taylor and Adoree
91 Gasped
92 Laudanum, e.g.
94 "Stompin' at the __"
95 Crinkled cloth
96 Fragrant rootstock
97 Golfer Stewart
98 Engraved pillar
99 __ blanche
101 Relevant: Lat.
102 Novelist Calvino
103 Worm: pref.
104 Talking tests
107 Part of MIT
109 Fish like a stick?
110 Mauna __

KHRUSHCHEVIAN COMMENT

by Alan P. Olschwang

ACROSS

1 Ovid's outfit
5 Liquid courses
10 Standing one in good __
15 Walked (on)
19 North Carolina college
20 Actress Dickinson
21 __ Haute, IN
22 Try to outrun
23 Lion's fare
24 Mexican Pancho
25 Lindros and Clapton
26 Place one's stake
27 Start of Nikita Khrushchev quotation
30 Formed whirlpools
32 Mach topper
33 Lobster eggs
34 La __ Opera House
35 Transfixes
36 German river
38 Brit's gun
39 Hindu groupings
41 Baxter and Bancroft
43 Part 2 of the quotation
48 New Jersey or California city
49 Scorch
50 John Jacob or Mary
51 At hand
52 Part 3 of the quotation
54 Golf score
56 Bear of the sky
58 Best pitcher
59 Tympanum
60 Musical interval
62 Irritated
64 CSA boy
65 Part 4 of the quotation
66 Part of NATO
67 Secret messages
70 Stretches tightly
71 Conveyance
75 Lyrical poem
76 Yacht pole
78 Begley and Begley, Jr.
79 Part 5 of the quotation
80 Brief note
82 Varnish ingredient
84 Large containers
85 Asian evergreen
86 Part 6 of the quotation
90 Ganders
91 Argyle repairman
92 Israeli dance
93 Stinging insect
94 Reinforced eyelet
97 Ascend
99 Gambler's marker
100 Long in the tooth
103 Embankments
104 End of the quotation
107 Dictator Idi
108 Thermoplastic resin
110 Lift
111 Roman tyrant
112 Exertion
113 Minneapolis suburb
114 Ova lobber
115 Harvest
116 Somme summers
117 Clan divisions
118 Pockmarks
119 Buyer-beware phrase

DOWN

1 Here-today employees
2 Imitation spreads
3 Net minder
4 Opposing
5 Rescuer
6 Chilling
7 Jamaican citrus fruit
8 Pillar set into a wall
9 Rap sessions?
10 Rip off
11 Urban porches
12 Home port in the War of 1812
13 Circle part
14 Permanent AWOLs
15 Exploits
16 Rajahs' wives
17 Two quartets combined
18 Frank Capra movie, "Mr. __ Goes to Town"
28 Vichy very
29 Yemen's capital
31 Comic Carey
35 Off the ship
37 Ill-starred lady of Celtic legend
38 Traveling carriage
40 Bring into harmony
41 Medicinal plant
42 Celestial explosion
43 Joyce Carol Oates novel
44 Heidegger and Balsam
45 Genuine
46 Intertwine
47 The __ Scott Case
49 Carp cousin
53 Lock
54 Nutritious substance
55 Set sights
57 Chilean-born pianist Claudio
60 Biographical play about Capote
61 Forerunner of the CIA
63 Lights
65 Suitable for a kosher meal
66 Spherical bodies
67 Hair splitter
68 River to the Baltic
69 Moore of "Ghost"
70 Innate ability
71 Carry
72 Pajama parties
73 Lupino and Tarbell
74 Ill-gotten gains
77 Noblewomen
79 Skater Lipinski
81 Sundries
83 Shopkeeper
84 Wordiness
87 Hunter's prey
88 Prop sound
89 Put one out of the park
90 Asian ox
93 Courters
94 Clearing
95 Send (money)
96 Sheeplike
98 Horne and Olin
99 Picture in picture
101 The king of France
102 Lets fall
104 Fall event?
105 Indication
106 Andes autocrat
109 Summer cooler

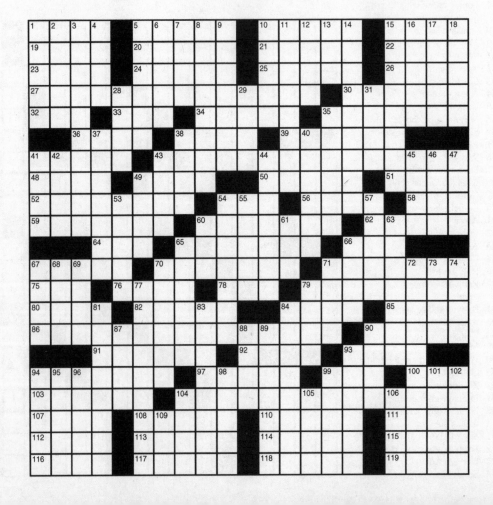

by Willy A. Wiseman

ACROSS

1 "Le __ du printemps"
6 Impressionist Edouard's paintings
12 Memento __
16 Needle-nosed fish
19 Cruelest month?
20 Legal writ
21 Uniform
22 Ulan-__, Russia
23 Diesis
25 Eavesdropper
27 Draft letters
28 Guitarist Paul
29 Bog substance
31 Fling with great force
32 Goes on the offensive
35 Skips
37 The Riddler on "Batman"
38 Black and Eastwood
39 "Bob & Carol & Ted & Alice" co-star
41 Way in: abbr.
42 Laments loudly
43 Stubborn
44 Feed-bag morsel
45 Afternoon receptions
46 Russ. or Lith., once
47 In working order
48 Period
49 Winter mo.
50 High-speed transportation
56 Mutilate
59 Hit by Jay & the Americans
62 Arledge of TV
63 More chancy
64 Animal
65 Eskimo
66 Cervantes' tongue
67 Loose tunics
68 "Beau __"
69 Saint __ of Lisieux
70 Small bays
71 Academic cap
73 Period
74 Cross or Kingsley
75 Prune
76 Uncle __
79 Import tax
81 Actress Dawber
82 Bony
86 Gage bestseller
88 Afr. nation
89 Sinclair Lewis novel
91 Work shifts
92 Dry gulches
94 Build up
95 "The End of the World" singer Davis
96 Semiconductors
97 Hebrew zither
98 Singer's syllable
99 Hospital area letters
100 +
102 High, thin shoe-lift
107 Math subj.
108 Foremost position
109 Phantoms
110 World according to Pierre
111 Japanese drama
112 Military force
113 Vertical fishing nets
114 Pot starters

DOWN

1 Likable losers
2 Twelve disciples
3 More gruff
4 Tease
5 Building wing
6 Early Persians
7 "__, poor Yorick"
8 Reverse pic
9 __ on (incite)
10 Items of men's jewelry
11 Extend
12 Run in the heat?
13 Egg: pref.
14 Do another take
15 Following the proper order
16 Rev it
17 Soprano Patti
18 Continues a lease
24 Wapitis
26 Hesitation syllables
30 Botanist Gray
33 Advice-columnist Landers
34 $ percentages
35 Popeye's Olive
36 __ tai cocktail
37 Pesky insect
39 North Carolina school
40 High time?
43 Grinding teeth
45 Large cup
47 "Star Trek" extras
48 Scale watcher
49 Opaque quartz gem
50 Assault and __
51 Capital of Transkei
52 Greek harp
53 Skin cream
54 Throw out of bed
55 Baker or Pointer
56 Accident
57 Tolstoy and Gorcey
58 __ Stanley Gardner
59 4th-century starter
60 Island group off Galway
61 Rake over
63 Upgrade machinery
71 Brief note
72 So-so
74 Taverns
76 Conscious
77 Go before
78 Governs ineptly
79 Poker-faced
80 French street-scenes painter
81 More matter-of-fact
82 Diffusions
83 Wiseacre
84 "__ the season..."
85 UFO crew
86 French season
87 Creative answer?
89 Mohammed's favorite wife
90 Has been
91 Card game for three
93 GI's garb
95 Spanish Mlles.
97 Robustelli or Williams
98 Marketing starter?
101 Hoofer's limb
103 Infamous Amin
104 Actor Chaney
105 Tumor: suff.
106 Title of respect: abbr.

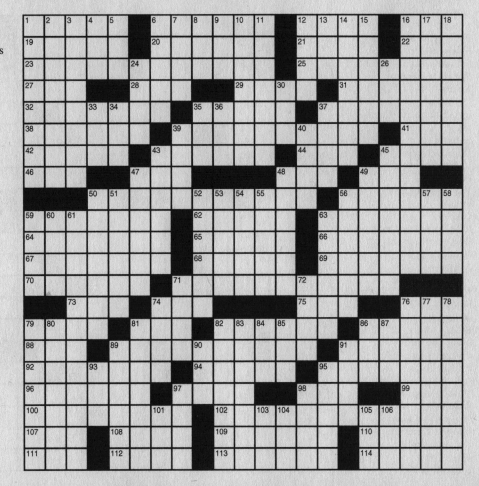

ACROSS

1 Fellows
4 "Queen Christina" star
9 Grade-B Western
14 Dulled by overindulgence
19 Year in the Yucatan
20 Use more lubricant
21 Doughy pastry
22 Ancient Greek coins
23 B&O and Southern Pacific
24 Guam capital
25 Mortise insert
26 Singer Gorme
27 Asleep
31 Noisy disturbances
32 Farrow and Hamm
33 Has intentions
37 Violent outburst
38 Proclamation
40 Stated
42 Gas: pref.
43 Asleep
47 Which person
48 As far as
51 Fork prongs
52 Unfortunately
53 Nice nothing?
54 Thick slice
55 Vitamin letters
56 Theatrical curtain
58 "Rebel Without a Cause" co-star
59 1988 presidential candidate
61 Foul-smelling
63 Lift one's voice
64 Friend from France
65 Asleep
68 __ Cruces
71 Linguistics writer Chomsky
73 Vigor
74 Leaves early
76 "Cosmos" author Carl
78 Dishwasher cycle
79 PC key
80 Monstrous creature
81 Feeble
82 Epic tale
83 Mile High Center architect
85 Coll. senior's exam
86 German article
87 Asleep
91 Mauna __ (Hawaiian volcano)
92 Departs
93 Of the eyes
94 Brag
98 Actor/director Ida
100 Composer Stravinsky
101 Falls
103 Asleep
108 "Medea" director Pier __ Pasolini
111 Physically lacking
112 Hades in Roman mythology
113 K.C. summer hrs.
114 Type of pear
115 Baseball theft?
116 Revere
117 Males
118 Monterrey money
119 Steed
120 Crimean resident
121 Afore

DOWN

1 "Meditations" author __ Aurelius
2 Captivated
3 Italian pronoun
4 Gloria of "The Bad and the Beautiful"
5 Norse sea god
6 Chestnut-and-white horses
7 Crooner Crosby
8 Norwegian king
9 Swift-running bird
10 Clear material
11 Curtis and Danza
12 Enough, old-style
13 "Aurora" fresco painter Guido
14 Eastwood film
15 Yawning chasm
16 Pentagon grp.
17 Actor Wallach
18 Gaming cube
28 City NE of Seville
29 Leaves out
30 Talons
34 Asleep
35 Sound of laughter
36 University of Maine town
38 Sicilian volcano
39 Anonymous John
40 Virgules
41 Composer Khachaturian
44 Forecourt
45 Archaic second person singular past tense verb
46 With caution
48 Govt. farm grp.
49 Damson
50 Asleep
53 __ Tin Tin
56 Cubic meter
57 Rocky outcrop
58 Baseball glove
60 Zen paradox
61 Feathers
62 Small guitars, briefly
63 Meals-on-wheels recipient
66 Janet and Vivien
67 Treble sign
69 Ambience
70 Leave text as is
72 Sturdy tree
75 Betrayed a cause
76 Expand
77 Vowels
78 Unit cost
79 Bk. of Revelation
82 Toper's honker
83 Opening bars
84 1501
87 Pyrogenic
88 Open-sided galleries
89 Disciple
90 Not as quick on the uptake
95 Don of "Cocoon"
96 Poet Gary
97 African fly
99 Icy abode
100 Surmise
101 Flamboyant tie
102 "Enterprise" crew member
104 Fanny
105 Toward the center
106 Castle ringer?
107 "The Ring of the Nibelung" character
108 Baby food
109 Sue __ Langdon
110 Trial-of-the-century inits.

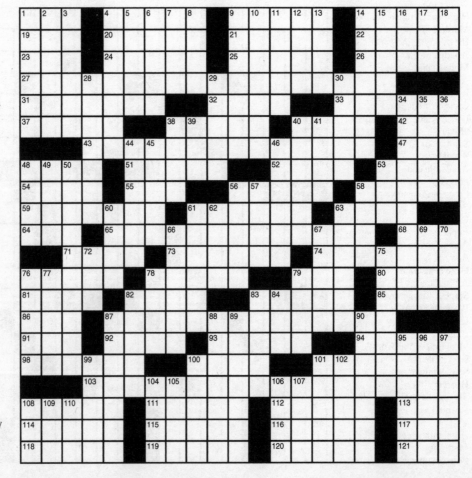

ALMOST INSTANTANEOUSLY

by Tom Pruce

ACROSS

1 Dipper
8 Seasoning plant
15 Feeling of anxiety
20 Pasta sauce
21 Weapons manufacturer
22 Electrician, at times
23 With 40A, very fast
25 Pleasant Island, today
26 Conrad and Barbara
27 Edgar __ Poe
28 Hosp. employees
30 Hollywood studio's letters
31 Exxon competitor
32 Seaweed
33 Peer Gynt's mother
35 Perfect place
38 Golf gadget
39 Provencal love song
40 See 23A
43 "48 __"
44 Adjective for Abner
45 Desert plants
46 Stat starter?
47 Cordon __
48 After: Fr.
49 Louvre Pyramid designer
50 Actor Alejandro
53 With 57A, very fast
57 See 53A
59 Eye
60 Posterior
61 Landlocked African nation
62 Beanery sign
63 "The Screens" dramatist
64 Swindle
65 Yang's counterpart
66 Theatrical curtain
67 Asian ox
68 Childhood taboo
69 French priest
71 For one
72 Very fast
74 Very fast
76 Tahlequah, OK school
77 Collide intentionally
78 Exclude
79 Desperate
80 Latvian capital
81 Arboreal ape, for short
82 CD's competition
83 Pointed end
86 Very fast
90 Bears' lairs
91 Single
92 Northern Ireland
93 Full of: suff.
94 Blackguards
95 Lather
96 PC key
97 Shortened bk.
99 Actor Reeves
101 Actress Dickinson
102 Indira Gandhi's wardrobe

105 Very fast
109 Sure-footed
110 Pacific islands language
111 Russian empress
112 Dominion
113 Transmuting power
114 Having no paddles

DOWN

1 Seventh day
2 Less overcast
3 Public positions
4 University of Maine town
5 Individual: abbr.
6 Dutch commune
7 Regal shade
8 Prentiss or Abdul
9 Killer whale
10 Govt. agent
11 Sweetie
12 Hesitation syllables
13 Parent, for example
14 __ Mawr College
15 Grain beard
16 Actress Long
17 Cranky folk
18 Director Leone

19 Roosevelt's successor
24 Russian saint
29 Secondary title
32 UFO crew
33 Performed
34 Roof-top cargo
36 Advertising gimmick
37 John's Yoko
39 Wholehearted
40 Glossy lacquer
41 Bitter
42 Foundling
45 Luxor or Mirage, e.g.
47 Short jacket
50 Bellowed
51 Lure
52 Sycophants
53 Bean
54 Water, water everywhere
55 Political pundit John
56 Avignon's river
57 Caan movie
58 Resolve
61 Bionic Woman, e.g.
64 Pause marks
66 Sudden gushes
68 Erie-Ontario connection
69 Composer Berg

70 Expressionless
71 Thais and Koreans, e.g.
73 Three-wheeler
74 Cliff dwelling?
75 Constituted
78 Charles Henry and Herbert Henry
80 New GI
83 Difficult problem
84 Cleveland team
85 Cordoba currency, once
86 Starlike object
87 Liquid lost during shipment
88 Croatian peninsula
89 Of a main artery
90 Actress Linda
94 Sideshow barker, e.g.
95 Entanglement
98 Crimson Tide, to fans
99 Actor Luke
100 Dutch cheese
101 Long way off
103 Not up to snuff
104 Theological sch.
106 Thoughtfulness letters
107 Doubter's exclamation
108 Explorer Johnson

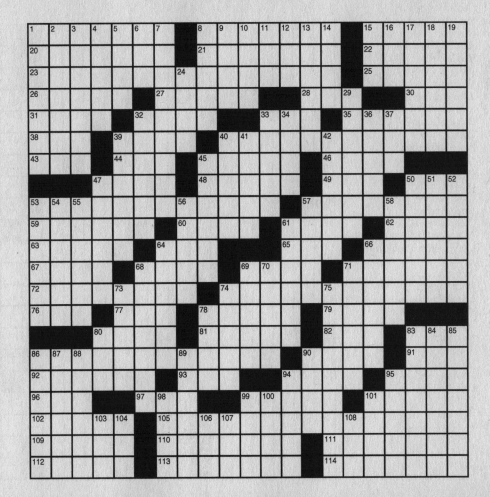

by Willy A. Wiseman

ACROSS

1 Alpine abode
7 Birthday number
10 Contingencies
13 "Lowdown" singer Boz
19 Henner of "Taxi"
20 Fem. address
21 Drunkard
22 Astaire film
23 Nocturnal flying mammal
25 Swiss peak
26 Off the boat
27 O.T. book
28 Cologne, to Germans
29 Unassuming
31 __ Royale
32 Gangster's rod
35 Marsh grass
37 Needle case
38 Move emotionally
39 Metal container
42 Very fast driver
45 London loos
46 Stritch and May
48 Nick and Nora's pooch
49 French impressionist
51 "Baby Don't Get Hooked on Me" singer
53 Gentlemen
55 Decorating again
58 Multi-lock opener
61 Of teeth
62 Embassy head: abbr.
65 Boisterously
66 Joys
68 Tuscany city
69 Tillis and Torme
71 Passover meal
73 Related on mother's side
75 Curving courses
76 Preceding in order
78 Administers narcotics
80 Across: pref.
82 His in French
83 Kitten family
85 Arizona lizard
88 Cultural values
90 Avant-garde art movement
91 Like envelopes and mason jars
95 French students
97 Mach+ jets
99 Lumet and Poitier
100 Belly muscles, casually
102 Winter-blooming shrub
105 Rustic inns
106 Act dejected
108 London district
109 Musical conclusions
111 Coll. Bulldogs
112 First ed.
113 Fortunate
115 Tiny pest
117 Nettle
120 Civil disturbance
122 Language suffix
123 Automobile of the '70s
126 Oder-__ Line
127 Place of confinement
128 "Norma __"
129 For one
130 __ up (totaled)
131 L.A. clock setting
132 Boundary
133 Pith

DOWN

1 CCCII multiplied by three
2 Golfer Jay
3 Dry brandy
4 Rim of a cup
5 Samuel's teacher
6 Upstart
7 Walks leisurely
8 Pop's pop
9 Approx.
10 Japanese golfer Aoki
11 Threw in one's cards
12 Heaven's gatekeeper
13 Based
14 Romaine
15 Garden pest
16 Undercover authors
17 Onionlike bulb
18 Takes the wheel
24 Goddess of the dawn
29 Encounter
30 Ancient region on the Euphrates
33 Corrosive substances
34 Japanese P.M. (1972-74)
36 Painter's base
39 President pro __
40 Stevedores' org.
41 City on the Loire
43 Become gloomy
44 Centering points
47 Stored, as grain
50 Ancient region in Asia Minor
52 Old sailor
54 Handled
56 Sportscaster Jim
57 Drinking vessel
59 Timorous
60 Longs (for)
62 Sufficient
63 Deserve
64 Noel Coward comedy
67 Balanced conditions
70 Yuccalike plant
72 Whip again
74 Call for
77 Repair a hem
79 Comic-strip soldier
81 Rarely
84 Called on again
86 Unleavened bread
87 Ayn and Sally
89 Firmly fixed
92 Deceiver
93 Caustic solution
94 Double bend
96 Lug laboriously
98 1952 Wimbledon winner Frank
100 Quantity
101 Third-largest island in the world
103 Villas and bungalows
104 Made a surgical incision
107 Excrete
110 Droop
114 Penny
116 Mine car
118 Puerto __
119 Recognized
121 Compass dir.
123 Billy Joel hit, "Just the Way You __"
124 Pollution patrol grp.
125 Russian space station

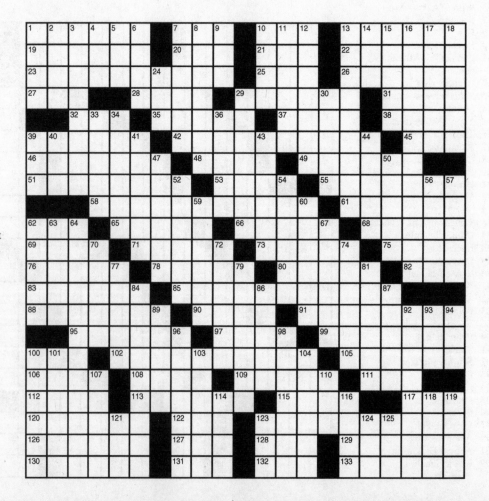

by Edgar Fontaine

ACROSS

1 Boxing match
5 Selects actors
10 Trajectories
14 Carpus
19 Tushingham or Rudner
20 Embellish
21 Greek letters
22 "__ la vista, baby!"
23 Setting of Durrell's quartet
26 More fit
27 Trellis
28 Chief
29 Schweitzer or Einstein
30 Having a thin metallic sound
31 Make a road
32 "The African Queen" screenwriter
33 Discolored
36 Other self
38 Biblical weed
42 Tippy transportation
43 "__ Maria"
44 Penny
46 Call for ewe
47 Business letter abbr.
48 Perspicacious
50 Waldorf-__ Hotel
53 Distress signal
54 __-de-dah
55 Lowest female voice
57 Standing room only
59 Saskatchewan or Alberta, e.g.
61 Bow of silent movies
63 Abilities
64 After expenses
65 Sworn foe
68 Ostrichlike bird
69 Of a pointed tool
72 Water nymph
73 Tells
77 Stepper
79 Sweats
81 Greek vowel
82 Help out
83 Click beetles
85 Millennia
86 Pithy part
87 Compass dir.
88 "Star Wars" princess
89 Lair
90 Self-indulgent spree
91 Reciprocal of a cosecant
93 Long-tongued mammal
97 Edited
99 Highland sweetheart
101 Jogger's gait
102 Baby beds
103 Relaxed
106 Portion
107 Make marginal comments
111 Pizzazz
112 Visa alternative
114 Signal interference
115 Ward of "Once and Again"
116 Close to cracking
117 Memorable periods
118 Glasgow or Barkin
119 Nagger
120 Skedaddles
121 Traditional tales

DOWN

1 Highland hillside
2 Lubricates
3 Sch. on the Rio Grande
4 Government levies
5 Dogtooth
6 Element of a total
7 Paltry
8 Dent or corn starter?
9 Trademark fruit drink
10 Greek
11 Poet
12 Contend successfully
13 Booming jet
14 Moby Dick, e.g.
15 Joining groove
16 Anglesey or Royale
17 Young or spin follower?
18 Tangy
24 Dress shape
25 Part of QED
29 Torments
32 Teen followers?
33 Resell tickets
34 Crimean resident
35 British P.M. (1955-57)
36 Declare
37 Logical start?
39 Best thing since sliced bread
40 1982 movie, "Eating __"
41 Bridge seats
43 Aftward
45 Speakers
48 Avoided defeat
49 Atahualpa, e.g.
50 Attentive
51 Pedestals
52 Ripped
55 Fortress
56 More sore
58 Capital of Peru
60 Constellation in Argo Navis
62 Embryonic sac
66 Canaveral or Fear, e.g.
67 Campfire whopper
69 Laurel and Musial
70 Singer Lopez
71 Let go
74 Occupant: abbr.
75 French floor
76 Overstuffed
78 Water falls
80 Look intently
84 Create lace
86 Troubadour
89 Perceives
90 Jazz style
92 Slip by
94 Merman and Waters
95 Noah's peak
96 Spelling or Amos
97 Tubb or Hemingway
98 Coquettes
100 Gray-faced
102 Tropical plant with brilliant flowers
103 Top-notch
104 Utensil
105 Distance-runner Zatopek
106 Hook's mate
108 Space starter?
109 Former Russian ruler
110 Latin I verb
112 Egyptian viper
113 NRC predecessor

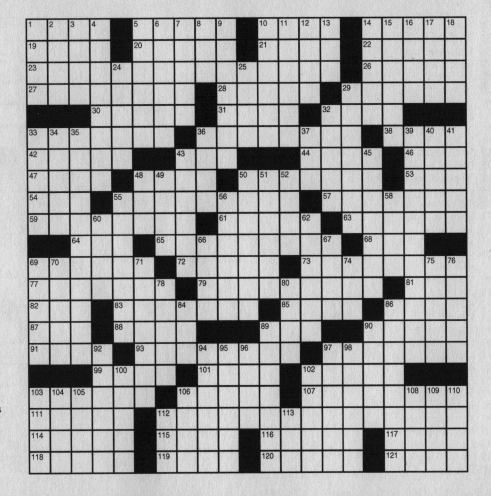

COMMUNICATION

by James E. Buell

ACROSS

1 Gather together
6 Place one's stake
10 Leases
15 Villainous
19 Villainous
20 Diving bird
21 Be nuts about
22 Turner of "The Postman Always Rings Twice"
23 Colossus
24 Tops
25 Bird call
26 Landon and others
27 Betrays
29 Gossips
31 Mournful poem
32 From a distance
34 Hires a hit man, e.g.
35 High-test conflagration?
38 "A Streetcar Named Desire" star
40 According to
41 Become larger
42 Dusting powder
43 Big __, CA
45 Two-time grand-slam winner in tennis
49 Pizza piece
50 Day's end
52 British flyboys
54 Casual farewell
55 Religious faction
56 Winning margin, sometimes
57 Small drink
59 Grandeur
61 Homer's hero
63 Pompous gait
65 Sportscaster Bob
66 Levels with
69 Stuck around
73 Dueling swords
74 Worthy of penance
79 Gets away
81 Edible tuber
82 Bridge support
83 Tie
84 Stink to high heaven
85 Quick swim
87 Wall art
89 Give the giggles to
90 Art holder
92 Black goo
94 Droops
95 Wordsmith
96 Oolong or Earl Grey, e.g.
98 Craving
100 Baggage handlers
101 Zanzibar's language
105 Tempo
106 Bundle
107 Reveals everything
109 Specifies people
114 Declare as true
115 Hit from the past
116 Panache
117 Tropical fruit
118 Country singer McEntire
119 Turns sharply
120 By oneself
121 Burstyn or DeGeneres
122 Cinch
123 German dadaist Max
124 Market
125 Smarting pain

DOWN

1 Ubiquitous insects
2 Primary
3 __ Spumante
4 Tell it like it is
5 Fold in rocks dipping inward from both sides
6 Maintain
7 Uproarious
8 Commotion
9 Tangles
10 Cane palm
11 "Victor/Victoria" director Blake
12 Christmas carol
13 Arduous journeys
14 Arranges in proper order
15 Gives details
16 Heroism
17 Jokingly
18 Goes on and on
28 Animal group
30 First murder victim
33 Confronts one's fate
35 Canvas coating
36 Like four-wheeled vehicles
37 Hot, in a way
38 Scourge
39 Your and mine
42 Scuffle
44 Collide intentionally
46 Expansive
47 R&B pioneer, __ James
48 Beams
50 Hit by the Cleftones, "Heart and __"
51 Becomes weary
53 Agent
56 Required
58 Place
60 Avildsen or Belushi
62 Dance move
63 Water vapor
64 Paths
67 Undercover agent
68 Shoshones
69 Barbra Streisand movie, "The Way We __"
70 Cruising
71 Chills
72 Accept responsibility
75 Confess
76 Beast
77 Intense beam
78 Pitchers
80 Take a load off
82 Summon
86 Beatnik's residence
88 Scarcity
89 Puts in order
91 Hawaiian garlands
93 Mends
95 Sorrows
97 Small recess
99 Most reasonable
100 Dissolving agent
101 Wound marks
102 Interlaced
103 One-celled organism
104 Sicker
106 Garment size
108 James Dean film, "East of __"
110 Cosmetics ingredient, often
111 Bamako's country
112 Level
113 Warbled

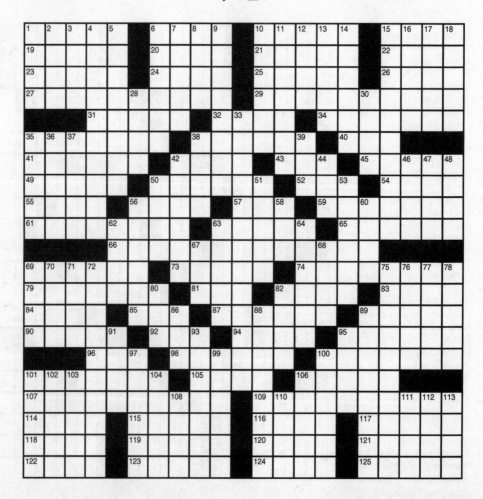

by Josiah Breward

ACROSS

1 Under ideal circumstances
7 Shea Stadium players
11 Best and Buchanan
16 New Deal grp.
19 Attached shed
20 Jazz state?
21 Arrowsmith's first wife
22 Venezuelan river
23 Wisconsin
25 Birdie game
27 NYC subway line
28 Water vapor
29 The king of France
30 West Coast sch.
31 Ancient temple
33 Cloy
36 Half a fly?
37 Chief ingredient
38 Marine mammal
40 Fictional mariner
43 "__ Haw"
44 Give too much money
45 Port __ cheese
46 French season
48 Vocal inflection
50 Speaks roughly
54 Ave. crossers
55 Mel and Hoot
57 "Feel Like Makin' Love" group
62 One full of oneself
63 Salami variety
64 Night-flying mammal
65 Last bio?
69 Transmits
70 Runaways
72 Idolize
73 Family plan?
74 Parseghian of football
75 Pavarotti or Caruso, e.g.
76 Titania's man
77 German spa
80 Fabrics for sheets
81 Kin of the FBI
84 __ and Gomorrah
85 Dear: It.
86 Opposite of NNW
87 Crevice
89 Type of general
94 Polish
96 New Mexico attraction
100 Military bigwigs
103 Turkish monetary unit
104 Friend from France
105 New York resort lake
107 Unemployed
108 Copycat
109 Word ending psalms
111 Hay units
113 Lamprey
114 Capital of Pakistan
116 South Dakota attraction
119 Brooks or Stottlemyre
120 Metal sheet
121 Cosmonaut Gagarin
122 Funeral speech
123 Draft letters
124 Dutch painter of "The Prince's Birthday"
125 Matched collections
126 Forced onward

DOWN

1 Unpigmented
2 Rip apart
3 Thoroughly evil
4 H.S. subj.
5 French religious figs.
6 Wrongful acts
7 Causing genetic change
8 Worsted cloth
9 Create lace
10 That ship
11 River of Hamburg
12 Lack
13 Knotty, as roots
14 Military forces
15 New World monkey
16 Kin of raspberries
17 X over
18 Musical performances
24 Annual cycles
26 Ancient kingdom on the Nile
29 Mother of Clytemnestra
32 Bishopric
34 Shortened bk.
35 Spigot
39 Coin-flip do-over
41 Neophyte
42 Grp.
46 Excrete
47 Woods on links
49 Canad. province
51 Brownish yellow
52 Hot tubs
53 One way to stand?
56 Back of a tape
57 Plead
58 Hill or Loos
59 Showered with love
60 Actor Michael
61 Call in the cantons
63 Fertilizer from ground fish parts
66 Bullwinkle's nemesis
67 Kite's clubs
68 Nerve-racking
70 Golfer Couples
71 Harry __ Zell
72 Soak up
74 Botheration
76 "__ Town"
78 Questions
79 Coll. hotshot
80 Sicilian wine
81 Praises
82 Tramps about
83 Charles and Eileen
85 Marijuana
88 Bow or Barton
90 "The Face is Familiar" poet
91 __ Marie Saint
92 Speech on Sun.
93 1955 Wimbledon champion
95 William Tell's canton
97 Volcanic rock
98 One-celled animals
99 Make wider
101 Heavy hammer
102 Generator element
106 Surrendered formally
110 Arabian seaport
112 Pronounce indistinctly
115 Brit. electees
116 Hardin and Cobb
117 Coloration
118 Clay, today

PRESENT ADVICE

By Alan P. Olschwang

ACROSS

1 Grappler's cushion
4 Swiss city on the Rhine
9 Aquatic, molelike mammal
15 Shrinking inland sea
19 Volcanic fallout
20 Ms. Rogers St. Johns
21 Whole
22 Golfer's call
23 Start of Stephen Ambrose quote
26 Highlands hats
27 Greek letters
28 Arab leaders
29 Apollo's twin
31 Dental exam?
32 Turns, as milk
33 Sun. talk
35 Dunne or Ryan
36 Like
38 Part 2 of quote
41 Part 3 of quote
47 Candidate Landon
48 Life's work
49 Nuzzled
50 Kid of jazz
52 Business
56 School supply item
57 Pique
58 French colonial administrator in Canada
60 Droop
61 Diplomat's asset
63 Unsolicited ms. enclosure
66 Bloodsucking parasites
67 R. Reagan's Star Wars
69 Part 4 of quote
72 Had dinner
73 Nielsen figures
76 Practice punches
77 Gumshoes
79 Shad delicacy
82 Tract of marshland
84 Make a choice
86 Request another hearing
88 Withered
89 Explorer Johnson
90 Finnish furniture designer
92 Sources
93 Half a dance?
95 Part 5 of quote
98 Part 6 of quote
102 Telescope part
103 __ Martin (James Bond's car)
104 Silent communication letters
105 Retract one's words
108 Shoshone tribe members
112 Austere
114 Neck part
116 Ladd or Lane
117 Yes indeed, Enrique
118 End of quote
122 Cleveland's lake
123 Certain organic compounds
124 Old World finch
125 Soda

126 Fewer
127 Erects
128 Mary-Kate or Ashley
129 '02 British Open winner

DOWN

1 Unleavened bread
2 Tribe of Israel
3 Greek letter
4 Sheep bleats
5 Madison Ave. offerings
6 Hits the road
7 Yale or Root
8 Light-show light
9 Escritoire
10 Seth's son
11 Actor Erwin
12 Old space station
13 Jockey on five Derby winners
14 __-do-well
15 Delayed reaction
16 Rambled
17 Giving weapons
18 Tenant
24 Gourmets' pride
25 Some sloths
30 Cultivate
32 __ Nevada

33 Slalom
34 Belgian painter
37 Forming thin, flat layers
38 Mine find
39 G-man
40 Singer Newton
41 High cards
42 Japan's first permanent capital
43 Don Garlits or Shirley Muldowney
44 College credits
45 Rocky peak
46 Consumes
51 Husband of Pocahontas
53 Intrinsic
54 "Norma __"
55 Harleys, e.g.
58 Service charge
59 Recipe measure
62 Tijuana houses
64 Coach Parseghian
65 Roll of papyrus
68 Personnel lists
70 Carbohydrate: suff.
71 One successor of Ludwig I
73 In medias __
74 "__ Maria"
75 Twilight, poetically

78 Jason of the NBA
80 Solemn promise
81 Otherwise
83 Roald and Arlene
85 Where copyrights are registered: abbr.
87 Chase
90 Simian
91 '50s candidate
94 Helpful information
96 Lubricate
97 Click beetles
98 Large quantity
99 Strive
100 Balance
101 Canal site
105 Coffee server
106 Words of denial
107 Sub-Saharan region
109 Brownish gray
110 Register: var.
111 Oozes
113 Way off
114 Biblical address
115 Snake's statement
116 Nora of "SNL"
119 A majority of V
120 49-ers' 6-pointers
121 For shame!

By Josiah Breward

ACROSS

1 G-men and T-men
5 In __ veritas
9 Sister of Laertes
16 FDR follower
19 Graven image
20 Biblical twin
21 Bring back to true
22 "Over There" cont.
23 Skedaddle!
24 Enthralled
25 Articles + vetch
27 Deer + fish
30 K-O connection
31 Old-time peep show
32 Provide with guns
33 AFL-__
34 Plummeted
36 "__ and Heloise"
38 More impetuous
40 Innate ability
43 McGregor of "Emma"
44 Makeshift stretcher
45 Drinking vessel
46 Condescends
48 NYC summer hrs.
51 Ruhr Valley city
52 Challenged
54 The gamut
55 Sundance's girlfriend
56 Sedge + correct
59 Cartoonist Wilson
60 Unpleasantly chilly
63 Newsman Rather
64 __ Stanley Gardner
65 Most up-to-date
66 Expression of regret
69 "Siddhartha" author
71 More covered in sphagnum
72 Ridicule
73 Mineo and Maglie
74 McKellen of "Gods and Monsters"
75 Pretoria's nation: abbr.
76 Goodnight girl of song
77 Herb + even
82 Vamoose!
83 Conrad or Barbara
84 Small, silvery fish
85 Adjutants
89 Follower of Attila
90 Heckle or Jeckle
92 Reverent wonder
93 Author of "The End of the Affair"
94 Dull, yellowish brown
96 At sixes and __
98 Trumpet blast
99 Strives
102 BMW rival
103 Storm center
104 "Cannery __"
105 Taking to court
106 Royal pronoun
109 Bamboo + competent
112 Hastened + Ram Das follower

115 Patron saint of sailors
116 Secret agent
117 & so on
118 Alpine singer
119 Aspersion
120 TV equine
121 Get it?
122 Poly follower?
123 Blackjacks
124 Cash drawer slot

DOWN

1 Like stocked lakes
2 "Apollo 13" star
3 Welcome sites
4 Narrow opening
5 Micrometer element
6 Man's name meaning "gift"
7 Snoozes
8 Not in the proper order
9 "Animal Farm" author
10 Shell-game item
11 Flax filament
12 Grade sch.
13 Tropical creeper
14 Elec. switch in a car
15 Wyeth and Mellon
16 Listen to + possessive pronoun
17 More confident
18 Arboreally cornered
26 Samoan cash
28 Sunflower seed
29 Bounded upward
35 Was first
37 Mercedes-__
39 Spin follower?
41 1997 20-game winner Denny
42 Church donation
45 Star of "Misery"
47 "I've __ a Secret"
49 Balanced states
50 Hindu mystic writings
52 6/6/44
53 Dons duds
55 Swallows
57 Knife blade
58 Tax letters
59 Neon or argon
60 Root for salads
61 Quick impression
62 Sported + part
65 Actress Anderson
67 Dryer trappings
68 Keats offering
69 Golfer Sandra
70 Shade tree
71 Groening or Damon

73 Flotilla members
74 Run in neutral
77 Playground pastime
78 Actress Plummer
79 Informative quality
80 Worked for
81 Menu plan
83 Ruth or Zaharias
86 River Rouge Plant city
87 Signer-upper
88 Wakame and kelp
90 Spotted South American wildcats
91 Gabor of "Green Acres"
93 Janet and Mitzi
95 Fruit's coat
97 Game played with 32 cards
98 Unite
99 Frank McCourt's "Angela's __"
100 Connecting rooms
101 Nobel-winning chemist Frederick
107 Cable subscriber
108 Vex
110 Singer Fitzgerald
111 Brief bullets
113 __ on your life
114 Barbie's beau

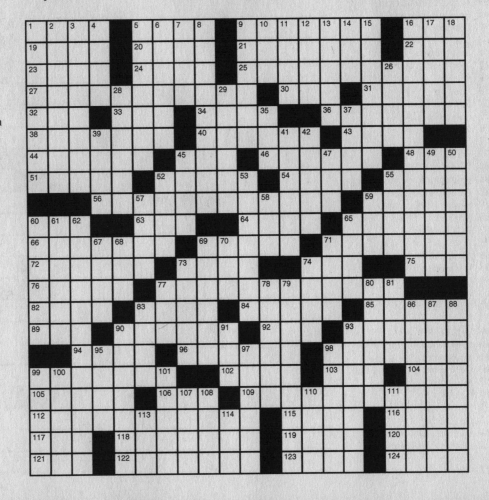

by Edgar Fontaine

ACROSS

1 Magic stick
5 E.T.s' vehicles
9 Renowned
14 Mohammed's birthplace
19 Jai __
20 Trading center
21 University of Maine town
22 Handled like a jug
23 Shameless
25 Expansive
26 Soft leather
27 Surfer's inhalations
28 King of France
30 Undertakings
32 Delhi dish
33 19th-century American poet
38 Kwik-E-Mart owner on "The Simpsons"
41 Tropical porch
42 Sequential
43 Harem
46 Coarse sieve
48 Squads
52 With 88A, end of 68A
54 Duped
55 Helmsley and others
56 Gauguin and Simon
57 Shucks!
59 Hindu title of respect
61 Be a stool pigeon
62 Dunderhead
64 Half of MVI
65 Building blocks
67 New Year in Vietnam
68 Poem by 33A (with "A")
73 Fond du __, WI
74 Site of the Louvre
75 Canvas cover, briefly
76 Toreador cheer
77 Addiction: suff.
79 P. Diddy's music style
80 Present starter?
81 Egg-shaped
85 Post-crucifixion depictions
87 Former LAX carrier
88 See 52A
92 Bench player
93 Separation into factions
96 More lustrous
97 In the interim
99 Of the ear
101 French born
102 With 47D, start of 68A
108 Feel ill
109 Castles' defenses
110 Expression of surprise
111 Whitewater
115 China from Stoke-on-Trent
117 Movie evaluator
119 Boozer
122 Mortise insert
123 Bad deeds
124 Earl Grey and oolong
125 Aloha in the Apennines
126 Upright
127 Heavyweight Marciano
128 Chinese: pref.
129 Sentry's command

DOWN

1 Armed conflicts
2 Toward shelter
3 California county
4 British Nobelist Paul
5 Parasol's kin
6 Air-travel watchdog grp.
7 Scrap of food
8 Breastbones
9 B-complex vitamin, __ acid
10 Altar constellation
11 Cemented
12 Prepare to fence?
13 Soft leather
14 Military dining companion
15 Water in the Seine
16 Articles of faith
17 Aromatic wood
18 An Astaire
24 Tanker's cargo
29 Elevator man
31 Barbie's boyfriend
34 Postal service
35 Organic compound
36 Navigational system
37 Butter substitutes
38 Hurry-up letters
39 Catcher Tony
40 Pakistani tongue
44 Book of maps
45 Scuttlebutt
47 See 102A
49 Ekberg or Loos
50 Horses' dos
51 Certain NCO
53 So long in Cancun
55 Stone: pref.
58 Objective
59 Clipped-off piece
60 Ocasek of the Cars
63 Headliners
64 Tap problem
65 Remove bridles
66 Athenian lawgiver and others
68 Oracular
69 More aloof
70 __ Angelico
71 Khaki shade
72 Denims
73 Cup brims
78 Torn tickets
80 Outstanding
82 Not."fer"
83 Fare-__-well
84 Raison d'__
86 Help on a heist
87 Religious
89 Fairy-tale monster
90 King of Norway
91 Mournful, musically
93 Attestor
94 Peso percentage
95 SAT section
98 Nobel prize winner, Le Duc __
100 WWII submarines
102 Sample
103 Windshield cleaner
104 Unchallenged
105 Dobbin-ish
106 Shout from the bleachers
107 Time period
112 Pieces of pelvises
113 Gauge face
114 Glaswegian
116 Disney dwarf
118 Wapiti
120 Wahine's gift
121 Is qualified to

SOME ASSEMBLY REQUIRED

by Willy A. Wiseman

ACROSS

1 Scales
7 Small whales
14 Expressionless
20 Secondhand transaction
21 Exploitation
22 Olympic discus legend
23 Like virgin ground
24 Relative assemblies
26 Greek column type
27 Contingencies
28 Creamier
29 Toasts
31 Stick-to-itiveness
33 Pillage
36 Indeed
37 Movie, as in "Variety"
38 Discomfort
39 __ de deux
40 Tightening snake
41 Highland assembly
46 Upgrade the circuitry
49 Part of LP
50 Bullriders' grp.
51 Highlanders
52 Bring to bear
53 DDE's rival
54 Pitcher's stat
56 Sun. homily
57 Coloring hippie-style
59 Political assembly
65 Jarreau and Jolson
66 Liqueur flavor
68 "The Flying Dutchman" soprano
69 Very wide shoe size
70 Casual assemblies
74 Another name for rickets
77 Fuss
78 Make do
79 Evergreen
80 Plains tribe
81 Swing jazz clarinetist Shaw
84 "Annabel Lee" poet
86 Secular
88 Buffalo Bob and Bubba
89 Annual female assemblies
93 "Foucault's Pendulum" author
94 Cart track
95 Windows to the soul
96 TV oldie, "__ Ramsey"
97 Part of UF
100 Removes from office
103 "Auntie Mame" co-star Peggy
104 Commencement of hostilities
106 Moving
108 Brief life story
109 Choreographer Cunningham
110 Festive assembly
114 Fate
115 Delphic prophet
116 Type of paint
117 Wacky
118 Little land masses
119 Lacking a rim
120 Intermediaries

DOWN

1 Loathsome
2 "The Raven" lady
3 Croatian peninsula
4 Cheech's surname
5 Local assembly
6 But, to Brutus
7 Very successful, in old slang
8 Gabor and others
9 Moon vehicle, for short
10 Swiss canton
11 Swallowing greedily
12 So far
13 Medical fluids
14 Hungarian dish
15 Last name in Communism
16 The Ram
17 That which can be preserved
18 DC VIP
19 Time meas.
25 List of lapses
27 Hankering
30 Web location
31 Advance
32 Horseshoes score
34 Anthracite, e.g.
35 Part of K.C.
38 Experts, briefly
39 Lowly mil. rank
41 Encircle with a belt
42 Legal writ
43 Speak pompously
44 Elbe tributary
45 "__ Mia"
46 Mark sale prices
47 Imposed absence
48 Littlest laddie
53 English princess
55 Marion or Diana
56 Distinct mus. tones
58 Venetian villain
59 Sneak a look
60 Tenor Caruso
61 Play lead
62 Camus play, "__ de siege"
63 Actress Janet
64 Go-aheads
67 Thin layer
71 Rear appendage
72 Keats' poems
73 Passes on
75 College assembly
76 Wife of Osiris
79 White lies
81 Venerable
82 Houston university
83 Hot and humid
84 Basis of operations
85 Not at home
87 Iowa State town
88 Clairvoyant
90 Some Louisianans
91 Co-founder of Dada
92 Stat starter?
97 "Amadeus" director
98 Giving off light
99 Mountain ridges
101 Preserved
102 Deep-blue paint
103 Spherical bacteria
104 Galvanizes
105 "Demian" author
107 Myth ending?
108 Woods in Paris
110 __-disant (so-called)
111 Alternatives
112 Part of a wd.
113 __-de-France
114 Korean car

by Robert H. Wolfe

ACROSS

1 Categorize
5 Old French bread?
10 Scottish Gaelic
14 Fido's org.
19 Start to date?
20 Detection device
21 Wry face
22 Orchid tuber
23 Brigand's order
26 Do-re-mi-fa-sol-la-ti-do
27 Concise
28 Attributed
29 Hannah and Hall
30 Computer key
31 Wading bird
32 Alternative to cola
34 Deg. with teeth?
35 Aits in the Aisne
37 LCD watch month
39 1980-93 Redskins receiver
42 Port on the Black Sea
44 Breathe
47 Five centimes, once
48 Minuteman's weapon
51 Dam-building grp.
53 1945 Nobel Prize winner Wolfgang
54 Doer: suff.
55 Certain Art Deco works
56 Abridges
58 Writer Rostand
60 Holy smoke!
61 Comic Herman
62 County cop
64 President pro __
65 Ste. Jeanne __
66 Cable-films stn.
68 Very French?
69 Passing fancy
72 Get ready
75 Cause of sympathy
77 Latvian port
78 Like an opera song
80 Changes into bone
82 Talking parrot
83 Uniting link
84 Atkinson of "Mr. Bean"
86 Scrimp
87 Politician's audiences
88 Trail behind
89 Channel
91 Buries
93 Inscribe
95 Vietnamese Nobel Prize winner, Le Duc __
97 Turn thumbs down
98 Touch gently
101 Turn back
104 Water bird: var.
106 Twenty fins?
108 Ringer?
110 Whopper
112 Biller's partner?
113 Be on cloud nine
114 Way of showing some films on TV
116 "Goodbye, Mr. Chips" star
117 Guinness of "Star Wars"
118 German mountains
119 Netting
120 Gibb and Griffith
121 Lairs
122 Requirements
123 Thirst quenchers

DOWN

1 Endured
2 Mean
3 Commences
4 Nerve-racking
5 __ Angelico
6 Western farms
7 Spout from a soapbox
8 Consumer advocate Ralph
9 Formulated beliefs
10 Exude
11 Wanders randomly
12 Nappy leather
13 Car's rear end?
14 Actor Armand
15 Posterior section of the pelvis
16 Get kissed in a kid's game
17 Con's quarters
18 Simians
24 Ridicules
25 Cruise ship
29 Rear ends
33 Colorado resort
36 Tennis do-over
38 Le Pew of cartoons
40 High time?
41 Resident of northern Iraq
42 Approved, for short
43 Affirm
45 Without: Fr.
46 Test limits
48 Encounter
49 Importune
50 Favorite haunt
52 Length times width
54 Bowling equipment mfr.
56 Evening in Milano
57 Music paces
59 Opposite of: pref.
61 Cover up, in a way
63 God of love
65 Some French?
67 Coffee shop
70 Seaweed product
71 Eurasian crows
73 Five-and-a-half yards
74 Son of Isaac
76 Heyerdahl's craft, "Kon-__"
77 Charlie Brown's exclamation
78 Fit
79 Horse shade
81 Pique performance
82 African nation
85 Lulu
87 Old hand, for short
89 Interviewer Dick and others
90 Oar holder
92 Sent by wire
94 Slo-mo shot
96 Raced faster
98 Consigned to a bad fate
99 Relaxed
100 Ship bunks
102 Inscribed pillar
103 Devoured
105 Weasel's kin
107 Field movie, "__ Rae"
108 Mother of Castor and Pollux
109 __ Hill, MD
111 Ranks above majs.
114 Young Scot
115 Page-bottom refs.

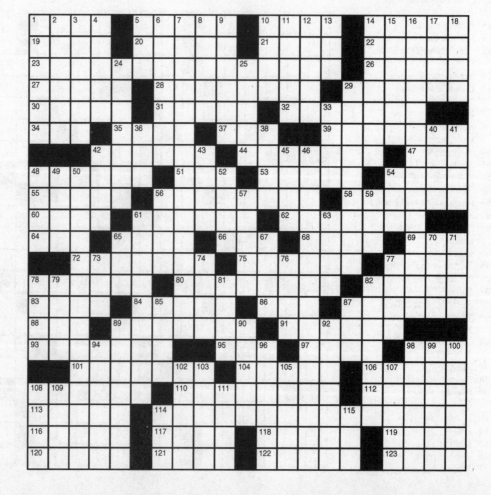

by Xan Lattimore

ACROSS

1 For Pete's __!
5 Book-jacket copy
10 Greek column type
15 Cry of distress
19 Stratagem
20 External
21 Time period
22 Bambi's folks
23 Eleftherios Venizelos to Mohamed V flight
26 Verve
27 Bankhead of "Lifeboat"
28 Calf meats
29 Fight, country-style
31 Caesar's date
32 Bing Crosby movie, "The Bells of St. __"
33 Tongue of Iran
34 Cinematic wolfman
37 Spanish priest
38 Neither high nor low
41 Hobbles
42 Cristoforo Colombo to Paradisi flight
44 Gardens of London
45 Gorby's nation
46 Louganis or Norman
47 Lyric poems
48 Commend
49 Night flyer
50 Chiang Kai-shek to Kimpo flight
54 Polite denial
55 Biko and King
57 Drug cops
58 French auto-race location
59 Muddies
60 Heroic tales
61 St. John Perse
62 After-market purchases
64 Regions
65 Avian joint?
68 Gauges
69 Cote d'Azur to Ben Gurion flight
71 Boxer Louis
72 Beaver projects
73 Levee
74 Fifty-fifty
75 Ky. neighbor
76 Blowup of a pic
77 Domodedovo to Charles de Gaulle flight
81 Giant killer
82 Computer displays
84 Cars
85 Chocolate browns
86 Glazier's need
87 Like a julep?
88 Presley hit of 1958
89 1999 U.S. Open tennis champion
91 "Gymnopedies" composer
92 Stored, as records
96 Beer ingredient

97 Sainte Foy to Benito Juarez flight
100 Salinger girl
101 Lead to seats
102 Secret
103 Medicinal plant
104 Practice boxing
105 British peers
106 Fax ancestor
107 Telescope part

DOWN

1 Lovers' quarrel
2 Ski resort in 7D
3 First chancellor of reunified Germany
4 Makeup item
5 "Father Dowling Mysteries" star
6 "Star Wars" director
7 Beehive State
8 In medias __
9 Swaggering behavior
10 Forestaller
11 Iridescent gemstones
12 Silver and Perlman
13 Trucking regulating agcy.
14 Pantomime game
15 Black Sea port

16 Vantaa to Butmir flight
17 "Hud" star Patricia
18 Caen's river
24 Life-drawing subjects
25 Yogi of the Yankees
30 Schedule abbreviations
32 Dog disease
33 Castro of Cuba
34 Woods' sticks?
35 Attacks
36 Schiphol to Santa Cruz flight
37 Chick calls
38 __ operandi
39 Climb aboard!
40 Pitchers
42 Broad smiles
43 Tackle-box items
46 Scottish Highlanders
48 Celestial transient
50 Dilutes
51 Jejune
52 Home-video show host
53 Rub out
54 Desert of Israel
56 Still places in rivers
58 "Sliver" author
60 Excellent, slangily
61 "She __ You"

62 Venomous snake
63 Actress Keaton
64 Galvanizes
65 Miles of jazz
66 Greek colony
67 __ a hand (helps out)
69 Down-and-dirty
70 "Bad, Bad __ Brown"
73 Fashionable shop
75 Characterized by ingenuity
77 Witticisms
78 Some servers
79 Of Carthage
80 Undertaking
81 Hawaiian singer
83 Light coat
85 Tailbone
87 Singer Mercer
88 Tee shot
89 Singer Ed
90 Shocked sound
91 Very German?
92 Leafstalk angle
93 Disgusting
94 Harrow's rival
95 Makes pink blue
98 Dos Passos work
99 Afore

by James E. Buell

ACROSS

1 Houston baseball player
6 Unhearing
10 Puppy feet
14 Uplift
19 Encore broadcast
20 Parisian diva Medeiros
21 Resting on
22 Shire of "Rocky"
23 Old hag
24 Large-mouth water pitcher
25 Utter indistinctly
26 Greenish blue shades
27 Establish speed
29 Assume control
31 "That'll Be the Day" singer Buddy
32 Lingerie purchases
34 Larger-than-life
35 Scroogelike
38 Gave rise to
40 Positive poles
44 Port on the Black Sea
45 Impudence
46 Hero, for short
48 Cunning
49 Supple
50 Wristband, e.g.
52 Hiatus
54 Keep in check
55 Dorothy's pup
56 WWII powers
57 Distress signal
59 Foods company, __ Purina
61 Storerooms
63 Room at the top
65 Nicaraguan snooze
66 Exercises authority
69 Sally Field role
73 Veered off course
74 Throbbing drums, in a way
79 Still in bed
81 __ excellence
82 Indiana city
83 Departed
84 Serb or Croat, for example
85 Cover crop
87 Mechanical men
89 Remove moisture again
90 Be silent, musically
92 Strike sharply
94 Automobile pioneer
95 Depressed
96 Move with a rushing sound
98 Lady of the house
100 Identify incorrectly
101 Peruse
103 Evaluate
104 Nascence
105 Provide direction
109 Bark commands
114 Lew of "Dr. Kildare" movies
115 Make reference to
116 Wading bird
117 Haloes
118 French measure
119 Copycat
120 Took the bus
121 Publish
122 Try hard to persuade
123 Lacking: suff.
124 Exploit
125 __-foot oil

DOWN

1 Trajectories
2 Withered
3 Swift pace
4 Make all decisions
5 Jerkwater
6 Profoundly
7 Ex-Bronco QB
8 One of the Baldwins
9 Bright meteor
10 Linguini and ziti
11 Map books
12 "The Winds of War" author
13 Spending frenzy
14 Engraving
15 Provide direction
16 Wing-shaped
17 Sound of a small bell
18 Alleviate
28 Blues great Fitzgerald
30 Money mgr.
33 Has full control
35 Sheds
36 Half-wit
37 Tussle
38 Machinery parts
39 Made a ditch
41 Low-fat and salt-free, e.g.
42 Ness of "The Untouchables"
43 Medicinal bush
45 Gruesome
47 Keep out
50 Skater's jump
51 Lugged
53 Turnover, e.g.
56 Chalcedonies
58 Informal family member
60 Bonet or Loeb
62 Sleeve cards
63 Fighting battles
64 Swindles
67 Sucker
68 Paddles
69 Blasts of wind
70 Relative by marriage
71 Northern constellation
72 Issue commands
75 Sweep away the dead wood
76 Hopper of Hollywood gossip
77 Actor Zimbalist
78 "Funny Girl" composer
80 Neither fish __ fowl
82 "The __ Must Be Crazy"
86 Edible tuber
88 Member of the thrush family
89 Hold back
91 African flies
93 Pittsburgh players
95 Turkish money
97 Scoffer's comment
99 Gale of football
100 Shot wide
102 Decorative transfer
104 Back of a 45
105 Aladdin's possession
106 Ogler
107 Comic Johnson
108 Clean off
110 Hautboy
111 Sky bear
112 Of ships and sailors: abbr.
113 Sandra and Ruby

CONTRADICTIONS

by Alan P. Olschwang

ACROSS

1 Cowardly Lion portrayer
5 Evaluates
10 Evening in Bologna
14 Spars
19 Curved molding
20 WWII marauder
21 Two of a kind
22 Octopus arms, e.g.
23 Toward the mouth
24 Baseball's Yogi
25 Formerly, formerly
26 Put away for a rainy day
27 More than gratified
30 Trap
31 Seeds used for oil
32 Behave humanly?
33 Let loose
35 Conifer
36 Blazing
39 Pick players
40 Beauty and the Beast?
44 Biographer of FDR
46 Bruins of collegiate sports
50 Capital of Tibet
51 Born in Burgundy?
52 Do beaver's work
53 Published in installments
55 Crossword solver?
56 Mosaic square
59 Short sleep
61 Balm
62 Gala
63 Coke or Pepsi
65 More limited
67 Potpourri
70 Fast-paced Olympic event
73 Final position
74 Shyly
76 Have top billing
77 Indiana city
79 Sheeplike
80 Theater-sign letters
82 Blackboard blur?
84 With what motive
87 Blush
89 Major or Minor
   constellation
91 Here in Le Havre
92 Nevada resort
94 Appear
95 City on the Ruhr
97 Withdraws from a contest
99 Any part of EAP
101 Most recent
103 Eliminate
104 Ready for graduation?
108 Opposing position
109 Third of a cohort
113 Umbel family plant
114 Meeting at the beach?
118 Tennille and Morrison
119 Semite
120 Benefactor Yale
121 Actress Swenson
122 Hersey novel,
   "A Bell for __"

123 Actress Moreno
124 Of musical sounds
125 Of the ear
126 Dominance
127 Former Russian sovereign
128 Choreographer Tharp
129 Night: pref.

DOWN

1 Plunders
2 Come to terms
3 Pays heed
4 Writes a revision
5 Elastic
6 Tasman and Muzorewa
7 British Conservative
8 O.K. Corral combatant
9 In a trite way
10 Guy with a simple
   weapon
11 Jug handles
12 Stairway part
13 Architectural style
   of the '30s
14 Irish and Spanish growths
15 Be oneself
16 Greek porticos
17 __ Haute, IN

18 Spirited mount
28 Copy
29 Important time
34 Runners' measures
36 "Rock of __"
37 Jason's objective
38 Distinctive flair
40 Layer
41 Pi follower
42 Vichy water
43 Breaks shrink-wrap
45 Hindu mystic
47 Eyelashes
48 Washes
49 Vigilant
52 Pygmalion's statue
54 Last letter of words?
57 To be in Toulouse
58 Propels with oars
60 Pittsburgh player
62 Added to the search
   subjects
64 Wing-shaped
66 Culture medium
67 Olfactory offenses
68 Embankment
69 Ammonia compound
71 Diplomat Vance

72 Banded venomous snakes
75 Female ruff
78 Greek wine
81 City on the Oka
83 Ella's forte
84 Which person
85 In what way?
86 Craving
88 Singing Diamond
90 Lunch counter
93 Computing sums
96 "The Philadelphia Story"
   Oscar winner
97 Keystone Kops creator
98 Stoker's sucker
100 Actor Liam
102 You, to Yves
104 Crimean resident
105 Battery terminal
106 Biblical mount
107 Day in Hollywood
109 Taj __
110 Patchy horse
111 Spock's forte
112 Participate in charades
115 Pro __
116 Look of love
117 Like Tarzan's jungles?

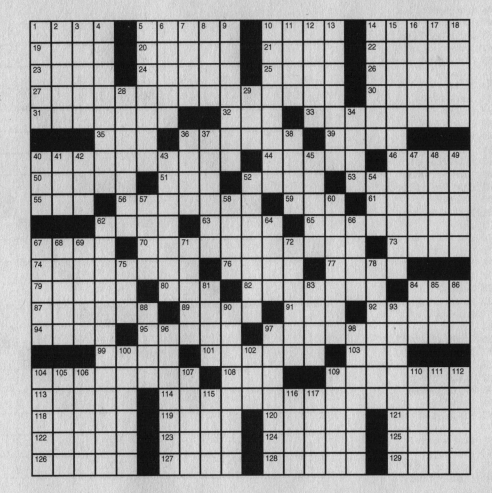

FICTIONAL CHARACTERS

by Xan Lattimore

ACROSS

1 Recipe meas.
5 Cass and Michelle, e.g.
10 Ice-cream flavor word
15 Education-minded orgs.
19 Elisabeth of "Leaving Las Vegas"
20 That is (to say): Lat.
21 Ho Chi Minh City dress
22 Truant GI
23 Zorba of fiction
26 Numerous
27 Bestowed lavishly
28 University girls for short, once
29 Spots
31 1990-92 French Open champion
32 Comic sketches
33 Free from a sty
34 Caravan rides
36 Sacred Christian book
37 Looks down on
40 Intoxicating
41 Jimson of fiction
43 Sardonic
44 Pound sounds
45 Home port in the War of 1812
46 Inning enders
47 Bucket
48 Followers of Davis Love?
49 Windermere of fiction
53 State capital meaning "wooded"
54 Authenticity
57 Turns sharply
58 Huddle
59 Seniors' grp.
60 Quart halves
61 Bucket in a car
62 Small compartments
65 Facetious tribute
66 Czar Ivan's sobriquet
70 Courtyards
71 Pooh of fiction
73 Truly
74 Cut, like lumber
75 "__ Zapata"
76 Shortened bullets?
77 Projecting rock
78 Ferocity
79 Smiley of fiction
83 Bullwinkle, e.g.
84 Ethnic
86 Lauder of cosmetics
87 Leather worker
88 "Star Wars" director
89 __ metabolism
90 Marriage announcement
91 Eavesdrop
93 Rot-resistant wood
94 "__ d'outre-tombe"
97 Letter-carriers' base: abbr.
98 Friday of fiction
101 Golda of Israel
102 Essence of roses
103 Heroic Horatio
104 Housewares brand name
105 Small stakes
106 Skedaddles
107 Neck of the woods
108 Profound

DOWN

1 Tongue-clicking sounds
2 Persian ruler
3 Corleones of fiction
4 Wakame and kelp
5 Corner joints
6 Carpentry tools
7 Fermented honey drink
8 Invite
9 Remain loyal to
10 Herbal quaff
11 Utterances
12 Caesar's date
13 Sally Field film, "Norma __"
14 Image
15 Spoon-feed
16 Finn of fiction
17 Top-drawer
18 Stone and Stallone
24 Poet Sachs
25 Dirties
30 Small European barracuda
32 Fathered
33 Solidarity
34 Dept. head
35 F.O.E. chapter
36 __ out (parachutes)
37 Framework posts
38 Move upward
39 "A Patchwork Planet" novelist Anne
41 Fresh and firm
42 Serengeti plaints
45 Water pitchers
47 Sophia Loren's Carlo
50 Lake Geneva spa
51 Intuit
52 Riga populace
53 Poppa pig
55 Prescription language
56 Okinawa port
58 __ Aconcagua, Argentina
60 Opposite in nature
61 Squalid
62 Simple
63 Hokkaido port
64 Napoleon of fiction
65 Alternative beau
66 Arizona city
67 Don Juan of fiction
68 Tenancy period
69 More than willing
71 Aluminum silicates
72 City where Erasmus died
75 Porches
77 Schemed
79 Clare Boothe or Henry
80 Audio-books personnel
81 Highway curves
82 Milky Way chart
83 Estate
85 Private teachers
87 Subduers
89 Become swollen
90 Plague (with)
91 Amorphous mass
92 Understanding words
93 Mennen after-shave
94 Factory VIP
95 It ends off, in the U.K.
96 Word in an octagon
99 List-ending abbr.
100 In the style of

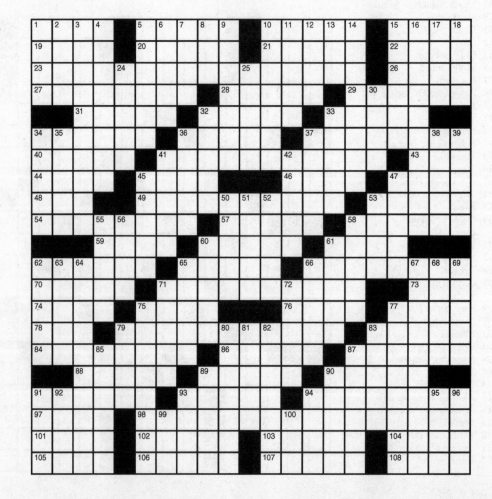

ANIMAL ACTS

by James E. Buell

ACROSS

1 Dreary
5 Pay out
10 Look forward to
15 The smallest bits
19 Diamond Head's island
20 Capital of Vietnam
21 Glisten
22 Soothing additive
23 Picos de Europa lake
24 Inert gas
25 Vast multitude
26 Cry out
27 Frolicking
29 Raising a false alarm
31 Rely
32 Holbrook or Roach
33 East of the Urals
34 Take pleasure in
37 Harry of "60 Minutes"
40 Tumbler
44 Town squares
46 Color changer
47 Twofold
50 Fuzzy fruit
51 Fired up
53 Talk back
55 Car grille protector
56 Heartthrob
57 Old-time rear seats
59 Golden glove?
61 Tangle up
63 Molten metal waste
64 One-half-step lower
66 Rex Stout's Wolfe
68 "Public Enemy" star
69 Getting down to the facts
72 Show up
76 Inkling
77 Husband of a countess
78 Carry on one's back
82 Sticky candy
84 Tall tale
86 Is on top of
88 1st letter
89 Make free (of)
91 Chamber
93 Legislative act
94 Moore of "Disclosure"
95 On __ (without guarantee)
97 Armed services grp.
99 Crabs
100 Point of view
102 At bay
105 Prods
106 Aggressive remark
109 Gangster's pistol
110 Comparable thing
112 Alternative to booing
   or hissing
116 Beating a sneaky retreat
120 Nose alert
121 Ruby Dee's Davis
122 Nincompoop
123 Run in neutral
124 Legal eagle Janet
125 Edmonton skater

126 French landlord's due
127 Actress Foch
128 Was privy to
129 Equals
130 Mystery award
131 Cogwheel

DOWN

1 Suffices
2 Relative status
3 Sailor's call
4 Proceeding insensitively
5 One-half-step higher
6 Valet, at times
7 Equipped with a motor
8 Lunch times
9 Fender flaw
10 Container for cinders
11 Having a pattern of spirals
12 Ethereal
13 Calcutta's land
14 Time between 12 and 20
15 Crossing illegally
16 Butter substitute
17 Ring recurrently
18 Ego
28 Infuse with oxygen
30 Musician's booking

32 Indulging in frivolous
   activity
34 Skewers
35 Rival of Polaris
   for brightness
36 Letter-lady White
38 Crease
39 Cause friction
41 Actor Quinn
42 Cursed
43 Zany
45 Old salts
48 "__ You Being Served?"
49 Primitive marine organisms
52 Ho-hum
54 Editor's command
58 H.H. Munro
60 Faithful
62 Pronounce
65 Word with sum or up
67 Viva voce
69 Highland cap
70 Neighborly?
71 Barbra's co-star in
   "A Star is Born"
72 Etching fluids
73 Board
74 __ ballerina

75 Accepting humiliating
   defeat
78 Showing off
79 Soft palate part
80 Given out in portions
81 Squeeze
83 Cup rim
85 Winning margin,
   sometimes
87 Ho Chi Minh City, once
90 Yule mo.
92 Searched for plunder
96 Hokier
98 Swordplay
101 Actress Carrere
103 Actress Mimi
104 Santee Sioux
107 Texas leaguer
108 Borden's cow
111 .264 gallon
112 Bottle stopper
113 Port of Yemen
114 Vocal inflection
115 Seagirt land
116 Nearly hopeless
117 Garfield's pal
118 Forearm bone
119 Sorrowful drop

by Robert H. Wolfe

ACROSS

1 Queequeg's captain
5 Disney deer
10 Mrs. Copperfield
14 "My Name Is __ Lev"
19 Frankie Avalon hit, "__ Dinah"
20 Off to one side
22 Inscribed stone marker
23 Shepherding president?
25 Zen paradoxes
26 Shorten
27 One of Tisiphone's cohorts
28 __ and Gomorrah
29 Proximity bombs
30 Probabilities
32 Painter Holbein
34 Circular ocean current
35 Shrink time?
36 Confidences
39 Code of silence
41 Buffoonish president?
45 Neath's opposite
46 Carpenter's supports
50 Pleat of lace
51 WWII arena
53 No-frills
54 Recipe meas.
56 Mountain lake
57 Sci-fi author of "Camp Concentration"
60 Monstrous
63 Lessen
65 Numero __
67 Younger Saarinen
68 Scand. country
69 Bearded president?
72 French wine
73 Take hold of
75 Sea eagle
76 Swann or Redgrave
77 Riviera resort
80 Gossipy woman
82 Mennen after-shave
84 South African golfer Ernie
86 Conger catcher
87 Ford fuel
88 Overwhelming defeats
90 Gilbert and Sullivan offerings
93 Volcanic fallout
95 President for dessert?
98 Morally pure
100 Perched
101 Spheres
105 Trolley
106 Smooth-headed
110 West and Murray
111 Frightening
112 Arrangement
114 Additional levy
116 Emotionally affected
118 V.P. Agnew
119 Wise up a president?
122 Forklike
123 Look
124 Kick back
125 Some lilies
126 Indigo and anil
127 KOs and TKOs, e.g.
128 "...see how __ run"

DOWN

1 Cartoonist Charles
2 Jazz pianist Hancock
3 Embellishes
4 Flocks of females
5 Small town
6 Deliver ending?
7 Twice DLXXV
8 Mayberry aunt
9 Unwelcome arrival
10 Remove from text
11 Spinachlike plant
12 Oscar de la __
13 After-market item
14 Queries
15 Stool pigeon
16 Prudent president?
17 Gregory Nava film of 1983
18 Sling more mud
21 1960 satellite
24 Begley and Wynn
30 Two quartets
31 Tom Courtenay film, with "The"
33 Five centimes, once
36 Sun. homily
37 Superman's letter
38 Sweet, white wine
40 TV's talking horse
41 "Turbulent Indigo" singer Mitchell
42 __ Victor, Broadway label
43 Drum with fingers
44 Reddish-orange dyes
46 Squishy
47 Clinton's backup, once
48 Belligerent president?
49 Encourage to hurry
52 Connection
55 Installment-plan phrase
58 1850's war zone
59 Military decorations
61 That girl
62 Zimbabwe's capital
64 Pigpen
66 Three-match connection
70 Guaranteed to get
71 Disengage
74 School org.
78 __-do-well
79 Veteran's abbr.
81 ADC
83 Wide, clumsy boat
85 Leopard feature
89 Leaf openings
91 Holiday lead-in
92 Primary color
93 Makes overtures
94 Card cheat
96 Lang. of Israel
97 Tricksters
99 Sound system
101 Inscrutable
102 Gung-ho
103 No-brainer
104 Australian city
107 Syrian leader
108 Like bad gravy
109 Hang in loose folds
111 Hoagie
113 Anglers' gear
115 Very pronounced French?
116 Diplomacy
117 Singletons
120 Journalist Hentoff
121 Org. of house-call RNs

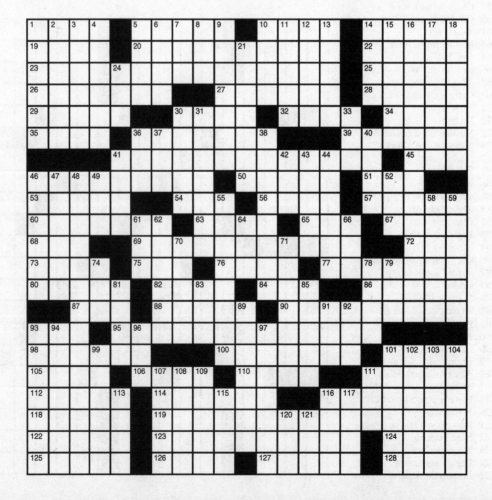

by Alan P. Olschwang

ACROSS

1 May celebrants
5 Home of Iowa State
9 Semitic people
14 Marsh grasses
19 Oriental nursemaid
20 Lead a nomad's life
21 Of the kidneys
22 Computer messages
23 Yemen's capital
24 Concerning
25 Biblical mount
26 Villechaize of "Fantasy Island"
27 Start of Evan Esar witticism
30 Like an old tree trunk
32 Send-ups
33 Look after
34 Part 2 of the witticism
35 Chameleons
37 Muse of lyric poetry
39 For one
43 Part 3 of the witticism
47 Besmirch
48 Rocks on the edge
50 Aussie hopper
51 Coupon presenter
53 Part 4 of the witticism
55 Floating fleet
56 La __, WI
58 Loads up
59 Wire spiral
60 Applauds vocally
62 Express a bias
65 Tolkien tree
66 Part 5 of the witticism
69 Writer Hentoff
72 Showy bloom
73 Hammerstein's forte
74 Inventor Elias
75 "Chinatown" director Polanski
78 Most reticent
80 Crownlets
82 Part 6 of the witticism
86 Send 22A
88 Knight's address
89 Pendant or stud
90 Bus. bigwig
91 Part 7 of the witticism
92 Plant containers
94 Product name
95 Dry gulch
97 Part 8 of the witticism
99 Wight, for one
101 Making lace
106 Peoria university
109 End of the witticism
111 Actress Blair
112 Old saw
114 Poi source
115 Pieces of pelvises
116 Change
117 Identify oneself to a computer
118 Melville's "Typee" sequel
119 Ancient Briton

120 Flash on and off
121 Biscuitlike pastry
122 Exercise counts, casually
123 Latin being

DOWN

1 Marina skyline
2 D-Day beach
3 "Olympia" painter
4 Puppeteer Lewis
5 Up and about
6 Unpaired X-chromosome
7 Merit
8 Ore processor
9 Fiery felony
10 Comet, Cupid et al.
11 "__ of Green Gables"
12 Sound sheepish?
13 More frail
14 Actress Ada
15 Materialize
16 Viscount's superior
17 Seedy bar
18 Luge
28 Expunged
29 Ballot option
31 City southeast of Nantes
34 London art gallery
36 Theft
38 Interpret, as dreams
40 Like the Gobi
41 Ice-cream holder
42 Coal scuttles
43 Barely detectable amount
44 Long-necked wading bird
45 Confess
46 Greenish blue
48 Adding pendent ornamentation
49 Wise lawyer
52 Manly in Madrid
53 Trumpet or cornet
54 Distant
57 Stephen of "The Crying Game"
61 "Star Wars" pilot Solo
62 Darting movement
63 Former power grp.
64 Panorama
66 On edge
67 Ogled
68 GPs
69 Bellini opera
70 Anticipate
71 Finals

72 __ the piper
74 Hodgepodge
75 Coarse file
76 Buckeye State
77 Trading center
78 Thin coating
79 Turning over to another
81 Altogether
83 Hold for later action
84 Orderly displays
85 Stuff
87 Turnips or beets, e.g.
90 Maker
93 Dispirit
95 Totality
96 Crude boors
98 Singer Petula
100 Play part
102 Two times
103 Wastes time
104 Simon and Diamond
105 Abrade
106 Spill the beans
107 Brooklet
108 Against: pref.
109 "Othello" villain
110 "Auntie __"
113 Disney dwarf

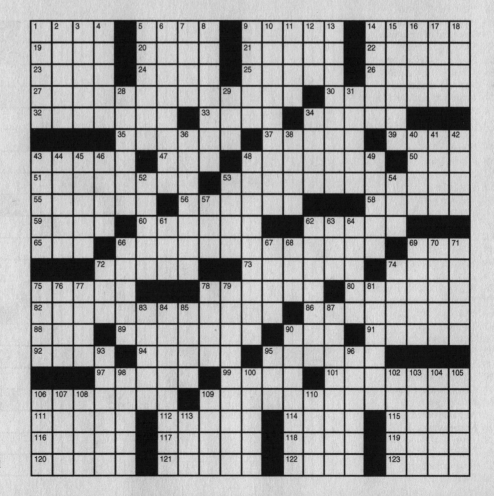

by Stanley B. Whitten

ACROSS

1 Eugene O'Neill play, "Desire Under the __"
5 Farm measure
9 Detest
14 __ Rica
19 Geezer
20 Support group
21 Sales circuit
22 "Bellefleur" author
23 Newspaper feature
25 Newspaper feature
27 In the advantageous position
28 Mall event
30 Goddess of sorcery
31 Poetic pasture
32 Lawmaker
35 Released conditionally
37 Gluts
40 Assemblage
42 Cover
43 Sticker?
44 Newspaper feature
49 Shout
50 Twisted sideways
52 Container with a tap
53 Decay
54 Withdraw
58 "Star Trek" extras
59 Polygonal projection
61 Stoppage of breathing
63 Sao Paulo suburb
65 Actress/director Lupino
66 Superlatively spooky
68 Newspaper feature
71 Attacks as questionable
74 Reverence
75 Gilbert and Sullivan offerings
79 "Semper Fidelis" composer
80 Pastoral poem
82 Period
83 Regardless
84 Online shorthand in reply to a joke
85 Compass pt.
86 Make lawn repairs
88 Ulan-__, Russia
89 Newspaper feature
94 Travel guide
98 WWII ration-book group
99 Huge
100 Worn out
101 Trinidad music
105 Close calls
107 Exist
108 Cure
110 City near Essen
111 City near Cleveland
115 Newspaper feature
118 Newspaper feature
120 Manipulators
121 Art school
122 Seaweed
123 Seine tributary
124 Searches for
125 Feeling of anxiety
126 Deli breads
127 Storyline

DOWN

1 Reverberation
2 Crazy bird?
3 Comic Sahl
4 Squealer
5 NCAA grouping
6 Church staffs
7 Go by again
8 "The Seven Year Itch" star Tom
9 Circle segment
10 Cries
11 Arm bone
12 Of the ear
13 Brief summary
14 Clique
15 Paddle
16 Yet
17 Conical shelter
18 Syrian leader
24 Asparagus unit
26 Soviet dictator
29 NFL team
33 Phone co. of yore
34 Folk song abbr.
36 Strange
37 Pelvic bones
38 Relevant: Lat.
39 Aromatic herb
41 Papal name
44 Revealing visual device
45 Turn to ice
46 "Rule Britannia" composer
47 Bucks' mates
48 Sports fig.
51 Eye element
55 Roman Hades
56 Rain not reaching the ground
57 Business subj.
59 Put two and two together
60 Narragansett baby
61 "Stormy Weather" composer
62 Reverence
64 St. Francis of __
65 Anger
67 Cornell or Pound
69 Nocturnal raptor
70 As far as
71 Small land mass
72 Disposition
73 Longhaired sheepdog
76 Blow with a blunt object
77 Hanoi dress
78 Brushed
81 Settlement
82 Sanitize
85 Pencil end
86 Hindu music form
87 Horsemanship demonstration
90 Plaything
91 Weigh heavily on
92 Touchdown
93 Hunters
95 Mil. training course
96 Vicinities
97 Computer model
100 In a desperate manner
101 "The Plague" author
102 Got up
103 Embankment
104 Symbol meaning last
106 Back tooth
109 Level
112 Stir up
113 Approximately
114 No, in Russian
116 Anger
117 Damp
119 German article

by Robert H. Wolfe

ACROSS

1 Tasman and Muzorewa
6 Pick out
10 U.S. tennis stadium honoree
14 Three-player card game
19 French landscape painter
20 Scat singer Fitzgerald
21 Getz or Kenton
22 Removes skin
23 "The Inhuman Condition" author Barker
24 Pitiful cry
25 Hearts or diamonds
26 Zodiac sign
27 Get a postponement stub at a horse show?
30 Delight
31 Utters suddenly
32 Nightmarish spirits
34 Mineral deposits
35 Native Alaskans
38 Regarding
39 Table extension
41 Negative horses?
45 Baseball Hall-of-Famer Juan
49 Light brown
50 Chris of tennis
51 Pindarics
53 Avignon's river
54 Give a bias to
56 Casual farewell
57 Gem weight
58 Site of the Duomo
59 NY's Crown or Washington
61 Shore
63 Muscle protein
64 Palmer of golf
67 Horse-colored waterway?
69 Impudent
70 Filmmakers Joel and Ethan
71 Writer Bierce
72 NYC arena
73 Portents
74 Honeydew, e.g.
75 Roman-fleuve
78 Catholic calendar
82 Change color again
83 Belgian composer
84 Shankar's instrument
85 Short jaunt
86 Nares
88 Horse's girlfriend?
91 Tortoise's rival
92 Harrow's rival
94 Invisible
95 Chomp
98 Singer Franklin
100 Usher after the interval
103 Takes on as one's own
105 Barn for newlywed horses?
110 Tippy craft
111 Ed or Early
112 Russian saint
113 Actress Black
114 Burns film
115 French girlfriend

116 Borscht ingredient
117 Sappho's Muse
118 Beery and Gordon
119 Actuality
120 "Jane __"
121 Force units

DOWN

1 $ in the bank
2 Gaucho's cowcatcher
3 Composer Satie
4 Florida pest
5 Furtiveness
6 Waste conduit
7 Braid
8 Ken and Lena
9 Dusting powder
10 Nod of the head
11 Wall covering
12 Japanese verse
13 Way in: abbr.
14 Milky gem
15 Richard Daley's horse?
16 Pipe type
17 Singer Della
18 Double curves
28 Winter apples
29 Snake speech
30 Jetty
33 Demolition expert
35 Ubiquitous bugs
36 News source?
37 "__ kleine Nachtmusik"
38 Fine work
40 Weather phenomenon
42 Gardner of "The Barefoot Contessa"
43 So far
44 Like pencil marks
45 Victor at Gettysburg
46 Winifred and Tim
47 Diarist Nin
48 Bruce or Wilkens
51 Mirage, maybe
52 Hammers home, as a nail
55 Milne's horse?
57 Leslie of "An American in Paris"
60 Mosaic piece
62 Sign on: var.
64 Future oak
65 Juliet's beau
66 Requirements
67 Wanderer
68 Hebrew measure and season

72 Theater projection
76 Had a bite
77 Boastful talk
79 Syngman __
80 Rest fitfully
81 Unwrap
84 __ Clemente
87 Gershwin and Levin
88 Land of Lot's descendants
89 Not invited
90 Sea at a river's mouth
92 Racial
93 Sandra Bullock film
95 Salted meat
96 Gem State
97 Nuku'alofa's country
99 Former forms of words
100 "The Life of __"
101 Lawn-care tool
102 List of candidates
104 Turner and Williams
106 Housecoat
107 Islamic republic
108 Pierre's head
109 Son of Seth
111 Former service branch: abbr.

by Alan P. Olschwang

ACROSS

1 Builder's maps
6 Away from the prow
9 Pretentious one
14 Glinted
19 Sublease a flat
20 Lea lament
21 Ghana's capital
22 Tapered off
23 Start of a Robert Frost quotation
25 Like the Arctic
26 Chekhov or Bruckner
27 Outer banana
28 Part 2 of the quotation
31 Six-line stanzas
33 Formerly, formerly
34 North or South China, e.g.
35 Miss. neighbor
36 Farm measure
38 Looking with disapproval
43 Part 3 of the quotation
49 Neither's partner?
50 "The Grapes of Wrath" character
51 Noblewoman
52 Small bottle
53 "It's a Wonderful Life" director Frank
55 Wash. neighbor
56 Southern breakfast dish
58 Quarter bushel
59 Places for public discussions
60 Reckless track
62 Part 4 of the quotation
64 Sentry's command
65 Martin and Pickford
66 Opposing position
67 Part 5 of the quotation
71 Looks at with favor
75 Rope knots for rustlers
76 Disencumbers
77 Scatterbrained
78 Docs' org.
79 Loudness units
80 Virginia's dance?
81 Shore bird
82 How my heartstrings went
83 Alfonso's queen
84 Part 6 of the quotation
88 Fundraising event
91 Goofs up
92 Comparative ending
93 Carnival city, briefly
94 Wight or Skye
96 Countersign
100 Part 7 of the quotation
107 Hula Hoop activator
108 More fit
109 North African antelope
110 End of the quotation
112 Martini's partner
113 Calvin of the PGA
114 Somme summer
115 Sweet, in Seville
116 Does ushering
117 Genders
118 Rocky peak
119 Deuce toppers

DOWN

1 Makes ready, for short
2 Embankment
3 Fugard play, "A Lesson from __"
4 "The __ Heart"
5 Actor Erwin
6 Out of order
7 Sucker
8 Singer Tennille
9 Wall coverer
10 Flat boats
11 Brilliance
12 Caspian feeder
13 Unilluminated
14 Gershwin song
15 Plane garage
16 In the know about
17 Light gas
18 Writer Buchanan
24 Tennessee gridder
29 Irish county
30 Oh yeah, right
32 Samuel's teacher
36 Slacken
37 Bounders
38 Claim
39 Org. of Flyers
40 Computer fodder?
41 __ Jean Baker
42 Lawn
43 Skyline element
44 Soup ingredient, perhaps
45 Disinformation
46 Quick flashes of light
47 Writer Waugh
48 Ice-cream tastes
53 Very dear
54 Golfer Palmer
56 Scowls
57 Death rattles
58 European capital
59 Finished, in France
61 The closer ones
62 Walk like a duck
63 Another name for sage
65 Architect Richard Alan
67 Map in a map
68 Nary a soul
69 Of musical sounds
70 Wooden cookware
71 Slavic-speaking Germans
72 Spinnaker, e.g.
73 Present starter?
74 Acts shrewish
77 Will of "The Waltons"
80 Greek letter
81 Minimum crowd
82 Commencement of hostilities
84 Horse arrester?
85 Old-fashioned messages
86 Drummer Starr
87 Roulette bet
89 Tubb or Truex
90 Baghdad's river
94 Directory
95 Do figure eights
96 Sign on a door
97 Ransack
98 Hot, in a way
99 __ Park, CO
100 Long, thin fish
101 Woodwind
102 Ingrid in "Casablanca"
103 Gullible dupes
104 __ fixe
105 Bard
106 Fascinated by
111 L.A. summer hrs.

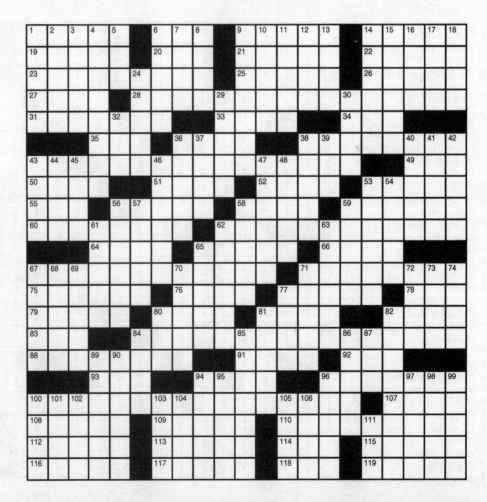

by Arlan and Linda Bushman

ACROSS

1 Temporary currency
6 Midway alternative
11 Adriatic seaport
15 Ovine cries
19 Fragrance
20 Deserves
21 Presley's middle name
22 Stage direction
23 Demolition derby excitement?
25 Soviet news agcy.
26 Assistant
27 Lady of "The Raven"
28 Charlotte of "The Facts of Life"
29 Crustacean rule?
31 Sole
33 Nominator
35 Magic stick
36 Michael of "Pole to Pole"
39 Keanu Reeves film, with "The"
41 Concerned with the whole
45 Revise for print
46 First-aid device
47 Planet
48 Cinder
49 Origami facial features?
51 Patches
52 Granary
53 Antithesis: abbr.
54 Paddles
55 Crystal-filled rocks
57 Fads
58 Incentives
60 Uses jargon
61 Goddess of sorcery
62 Wall Street malady?
65 Garland
68 Spooned
69 Like winds and rivers
73 Rio Grande feeder
74 Actress Elizabeth
75 Rigging support
76 Pinch
77 The Zombies' hit, "__ Not There"
78 J. Paul or Estelle
79 Eve?
81 Slip up
82 Patsy Cline hit
83 Twists together
85 __ thin air
86 Fine distinction
88 Creatures
89 At right angles to the keel
90 Millennia
91 Prevention measure?
92 Vague amount
94 Starchy buildup?
98 Crone
100 Trademark fastener
104 Lawman Wyatt
105 Actress Neuwirth
106 FDR's chapeau?
108 One of the Cosby kids
109 Lascivious look
110 Playful aquatic mammal
111 Upright
112 Sheep fat
113 R & B singer James
114 Deep voices
115 Path starter?

DOWN

1 Satirist Mort
2 Algonquian language
3 Horse shade
4 Rude
5 Customer
6 Bruins great Bobby
7 Filament
8 Legendary island
9 Study anew
10 Curving shape
11 Ulan __, Mongolia
12 Yemeni or Saudi
13 Perot's speeches?
14 Loads, as software
15 Growths of ZZ Top
16 Leafstalk angle
17 Verdi work
18 Fret
24 Coop layer
29 Latin law
30 Oklahoma city
32 Charlatan
34 Sch. near Harvard
36 Squash
37 Change with the times
38 "Adoration of the Magi" painter
40 Yodeler's range?
41 Frank
42 Subarctic forest
43 Ait
44 Picked
46 Skier's zigzag
47 Crammed (in)
50 Sales trails
51 Word with bars or business
52 Goldman's Wall Street partner
55 Willingly
56 "Guitar Town" singer Steve
57 Vacation spot
59 Windows basis, originally
60 Wiseacre
61 Beleaguer
63 Clumsy
64 Subjugate
65 Basilica features
66 Jawaharlal of India
67 Sour tasting, old-style
70 Vacuous
71 Panorama
72 __ salts
74 Electric blanket?
75 Warble
78 City on the Isere
79 Painting, sculpture, etc.
80 Liars in print
82 Coagulate
83 Bo's number
84 Campbell hit, "__ Lineman"
87 __ Dome (1921 scandal)
88 Clear tables
89 Painter Modigliani
91 La Scala production
93 Egg: pref.
94 Cats and cockatoos, e.g.
95 Honolulu's island
96 Family chart
97 Yeah, sure
99 Lift-off pressure
101 Newsman Huntley
102 Track contest
103 Eight: It.
106 Pocket-watch accessory
107 __ Lanka

by Josiah Breward

ACROSS

1 "Two Years Before the __"
5 Theater sec.
9 Lupino and Tarbell
13 Los Angeles suburb
19 Utah ski resort
20 Hillside by a loch
21 Palm thatch
22 First Japanese-American congressman
23 Male chauvinist policy
26 Go-fer
27 Moore of "Arthur"
28 Lag behind
29 Actor Estevez
31 Paraffin-coated cheese
33 "Delphine" author Madame de __
35 Heraldic beast
38 Chips off the old block
41 First public park in North America
44 School in Fort Worth, TX
45 On the __ vive
46 Hebrew month
47 Alaskan island
48 Lower or under
50 Stingy
54 PA nuclear reactor in 1979 headlines
56 Ostrich relatives
57 Was sore
58 Inadequate
62 Venetian ruler
63 Superfluous
65 Oil: pref.
66 Dutchman's dagger
68 Notes of scales
69 Monks' hoods
71 Actress Madeleine
73 Three-bean or Waldorf
75 Class for U.S. immigrants
77 Tune
79 Sharif and Epps
81 Yucatan capital
84 Stay in the army
86 Beyond scientific explanation
89 Creepers
90 Truman's V.P. Barkley
92 Fish like a stick?
93 "China Beach" star
95 Episodic TV show
97 Pocketed bread?
100 Speaker of Cooperstown
101 66 or 1, e.g.
102 Logical starter?
103 Usually
107 Part of DOS
108 Flummoxed
110 Hackneyed
111 Puget Sound whale
113 Mother __ of Calcutta
115 Mosaic pieces
117 Old World
121 One who tolerates
123 Inured
126 Tropical fruit
127 S-shaped molding
128 Fuel-line element
129 Rocket cap
130 Button holder
131 "The __ of the Rings"
132 Has debts
133 Thug

DOWN

1 Road safety grp.
2 Moises or Felipe of baseball
3 Ornamental button
4 Data displays
5 Like commands
6 Amtrak and B&O
7 American suffragist
8 Kidnapped heiress
9 Notre Dame's state
10 Local lingo
11 Showery mo.
12 "Smooth Operator" singer
13 Crude metal ingots
14 Short joke
15 Recurrent theme
16 Unusual
17 Comic Louis
18 Gas: pref.
24 Guided
25 W. alliance
30 Hollywood studio's monogram
32 Grieve
34 Numbers game
36 Long, cold period
37 Hospital workers
38 Athletic team
39 Light weight
40 Stand-up act
42 Beach Boys hit, "__ John B"
43 Inflammatory disease
46 Provides funds for
49 Religious deg.
51 Younger Saarinen
52 Shoshones
53 Place in New York City?
55 Woosnam and Fleming
59 TV teaser
60 On the way to
61 Twenty quires
64 Drop heavily
67 French students
70 Unforeseen obstacle
72 Columnist Bombeck
74 Seed coat
75 Expunges
76 Pick
78 Quantitative diagram
80 __ Cruz, CA
82 Fender flaws
83 To this point
85 Can. province
87 Zodiac ram
88 Key __, FL
91 Synthetic rubber
94 Double dots over letters
96 Look down on
98 Squealer
99 Helped
104 6-pointers
105 Cinder ending?
106 Say again and again
107 Wraparound skirt
109 Winner's token
112 Sever
114 Runaway GI
116 Flat-bottomed boat
118 Melville novel
119 Miguel's money
120 Paradise lost
121 Fortas or Vigoda
122 Howl
124 I problem?
125 Manipulate

by Robert H. Wolfe

ACROSS

1 Northern Native American tribe members
8 Husky
14 Close a purse
20 Winfrey's peer
21 Stir to action
22 Beethoven's Symphony No. 3
23 Obvious
24 Roaster of an Indiana school?
26 Veteran's abbr.
27 Lawyers: abbr.
29 Germ
30 __ after (desires)
31 Of a pointed tool
33 Taskbar images
35 Author of "The Republic"
38 Filer in an Atlanta school?
42 Weaving machine
46 French historian
47 Carefree, lively outings
48 Choice: abbr.
49 Writer Bontemps
50 Ask
52 Leftover piece
54 Piano student's pieces
56 Computer in Orono?
58 In the style of
60 __ we all?
61 Class for new U.S. immigrants
62 66 and 1, e.g.
63 Added fat
66 Gridiron demarcations
67 Bear of the sky
68 Parallel bands
69 Wire measures
71 "Adoration of the Magi" painter
74 Of a stage
76 John Doe's dog?
77 Half an African fly?
80 Licorice flavoring
81 Pre-college exam
82 Treats roughly at an Illinois college?
85 Way up or down
87 Make rough
90 Expressed delight
91 Dispatch
92 Northern sea bird
94 Find a new lair
96 Set to rest
97 Shaving-cream additive
98 Slips in a Brooklyn school?
100 "Mr. __ Goes to Town"
101 Malicious ill will
102 Hunting dog
104 New Jersey city
108 Politician Perot
112 "Take Her, __ Mine"
113 AL or NL honoree
116 Road to a Louisiana university?

119 Country once part of Greater Colombia
121 Makes amends
122 Crescent-shaped
123 Perilous surface
124 College in Geneva, NY
125 Overacts
126 Emilio of "St. Elmo's Fire"

DOWN

1 Polish-German border river
2 Chief Roman god
3 Laverne's L, e.g.
4 Unpleasant
5 Dog of a Massachusetts college?
6 Ma's sister
7 Comes to rest
8 Cool or groovy
9 Burden
10 Field measure
11 Hound
12 Workroom
13 Wide shoe size
14 Manipulate again
15 Gray and Moran
16 Punch
17 Reebok rival
18 Perfect server
19 Kitchen utensils
25 Task
28 Dominant tennis player of the '90s
31 Blot
32 Music critic Ned
34 Elsinore, e.g.
35 First in quality
36 Horne and Olin
37 Blacksmith's block
39 Thaws again
40 Hankering
41 Youth org.
42 Dern and Ashley
43 Alphabetize
44 In an upright position
45 Spars with sails
51 Immature newts
53 Zilch
55 Indiana university outfit?
57 Harvests
59 Blend
64 Jackie's second
65 Two-wheeled transport
67 Advantageous aspect
68 Japanese P.M. (1964-72)
70 Lupino and Tarbell
71 African fever
72 Pentium makers
73 Spinet, e.g.
75 Cut carelessly
76 Caresses
77 Veil material
78 Slammin' Sammy
79 Arnold and Diaz
83 Simon and Young
84 Crude workman
86 Most sugar-coated
88 Craftsmanship
89 Ring off.
93 "Vega$" star
95 Affected lover of beauty
99 Arthropod's body segment
101 More rational
103 Support-line employees
104 Egyptian god
105 Biography beginning?
106 Mess maker
107 Yemen's capital
109 Phrase of distress
110 Thwack
111 Fill completely
113 DCCLII doubled
114 Sotto __ (in an undertone)
115 D.C. honcho
117 __-de-France
118 OK
120 Dijon donkey

TOUR BY TUBE

by Ed Voile

ACROSS

1 Cut and splice
5 Camper's shelter
9 Pub drinks
15 Lovers' quarrel
19 __ fide (authentic)
20 "Dies __"
21 Common mushroom
22 Scrabble piece
23 Monarch's residence
26 Corrosive substance
27 Globes
28 Peas' package
29 Affected by pathogens
31 Shakespearean contraction
32 Eclipse revelation
35 Synagogue scrolls
38 Archaeologist Harriet
41 Location of the Turner Wing
44 Buck's mate
45 Revealed oneself
47 Put to sleep
48 City on the Arno
49 Harvest goddess
50 One of the Finger Lakes
53 Customary extras, briefly
54 Grade sch.
55 Tennis player Korda
57 London landmark
60 Legendary football coach
61 Childbirth innovator
63 Calyx segment
64 Misbelief
66 Alonso and Silverstone
68 Sacred ceremonies
70 Wind from the Sahara
73 Unclaimed
75 Peter and Franco
77 Boston team
78 Medea's husband
80 Venue of the Promenade Concerts
83 Senior dance
84 Bus. letter directive
85 Myth ending?
86 Part of USSR
88 3-mvmt. musical piece
89 __ van der Rohe
90 Plump
93 Heirlooms
95 Bklyn. or Bx., e.g.
96 Thames spanner
99 Ballet __ of Monte Carlo
100 Vacuum-cleaner attachment
102 Scottish alderman
103 Chinese Chairman
104 Inters
107 Brown with a band
108 The blues
112 Lofting shots
114 Christopher Wren masterpiece
118 Region
119 Travel with difficulty
120 Gen. Bradley
121 Bullets, briefly
122 __ Mawr College
123 Detection device
124 Wise person
125 Sail support

DOWN

1 Wanes
2 Fasten, as buttons
3 Foot twelfth
4 Rest
5 Fork prongs
6 Work units
7 Slangy negative
8 __ Dome (Harding administration scandal)
9 Toadies
10 __ Khan IV
11 Babe
12 Periods
13 Eastern staple
14 British sovereign's staffs
15 Step
16 Location of Eros
17 The Greatest
18 Tycoon Turner
24 Garden blooms
25 Extra
30 Plaything
32 Pranks
33 Stirling negative
34 Rot-resistant wood
36 Book before Joel
37 Cloth connections
38 To-do
39 Second trial
40 Site of Chaucer's tomb
41 Sushi fish
42 Spring lock
43 Engraves
46 Humiliate
48 London fog
51 Pers. with a handle?
52 Of high mountains
56 Masked carnivores
58 Diner patron
59 Periods of readiness
60 Frankfurt mister
62 Promised land
65 Lamb cut
67 Manatee or dugong
69 London district
71 $100 bills
72 Pass through a membrane
74 Roofer's stone
76 Ferocious
78 Door columns
79 Tempt ending?
81 Book-jacket copy
82 Bit of dialogue
85 O. Henry and others
87 Fulmination
91 Cagers' org.
92 Dentist, at times
94 One-time
96 Rocky crag
97 Aits in the Seine
98 Dance clubs
101 South Korean seaport
103 Olympic skier Phil
105 Raison d'__
106 Rotated
108 Dateless
109 Humorist Bombeck
110 Houston and Donaldson
111 Coin channel
112 Practical sci. class
113 Bobby of the NHL
115 Madison Ave. output
116 Italian actor Tognazzi
117 Group of docs

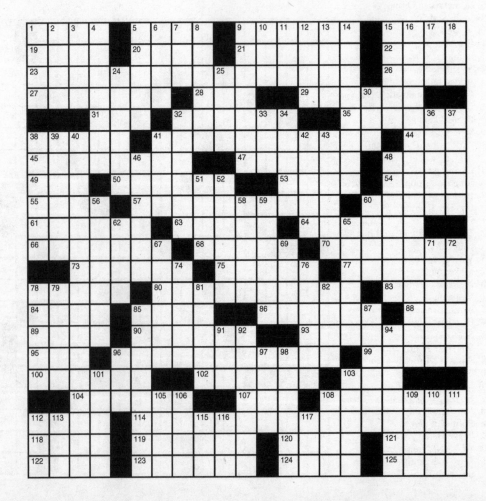

EASTER HUNT

by Edgar Fontaine

ACROSS

1 Young elephant
5 Rolling stone's lack
9 Florida raptor
15 Hog fat
19 Melville's "Typee" sequel
20 Pieces of pelvises
21 Conditional release
22 Lamb's pen name
23 Natl. possession
24 Former Celtic
26 Talent
27 Elbow grease
29 Lets fall
30 Dicker
32 Memorable periods
33 Dershowitz and Greenspan
34 Foretold
35 Nocturnal marsupial, casually
38 "Golden Boy" dramatist
39 Part of Wessex
40 Bring joy
41 Sound asleep?
42 Three-sided figures
46 Carried a tune
47 Seasoning plants
48 Feather scarves
49 Large truck, briefly
50 Set too high a price on
52 Safecracker
55 Help out
56 Gutters' location
57 Chinese: pref.
58 Baby-bottle feature
60 Slow
63 Half a score
64 Hatted, say at Easter
66 Toy weapon
67 Depend
68 Twisted and squeezed
69 Birthday figure
70 Brain
73 Dawdles
77 Chinese secret society
79 Fruity coat
80 King of Crete
81 Noel
82 Natural ability
85 Pie nut
86 Many times
87 Mountain nymph
88 Informers
89 Flew alone
90 Alternative to here
93 Sloughs off feathers
94 Canaveral or Fear
95 Montana capital
96 Gibbs of "The Jeffersons"
97 Earthquake phenomena
101 __ fixe (obsession)
102 One of Cher's exes
105 Keen on
106 Part of LP
107 Worker
108 Expel
109 March Madness org.

110 Catch
111 Flattens on impact
112 Western tribe
113 Blathers

DOWN

1 Sheep shelter
2 Credit-card comp.
3 Traditional tales
4 Canton Hall of Fame member
5 South African singer Makeba
6 Butter substitutes
7 Indication
8 Droop
9 Drive
10 Beauty parlors
11 Makes ready, for short
12 Horizontal series
13 Samuel's teacher
14 Judaic school
15 Children's warm outerwear
16 Make straight
17 Ransack
18 Passe
25 Couch potatoes
28 Make square

31 Makeup marketer
33 Homemade brick
34 Belief in a god
35 Mexican money
36 King of Norway
37 In one's right mind
38 Forward flow
39 Retarding force
41 1990-92 French Open Tennis Champion
42 West African country
43 Jumped
44 French writer Zola
45 Faceted
47 Possessing
48 Funny Jack
51 Inexplicit
52 Concede
53 Invalidates
54 Airhead
57 Standing one in good __
59 1978 Olympic gold-medal skater
60 Sudden flow
61 Identify oneself to a computer
62 Make vertical
64 Respectful African titles

65 Acrylic fiber
67 Become a lessee
71 __ Barrier Reef
72 Rear
73 Ice-cream tastes
74 Mobile starter?
75 Happiness
76 E-mail
78 Zilch
80 __ telepathy
83 Small, brown bird
84 Households
85 __ of Hercules
86 Sorry 'bout that!
88 Disregard on purpose
89 New Orleans team
90 Collins and Donahue
91 Pre-surrealist painter
92 Barcelata tune, "Maria __"
93 __ Carta
94 Discontinue
96 Blackbird
97 Sooty matter
98 Andes people
99 Use a stiletto
100 Extinct birds
103 __ across the knuckles
104 Bud's buddy

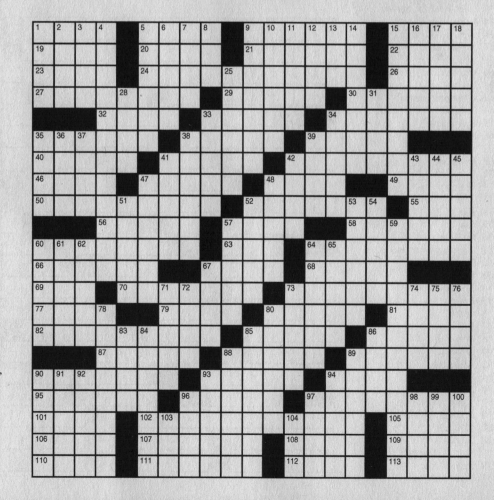

ACROSS

1 Turner of "Imitation of Life"
5 Hey, over here!
9 Musical staff sign
14 Make merry
19 Seed cover
20 External: pref.
21 World's busiest airport
22 Gimme putt
23 Tree in Florida?
25 Tree in New York?
27 "Goblin Market" poet
28 Borden's cow
29 "__ the fields..."
30 NJ inventor's initials
31 Ravel's "Daphnis and __"
33 Annoys
37 Nose-and-throat problem
41 Tree in Wisconsin?
44 Daffy bird?
45 Sharif and Epps
46 Tapestry in "Hamlet"
48 Tears
49 "Mysteries of the Virgin" painter
50 Witticisms
51 Cultivated plants
52 Daughter of Elizabeth II
53 Coen brothers movie
54 Hosp. area
55 Tree in California?
57 A point ahead
58 British emcees
60 Cinnabar and bauxite
61 Barrow and Drexler
62 Computer image
63 Morsels
65 Spicy stew
66 Sandhill and whooping, e.g.
69 Extra
70 In a faint
74 Honey plants?
75 Tree in California?
78 Karel Capek's sci-fi play
79 Clayton Powell and West
80 Links grp.
81 Highway components
82 Conflagration
83 Vegas rival
84 Church recess
85 Boring tool
86 Girlie
87 Ballerina's skirt
88 Tree in Brooklyn?
90 Cuts slits
92 Lathe axis
94 Riyadh resident
96 Alternatives
97 __ the line
98 Postage
100 My fault
105 Tree in Iowa?
109 Tree in Illinois?
110 State as true
111 I want in!

112 "A Death in the Family" writer
113 Work on manuscripts
114 Paints a word picture
115 Embellish
116 Funny Foxx
117 Be mouthy

DOWN

1 Bert the Cowardly Lion
2 End of a buck?
3 Swedish inventor, __ Gustaf Dalen
4 League's best players
5 Gray shade
6 Glaswegian
7 Cicero, e.g.
8 Pioneer filmmaker Browning
9 Small portions of meat
10 Sculptor's tool
11 "Lift Every Voice" author Guinier
12 Mahler's "Das Lied von der __"
13 Cost to participate
14 Singer Waters
15 Tree in California?
16 Car-payment fig.

17 "__ the season..."
18 Absorb ending?
24 Full calendars
26 Middays
28 Half of UTEP
32 Marx brother
33 Gloomily sulky
34 Piloted a glider
35 Language
36 Uses too much nose
37 Jokester
38 Exxon rival
39 Actress O'Neal
40 Toughen
42 Els and Kovacs
43 Color shades
47 Horizontal series
51 Caribbean food fish
52 Farmland unit
53 Page numbers
55 Niche
56 __ on (pampers)
59 Tree in Georgia?
61 Stoppages
63 Ray the Scarecrow
64 "My Friend __"
65 Deed holders
66 Presentation graphics
67 Arrive on horseback

68 Lemmon movie
69 Weighty
70 Trigonometric function
71 Lucky people?
72 OR or ER staffer
73 Joel and Jennifer
75 Contents of cocoons
76 Fill in
77 Spoke angrily
82 Splits
84 More fit
85 "Born Free" writer
86 Mr. Polo
89 Man's name meaning "gift"
91 Idled
93 Frosh residences
95 Picture in one's mind
98 Made haste
99 Josip Broz
101 Scraped (by)
102 Spartan queen
103 Greek letters
104 Lawyers: abbr.
105 Quarter M
106 Inventor Whitney
107 Hoover, e.g.
108 Group of docs
109 Paddle

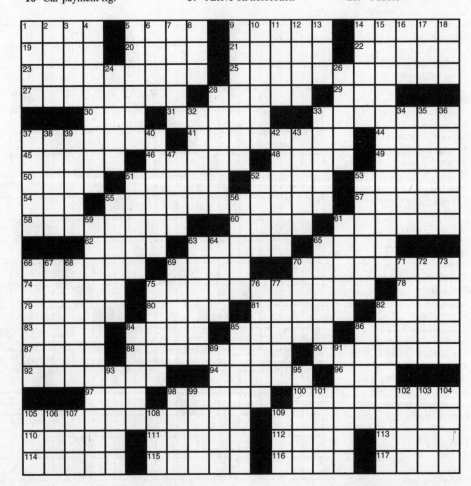

by Sheryl Scott

ACROSS

1 In the manner of
4 Showplace for antiquities
10 Some NCOs
14 Argentine grassland
19 Branch of Buddhism
20 5th-century leader
21 Dismounted
22 Actor Merlin
23 Former station from Tenn.
24 Navigational system
25 Pheasant's brood
26 Pairs of draft animals
27 Letter after zeta
28 Frankenheimer film of 1964
31 Describe as similar
33 Got to one's feet
34 Kin of birches
38 Leo's mo., usually
39 Artist Salvador
41 Fully developed
43 Sass
44 Wings hit of 1977
49 Turndown vote
50 "Born in the __"
51 Reuthers org.
52 "Full House" co-star John
53 Standing by
55 Lemon drinks
56 Possible prince?
58 __ and terminer
59 Black currant liqueur
60 Set duration
61 Tennille and Morrison
63 Texas oranges
65 Basketry willow
67 Fix indelibly
69 Weighed down
71 Highest possible
75 Redgrave and Swann
77 Singer Julius
79 Hebrew letter
80 H.H. Munro
83 Flying dish?
85 Comic Martha
87 Rote or Petty
88 Copse element
89 Assign blame to
90 Brown shades
92 Open container
93 Harem room
94 Bro's sib
95 Denver before Gilligan
98 Charged particle
99 Lounge lizard
101 Caen's river
102 Last of cash?
103 Defoe hero
105 Moolah
107 Challenges anew
111 Lead singer of the Impressions
115 Singer Sumac
116 Printer input
119 Needle case
120 Strength of character
121 Water damage
122 Make right
123 "You've Got Mail" director Ephron
124 Not so tough
125 Part of TGIF
126 Ended widowhood
127 Arduous journey
128 Laundry machines
129 Woad or anil

DOWN

1 Nahuatl speaker
2 Slowly, in music
3 "The Thief of Bagdad" co-star
4 Muscle treatments
5 Father of King Arthur
6 Kitchen appliance
7 Emerald Isle
8 __ Bator, Mongolia
9 Geometric Buddhist designs
10 Sony competition
11 Gliding steps
12 Made neat
13 Anna of "Nana"
14 Allegiance
15 Harold of "Safety Last"
16 Question
17 Born in Bordeaux
18 Switch positions
29 Neighbor of N. Mex.
30 Location of Kuala Lumpur
32 Tavern by a tube station
35 Duck past
36 Stairway past
37 Charley horse, e.g.
39 Titled ladies
40 Lacking values
42 Still resolute
44 Civilian dress
45 Copland or Spelling
46 Simpson trial judge
47 Thick, rich dressing
48 Pencil end
54 Japanese volcano
55 In jeopardy
57 Missy
59 Aromatic wood
62 Pronounce
64 Ore of lead
66 In-house #
68 Team leader, e.g.
70 Shark on the golf course
71 Ken Berry sitcom
73 Extemporize
74 Mortgage attachments
76 Baltimore newspaper
78 Buffalo hockey player
80 Seemingly indifferent person
81 Zeal
82 Actor Reeves
84 Equanimity
86 Work unit
90 Like some poetry
91 Log haulers
94 Used elbow grease
96 Hindu discipline
97 FDR group
100 Newspaper bigwig
104 Spectacle
106 Inuit craft
107 Bind again
108 Carl of the gridiron
109 University in Atlanta
110 Composer Erik
112 Tepee or yurt
113 Cold feet
114 __-bitsy
116 Golf norm
117 Put on the feed bag
118 MIA verified

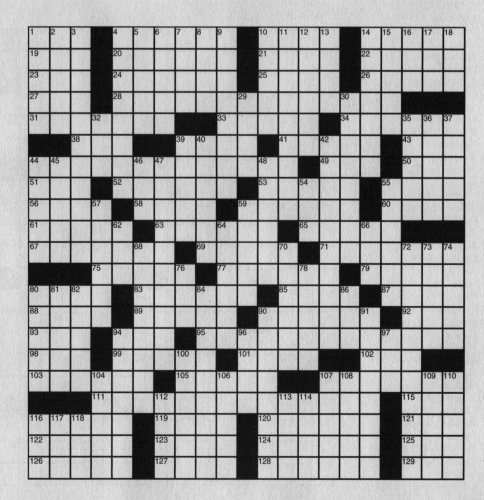

MOTHER'S PRIDE

by Josiah Breward

ACROSS

1 Discharges of pent-up emotions
10 First world chess champion Anderssen
15 Unstated
20 Ultimate combo of athletes
21 Subsequent
22 Enthusiastic cheer
23 Rachel Kempson's daughter
25 Long narrow region
26 Stevedores' grp.
27 "__ Haw"
28 Stand
30 Angry states
31 Chicago singer Peter
36 Shirley Jones' son
40 Tearful whiner
42 Row's opp.
43 Rocky ridge
44 Italian appetizer
46 Capital of Italia
49 Lane-crossing turns
52 With 87A, Blythe Danner's daughter
53 Maureen O'Sullivan's daughter
57 NYC subway line
58 Third grade
59 Hep dude
60 Parathyroid malady
61 Big __, CA
62 Parts of shoes
65 Fly apart
67 Actor Richard
68 Encourage to hurry
69 Wallach and Whitney
70 Mary Martin's son
73 Monster's loch
74 Hot shot
75 Importunes for payment
76 Psychologist Havelock
77 Damages
78 Actress Gardner
79 Alimentary canals
82 DDE's rival
83 Singer Rawls
84 Jewel
85 Diane Ladd's daughter
87 See 52A
91 Writer Jong
93 Ward of "Once and Again"
94 Superlatively durable
96 Song for nine voices
99 Candler of Coca-Cola
101 Wright and Moody
102 Roxie Roker's son
106 Frosh cap
107 With, in Arles
108 Type of plum
109 Thurman of film
111 Rehan or Huxtable
114 Odometer figures
116 Daughter of 23A
123 Rand McNally book
124 Be as one
125 Like the greenest pond

126 Crakes
127 Snouts
128 Navigational devices

DOWN

1 CCIII doubled
2 Asian sea
3 Doggedness
4 Possess like a Scotsman
5 Mornings: abbr.
6 NFL linemen
7 Body of water
8 Aviator Amelia
9 Hook's mate
10 Math subj.
11 Patriotic grp.
12 Hokkaido port
13 "Sliver" author
14 Soft-drink brand
15 Recipe abbr.
16 Pretentious performer
17 Debbie Reynolds' daughter
18 Like college walls
19 Turvy preceder
24 Offspring: abbr.
29 Corn serving
32 Manifests

33 Conical shelters
34 Make joyful
35 Hebrew letter
37 Israeli dance
38 Overhead
39 Cambridge college
40 Droop
41 Opposite of SSE
45 Astrologer Sydney
47 West of Hollywood
48 Apollo's twin
50 Maxim
51 Accent
54 Teensy
55 Hindu tunes
56 Judah's son
59 Swearers
62 Disposal problem
63 Writer Goldsmith
64 Judy Garland's daughter
65 Language group of Swahili
66 "__ Other"
70 Moon goddess
71 Wing-shaped
72 Valleys
73 Spiral-shelled mollusks
75 Sci-fi author of "Dhalgren"
77 Choke back

80 "Norma __"
81 '50s candidate Stevenson
83 Newly-hatched stage
86 Bridge hand
87 Immaculate
88 Lets go
89 Carbohydrate: suff.
90 Heaviness meas.
92 Camouflage
95 Smoking mixture
97 Heart-chart letters
98 Nerva's successor
100 Cote d'__
102 Truman's Missouri birthplace
103 Madonna title role
104 Lively dancing
105 Turns sharply
110 Gen. category
112 Medication unit
113 Acacia crawlers
115 Draft letters
117 Grant's opponent
118 Nodding response
119 Run smoothly?
120 Unit of elec.
121 Sandhurst sch.
122 Not: pref.

SIMILARITY

by Ed Voile

ACROSS

1 "Heaven Can Wait" star of 1943
7 Mickey Spillane novel
15 Parking-lot attendant
20 Meg of the LPGA
21 Certain brewer
22 "Fear of Fifty" author Jong
23 Identical
26 Boris Karloff classic
27 Abrasive tool
28 Zilch
29 Heckerling and Irving
30 __ Mawr College
32 AMA members
33 Neighbor of Tunisia: abbr.
36 Spawn of an oyster
39 Former Dolphin Marino
40 Marsh of mysteries
42 Pearl Harbor garland
43 Look like
50 Enzyme: suff.
51 John and Tyne
52 Window catches
53 B. Thomas play, "Charley's __"
54 RR stop
55 Corrosive substance
56 Segments of a whole
57 Composes epistles
59 Golf-hole starting point
60 "Smooth Operator" singer
61 Opposite of aweather
62 Impartial
63 Every practical sense
70 Coarse grass plant
71 "__ It Romantic?"
72 Sailor's saint
73 One of T. Turner's stations
74 Grinding teeth
77 Smug puritans
78 Skinner or Redding
79 Organic suffix
80 French state
81 Capt. Queeg's ship
82 Forward section
83 Part of AT&T
84 Identity proviso
89 Soggy
90 J.R. of "Dallas"
91 Beat or Jazz, e.g.
92 Government farm grp.
93 Hindu title of respect
94 Match up
95 Highland group
97 Move little by little
100 Big __, CA
101 __ the Clown
103 Made too many bookings
107 Find no difference
113 Bay window
114 Top vote getters
115 Earth pigment
116 Serengeti plaints
117 Genesis craft
118 Implant firmly

DOWN

1 Amo, amas, __ ...
2 Alda sitcom
3 "Vogue" rival
4 Meteorological conditions
5 Malarkey
6 Adversary
7 __-bitsy
8 Hanoi holiday
9 Turn left!
10 Atlanta university
11 Glossy lacquer
12 Small guitars, briefly
13 Gather in
14 Time meas.
15 Deer meat
16 Asian sea
17 Rim of a cup
18 "The Name of the Rose" author
19 Small amount
24 Morning hrs.
25 Pakistan's neighbor
30 Bengal and Biscay
31 Cellular letters
32 Red planet
33 Native Alaskan
34 Sierra __

35 Presents
36 Mount in the Cascades
37 Delicate hue
38 Golf course of the Kemper Open
39 Restoration poet
40 Built a home
41 Interruptions of continuity
44 "Lou Grant" star
45 Leaves empty
46 Slurred over
47 Infantry formations
48 Mom and dad
49 Egypt's capital
56 Going by
57 Reheating
58 Witty reply
62 Steamboat man
64 Furious
65 Growing weary
66 City on the Illinois
67 Social standing
68 Group of nine
69 "A Streetcar Named Desire" role
74 Cat calls
75 Marine mammal

76 Actress Christine
77 Discomfort
81 Voucher
82 Plant with fronds
85 Gets more gas
86 Spin
87 Actress Arthur
88 Seeker
95 Prague resident
96 Garrets
97 __ Marie Saint
98 Thick
99 Type of vault
100 End of a pun?
101 Philippine machete
102 Draft classification
103 City on the Irtysh
104 Exclamation of distress
105 Comic Jay
106 Euphemistic oath
107 Neither fish __ fowl
108 Spanish gold
109 Spanish aunt
110 Author Deighton
111 Stephen of "The Crying Game"
112 Above, in poems

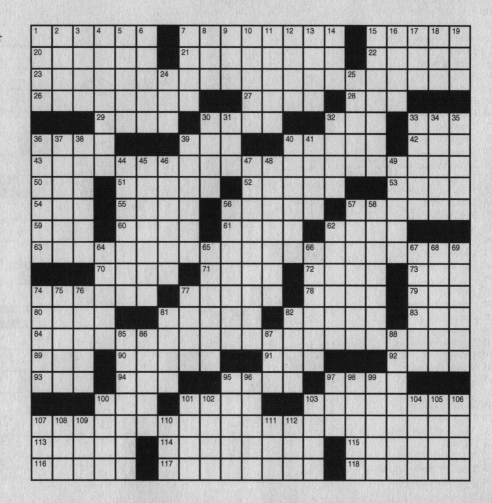

MEMORIAL DAY MESSAGE

by Alan P. Olschwang

ACROSS

1 Old hat
6 Leg-up
11 Wing-shaped
15 Nob Hill cops: abbr.
19 Tabernacle table
20 Muse of lyric poetry
21 Right-triangle ratio
22 Followers of tra
23 Extensive
24 Devoured
25 Gaffe
26 Poetic name for Ireland
27 Stead
28 Start of Will Rogers quote
31 Mountain lake
33 Clairvoyant's letters
34 Roast hosts
35 Louis of "The Steve Allen Comedy Hour"
36 Remove from a box
39 Flock youngster
41 __ up (set to drive)
43 Part 2 of the quote
50 Lift
51 Comprehend
52 Shakespearean contraction
53 City on the Dnieper
54 Opposite of WSW
55 Track tipster
56 "The Egotists" author Fallaci
59 Gaming cube
60 Do-over sprint
63 Burn slightly
66 Bee entrants
68 Part 3 of the quote
72 Pretender
75 Virginia's dance?
76 Taylor and Adoree
80 Instigate litigation
81 Flourish
83 1966 batting champion
86 Letters for 41
87 Part of VMI
89 Sure shot
90 Piano adjuster
92 Chelmsford's county
94 Part 4 of the quote
99 Architect Pei's first name
100 Take care of
101 Gordimer and others
102 Hole-making tool
104 Open __!
107 Superlative ending
110 Crowd
111 End of the quote
115 Largest island in the Marianas
118 Musical Horne
119 Discomfort
120 Stop, look and look?
121 Vibrant
122 Circle parts
123 Quod __ demonstrandum
124 Neighbor of Japan
125 "John Brown's Body" poet
126 Dates regularly
127 Crime-stopper Eliot
128 Sugary
129 Consumers

DOWN

1 Gloomy atmosphere
2 Jai follower?
3 More flexible
4 Considerable cacti
5 Afore
6 Complaint
7 Speak one's mind
8 Solemn promises
9 Church tops
10 Theatrical award
11 Model maker
12 Spring bloomer
13 Old-womanish
14 Stuffed full
15 Offed
16 Everywhere
17 Author of "Historia Naturalis"
18 "Divine Comedy" poet
28 __ thin air
29 San __, Italy
30 North Sea feeder
32 Lose control of a tirade
36 Father of King Arthur
37 Nary a soul
38 Hence
40 Eurasian viper
42 Inuit: abbr.
44 Play about Capote
45 Break out of one's shell?
46 Believer in God
47 Not right
48 Presumptive preceder
49 Actor Montand
55 Tithe amount
56 Heraldic band
57 Former Indian leader
58 To shelter
61 Pother
62 Expense
64 Roll-call response
65 Nautical assent
67 K-O connection
69 Pentateuch
70 Instant
71 Large antelope
72 Egyptian goddess
73 Oscar winner of 1936
74 Fatal epidemic
77 Lacking blood
78 Sartre as a student?
79 Crapshooter's boxcars
82 Gowns of office
84 Brown of music
85 Algerian port
88 Even score
90 Beach acquisition
91 Seaward pull
92 Icelandic saga
93 Roofing pieces
95 Rocket cap
96 Annual golf event
97 Abound
98 Hungarian leader Imre
102 Rand novel, "__ Shrugged"
103 In what place?
105 Bowler's conversion
106 Also known as
108 Panic
109 Minimum crowd?
112 Craps option
113 Pops the question
114 Rhythm
116 Affirm
117 N.L. team
121 __ Simbel

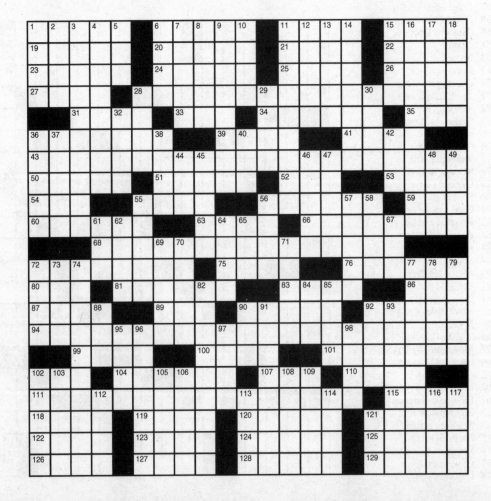

SHADY CREATURES

by Arthur S. Verdesca

ACROSS

1 Bucks' leader?
5 Destiny
10 Watered, as a lawn
15 __-in-the-wool
19 Surrounded by
20 False name
21 Essence of roses
22 Facility
23 Mirrored tarpon?
25 Pale ride?
27 Cinematic teasers
28 Barker's customer
30 Assented silently
31 Of sound mind
32 Paint additives
33 Numbers pro
34 Marsh wader
37 Fawning sycophant
38 Icy dessert
42 Copycat
43 Drunken
45 Christian celebration
48 "Coppelia" composer Delibes
49 Torso
50 European white-tailed eagle
51 Roe source
52 Military theorist von Clausewitz
53 Dog tags, e.g.
54 Envious simian?
58 Rhodes of the scholarships
59 Agave drinks
61 Like some college walls
62 Studebaker stoppers
63 Not invited
64 Product name
65 Arboreal ape, for short
66 Up and about
68 Take care of
69 Quality
72 Daughter of Ops
73 Midas' bird?
75 Magnetite or hematite
76 Ludwigshafen mister
77 Number of votes cast
78 Small bottle
79 Performing couples
80 Suffix for a language
81 Stevedore, at times
83 "Broadway __ Rose"
84 __ Royale, MI
85 Shoulder muscle
87 Slur over
89 Intuits
90 Mo. for Leos
91 Mountainous
93 Man of the Peacock Throne
95 Soviet dictator
98 Nothing __!
99 Beverage servers
103 Top-notch fish?
105 Well-tanned fish?
107 Medicinal plant
108 Signal interference

109 Was under the weather
110 Information
111 Tear
112 Lugged
113 Eldredge and Woodbridge
114 Affront

DOWN

1 "Two Years Before the __"
2 Umm al Qaywayn leader
3 Monster of the Mojave?
4 Warning
5 Singing Carpenter
6 Actress Woodard
7 Jacob the journalist
8 Grad. degrees
9 Butt collector
10 Iowan
11 Different
12 Moves emotionally
13 Snack
14 Thoroughly wet
15 Himalayan cedar
16 Scotland __
17 In __ (in actual being)
18 Exploit
24 Enthusiastic vigor
26 Optimist

29 Lend a hand
32 Twelve
34 Sister's clothes?
35 Lyric poem
36 Blushing rodent?
37 Shades
38 Stick around
39 Night bird?
40 Eldritch
41 Road charges
43 Composer of "White Christmas"
44 Mountain nymph
46 Made a request
47 Cast off
52 "The Family Circus" cartoonist
54 Sarcastic taunts
55 Bogged down
56 Egg-shaped
57 Lightweight fabric
58 __ myrtle
60 Family name of several Indy winners
62 Bumbershoot
64 Ball VIP
65 Body part
66 Yearned (for)

67 "Harlem Nights" co-star
68 Auctioneer's last word
69 "Common Sense" author
70 Fairy-tale villain
71 Affirmatives
73 Stimulate
74 Get around
77 Moving
79 Bitter-enders
81 St. __ Cardinals
82 Fretted
83 Typographical ornament
86 Spoke
88 Vietnam Memorial artist
89 Undeniable truth
91 Allow in
92 Set free
93 Stitched
94 Rounds of applause
95 Practice boxing
96 Mah-jongg piece
97 Soon
99 Spilled the beans
100 Horse color
101 Ballet skirt
102 Wild guess
104 Old card game
106 Carnival city, casually

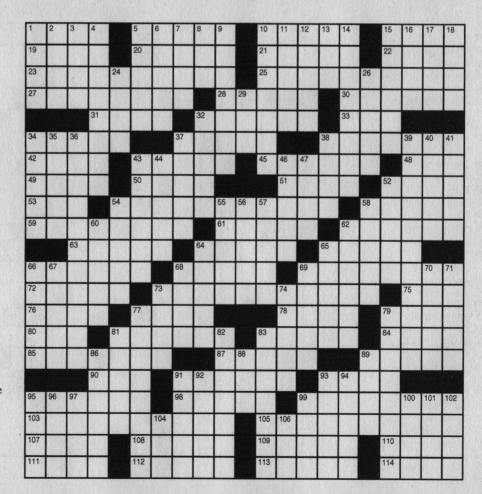

YOU ARE WHAT YOU WEAR

by Josiah Breward

ACROSS

1 Tex-Mex menu items
9 Stopper for a cask
13 Man who made a Mexican purchase
20 Take back into custody
21 Zeno of __
22 Transparent material
23 Co-star of "Dr. No"
25 Carnivorous fish
26 Golden glove?
27 Has intentions
29 Actress Blythe
30 "__ Cannonball"
33 Paquin of "The Piano"
34 River inlet
36 Pastoral poems
37 Portents
38 Floating jail?
39 Half quart
40 Part of a tour
41 Campus military org.
42 Author of "Deliverance"
45 "Lohengrin" lady
48 Arnold's crime
50 Poetic meadows
51 Moselle tributary
53 Resistance measure
54 Servings
56 Seaweed
58 "__ Doubtfire"
59 By way of
60 Position properly
62 Brewer's grain
64 Identifiers
66 Cotton of poor quality
69 Girl of "Our Gang"
72 Peeves
73 Procreates
76 Moolah
77 Trademark antidepressant
80 Eur. nation
81 Contented comments
83 House servant
85 Lunch counter
89 Verse opener?
90 Qatar's capital
92 Ancient temple
94 Getty of "The Golden Girls"
95 Seaport on Okinawa
97 Antiapartheid activist
100 Affirmative votes
101 Kin of the FBI
103 Gray and Candler
104 Oroville and Aswan
105 Chic
106 Correct: pref.
108 Moroccan city
109 Marine shockers
110 Captivates
111 Extrusion gadgets
113 Surgical thread
115 Island group off Galway
116 Island country near Florida
118 "Star Trek: Voyager" star
123 Repeat
124 Dullea of "2001: A Space Odyssey"
125 Unequivocal
126 Mini-pie
127 Lemon drinks
128 Fuel measuring device

DOWN

1 Play about 4D
2 "__ the fields..."
3 Swed. flyers
4 Author of "In Cold Blood"
5 George of "Disraeli"
6 The Grim Reaper
7 Space weapon abbr.
8 RR stop
9 Waters north of the Aleutians
10 Muslim scholars
11 Capone's nemesis
12 Of the stomach
13 Pass
14 Word with rock or rain
15 Jump the tracks
16 Straphanger
17 "Lethal Weapon" star
18 One Barrymore
19 Approaches
24 Book before Hosea
28 Sty comments
30 Value
31 Dean Martin hit, "That's __"
32 Narcotic nut
33 Branch
35 Mr. T's group
38 Slammed
39 Another name for Mount Nebo
42 "Turbulent Indigo" singer Mitchell
43 Spotted dog
44 Campfire whopper
46 Avoid work
47 Pile up
49 Knight's title
52 Pretoria's nation: abbr.
55 Unforeseen obstacle
57 Hanging to one side
61 Neat and tidy
63 Rocky pinnacles
65 Yankee 7
66 Unrestricted weapon
67 Athlete's job site
68 "Lois & Clark" star
70 Gaucho's plains
71 Ukraine river
74 Man of the house
75 Like broken horses
78 Actress Pitts
79 Perform
82 Bundle
84 Unsteady walkers
86 Dim with tears
87 Frighten
88 Pauses
91 Boobs
93 More old-hat
96 Fundamentally
98 Polish dance
99 Hesitation sounds
102 Prom dress
105 __ aleichem!
106 Planetary path
107 Rodeo rope
109 Composer Blake
110 Salad green
112 Fill too much
114 Hammered on a slant
115 Eban of Israel
117 Matched collection
119 Chasing game
120 Cart track
121 Had a bite
122 Saul's uncle

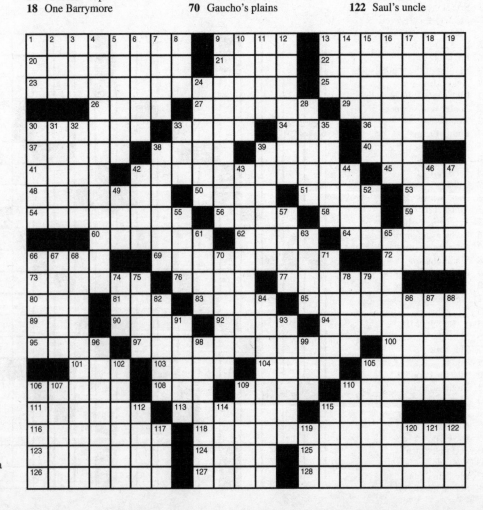

by Ed Voile

ACROSS

1 Dianne of "Hannah and Her Sisters"
6 Dined in a restaurant
12 Teddy Roosevelt's home, __ Hill
20 Relative by marriage
21 Group of Italian islands
22 Wearing a Muslim headdress
23 Start of Peter De Vries quote
26 Abode of buzzers
27 GM make, briefly
28 City near Cleveland
29 Evergreen
30 Grp. for mom-&-pop stores
31 Dos Passos trilogy
32 Word with acid or oxide
33 Castro of Cuba
34 Tennessee team
36 Part 2 of the quote
38 Removes blocks
39 Expiate
40 Jimmy and Tommy of jazz
41 Gardener's tools
42 Nebbish
43 Egyptian dry measure
44 Flat fish
45 Learning org.
48 Deg. with teeth?
49 Small ice field
50 Ballyhoo
53 Sound stages
54 Leak slowly
55 Had desires
57 Travels by glider
58 Part 3 of the quote
63 Radioactivity unit
64 Pizza slices, perhaps
65 Shakespearean lament
66 1996 Tony-winning musical
67 Counsel
68 Clipped-off piece
69 Tatami
72 U.S. Open golf champion of 1994
73 French cheese
74 Wear away
76 "The __ Ranger"
77 Keep in check
78 Food evaluators
81 Philippines machetes
82 Hosted
85 Part 4 of the quote
86 Bly or Bloch
87 Floorboard support
88 Unit of volume
89 Musician's booking
90 TV oldie, "__ Ramsey"
91 R & B pioneer, __ James
92 Antenna
93 Artist Mondrian
95 Printer's measure
96 End of the quote
100 Woody?
101 Dwarflike creatures
102 Kukla's friend
103 Most prone to be impudent
104 Contents of a will
105 Compact __

DOWN

1 Resist
2 Restrained
3 Lifts
4 Set aside
5 Northwest rival, once
6 Wing part
7 Deadlocked
8 Poetry collection
9 Lummox
10 Variety of hornblende
11 Hay grass
12 Nautical passage
13 Of gold
14 Toothy smile
15 Lawyers' grp.
16 Chatterers
17 Lake near Utica
18 "The Jerk" director
19 Ford flops
24 Profit's partner?
25 "Hamlet" tapestry
31 One to Therese
32 Plane-crash investigation grp.
33 Take off
35 In addition
36 Protuberance
37 Mine output
38 Coke or Pepsi
40 Paid a surprise visit
41 Make a manual connection?
43 Pub orders
44 On __ (without guarantee)
45 Approach
46 Tours to be?
47 Org.
49 Gala
50 Terre __, IN
51 Theater sec.
52 Singles
53 Puts in turf
54 Narrow cut
55 Berra of baseball
56 Old English letters
57 Hand blow
58 Pasture measure
59 Two-man fight
60 Coffee servers
61 La __ gauche
62 Nastase of tennis
67 Parched
68 Classify
69 Potential mountains?
70 Lacking appetite
71 Likely legal precedents
73 Borscht ingredient
74 Of a people: pref.
75 Actor Stephen
76 Lofting shot
77 Used-goods transactions
78 Dutch flower
79 On the loose
80 Ground-hugging stems
81 Marshland
82 Expels
83 Japanese monster
84 Urban centers
85 London borough
86 Moreno or Rudner
88 Some carnival performers
89 V-formation flock
92 Racer Luyendyk
93 Cougar
94 "New Jack City" co-star
95 Longhaired sheepdog
97 Half of MCII
98 E-mail period
99 Pentagon grp.

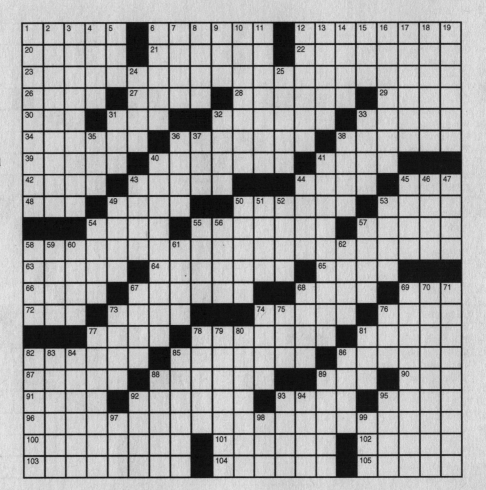

by Robert H. Wolfe

ACROSS

1 Without-delay acronym
5 Vilify
11 Czech or Slovak
15 Israeli port on the Bay of Haifa
19 Expose
20 Painter Modigliani
21 Ivy League school
22 Space
23 CC in the military
26 Naked
27 Rustle
28 Bad time for Caesar
29 Monotonous speaker
31 Live oak
34 Actress Lollobrigida
36 Entertainer Zadora
37 Gear tooth
38 Cheerleader's cheer
39 CC to a mechanic
45 "Thou __ not..."
48 Currently occupied
49 Of milk
50 Gentler
51 Spanish article
52 Stellar whale
53 Prescribed amount
56 Prejudices
58 Alluring women in Islamic paradise
60 Woven fabrics
61 Sugar bowl's companion
63 __ wheel
64 Team's charm
65 His companion?
66 CC to a banker
69 Otto I's realm
70 Weather-map line
72 Miniature whirlpools
73 Thoroughfares
75 Table
76 Remnant
77 Donahue of "Father Knows Best"
78 Customary extras, briefly
79 Canned
80 Memo acronym
81 Host
84 Runniest and squishiest
86 Marker made of stones
88 Swat again
89 CC to an educator
93 180 degrees from WSW
94 PC maker, once
95 Northwest Indian flat bread: var
96 "Dies __" (day of wrath)
97 Discordant sounds
100 Intervene
102 Work for
104 Kemp of the NBA
106 Ringlet
107 CCs to a nurse
114 Drugstore chain
115 Israel's airline
116 City in northern Spain
117 "Limp Preludes for a Dog" composer Satie
118 Future plant
119 Lairs
120 Full-width headline
121 Gentlewoman

DOWN

1 Letters openers
2 __ Paulo, Brazil
3 Upper limb
4 Coke rival
5 Raving lunatic
6 Heckerling and Irving
7 Walesa of Solidarity
8 Bride's vow
9 Valued person
10 Election hopeful
11 "Auld Lang __"
12 Young Scots
13 Ginger __
14 Jury findings
15 River of Florence
16 CC to an ecumenist
17 Western events
18 Become apparent
24 Arista
25 Hebrew month
30 Garden tool
31 Former, once
32 Okinawa port
33 CC to a merchant
34 Wildebeests
35 "__ a Wonderful Life"
36 Hocus __
40 Crude workers?
41 __ cuantos (a few)
42 Pastors, rabbis, priests et al.
43 Somewhat past due
44 Splashes in the shallows
46 "Star Wars" princess
47 Mine vehicle
52 Execrable
54 Mall unit
55 Photorealist painter
57 Scorch
58 Paid attention to
59 Senator Hatch of Utah
60 Alarm clock, e.g.
61 Scold mildly
62 Change an alarm
63 Unable to sit still
64 DLIII doubled
67 Kidnapped heiress Patty
68 London borough
71 Broom of twigs
74 Alaska town
76 Advertising connection
77 Australian lake
79 Provided backing
80 Organized record
82 "__ kleine Nachtmusik"
83 French summers
85 Pueblo dwellers
86 Pipe type
87 Just like
89 Whitefish kin
90 Not sharp
91 Round line: abbr.
92 Sweet-talk
98 Be beholden
99 Pentium makers
101 Proceed slowly but surely
102 Abba of Israel
103 Feels poorly
104 "Nana" star Anna
105 Conceal
108 Caps ending?
109 Actress Gabor
110 Diarist Anaïs
111 Period
112 Disencumber
113 Cloud cover

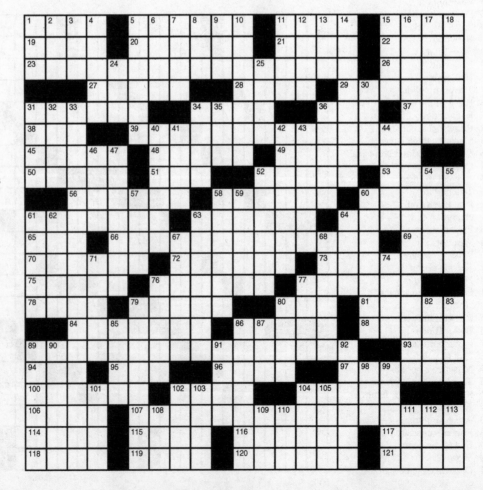

By Robert H. Wolfe

ACROSS

1 Comic Foxx
5 Revolve
9 Evergreens
13 Buddhist tower
19 Nastase of tennis
20 Switch tail?
21 Pierre's girlfriend
22 Of great suffering
23 Part of an alluring siren's figure?
26 Most rational
27 Hurricane heart
28 Classic Pontiac letters
29 Soup dish
30 Breathy utterance
31 Remove sails
33 Distress signal
35 Eat at a restaurant
38 Harass
40 Printer's spaces
41 Mortise insert
44 Frank Herbert sci-fi classic
45 Holy war
47 Asian apes, casually
49 Edge
50 Apiece
53 Kind of skirt
54 Winter destination, often
55 Dad
56 Scrooge exclamation
57 John or Sean
58 Exchange charge
59 Out-and-out
61 Highland child
63 Our lang.
64 Stat starter
65 Neet competitor
66 Cowboy bars
68 Swed. flyers
69 Indicate
72 Silver peso
73 Anna of "Nana"
75 Actor Mineo
77 Serviceable
78 Northern
80 Old Capri cash
81 Holmes hints
83 Actress Long
84 Before, briefly
85 Type of energy
87 Injure
88 Lab gel
89 Multi-computer syst.
90 Co-founder of "The Tatler"
91 Pompous speech
93 French state
95 French heads
96 Moody or Silver
97 Untie
101 Covered (a roadbed) with broken stones
103 Kind of race
105 Beast
106 Rx place
107 Quick squirt
110 Libation station potation
112 Media business grp.
113 Virgules
115 Maintain conservatism?
118 Typewriter roller
119 Bancroft or Boleyn
120 High time, clockwise
121 Stagger
122 Setting down
123 Subsequently
124 Son of Seth
125 Jacuzzi effect

DOWN

1 Arrive on horseback
2 Comic Boosler
3 Restaurant patrons
4 U. acquisition
5 Spanish artist
6 Validation
7 Valuable note
8 Complete lack of status?
9 "Penelope" composer
10 Nagy of Hungary
11 Split
12 Observed
13 Quarterback opening?
14 Once more
15 Rang a big bell?
16 Teen make-out limit?
17 German article
18 Highway-sign abbr.
24 Ova lobber
25 Blaspheme
32 Hankering
34 Intro
35 Over
36 Marriage
37 Lure
39 Sailors' drinks
41 Rowdy thugs
42 Sgt. Bilko
43 "Star Wars" prequel planet
46 Places
48 Low-altitude cloud
50 Flows back
51 Honor student's grades?
52 Kids in the theater?
54 New York resort lake
57 Parkas
60 Massive public unrest
62 Libertine
67 Kitty, you can't give birth here!?
68 Episodic television show
69 Dust-jacket info
70 Charles Lamb
71 Get closer
73 Wintry forecast
74 Championship
75 Fish area?
76 Woman grad
78 City on the Amazon delta
79 Spout off
82 & others
86 Be without
88 Idol follower?
91 Royal George
92 On the wagon
94 Papeete's location
98 Increased suddenly
99 Marked with acid
100 In an orderly way
102 Carrying a burden
103 Grow on the vine
104 Web name
107 Three-hand card game
108 Phnom __, Cambodia
109 Russo or Descartes
111 Eye part
113 1-of-a-kind
114 Cup or pay attachment?
116 Heavy weight
117 Rage

FREEDOM OF SPEECH

by Alan P. Olschwang

ACROSS

1 Walks worriedly
6 California wine county
10 Napoleon victory site
14 Medieval trade association
19 Soap substitute
20 Thoroughly corrupt
21 Biographer of Henry James
22 Cacophonous
23 One of the Philippine Islands
24 Hit on the head
25 Pueblo dweller
26 Speech impediments
27 Start of Evan Esar quote
31 Winter hrs. in Boston
32 Tallinn's land
33 Czech or Slovak
34 Dripped
36 Rue
38 Bathe
40 System of import duties
43 Hindu music form
46 Part 2 of quote
49 Incarnation of Vishnu
52 Old Testament boat
53 Ball-shaped hammerhead
54 Mailed
55 Actress Bertinelli
57 Wide shoe width
60 __ Spumante
62 Entirely
63 Snorer's peril
66 Whiskey shot
69 "__ Gay"
73 Part 3 of quote
78 Boredom
79 Deion's nickname
80 Diarist Nin
81 City in central Israel
82 Normandy town
85 Military science
87 Proposition
89 Navy mascot
92 Words of realization
95 Unrefined mineral
98 More hackneyed
99 Part 4 of quote
104 Meeting: abbr.
105 Simoleons
106 Marmara and Galilee
107 Exhibit a short fuse
110 Mortar's partner
112 Radar image
114 Beatles movie
118 Cool dude
120 End of quote
123 Small antelope
125 Competent
126 Urban renewal target
127 Frighten
128 1988 Olympic Games city
129 Builder's map
130 Ms. Fitzgerald
131 Medicinal plant
132 "Driving Miss Daisy" star Jessica
133 Stitches
134 Munich's river
135 Photorealist painter Richard

DOWN

1 Cheap jewelry
2 Indian nursemaids
3 Solar-system transient
4 Rich in detail
5 Tranquil
6 Hummingbird sips
7 Declare
8 Pyramidal tree
9 Monovalent radical
10 Christian God
11 Dead Sea kingdom
12 Katmandu tongue
13 Analogous
14 Legal part of the Talmud
15 Jackie's second
16 Steep descent
17 Gullible dupes
18 Formerly, formerly
28 Italian Mr.
29 Bath powder
30 Theophilus and Mark
35 Expunging
37 Nature grp.
39 Bigwig's letters
41 Bog
42 Overweight
43 Damage severely
44 King Arthur's paradise
45 Unit of volume
47 Stretch (out)
48 Darjeeling, e.g.
50 Persian Gulf peninsula
51 Finished growing
56 Part of the U.K.
58 Minneapolis suburb
59 Sea eagle
61 Playful prankster
64 German article
65 Dijon donkey
67 Turkish title
68 Douglas' isle
70 Limestone grain
71 Unleashes
72 Vipers
74 Malleable
75 At present
76 Siesta
77 Soil
83 Half a quarter
84 Advisory grp.
86 Asian nation: abbr.
88 Calls incorrectly
89 Jewel
90 John's Yoko
91 Ratification
93 Coordinated outfit
94 Dutch commune
96 Uses new letters?
97 Ending for car or cant
100 With mean intent
101 Alternative to capsules
102 Christiania, today
103 California observatory peak
108 Game counter
109 Relaxed
111 Bounds
113 Japanese immigrant
115 U of the U.N.
116 "Games People Play" author
117 Bombeck and others
118 Amount paid
119 Region
121 Talon
122 City south of Moscow
124 Flower at first

LUNAR CLIPS

by Sheryl Scott

ACROSS

1 Maintains one's subscription
7 Tributes
14 Fight, in Dogpatch
20 Decorative bush
21 Serving trolley
22 "Sense and Sensibility" heroine
23 Jules Verne classic
26 Isl. of Australia
27 Maglie and Mineo
28 __ Paulo, Brazil
29 Last letter
30 Grass bristles
31 Ambiance
32 Sick and tired
34 Take it on the __
36 Small portion
37 Author of "Blue Highways"
43 Eskimo
44 Giant Mel
45 War casualties grp.
46 Sculptor Oldenburg
48 Carp and minnows
49 Ex-Cub Sandberg
51 Rural
54 Old Gaelic
55 Wide smile
56 Wonder
57 Mil. rank
58 Racetrack shape
60 Summer hrs. system
61 Abnormally located, as of an organ
63 "I Love Lucy" production company
65 Make free (of)
67 1961 hit by the Capris
73 Hindu title
74 Straying
75 Vilifier
76 Individual Apples
79 Bus. letter abbr.
81 Some MDs
82 Go, in Glasgow
83 Petty of "A League of Their Own"
84 French cop: slang
86 Author of "The Horse You Came In On"
88 Whey's partner
89 Togo's capital
90 Walk-on part
92 Numero __
93 Drivers' org.
94 Cut off
95 Robert A. Heinlein novel, with "The"
101 Our sun
102 "__ bin ein Berliner:" JFK
103 Murdered
104 Brief periods
105 Vicinity
107 Men
109 K-O connection
110 Blackbird
111 Radicals of the '60s
114 Eugene O'Neill play, with "A"

119 Sand trap
120 Aromatic tropical shrub
121 The Continent
122 Puts to a test
123 Gardeners, at times
124 Conceive

DOWN

1 Flat float
2 Cornell or Pound
3 Ancient temple
4 Shade tree
5 Diver's outfit
6 African expanse
7 Somme summers
8 Teachers' org.
9 Bucket in a Buick
10 Groups of eight
11 Elephant rider
12 NYC subway line
13 The gamut
14 Prepare leftovers
15 Pub pint
16 Lower layer of Earth's outer crust
17 Winter ride
18 Silly stuff
19 German dadaist
24 Oater actor Jack

25 __-Jaffa, Israel
31 Those who transfer property ownership
32 Outdoor gala
33 Advanced degs.
35 CCX x X
37 Small device
38 Graft a plant while still growing
39 Trademark thermoplastic
40 Wolf modifier
41 Dine al fresco?
42 Corrida cheer
47 Sun's fall
49 Bringing up
50 Org. founded in 1858
51 Fastens again
52 Labor groups
53 Collided and rebounded
57 One Gershwin
59 Queue
62 Dumas __
63 Of gold, in France
64 Iranian desert, Dasht-e __
66 U.K. rotary-phone users
68 Actress Mercouri
69 Russian ruler
70 Channel
71 Mythological messenger

72 Attempters
76 Low mil. letters
77 Vociferous
78 Moolah
80 Subduer
82 Marianas island
85 Bus. bigwig
87 Scale for minerals
88 "High Hopes" lyricist
91 Sailors' admin.
93 Stupid
94 Kissimmee's neighbor
96 Wound discharges
97 Maintain
98 Butted
99 A-ha!
100 Prokofiev or Rachmaninov
101 Dance in duple time
106 "Diana" singer
108 Fricassee
110 Post-grad degs.
111 Greek colonnade
112 Part of N.Y.P.D.
113 Dundee dagger
115 Eccentric
116 Dimension of color
117 Knight's title
118 Three in Italia

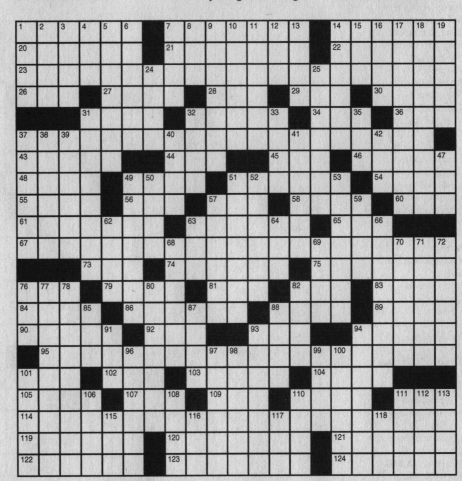

CASUAL ROBERTS

by Josiah Breward

ACROSS

1 Event official
8 Altered to suit
15 Remove hidden ears
20 Aquarium need
21 Beer choice
22 Entertainer Massey
23 Famed Edinburgh dog
25 Composer Berg
26 Killer whale
27 Beatles song, "__ Blues"
28 Scottish Gaelic
29 Unsaturated hydrocarbon
30 City on the Ganges
32 Trip in the bush
35 Mesabi Range product
36 Gets up
38 Horse somebody bet on?
41 Out of the bus.
42 Vietnam Memorial artist
43 RR stop
45 Occupant: abbr.
46 Simon or Sedaka
47 Young Scots
48 Bethlehem visitors
50 Top-drawer
52 Gather strength
53 Baby's seat?
54 Early Sinatra fans
58 Pursue with gusto
61 Kin of cleats
64 Spanish painter
65 Brightest star in Auriga
66 Yucatan year
67 Abscond
68 Balin or Claire
69 Focal points
70 German article
71 Mates of the little women?
73 Disney sci-fi flick
74 O. Henry and others
76 Impose a fine
77 Doohickey
79 __-de-dah
80 Disinformation
81 Maglie and Mineo
82 Milky Way maker
86 Prophet
88 Schism
89 Pouchlike structure
91 Stitch
93 One Tweedle
94 Dancer Charisse
95 Friend of Howdy Doody
98 "Canto General" poet
100 Leading lady
102 TNT
104 Singular performances
105 John and Maureen
106 Vocal inflection
108 "To Have and Have __"
110 Island east of Java
111 Crazies
112 In a state of confusion
116 Coeur d'__, ID
117 Weapons stockpile
118 Sea otter's meal
119 Make fairway repairs
120 "Mommie __"
121 Vacation spots

DOWN

1 Tropical cycad
2 Lizard containers
3 Putting up
4 Keenen Ivory or Damon
5 Booze, butts and bullets bureau
6 Actor Calhoun
7 Helps with the dishes
8 Showery mo.
9 City lawyers, for short
10 Einstein and Gore
11 City on the Illinois
12 Bar bills
13 European river
14 "L.A. Law" co-star
15 Conversation
16 Burstyn or Barkin
17 Participate in a Halloween game
18 Not yet broadcast
19 Solans
24 Part of U.A.E.
29 Verbal
31 DDE's opponent
33 Front parts
34 Burrows or Fortas
35 Laverne's L, e.g.
37 Stationary sculptures
39 Like some gases
40 Lacking: suff.
44 Titled folk
47 Word before duck
49 Arabic Mac
51 Wall St. abbr.
52 Called back
53 Actor/director Ida
55 Clumsy
56 Egyptian judge of the dead
57 Atomic number 54
58 Author of "Marie Gubbe"
59 Came to earth
60 Brown shades
61 Sarcastic chuckle
62 Millstone
63 Olympic events
65 Reef formers
69 __ bean
72 Tolerate
73 Eighth Greek letter
75 Big Blue computer?
77 Lovers' spat
78 Fancy cravat
80 Longest sentence?
83 Worshipper
84 Aromatic
85 Coasts
86 Learned one
87 One of two mask features
88 Operates
89 Any individual
90 Arab robe
92 Director Craven
95 Showing a preference
96 Certain cavalryman
97 U2 singer
99 Snook
101 University of Maine town
103 Of the lungs
106 Become weary
107 Peak in Greece
109 Hollow cylinder
112 Pa
113 Pas' mates
114 3-letter sandwich
115 Spanish article

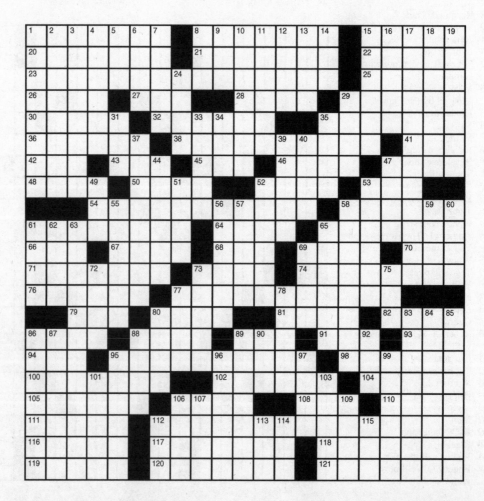

DOWN UNDER

by Edgar Fontaine

ACROSS

1 Links activity
5 "J'accuse!" author Zola
10 Fine-tune
15 R & B singer James
19 Alternative to butter, for short
20 Sophia of "Two Women"
21 Italian white wine
22 Seed cover
23 Olfactory trigger
24 World's largest coral colony
27 Landed
29 Boardwalk extensions
30 Cabbage salad
31 Borderline
35 Endeavors
37 Beatles drummer Starr
41 Chills and fevers
42 Russian money
44 Business operators
47 Flesh of coconuts
49 Creation mythology of 59A
51 Quid pro quo
52 Belligerent god
53 Sleeper spy
55 Vote in
57 Knight's address
58 Open hostilities
59 Indigen of 84A
63 Organic compound
65 Device to regulate spring tension
68 Commands
70 Timid
71 Trading centers
72 Pink-legged wading bird
73 Calibrated glass tube
75 Purple hue
77 Encapsulate
79 Starves
82 Wind off
84 Site of Fort Jackson penal colony
86 Compass dir.
87 Showing embarrassment
88 Imminent danger
90 Pioneer director Fritz
91 Jose's home
92 Love of Don Quixote?
94 Eucalyptus consumer
98 Even badder?
100 Certified
102 Keaton and Feinstein
104 Correct
105 Likable loser
106 Relish
108 Maladies
110 Move very slowly
113 Financier Green
115 Guam or Yukon: abbr.
116 Jorn Utzon's masterpiece
121 Surprise attack
125 Leader
126 Shuts with force
127 Icelandic currency
128 Simply

129 Remnants
130 To the point
131 Parts of speech
132 Reebok rival

DOWN

1 Moo __ gai pan
2 Like MacDonald?
3 August sign
4 Rummagers
5 Cager Baylor
6 Portable cannon
7 Rage
8 Bound upward
9 Give a right to
10 Former Russian system
11 Of less quality
12 Dumbo's wing
13 See 26D
14 Bow-stern connection
15 Silverfish relatives
16 Uno, due, __...
17 Deadlock
18 Candidate Landon
25 Cleveland suburb
26 With 13D, unique person
28 One Simpson
31 Showy parrots

32 Spartan markets
33 Media mogul from down under
34 Suburb of Springfield, MA
36 Grinner
38 Sydney's state
39 Cereals
40 Fish hawk
43 Fox's title
45 Pierre's soul
46 Narrowest stretch
48 Brainy
50 Fundamental principle
54 More than well-rounded?
56 Cadences
60 Scintillas
61 Ground cereal
62 Layabout
64 Lower digits
66 Squirrel away
67 Lounge lizard
69 "Lady of __"
72 Stern oar
74 Mental picture
75 Wall art
76 Listless and weak
78 Water nymphs
79 Burst into flames

80 Jewish mystic
81 Stretches of grassy turf
83 Birds' display areas
85 Mr. Dershowitz
89 Lobster eggs
91 River of the Oklahoma panhandle
93 Stirs memories
95 Contrary
96 Flora and fauna of a region
97 Made of baked clay
99 Swerve
101 Nary a one
103 Participates as a visitor
107 Attention getters
109 Prognosticators
111 Saclike structure
112 Perforation
114 Spinning toy
116 Haggard novel
117 Hankering
118 Man of the house
119 __ for the course
120 S. Amer. nation
122 Communal cuckoo
123 Kind
124 Woad or anil

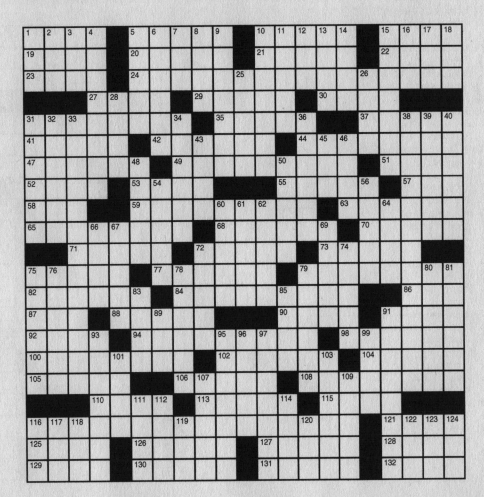

GET A GRIP

by Ed Voile

ACROSS

1 Spirit away
7 Verdi opera
13 Moral
20 Barely sufficient
21 Jeanne of "Jules et Jim"
22 Aquamarine
23 Evidence desperation
25 Sentence analysis
26 Swenson of "Benson"
27 Pen fill
28 Louis and Bill
30 Tears
31 Seize suddenly
32 24-hr. info stn.
33 Contribution to the pot
35 Raising (the pot)
38 Eyelike window
40 Available to anyone
42 Thermoplastic resin: abbr.
45 Bones in forearms
46 Iridescent gemstones
47 "Quando rapita in estasi," e.g.
48 Film spool
49 Matched groups
50 Quantum theorist
51 Trebek of "Jeopardy!"
52 Form of bingo
53 Carpe diem!
57 Slick and Kelly
58 Easy as __
61 Put to sea
62 Pub drinks
63 Two-syllable foot
64 Backslid
66 Hesitation sounds
67 Bestowers
68 Guillotined poet Andre
69 Coagulate
70 Fluff
71 Booming jet, for short
72 Door elements
73 Primary resident
76 Anvil in the ear
77 Dimwit
78 Competent
79 French female friend
83 Old English letters
84 Present starter?
85 Vaults
87 Maliciously derogatory
88 112.5 degrees from W
89 Vital singles, for instance
91 Dressmaker
92 Menial worker
94 St. Louis bridge
95 Bagel topper
96 Frazier's foe, often
97 Morley of "60 Minutes"
99 Bellow
101 Corn unit
102 Nabokov novel

103 Snobbery
106 Economic pressure
110 Milan's opera house
111 Extreme panic
112 Czar's edicts
113 Pollen-bearing organs
114 French detective Lupin
115 Conger catchers

DOWN

1 Of chest pains
2 Nautical hanger-on?
3 Attempt for an infield hit
4 Bear of stars
5 Police officer
6 Mark and Shania
7 Trans-Siberian RR stop
8 Young 'un
9 Make a mistake
10 Canted sheds
11 Attorney
12 River into the Wash
13 6th sense
14 Oolong or Darjeeling
15 Singer Emmylou
16 "Ghosts" dramatist
17 Canned-fruit choice
18 Dad's sister

19 Pants parts
24 Former station from Tenn.
29 English poet executed for treason
32 Pool tool?
33 Isolated
34 Org. of Giants and Titans
36 Be quiet, Pierre!
37 Kin of PAL
39 Highland honey
40 Supported
41 Celebrations
43 Thin surface layers
44 Nearest
46 More squishy
48 Show shock, e.g.
50 Prejudices
51 "__ Fideles"
52 Author of "Jane Eyre"
54 Catches sight of
55 Use a pulley
56 "St. __ Fire"
57 Rio __
58 Moore and Griffin
59 Rear ends
60 Defiant gesture
63 Warbles
65 Novelist Wilson
67 Spheres

69 Humorous or humorist
73 Intimater
74 Weapon handles
75 Hindu princess
77 Self-satisfied
80 Northern Italian cuisine
81 Worshipper
82 Unnatural aura
84 Ancient
85 Generous folk
86 Assistance
87 Jazzy instrument
89 Roman political subdivisions
90 Listener
91 Twisting force
93 Gag
95 Spanish article
97 Actress Ward
98 Greenspan, once of the Fed
100 Eight: pref.
101 To be in Toulon
102 Ring
104 Camera letters
105 Pas' mates
107 Rapping Doctor
108 Charged particle
109 Luau instrument, for short

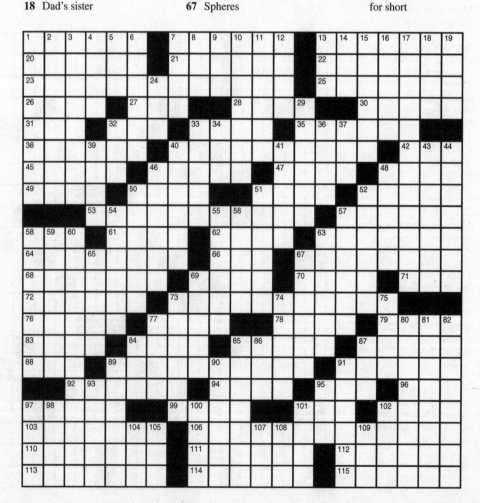

by Alan P. Olschwang

ACROSS

1 Bit of bread
6 The nearer one
10 Fete
14 Spoken examinations
19 Flaxlike fiber
20 Casa component
21 Serengeti sprinter
22 Twofold
23 Promenade
24 Without coverage?
26 Virgo's brightest star
27 Start of Cary Grant quote
29 Handcuff
31 Independent gov't agcy.
32 Jacob's first wife
33 Rajah's wife
35 Solidarity
36 Capital of Belize
38 Fowl choice
40 Too
43 Under the weather
44 Part 2 of quote
49 Less affluent
52 Sudanese gazelles
55 Double LIII
56 Piccadilly Circus statue
57 Part 3 of quote
59 Variety of melon
61 Create a fold
63 Viper
64 Runaway lovers
66 Mine find
68 Li'l man
69 Bobby of the NHL
71 Part 4 of quote
73 Ryan of "You've Got Mail"
74 Clinton cabinet member
76 Former name of Tokyo
77 Grasslands
79 Lending organ?
82 Steers
84 Collagen component
   of bone
86 Part 5 of quote
88 Tours to be?
89 Computer of "2001..."
91 Off-the-cuff comment
93 Comments to the audience
94 Part 6 of quote
97 __ Lanka
99 Collapsible shelter
100 Capers
101 Approximation
105 A NYC university
109 Ginger cookie
111 "Pursuit of the Graf __"
112 Fort Peck or Oroville, e.g.
115 Toxins, e.g
117 End of quote
120 Cogs
121 Fellow of independent
    means
123 Relish
124 Put up
125 One of HOMES
126 Orange coat

127 Imposed absence
128 Last year's frosh
129 Tree juices
130 Summers on the Somme
131 Irritates

DOWN

1 Biggio of baseball
2 Freeway exits
3 Shade
4 Distance measure
5 Scarab
6 Tidal wave
7 Straphanger's grip
8 Nastase of tennis
9 A Dee
10 Hypothetical particle
11 Expose to public scrutiny
12 Leopold's cohort
13 Soviet politician Yuri
14 Indecent
15 Age
16 Old-womanish
17 Adds some spirits
18 Blind strips
25 The Man
28 Sniggler's prey
30 Socially unstable

34 Word before bag or box
36 Max of quantum mechanics
37 Make-believe medications?
39 Nematode worm
40 Western Samoa's capital
41 Cattle calls
42 Daytime drama
44 Baden-Powell's org.
45 Bathysphere explorer
46 Summer cooler
47 Prescribed amount
48 North Sea feeder
50 Always, in a poem
51 Sis or bro
53 Stable denizen
54 Took upon oneself
58 Overplay the TLC
60 Plant person
62 Exodus pharaoh
65 City of Lenin's
   collaborations
67 Race in "The Time
   Machine"
70 Metal bolt
72 A Diamond
74 Aid in wrongdoing
75 Adam's youngest
78 Pugilists' grp.

80 The last word
81 Remainder
83 Pulley wheel
85 __ Juan Capistrano
87 Issue a ticket
90 Puts in place
92 Australian city
   on Moreton Bay
95 Predicaments
96 CIA predecessor
98 Is about to take place
101 British noble
102 Orb
103 NRC predecessor
104 Conundrum
105 "The Dresser" director
    Peter
106 January in Juarez
107 Much inclined
108 Pitfall
110 Pays heed to
112 Beelzebub
113 Soap substitute
114 Poetic ponds
116 Evening in Roma
118 Give off
119 Ankle-length skirt
122 Tuck's partner?

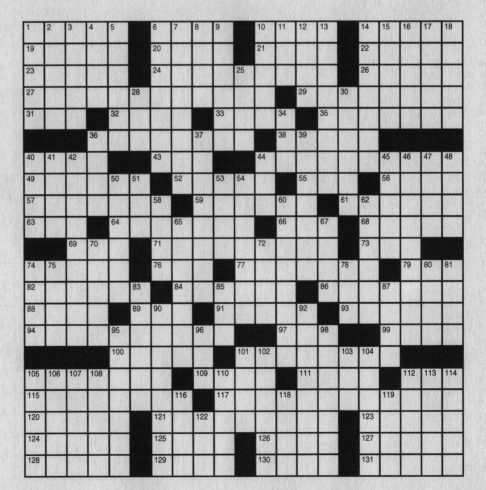

PERPS

by James E. Buell

ACROSS
1 Steeplechase or marathon
5 Of the Vatican
10 Bid
15 Slightly open
19 Astronaut Shepard
20 City southeast of Rome
21 Fielder's equipment
22 "__ Only Just Begun"
23 See regularly
24 Correct a clock
25 Drag through the mud?
26 Dumbfounded
27 Food of the gods
29 Quahogs
31 Interviewers
33 Rub the wrong way?
34 Knickknack spot
35 Oust
36 Tire holders
37 "This Is __ Tap"
38 Return of "Discovery"
41 Hourly payment
43 Floating on water
45 Bestow upon
47 Step on it!
48 Troubles
49 In the midst of
50 Iowa State city
51 Printer's measure
52 Drink for two?
53 Reeked
54 Low-cut shoe
55 River feeders
57 Like a worn LP
59 Editor's mark
60 Equip
61 Cries of contempt
62 Calculator power, often
63 Wind blast
64 Strive toward an end
67 Yarns
68 Armored-car item
72 Scolder
73 Great distance
74 Components
75 In the manner of
76 NFL receiver Jerry
77 Choppers
78 Extent covered
79 Uppity one
80 India or indelible
81 Subject
83 Wood facing
84 Squeezes (out)
85 Keep from keeping
87 Slowed one's horse
89 Consternation
91 Paddled
92 "__ of God"
93 Actor's role
96 Scoffer
98 Henry James novel, "The Turn of the __"
99 Reside beside

100 Sommer of "A Shot in the Dark"
101 Exchanged words
103 Terminate
105 Woodwind
106 Lascivious look
107 Assistants
108 Former nit
109 Use for a fee
110 Small fries
111 Has on
112 More reasonable
113 Highland tongue

DOWN
1 Velocity detector
2 San Antonio landmark
3 Second-story man
4 Strengths
5 Bagman?
6 Dined at home
7 City on the Arno
8 Opening-day pitcher
9 Throwing a deadbolt
10 Black Hills native
11 Silver-tongued bandit?
12 Watch guards
13 Plumb or Arden

14 Easy-chair occupant
15 Come to one's senses
16 Icebreaker?
17 Declare as true
18 Cincinnati's nine
28 Resistance measurement
30 Period after Mardi Gras
32 Risked a ticket
34 Paddle
35 Noteworthy periods
37 Abounding in rocks
39 Talk-show host Lake
40 Fermenting agent
41 Mental ability
42 Smart guy?
44 Oriental nursemaids
46 Sobbed
50 Distinctive atmospheres
51 Minor
53 Look with a wide-eyed gaze
54 Weaker in color
55 Moneymaker?
56 Artifices
58 Put up with
59 Coke and Pepsi
62 Yegg
63 Deep ravine

64 Bitterly pungent
65 Waxing result
66 Dip
67 Travel before takeoff
68 Locked like a lion
69 Heistmeister
70 Hand-cream ingredient
71 Chatters
74 Window subdivisions
77 Imitated
78 Subscription extensions
79 Coast
81 Lose will
82 Supervised
83 Climbing plant
86 Leaf collectors
88 Emergence
90 Unit of energy
93 Intrinsically
94 Middays
95 Narrow mountain ridge
96 Thaw
97 Bread spread, for short
98 Pop
99 Person, place or thing
102 Heavenly dessert?
104 Long, feathery scarf

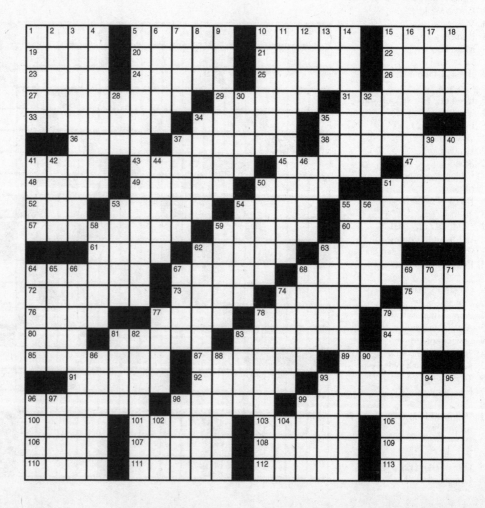

by Josiah Breward

ACROSS

1 Carte du jour
5 Crude
10 Cabbage salads
15 Hoover Dam lake
19 Stratford's river
20 Financial checkup
21 Vowel sequence
22 Furthermore
23 Anglican cathedral city
25 Body of water near Carson City
27 Feeling poorly
28 Lumberjacks
30 "Purple People __"
31 Stacks
34 More ribald
35 Looks back on
37 Cupid
38 Politician's wealthy supporter
39 Bread units
41 Sucker
42 "The Blue __"
43 Shared a boundary with
47 Short joke
49 "Moon River" composer
50 After a fashion?
51 Fabric treatments
52 Exude
54 Loathe
55 Liquid sample
56 Pen fluids
57 Prods
58 Carole King hit, "__ Too Late"
59 Use an ax
60 Emcees
62 Meadow of the Magna Carta
64 Airheaded
65 One on one's side
66 Metal container
67 Twixt 12 and 20
68 Exist
69 Actress Lupino
70 "Death in Venice" author
71 Come down to earth
72 Nickname
75 Writer Kesey
76 One who shows up
78 The self-centered 1970's
79 Emphasizes
81 Came up short
83 Compete
84 Yes man
85 Ball lasses
86 Singer Jagger
87 Follower of Mussolini
90 "__ Bailey"
91 Strongholds
92 Nile dam
93 Country once part of Colombia
95 Debt letters
96 City in the Caucasus Mountains

99 Town in central New Jersey
104 Genealogical diagram
105 Ward off
106 "Tomorrow" musical
107 September's number
108 Barflies
109 Removes skin
110 Abrupt inhalations
111 Work hard

DOWN

1 Prefix for Scottish names
2 A Gabor
3 __ compos mentis
4 Frees from restraint
5 Sandburg or Sagan
6 Cause friction
7 Idolizer
8 Wind from the Sahara
9 __ Ferryman (Charon)
10 Lumberjack, at times
11 Cordelia's father
12 Is not well
13 Chinese pan
14 Instigate litigation
15 Blahs
16 Bring joy
17 Awry
18 Accomplishers
24 Golfer Ernie
26 Abstracted musing
29 Obtain
31 Mexican coins
32 Tehran resident
33 Neighbor of Vancouver
34 Burns wildly
35 Emerge in waves
36 Occurrences
38 Viper's weapons
39 Actor Chaney
40 Corsage flowers
42 Connections
43 Baseball sluggers
44 Desert in Iran
45 Medleys
46 Fuzzy or frizzy
48 Full of fluff
49 June and July
52 Geological time period
53 Shelves over fireplaces
57 Revving
59 Municipal
60 Japanese verse form
61 Bygone
62 Got out of control
63 Final one
64 Had a meal

66 Moya or Baerga
68 Veins of riches
70 Hingis of tennis
72 Brawl
73 Proclamation
74 Stinks to high heaven
77 Sign of victory
78 Races in streams
80 Gets away
81 Dobbin's lunch pail?
82 City in the Allegheny Mountains
85 Actress Benaderet
86 Grieves
87 Abstains from eating
88 "The Jetsons" dog
89 Sugary
90 Sacrifice plays
91 Watch pocket
93 At any time
94 Feel concern
95 March 15th, e.g.
97 Snooze
98 Gardner of "The Killers"
100 Chill
101 Texas tea
102 Lennon's widow
103 Beer barrel

OLD WIVES' TALE

by Alan P. Olschwang

ACROSS

1 Holiest of cheeses?
6 Brits' raincoats, briefly
10 Ralph Ellison or Ralph Emerson's middle name
15 Vault
19 Member of the Italian nobility
20 Medicinal plant
21 Locales
22 Pause in the action
23 __ of roses
24 Evening along the Tiber
25 Buy new weapons
26 Molecule part
27 Lassos
29 "Honest" politician
31 Flows copiously
33 Start of Agatha Christie quote
37 Rat race
38 Spotted infrequently
39 Bottom line
40 Sexual equality grp.
43 Part 2 of the quote
50 Seuss or Spock
52 At the outer limits
53 Old Spanish bread?
55 A ship to remember
56 More wintry
57 Potent hallucinogen
59 Part 3 of the quote
61 Small, tropical lizards
63 Excuses
68 Taper off
69 Fraternal group member
70 Part 4 of the quote
73 Letter additions: abbr.
76 Paper quantity
78 Seattle pros, casually
79 Nautical passage
82 Part 5 of quote
86 Ad __ committee
88 Course taken
89 Lasso
90 Go back over old ground?
95 Of iris rings
97 Check
99 Part 6 of the quote
101 Preferred one
102 Sesame
104 First grandfather
105 Exclamation of discovery
106 End of quote
115 Fragile
117 157.5 degrees from S
118 Small cooking mold
119 Corrosive substance
120 Sea-going
123 Sorrowful drop
125 Potts or Oakley
126 Distinct region
127 January in Central America
128 R & B pioneer, __ James
129 Hubbubs
130 Art print: abbr.
131 Aleppo's country
132 Child's toy
133 Descended on the mother's side

DOWN

1 Puccini's stairway
2 Odin, to some
3 Mural beginning?
4 Step
5 Crevasse pinnacle
6 Rubdown pros
7 Pub potable
8 Reef material
9 Carried on ocean waves
10 Open hostilities
11 Exist
12 Smallest number
13 Australian city
14 Gradually absorbed
15 Cut a slit
16 Genuine
17 Icefield
18 Shade providers
28 Drum with fingers
30 Yikes!
32 Cushioned footstool
34 NYC gambling center
35 "Dies __"
36 Transmitted
41 Ms. Chaplin
42 Small songbird
43 Light tan
44 Surpass
45 Affix
46 Odyssey
47 Deli delight
48 Macintosh computers
49 Nautical lurch
51 Sugar source
54 Scatters seeds
58 23rd Hebrew letter
60 Murray and West
62 Roe source
64 Nigerian, perhaps
65 Cross or Crenshaw
66 Here in Le Havre
67 Perfumed packet
71 __ Rev.
72 PFC's entertainment
73 Sao __, Brazil
74 Ravi Shankar's instrument
75 Cubic meter
76 Memory method
77 Stretchable
80 Kilmer subject
81 Chamber
82 Snare
83 Engage
84 Human being
85 In medias __
87 Principal church
91 Can you beat __?
92 Counsel
93 Larry Storch on "F Troop"
94 Glued
96 Valerie Harper sitcom
98 Herbal infusions
100 Drunkard
103 Prayer
107 Down source
108 Absolutely not!
109 Take care of
110 Raging
111 Sheer rayon fabric
112 Japanese car maker
113 T.S. or George
114 Actress Della
115 Stun
116 Wharton School subj.
121 Jackie's #2
122 Mauna __
124 City in GA

FILM NEGATIVES

by Ed Voile

ACROSS

1 Vanzetti's cohort in anarchy
6 Manage
10 Language suffix
13 Keaton and Sawyer
19 Prof. Higgins' student
20 Impersonator
21 Teaching grp.
22 On cloud nine, perhaps
23 1955 Frank Sinatra movie
26 Passing stages
27 Amphitheater level
28 Floppy storage device
29 Two under par
31 Pile up
32 Firedog
34 One side of a leaf
35 Make lawn repairs
37 1968 Doug McClure movie
41 __ Lanka
44 Existing naturally
47 N.E. school
48 Having an asymmetric shape
50 Performing couples
51 Starting center?
52 Seed cover
53 At some prior time
54 European eagle
55 1965 Jim Hutton movie
60 Matures
61 Western Hemisphere
63 Daybreak song
64 Double bend
65 Sex drive
66 Fall bloomer
67 Imitative
70 Shoshone
71 Hindu groupings
73 Ridiculing
75 One of the Aleutian Islands
77 1978 David Janssen movie
79 First name of a canine star?
80 Brent Spiner on the "Enterprise"
81 "Dies __" (day of wrath)
82 One to Therese
83 Feds
84 Olympians
86 Principal artery
89 Materials for girders
91 Marsh or West
92 1964 Ivan Dixon movie
95 Sportscaster Musburger
97 Purple seaweed
98 Peter Weller movie
102 U.S. Grant's original first name
104 War-hero/actor Murphy
106 Take a look
108 Siamese, today
109 Gum arabic tree
111 1937 John Loder movie
114 Embankments
115 Com preceder?
116 On the waves
117 Binge

118 Port on the Black Sea
119 Alternatives
120 Tints
121 Plucks plant pests

DOWN

1 "The Flying Dutchman" girl
2 Laxative from aloe
3 Commended
4 Russian rulers
5 NATO cousin
6 Luxor or Mirage, e.g.
7 Makes a decision
8 Fringe benefit
9 Period
10 Books
11 Folk singer Pete
12 Justice Warren
13 Chip scoop
14 Too quickly
15 Texas mission
16 1950 Margaret Sullavan movie
17 Nights before
18 Hr. with a shrink
24 Sun-dried brick
25 Certain tides
30 Religious recluse

33 Decompose
34 O.T. book
36 French school
38 Con man's victims
39 Norse giant
40 Capacitance unit
42 Houston school
43 __ of March
44 Standard of perfection
45 The Flying Finn
46 1965 Frank Sinatra movie
49 Speaks too proudly
51 __ Marie Saint
52 Wing-shaped
55 Pheasant's brood
56 Writer Umberto
57 Savor
58 TV classic, "The __ Limits"
59 Way overweight
62 Ceremony
64 Actress Moran
66 U.S. tennis star
67 Island group in the Moluccas
68 One archangel
69 Redgrave and Swann
71 King's widow
72 Flooded

73 "Goodbye, Mr. Chips" star
74 Afore
75 First person?
76 See-ya!
77 Radon, originally
78 Ballerina's skirt
83 Parental hereditary transmission
85 Foes
86 Applies oils
87 Hideous monsters
88 Baseball stat.
89 Fire giveaway
90 Can opener?
93 Homebound
94 Sports venues
96 Tries to outrun
99 Domestic task
100 Having paddles
101 __ Peak
102 Ring around the moon
103 Chilled
105 Disassemble
106 Bouquet
107 Fencing tool
110 Botanist Gray
112 Little bit
113 Compass dir.

by Robert H. Wolfe

ACROSS

1 Pineapple brand
5 Twosome
9 Harvests
14 Port __ cheese
19 Harbinger
20 Until
21 Be jubilant
22 Upper crust
23 How dare you!... powerfully?
26 "Gorillas in the Mist" director
27 Double curve
28 Author of "The Gods Themselves"
29 Fact fabricator
30 Laments
31 Tire/axle fasteners
33 Silent, in music
35 "M*A*S*H" co-star
36 Kiss
37 Yothers and Louise
38 Aircraft carriers
42 Comic Louis
43 Ex-superpower
44 Tractor maker
45 __ Schwarz (toy store)
46 Eight: It.
49 Shoulder of the road
51 Laotian or Mongolian, e.g.
53 Rudner and Moreno
55 College cheer
56 Swann or Redgrave
57 Accepted a humiliating defeat
59 Auto-racing org.
60 Transparent material
62 Arthur C. __
63 Oh yeah, right
65 Find
66 More glistening
67 Baby-bottle feature
70 Stat starter?
71 Over thar
72 Inevitable
73 End of a buck?
75 Threadbare
77 No __, no fuss
78 AFL-__
79 Made bovine noises
81 Thorax
82 Small quantity
83 Roof-rack tote
84 Newsman Rather
85 __ Hebrides
87 "__ It a Pity?"
89 Peacock network
91 Claims manager
93 Group of eight
94 Low cards
98 Theater sec.
99 Capital of Senegal
100 Fatty
101 Divers' acronym
103 Channel island
105 Hume of "Cocoon"
107 Ave. crossers
108 Like the Arctic
109 No way!...speedwise?
112 Remedy
113 Sadat of Egypt
114 Pheasant's brood
115 Le Pew of cartoons
116 Floral gift
117 Country east of Fiji
118 Lower digits
119 Off. underling

DOWN

1 Wooden pegs
2 Cow's third stomach
3 Shall we be off?
4 Way in: abbr.
5 Asks for money... for a computer?
6 Garden pest
7 Gossip column bit
8 Mechanical performance
9 Std.
10 Banishes
11 Financial exam
12 Not guilty or guilty
13 Midnight twinkler
14 Ocean fill
15 Trumpeter Herb
16 Group honcho... by volume?
17 Sch. on the Rio Grande
18 Turner and Knight
24 Pert
25 Bunin and Lendl
32 Childhood taboo
34 Reward-penalty ploy... by weight?
35 Much removed
37 Chance to play
38 Scaredy-cat
39 Host after Carson
40 Host before Carson
41 Homer-hitter Sammy
44 Bargain
46 By mouth
47 Tex-Mex order
48 English valuables... energywise?
50 Compass dir.
52 Episodic TV show
54 Bungling
56 Recently deceased
57 Skirt styles
58 Entertains...forcefully?
61 Lake in the Sierra Nevada
62 Irritability
64 Knights' titles
66 Overlap chamfered edges
68 XXVII + XXVI
69 Son of Seth
72 Incision
73 "M*A*S*H" star
74 Highway or byway
76 Complexion woe
77 Feminist Lucretia
80 Throws away
82 Infallible
83 Brown-and-white porgy
86 Ultimate degree
88 Actor Keach
90 Sartre's "__ and Nothingness"
92 Effortlessly gracious
93 Poster material
95 Uses a blackjack
96 Bars legally
97 Six-line poem
99 Engulf
100 Battery electrode
101 Prepare for a fight
102 Lake in Lombardy
103 Three-handed card game
104 Part of A.D.
106 Hodgepodge
110 Half a bikini
111 Rejuvenation resort

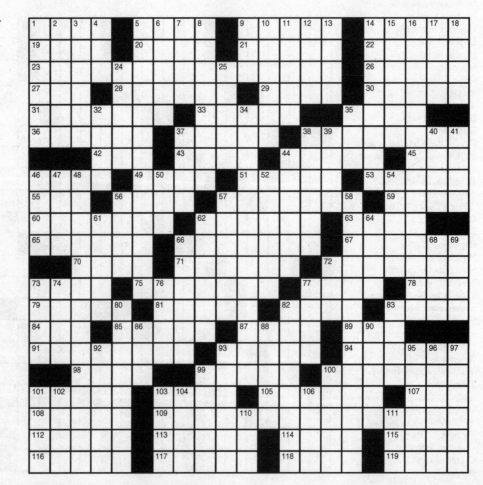

by Josiah Breward

ACROSS

1 Baffler
8 Blood-bank menu?
15 Richard of "Hot L Baltimore"
20 Ornate wardrobe
21 Structure for climbing plants
22 Dress shape
23 Index
25 Splits apart
26 Butter's brother?
27 Big __, CA
28 Guy's sweetie
29 Copse
31 Drug cops
33 Portuguese colony in India
35 Restraint in action
38 Queen's letters?
39 Higley/Kelly song of 1904
42 Andalucian gold
43 Gangster's gun
46 Demons
47 Rehan or Huxtable
48 Oater actor Jack
49 Aural buildup
51 Post fresh troops
54 Conceal
57 Opera songs
58 Charge
60 Precisely defined quantity
62 Presbyterian parsonages
63 Golf-ball holders
64 Alien craft
67 Commercial pieces
68 Courtenay film, "Billy __"
69 Old Testament book: abbr.
70 Tennessee Ernie Ford song, "Sixteen __"
71 NYC arena
74 Traveler's choice
77 Track
78 Place side by side
81 Continental currency
82 Scrap of food
83 Worsted cloth
84 Whippers
86 Active starter?
88 Lengthy periods
89 Soaks up rays
90 Guys
92 Break out
95 CIA forerunner
96 Fractional ending
97 Cause of continental drift
102 Actor Stephen
103 Fast month of Islam
104 Red or White team
105 Scrawny person
109 Southwestern saloon
111 Apron element
113 Asian car make
115 Half: pref.
116 "The Age of Anxiety" poet
117 Make a powerful impression on
122 Find a new tenant for a flat
123 Printed lies
124 Aldiss novel, "Frankenstein __"
125 Perfect places
126 Joy bringers
127 Like a family of girls

DOWN

1 Squelched
2 Refrain sounds
3 Brown shade
4 Phoenician god
5 __ a la mode
6 Cupid
7 Political exile
8 Arafat's grp.
9 Director Fritz
10 Affix
11 Inscribed slabs
12 Hr. fraction
13 Perform on stage
14 Provencal verses
15 Leatherneck
16 Smart guy?
17 Natural depressions
18 Fail to appreciate
19 Care facilities
24 Sing
30 Overeater
32 Seats for several
34 Gromyko or Sakharov
36 Muse of astronomy
37 Little bit
40 Shuffle
41 Mao __-tung
43 Ranch name in "Giant"
44 Paddled
45 Helps with the dishes
48 Sea eagles
50 Existed once
52 Perp's pic
53 Handlelike parts
55 Revise
56 Train units
58 Antiaircraft fire
59 Eagle's nest: var.
61 Teach
64 Pink-slip dispenser?
65 British saltpeter
66 Layer
68 Misplace
71 Mr. Polo
72 Audible breaths
73 Actress Sharon
74 Hope movie, "The Seven Little __"
75 Suckled
76 Perches
77 Old Olds
78 Convalescent treatment
79 Leveled off
80 Feature of Florida or Oklahoma
83 Bifocals, casually
85 Susceptible to guilt
87 Proof of purchase: abbr.
88 Center leader?
91 Greek letter
93 TV host Alistair
94 Worried
97 Writes letter by letter
98 Computer hookup, briefly
99 Type of pill
100 Isolate
101 Training center
106 Musical show
107 Prayer endings
108 Dons a belt
110 Young adult
112 Dutch South African
114 __ Domini
118 Lubricate
119 Ring grp.
120 ER workers
121 Naut. direction

by Willy A. Wiseman

ACROSS

1 Actress Gaynor
6 Poetry
11 News services
16 Plunk starter?
19 Blood of the gods
20 Of the intestines
21 Drury and Freed
22 Ill temper
23 J.R.R. Tolkien title
26 C. Heston's old org.
27 Tippy vessel
28 Poet Dove
29 Dakar's country
31 __ de la Plata
33 Kind of energy
35 Kinds
38 Be too kind
39 Bread bits
42 Porthos, to Athos
43 Proud step
44 From a distance
45 Craze
46 Papal bull, e.g.
48 "__ the season..."
49 D.C. summer hrs.
50 Firth or Finch
51 Rand of writing
52 Mezzo-soprano Marilyn
54 Lacking coolness?
57 Lennon's widow
58 Russ. jet fighter
59 Lindros and Clapton
60 Louis Prima's singer Smith
61 Candidate Landon
63 Light gas
65 Flavor enhancer
66 Prepared coffee, one way
67 __ de plume
68 Deflected
69 Orinoco tributary
70 Buzz off!
72 Alternative to sweet-'ums
73 French star
75 Surround
77 Individuality
78 Singer Sumac
79 Saki, really
80 Actor Alain
81 Network of "Nova"
82 Flow back
84 Start of a path?
85 Relating to a pelvic bone
86 __ longa, vita brevis
87 Showplace
90 Yore
91 Jazzy instrument
92 Spooky
94 Less common
95 Killer whale
97 Maori figurines
99 Young Scot
100 Armstrong, __ and Collins
101 Mountain lake
102 Lethargic
103 Cagney of "Cagney & Lacey"

105 __-de-France
106 Plain to see
108 Off kilter
110 "Mrs. Dalloway" writer
113 Fleur-de-__
114 John Webster title
120 D-Day transport
121 Nostrils
122 Much less cordial
123 Plain to see
124 Ah, I see!
125 Perplexed
126 Propounded
127 Mirage image

DOWN

1 Cambridge sch.
2 "__ bin ein Berliner": JFK
3 Alexandre Dumas title
4 Author of "Germinal"
5 Pig or cast follower
6 Part of DVD
7 "Evil Woman" rock grp.
8 Changing crop marks
9 Mock-heroic
10 For real: Ger.
11 Disfigure
12 Wallach of "The Magnificent Seven"

13 Ballerinas
14 Consume
15 Grp.
16 Rudyard Kipling title
17 Listed mistakes
18 More authentic
24 __ Ice Shelf
25 Swallows
30 "Lou Grant" star
31 Dudley Do-Right's grp.
32 "Dies __"
34 Raymond Chandler title, with "The"
36 Of element at. no. 39
37 William Goldman title, with "The"
40 Appearance
41 Joseph Cotten title
46 De Valera of 74D
47 Niccolo Machiavelli title
49 Gene Chandler title
53 Hunter of the stars
55 Terminal portion of the small intestine
56 Site of Roman defeat of Perseus
61 Wind: pref.
62 Water lily
64 Wide shoe width

65 Pacific island group
66 D.C. old-timer
71 "Siddhartha" author
74 Politically divided island
76 Magic potion
80 Digs up
81 Inability to move
83 Hall or Pitt
88 A Diamond
89 "Rule Britannia" composer
93 Spanish painter born on Crete
95 Verdi opera
96 Enrapture
97 Helmet
98 Distinct musical tones: abbr.
100 From
104 Saber or rapier
107 Sicilian volcano
109 Lash lead-in
111 Melville's "Typee" sequel
112 Kilauea flow
115 One of the Tweedles?
116 New World country: abbr.
117 Get it?
118 Part of TGIF
119 Part of TGIF

POINTING A FINGER

by Alan P. Olschwang

ACROSS

1 Lanchester and Schiaparelli
6 In the sack
10 Private dining room?
14 Remove bridles
19 Snitch
21 Celebes ox
22 New Hampshire city
23 Start of Evan Esar quote
26 Limb
27 Banned insecticide's letters
28 Ludicrous
29 Inconsequential
30 Classic car
31 Pompous ass
33 Uris or Trotsky
34 Trigger's lunch
35 Pinnacle
38 Salary boost
40 Storyteller
42 Part 2 of quote
45 Family name of several Indy winners
48 Eurasian ruminant
49 Vote in an incumbent
53 In the manner of
54 Class for U.S. immigrants
55 Russian empress
59 With the fingers
61 Medley meals
63 Ham it up
65 Morning in Marseilles
66 Newbie
67 Part 3 of quote
70 Without: Fr.
74 Plains tribe
76 Mild-flavored seaweed
77 Presley's "Love Me Tender" co-star
78 Seaside walkway
82 Very hot under the collar
85 Bladed pole
86 Tibetan gazelle
87 Italian city founded by Spartans
89 Creepy count?
91 Highly unconventional
93 Part 4 of quote
97 Popular purple perennial
101 Left bed
102 "__ kleine Nachtmusik"
103 Southeast Asian nation
105 "The Umbrellas of Cherbourg" director
106 Distinctive flair
107 Espied
109 Jamaican citrus fruit
110 Worsted cloth
112 Our star
113 RR stop
116 End of quote
121 Take-out item?
122 Highway subdivision
123 Workers' association
124 __ Domingo
125 WWII landing crafts
126 Identical
127 Small pies

DOWN

1 Kett of comics
2 Cowardly Lion
3 Staunch
4 $ dispenser
5 Ex-senator Gorton
6 Element fig.
7 __ humbug!
8 "Do Ya" grp.
9 Open condemner
10 Provides the crew
11 Preserved fodder in a way
12 Melancholy
13 Mariner
14 A. Godfrey's instrument
15 Our satellite when invisible
16 Dry run
17 Like a couch potato
18 Hereditary units
20 Sanctions
24 Islet
25 Horne of music
30 Tear apart
31 Yucatan uncle
32 Compass dir.
35 Motionless
36 Large-busted
37 "For the Boys" star
39 Taj Mahal site
40 Compass point
41 All, in music
43 Obtains
44 Sacred pageants
46 Building addition
47 Beam
50 Supple
51 Equal in Paris
52 Lincoln or Gary
56 Mignonette
57 Rascal
58 Asta's mistress
60 Latin handle
62 Something to gather?
64 Israeli Abba
67 Ms. Mandlikova
68 Culture medium
69 MDs' org.
71 Tropical rodent
72 Kevin of "Weeds"
73 Fire from a low-flying aircraft
75 Fills completely
77 Wampum
78 Creative drive
79 Old French coin
80 Beat cop
81 Delight
83 Fusses
84 Causing repugnance
88 Palindromic pharaoh
90 Masticate
92 Most in the pink?
94 Abilities
95 Musical syllable
96 Term of endearment
98 Utopia
99 Pass gossip
100 Poncas' relatives
103 Strong cravings
104 Greek market
106 Alfonso's queen
108 Native Alaskan
111 Cools down
112 Marquis de __
113 Recipe direction
114 Palindromic honk
115 Miller and Jillian
117 Exclamation of discovery
118 Bikini part
119 Escape from jail
120 Actress Claire

TOO MUCH VIOLENCE

by Josiah Breward

ACROSS

1 Portuguese wine
8 Timeless
15 Musical endings
20 Chafer
21 Capital of Cyprus
22 Venture a thought
23 Libido
24 Boxer's fists?
26 Devitalizes
27 Conquistadors' quest
29 Lobster eggs
30 Unsightly sights
31 Religious deg.
32 City in the San Joaquin Valley
34 Sutter and Spiner
35 __ Dawn Chong
36 I've gotta have it!
39 Guessed figs.
43 Islamic scholars
45 Yucatan uncle
46 Mom's mom
47 Overused
49 Qatar's capital
51 __-Saxon
53 987-65-4321 group
54 Volga tributary
55 Jungle cat
58 Legendary baseball hall-of-famer
62 Rock composer Brian
63 Warble
65 Like rhymes and verses
66 Assassinated Egyptian leader
67 '60s continental hairstyle?
69 Supporting pieces
71 Very dry
73 Gordie of the NHL
74 Musical repeat signs
76 Turkey's capital
80 Soundstages
82 Armed conflict
83 Done up to the nines
86 Dana and Ron
88 Year in the Yucatan
89 Notes of scales
90 Penetrate
92 Indira's garb
93 Estee of cosmetics
95 Grafton and Miller
97 Mil. rank
99 Outlets
102 Otherwise
103 Alluring woman
106 Air-travel watchdog grp.
107 Deviations
110 Andes herd
111 End-of-season baseball event: abbr.
112 Military shoulder ornaments
115 Partner of to
117 Edge
118 Thin strip of wood

119 Four-and-twenty blackbirds?
122 Part of the Czech Republic
124 Digestive disorder
125 Turned on a point
126 Senselessly
127 Athletic activity
128 Theater companies, basically
129 Map volumes

DOWN

1 Eminent conductors
2 Isaac's father
3 A knockout!
4 Has a bite
5 Infamous Amin
6 Club Med, e.g.
7 End of a couch
8 Blowup of a pic
9 Steering linkage piece
10 External: pref.
11 Mies van der __
12 DC advisory grp.
13 Wing flap
14 Attorney
15 Seashore
16 Was contrary to
17 Fashionable Christian
18 English princess
19 Hr. with a shrink
25 Hallow ending?
28 Port of Rome
32 Catches rays?
33 Nary a soul
34 Designer's deg.
37 Ice palace?
38 Irregularly notched
40 Rebuffed dramatically
41 Remove
42 Golf-course employees
44 Afr. country
47 Cowboys' sch.
48 Straggles
50 So to speak
52 Country's $ output
53 Worthy of reverence
55 Sara the poet
56 Diabolical
57 J.C. and Sammy
59 Rel. figures
60 Disinformation
61 Exclamation of doubt
64 Fella
68 Switch positions
70 Ring decision letters
72 Tours summers
75 Small geographical unit

77 Olajuwan of basketball
78 Dishwasher cycle
79 Road-sign abbr.
81 Unpaid servants
84 Serving of corn
85 Lawful
87 Exist
91 Make roof repairs
94 Bamboozler
95 Is so minded
96 Hesitation sounds
98 Windhoek's location
100 Perceptible by touch
101 Flounces
103 Camera settings
104 Bloom
105 "Sanford and Son" son
108 State of readiness
109 According to
112 Flightless birds
113 "__ Fiction"
114 Shell rival
115 Potential prince?
116 Memory method
118 Musical Horne
120 NW dam-builders
121 '60s radical campus group
123 Actor Linden

by James E. Buell

ACROSS
1 Nincompoop
5 Shoot-out signal
9 Porgies
14 Single
19 Switch position
20 Comfort
21 Of musical sounds
22 Home of the Dolphins
23 Pop, perhaps
26 Hit by the Rolling Stones
27 Recesses
28 Places side by side
30 Morays or congers
31 Wide-mouth pitcher
32 Deodorant applicator
34 Tighten an oxford
36 Rusty of "Make Room for Daddy"
38 Mind a mansion?
40 Deep pinks
43 Yikes!
44 Sticking stuff
45 Book before Nehemiah
47 Waterwheel
48 Biblical boat
49 Have supper
50 Pop, perhaps
52 Staggering
54 Lyric poem
56 George Eliot novel, "__ Marner"
57 Greek letter
58 Infer
59 Spoils
61 Poe story, "The __ and the Pendulum"
62 God of love
63 Pop psychology?
67 Identical
70 Decompose
71 Spooky
72 Lassos
76 Oklahoma town
77 Chicago team
79 Vietnamese holiday
80 Announce
81 Pop, perhaps
84 Choice spot in the road?
85 Sault __ Marie
86 Ciao on Kauai
87 Responding easily to the helm
88 Makes headway
90 Actor Tamiroff
91 Most secure
93 City between Houston and Austin
95 Top points
96 Monopoly purchase
98 Mixes together
99 Twelve-point measure
100 Like broken horses
102 Mild discomfort
104 Jellyfish
107 Sots

109 Pop, perhaps
112 Greek marketplace
113 Terminator
114 Pilot starter?
115 Extra-wide shoe size
116 Let fly
117 VCR button
118 Hive population
119 __ Scot decision

DOWN
1 Qatar's capital
2 German auto make
3 Pop, perhaps
4 Gifted
5 Postpone
6 Darn it!
7 Volcanic fallout
8 Itsy-bitsy
9 Principal commodity
10 ASCAP member
11 Organizes workers
12 Sidekicks
13 Slicker
14 Ms. Thurman
15 Club for short shots
16 Pop, perhaps
17 "__ and the Detectives"
18 Passes away

24 Completed
25 Trumped-up
29 NYSE watchdog
32 Flower with hips
33 Extinguished
35 Tennille and Morrison
36 Got wind of
37 See eye to eye
38 Suspend
39 Gad about
41 Remain stationary facing into the wind
42 Gilbert and Teasdale
44 Cone bearer
46 Improvise
49 Opera star
50 Publisher Cerf
51 Sprinklers
53 Biography subject
54 "__ Town"
55 Levee
59 Repeat hearing
60 Nursing a grudge
62 & others: Lat.
64 "Lazy Bones" composer Carmichael
65 Comic
66 Nauseated
67 Epic tales

68 Ms. Rogers St. Johns
69 Pop, perhaps
73 Pop, perhaps
74 Clarinetist Shaw
75 Appears
77 Bang-up time
78 Stately dances
80 Over with
82 President Roosevelt
83 Nightgown
84 Dried fruits
88 Yiddish thief
89 Word in partnerships
90 Jodie Foster film, with "The"
92 President pro __
94 Vacation spot
95 Opera set in Egypt
97 Los Angeles hoopster
99 Rio Grande tributary
100 Thwack
101 Lofty
103 Checkout formation
104 Distribute
105 Toward shelter
106 Burpee kernel
108 Spotted
110 Slot-filler
111 Tint

ACROSS

1 Blindfolded children's target
7 Votes in
13 Period after surrender
20 All gone
21 Helmet
22 Surplus
23 Society Islands plants?
25 Maines of the Dixie Chicks
26 Turner film, "__ X"
27 Fathered
29 Missile berths
30 Light touches
33 French pal
34 Ump's cohort
35 Eye part
37 __ the tentmaker
38 Westminster 10K?
41 Part of WWW
44 French sculptor
46 Light gas
47 Watching one
48 Abnormal respiratory sound
49 Nike rival
51 HST follower
53 Parts of brains
55 Abdul Aziz __ Saud
56 Downtown NYC dance club?
60 Like flowers with calyxes
61 Slot fillers
63 Kemo __
64 Training rms.
67 Bushnell and Ryan
68 Exclamation of discovery
70 Spanish painter Joan
72 Easy stride
74 Member of 54D
75 Singer Pia
78 Russian ruler
80 Longest river
82 Word after Scotland
85 Lake at the entrance to Hades
87 Leatherwood of Viti Levu?
90 Qns. or Bx., e.g.
91 Sodium __ (truth serum)
94 Disney dwarf
95 Mutual-assistance network
97 Talk to God
98 Earl "Fatha" __
100 Prego rival
103 Jungle vine
104 City in GA
105 Kowloon tune?
108 Winter glider
109 Scrubs, as a mission
111 "The Bells" poet
112 Rapping Doctor
113 Man behind filmdom's moral code
114 Ballplayer Guerrero
116 Japanese seaport
118 Newspaper bigwig
120 Leakeys' African gorge
122 Samoan dance?
127 Carl and Rob
128 More vacuous
129 Vocal supporters
130 Fit of pique
131 Stupefied with liquor
132 Likes and dislikes

DOWN

1 Belgravia bar
2 Late starter?
3 Saul's uncle
4 Tracy/Hepburn film
5 Brass instrument
6 Footless
7 Worsted cloth
8 Unending sentence?
9 Bigger pic
10 Selected
11 Customs duties
12 Matinee idol
13 Meditators
14 Cato's eggs
15 Becomes entrenched
16 Work out
17 Hebrew mysticism in Washington?
18 Exchange fee
19 British Astronomer Royal, Martin __
24 Actor Novarro
28 Els or Kovacs
30 Dickens' "Little __"
31 Single-celled organism
32 Boy with a lamp in the Black Forest?
34 Last movement of a sonata
36 Stew dish
39 California team
40 Product bars, in brief
42 DeGeneres series
43 Necklace units
45 Negative votes
48 In truth
50 Boxer's stat
52 Easter item
54 Fraternal org.
57 Scenery chewer
58 Funeral info
59 Popeye's Olive
62 Elmore Leonard novel, "Get __"
65 Seles and Vitti
66 Roasting stick
69 Pisa's river
71 Lummox
73 Lilly or Wallach
75 Mothers of Invention leader
76 Prevent
77 Writer
79 Disencumber
81 Ike's arena
83 Andy of "60 Minutes"
84 Wood nymphs
86 Religion of Japan
88 Writer Borges
89 Feeling peaked
92 Feeling of anxiety
93 Courtship display area for birds
96 Kitchen cleaners
99 Female voice
101 __ Space Flight Center
102 Remove bridles
105 President elected in 1928
106 Honey-and-nut paste
107 Leave at once!
110 Main impact
114 Left, aboard
115 Zeno of __
117 Sacred bull
118 Edgeless sword
119 Other: Sp.
121 Indonesian islands
123 Toronto's prov.
124 Profit figure
125 Coll. seniors' test
126 CIA's predecessor

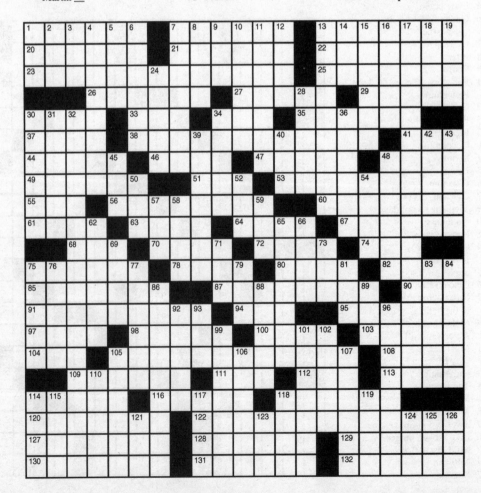

by Edgar Fontaine

ACROSS

1 Contemporary
7 Bactrian and dromedary
13 Network of "Sesame Street"
16 Poetic offering
19 Manufacturing statistic
20 Slowly, in music
21 Temptress
23 Former mayor of Cincinnati
25 Explanations
26 Draft classification
27 __ Cruz, CA
28 Makes insane
30 Renown
32 Little piggy
34 Unlikely winner
38 Is next to
41 1970 candidate for the Senate
43 Actress Meyers
44 Ringlet of hair
45 Earl __ tea
46 Moselle tributary
47 Tel __-Jaffa
48 Signal for help
49 Shinbone
52 Distinctive flavors
53 Wall St. abbr.
54 1994 U.S. Open golf champion
55 1998 candidate for Congress
58 Georgia city
59 Pub preference
60 Part of YMCA
61 Tapestry in "Hamlet"
62 Mounds of stones for memorials
63 Contending
65 Fabric
66 Authority to decide
67 Author of "Our Man in Havana"
69 Dishes
70 Common rail
71 Numbers pro
74 Tropical porch
75 Former Iowa congressman
77 Bruce Lee's original surname
78 Newts
79 Hag
80 L'chaim or prosit
82 CBS logo
83 Maritime: abbr.
84 Legendary Detroit Red Wing player
85 Bough
87 Frequently
89 Strauss opera, "__ Rosenkavalier"
90 Former California congressman
92 Stung
94 Menu option
96 In-house #
97 Scold mildly
98 Single-handed
100 Handled like a jug
102 Therefore: Lat.

106 Idle talk
109 Former mayor of Carmel-by-the-Sea
112 Resident of Indiana
113 Black currant liqueur
114 Swapped
115 Lamprey
116 Pompous fool
117 Clown Kelly
118 Dorothy of mysteries

DOWN

1 Stephen King's dog
2 Unwrap
3 To be in Toulon
4 Domineering women
5 Writer Tan
6 "A __ from Aloes"
7 Sideshow barker
8 Mine entrance
9 Aquatic mammal of Florida
10 Faberge item
11 German songs
12 Tender
13 Lineage
14 Liquefiers
15 Christian or Helen
16 Gold in Madrid
17 Bear's lair
18 Hesitation syllables
22 Gorby's nation
24 Golf scores
29 Ninja turtles?
31 Itemization
33 Moronic start?
35 Former Tennessee congressman
36 Prayer
37 Things taken for granted
38 Perplexed
39 Whimsical
40 Governor of Minnesota
41 Golf hazard
42 Hebrew prophet
45 Hodges and Gerard
47 Diarist Nin
50 Dancing Castle
51 Explosive report
52 Dental coating
56 Halogen compound
57 Inappropriate
58 Belize people
60 Skirt type
62 Middlecoff and Grant
64 Leavening agent
65 Bush's veep
66 Scotch companion
67 Jackson of "Women in Love"

68 Dominican dictator Trujillo Molina
69 Enthroned
70 Stuffed shirt
72 Check recipient
73 Correct
75 Limits of knowledge
76 Sphere starter?
79 Protestant hymns
81 Natterjack
85 Smoked salmon
86 Deeply felt
88 Highway without tolls
90 Albuquerque crest
91 Chaos
92 NL stadium
93 Centers
95 Cows' chews
97 Wave top
99 __ homo (Behold the man!)
101 Arguing
103 Took a horse
104 Fast horse
105 Track stats
106 Definite article
107 Heartache
108 Major ISP
110 Doctrine
111 La-la lead-in

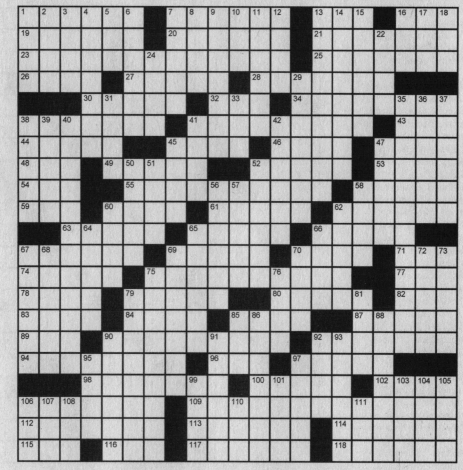

BIRD TAILS

by Stanley B. Whitten

ACROSS

1 Stadium roof
5 Nonsense
9 Potential raisin
14 Pee Wee or Della
19 Frigg's husband
20 Woody's son
21 Hunt or Alexander
22 Eero Saarinen's father
23 Prairie State avifauna?
25 Empire State avifauna?
27 Sacred Egyptian beetle
28 Way down
30 Art stands
31 Flask
33 Traditional tales
34 Cleansing ritual
35 Prairie State avifauna?
40 Buckeye State avifauna?
44 Scads
45 Tight spot
46 Swindles
47 '52 and '56 candidate
48 7-time A.L. batting champion
50 Harbor craft
51 Chelsea apartment
52 Sports infractions
54 Schedule info
55 Washington's vice president
57 Butcher's offering
58 Golfer's porter
59 Madrid maiden
61 Verse
62 "The Time of Your Life" playwright
63 Hoosier State avifauna?
66 Small pieces of computer code
69 Coffee servers
70 Ring-necked bird
74 Lusters
75 Culturally pretentious
76 Kasparov's game
77 Food from taro
78 Quantities of wood
79 Overtake
80 Angler's bait
81 Object
83 Sailors' admin.
84 Trading center
85 Upolu resident
87 Noun-forming suffix
88 Buckeye State avifauna?
91 Peach State avifauna?
93 Make over
94 Bad to the bone
95 Old
96 Become apparent
99 Strips blubber
102 Principal ore of lead
106 Lone Star State avifauna?
108 Empire State avifauna?
110 School for Stendhal
111 Trial's locale

112 Bank transaction
113 Campbell of "Scream"
114 Feel
115 Tacked on
116 Safecracker
117 Tie

DOWN

1 AMA members
2 Like Pindar's poetry
3 Complex silicate
4 Devitalize
5 Bombax trees
6 Globe
7 Skidded
8 Sharpen
9 Blood sugar
10 Scorers
11 Ammonia derivative
12 Treaty
13 Period of note
14 Estimate a new age
15 Hebrew prophet
16 "__ kleine Nachtmusik"
17 Emblem
18 Pipe bends
24 Train track
26 Raises

29 Food for a pig out?
32 Produces milk
34 Deflected
35 Carps and minnows
36 Make joyful
37 Islamic text
38 Roosevelt's successor
39 Cartoon tiger
40 Gravy or love follower
41 Tastelessly showy
42 Sand novel
43 City on the Ruhr
46 Gripping device
49 Rabbit colonies
51 Nourishes
52 Orient
53 Smells
56 Weight-loss plans
57 Absent-minded
58 "__ and Ale"
60 Eyed covetously
61 Sailors' stopovers
62 Outlines
64 German sausage
65 "Sleepless in Seattle" writer Nora
66 Flamboyant tie
67 Graph starter?

68 Imminent danger
71 Imitating
72 Time being
73 Woods of links
75 Rhine tributary
76 Suspended consciousness
79 Peacock constellation
80 Places for murals
82 Promontory
84 Computer communicator
85 Was sparing with
86 Pestering
89 Flynn and others
90 Relative intensity
91 Line of inquiry
92 Close at hand
94 African antelope
96 Woolly females
97 Knight's weapon
98 Financial subj.
99 Mr. Rogers
100 Slithery
101 Blackthorn
103 At all times
104 St. Petersburg's river
105 Once again
107 Cato's eggs
109 Periodical, briefly

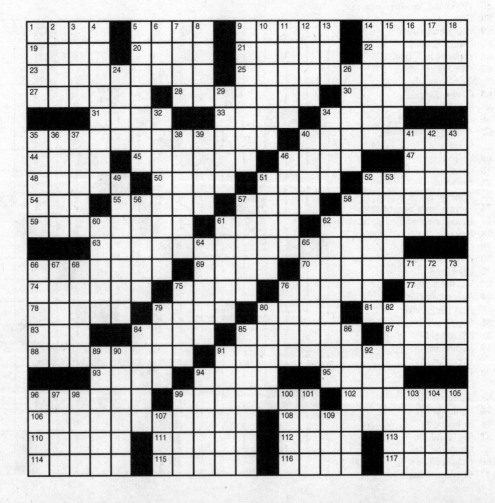

ANAGRAM ACTION

By Alan P. Olschwang

ACROSS

1 Dame Edith or Dale
6 Smelting residue
10 Ski lift
14 Squabbles
19 Taylor of "The Nanny"
20 Glass piece
21 For certain
22 __ Haute, IN
23 Hollywood statuette
24 Cato's way
25 Part of U.A.E.
26 Like some buckets
27 Retrogression of PETS?
30 Put into action
32 Letter on Superman's chest
33 Come to regret
34 River nymph
36 Rewrites
37 Lag behind
40 Double DI
41 Lothario's cousin?
43 DRAPES all over?
47 Is present throughout
52 Spinach substitute
53 Lead a nomadic life
54 Observed
56 Grenoble's river
57 People before Aztecs
59 Take upon oneself
61 Ballerinas
63 Olfactory triggers
65 Command to Rover
66 Shackle
67 Promos
70 Spin RITES?
74 "Turn to Stone" rock grp.
75 Some Louisianans
78 Russian space station
79 "Fear of Flying" author Jong
82 Impair steadily
83 Isolated mountain
86 Kiner and Ellison
90 Gads about
91 Explorer Heyerdahl
93 Summers on the Somme
95 Insertion mark
96 Heretic
98 Set-to with ACTIONS?
101 Staff signs
103 Belief system
104 __ acids
105 Capture in a snare again
109 Burglar
111 Hindu title
112 Aeronautics watchdog grp.
115 Deplete
117 Meaningless SWORD?
121 Dumbfounds
122 Has a deed
124 Aussie hoppers
125 Black-and-white treats
126 Debate
127 Memory method
128 Ballerina's skirt
129 Shrine at Mecca
130 Stingers
131 Settle down and raise chicks
132 Uriah of fiction
133 Concluded

DOWN

1 Irregularly notched
2 Waistcoats
3 Immemorial
4 Lowest high tide
5 Belgrade resident
6 Like sponges
7 Potato pancake
8 All over again
9 Cranesbill plants
10 Hebrew letter
11 College treasurer
12 Altar of stars
13 "I Know How He Feels" singer
14 OPTS to stand still?
15 U.S. painter Rembrandt
16 "Catch-22" star
17 Trapped in branches
18 Transmits
28 Saharan
29 Precipitation
31 Equal
35 Ninny
38 Right-hand page
39 Exclaimed in pleasure
40 Extinct birds
42 Busybody
43 Drunkard
44 In favor of
45 Cook with dry heat
46 Relinquish
48 Fungi sacs
49 Tractor maker
50 Flynn of film
51 CNN newsman Frank
55 Himalayan bigfoot
58 Hollowed, as apples
60 PC operators
62 Norse gods
64 Badge of honor
67 Ghana's capital
68 Sag
69 Motor or mechanism starter
71 Shortened bullets?
72 Pope's triple crown
73 Attribute
76 Mine finds
77 Misplaced SAUCES?
80 Desert growth
81 French actor Delon
84 Proposes
85 News piece
87 Check text for errors
88 Biddy
89 Aves.
92 Determine weight by lifting
94 Gathers using ingenuity
97 Yodeler's range?
99 Willingly, old-style
100 In the thick of
102 Railroad switches
105 Shorten a plank
106 Additional
107 Mob enforcers
108 Increased
110 Map in a map
111 Struck powerfully
113 Sun-dried brick
114 Syrian VIP
116 Ripped
118 Rake
119 Left dreamland
120 Algerian port
123 Misery

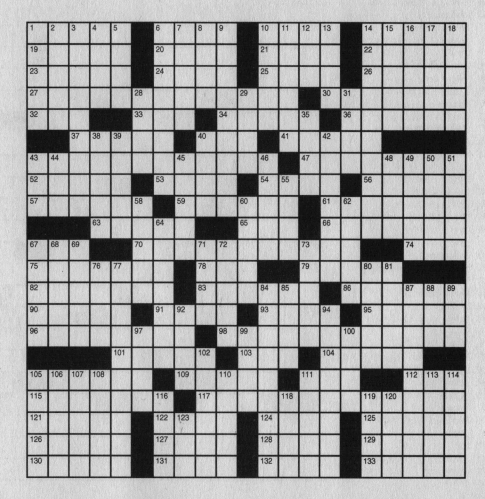

BIG NUMBERS

by Josiah Breward

ACROSS

1 Mauna __ volcano
4 Rub with liniment
13 Deep-fried Japanese dish
20 Ending for a belief
21 Aristocracies
22 Short opera solos
23 Sprint rival
24 1985 Richard Pryor movie
26 Rhizome
28 On a cruise
29 Heckart or Herlie
30 Mama Cass
33 Mark and Shania
36 Packs away
40 Crake
43 Apron element
44 Lowly mil. rank
47 Agitated state
48 Ike's arena
49 Rarity
53 "Telephone Line" rock grp.
54 Say it ain't so
56 Marquis de __
57 Ustinov autobiography
58 Bub
59 Sch. trainees
61 Economical plane fare
64 Performed
65 Press coverage
66 With 81A, big-money game show
70 Questioning interjections
71 "Paper Lion" star
72 Extravagant publicity
73 Twenty
75 Like the nobility
77 Country hotels
78 Animal's gullet
81 See 66A
84 Foot's end
85 FDR's money?
87 Lugosi and Bartok
88 Full-house letters
89 South African golfer Ernie
90 One-sixth of an ancient drachma
92 Golden calf, e.g.
94 Machu Picchu honcho
97 What say?
98 Profitable book
102 Distant
103 Palme of Sweden
105 Gas: pref.
106 Beat follower?
107 Legal right-of-way
109 Ballet skirts
111 School papers
114 "Citizen Kane" co-star Everett
115 Writer of "Dialogues of the Dead"
118 Be first
121 1982 Disney sci-fi film
122 1939 Betty Grable movie

129 RR stop
130 Annually elected Roman magistrate
131 Set too high a price on
132 Actress Arthur
133 Conceal
134 Doing clumsy repairs
135 Music collection letters

DOWN

1 Made flexible
2 Kiss
3 Fat chance
4 Flow back
5 Spoil
6 La __ Tar Pits
7 Brawls
8 Beginning
9 College in Salisbury, NC
10 Long, long time
11 Part of Canada's Y.T.?
12 City on the Ruhr
13 Caudal appendage
14 Perry's penner
15 Odometer figures
16 Dots
17 It brought Hope to soldiers
18 Howard of "Happy Days"
19 Dunderhead
25 Lose
27 Puppeteer Baird
31 Seller's $ equivocation
32 Metal containers
34 Goal
35 Footnote abbr.
37 1966 Raquel Welch movie
38 Mats of tennis
39 Military jail
41 Show shock, e.g.
42 Antics
45 Scottish estuary
46 Revives
50 __-foot oil
51 Poetic meadow
52 Actor Beatty
55 Sharp cries
60 Actor Mineo
62 Comic Imogene
63 Weapon of mass destruction
66 Glowing brightly
67 Pearl Harbor location
68 Windhoek's nation
69 Great Lake
71 Video-game pioneer company
74 Songwriter Greenwich
76 Green-card org.
79 Soap substitute
80 Bookish
82 Soup server
83 Luigi's island
85 DiMaggio of the Red Sox
86 __ generis: Lat.
91 "All My __"
93 A smaller amount
95 Stood for
96 Aerials
99 Actress Long
100 Bird known to sing while flying
101 Fam. member
104 Architect Buckminster
108 Witticism
110 Connecting rooms
112 Honker
113 Suffice
116 Geezer
117 Concerning: Lat.
119 Winglike
120 Sandwich shoppe
122 Brit. electees
123 Wrath
124 Fond du __, WI
125 Fifth of CCLXXX
126 Ex-QB Dawson
127 .38 Special, e.g.
128 Portion: abbr.

ORDINARY ORDINALS

by Frances Burton

ACROSS

1 Tempest in a teapot
5 Roman __ of Caracalla
10 Ed of "The Mary Tyler Moore Show"
15 Bellicose deity
19 Black-and-white cookie
20 System of moral values
21 Let live
22 __ carotene
23 Home plate?
25 Rest period?
27 Starve oneself
28 Dried plum
30 Slobbers
31 Delta deposit
32 Commence
33 __-do-well
34 Like house plants
37 Spectacle
38 Touched tenderly
42 Sore spots
43 Wound reminder
44 Flitted
46 Time of note
47 "American Pie" actress Tara
48 Related (to)
49 Enjoy a book
50 Flip through
51 Besmirch
52 Double-date extra?
56 "__ Life Is It, Anyway?"
57 Auto racer Mario
60 Gray and Moran
61 Lifting devices
62 Winfield and Brubeck
63 Coronet
64 Scottish landowner
65 Crafty
67 Squander
68 Hermetic
71 Alternative to ale
72 Intuition?
74 Former Mid east nation
75 Blunders
76 Get along
77 Foundry form
78 Inconsequential
79 Historic period
80 Go back
82 Program instructions
83 Itemized accounts
84 Made additional cuts
86 Colorful variety of chalcedony
88 Affectionate greetings
89 Ardently eager
90 Irish county
91 Is not well
92 Hangman's knots
95 Spicy dip
96 Fred and Adele
100 Do?
102 Pre-school?

104 Model Macpherson
105 Soothes
106 Eero Saarinen's father
107 In the past, in the past
108 Soaked in woad
109 Shy
110 List of candidates
111 Notices

DOWN

1 Bean curd
2 Pig or cast follower
3 Internecine conflict
4 Woodsy
5 Laid eyes on
6 Ready to swing
7 The one there
8 "__ Girl Friday"
9 Symbol of regal power
10 Removed doubts
11 All in
12 Church area
13 Afore
14 Depicted
15 Loathes
16 Second chance
17 & others: Lat.
18 Pronounces
24 Makes an effort
26 Arboreally cornered
29 Sought office
32 Meager
33 Part of South Africa
34 Correggio's city
35 Body of water
36 Ph.D.?
37 Where you might find E.T.s
38 Canadian tribe
39 Bettor's pick to place?
40 Tape over
41 Copenhagen populace
43 Comic routines
45 Showplace
48 Subsequently
50 Puppeteer Lewis
53 Bank job?
54 Ire
55 Expands one's staff
56 Formal legal document
58 Utters in a frenzy
59 Of all time
61 Showed concern
63 Government role?
64 Extra-strong cotton thread
65 Jump, as a fence
66 Colossal

67 Belushi biography
68 Positively charged electrode
69 "The Lost Galleon" poet
70 Ringlet of hair
72 Rescued
73 Act the ham
76 Magical objects
78 Projectiles
80 Metal bolt
81 Most lofty
82 Decanters
83 Purple shade
85 Ran fast
87 Neon or radon
88 1983 A.L. Rookie of the Year
90 Supply the food
91 Cash in hand, e.g.
92 Poverty
93 Unctuous
94 Look long and lustily
95 Mediocre
96 "Stride la vampa," e.g.
97 Like hens' teeth
98 Latin being
99 Mach+ jets
101 Slangy negative
103 __ be seein' ya!

by Robert H. Wolfe

ACROSS

1 First of a series
6 Consecrate
12 Greek portico
16 Mrs. in Madrid
19 Show-biz notable
20 Forbidden acts
21 Off kilter
22 Family dog
23 Muppet song, with "The"
26 Addams Family member
27 "__ Gotta Be Me"
28 Idolizes
29 CIA's predecessor
30 Seed protector
31 __ Plaines, IL
32 Saturn's daughter
33 Industrious insect
35 Series of related rock formations
38 Opps. of antonyms
39 Let loose
40 Armpits
41 Tex-Mex order
44 Belly
47 Unbeatable foes
48 Show clearly
50 Large hospital room
51 Firefighter's connection
53 Less common
54 Prove false
55 Catnap
56 Spoken
59 O.T. book
60 Effective
62 Principle of good conduct
64 Mrs. Eddie Cantor
65 Bedridden
66 Coffee server
67 Onassis, to pals
69 Perfect game box score
70 "Man on the Moon" group
71 French born
72 Foot control
75 Basketball pass
78 Lid
79 False god
81 Provoke
82 In plain sight
83 Uplift
85 Cats
87 Appearance
88 Up for the day
89 Open insult
91 Suitability
93 Turner and Knight
94 Smooth by rubbing
95 Pain in the neck
96 Cash in Pisa, once
98 Property recipient
99 Teensy
100 Cutting edge
102 Banned insecticide's letters
105 Tip or spin follower?
106 Aussie hopper
108 Jets and gliders
109 Profound dread

110 Sweet 'ums
111 Completely
116 Stop
117 Cricket pitch
118 Medium meeting
119 Distributes cards
120 Three satisfactory grades
121 Arp's art
122 Shaper
123 "Guitar Town" singer Steve

DOWN

1 Bitter
2 Depart
3 Ballet movements
4 Farm layer
5 Rights of a monastery's leader
6 Under the most negative circumstances
7 Mother-of-pearl
8 Double-reed woodwinds
9 Charged particles
10 __ sequitur
11 Either part of a fly?
12 800 exams
13 1964 hit by the Beatles
14 Gold in the Sierra Madre
15 "Atlas Shrugged" author Rand
16 Steps in a tight space
17 Parts of eyes
18 British P.M. Clement and family
24 Hans Christian Andersen's birthplace
25 Dove shelter
30 Harold and Michael
33 Paris landmark
34 Bk. after Ezra
36 Elbow grease
37 "Green Mansions" girl
38 Loudness unit
39 Fine meal
41 Ends of the lines
42 Benefited
43 One's cronies
45 Debtor
46 Prop starter?
49 Larynx ailment
51 Otto I's realm
52 Thus far
54 Highway course correction
57 Imagined
58 Wets
61 Wet beforehand

63 Programmer
68 Ask
73 Ginger __
74 The in French
76 __ there, done that
77 Birthplace of Camembert
80 "Brigadoon" lyricist
84 Low-cal
86 Meat cut
88 Sotto voce remarks
89 Disconcerts
90 __ folly
91 Dead-eye
92 Character assassination
95 Gone GI
97 Live
100 Wishy-washy
101 Spear
102 Senegal's capital
103 Live
104 Brief
107 Neighbor of Colo.
108 Ring out
111 Brick carrier
112 Caesar's eggs
113 Ideology
114 Natal starter?
115 Learning org.

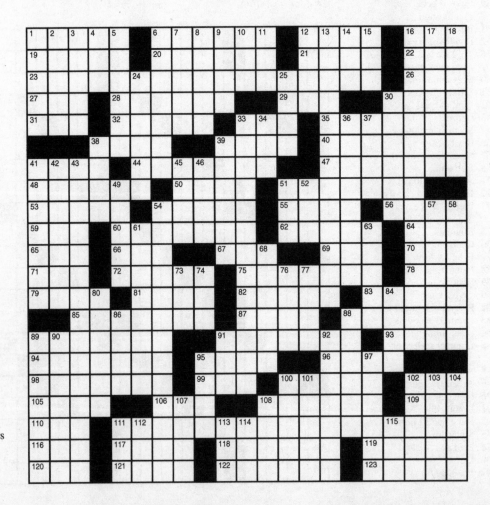

ACROSS

1 Grand __ Island
7 Pale
10 Nom de guerre of Ernesto Guevara
13 Canine
19 Greek marketplaces
20 Red-faced
22 Lake near Syracuse
23 Ernie of the Football Hall of Fame
24 Start of Evan Esar quote
25 Better arranged
26 Grandmother's sister
28 Photographer Adams
30 Selling point
31 Lat. or Lith., once
32 One to Therese
33 R-V connection
34 Movie pooch
36 Part 2 of quote
45 Fugue finales
47 Takes care of
48 Main course
49 Chicago hub
50 Carp and minnows
52 Formerly
54 Arthur of "The Golden Girls"
55 Part 3 of quote
57 Makes all better
60 Stationery tablets
63 Made a lap
64 __ the line (obeyed)
66 Brogan binders
68 Remove lather
69 Part 4 of quote
73 Plant pest
76 Ancient region of Asia Minor
77 "__ we forget..."
78 Comparative suffix
81 Of a lens measurement
83 Explorer who claimed New Mexico for Spain
85 Part 5 of quote
88 "The Ipcress File" author Deighton
89 All over again
91 Turkish bread?
93 Vacuous
94 Eugene O'Neill play, "The __ Cometh"
97 Headlands
100 Muddies
102 Part 6 of quote
105 Artifice
106 Qty.
107 One of Santa's little helpers
108 Mobster's rod
111 Type of cigar or sandwich
114 Unit of magnetic flux density
117 Entreaties
120 Order of business
122 End of quote

124 Occultism
125 Like Brinker's skates
126 What's left over
127 Newspaper employee
128 Indian instruments
129 NYC hours
130 CIA forerunner
131 Repairs stitches

DOWN

1 Forehead fringe
2 Teen followers?
3 Air-cushion vehicle
4 Length x width
5 Trading center
6 Battery mate?
7 Composer Richard
8 Fence the loot
9 Natalie's father
10 Calisthenics of a kind
11 Multiple layers?
12 Rim
13 Swindle
14 Left on the plate
15 Ocean extract
16 Low places
17 __ fixe (obsession)
18 Pub projectile
21 Eros in Piccadilly Circus

27 Dismantled
29 Long.'s counterpart
33 Villain's look
35 Thin layer
37 Deli sub
38 Cato's way
39 Portuguese currency
40 Ice-skater Midori
41 Inferior poet
42 Citified
43 City near York
44 Term of tenancy
45 Weepy gasps
46 Train of song?
51 Type of torch
53 Expenses
56 Somme summer
58 Violinist Mischa
59 Spring runner
61 Sea eagle
62 Litter dropper?
65 Ottoman dynasty founder
67 Religious extremism
69 Gratuity
70 33rd president
71 Carnival city
72 Addams Family cousin
73 Improvise
74 Part

75 Sharpened
78 Fertilize
79 Kitchen addition?
80 Acuff and Rogers
82 Talks wildly
84 Watchful
86 Blood: pref.
87 Bahrain leader
90 Director Craven
92 White poplar
95 Satellite of Uranus
96 Into pieces
98 Most passe
99 Mogadishu resident
101 Obliterator
103 __ up (excited)
104 Ball attendees
109 Having the look of love
110 Russian rulers
111 Hacks
112 Jamaican fruit
113 Rhythm
115 To be in Toulon
116 Females
117 Added benefit
118 Miami-__ county
119 Bird of Egypt
121 Promos
123 Japanese vegetable

AULD LANG SYNE

NOTE: This puzzle originally appeared on 12/31/00.
No clues have been changed.

by Willy A. Wiseman

ACROSS

1 Speculative genre, briefly
6 On __ (without guarantee)
10 Muckraker Tarbell
13 Passover participant
19 Bonheur and Parks
20 See-ya!
21 Tatami
22 Bun seed
23 With 43A, film for tomorrow?
26 Bunchberry
27 Author of "The Nazarene"
28 Minnesota twins?
29 Forum robe
30 Weighty weight
31 Mod or glob ending
32 Trademark jeans
34 Upkeep
35 Train unit
36 Fruitless
37 Corkscrew shape
39 Dine at home
40 Can. province
41 Gershwin and Levin
42 Bee and Em
43 See 23A
46 Deferential gesture
48 Actress Arthur
49 Red beginning?
52 One Osmond
53 Coke rival
56 Potts and Lennox
57 Globes
60 Lurch and swerve
61 Gets into one's head
62 Ms. Zadora
63 Tonight
66 Bering or Ross
67 Vicuna's cousin
70 Degrades
71 Brought to bear
74 Lassoers
75 Cash penalties
76 Animate
77 "Funny Girl" composer
78 Org. of Argonauts
79 Does certain caretaking
83 What begins tomorrow
88 Childhood taboos
89 Book of "The Alexandria Quartet"
91 Language suffix
92 Believer in God
93 Individuals
94 Statutes
95 Pre-World Series abbr.
96 Cotton separators
97 Waste piece from metal casting
98 Whatever
99 Brief life story
100 Scrabble piece
101 Greek cross
102 Leatherwood
105 Act parts
107 Zero hour, in a way
110 Forms beads
111 NATO cousin
112 Mr. Knievel
113 Fla. State players
114 Horizontal layers
115 Hrs. in Salt Lake
116 Painter Holbein
117 Adversary

DOWN

1 Mlle. from Madrid
2 Intimidates
3 Tightly folded rock layers
4 Tonight's VIP
5 Sort of ending?
6 Knocks for a loop
7 Decline to bid
8 Zeta follower
9 Musical composition
10 Sid's comedic sidekick
11 Comic Carvey
12 Lunched
13 Shepherds
14 Uris or Trotsky
15 Neighbor of Syr.
16 Start of 83A
17 Feminist Bloomer
18 Hunt and Reddy
24 Eye in Aix
25 Ancient Greek dialect
30 Singer Tucker
33 College in Poughkeepsie
34 Dracula's wrap
35 Opium-based cough suppressant
36 Capital on the Danube
37 __ Tome and Principe
38 Tavern by a tube station
39 Last of coal?
43 Herb with aromatic seeds
44 Preoccupy
45 Reciprocal of a cosecant
47 Sports venues
50 Taylor of "The Nanny"
51 Syrian leader
53 Song of praise
54 Wipe memory
55 Former Israeli P.M.
56 Model Kim
57 Tunes up for a bout
58 Flier
59 A wish to all!
60 Shepherd of "Moonlighting"
64 Brunch choice
65 Soft palate
68 Virgil's hero
69 Work gang
72 More level
73 Tonight's pledge
76 August in Paris
78 Kid of the west
79 Serpent's warning
80 Obtain by cajolery
81 Sock end
82 Draft org.
84 Singer Etheridge
85 Uneasy to the max
86 "Jurassic Park" star Sam
87 Assyrian capital
89 Holds tight
90 Surgical knife
93 Potato
97 Windmill blades
99 Encircling route
100 "__ the night before..."
101 Fed. agents
103 Those folk
104 __-bitsy
106 Gun lobby's letters
107 Mister turkey
108 Gabor sister
109 Compass dir.

by Willy A. Wiseman

ACROSS

1 Changed the proportions of
9 Herald
17 Patriotic men's org.
20 Composer Respighi
21 Harvey or Olivier
22 Resembling: suff.
23 Catch forty winks in cyberspace?
25 Business letter abbr.
26 Stitch
27 Pasturage grass
28 Jack of "Barney Miller"
29 Of part of a foot
31 Fido rider?
33 PBS sister station
35 Long or Peeples
37 Singer James
38 Indian state
41 Spanish dish
44 WWII craft
47 Judgment
49 Farmer's fantasy?
52 Fox's title
53 Mineral vein
55 Henry VIII's last Catherine
56 Fairy tale opening
57 S-shaped curve
58 "The Flying Dutchman" girl
61 Ancient temple
63 __-friendly
66 Foundation stones
68 Very dry
70 Treason, e.g.
73 Old French coin
74 Rip van Winkle's time in the sack?
77 Mom-&-pop store grp.
78 Containing element #73
80 Fleming superspy
81 Of spiritual knowledge
83 "God's Little Acre" co-star Ray
84 Annan of the U.N.
86 Alleviates
88 American suffragist
89 Wallach and Whitney
92 Orderly
94 Gold in the Sierra Madre
95 In the know
96 Take some time off?
101 Songsmith Johnny
103 Bettered
104 Used a strainer
106 Equals
107 Holy Roman emperor
108 Billy Joel hit, "Just the Way You __"
111 Part of 93D
112 Danube tributary
114 Formal, casually
117 BPOE member
119 Abraham's son
121 NFL scores
124 Damage
125 Worth staying awake for?
130 Puncture starter?
131 Chafe
132 Sweet, white wine
133 Reverse pic
134 Balanced on the brink
135 Tallinn man

DOWN

1 Anglers' gear
2 Nice to be?
3 Pack cargo
4 Heifer
5 Horace work, "__ Poetica"
6 Hamlet, to Horatio
7 Lure
8 Capital of Qatar
9 Easily shaped
10 Flowed
11 Inning enders
12 Antigone's uncle
13 "__ Soleil" (The Sun King)
14 Writer Beattie
15 "Rhyme Pays" rapper
16 Change: pref.
17 Unwillingness to nod off?
18 Lipstick tree
19 Get a better grip
24 Burning coal
30 Happen again
31 More equable
32 K-O connection
34 Give a hand
36 Exactly suitable
38 Gardens of trees
39 Like operations
40 Nod off beneath a lap robe?
42 Port of Yemen
43 Garnished with almonds
45 Not withstanding that, informally
46 Actor Stiller
48 Unquestioned principle
50 __ pro nobis
51 Expression of displeasure
54 Astronaut Judith
59 Old sailor
60 Breed of horses
62 Birth-control pioneer
64 Excite hate
65 Nuclear power sources
67 Turkish title
69 O.J. trial judge
71 Captive's cost
72 Nav. enlisted rank
75 Bargain model: pref.
76 Harem room
79 Cities in Ohio and Spain
82 Olympics official
85 Pot-au-__
87 Sound unit
90 Late starter?
91 RR stop
93 Wage-slave's letters
96 John or Dody
97 Travel faster
98 Indeed
99 Earned
100 Dispatch boat
102 Anti-pollution grp.
105 Dors and Ross
109 Swat again
110 Privileged few
113 Trailblazer
115 Agitated state
116 Olden days
118 Trunk bulge
120 African fox
121 Actress Hatcher
122 Comic Carvey
123 British gun
126 Three in Italia
127 Phone co.
128 Of the ear: pref.
129 Branch of Buddhism

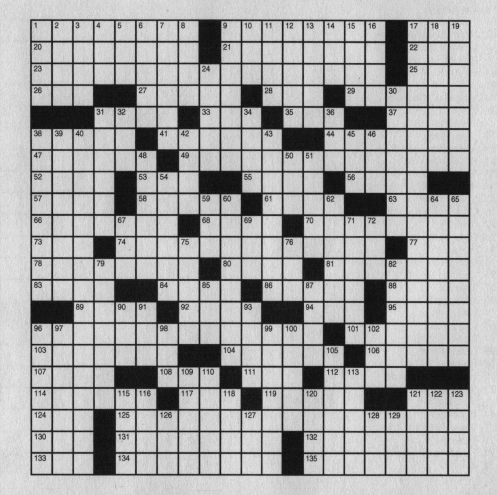

WRITE RHYMES

by Josiah Breward

ACROSS

1 Last
6 Grounds of colleges
14 "Two Mules for __ Sara"
20 Capital of Guam
21 Estrange
22 Laud
23 Sir Penitent?
25 Butted
26 Edwardian or Victorian, e.g.
27 Morse symbol
28 Former name of Exxon
29 In __ (in position)
30 Not fulfilled
32 Islamic sect's ceremony?
38 Too lit?
44 Having the necessary skill
45 Blue dye obtained from indigo
46 Felix and Polly
47 Adenauer's nickname
49 Composer Shostakovich
51 Draws
52 Swashbuckler
53 District
55 Feed
56 Literary leftovers
57 Stephanie Zimbalist's father
59 Thaw twice
61 Compass pt.
62 Makes additional prints
64 Brown shades
66 Droning insects
68 Big Stick policy
71 Verve
74 Vizquel or Khayyam
75 Printed matter of mere passing interest
79 __-de-France
80 And others: Lat.
82 Huntley and Atkins
83 "I __ a Male War Bride"
84 Useful bit of information
85 __ bene (This is important!)
86 Comaneci and others
89 Clamors
90 Daytime serial drama: slang
92 Fix indelibly
94 Medium meeting
96 Gudrun's victim
97 Typeface
99 1985 Roddy McDowall movie
101 Prism input
104 Smoky deposits
105 Lost traction
106 Evaluate
110 Cheer for the matador
111 Short, straight, stiff piece of wire
114 Unkempt
117 Minor dental imperfection
121 Creamy
122 Tenement for biddies?
123 Relieves

124 Lever moved by contact
125 Bird enclosures
126 Fluid ounce fractions

DOWN

1 Go up against
2 "Prince __"
3 Anna Sten film
4 Porch raider
5 Author of "You Know Me, Al"
6 Author of "O Pioneers!"
7 Pub potable
8 Audio pickup
9 Ballpoints
10 Les Etats-__
11 Asian starches
12 Numerical ending
13 Put in position
14 Elfin treat?
15 Full of wrath
16 "The Seven __"
17 Daggett or Curry
18 Language ending
19 Carmine
24 Prosodic feet
29 Part of RSVP
30 Colorado tribe
31 Most orderly

33 Role indicator
34 Girder piece
35 Mean
36 Albanian capital
37 Best of the best
38 Land of Doha
39 City near Venice
40 Of the intestines
41 Pathogen
42 Govt. med. grp.
43 Make lace
48 "My Fair Lady" lyricist
50 Corresponds exactly
52 Warm beforehand
54 Cookbook makeup
57 Unmanly
58 Instinctive reaction
60 Road curve
63 Tumor: suff.
64 Domesticating
65 Alias letters
67 Letters of a money dispenser
69 Me, in Marseilles
70 Repositions pictures
71 Lumberjack's two-man tool
72 Big Dipper star
73 Katmandu tongue

76 J.R. of "Dallas"
77 Southfork of "Dallas"
78 Plus feature
81 "Knots" author
82 Roman 103
87 Barking sound
88 __ es Salaam
89 Podium
91 Indy break
93 To the __ degree
94 Shoulder warmer
95 Went in
98 Resembling: suff.
100 Places for horseshoes
102 Exhilarate
103 Singer Lopez
107 Eastern potentate
108 God of thunder
109 Pin box
111 Tuscany city
112 List unit
113 Scottish loch
114 Q-U connection
115 Docs' org.
116 Republicans, with "the"
117 __ Na Na
118 "My Name Is Asher __"
119 Full of: suff.
120 Saloon

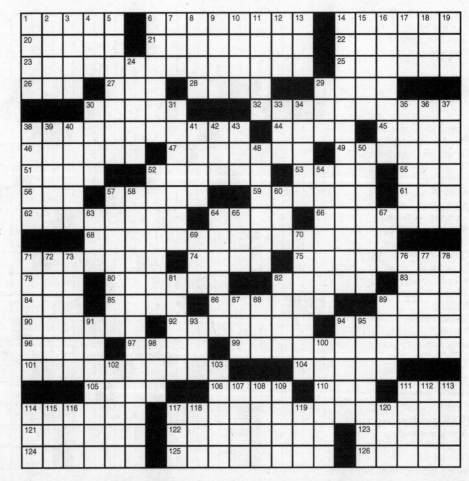

159   EMPTY HONORS

by Alan P. Olschwang

ACROSS

1 Surrealist painter Max
6 Barley used in brewing
10 Trunk
14 Cryptic
19 Lixiviate
20 Sturdy cart
21 Major golfing event
22 Old-womanish
23 Start of Anna Quindlen quote
26 __ fours
27 Give confidence to
28 Elementary lepton particles
29 "Faust" poet
30 Rents
32 Agree silently
33 Part 2 of Quindlen quote
36 Greek X
39 Robin's leader
41 Backslide
42 More isolated and dejected
44 More fit and robust
45 Barrymore or Carey
49 Part 3 of Quindlen quote
54 Jackie's second husband, for short
55 Currency in Chihuahua
56 Guilty and not guilty
57 Footless
59 Crowd stirrer?
62 Believer in an esoteric Hebrew sect
64 Part 4 of Quindlen quote
71 Maladies
72 Kind of fuel
73 Worked very hard and doggedly
74 Main impact
76 Ninny
81 Sty
82 Part 5 of Quindlen quote
88 Roush and Hall
90 Esther of "Good Times"
91 Time to serve
92 Features
95 Spiny-finned marine fish with thick lips
97 That girl
98 Part 6 of Quindlen quote
101 Pizza order
102 Beer buys
104 Region united with Castile to form Spain
105 Fall guy
107 Exchanges
111 Mushroom with a brown spongy cap
112 End of Quindlen quote
116 In unison
117 Sacred bird of ancient Egypt
118 Polynesian pantomiming dance
119 Past, present or future
120 Easter forerunners
121 Unit of capacity
122 Sharp cry
123 Bordered

DOWN

1 Director Kazan
2 Ump's cohorts
3 Those opposed
4 Scrub
5 Liturgical censers
6 AMA members
7 Cuckoopint
8 Gap in manuscript
9 Magnate
10 Supervisor
11 Saturn's wife
12 Floral loop
13 Printers' measures
14 Fowl choices
15 Like two jacks
16 Me too
17 Root or Yale
18 Frighten off
24 Make right
25 Bring to closure
29 Political elephant's letters
31 Arrest
33 Gwyn and Carter
34 Bread spread
35 Poi source
36 Horse hoof sound
37 Gordie of hockey
38 Hostelries
40 "__ Robinson"
41 Pro __
43 DDE's command
44 Ancient Greek temple slave
46 Brit's wireless
47 Expunge
48 Droops
50 __ dixit
51 Took wing
52 Afghanistan's capital
53 Altercation
58 Long in the tooth
59 Musical composition
60 Giant slugger
61 Hesitator's sounds
62 Program media, briefly
63 An honest man?
64 Quebec peninsula
65 Lubricated
66 Chan portrayer
67 License regulators: abbr.
68 Adolescent
69 Saturn feature
70 Zeus' consort
74 Clobbers
75 Fam. members
76 Blend
77 Color
78 Charged particles
79 Toe-stubber's cry
80 Trap in an oak
83 Waste allowance
84 Centering points
85 Explorer Johnson
86 Escritoire
87 Maps in maps
89 Dick or John Singer
93 Long scarves
94 Brooch
95 "__ Woman"
96 Save from a pickle
98 Muslim porter
99 Irregularly notched
100 Moses' brother
101 City near Bayonne
103 Cloyed
105 Hey, over here!
106 Caterwaul
108 Mild expletive
109 Otherwise
110 Luge
112 Tuck's partner?
113 Sapporo sash
114 Soft metal
115 Drain

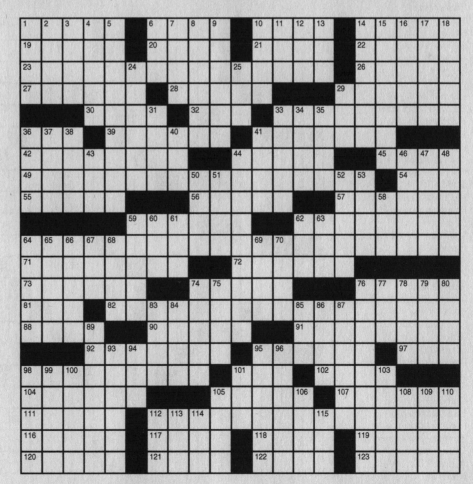

GOING DUTCH

by Edgar Fontaine

ACROSS

1 Dutch South African
5 Netherworld
10 Glances
15 Soup du __
19 "Clair de __"
20 Spartan market
21 White heron
22 Bear in the sky
23 Milanese eight
24 The Flying Dutchman of baseball
26 20% of CCLXV
27 Lyric poem
28 Pizzazz
29 Dutch uncles, e.g.?
31 Fable's lesson
33 Addams Family cousin
34 In the past
36 Weird
37 Corn varieties
39 Tropical tree
41 Writer Rand
42 Paintings on plaster
45 Nab
47 Help hoods, e.g.
51 Tunes in
52 Tarzan's mate
53 Polanski film
56 Nice summer?
57 Means of entry
58 Notes
59 Add breath to pronunciation
61 Pub pint
62 In front
63 Dutch brew
64 Daytona 500 winner Waltrip
67 Apparition
69 Dutch actress in "An American in Paris"
72 Warning signal
73 Tattle
77 Me, myself and I problem
78 Phonograph needles
79 Dour
81 Took first
82 Pealed
83 Bit of news
84 Pool adjuncts
85 Elder or alder
87 Trough along eaves
89 Edible roots
90 Occupant: abbr.
93 Periods
94 Hit hard
95 Processes seawater
99 Impressive skill
100 One to Therese
101 Postage
105 Hans Brinker's transportation
107 Numbers at the pump
110 Open hostilities
111 "Cheers" barfly
112 Holland

114 African nation
115 Baseball family name
116 Throws down the gauntlet
117 Remove the cover from
118 Repast remnants
119 Shapes with an ax
120 Luges
121 Hollywood Noah
122 Dutch cheese

DOWN

1 Tulip, e.g.
2 Surpass
3 Computer key
4 Old-time motorcar
5 Sarcastic chuckle
6 Suffers
7 Gives
8 Belches
9 Window element
10 Round legume
11 Chinese appetizer
12 European sea eagle
13 __ over (collapses)
14 Layers
15 Dutch queen (1948-80)
16 Belted hunter
17 Employing
18 Salary boost

25 Armed
28 Locations
30 Attempt
32 Dutch capital
35 Strong winds
38 Charged atoms
40 Dutch spy
42 Loose weight?
43 Oriental staple
44 Evan's end?
45 Kiel or Caledonian, e.g.
46 Begrudge
48 Honker
49 Back end of a kitchen?
50 Adolescent
52 Schumacher or McCrea
54 Roasting stick
55 Chinese: pref.
58 Dutch seat of government
60 Dutch painter of "The Anatomy Lesson of Dr. Tulp"
62 Curving
65 Way off
66 Columnist Barrett
67 Tradesman
68 Steering mechanism
69 Salamander
70 Frankenstein's assistant

71 Zippo
72 Witness
74 Burt's ex
75 PDQ
76 A Truman
78 Shankar's instrument
79 Trading center
80 Preoccupy
84 Datebook
86 Dutch writer of "In Praise of Folly"
88 Vandalized
89 Catholic sacrament
91 Wapiti
92 Pedestals
94 Lighter fuel
95 Shore or Washington
96 Eleve's place
97 Sikkim antelope
98 Purloin
102 Bestow upon
103 Valletta's nation
104 Spectrum maker
106 Raison d'__
108 Simple weapon
109 Catch sight of
113 Snaky turn
114 Leader of the Three Stooges

CRIMINAL ELEMENTS

by Ed Voile

ACROSS

1 "Ethan __"
6 Audience
11 Kinnear of "As Good as It Gets"
15 Bipartisan coalition
19 Greek storyteller
20 Sharpener
21 Car
22 Stanton film, "__ Man"
23 Methods used by corporate pirates?
26 Of a people: pref.
27 Concerning: Lat.
28 Tickle Me __
29 Welsh valley
30 __ and yon
32 Long and Peeples
33 Driver's peg
34 Half a fly?
35 Sicilian wine
36 State off.
37 Group of blackbirds in "The Birds"?
41 Top
42 Alternative part
44 __ sequitur
45 Take a gander
46 "__ brillig..."
47 Prevented
50 Ancient temple
51 Coloration
52 Sierra __ Mountains
55 "And I Love __"
56 Black widow?
60 Taj Mahal site
61 Language of Bangladesh
63 Ashe Stadium event
64 Corrida shouts
65 Guinness and Sellers in '55 film
69 Acuff and Rogers
70 Dwell
72 Recollects vividly
73 Fascinated by
74 I've gotta have one!
78 Barbie's guy
79 More contemptible
80 Wide shoe width
81 Midday
82 Pensively sad
84 Olympus populace
86 January honoree
87 "__ of the Pink Panther"
88 Novelist Le Guin
92 Play part
93 Legendary baseball hall-of-famer
97 Family dog
98 German dessert
100 Press coverage
101 Major ISP
102 Seed coat
103 Scott of "Quantum Leap"
104 Max of "The Beverly Hillbillies"
106 Grimm beast

107 Diva Ponselle
108 Rara __
109 Too good-looking
113 Moolah
114 Morays
115 Phrygian king of lore
116 __ nous (just between us)
117 Maglie and Mineo
118 Calendar unit
119 Actor Davis
120 Lets up

DOWN

1 Surface layers
2 Gathering of the clan
3 Czech city
4 Small specks
5 N.T. book
6 Irritability
7 Rambled
8 Aware of
9 Moist
10 Moves too slowly
11 Walled-city entrance
12 Undoing
13 & so forth
14 Falconry bird
15 Harte and Saberhagen
16 Boxer's fists?

17 Laertes' sister
18 Joseph and Robert
24 Make piano corrections
25 Pitch symbol
31 Tax grp.
34 Stepped (on)
35 Bullwinkle, e.g.
37 Make a motion
38 Vitality
39 Littleneck, e.g.
40 Chamber
43 Bloodsuckers
46 Software teaching aids
48 Ostrich kin
49 Take care of
50 "Jurassic Park" star Sam
51 Is down with
52 Polynesian New Zealander
53 Shoelace tip
54 Packing heat?
56 Aviator
57 Needless activity
58 Philippines island
59 Nightmarish Belgian artist
61 Used leeches
62 City near Cleveland
66 Taste
67 Nights before

68 1996 Tony winner
71 John or Jane?
75 Bulge at the back of the head
76 Ages and ages
77 Obscuring hazes
79 Hamilton's opponent
82 "The Caine Mutiny" author
83 Flying gas station
84 Windy speakers
85 Daughter of Claudius
86 Stretched and pounded
87 Riviera resort
89 Prepares for transplanting
90 Spare time
91 Map collections
93 Building add-on
94 Manufactured baloney?
95 Old Testament book
96 Cylindrical
99 Strong cravings
102 Hippodrome
104 Take off quickly
105 Altar area
106 Chances
110 FDR group
111 Greenish sloths
112 Whiz lead-in

ACROSS

1 Eschew
5 Ascend
10 Brazilian dance in duple time
15 Gone by
19 Weight of one silver rupee
20 Emulsifying agent
21 Zodiac sign
22 __ of Dogs
23 Present starter?
24 Glare with fury
26 Fictional sleuth Charlie
27 Ground grain
28 Concurred
29 SSS classification
30 Hrbek or McCord
31 Affected person
33 John Quincy or Samuel
35 School kids
37 Helps with the dishes
39 Arena cheers
41 Lost traction
42 French pets
45 Shipshape
47 Figurative uses of words
51 Norway's capital
52 Shepherd's stick
56 Leprechauns' land
58 Sidestep
59 Shoulder wrap
61 Potted household favorite
64 Sicilian peak
65 Browned
67 Neighborhoods
68 Frozen dessert
70 Composer Satie
72 Wapiti
73 Mexican bread
74 Lounging attire
78 Hideaways
80 Writer Ellison
85 Taj Mahal city
86 Located exactly
89 "Moonlight Gambler" singer
90 "I Can't Make You Love Me" singer Bonnie
92 Actress Ward
93 Jewish feast
95 Westerns author Grey
96 Dieter and Lou
98 Carpenter's groove
100 Studied, but not so much?
102 Customary time
104 Socially inept loser
106 More mature
107 Rights to enter
111 Salary increase
113 Satellites' paths
117 Overwhelming defeat
118 Against: pref.
120 Gaps
122 Med. sch. course
123 Sci. or math, e.g.
124 Embroidery on canvas

126 "__ Mia"
127 Popular cookie
128 Recently
129 Singer Fisher
130 Half hitch or bowline
131 Crash-site grp.
132 Mississippi quartet?
133 Marsh grasses
134 Soundstages

DOWN

1 Trample
2 Path starter?
3 Bones in forearms
4 Established conclusively
5 Compensations
6 Block up
7 Greek marketplaces
8 Enjoyed
9 Make beloved
10 Give in to gravity
11 Jason's ship
12 Bearings
13 Crushable hats
14 1946 Triple Crown winner
15 Examined item by item
16 Deathly pale
17 Particular bias
18 Campers' residences

25 Clio Award winner
32 Internet address: abbr.
34 Diplomas casually
36 Nearly hopeless
38 Guessed figs.
40 Put to sea
42 Work station
43 Employee protection agcy.
44 Heroine of "The Good Earth"
46 Meandered
48 __ de foie gras
49 "So Big" and "Show Boat" author Ferber
50 Connection line
53 Stirred from sleep
54 In favor of
55 Gravy-train passenger
57 Noun-forming suffix
60 Lascivious look
62 __ Lama
63 Pianist John
66 Hit the dirt
69 Fossil fuel
71 Sacred bird of ancient Egypt
74 Fishhook feature
75 Lab gel
76 Small combo

77 Crude effort
79 66 or A1A, e.g.
81 Semiwild hogs of the southeast U.S.
82 Fictioneer
83 "__ of Green Gables"
84 Have not
87 Blueprint
88 Moore of "Disclosure"
91 Boxing decisions, in brief
94 Comebacks
97 Philosopher Langer
99 Pope's fanon
101 Saul's uncle
103 Taylor and Adoree
105 Laundry stinker
106 Live
107 Fiery crime
108 Woo
109 Dice, e.g.
110 Medley meals
112 Josiah's porcelain
114 Lacking sense
115 Fortuneteller's cards
116 Sports pages figs.
119 Unemployed
121 Oklahoma city
125 Fleur-de-__

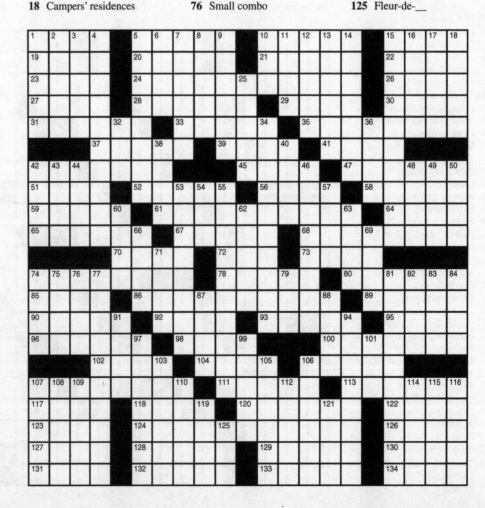

by Sheryl Scott

ACROSS

1 Seat of power
7 Army posts
12 Binding bandage
20 Unseal
21 Lethargic
22 Alone
23 Drawer, e.g.
24 Palace of Tiepolo's frescoes
25 Lotion ingredient
26 Wet peak in the Cascades?
28 Put on the canvas, for short
29 Scheme
30 Brief skirt
31 Puppy bark
32 Least desirable portion
34 Steering devices
36 Not from either side
38 Sch. near Harvard
40 Sell-out letters
41 Carson's predecessor
42 Listed to one side
44 Bottom line
46 Mutual good will
48 __-o'-shanter
51 Actress who's all wet?
55 Mediocre
56 Suitcases
60 Courteney of "Friends"
61 Acquired
63 Hungarian violinist Leopold
64 Abreast of
67 Harvest
69 Hedren of "The Birds"
70 Wet prose style?
75 Four-bagger
76 Golfer's cry
77 Swiss marksman
78 Work on text
79 Smallest species subdivisions
82 Avant-garde French sculptor
84 Needlelike
86 Baseball scores
87 Sinatra movie that's all wet?
91 But, to Brutus
92 __ China Sea
93 Even score
94 Rocks of Montmartre
99 Coke or Pepsi
100 __-CIO
103 In favor of
105 Brandon de Wilde's cinematic cry
106 Author of "Little Women"
109 Approximately
111 4/15 addressee
113 Art Deco designer
114 Ananias, e.g.
115 Exactly suitable
117 Wet, small brownish tree frog?
120 Cypriot saint

122 Drunkard
123 Garlicky poisonous gas
124 Account for
125 Peruvians of yore
126 Falls as ice
127 South African jazz trumpeter Hugh
128 Looks suggestively
129 Untidy situations

DOWN

1 Fowling net
2 Leading lady
3 Domed room
4 Judgment
5 Viper collective
6 Doorway, e.g.
7 Tagalog speaker
8 Son of Judah
9 Bridge action
10 Attempters
11 Rubbernecker
12 Ice-cream tastes
13 Japanese golfer Aoki
14 All wet politician?
15 Miss. neighbor
16 Interfere
17 Functional
18 Of the kidneys

19 Perfect places
27 Objective
33 Objective
35 Fodder
37 River to the Gulf of Finland
39 Sundial X
41 Mountain-dwelling lagomorph
43 Remove sticky stuff
45 Facial twitch
47 Heckle or Jeckle, e.g.
48 Sub weapon
49 Disease-free condition
50 Fashion designer
52 Collection biz
53 Intersection elements
54 Choppers
55 Net user
56 Harsh critics
57 Deejay's gimmick
58 Jack of the "Baltimore Sun"
59 Says howdy
62 PMs
65 Counterbalance
66 Sgt., e.g.
68 Deed
71 Back of station?
72 Algerian port

73 Norwegian saint
74 Digestive-system malady
80 Wet furniture?
81 S. Amer. nation
83 Classroom favorite
85 Slaughter in Cooperstown
88 Melville's captain
89 Durocher feature
90 Unnatural aura
92 Barstool drop-off
95 Brie and gouda
96 Loathsome mythological monsters
97 Cooperative agreement
98 Sibyl
99 Part of an eye: Fr.
101 Paleontologist's find
102 Patti of Broadway's "Evita"
104 Assoc.
106 Photo collection
107 Vine
108 Jacks and jokers
109 Confused
110 Armistice
112 Charley horse, e.g.
116 Jack's tote
118 Munich's river
119 Perry's creator
121 Noah's craft

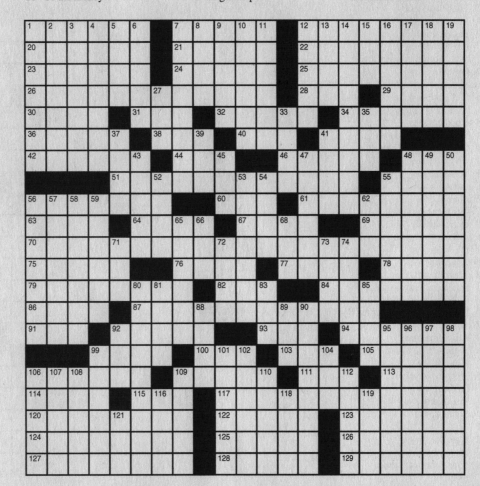

by Arlan and Linda Bushman

ACROSS

1 Rhubarb
5 Carvey and Ivey
10 Lace end
15 Bedouin
19 Rio makeup?
20 Maine campus site
21 Effervescent tonic
22 Cleanse
23 Pratfall?
25 Cockroach plea?
27 Vine support
28 Pop vocalist Bryson
30 Pioneer French feminist de Beauvoir
31 Intellectual pursuits
34 Ambrosia ingredient
35 Parti-colored cat
39 Foot: suff.
40 Impassive
42 His, in Hyeres
43 Invigorating
44 Back talk from a psychoanalyst?
47 Organic compound
48 Goodyear billboard?
49 Superabundance
50 Gillette shaver
54 Bobby Brown hit of 1989
55 Wishes undone
56 Macrame feature
57 Zodiac earth sign
59 Animal tracks
61 Fully versed concerning
62 Oyster or clam
63 Sound of irritation
65 Philosopher Adler's least promising pupil?
68 $ percentages
69 West Point, for one
71 "Pursuit of the Graf __"
72 Go on a sortie
74 Temptresses
75 France, once
76 Zeal
77 European capital
80 Concert halls
81 H.S. math course
82 Pitching coups
83 Small bit
84 Treats from a St. Petersburg baker?
88 Garlic unit
89 Midsection muscles, casually
92 Below, in poems
93 Power measure
94 Wyoming city on the North Platte River
95 Stringed keyboard instrument
97 Single guy
99 Soundtracks
100 Separate
102 Checks
107 Inattentive Cincinnati player?
109 Miss America's prize money?
112 Man or Dogs
113 Fritter away
114 Relish
115 Sushi choice
116 Woad and anil
117 Endured
118 Kick back
119 Skittish

DOWN

1 Diplomacy
2 Mr. Stravinsky
3 Get hot under the collar
4 Give out
5 Square-dancing movement
6 Pretentious
7 "...__ gloom of night..."
8 Black cuckoo
9 Absorbed
10 __ the Great, Shah of Iran
11 Chow
12 Brand symbol
13 Printing measures
14 Planting layer
15 Dollar rival
16 Synthetic fibers
17 Means of access
18 Brimless toppers
24 Use a stopwatch
26 Christina of "Sleepy Hollow"
29 Sized up
32 Most lively
33 Looks so
34 Outlay
35 Radio enthusiast
36 Florence river
37 Furry pet for Leo?
38 Long Island township
40 Stylish businesses?
41 Hardware doodad
44 Light snowfall
45 Pay no heed to
46 Artist Cezanne
48 Simple sweepers
51 Low overpass scraper, perhaps?
52 Pipe problem
53 Inquires
56 Prepare to be knighted
57 Rich cakes
58 TV doctor portrayer
60 Writing on the wall
61 Throw mud at, figuratively
62 Brighton lengths
63 El __, TX
64 Base neutralizer
66 Hebrew prophet
67 Natural simplicity
70 Honey
73 Embers
75 Stick-to-itiveness
76 Firm belief
78 Treasure
79 Passover offering
81 Russian ruler
82 Keyboard feature
85 Labor group
86 Waffles
87 Tchaikovsky bird
88 Shoulder
89 Tick or mite
90 Like Bessie Smith's singing
91 Bike seat
94 Gray matter
96 Clamps
97 Tunneled
98 First Lady's first
100 Lhasa __
101 Mother of Apollo
103 Ferrara family
104 Tater
105 Chinese secret society
106 Don't leave me
108 Superficially complete
110 Dutch commune
111 Popular ISP

NON-FICTION

by Bill Swain

ACROSS

1 Narrative events
9 Specifies distinctly
16 Paper tablets
20 Computer bank
21 School
22 Cain's victim
23 Gerald Green book about Cain?
25 Dry by rubbing
26 Neighbor of Syr.
27 Standoff
28 Prickling sensation
30 Depression era agcy.
33 "Downtown" singer Clark
36 Proust volume, "__ a Budding Grove"
40 Kiddy
41 Priest's vestment
42 Anna Quindlen book about a lie?
44 Vein to mine
45 Hindmost part
47 __ sequitur
48 One who pretends
49 Marry
50 Don vestments
53 Job shift
55 Novelist Uris
57 Changes the machinery
59 __ de Saint-Exupery
63 Deftness
66 Water depth: abbr.
67 Prohibits
69 Hoisted
70 Mount of Moses
71 "O don fatale," e.g.
73 Explosive liquid, briefly
75 French floor
77 Poultry output
78 Horne and Olin
80 Group of five
82 "Symphonie Espagnole" composer
84 Way in: abbr.
85 Camus play, "__ de siege"
86 Made possible
88 Abstracted musing
90 Actor Corey
92 Cruise ship
94 Quarterback Troy
95 "Norma __"
97 Terhune book
101 Island near Naxos
103 Stand open
104 Pixie
105 Tom Wolfe book about switched luggage?
109 "All Things Considered" net.
110 Physicians' org.
111 Scored two under par
112 Different ones
113 Affirmative reply
114 Cure
116 Department of Justice agcy.
117 One-time link
119 Composer Satie
120 Theodore Dreiser book made into a sitcom?
130 Khartoum's river
131 Oscar contender
132 Naval might
133 Calendar units
134 Unfathomable chasms
135 Master openers

DOWN

1 NYC summer hrs.
2 Contemptuous exclamation
3 Inhabitant of: suff.
4 Moroccan port
5 San Luis __, CA
6 "Gidget" co-star James
7 Superman's letter
8 Confirmed
9 Repudiation
10 Verge
11 Coati's coat
12 Frigid
13 SE Asian war
14 Zeta follower
15 Watchman
16 Hock
17 John le Carre book about the boom of Bonn?
18 Condemn
19 Fell as ice
24 City once called Terminus
29 Right to enter
30 Cascade
31 Sycamore
32 Agee book about a blessed event?
34 Decimal base
35 E.T. vehicles
36 John Steinbeck book about Mae portraying Eve?
37 Part of TGIF
38 Calendar watch abbr.
39 That man
43 Pierre's health
46 Old card game
51 Move up and down
52 Spirited vigor
54 Truman Capote book about a crime of passion?
56 "The Grapes of Wrath" character
58 Shoot from hiding
60 Addams Family cousin
61 Schon or Cassady
62 Mystery award
64 Promotional gift
65 Radio audience
68 Anna of "Nana"
72 Perfect report card
74 Cytoplasm letters
76 Zeno of __
79 Contrived
81 True up
83 Egg: pref.
87 Of God the Creator
89 Med. lines?
91 Buddhism school
93 Type of IRA
95 Back part
96 Spanish port
98 U. acquisition
99 Pointed tool
100 Rapping Dr.
102 Writer Miller
106 Spiny fishes
107 Brouhaha
108 Camera settings
115 Just gets by
116 Liberate
118 Out of control
121 Frisco hill
122 Writer Tan
123 Wrong: pref.
124 Annapolis grad.
125 Egyptian viper
126 Teachers' grp.
127 Female sheep
128 "L.A. Law" co-star
129 Time meas.

by Lee G. Barrow

ACROSS

1 Max of quantum mechanics
5 Pulitzer Prize winner Ferber
9 Ascend
14 Imminent danger
19 Shaving-cream additive
20 In good shape
21 Of harmonic sounds
22 Borg or Sorenstam, e.g.
23 Spills the beans
27 Dogma
28 Perot's middle name
29 Nag
30 Fed. transport agcy.
31 Singular performances
32 Staffs
34 1955 Pulitzer Prize-winning drama
40 Loose-fitting garment worn by Arabs
43 Hogwash
44 Stood
45 Boot out
46 Complacent
47 Screen parts
48 Marshland
49 Enormous
50 Item in a squirrel's cache
51 Harbinger
52 Toys with one's victim
56 Bonkers
57 Felt regret
58 Kitchen knife
59 Scrubs, as a mission
60 Bad luck charm?
61 Exactitude
62 One-liner
63 St. Francis' birthplace
66 French social philosopher
67 Football kick
68 Relative pronoun
71 Sitting pretty
74 Baby bed
75 1842 Nikolai Gogol novel, "__ Bulba"
76 Get the job done
77 Yell
78 Isolated
79 Caked deposit
80 Fed
81 Lost traction
83 Groups of trees
84 Stitched border
85 Why so quiet?
88 Young adults
90 Sean of "Dead Man Walking"
91 Atom with a charge
92 Lofty
95 Galvanizing metal
96 Exits
101 Smiles broadly
105 Door hardware
106 Singer Page
107 Pot sweetener
108 Shuttle grp.
109 Cherub
110 French writer Madame de __
111 Thomas Hardy novel, "__ of the d'Urbervilles"
112 Deuce beater

DOWN

1 Hairless
2 Margarine
3 Sch. mil. org.
4 Snug retreat
5 Moral
6 Soak
7 Considerate
8 Physicians' org.
9 Squealer
10 "My __ Vinny"
11 Social insects
12 Buddhist Thai
13 Sprite
14 Shucks!
15 Water pitchers
16 Country singer McEntire
17 Lupino and Tarbell
18 Chair supports
24 Groups of three
25 Jogs
26 Larceny
31 Unemotional
32 Mercury model
33 Al of the '50s Cleveland Indians
34 Type of portable memory
35 Bouquet
36 Like many showers
37 Pizzeria fixture
38 Mountain nymph
39 Milling tool
40 Illicit love affair
41 Fireworks explosion
42 "__ of God"
46 Ice cream unit?
48 Bend
49 Arlen or Lloyd
50 External boundary
52 Carthaginian
53 Soul
54 NBA player
55 Discourage
57 Upslopes
60 Holy war
61 Dressing a judge?
62 Wharf
63 Gee follower
64 Trap
65 Banjo beat
66 Ermines in brown coats
67 Marcel Proust's "A la recherche du temps __"
68 Injustice
69 Caste member?
70 Corpulent
72 Typical Clio Award winner
73 Heir
74 Family group
78 One who makes amends
80 Immune system member
81 Mold's kin?
82 "Twin Peaks" director
83 Skyscraper figures
86 Narcotic
87 Legal claims
88 Barest trace
89 Stand for art
92 Turkish honorific
93 Poet's Ireland
94 Marriage token
95 Greek letter
96 Medieval slave
97 Dispatched
98 Wound reminder
99 Alleviate
100 Remain
102 Tape-counter abbr.
103 Krazy __
104 Devour

by Josiah Breward

ACROSS

1 Stately display
5 Twirl
11 Allen and Blanc
15 God of war
19 Myth ending?
20 Enclosing line of people
21 Jai __
22 Actress Campbell
23 Display one's wealth
25 Very competitive
27 Gage bestseller
28 Veteran sailor
29 Pariahs
30 Shade tree
31 Liked from the start
33 Virgil's shepherdess
35 Makes mistakes
36 Holiday lead-in
37 Columnist Bombeck
39 Fender flaws
41 Sedating guys?
43 Sword lily
47 Be __ as it may...
49 Helper: abbr.
50 CD-__
51 Needlessly selfish person
57 United
59 Stallion's mate
60 Astrologer Sydney
61 __-CIO
64 Goose on Oahu
65 Hand-launched bombs
68 Lack of success
70 Really weary
72 Mauna __
73 Favorite of the gods
74 Alternative to a thumbtack
75 The garment industry
77 Enrage
78 Lawyer: abbr.
79 Bristles
81 Gardener's tools
82 Polio vaccine developer
83 Hyped up presentation
87 Math letters
88 Urn
91 God of France
92 Affected appearance
94 Spielberg epic of 1997
98 Mexican moola
101 "Rule, Britannia" composer
102 Tour segment
103 Assert positively
105 Tears
107 Part of speech
111 Rural stopover
112 Bunting and Rathbone
114 Statutes
116 Flower parts
117 Miserably unhappy existence
119 Degenerate
121 Pianist Peter
122 Meal scraps
123 Metcalf of "Roseanne"
124 Toward shelter
125 Golf-course hazard
126 Highland loch
127 Put between
128 Guitarist Lofgren

DOWN

1 Calibrated tube
2 Eye: pref.
3 San __, CA
4 Dropped abruptly
5 GI
6 Wonderstruck exclamations
7 Tire pattern
8 Muddled
9 Play a flute
10 High school subj.
11 Manufactured
12 Wed on the wing
13 Pub drinks
14 "High __"
15 Picnic pest
16 Buys back
17 Develops changes gradually
18 Subdivision
24 Ammonia or fertilizer
26 Org.
29 Shop machine
32 Melville's "Typee" sequel
34 Out of favor with one's wife
38 Math subj.
40 Island of Epicurus' birth
42 __ es Salaam
43 Pop's pop
44 Fail to achieve an expected gain
45 In the company of
46 Set sights
48 Highland cap
52 Fabray, casually
53 Musical refrain
54 Arabian desert
55 Meal prayer
56 Actor Estrada
58 Holland: abbr.
61 Out loud
62 Carefree times
63 Romanticized myths
65 Norwegian composer
66 Oscar de la __
67 Jackson's Secretary of War
69 Vega's constellation
71 __ facto
73 African fever
75 Load more salsa on one's chip
76 "The Bridge of San Luis __"
80 Plus
82 Defraud
83 __ Moines
84 Jury makeup
85 Govt. med. grp.
86 Other: Sp.
88 Brave
89 Person with corrections
90 Milano Mrs.
93 Reno resident
95 Slot fillers
96 King Arthur's paradise
97 Want
99 Borrowed
100 Social standing
104 Fissures
106 Cursed
108 "Christ Stopped at __"
109 Star in Orion
110 Military locations
113 Subtraction word
115 Mix
118 The Republicans
119 The: It.
120 __ up (excited)

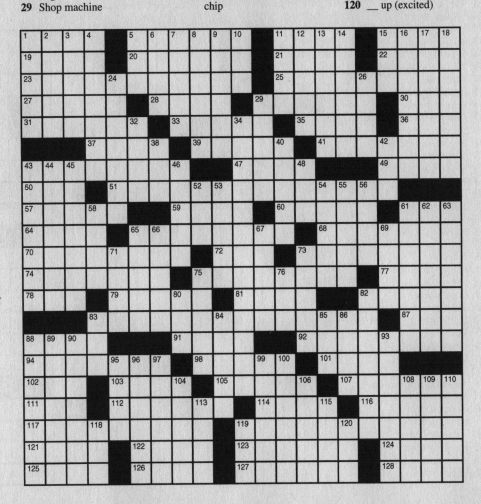

LOST LOVES

by Willy A. Wiseman

ACROSS

1 1996 Tony-winning musical
5 Spanish cellist Casals
10 Comes up short
15 Lends a hand
19 Frankenstein's assistant
20 Estuary
21 Lowest deck
22 Sink one's teeth into
23 Elixir without love?
26 Garfield's buddy
27 Instruct privately
28 "Star Wars" princess
29 Pleasure sail
31 Lazybones
34 Judged
36 Small quantity
37 Close
38 WWI battle site
41 Rome's airport
44 Isl. off Australia
45 U.S. fashion without love?
48 Scoundrel
49 Military training
   course: abbr.
50 Send an overdue notice
51 The one __ got away
52 Whittle
53 You, to Yves
54 "__ and Ivory"
55 Substantially made
57 Russian saint
58 Type of general
60 "You Send Me" singer Sam
61 Farm towers
62 After a sex change
   without love?
67 Cheap West Indies rum
70 Breaks from a habit
71 Byzantine portico
75 Woe is me!
76 Mommy's mommy
78 Job shift
80 Ginger __
81 Building wings
82 Train track
83 Parrot
84 Black goo
85 Solidify
86 Marvel character
   without love?
89 Make work
90 Serving to make one
92 Lift
93 Ditty
94 Cleopatra's river
95 Cash in
97 Landscape dips
98 Massachusetts city on the
   Merrimack
100 Govt. farm grp.
101 Pompous fools
104 Oklahoma city
105 Beach message
   without love?
112 Import tax

113 Outmoded anesthetic
114 Musician Shaw
115 Pin box
116 U.S. tennis stadium
117 Fragrant bed?
118 Uncanny
119 Allow to use

DOWN

1 Tear
2 I problem?
3 "It's __ Unusual"
4 More hackneyed
5 Half quart
6 Part of A.D.
7 Obscure
8 Moon vehicle: abbr.
9 Gambling parlor's letters
10 Crew leaders
11 Golfer Palmer
12 Homeric epic
13 Chaney of "The Wolf Man"
14 Strong suit
15 Tropical rodent
16 Telephone to Delhi
   without love?
17 Speaker's platform
18 Popeye's nephew, __ Pea
24 "__ Town"
25 "Maria __" (1932 hit song)
30 Travel about
31 Altogether
32 Church leader
33 Movie dog
34 Lace mat
35 Bus. letter abbr.
38 One-celled organisms: var.
39 Given new life
40 Toothy smile
41 Two regarded as a pair
42 Hold contents
43 Concepts
45 Singer Franklin
46 German plane
47 Flung
52 Tapered end
55 Cher's ex
56 Fling
59 Cheese choice
60 "Thief" star
61 "No Exit" dramatist
63 Anticipate
64 __ Park, NJ
65 Edible bulbs
66 Equestrian school
67 South Korean city
68 Witty Woody
69 Join a gang without love?

72 "A __ of Rain"
73 "Seinfeld" role
74 Persian victor at
   Thermopylae
76 Cringing crawler, in the
   U.K.
77 Quickness contest
78 Go away!
79 Bangkok resident
83 Tours to be
86 Seasoning herb
87 Aircraft guidance devices
88 Stalk of asparagus
91 Color fabric, '60s-style
93 Hanging frill
95 Bader Ginsburg and Buzzi
96 Lauder of cosmetics
97 Winner's letter
98 Clytemnestra's mother
99 Encumbrance
101 Against
102 Move, emotionally
103 Storage building
106 WWII arena
107 Spotted
108 Dander
109 Devoured
110 Holy sister
111 Accomplished

CHICK FLICKS?

by Ed Voile

ACROSS

1 Pekoe or hyson warmer
8 Porch of a penthouse
15 The ones here
20 African javelin
21 Fleet commander
22 Return in kind
23 1967 Elke Sommer movie?
26 Slaughterhouse adjuncts
27 Inasmuch as
28 Asian inland sea
29 Max of "The Beverly Hillbillies"
31 Calendar increment
32 Brown with a band
33 Comforting letters
35 901
36 Extinguished
37 Fedora feature
39 1940 Edward G. Robinson movie?
42 Candidate not on the slate
44 __ Na Na
45 Pagliacci
46 1947 Gregory Peck movie?
50 Shakespeare's "__ Andronicus"
54 Chicago tower
55 Levin or Gershwin
56 Crocodile __
59 Bounding gait
60 Sacred image
63 Scathing review
64 Moveable wing surface
66 1951 Spencer Tracy movie?
73 Stirs to action
74 Dolores __ Rio
75 Med. sch. subj.
76 Period in office
77 Tennille's Captain Dragon
79 "The Joy Luck Club" author
81 Wrist bones
86 Bangs shut
88 1948 Edward G. Robinson movie?
92 Chair designer Charles
95 "Another 48 __"
96 Author of "A Bend in the River"
97 1943 Spencer Tracy movie?
102 Recipe meas.
103 Opposite of SSW
104 "To Have and Have __"
105 511
106 Goddess of the dawn
107 Racket
108 Makes haste
109 Suffix for adherents
111 Privalova or Vorobyeva
113 Golf club metal
116 1998 Leonardo DiCaprio movie?
121 Russo and Auberjonois
122 Conveyance
123 John Tyler's First Lady
124 Machu Picchu locale
125 Brennan and Heckart
126 Pitcher's trick pitches

DOWN

1 Small boy
2 Wind dir.
3 Foul-smelling natural medication
4 Relinquisher
5 Eye covetously
6 Stated
7 Giving in
8 Shabby
9 Old English letters
10 Sandhurst sch.
11 Removes suds
12 Drawer, e.g.
13 Lyricist Sammy
14 Part of EKG
15 Three in Trieste
16 Blood: pref.
17 Orthodox bishop
18 Genoese specialty
19 Peeper protector
24 Ramble
25 Big-time criminal
29 Soup servings
30 Haloes
32 Actor Neeson
34 R. Ebert, e.g.
37 Smith and Coleman
38 Narrow inlet
39 Flushing stadium
40 Kett of comics
41 Like a snake ready to strike
43 Son of Odin
44 Speech on Sun.
47 Brooklet
48 & others
49 Oahu goose
51 Barreled (along)
52 Current
53 Dispatch
57 Downpour
58 Indian deity
61 The __ Scott Case
62 Pelion's partner
63 Jim Bakker's org.
65 Chinese fruits
66 Tangled masses
67 Pitcher Hershiser
68 One-third of a WWII movie?
69 Composer Johann Nepomuk __
70 Pastoral poem
71 Spill the beans
72 Carvey or Delany
78 Demolish in London
79 Bentley wheel
80 Brief commercials
82 Org. of Sampras
83 Bring back to life
84 Former plum
85 Man and Dogs
87 Smooth wood
89 Conductance units
90 Removes tangles
91 Hiatus
93 Saying
94 Abu Dhabi or Fujairah
97 "Peer Gynt" role
98 Land o' __!
99 Go to
100 Repudiation
101 Actress Woodward
102 S. Amer. monkey
107 Weight-loss plans
108 Hot and sticky
110 Popeye's __ Pea
112 Cross inscription
113 Watery
114 Christmas song
115 Former Peruvian currency
117 CIA's predecessor
118 Half a fly?
119 Knight's address
120 Egyptian souls

PGA PAIRINGS

by Josiah Breward

ACROSS

1 Iron oxide
5 One who tolerates
11 Light touches
15 Surefire shots
19 Con
20 "__ X"
21 Writer Harte
22 Pound or Frost
23 PGA pairing is a rookie?
25 Sacred text
27 PGA peg
28 Lilly or Wallach
29 Lobster pot
31 Devil's domain
32 __ in the sky
33 Change one's stance?
35 Enroll
37 Fastener attacher
39 Baldwin and Guinness
40 Unspecified amount
41 Store of valuables
43 Concavity
44 Wry face
45 __ on (victimizes)
46 Medicinal quantities
49 Wynn and Wood
50 Supermarket carriage
51 Crop up
52 Mini-wave
53 PGA pairing from Canada?
55 Irrigated
56 Satellite connection
59 Closely confined
60 Swaddle
62 In-person
63 Instant
64 From 570 to 240 million years ago
66 Digestive disorder
67 SAT test section
68 Ratchet part
69 Foot woe
70 Primps
71 Footstool
73 PGA pairing forms a small dam?
76 Merchant
77 Elevating footwear
78 Holm and McKellen
79 Evergreen
82 Hank of hair
83 Carnivals
84 Edges
85 Stick in the mud
86 Sitcom eponym
88 Practical jokes
89 Waldorf or Caesar
90 Former Georgia senator
92 Zsa Zsa and Eva
94 Danny of "Radio Days"
95 Alias letters
96 Bygone
98 Exploit
99 Bank pymt.
100 Brooks or Blanc
101 Upgraded Brownie

104 PGA pairing is Kubrick title character?
107 Gaelic tongue
108 London subway
109 Sandal straps
110 Emerald Isle
111 Collegiate cheers
112 Ollie's partner
113 Group of seven
114 Swell guy

DOWN

1 The garment industry
2 Removed from a spool
3 Increases inclination
4 Equal score
5 Enough
6 Indonesian island east of Java
7 Muckraking journalist Tarbell
8 Sunrise to sunset
9 Materialize
10 Aired again
11 Network of "Sesame Street"
12 St. Louis landmark
13 Wright and Brewer
14 Wading birds
15 Suitable
16 PGA pairing of a discount for two?
17 Hair-raising
18 Handle the helm
24 Capone's nemesis
26 Enthusiastic approval
30 Foul-smelling
34 Tenth mo.
35 Lefty
36 Printing operation
38 Airscrew
40 Classify
42 CBS logo
44 Golfer Calcavecchia
45 Standards of etiquette
47 Tenth of one-ten
48 Passover repasts
50 Ice cream container
51 First-class
52 Getting handed a bum __
53 Jack of "Chinatown"
54 Salubrity
55 Female GI, once
56 Extreme
57 Viennese park
58 PGA pairing forms a smaller swamp?
61 Lather removals
64 Kitchen utensil

65 Animal displays
66 "Exodus" writer
68 Average score
70 Farm enclosures
72 Blunders
74 Double-check text
75 Rolls of bills
77 Solo of "Star Wars"
79 13th President
80 "Rosemary's Baby" author
81 Aromatic
83 Disperses
84 Aural medication
85 West of "She Done Him Wrong"
87 Makes into law
88 "Faust" poet
89 Web location
90 Wiser
91 "The Seven Samurai" director Kurosawa
93 Outdoes
94 Feeling of apprehension
97 Big band tote
99 "Picnic" playwright
102 Paul of guitars
103 X
105 Industrious insect
106 Part of a journey

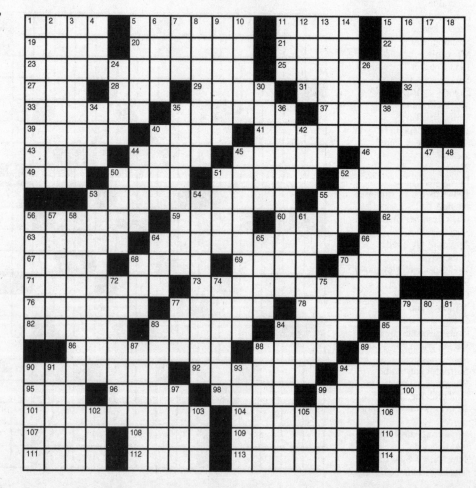

by Stanley B. Whitten

ACROSS

1 Bakery items
6 Brown tint
11 Minute arachnids
16 Director/actress Lupino
19 Elite social category
20 Boorish
21 Beginning
22 Taxi
23 __ Cruz, CA
24 Suburbanized L.A. hoopsters?
27 Constriction
29 State: Fr.
30 Low hisser
31 Big Bird's street
32 H. Ross and family
34 Actress Uta
35 Calendar abbr.
37 Bar selection
39 Requirement
41 Jacket slit
42 Fugard play, "A Lesson from __"
44 Cobbler's task
46 Cash penalty
48 Poker-pot increasers
51 Turning part
52 Christopher or Brenda
53 Crazy
56 Traveler's stop
57 Fowl perch
59 Hard, dark wood
61 Old saw
63 Shakespeare's "__ Night, or What You Will"
65 "Whip It" group
66 Purloined
67 Austen novel
69 Musical piece
71 Landing place on a river
73 Lyric poems
74 Feudal lords
76 Ballpoints
78 Smear with dirt
80 Heavens to __!
81 Jackson or Owens
82 French student
83 Grab hold of
86 Ques. response
87 Sun Devils' sch.
89 Spirited board?
91 Happen again
93 Danube tributary
94 Chorus members
96 Step up the pace
97 Slot fillers
100 Secretarial mistake
102 Store fodder
105 Connery of "The Russia House"
106 Haughty
108 Disks of unleavened bread
110 Golf-ball material
112 Fashion
113 Yoko's family
114 Female anchors

117 Suburbanized 1940 Cukor film?
121 Enough
122 End of a ballad?
123 Native Alaskan
124 Actor Davis
125 WWII surrender site
126 Prosecutors, for short
127 Full of fluff
128 Javelin
129 What to do for success?

DOWN

1 Throw
2 Jai __
3 Suburbanized 1969 World Series winners?
4 Affected lovers of beauty
5 RBI and ERA
6 Outline
7 Pencil ends
8 Fido's feet
9 Adherent's suffix
10 Baseball bat wood
11 Suburbanized Super Bowl XX winners?
12 Existing naturally
13 Sleeping-sickness spreader
14 Conger
15 Secret store
16 Cold epoch
17 Make gloomy
18 Missing
25 "__ the ramparts we watched..."
26 Rascal
28 Doze
32 Game played on horseback
33 Corrected manuscript
35 Delhi dress
36 Verve
38 Suburbanized 1979 Nolte film?
40 Board-game cube
43 Very dry
45 Dynamite man
47 Orderly
49 Dramatic parts
50 Gentle
53 Suburbanized bakery item?
54 "The African Queen" screenwriter
55 Lairs
58 Warm compress
60 Innovative
62 Ruinous fate
64 Droll fellows
66 Wait on
67 Napoleon's first isle of exile
68 Bearing

70 Follow logically
72 Elbe tributary
75 Unfledged bird
77 Net man
79 Architect Pei's first name
81 Female panel members
84 Atmosphere
85 __ Mawr College
88 Formed a lap
90 Bon Jovi or Voight
92 Patron
93 Luigi's island
95 Location of Lake Baikal
97 Sampled
98 Gibson of tennis
99 Third basemen Ken and Clete
101 Come to fruition
103 Attorney
104 Golfer Ernie
107 Wild
109 Compass pt.
111 Oscar, e.g.
114 Proboscis
115 O'Neill's "Desire Under the __"
116 Highland loch
118 Half of MCII
119 Distress letters
120 Recipe abbr.

by Robert H. Wolfe

ACROSS

1 Louvre Pyramid designer
4 Former Dolphins' coach
9 Talked idly
15 Aleutian island
19 Operate
20 Propelled a punt
21 Dahl or Francis
22 Holier-__-thou
23 Do something
24 Muse of poetry
25 Neighbor of Kenya
26 Blackbird
27 Lawrence Welk's singing boys?
31 Chowed down
32 Slipped up
33 Turndown vote
34 Fancy button
35 Mountain lions
37 Carnal
40 Even more yucky
42 Temptresses
43 Tomfoolery
45 Hurried along
46 Tierney and Tunney
47 __ Mahal
50 Malay isthmus
51 "Wheel of Fortune" request
52 Business deal
53 __ Diego
56 "__ Gay"
59 __ by (just managing)
61 Lists of charges
62 Resident of: suff.
63 Porthos' pal
64 Trademark wafer
65 Wile E. Coyote's supplier
66 Powell-Loy co-star
67 Arantxa __ Vicario
69 Seem suitable
71 Judge
73 Cogito __ sum
74 Buddy
76 Got up
78 Dunne or Ryan
79 Luau garland
80 Chocolate bits
81 Matisse or Rousseau
82 Dweebs
83 Lat. or Lith., once
84 Millennia
85 Part of mph
86 Tempe sch.
88 Mach+ flier
89 Took on cargo
91 Singer McEntire
92 Bellini opera
95 Scaredy-cat
97 Legislative body
99 "Made in America" co-star
103 Video-game pioneer company
104 Roman 103
105 Bus. letter abbr.
107 Cowboy event
108 Lon __ of Cambodia
109 "My Life with Martin Luther King" authoress?
114 Lug
116 Writers
117 Angers farewell?
118 OK school
119 Carolina college
120 Renter
121 A votre __!
122 Boozer
123 M. Descartes
124 Biases
125 Ms. Lauder
126 Nav. rank

DOWN

1 Chatters
2 Game played with 32 cards
3 Practical trainee
4 Accelerate
5 Trumpet or cornet
6 __ Bator, Mongolia
7 Give the game away
8 Sacred name of God
9 Asian ox
10 Merchant fleets
11 Uttered without thinking
12 Blockbuster of 1959
13 Brought to closure
14 Cherished
15 $ dispenser
16 Sibling chanteuses of the '50s?
17 Scottish clan pattern
18 If not
28 A smaller amount
29 Accidentally
30 Backbones
36 End of a post?
38 In working order
39 "My Funny Valentine" lyricist?
41 Solomon's tempter?
42 Merchant
44 Unreal
46 TV's "Wild Bill Hickok" chick?
47 Nap-making devices
48 Scorpio's brightest star
49 Role for Ms. Richard Thomas?
52 __ transit gloria mundi
54 Goes to
55 Closest
57 Start of a motive?
58 Fire residue
60 Weapons limited in SALT talks
61 Conductor's stick
66 Last of a million?
68 Parroted
70 Repeats
72 Open receptacle
75 Boom times
77 Algerian port
80 Pioline of tennis
85 Remorseful one
87 William Tell's canton
90 Berne's river
91 "Ghostbusters" director
93 Theater projection
94 Baseball family name
95 Easy gallop
96 Star of "My Favorite Year"
97 Earth pigment
98 Put in a box
100 Danish port
101 "Schindler's List" star
102 Run amok
104 Angler's tote
106 Musical conclusions
110 Makes a decision
111 Swarming insects
112 Color shade
113 Place for a chapeau
115 U-turn from WSW

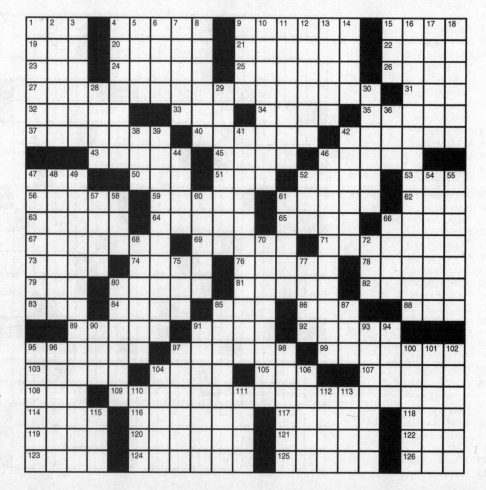

LETTER BY LETTER

by Arthur S. Verdesca

ACROSS

1 Sea of France
4 Daddy
9 Change for the better
14 Spanish cellist Casals
19 One in Guadalajara
20 "The cruellest month"
21 Flood protection embankment
22 Vegetable to cry over
23 Fraction letters
24 Horse checkers
25 Silvery European fish
26 Slight trace
27 G
31 Gad about
32 Leave out
33 Detest
37 Feel
38 Father children, once
40 __ Parker Robinson Dance Ensemble
42 __ populi (popular opinion)
43 T
47 Crude shelter
48 Norse mischiefmaker
51 Flexible footwear
52 Umps' cohorts
53 No great shakes
54 Norwegian saint
55 Alternatives
56 Ermine in a light coat
58 City where Erasmus died
59 Pedigree
61 Shiny fabrics
63 Ink spot
64 __ Gatos, CA
65 I
68 Poetic meadow
71 Presently
73 Repudiates
74 Unfair treatment
76 Analyze chemically
78 Cheapskate
79 Herbert of "The Ladykillers"
80 Ancient people of the Andes
81 Traveling carriage
82 Bit of data
83 Lift and toss
85 Aahs partners?
86 Old French coin
87 B
91 Grain beard
92 Fruit drinks
93 Conger catcher
94 Stable mothers
98 Altogether
100 Skin problem
101 Comestible item
103 P
108 Enthusiastic appreciation
111 Former Yankee slugger Roger
112 Acclamation
113 Publicize
114 Quaker of the forest
115 Long for
116 Elbow
117 Half a fly?
118 Cogwheels
119 Vaulted recesses
120 Pulled
121 '40s arena

DOWN

1 Cash penalties
2 Additional performance
3 Dennis of the NBA
4 Balcony railing
5 Bids first
6 Lion clan
7 Quart fraction
8 Plus
9 Egg protein
10 James __ Ives
11 Occurrence
12 Approach
13 Moore of "Indecent Proposal"
14 Lid lifter
15 "Hotel du Lac" author Brookner
16 Open container
17 Record
18 United
28 Letter
29 Forum dress
30 Highland valleys
34 J
35 Family dwelling
36 Glorify
38 Tampa Bay's eleven
39 Wapiti
40 Sharp fold
41 Elevator in Harrods
44 Geometric figure with equal sides
45 Mushroom selection
46 Worker bees
48 Kick back
49 Medley
50 M
53 __ Paulo
56 One step
57 Point of a fork
58 Muffed
60 Gob's hail
61 Cancun snooze
62 __ of Cleves
63 Finger pointer
66 Decrees
67 Took the wheel
69 Per person
70 Worrier's word
72 No vote
75 3-D miniature scene
76 Brazilian palm
77 Displayed
78 Knight's weapon
79 Cowardly Lion portrayer
82 Made a meal of
83 "When It's Love" group, Van __
84 Tours summer
87 Countries
88 Take delivery
89 Very beginnings
90 Sent forth
95 Partial refund
96 Join up
97 Multi-speaker system
99 River frolicker
100 Tapestry in "Hamlet"
101 Love-lit
102 Be off
104 Athletic org.
105 "The World According to __"
106 Waistcoat
107 Narcissus' lover
108 Obstacle to free speech?
109 Take advantage of
110 Rejuvenation center

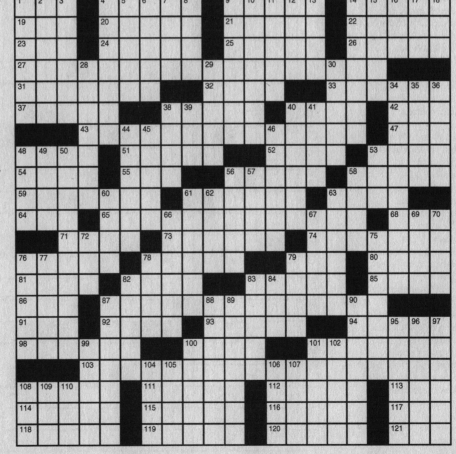

ACROSS

1 Parks and Lahr
6 Greek Mars
10 Small commune on the Iowa River
15 Ringer
19 Lethargic
20 Power
21 Market figures
22 La Scala highlight
23 Gossip
24 Succeds in an insurrection
26 Mini drinks
27 Instants
29 Expanse
30 Most shoddy
32 Start of Benjamin Franklin quote
35 Moslem prince
36 High level D.C. grp.
37 ID info
38 Julius Caesar's eggs
41 Disencumbers
44 Fissure
47 Edges
50 Set of values
52 Boyfriend from France
53 Part 2 of quote
57 Operatic tenor Peerce
58 Remove violently
59 Contribute one tenth
60 Pete of baseball
61 Tropical American lizard
63 Type of poker
65 Comic Johnson of "Laugh-in"
67 Part 3 of quote
76 Nice nothing?
77 Lah-de-dah ways
78 Couch potato
79 Tanguay and Gabor
82 Laurel and Musial
86 Pine tar derivative
89 Early bird?
90 Part 4 of quote
93 Important time
94 Asparagus unit
95 Verifiable
96 City north of Santa Fe
97 Related
98 112.5° on a compass
99 Addams Family member
102 Sis or bro
104 Cover from overhead
106 End of quote
114 Novelist Anne Porter
117 Cube inventor Rubik
118 Photographs
119 Nastase of tennis
120 Stamp collectors' delights
123 Reveal
124 North American rail
125 Queenly headwear
126 Withered
127 Worn away unevenly
128 Oracle
129 Assassinated Egyptian leader
130 Allowance for waste
131 Right-triangle ratios

DOWN

1 Nativity
2 Harden
3 Pay the piper
4 Small lozenges
5 Flow past
6 Pother
7 Beau number two
8 Juan's winter month
9 Scattered
10 Fire residue
11 Mr. Polo
12 Hawaiian hello
13 Handrail posts
14 Set taxes
15 Mooring area
16 Ashtabula's lake
17 Kissers
18 Final
25 Mortarboard's ornament
28 Agitate
31 Tendon
33 Pipe material
34 Is able, to Shakespeare
38 The Buckeye State
39 Damone and Morrow
40 Pain
41 Indian prince
42 Pol's concern
43 A Shore
45 Chilly coating
46 Fidelity
48 Intoxication citation: abbr.
49 Make a lap
51 Characteristic of a screw
53 Resembling
54 Needle case
55 Mumford or Busby
56 Protagonist
62 Actress Mason
64 Genetic letters
66 Pickpocket
68 Brooding place
69 Aware of
70 Pink baby?
71 Trick alternative
72 Rome's port
73 Glossy
74 Pola of the silents
75 Body part
79 Scottish Gaelic
80 High muckamucks
81 "A Death in the Family" author
83 Play part
84 Neither's partner
85 Blue character
87 "__ Arden"
88 First generation Japanese-Americans
91 Rubbish
92 Kitchen implement
97 Italian playwright Conte Vittorio
100 Reading decks
101 Minutiae
103 Greek harpist
105 Pita fibers
106 Fleece
107 Work the dough
108 Missionary Junipero
109 "__ Sanctum" radio show
110 Dame's leader?
111 City near St. Louis
112 Glenn of "Jagged Edge"
113 Feudal serfs
114 Buss
115 Medicinal plant
116 Exhaust
121 Light touch
122 Sun's fall

WAR IS OVER

by Ed Voile

ACROSS

1 Traveler's stopover
6 One of the Apostles
14 Make a mistake
20 Refuges
21 "Goblin Market" poet
22 Female graduate
23 Resolve a quarrel
25 Relishes
26 Japanese watch
27 "My Life as a Dog" director Hallstrom
29 Confiscates
30 Texas/Louisiana border river
33 Flip through
35 Rapping Dr.
37 Starting center?
38 Zeno of __
39 Calm the citizenry
44 Chinese way
45 "The George and __ Show"
47 Sedan's river
48 Seethe
49 Vandyke site
50 Rough protuberance
51 Burglar
53 Top-notch
54 Molts
55 Eggs
56 Re-establish security
59 __ d'etat
60 Dog's first name
61 Popeye's nephew __ Pea
62 Dimensions: abbr.
63 Evening receptions
66 Ancient temple
68 Neither Rep. nor Dem.
69 Brief photo
70 Computer game character
71 Scruff
72 Actor Gould
74 Island east of Java
75 Leaning precariously
77 Today's OSS
78 1st letter
79 Suspend the hostilities
81 NYC hours
82 Went spelunking
84 Ripped
85 Facetious tribute
86 Jim Bakker's org., once
87 Tavern orders
88 Gordie of the NHL
89 Struggler's sound
91 Writer Zola
93 High-lofting tennis shot
94 Make friendly forays
97 Simians
98 German definite article
99 Internet address: abbr.
100 Slightly blue
101 "Rainbow After a Storm" artist
103 Dame Edith or Dale
105 Astronomer Carl
108 Vietnamese dress

110 Soprano Tebaldi
112 Disarm
118 Bowman
119 Trifling annoyance
120 Earthy materials
121 Largest desert in the world
122 Pilchards
123 Former Israeli P.M.

DOWN

1 Queen of the fairies
2 Buckeyes' sch.
3 Son of Odin
4 Blissful
5 Pass, as time
6 "Star __"
7 Holiday chuckle
8 Botanist Gray
9 Hrs. of summer
10 State
11 Natural gas constituent
12 Shoshones
13 Stays idle
14 Mothers
15 Click beetle
16 Fiji's capital
17 Become allies
18 Still outstanding

19 Boundless enthusiasms
24 Holy: pref.
28 Jockey Arcaro
30 Carried on ocean waves
31 Of a flood plain
32 Wave a white flag, in a way
33 Pack a capacity
34 Romaine
36 Theol. belief
40 Noteworthy
41 Ranked at Wimbledon
42 Orchestra members
43 Leibman and Howard
46 $$ dispensers
49 Butter maker
52 Mercury vapor lamp inventor
53 Gum tree
54 __-disant (so-called)
57 Stick on a stick: var.
58 Actor Sam
59 Funny pages
63 Position
64 St. Paul's letters
65 Like a loser in musical chairs
67 Trigonometric functions
70 Tropical wrap

73 Resembling: suff.
74 Exposed
76 Sampras or Rose
79 Monk's hood
80 Nickname for Ederle or Stein
82 Volcanic craters
83 Medicinal houseplant
84 Works hard
88 "Ben-__"
89 Pop's pop
90 Singer Ocasek
92 Third of a cohort
94 Actor Keaton
95 Ink roller
96 Team
102 Afr.-Amer. org.
104 Port on Okinawa
106 Landon and others
107 Festive
108 Chip in chips
109 Has debts
111 Parseghian of football
113 Oriental sash
114 Victory
115 Paddle
116 "Bill __ the Science Guy"
117 Draft letters

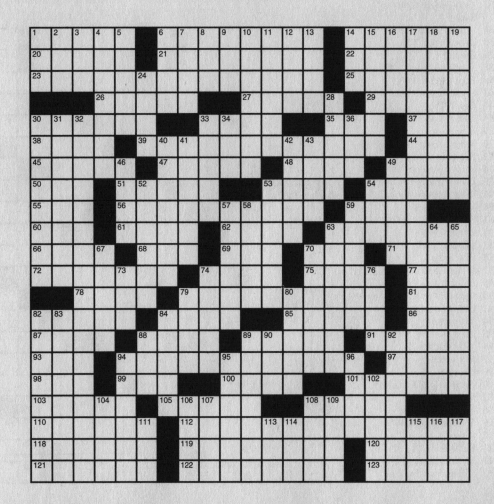

WHAT'S MY LINES?

by Sheryl Scott

ACROSS

1 Non-believer
8 Did, but doesn't now
14 Onionlike seasonings
20 Resident
21 Comaneci and others
22 Recorded books, e.g.
23 Invitation to a game-show contestant
26 Turkish honcho
27 Certain believers in God
28 Film holders
29 South American monkey
31 Vertical fishing nets
32 Cotton separators
33 Italian sky color
36 With 46A, panelist's classic question
38 Italian actress Eleonora
39 Feel rapture
41 __ compos mentis
42 19th-century actress Menken
43 Comics Abner
44 Equilateral parallelograms
45 Too much for Yvette
46 See 36A
50 Toward the tail-end
53 Avant-garde composer Satie
54 "Faust" poet
55 Lyon's river
56 Bumpy
58 Star Wars letters
59 Beer ingredient
63 Contestant's request
67 Regarding
68 USNA grad
69 Singer Vic
70 Mom's sister, informally
71 Regulars' orders
74 Painter Holbein
75 Uses swearwords
76 What to say to Groucho
80 Venetian ruler
81 Fingers of baseball
82 Chill
83 Theater sec.
84 Blackguard
87 McBeal and others
88 Individual: abbr.
90 Invitation to a contestant
93 Old-time singer Sumac
94 Youngsters
95 Go by again
96 __ podrida
97 Hoosegow
99 Coercion
100 Dropout's 2nd chance
101 Host's ultimatum
108 Of the nostrils
109 Sentence segment
110 Rise
111 Backbones
112 Mooring rope
113 Dilapidated dwelling

DOWN

1 Military asst.
2 A couple
3 Decomposed hemoglobin
4 Legal writ
5 Parts of pelvises
6 Bigwig in DC
7 Import-export difference
8 Water spirit
9 One prone to back talk
10 Blue-pencils
11 Expands a pit
12 Beach acquisition
13 Husband of Isis
14 May and Ann, e.g.
15 Outer covering
16 March middle
17 By way of
18 Dawn goddess
19 Compass dir.
24 Whinny
25 Goose on Oahu
29 Malleable metal
30 Late starter?
31 Phoenician city
32 "The __ Archipelago"
33 Broadway flop
34 Gray wolf
35 DOS rival
37 Hogshead, e.g.
38 Ruckus
39 Persian ruler
40 Writer P.G. __
43 Sierra Nevada resort
44 Networks
45 Flimsily
46 Long journey
47 Lived like a bee
48 Petty officers
49 Re-change color
50 Largest continent
51 Adages
52 Whistle blast
53 Isolate
56 Of an arm bone
57 Slugger Garciaparra
60 Has
61 Server Sampras
62 Stone and Stallone
64 Low card
65 Fleming's spy
66 Slugger Mo
72 Six in Seville
73 Moves emotionally
75 Chanel and others
76 Waiter's aid
77 Celeste or Ian
78 Fitzgerald of scat
79 London loos
80 Actress Marie
83 Ruminants' belly parts
84 U.S.-U.S.S.R. standoff
85 Pointed tool
86 Genetic letters
88 Like some woods
89 Former NY mayor
90 Vivid purplish red
91 Kitchen gadget
92 Refuses to
94 Flying toys
95 Choate or King
97 What to keep up
98 Bowling alley
99 Sketch
100 Pesky insect
101 __ and outs
102 Dolt
103 Cycle starter?
104 Tail of a fib?
105 MDs' group
106 Greek letter
107 Corded fabric

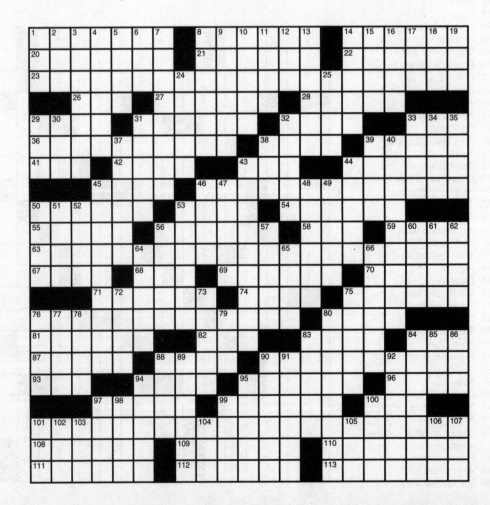

COMMUNICATION BREAKDOWN

by Robert H. Wolfe

ACROSS

1 Periods
5 Pronto acronym
9 Habitual practice
15 Fords and Dodges
19 Nautical side
20 Tardy
21 Punctual
22 Came to earth
23 Nastase of tennis
24 Move laboriously
25 View a film
26 Church leader
27 Dick Tracy watch updated
29 Non-arachnid creation
31 Most rangy
33 Arista
34 Outlanders
35 Episcopal cleric
38 Short putt
40 The Greatest
41 King of the Visigoths
43 Brad of the PGA
44 Able to read
49 Man's title
50 Wool fat
52 Get up
53 Done
54 Asian holiday
55 Abides by
56 Southern solecism
58 9th month
59 Regulations
60 Pensioner
61 Forest unit
62 Select
65 Part of WASP
66 Handbags
68 "Murphy's Romance" co-star
69 Old-style photograph
72 Journalist Alexander
74 French pronoun
75 Even badder?
76 Foolish folk
77 Omelet item
80 At any time
81 "Symphonie Espagnole" composer
82 Otitis
84 Give the ax to
85 Lamp oil
87 Tea from India
88 White powder used in incandescent gas
90 Med. feeders
91 Syrian leader
92 Ridicule
93 Donna of the LPGA
97 Archaic: abbr.
98 Blue-striped target
102 Cloudy communication
105 Dots and dashes
109 Sound of a well-tuned engine

110 One of the Mandrell sisters
111 Gardner and others
112 Caspian feeder
113 On a cruise
114 Code of silence
115 Furor
116 God of war
117 Beatty and Buntline
118 Former Egyptian leader
119 Beer barrels
120 Dunfermline dagger

DOWN

1 Heroic saga
2 Part in a play
3 Seed protector
4 Of constellations
5 First of a series
6 Beauty parlor
7 Make right
8 Bases for structures
9 Expense
10 Remove shackles
11 Scattered
12 Connection
13 Portent
14 Occult exchange
15 Italian isle
16 Isolated
17 Age
18 Editorial instructions
28 Risky
30 Nobel winner Wiesel
32 Cab
35 Extensive
36 Tennis' Nastase
37 Supermarket shopper's aid
39 Horseback post
40 Audience divider
42 Multi-station system
43 1955 Bob Hope movie, "The Seven Little __"
44 Pinocchio or Ananias
45 Forum platforms
46 States with conviction
47 Conical shelter
48 Certain Art Deco works
51 Born in Bordeaux
52 Destroy
57 Sioux tribe
59 Actor Cesar
60 Actress Martha
62 Effrontery
63 Make two
64 Edmonton hockey player

65 French town near Caen
67 Make uneasy
70 Lendl and Reitman
71 Aswan's river
72 Did the butterfly
73 __ jacet
76 Product's symbol
77 Cream shade
78 Advance
79 Pesky insect
83 SDI weapon
86 Right-triangle ratio
87 "Gotti" star Armand
89 Dusting powders
91 Doubleday and others
93 Channel of politicos
94 Make laugh
95 Like leaves and skin
96 Vegetables for gumbo
97 Eyes flirtatiously
99 Exploding stars
100 Fort __, North Carolina
101 Saps
103 "__ la Douce"
104 Shakespearean king
106 Algerian port
107 Challenge
108 What __ can I say?

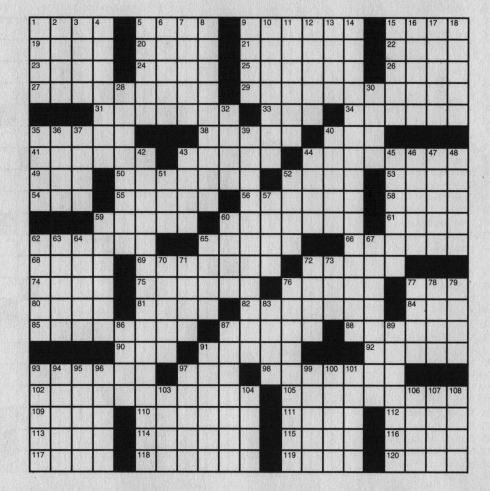

YOU CAN SAY THAT AGAIN

by Josiah Breward

ACROSS

1 Snatches
6 Threaded fasteners
12 Invites
16 Exclamation of discovery
19 Hindu prince
20 Pierre's horse
21 Check horses
22 Downswing
23 Former name of Guam's capital
24 Prefix meaning different
25 Hallucinatory
27 "Rio" singers
29 City in the Black Forest
31 Disinformation
32 Bk. of the Old Testament
34 Cariou or Berman
35 For fear that
36 Mas' mates
39 William Faulkner novel
44 Too colorful
46 Kennedy or Williams
47 Aid a criminal
48 Smells
52 Quibble
54 First golfer to win all four majors
57 Identify incorrectly
58 Commences
60 Mexican money
61 Venice beach
62 Black shade
63 With 74A, Norman Lear series of the '70s
65 Create lace
66 Hit on the head
67 Physically gratifying
68 Evergreen with aromatic wood
71 Duct or lung starter
73 April 15 org.
74 See 63A
77 Drag
78 Supporters
80 Entity
81 Ritzy residence
82 Creating a prejudice
84 "The Hostess" and "Mobile," e.g.
86 Toy soldier
87 Discord
88 Bamako's land
89 & so forth
91 North of Paris
92 MGM Grand's Las Vegas neighbor
97 Med. personnel
98 Highly excited
101 Old name of Tokyo
102 Fuss
103 Director Bunuel
105 Ben Hecht play
109 Stanley Donen film
114 Subscription continuers
115 Escaped
117 Reckon

118 Wapiti
119 Dollar fraction
120 Hereditary
121 "The Prince of Tides" star Nick
122 Tee preceder
123 African fox
124 Like post-rain streets
125 Pope's fanon

DOWN

1 Alum
2 Prego rival
3 Open a bit
4 Trite
5 Singer Twain
6 Skis
7 "Moonstruck" star
8 Sell direct
9 Nevertheless
10 Simple card game
11 Mess maker
12 Maximally dry
13 Tejano superstar
14 Hot box
15 Affront
16 Stage whisper
17 Fortunate ones
18 Spy
26 __ P. Chase

28 Obligation
30 Harry's veep
33 Aggressive giantess
36 Tissue: suff.
37 Bloody passage
38 Hit by the Archies
40 Compatibility devices
41 Lincoln and Fortas
42 The best __ plans...
43 Thereabouts
45 Actor Dan
49 "Catch-22" character
50 Iowa college town
51 Cain's brother
53 Of a people: pref.
55 Twin of Romulus
56 Gray and Candler
57 Cager Richmond
59 Swed. flyers
61 Queen of England for nine days
64 Regretting
65 Metal roofing material
66 Noted painter of Native Americans
68 Foray
69 "The Gold Bug" monogram
70 Retarding force
71 Clerical vestments

72 Say uncle
74 Greek actress Mercouri
75 Future oak
76 Necessities
78 High-pitched flute
79 Once again
80 Pitcher's error
83 Unmarried
84 Christmas song
85 With little emotion
88 Fashion designer
90 Motley __
93 Pines
94 Spenser or White
95 Full of trees
96 Geisha garb
98 Concur
99 Scottish Highlanders
100 Sty cries
104 Deep, unnatural sleep
106 Religion-based org. founded in 1858
107 Lift-off pressure
108 Sharp, shrill bark
110 Calf meat
111 WWII Solomon Island locale
112 Abbr. in airport names
113 Extra-wide shoe size
116 Bei or Yuan

by Frances Burton

ACROSS

1 Grange
5 Surrenders by treaty
10 Playful prank
15 Fling
19 Guinness of "Star Wars"
20 Fight site
21 Because of
22 Apiece
23 Take the train
24 Song for nine voices
25 Minnie?
27 Belle?
29 Collection of students
31 Calm
32 Replacement tooth
33 Ignominy
34 Equipped with claws
35 NY subway line
36 Goblet elements
37 Rolls dem bones
38 Mother-of-pearl
41 Shoulder wrap
42 Honey farmer
46 1975 Wimbledon champ
47 Eyeglasses: slang
48 Whopper peddlers
49 Gardener's implement
50 RR depot
51 Liquor container
52 Duck's relatives
53 Star of "Captain Blood"
55 More accessible
57 Dracula's conquests
59 Fluffy dessert
60 Diacritical mark
61 Portentous bird
62 One half of Hispaniola
63 Words for liqueurs
65 Nodded off
66 Bugs
69 Reprobates
70 Encrusted
71 Small land mass
73 Debt letters
74 PAU's successor
75 Apple centers
76 States of agitation
77 Uncommon
78 Mothballs or brine
81 Green years
82 Collapsible shelters
83 Made an effort
84 Moral failings
85 Chow down
86 Letterheads
89 Ulan __, Mongolia
90 Crated
94 Add to the beauty of
95 Wise lawyer
96 Sue?
97 Tracy?
99 Voice one's opposition
101 Shucks!
102 Wedding shower
103 Night hunter of the future

104 Slur over
105 Gannon College city
106 Unpack
107 Approaches
108 Beneficiary
109 Barely passing grades

DOWN

1 Unit of capacitance
2 Wanted-poster option
3 Pre-surrealist painter
4 Reba's last name
5 False report
6 Wear away
7 Withhold
8 Compass dir.
9 Tote bags
10 Macabre cartoonist Charles
11 HMO employee
12 Driving gadgets
13 For what __ worth
14 Riders from the steppes
15 Yellowish pink
16 Like the old bucket of song
17 Act subdivision
18 Faint trace

26 Donnybrook
28 "Clair de __"
30 Feeble
33 Cher?
34 Stadium levels
36 Fr. religious figs.
37 College leaders
38 "The Face is Familiar" poet
39 Dog in "The Thin Man"
40 Carol?
41 Extra
42 Jean?
43 Patience?
44 Long, long time periods
45 Russo of "Get Shorty"
47 Iditarod rides
48 Waterproof wool cloth
51 "The X-__"
52 Furiously angry
53 Compel to accept
54 Pear-shaped instrument
56 Pocket change
58 Demolishes
59 Lions' hairdos
62 Handles of weapons
63 Rider's whip
64 Pride signal

65 Challenged
67 Grounds for a suit
68 Instigates litigation
70 Small bays
72 Evildoings
75 "Jurassic Park" author
76 Added support to
77 Caused delays
79 Endeavored
80 "Fear of Fifty" author Jong
81 Josip Broz
82 Mexican menu item
84 Male servants
85 TV dinner element
86 Publishable copy
87 Tear open
88 Fanny of vaudeville
89 Actor Charles
90 Musical piece
91 Trap
92 Macabre
93 Units of force
95 Ward of "Once and Again"
96 Ugandan despot
98 Flock female
100 "Do Ya" rock grp.

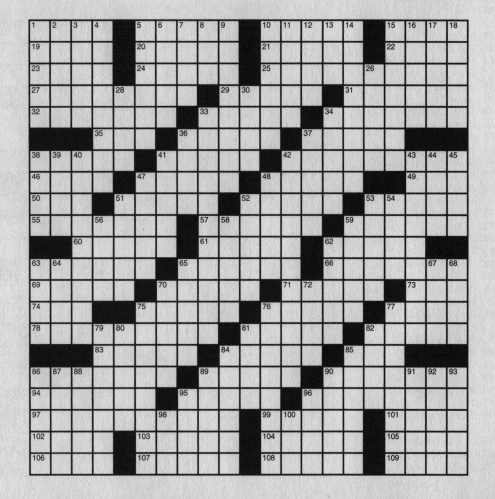

by Robert H. Wolfe

ACROSS

1 Casual coinages
6 Still part of a stream
10 Small, grotesque Japanese figurine
15 Expand
19 Choir part
20 Annapolis sch.
21 Gothic arch
22 Second chance
23 Mrs. Gorbachev
24 1938 Robert Donat film
26 Fencer's weapon
27 Muscle protein
28 Writer Hentoff
29 Absolutely not
30 Cogwheels
31 Wife of Theseus
33 Declaim
35 Mawkishly sentimental
37 Ham's brother
38 Black gold
39 Close companion
42 Catcher Howard
45 1987 Edward Woodward film
48 Understand
49 Examination subject
51 Short-tailed rodent
52 Cove
53 Canines
55 Paddle
57 Light beams
58 "Magnificent Obsession" director
59 Stephen of "The Crying Game"
61 Sue __ Langdon
62 Singer Mitchell
63 Port beginning?
64 1996 Diane Keaton film
67 Trans-Siberian RR stop
71 Shine brightly
73 Switch positions
74 Compass dir.
75 Old-womanish
76 Stableman
79 Vallee and Tomjanovich
81 Family members
83 Crevasse pinnacle
84 Centering points
85 1992 Wimbledon champion
87 Post-dusk
88 1983 Michael Douglas feature
91 Wiseacre
93 Rubbed-out spots
94 Charged particle
95 Carson's predecessor
96 Rock or Schenkel
97 Talk idly
99 Brennan and Heckart
103 Nevada resort
105 Insertion mark
107 Author Amy
109 Leaflike layers

110 Cordon __
111 1942 Bing Crosby film
113 True up
114 Broadcasts
115 Squalid
116 External: pref.
117 Demolished
118 Comic Martha
119 Rubbish
120 Org.
121 Four-time Indy winner

DOWN

1 Thong
2 Lixivate
3 One of the Pointer Sisters
4 Ultimate quidnunc
5 1932 Greta Garbo film
6 Israel of Bunker Hill
7 Workplace injury grp.
8 In matched pairings
9 Fond du __, WI
10 Sacred song sung a cappella
11 Century plant
12 Author of "The Immoralist"
13 Conquer
14 __ Aviv-Jaffa

15 1959 Audrey Hepburn film
16 Like a loan
17 __-Neisse line
18 Sorrows
25 Total
30 Spartan or Athenian
32 Taylor of "The Nanny"
34 Chops very fine
36 Positive hand signals
39 Egg feature
40 Level
41 Ways in: abbr.
42 Excrete
43 Philippines island
44 Make off with
45 King Arthur's father
46 Dame Edith or Dale
47 Skin creams
50 Barn bedding
54 1972 Alan Alda film
56 Flower with velvety petals
57 Actor Herbert
60 Affirm
62 Human dewlaps
64 N. African nation
65 Neighbor of China
66 Academy Award
68 Silent performer

69 Ice fall
70 Ill-fated "South Park" kid
72 Professor's spiel
75 1955 animated feature
76 Bone: pref.
77 Very German?
78 Perfidy
79 Mythical birds of prey
80 Wooden shoe
82 Brazilian palm
84 Wall painter
86 Heredity
89 Onassis, to pals
90 Mazda model
92 Interstices
95 Banner on a lance
97 Groom oneself
98 Change color again
100 Prof. Higgins' pupil
101 Niamey's nation
102 "__ of Iwo Jima"
103 Skier's ride
104 Inter __ (among other things)
106 Jai __
108 Picnic crawlers
111 33rd president
112 Vote for

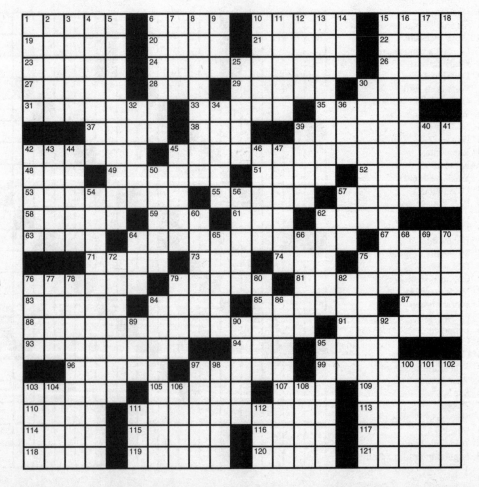

181

HOW WOULD YOU FEEL...

by Arlan and Linda Bushman

ACROSS

1 Aspect
6 Dude from Dubuque
11 Luge
15 Categorize
19 Love Italian-style
20 Tragedy
21 Marine shockers
22 Toot one's own horn
23 ...landing a space shuttle?
25 Mine entrance
26 End of all roads
27 Building wings
28 Totaled
29 Buzz off!
30 Stupid mistake
31 Author of "Delphine"
33 ...leaving downtown Chicago?
36 Mrs. Gorbachev
39 Soft-toy stuff
40 To a man
41 ...conducting a seance?
46 Beef cut
50 Seemingly forever?
51 Tent peg
52 Leave the Union
54 Mil. address
55 Clementine's dad, e.g.
57 Pen points
59 Side order, for short
60 Morally smug person
61 Flaw
64 Song for two
66 Mexican resort
68 ...visiting Santa's workshop?
71 Suitable target
74 "M*A*S*H" co-star
75 Teases
79 Russian-born Art Deco designer
80 Attire
82 "Doctor Zhivago" heroine
84 Type of skirt
85 Golfer Trevino
86 Bassett or Lansbury
88 Young horses
91 Med. readings
92 Thin layers
94 ...deep-sea diving?
97 Army bed
98 Lyons head
99 Make cloth gathers
100 ...meeting one's clone?
105 Single
110 Sierra __
111 Ticks off
112 Get out of line
115 Fanfare syllables
116 Cleveland's lake
117 Morales of "Bad Boys"
118 ...touring the Capitol?
120 Is not well
121 Lacoste or Levesque
122 "The Many Loves of __ Gillis"

123 Chip maker
124 Hardy girl
125 Part of B.A.
126 Pounds
127 Cacophonous

DOWN

1 Lost brightness
2 Soap plant
3 Monk's hoods
4 Dadaist Max
5 Vietnamese holiday
6 Utopian
7 Algerian port
8 Viral lump
9 Retort to "Are not!"
10 Slangy negative
11 Marine herd
12 Went first
13 Author of "Adam Bede"
14 Summer hrs.
15 Moves a document in a window
16 University of Maine town
17 Faithful boyfriend
18 Twit
24 Mountain nymphs
29 Editorial directives

30 Contradict
32 Orinoco tributary
34 Cycle beginning
35 Computers
37 Breadth
38 Nonresistance self-defense
41 Metrical foot
42 Moonwalker Armstrong
43 Left
44 Spears' "...Baby __ Time"
45 Blunt refusal
46 Guiding light
47 Malden or Malone
48 Monumental
49 Lome's land
53 Talon
56 Call up
58 Of bristles
60 Wet potholes
62 Lie fallow
63 Act of fealty
65 Ancient Balkan region
67 Supplication
69 French father
70 Misplays
71 Plummeted
72 Region

73 Agenda topic
76 In __ of
77 Art print: abbr.
78 Mobutu __ Seko of Zaire
81 1927 song
83 Xanadu's river
86 Battery electrode
87 Pot builders
89 Declarations of praise
90 Angel of the first order
93 Frigidity
95 2nd-smallest state
96 Imminent grads
98 Dictator
100 Lamb's lament
101 Spooky
102 Dirties
103 Tightwad
104 Friendly regard
106 Of a people: pref.
107 One half of Hispaniola
108 Waits at the light
109 Score
113 Philippines island
114 Prune
117 Age
118 Quirky
119 German article

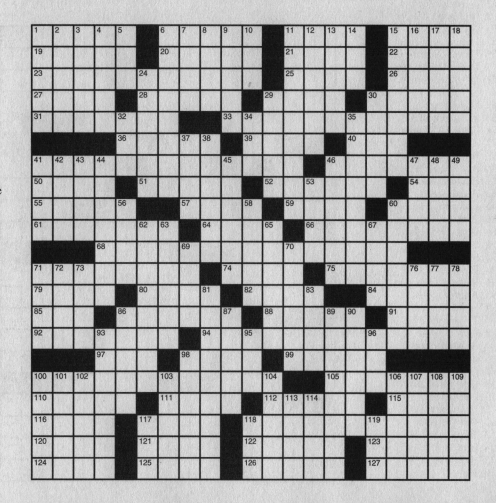

by Willy A. Wiseman

ACROSS

1 Par
5 Aluminum company
10 Vanzetti's cohort in anarchy
15 Classic saga
19 Tony's cousin?
20 Spasmodic
21 God's blood
22 Astronaut's negative
23 Mil. group
24 Ere
25 Hypothetical particle
26 Money __ everything!
27 Start of a quote from Sue Grafton's "O is for Outlaw"
31 "The Maltese Falcon" co-star
32 Fired
33 Actress Suzanne
35 Spurn
39 Those with an anti-seniors bias
43 Founded
44 Italian pronoun
47 Alphabetical quintet
49 Being decided in court
51 Draft letters
52 __ out (scrape by)
53 Broken-bone support
55 Conjectures
57 Rein in
59 Former Supreme Court Justice O'Connor
61 "The Confessions of __ Turner"
62 Drawstring
66 Part 2 of quote
71 Former D.C. hostess Perle
72 Lanchester and Schiaparelli
73 Bridal path?
74 Part 3 of quote
81 Sandwich shoppe
82 Easy dessert?
83 Listen to an appeal
84 Damage
86 Dining room linen
90 Send again
92 Sephia maker
93 Bigwig in D.C.
96 Volcanic formation
98 Arledge of ABC
99 Writer Umberto
100 To have in Le Havre
102 Lady of Spain
104 Blue dye plants
106 Frankness
108 "Barney Miller" character
110 Italian architect Aldo
114 End of quote
121 Hawaiian port
122 News services
123 When actors enter
124 Flag down
125 Galba's egg
126 Hen

127 __ Buena Island
128 Bancroft or Boleyn
129 One Truman
130 Desert springs
131 Some quiz answers
132 Tongue-clicking sounds

DOWN

1 Bellini opera
2 Abides by
3 Just
4 Luminous trail in the sky
5 Close to closed
6 Took off
7 Exult blatantly
8 Gumbo veggies
9 Mohammed's favorite wife
10 Spotting
11 Rights grp.
12 Buddy
13 Chicken quarters
14 Bird life of a region
15 Mystery
16 Have
17 Disregards
18 Camp bed
28 Neighborhoods
29 Fast-food option

30 Majestic
34 '60s radical grp.
36 Coke rival
37 Israeli seaport
38 Cuts of meat
40 R-V hookup
41 The way things are going?
42 Agave plant
44 Min. part
45 Purvis' instrument
46 Type of spray
48 Cause for a downfall
50 Italian wine center
54 Genuinely
56 Santa's ride
58 Interrupt rudely
60 Goose classification
63 Being risked
64 Like swimming pool water
65 Wide shoe width
67 Morse symbol
68 Chicken caller
69 Swimmer Williams
70 Alternative to KS
71 1,400 in letters
75 Actor Omar
76 Northern India monotheists
77 Clear a windshield

78 Plant new seeds
79 Loudmouth
80 Privalova or Vorobyeva
85 China's Chairman
87 Hammerin' Hank
88 __ compos mentis
89 Winter school closings
91 __ of Aragon
93 N.A. defense grp.
94 Intentionally noncommittal
95 Bewilder
97 Switch tail?
101 Language quirks
103 Four-time Indy 500 winner
105 I couldn't care less
107 Stallone character
109 Property holder
111 Penn and Young
112 Move furtively
113 Man and Dogs
115 Solo's princess
116 Vegas quote
117 Right-hand man
118 Beige shade
119 Hollow cylinder
120 Pekoe and oolong
121 Fireplace shelf

TRAVELING IN RHYME

by Ed Voile

ACROSS

1 Alamogordo headline word
6 Drive
11 On deck follow-up
16 Alternatives
19 Make road repairs
20 One-bit-per-second units
21 Singer Lopez
22 Abu Dhabi, Dubai et al.
23 Destination in Peru
25 "Siddhartha" author
26 Easy letters?
27 Conundrums
28 Intuited
29 Hood's heater
30 Inventor with protection
33 Heroic
34 Boater and bowler
35 In the past
36 Destination in Somalia
39 Flower garden
40 Faded the most
44 Make insane
45 Cylindrical
48 Punishes with arbitrary
   penalties
50 Cruise and Mix
51 Circumvent
53 Destination in Belgium
55 Destination in Nepal
57 Band's booking
58 Facial disguises
60 Lagerlof and Diamond
61 Method
62 Humor ending?
65 Contends
67 Chest bones
68 Reprobates
69 Southern constellation
70 Luxurious country houses
72 Endorsed, as a passport
74 Hindu title
75 Destination in Hawaii
77 Destination in Mali
81 "Break, Break, Break" poet
83 Tim of "Star Trek:
   Voyager"
85 Sam & Dave hit
86 Fixed outcomes
87 Seethe
89 Cooks in vapors
90 Bustle
91 Destination in Michigan
94 Narrow inlet
95 Bowling alley
97 Grave crime
98 Somewhat
102 Muckraker Tarbell
103 "Sunrise" and "Water
   Lilies," informally
104 Wrap in bandages
106 Cake of soap
107 Land of Luxor
108 Vietnam destination
112 Psyche division
113 Yawning wide

114 __ acids
115 100-eyed giant
116 Lion's name
117 Church council
118 Aviator Post
119 Mazda model

DOWN

1 Upper limb
2 Actress Arthur
3 Stock-market abbr.
4 Olympic skier Phil
5 Boston hockey player
6 Footnote word
7 Gavin of "The Love Boat"
8 Purplish brown
9 Old English letters
10 Baton Rouge sch.
11 Nonbeliever
12 Sapper's creation
13 Guinea-__
14 Photographer Adams
15 Deadlocked
16 Destination in Burkina Faso
17 Capital of Morocco
18 Religious factions
24 L.A. summer hrs.
28 Single woman

30 Yellow-fleshed fruit
31 Old World lizard
32 For rent, in London
33 Swellings
34 Sub
37 Acquire
38 Berserk
39 Brian __ of Ireland
41 Passage to Hades
42 Cliff-base debris
43 Brain tissue
45 Small amounts
46 Derisive
47 Advantages
49 Mira of
   "Mighty Aphrodite"
51 Ploy
52 Jackie's Aristotle
54 Artist Redon
56 DXXVII doubled
59 Peddle
61 Standard unit
62 Bridge positions
63 Romp
64 Destination in Mexico
66 Lizards
68 Try to disprove
70 Patrick White novel

71 Squalid
73 Follower of Joel
75 Syringe, for short
76 West Point sch.
78 S.S. Kresge store
79 Sri Lankan separatist
80 Retract one's words
82 Au naturel
84 Oh yeah, __ who?
87 Assigned a position
88 "Seven Year Ache"
   singer Cash
91 Kip Keino, e.g.
92 Ancient Syrian city
93 Eton alum
95 Calumny's kin
96 Proverb
97 Vague
99 Dictator Amin
100 Reflected light
101 Painter Matisse
103 Dimensions: abbr.
104 __ Valley, CA
105 __ An Rhein
108 European crow
109 Links org.
110 Crude shelter
111 "Born in the __"

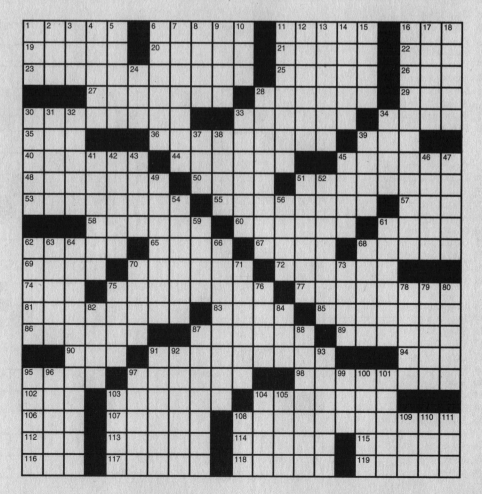

VERBS OF A FEATHER

by Ed Voile

ACROSS

1 Cultivate
5 Posters
11 Mahler's "Das Lied von der __"
15 Wight or Skye
19 Miscellany
20 Occurrences
21 Banana wrapper
22 Roe source
23 CHAT
26 Eye shades?
27 Remove from office
28 Distress signal letters
29 Pray in Notre Dame
30 __ Juan Capistrano
31 Visualize
32 Hearsay
34 Silent, in music
35 Last letter from Greece
38 QUAIL
41 William Tell's canton
42 Egyptian tomb
45 Showery mo.
46 Pooh-poohed
48 Theater employees
49 Hindu title
51 Unit of work
54 Wistful
55 Good loser
56 Billy Joel song, "__ Always a Woman"
57 Extra-wide shoe size
59 Scintillas
60 Laptop image
61 Make even
63 Actress Bening
65 Garfield or Felix
66 DUCK
68 Point: pref.
71 "__ and Johnny"
73 Chinese dumplings
74 Lupino and Tarbell
75 Tahitian lava-lava
77 Sicilian resort
79 Half of MVI
80 "Crazy" singer
81 On the plane
83 Lat. or Lith., once
84 Part of TGIF
85 Word after double or pot
86 Caesar's time
88 Full-house sign
90 Juicy fruits
91 Slangy negative
92 HAWK
97 Barcelona buddy
99 Privalova or Vorobyeva
100 Total
101 Country $ output
104 Pop
105 "Slaves of New York" author Janowitz
106 Air-safety agcy.
107 More squishy
109 Dismal
111 GROUSE
114 Top-drawer
115 "Dies __"
116 Change with the times
117 Caen's neighbor
118 Table supports
119 Off. underling
120 Add grass to greens
121 __ she blows!

DOWN

1 Adjust binoculars
2 Isolated
3 Dishwasher cycle
4 Relocate
5 Makes anxious
6 Med. feeders
7 Actor Liam
8 Open, as wine
9 Sch. orgs.
10 Draft letters
11 Eastern Orthodox bishop
12 Charitable aid
13 Takes out text
14 Culbertson of bridge
15 Muslim faith
16 FLICKER
17 Highland boy
18 McBain and McMahon
24 Aviator lost in 1937
25 Trapped in branches
30 College organization
33 Hamm of soccer
34 Pointed end
36 Scacchi or Garbo
37 Helpers
38 Strict
39 Belt positions
40 Play part
42 "The Sound of __"
43 Source of the fam. mutt
44 SNIPE
47 Mob violence
49 Certain winners
50 Resumes business
52 Let back in
53 Source
56 Fire giveaway
58 Tedium
61 RR stop
62 Paul Newman movie
64 Nightmare street?
66 Jurassic dinosaur
67 "Play It As It Lays" author
69 Capital of Crete
70 Consumers
72 Gather in
74 Of a pelvic bone
75 City on the Ganges
76 At a right angle to the keel
78 Weapons stockpile
80 Flier's backup
82 Rapping Dr.
85 Cast votes
87 Magazine staffers
89 Long, narrow estuary
90 Law enforcement support grp.
93 Theatrical works
94 Clinging mollusk
95 Baldwins and Steinways
96 Incompetent
98 Competitive activities
101 Circumference
102 "Gianni Schicchi" soprano role
103 "Silver Streak" co-star
106 V
108 Piquancy
109 Four qts.
110 Lobster eggs
111 OSS sucessor
112 Gas: pref.
113 __ been had!

REVERSIBLE FIRST NAMES

by Josiah Breward

ACROSS

1 Hooded coats
7 Transkei capital
13 Eurasian bird of prey
20 Marilu on "Taxi"
21 Grossed
22 Struts like a steed
23 Actor and gymnast with reversed first names
25 Autobiography
26 Hesitation sounds
27 Normandy town
28 Seven of Siena
30 "Aida" or "Tosca"
31 Fifths of a five
33 Window part
35 Silent comic and talk-show moderator with reversed first names
38 Of ocean motion
40 Pekoe or hyson
42 Supplies food for
43 Slangy negative
46 Botanist Gray
48 "Kidnapped" auth.
49 Names
53 Manners expert and singer with reversed first names
59 Mile High Center architect
60 ___-Magnon
61 Deck officer, for short
62 Church projection
63 Copter port
65 Capital of Italia
67 Element #80
69 Mint or sage
71 Flow measurers
72 Baseball players with reversed first names
76 Dull finishes
77 Loamy fertilizer
78 Cinder ending
79 Weapon in a silo
81 Adjusts pitch
83 Sacred ceremony
85 The two
87 End of a fib?
88 Stadium levels
89 Marshal and actor with reversed first names
93 Height: pref.
94 Once owned
95 Sawbones
96 Charlotte Bronte's "Jane ___"
97 More pleasant
100 Used chairs
102 Ivan of tennis
106 Actress and writer with reversed first names
111 Ballplayer Ruth
114 Authentic
115 Render harmless
116 More mature
118 Actress Patricia
120 Worldwide help grp.

121 Medicated liquids
124 Playwright and Bolshevik with reversed first names
127 Political winner
128 African fly
129 Liberated
130 Poet Siegfried
131 Small river
132 Dirty looks

DOWN

1 Connecticut tribe
2 Degree holders
3 Lifted
4 Clan members
5 Blyth and Jillian
6 Offshoot groups
7 Extreme
8 Extinct bird
9 Oodles
10 Cager Olajuwan
11 Toe lead-in?
12 "Peer Gynt" dancer
13 Letters in record time
14 Afore
15 Runyon and Berryhill
16 Big name in publishing
17 Much less cordial
18 ___ Haute, IN
19 Class paper
24 Pay attachment?
29 Additional
32 Hourglass fill
34 Make sound
36 Actress Raquel
37 Tax grp.
39 Leopold's cohort
41 Nora's pooch
44 Make a pledge
45 "Barnaby Jones" star Buddy
47 Paved
49 Composer Shostakovich
50 Knockout punch
51 Not intolerable
52 Caesar and Luckman
53 TV add-on
54 Fragrant
55 Regardless of
56 Against a thing, in law
57 Exploiter
58 Choreographer Cunningham
59 Ends of small intestines
64 Fellow feeling
66 Conductor Toscanini
68 Russian rulers
70 Hobbit Baggins
73 Sawbucks
74 Indomitable spirit

75 All by oneself
76 ___ Hari
80 Damage
82 Petty
84 Aphrodite's boy
86 Fling
90 Milk snake
91 Wound cover
92 ___-do-well
94 Word on a towel
97 P. Lorre character
98 Ousts
99 Retaliatory action: var.
101 Two-seater
103 Oder-___ Line
104 Closer to black
105 Insurance group
106 Stubborn beasts
107 Harrisburg suburb
108 Director Peter
109 Idle and Ambler
110 Dated later
112 Gambler's risk
113 British peers
117 Cost per unit
119 Daffy bird?
122 Natal lead-in
123 Bigwig in D.C.
125 N. Mandela's land
126 Front of a shoe

by Alan P. Olschwang

ACROSS

1 Perform an usher's job
5 Soft drink
9 Stake
14 Perform an ore analysis
19 Lofty
20 Canned
21 Circumvent
22 False alarm
23 Mythical monster
24 Cordelia's father
25 Swift, vigorous attack
26 __ and Gomorrah
27 Start of Ruth Brown quote
30 Unique
32 Harsh
33 Feudal serf
34 Man from Memphis
36 Truly
38 Live on
40 Opinions
41 In the past
44 Part 2 of quote
52 Speed-regulating device
55 Cubic meter
56 Put into service
57 Narrow mountain ridge
58 Neither fish __ fowl
60 Belgrade population
63 Info from schedules
64 Seek office again
65 Tooth covering
68 In medias __
70 Imminent grads
71 Part 3 of quote
76 Badly, in Limousin
78 Confirmed
79 Abandon
80 Term of tenancy
83 Arabian port
85 Catalyzing enzyme
88 Wahine's garland
89 Stable females
90 Stared open-mouthed
92 Large, red hog
95 The ones that got away
97 Part 4 of quote
101 Sell-out letters
102 Cosby kid Lisa
103 Holiday forerunner
104 End of a ballad?
107 Member of the ruling class
112 Ids' companions
115 Drug cops
119 "Immaculate Conception" painter
120 End of quote
123 Lessen
124 Prepare for the counterattack
126 Mah-jongg piece
127 __ vincit omnia
128 Earl "Fatha" __
129 Beyond
130 Seth's son
131 Palm fruit
132 Loses traction
133 Painter of "Flemish Feast in an Inn"
134 Parking lot souvenir?
135 In a fresh way

DOWN

1 Gunfire
2 Five after three
3 Come to terms
4 Conjecture
5 Telephone
6 Type of daisy
7 Bounds
8 Gland on a kidney
9 Networks
10 Parcel out
11 Lancelot's love
12 NYC summer hours
13 Changes building restrictions
14 Evaluator
15 Hebrides populace
16 __ Hawkins Day
17 Smell
18 Neighbor of Saudi Arabia
28 180 degrees from SSW
29 Host Philbin
31 Salamander
35 SF gridder
37 Arista
39 Superlative ending
41 Culture medium
42 Tipper's last name
43 Awoke late
45 The best policy
46 Maine college town
47 Units of magnetic flux density
48 Speller's contest
49 Looks longer
50 Russian ruler
51 Pianist Myra
53 Needle case
54 Tears
59 Brit. flyboys
61 Barbaric
62 Theology sch.
66 Mexican president (1911–13)
67 Chemical suffix
69 Alabama town in '60s headlines
72 Sniggler's prey
73 Sis or bro
74 Welcome
75 Kind of tide
76 Creche threesome
77 Rehan and Huxtable
81 Diviner
82 Exxon, formerly
84 O.T. book
86 Contemporary of Freud
87 Oman, for example
91 In the black
93 Be in the red
94 Musky cat
96 Mediocre grade
98 Hoodwink
99 Additional performances
100 Nullified
105 Absorb ending?
106 Chain of inns
107 Indian nursemaids
108 Toy-cube inventor
109 Shiraz resident
110 Situated
111 __ Haute, IN
113 Express a view
114 Permanent place
116 Post fresh troops
117 Twenty fins?
118 Scatter about
121 Marvel superhero
122 Remainder
125 In-house #

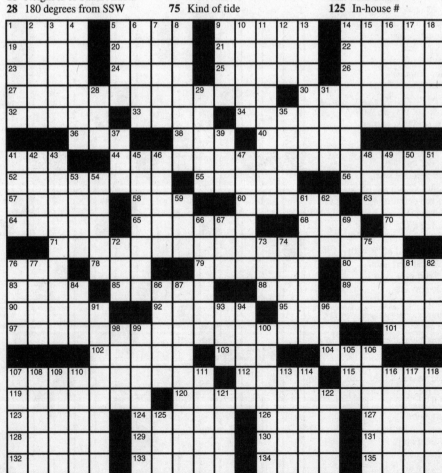

by Robert H. Wolfe

ACROSS

1 Favors one leg
6 Plummet
10 Wind blast
14 Donahue movie, "Susan __"
19 Bay window
20 S-shaped molding
21 Mimic
22 Brother of Moses
23 Look all over for things
25 Genealogical chart
26 Early 21st-century date
27 Sapped
28 Show great vigor
30 Ayres and Wallace
31 Page number
32 4 on the phone
33 Projections at the east ends of churches
36 Feeds on living grass
38 Use a broom
42 Dugout stack
43 Make in a hurry without care
46 Actress Merkel
47 Muffs it
48 Abductor of Helen
49 With seriousness
51 Garland of flowers
52 Primary
53 Place of worship
56 Part of USMA
57 Asian car maker
59 Homemaker, in a way
62 Loren of "A Countess from Hong Kong"
64 Looks __ everything
66 Partake of fast food?
69 Prepared
70 Attached shed
72 Derived from
73 Grp. of D.C. advisors
74 Motor add-on?
75 NBAers
78 Honshu port
80 Albanian money
83 With a feeling of distaste
85 Old hat
87 Sound of pain or pleasure
88 __ culpa
89 Work continuously on
93 Land unit
94 City on the Loire
96 Oval nuts
97 Low joint
98 __-fi
99 Military trainee
100 Speak roughly
102 Travel without a plan
106 Some reproductive cells
111 Actor Williamson
112 Qualified
113 Reach the end of one's endurance
114 Earthy color
115 Very in Vichy
116 Kett of comics

117 Swing a thurible
118 Aptitude determiners
119 800 exams
120 Shoot wide
121 True's partner?

DOWN

1 Long stride
2 Pressing need
3 Myers or Nesmith
4 Unique
5 Unpaid servants
6 __ the bill (pays)
7 Malarial sign
8 Furnish conditionally
9 Was in front
10 Type of table
11 Elevate
12 Take care of
13 Transit-loss allowance
14 I'll have what he's having
15 Term of affection
16 Piece of Puccini
17 Slay
18 OK city
24 Unpleasantly chilly
28 __ the Clown
29 "The Time Machine" author

31 Singer Domino
33 First victim
34 Make cuts
35 Negotiate successfully
36 First Roosevelt VP
37 Upstate NY school
38 Oxford or brogue
39 Log in at the job
40 Like carpet still in a store
41 Time for wages
43 Hot tub
44 R.D. of psychology
45 Recipe amt.
50 Welsh poet
52 Dillon of "Drugstore Cowboy"
53 Social rank
54 Cupbearer of the gods
55 Very dry
58 __ Hebrides
60 Kemo __
61 Slope device
63 Birthplace of Camembert
64 City near Palermo
65 Marauder old-style
67 Hungarian wines
68 "__ Gay"
71 South Pacific area

76 Charity
77 Training room
79 Risk
81 Justice Warren
82 Joint with a cap?
84 Fetters
85 Thwack
86 "The Joy Luck Club" author Amy
87 Available workers
90 Shoulder fringe
91 Inflammation sign
92 Served perfectly
95 Companion
97 Facet
99 Hooded snake
100 Duty lists
101 Silver-gray color
102 Square or granny
103 Pleasant
104 Folk singer Phil
105 Curses!
106 Type of pasta
107 Ballplayer Mel and others
108 Hindu princess
109 Different
110 Snow-day ride
113 Stitched border

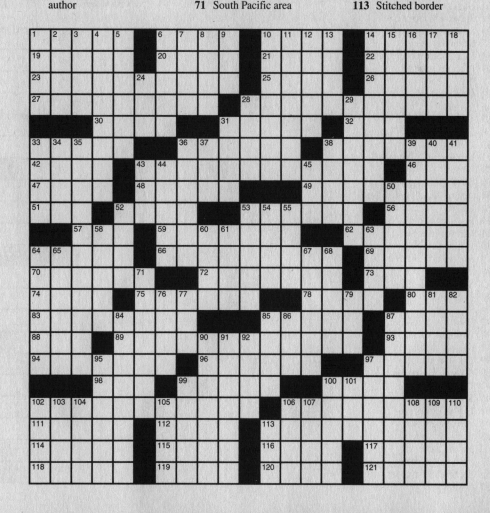

by Sheryl Scott

ACROSS

1 Wet impact
6 Team's good luck charm
12 Wrong moves
20 Laughing predator
21 Baltimore ballplayer
22 Loathed
23 Winner of four Masters titles
25 Topographies
26 "Agnus __"
27 City on the Oka River
28 Average score
29 Excitingly strange
30 Foch and Simone
32 Lamp resident
34 Trademark fastener
37 Florida raptor
39 Bond foe
42 Book following Exod.
43 Standing one in good __
44 Lion's name
45 Duck down
46 Old hat
48 Bank deal
49 1976-80 Wimbledon winner
50 Unseal
52 Switchboard pers.
53 National tree of the U.S.
54 Polyester fabric
56 Smelting residues
57 School orgs.
58 Pincus Leff's stage name
60 Pond scum
61 San __, CA
62 Grade over max
65 __-relief
67 Transplant recipient
68 Belgian composer Jacques
69 Claire and Balin
73 Diminutive folklore hero
78 Actual
79 Change one's offer
81 "Blue Moon" lyricist Hart
82 Clique
85 Homestead plot
86 Old World lizards
88 Identical
89 Continental currency
90 Pointers
92 School for Sartre
93 Fi preceder
94 Of cities
95 Peer Gynt's mother
96 American Dance Theater choreographer
99 Existing naturally
100 Stick one's nose in
102 Dimensions
103 Small harbor
104 Lifting devices
107 Abner's partner
108 A single time
109 Harem room
112 So it would seem
114 USA-USSR trade pioneer
117 Minuteness

118 Nastier
119 Pizza piece
120 Most composed
121 St. Francis' birthplace
122 Rubes

DOWN

1 Roe source
2 Pile of combustibles
3 Highest point in the Alai Mountains
4 Yucatan year
5 Having claws
6 Acts down in the dumps
7 Asian inland sea
8 Part of RSVP
9 Force
10 Rosebay
11 Frightens
12 Life partner
13 Wild goat
14 Tuesday before Ash Wednesday
15 Some postal workers
16 Bring up the rear
17 Guitarist known as Slowhand
18 Ballpoint, e.g.
19 '60s radical group

24 Sturdy cart
31 Land of Isfahan
32 Very large number
33 Phantoms
35 Liberate
36 Supervise
37 Norway's capital
38 Greek portico
39 Saxophonist Mulligan
40 Himalayan kingdom
41 Shorthand system
44 Security device
47 CEO, e.g.
49 Forbid
51 D.C. advisory grp.
54 Roman Pluto
55 Whippoorwill bill
58 Young hen
59 What to do at Joe's
62 Isaac's father
63 Exact
64 "The Spirit of Liberty" writer
66 Our sun
67 Buffer area in a war: abbr.
69 Lyricist Gershwin
70 Israeli desert
71 Oriental adders

72 Carly and Paul
74 Irish and Spanish growths
75 Austin of tennis
76 Half: pref.
77 Nice one?
80 Tibetan leader
82 Like elementary particles
83 Part of Q.E.D.
84 Vocal inflection
87 Epilepsy attacks
89 Sea eagle
91 Noticeable
94 Free
97 Tenant
98 Subsidiary propositions
99 Move very slowly
101 Andrea, the dictator of Genoa
103 Madagascar primate
105 Pravda source
106 Part of DOS
108 Smallest bills
110 Orlop or poop
111 Bellicose deity
112 __ in the bag!
113 Bite the dust
115 Colonial cuckoo
116 1051

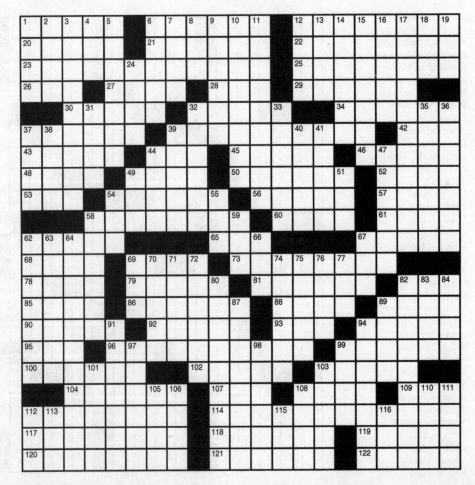

by Ernest Lampert

ACROSS

1 Name-droppers
6 Contracted, as one's lips
12 Dunderhead
15 Italian auto maker Ferrari
19 Divining card
20 Ultimatum phrase
21 2nd letter add-on
22 Prepared to drive
23 Vacuum
25 Archaeological fragment
27 Wicked
28 Can. province
29 Granular seasoning
31 Poi ingredients
32 "Cabin in the Sky" star
35 Joy
37 Crowd stirrer?
38 Make an X with weapons
42 Music practice pieces
45 Draw
47 Art __
48 Steve Martin film, "__ of Faith"
49 Condemn
53 Oroville and Aswan
55 Hendrix album, "__ You Experienced?"
56 Fortas or Vigoda
57 Big __, CA
58 January honoree
60 Did electrician's work
62 Ann of burlesque
65 Waikiki garland
67 Disinformation
69 First name of a canine star?
70 Make Waldorfs?
73 A-line or sack
78 Cousin of Gomez Addams
79 Periods
81 Gabor sister
82 Twisted sideways
83 Reflexive pronoun
87 Humdinger
89 "All About __"
91 Tom Hanks movie
92 Gardner of film
93 Trompe l'__ (photorealism)
95 Retailer's ploy
99 Acts shrewish
101 God of war
103 Crow comment
104 Finnish baths
105 Metamorphic rock
108 Practical trainee
111 "Grumpy Old Men" star
112 Shift in loyalty
116 Fraternity letter
119 One causing damage
122 Game room, for short
123 Chevron rival
124 Time between
126 Orchestral division
129 Former Russian ruler
130 Bigger pic
131 Spots

132 Sandal strap
133 Impudence
134 Big name in ice cream
135 Catch sight of
136 Cassia family plant

DOWN

1 French writer Madame de __
2 Inexperienced
3 Senator Hatch
4 Wharf posts
5 Sault __ Marie
6 Baffling problems
7 Bearlike
8 Agt.
9 Happy starter?
10 Last of coal?
11 More profound
12 Pacified
13 Racing vehicle
14 Fast jet's letters
15 Alternative fuel
16 __-do-well
17 Goose egg
18 Vegas quote
24 Husbands and wives
26 Pack
30 Proceed slowly but surely

33 Gardener's tools
34 Pseudonym of Romain de Tirtoff
36 Chemically similar substances
38 Fielder or Cooper
39 Hind part
40 Act boldly
41 Made haste
42 Solar-lunar calendars differential
43 Prohibition
44 Operators
46 Squid's defense
50 __ and void
51 Trample
52 Novelist Bagnold
54 Geneva's people
59 "Pretty Woman" co-star
61 Part of IBM
63 Mother of Horus
64 Start of a path?
66 Teen heartthrob
68 Cut off
71 By my lowest estimation
72 Ornamental button
74 Set aside
75 Coffee brand
76 Goldoni of "Shadows"

77 Perimeters
80 Pizza piece
83 Dangle
84 Novelist Hunter
85 Furor
86 Directly
88 "Born in the __"
90 Intrinsic nature
94 With deadly force
96 Pompous ass
97 Gilbert of "Roseanne"
98 Bask
100 Smiles coyly
102 Fly like an eagle
106 German industrial basin
107 Made insensitive
109 Suckling babe
110 Having luxuriant locks
113 Hunter of stars?
114 Sch. in Storrs
115 Pacific island country
116 Models in parts
117 Latin handle
118 Sch. orgs.
120 Old Gaelic
121 Knocks lightly
125 Victory sign
127 Get 'em, Fido!
128 Small change

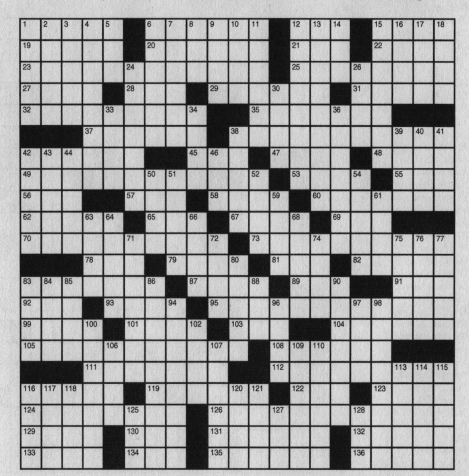

SUPERLATIVES

by Robert H. Wolfe

ACROSS

1 Accumulates
8 J. Hancocked?
11 Composer Alban
15 Thompson of "Peter's Friends"
19 Vatican chapel
20 You, to Yves
21 Actor Sharif
22 Burden
23 Lighted, poetically
24 Perfect fastball?
27 Bought the farm
28 Tumbler
30 Erie Canal mule
31 Possess like a Scotsman
32 Wide shoe width
33 Cornerstone abbr.
35 Actor Armand
37 Make a blunder
38 Wimbledon arena?
41 Nothing in Nogales
42 Caviar
43 Sailors' admin.
44 Merchandise label
45 City on Baranof Island
47 Hebrew musical instrument
48 Office asst.
51 Spins rapidly
54 Bearing
55 Bakery buy
56 Nasal applicator
58 Of the back of a tooth
60 Lawman Wyatt
62 Cut to fit
64 Add more luster
66 Santa's helper
69 Bomb blast, in headlines
70 Long and Peeples
73 Young adult
74 Bibelot
76 Gridiron zebra
77 Rough struggles
80 Sale of church preferments
82 Organic compound
84 Hit one's drive
87 Lemonlike fruits
88 Two eleven
90 Russian emperor
92 Illegal activities
94 Highland Gaelic
95 Gardener's tools
96 Takes five
98 Dos Passos trilogy
99 Reverent wonder
101 Bus. letter abbr.
102 Prot. sect
103 Remaining true even when intoxicated?
109 Sun Devils' sch.
110 Singer Gloria
112 Tight spots
113 Make up facts
114 Place
115 Female deer
116 Major soccer mistake

118 Pepsi or Coke
119 Superpower?
122 Involves by necessity
125 Golfer Ballesteros
126 Emphatic typeface: abbr.
127 Italian three
128 Mini-pie
129 Deuce topper
130 Luck of the Irish
131 The Loop loopers
132 Dynamo pivots

DOWN

1 Stage whispers
2 Environment
3 Napping
4 Type of poker
5 Fig. of speech
6 U-turn from WSW
7 Serenely deliberate
8 Right-hand side of a ship
9 Faline's brother in "Bambi"
10 Exclude
11 Charges off
12 Ostrich cousin
13 Nonvenomous serpent
14 Bohr and Borge?

15 Actor Wallach
16 Mrs. America contest winner?
17 Almond/coconut cookie
18 Ones that stick
25 Tobacco kilns
26 Entreaty
29 Water-storing plants
33 Shakespearean contraction
34 One inflicting heavy blows
36 West Indies islands
39 Kansas City team
40 Jamaican fruit
46 Likeness
47 Shortened bk.
48 Shankar's instrument
49 Related on mother's side
50 Owner of Kansas City team?
52 Small songbirds
53 Ukr. or Lith., once
57 State gambling game
59 Hanoi holiday
61 Fancy cravat
63 Aversion
65 Preserved for later
67 Mortgage attachments
68 "All That Jazz" director

71 Warn
72 Understand
75 Empty a spool
78 Top Seattle cager?
79 Assn.
81 Get a wrong total
83 City in Serbia
85 Dance of the '60s
86 Peril of salmon
88 Costing the least
89 Marketing figure?
91 Group of seven: var.
93 Crime syndicate
97 Oboe's ancestor
100 Director Craven
102 Anglo-Saxon theologian
104 Existing naturally
105 Small bays
106 Philippines port
107 Gardener, at times
108 Leavening agents
111 Ninnies
117 Pink baby?
118 American suffragist
120 Napoleon's marshal
121 "__ Kapital"
123 Writer Hentoff
124 Refrain syllable

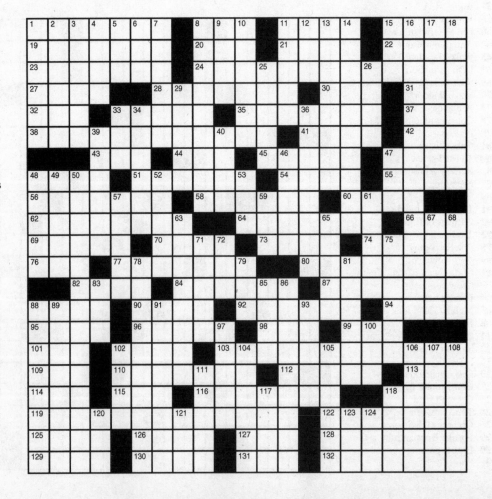

by Frances Burton

ACROSS

1 Disengage from a habit
5 Rascal
10 "Cheers" barmaid
15 Young cow
19 Choir voice
20 Mistake
21 Once more
22 Smell
23 Mob melee
24 __ Dame
25 Chuck Berry song
27 Nat "King" Cole song
29 Center of Minoan culture
31 Croquet stick
32 Fatty tissue components
33 Trumpet blast
34 Duplication devices
35 Inhabitant of: suff.
36 Sao __, Brazil
37 Added shading
38 Titled ladies
41 Set
42 Returns the incumbent
46 Periods
47 Ice-cream cake
48 Price proposals
49 Small islet
50 Segment of a journey
51 Light wood
52 Mexican farewell
54 Vocalist Eydie
56 Atoll bays
58 Disentangles
60 Weasel's kin
61 Cove
62 Spirit of "The Tempest"
63 First-generation
   Japanese-American
64 Puts up
66 Deli sausage
67 Lacking guile
70 Singer LeAnn
71 Assign blame to
72 Get the lead out?
74 Miss. neighbor
75 Actress/director Lupino
76 Mass. neighbor
77 VCR function
78 Cinch
79 Wedge-shaped piece
82 Catching a few Z's
84 Sacrifice plays
85 Flung
86 Foot control
87 Currency of Albania
88 Worshippers
91 Imbecile
92 Most bloody
96 Prefix meaning monster
97 Lyricist Carole Bayer __
98 Buddy Holly song
99 Four Tops song
101 Surrounded by
103 Largest continent
104 Very dry
105 Select few

106 Barbizon School
   painter Jules
107 Berry and Branagh
108 Hamilton bills
109 Painful spots
110 Basketry willow
111 "Bus Stop" playwright

DOWN

1 Reheats
2 J. Alfred Prufrock's creator
3 Expiate
4 Official witnesses
5 Doddering
6 Span
7 Gulf of the Ionian Sea
8 N. African nation
9 Make impossible
10 Diaz of "My Best
   Friend's Wedding"
11 Striped gem
12 Martha of "Monsieur
   Verdoux"
13 Ad follower?
14 Windflowers
15 Make an impact
16 Fred's dancing sister
17 Solitary one

18 Is vexed
26 Collar extension
28 Scads
30 Death rattle
33 Beach Boys song
34 Female students, once
36 Dawber and Shriver
37 Threesomes
38 Secluded valley
39 Location
40 Rod Stewart song
41 "The Planets" composer
43 The Hollies song
44 Duration
45 Leave text as is!
47 Deadly poisons
48 Michael Jackson song
51 Charges off
52 Of birds
53 View as
54 "The Last Remake
   of Beau __"
55 Pitcher Hershiser
57 In the past
59 Alice's Restaurant patron
60 Initial
63 Integration grp.
64 Estrada of "CHiPs"

65 Hound
66 Tendon
68 Louver
69 Gullible dupes
71 Cornmeal concoctions
73 Scottish dance
76 Deteriorates
77 Place of fabulous wealth
78 Japanese dish
80 Locks of hair
81 Brain wave of the
   semiconscious
82 Highest points
83 Bone dry
84 Ice mass
87 Lumberjack
88 Ready for the pitch
89 Tractor man
90 Senator Hatch of Utah
91 Dull surface
92 Art school
93 Ruhr Valley city
94 Taking to court
95 Needle
97 Mix
98 Alan Arkin movie
100 "Evil Woman" grp.
102 Greek letters

ENGAGEMENT CARDS

by Alan P. Olschwang

ACROSS

1 Ear part
5 Extra-strong cotton thread
10 Transfer image
15 Stable tyke
19 "Roots" author Haley
20 Charged particle
21 Greek marketplace
22 Look long and lustily
23 Without ice
24 Come to pass
25 Copy machine additive
26 Goad
27 Start of Evan Esar quote
30 Merchandise label
31 Raise
32 Organic compound
33 Choose
34 Fight back
36 Terribly timid
38 Aspirations
40 Metamorphic rock
44 Part 2 of quote
47 Part 3 of quote
49 Live on
50 All tuckered out
53 Jacob's twin
54 Infamous hotelier Helmsley
55 Facet
57 Tarzan's son
58 Samuel's mentor
59 Maturing agent
61 Part 4 of quote
64 Position of superiority
66 Greek goddess of the moon
67 Part 5 of quote
69 Franz Joseph and Kevin
74 Stag
76 Part 6 of quote
78 West Indies island
82 Altar constellation
83 Drinking vessel
84 Epps of "The Mod Squad"
85 Like the pounding surf
86 Nemesis
88 In verse
91 Cockney aspiration
92 Part 7 of quote
95 Part 8 of quote
97 Dancer Ruby
98 Feeds the pot
99 Cass and Michelle, e.g.
101 English Channel swimmer Gertrude
103 Kitchen gadget
105 Point in question
109 Sacred image
112 Exclamation of discovery
113 End of quote
115 Unconscious state
116 Australian wild dog
118 Star in Orion
119 Fontainebleau residents
120 Tied up
121 Come in!
122 City south of Gainesville
123 Dancer Tommy
124 Transmit
125 Diplomat Silas
126 Scandinavian
127 British gun

DOWN

1 Judge Ito
2 Margarines, briefly
3 Lulu
4 Outermost
5 Vietnam neighbor
6 Small distances
7 Mediterranean island
8 Jeweler's glass
9 Added nutrients
10 Computer input
11 Psyche division
12 Italian noblewoman
13 Localities
14 Kind of big
15 Third green follow-up
16 Fairy-tale monster
17 Pond growth
18 Suggestive look
28 Move as a group
29 Greek portico
34 Greek wine
35 Surgeons' knives
37 E.T. craft
39 Early matches, briefly
41 Victor's cry
42 Rational
43 Russian ruler
44 Pants
45 Nimble
46 Winner's token
47 Attention getter
48 Chance to play
51 Oriental sash
52 Puerto Rican port
56 Scope out
58 Ancient Syrian city
60 Gooey
62 Countersigned
63 New or raw follower
64 Hillary's hill
65 Provide with a characteristic
68 Protein constituent
70 __ Jima
71 "Star Trek" co-star
72 Day's march
73 Faint trace
75 No-no
77 Suitable
78 Short nail
79 Heraldic band
80 Lecherous man
81 Mesa
83 Intimidate
87 Mythological runner
88 Antielectron
89 Tape meas.
90 Assert
93 Coated with crumbs
94 Florentine glassmaker Antonio
96 Classifies
99 Civil rights martyr Evers
100 Sharon and Durant
102 River of Cologne
104 One of Harpo's brothers
106 Nose
107 City near Trieste
108 German industrial city
109 Freezes
110 Peace advocate
111 Sign of things to come
113 Sported
114 Winglike structures
117 Mil. rank

BRIGHT MOVIES

by Robert H. Wolfe

ACROSS

1 Arctic goose
6 Actress Thompson
10 John and Denny, e.g.
15 Off. underling
19 Travail
20 Roger Rabbit, e.g.
21 Hersey's bell town
22 Small parasite
23 Courtyards
24 __ soit qui mal y pense
25 Actress Nita
26 Cart-pulling pair
27 1971 Sandy Duncan movie
30 Western tribe
31 Wee bit
32 West Point code
33 French river
34 French pancake
35 Duncan's dagger
37 Actress Campbell
38 PGA member
39 Treacherous ones
41 Varnish ingredient
43 Borden bovine
45 Russian sovereign
46 Lepidopterist's equipment
47 Convert from code
51 Former capital of Scotland
53 On __ (without guarantee)
55 Light gray
56 Garment with bloomers
58 Breather
60 Pops
63 Climb
65 Lay asphalt
66 Histories
67 Break suddenly
68 Son of Osiris
69 Timber-to-be
70 S. Amer. nation
71 Ballplayer Guerrero
72 __ go bragh!
73 Chestnut-and-white horses
74 __ Oreille Lake
75 Glasgow or Barkin
76 Greek portico
77 Pakistani tongue
78 Elevate
80 Work unit
81 Fall event?
83 Venture a thought
85 Native American game
87 Distress signal
89 Back part
91 Early Persians
93 Buckeyes' sch.
94 Creamy whites
96 Hot tub
97 Night: pref.
99 Small land mass
103 Lounge furniture
104 Countertenors
106 "Operator" singer
108 Tablet
109 Spat
110 1977 Richard Pryor movie

113 Prune text
114 "Barnaby __"
115 Leisure
116 From this day on
117 Less common
118 Infamous Hiss
119 Baking chamber
120 Stamp pad
121 Frome's vehicle
122 Nourishes
123 Snug home
124 Plays' players

DOWN

1 Explosions
2 Cane palm
3 Wear away by friction
4 Roulette bet in Monte Carlo
5 Curbside pile
6 Fuel ingredient
7 1988 Richard Dreyfuss movie
8 Mixed breed
9 Indigo dye
10 Exploiter of lower tastes
11 Slowly, in music
12 "Hemingway's Chair" author Michael
13 Wyeth and Jackson
14 Farmland
15 Illicit love affairs
16 1984 Molly Ringwald movie
17 Spire holder
18 Most on edge
28 Worn blanket?
29 Spots
34 Beef and moan
36 Wallach of "The Good, the Bad, and the Ugly"
40 Bridge seats
42 After, in Tours
44 Binges
45 1957 Tyrone Power movie
47 Hurries away
48 Accompany
49 1981 Ian Charleson movie
50 Caveat __
52 Missing-persons investigator
54 Short-lived Ford model
57 Get back to level
59 The Colosseum et al.
61 Chicken callers
62 Mooch
64 Part of LEM

66 __ up (invigorated)
71 Jury makeup
73 Indian bread?
78 Disquiet
79 Word with pine or tape
82 Garden bloom
84 Those taking unfair advantage
86 Assent, in Bordeaux
87 Nuns
88 Shaped like an egg
90 Generally
92 Isolated ethnic community
95 Traveled like Huckleberry Finn
96 Enacted
98 Convincing
100 Heavyweight boxer Leon
101 Surgical cutter
102 Lawn-finishing tools
105 Rocky outcrop
107 System of moral values
110 Seven-time Wimbledon champion
111 "Love Makes the World Go Round" singer Jackson
112 "99 Luftballons" singer

by Xan Lattimore

ACROSS

1 Flat-bottomed boats
6 Tennis star Monica
11 Geezer
15 Workplace safety grp.
19 Chicago airport
20 Skirt fold
21 Oriental nanny
22 __ there, done that
23 Mamet's "A __ in the __"
25 Mailer's "The __ and the __"
27 Dutch painter
28 Surround
30 Full blast
31 Presage
34 __ lazuli
35 __ vincit omnia
36 Jergens and Astaire
37 Bogged down
38 Chewy candy
42 Heads of France
43 Jewison's "In the __ of the __"
46 Old hat
47 Burden
48 Mournful sound
49 Lion's den
51 Covetousness
52 Neighbor of Leb.
53 Wyndham's "The __ of the __"
58 Obtain
59 Able to perceive
61 French interjection
62 Poe's lady
64 Life-drawing subjects
65 Permeate
66 Computer language
67 Former Israeli P.M.
69 Black-and-white treats
70 Clean dirty money
73 Strike
74 McCullers' "The __ of the __"
78 Actress Gabor
79 Parched
81 Singer Celine
82 Wood and Silver
83 Some time hence
84 Cathedral areas
86 R.E. Floyd's "__ in the __"
90 Slap on the buttocks
91 Patriotic song
93 Save for future use
94 Forever, in poems
95 Rehan and Huxtable
96 Whimpers
97 Frightened
98 More nervous
101 "St. __ Fire"
102 Film critic Roger
103 Hersey's "A __ for __"
105 Sergio Leone's "The __, the __, and the __"
110 Out of the wind
111 Latin "ditto"
112 Els or Kovacs
113 Pontificate
114 Requirement
115 Beatty and Buntline
116 Tree houses?
117 Card-game displays

DOWN

1 Our star
2 "The Sweetheart of Sigma __"
3 Lummox
4 Grapples
5 Small sofas
6 Pace
7 Spirited vigor
8 Allow to
9 Aviator Amelia
10 Trend upward
11 Caesar's dog
12 Arabian sultanate
13 Sturdy tree
14 "__ & Louise"
15 Hardhearted
16 Potential plant
17 Make sound
18 Griffith or Rooney
24 Biddies
26 Cabinet features
29 South of France
31 Jargon
32 Danish seaport
33 Hardy's "The __ of the __"
34 Jungle vine
35 Muscle protein
37 Repast
39 Algren's "The __ with the __"
40 Glass eel
41 Philippines island
43 Doughnut centers
44 Angry look
45 Scenery chewers
48 Beveled edges for joining
50 Gives again, temporarily
53 "Barbarella" director
54 Enthusiastic player
55 Nudge
56 Wet thoroughly
57 Remove listening devices
60 Total
63 __ sequitur
65 Goddess of peace
66 Singer Black
67 Journalist Alexander
68 U.S. Grant's first name
69 Woodwind instrument
71 Goolagong of tennis
72 Positioned in order
75 Golden-touch king
76 Olive __
77 Flat-bottomed rowboat
80 Jumped the tracks
83 Opening
85 Part one of a tape
87 Jack Horner's find
88 Bulb type
89 Blight on the landscape
90 Hollywood success
92 Designer Pierre
94 Zeno of __
96 Walks heavily
97 French clerics
98 Israeli diplomat Abba
99 Cut text
100 Happiness
101 Novelist Bagnold
102 Work on manuscripts
104 Justice Fortas
106 Switch positions
107 Guy's sweetie
108 Inc. in Liverpool
109 Positive reply

by Willy A. Wiseman

ACROSS

1 Put to sea
8 Bow and Barton
14 Superlatively down in the dumps
20 One who knows his food and drink
21 Find a new tenant
22 Mesh foundation for lace
23 Exploit an upper hand
25 Chant
26 Charlie Chan portrayer
27 500-mi. race
28 Major stars
30 Goblet part
31 Crack shots
33 Floor squares
34 Pop
35 Piece of advice
39 Infamous Helmsley
41 Jim Bakker's former org.
44 "Don't Bring Me Down" grp.
45 Earth tone
46 Ventilation shaft
47 Small antelope
49 Kept talking
51 Enters
53 Reebok rival
54 ASAP
55 & so forth
56 U.K. honor
57 Distinct musical tones: abbr.
60 "Mashed Potato Time" singer Sharp
62 Advice to Skywalker
66 Med. care plan
67 Approx.
68 Make off with
70 Scents
71 Corn serving
72 "Cannery __"
73 Sewers' gatherings
77 Portuguese seaport
79 Elitist
81 Opposite of SSW
82 Lon __ of Cambodia
83 Nautical swerve
85 Murder
86 __ up (paid)
88 Slithered
90 Get going
91 Melonlike fruit
93 Writer Gertrude
94 Thai's neighbor
96 German article
97 Rainer of "The Great Ziegfeld"
98 Stage signals
102 Coffee server
103 Pipe root
104 Way of walking
105 Military grp.
109 Most contemptibly small
112 College cheers
114 Dry-heat bath
115 Toddler
116 Ecdysiasts
120 Plaza Hotel girl of the comics
121 Slip by
122 Head-to-head fighter
123 Gilda of "Saturday Night Live"
124 Intuited
125 Casual shirts

DOWN

1 Splinter groups
2 Disney World attraction
3 Book datum
4 Preliminary draft
5 Hungarian violinist
6 Novelist Levin
7 Was in front
8 Rhode Island city
9 Advance
10 Bohemian
11 Stephen of "The Crying Game"
12 More furious
13 Hard like metal
14 Military jails
15 Filmmaker Riefenstahl
16 Org. of court players
17 Song from "The Wiz"
18 Guitarist Carlos
19 Weld in movies
24 Contended
29 Actress Susan
31 Leading ISP
32 Audience
33 From that place
36 Huang tributary
37 Band of eight
38 Egyptian god of wisdom
39 Fleur-de-__
40 Goddess of discord
41 Mulls over
42 Dons to test fit
43 Similar
46 Accepted a humiliating defeat
48 Plot for roses
50 Matched
51 So long
52 Spanish river
54 Porky's girlfriend
58 Passionate
59 Alternative to a medical examiner
61 Honorific title: abbr.
63 Most remote, briefly
64 Watch pocket
65 Psychic's letters
69 German article
74 Insect stage
75 Song for nine voices
76 Egg white
78 Keats offering
80 Feathery scarves
84 Dwight's rival
87 Comic Louis
89 Honored royally
90 He speaks, in Lat.
91 Actress Amanda
92 Halo
93 Washington city
95 PC key
98 Italian three
99 Snake speech
100 Players
101 Cowers in fear
103 Mosquito or flea, e.g.
106 1957 hit, "Wake Up Little __"
107 Fidgety
108 Abstains from eating
110 Joyride
111 __ majesty
112 Tears
113 Altar area
114 Hip ending?
117 Operated
118 Pt. of speech
119 Road to Rouen

ELECTABLE CANDIDATE

by Alan P. Olschwang

ACROSS

1 Handhold
5 Plantation machine
10 Benson novel, "__ and Lucia"
14 Homegrown
19 Incarnation of Vishnu
20 Speak one's mind
21 Runner Zatopek
22 Tropical lizard
23 TV sports award
24 Pelvic bone
25 One Simpson
26 Uses a stopwatch
27 Start of H.L. Mencken quote
30 Abodes
31 Power and Guthrie
32 __ Hashanah
33 Peace goddess
35 Small amount
36 Belle and Bart
39 Eurasian viper
40 D.C. advisory grp.
43 Garland for the head
46 Part 2 of quote
50 Permit to
51 Pastry topped dish
53 Dander
54 Feudal lord
55 Dictator Amin
56 Stumble
57 Melvil and Thomas
60 Provide with income
61 Now, without further __
62 Despises
64 Way cool!
65 Whale school
66 In one's right mind
68 Part 3 of quote
72 Shoshones
76 French possessive pronoun
78 Addams Family cousin
79 Spanish cowboy's lariat
81 Table scrap
82 Sri Lankan separatist
85 Stop at several saloons
88 Currier's partner
89 One to Therese
90 Total
91 An honest man
92 Penske and Vadim
94 Cravat
95 Part 4 of quote
99 Abrupt
101 Downcast
102 NYC hours
103 Wrinkled
105 Female sandpiper
106 Third rock
109 Gull's cousin
110 Mid-ocean
114 Finnish currency unit
116 End of quote
120 True up
121 Lamb's pen name

122 Cook unshelled eggs
123 Old Thailand
124 Window parts
125 Males only
126 "Guitar Town" singer Steve
127 Kett of the comics
128 Viewpoint
129 Perforation
130 Endearing
131 Witnessed

DOWN

1 Extensive
2 Gravelly
3 Tariff target
4 Warhead's contents
5 Small nightclub
6 George of "Disraeli"
7 Noncleric
8 Needle case
9 No longer an ex
10 "Come to My Window" singer Etheridge
11 Anabaptist sect
12 Tilting tower town
13 Hammers metal to smoothness
14 Wood-shaping machine
15 Leek cousin
16 Began
17 Shelterward
18 Fewer
28 Thorough
29 Comic Crosby
34 Troy, NY school
37 Valve attachment
38 Black cuckoo
39 Askew
41 Food thickener
42 Once again
43 False name
44 "Pagliacci" role
45 Quagmire
47 German songs
48 Nile queen, casually
49 Brahmanist
52 South American monkey
58 Muse of poetry
59 One-time female mil. group
63 After-dinner party
65 Roberta or Bernadette
67 Post of etiquette
69 Utmost
70 Stable sounds
71 Grotto
73 Right now, Pierre!

74 Banks of the Cubs
75 "Village Wedding" painter
77 French she
80 Confidence builder
82 Barcelona aunts
83 Paquin of "The Piano"
84 Infuriating
85 Tip to expedite service
86 Fence the loot, e.g.
87 Outlooks
93 Of the ear: pref.
96 Hanoi holiday
97 Foretell
98 Bacharach or Young
100 Removes from office
104 English Channel swimmer Gertrude
107 Broadway backer
108 Washer cycle
109 Test run
111 Wading bird
112 Related on mother's side
113 Madison Ave. guy
114 Hemingway's sobriquet
115 Distinctive flair
117 Choir member
118 Melt
119 Place on the payroll

B MOVIES

by Josiah Breward

ACROSS

1 Employment summaries
8 Sailor's saint
12 Send to press
20 Distant settlement
21 Burden
22 Tete-a-tete
23 Sweeping saga starring the Marx Brothers?
25 The Captain's Toni
26 Swiss capital
27 Misfortunes
28 Breezy exchanges
29 Hungry Horse or Hoover
30 Eisenhower
31 Getz and Kenton
33 Loving stroke
35 Kimono sashes
36 Toward the rising sun
38 Wages
39 AFL-__
40 Film about a fight between squirrels?
42 Corals, e.g.
45 Shuts out
48 Open, as toothpaste
49 Marino or Fouts
50 Monk's title
51 Grenoble's river
52 Guy's date
54 Derision
56 Beam
57 Hot tubs
58 Applelike fruits
62 Huber of tennis
63 Worldwide workers' grp.
64 Glutton
65 Curve movie?
67 One in Emden
68 Class for U.S. immigrants
69 Hershiser of baseball
70 Rocks on the edge
71 Sicilian resort
72 Compete
73 Not at any time
75 Wash. or Jackson in NYC
76 Rot-resistant wood
77 UFO pilots
78 Retirement grp.
79 Water bottler
83 Port on the Black Sea
84 Chinese fruit
86 Film starring a snake?
89 Cycle starter?
90 Delicate hue
91 Idealists
95 College sports org.
97 "Honor Thy Father" author
98 Like some gases
99 Mauna __
100 No spring chicken
101 Shopping complexes
102 MIT grad
103 South of France
104 Cornmeal bread
106 Film about masochist Dufy?
110 Stated clearly

111 "Jane __"
112 Peter or Paul, but not Mary
113 Caries spotters
114 Jodie Foster film
115 Locked closed

DOWN

1 Alternative to Bob
2 I've got it!
3 Provisions
4 Resting atop
5 "Mr. __"
6 Part of CBS
7 Rod of rock
8 Pixies
9 Superman's girl
10 Bub
11 Keats opus
12 Seasoning plant
13 Anxious
14 Temporary shelters
15 Scads
16 Sailors' admin.
17 Film about daring beaus?
18 Zhou of China
19 Judges
24 Sonata's last movement

28 Spasmodic muscular contractions
31 Vowed
32 Greek crosses
33 Math subj.
34 Inter __ (among other things)
35 Lubricate
37 Ski-slope rides
38 __ Jose, CA
39 Swindled
41 Latin negative
42 Winter coats
43 Pecan treats
44 Osaka farewell
45 Throw into disorder
46 Phil of the NHL
47 Snoopy vs. the Red Baron movie?
49 Philanthropists
52 City on Seneca Lake
53 Muddle
55 Insertion mark
58 Slightest
59 Away from the prow
60 Hwy. sign abbr.
61 Thar __ blows!
65 Dwarfed tree
66 Of a people: pref.

71 Gage bestseller
74 Pee Wee and Della
76 Proficient
80 Big barrels
81 Oh yeah, right
82 NL Braves
83 Redolence
85 Actress Merkel
86 Sentimental songs
87 Mold, mildew and smut
88 Timeless
90 Portable platform
92 Star in the Big Dipper
93 Protuberance
94 Left port
95 Well-known
96 Genetic duplicate
97 After-shower powders
98 Pentium makers
101 Short skirt
102 Noble rank
103 Male: abbr.
105 Steve Martin song, "King __"
106 Blue or Cross
107 Scope out
108 College student's letters
109 Water damage

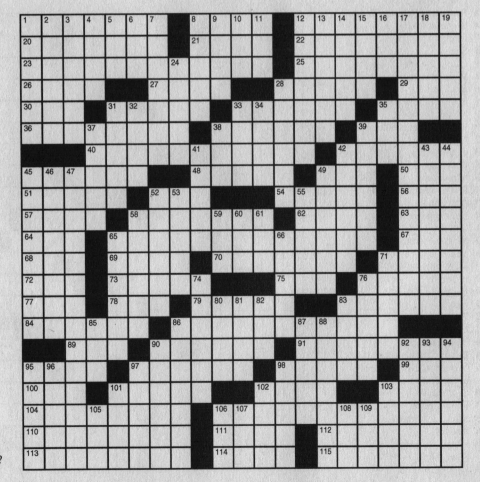

By Willy A. Wiseman

ACROSS

1 "Blue" singer LeAnn
6 Lug laboriously
12 Liquid sample
15 Assns.
19 Fanon of the pope
20 Soviet newspaper
21 Lower digit
22 Criminal, to a cop
23 Hints on skewer use?
25 AAA suggestion
26 Even one time
27 Sundries
28 Make off with
30 Santa Maria's sister ship
31 __ Plaines, IL
32 Biddies
33 Real strong java
36 Non-clerical
37 Goes to a diner just for cake?
39 Obstruct
41 "Studies in the Psychology of Sex" author Havelock
44 Bizarre
45 More sedate
46 Black of Burgundy
47 Member of a Catholic order
50 Broccoli piece
51 National syst.
52 Feudal serf
53 Bennett of Random House
54 Guitarist Atkins
57 Employ
58 Snap up
59 Star in Cygnus
62 Without coercion
64 Rock shelf
66 Prize for the best marijuana?
69 Mystery award
70 Behaves coquettishly
72 Never existed
73 Tiny amount
75 Rationers of WWII
76 "Auld Lang __"
77 Part of a hammerhead
79 Arm bone
80 Deck officer
81 Call for
83 Most substantial
86 Yemen port
87 Magazine staffers
89 Imperial
90 Flippant
91 Renter
92 Parlors frequented by moles?
96 Work unit
97 Russian empresses
99 Garr of "Close Encounters of the Third Kind"
100 Scot's cap
103 France, once
105 Rib-eye alternative
106 Abuses
108 Inter __ (among other things)
109 Groovy, updated

110 Anubis?
113 Crash-site grp.
114 Simpson grandpa
115 Baseball bird
116 __-Saxon
117 Golf shop purchase
118 Golf standard
119 Pestered
120 Bellow and Kripke

DOWN

1 Dressed as a judge
2 Steamed
3 Cohn and Connelly
4 Dresden's river
5 Boils
6 Rejects with disdain
7 Pleat
8 Toppers
9 Gladiators' 56
10 Key-punch bus.
11 Travel document
12 Thoroughfare
13 Scintillas
14 Strips for bed?
15 Broad-minded
16 Issued a strong product condemnation?
17 Marine pineapple?

18 Hose attachment
24 Middling marks
29 Verifiable
33 Pin box
34 Mach-breakers' letters
35 Sharif of "Lawrence of Arabia"
37 Gossip
38 Function
40 __ together (connected)
41 Overwhelms
42 In a vague way
43 Masqueraded as Satan?
45 Letters on cameras
47 RPM part
48 Urgent letters?
49 Still standing
50 Feverish
53 Govt. financial grp.
55 Slips by
56 Absolute power
58 Retrieve
59 Med. personnel
60 Post-dusk
61 Part of Can.
63 Stephen of "The Crying Game"
65 Welcomes
67 Soak up rays

68 Puts on
71 Extra thong?
74 Create lace
78 Tennis doubles?
79 Hideous
80 Sheep bleats
82 Champagne choice
83 Gained support from
84 Water of Mexico
85 Blast it!
87 Grand
88 Adenauer
89 Check horses
90 Bridal wreath and meadowsweet
92 Washington Post journalist David
93 Smother
94 Tried
95 Correct: pref.
98 Addis __, Eth.
100 South Korean city
101 Not the least bit
102 IBM feature from 1981
104 Sci. classes
106 Synthesizer maker
107 Author Ferber
111 __ pro nobis
112 Musician's booking

HE, OR SHE, WHO LAUGHS LAST...

by Alan P. Olschwang

ACROSS

1 Start of Evan Esar quote
6 City in the Sawatch Range
11 Leer at
15 Incarnation of Vishnu
19 Avid
20 Binge
21 Flamingo lily or elephant's ear
22 Ancient kingdom south of the Dead Sea
23 Worn away unevenly
24 Worker
25 Lucknow wraparound
26 See ya!
27 Compressor component
29 Wrigley greenery
30 Part 2 of quote
32 Monarch's loyal subject
34 "__ we forget..."
35 Iron
36 Take back
40 Korean dictator Syngman
42 Family car
45 Part 3 of quote
48 Lynn of country music
52 Ginger cookie
53 Black Sea port
54 Worker on walls
56 Biblical stories
58 Run off to get married
59 Opposite of WSW
60 Pres.'s financial grp.
61 Frosh caps
64 Shock or lock
66 Part 4 of quote
71 Banquet
72 Ornamental hangings of rich fabric
73 __ Alamos, NM
74 Tee preceder
75 Intuit
76 Letters
81 Prohibition
84 Diacritical mark
87 Ontario or Michigan
88 Sack
89 Part 5 of quote
92 Lubitsch or Zermelo
94 Islands in the Seine
95 St. __ of Avila
96 __ we all?
99 Cerise and crimson
101 Palliates
103 Part 6 of quote
106 Cassowary's cousin
107 Play producer
112 Fed. watchdog agcy.
113 Vegas quote
114 Lees
116 Ham it up
117 Consumer
118 Enclosure for confinement
119 Cancel
120 Amassed
121 High crags
122 The last word?
123 Make a second attempt
124 End of quote

DOWN

1 Show sorrow
2 Spy Mata
3 Self-images
4 Brooding place
5 Of iris rings
6 Egyptian viper
7 Branchlet
8 Pithy sayings
9 Slithery
10 Born in Nice
11 Sahara setting
12 Surgical implants
13 Entice
14 Actor Jannings
15 Frequenter
16 Pithy saying
17 Fluttery fliers
18 Pile up
28 Harold or Fayard
30 Unwanted plant
31 Separated
33 Music class piece
34 Olin or Horne
36 Coarse file
37 Sicilian volcano
38 __ she blows!
39 Puts back in the carton
41 Possesses
43 Pass
44 Apothecary measure
46 His: Fr.
47 Challenging spares
49 Acacia and baobab
50 Past, present or future
51 War god
55 "Stay (I Missed You)" singer Lisa
57 Sugar source
58 Organic compound
61 Actress Jacqueline
62 Latin being
63 Collection of anecdotes
64 Pueblo in New Mexico
65 Steer stealer
66 Jackson or Owens
67 Tobacco ovens
68 Paradigms
69 Chinese mob
70 Makes final
71 Fodder
75 Joyride
76 Go wrong
77 Bards
78 Bathe
79 Scrapes (by)
80 Evening in Padua
82 All-you-can-drink situations
83 __-cochere (covered entrance)
84 Blanc and Blount
85 Pro vote
86 Type of window
90 Take cover
91 Pearson and Flatt
93 Plod
96 Regarding
97 Actress Rene
98 Former anesthetic
100 City on the Ruhr
102 Soothsayer
104 Zany Imogene
105 First gardener?
106 Sea eagle
108 Oriental nanny
109 No longer present
110 Needle case
111 Agts.
114 __ es Salaam
115 Shifty

THE GANG'S ALL HAIR

by Robert H. Wolfe

ACROSS

1 Chic
6 African fever
11 Barley bristles
15 Arthur of tennis
19 Trimmer
20 Open positions
21 Spike or brad
22 Sci. branch
23 Reappear
25 Writer Buzzati
26 Pack down tightly
27 Soprano Gluck
28 Main commodities
30 Spike or Brenda
31 Unattractive fruit?
32 Port of Iraq
34 Off-course wanderer
36 Animal with a long snout
37 Terra __
38 Big birds Down Under
40 Synecdochical prison
41 Make amends
42 Jackie's second
43 Clan pattern
45 AMA members
46 Words used figuratively
47 Take on, figuratively
50 Star such as ours
51 Three on a par five
52 Part of VMI
53 Dawn goddess
54 Actress Taylor
57 Eatery furniture
60 Nevada resort
62 Philosophies
64 Break bread
65 Ring in the ocean
66 Rams on purpose
68 Tractor maker
69 Mug in the shape
   of a stout man
70 Male moose
71 Angel in Aix
72 Optical devices
73 Bowling equipment mfr.
74 Young goat
75 Touch against
77 Elicit
79 Ken and Lena
81 Assume the fetal position
86 Copland and Burr
88 Is not well
89 Tubular worm
90 Reed or Rawls
91 Great __ Lake
92 Merciless character
93 Berry and Venturi
94 Render harmless
96 Treatise or essay
97 Neighbor of Libya
99 Prevailing tide
100 Gremlins
101 Pay dirt
102 Settle down
105 Tra follower

107 Part to play
108 Pass on male genes
110 Go ga-ga
112 Notion
113 Overwhelm with flattery
114 Incorrect
115 Drive in Beverly Hills
116 Cozy home
117 Top-notch
118 More timid
119 Growls

DOWN

1 Source for the fam. pet
2 Music school in Vermont
3 Fragrant
4 Feast
5 Play about Capote
6 Would-be atty.'s hurdle
7 Kelp, e.g.
8 Lather
9 Individual elevators?
10 TV's Mr. Grant
11 Also
12 Bob Marley's band
13 S.F. gridders
14 Blackthorn
15 Disk drive mechanism
16 Train in the field
17 Height of fashion?
18 Imperial realms
24 O.T. book
29 Wooden shoes
33 "Sistine Madonna" painter
35 Pleasure sailing
36 "__ Bulba"
37 30th president, for short
38 Justice Warren
39 Twenty Questions
   classification
44 Records of progress
45 Mesozoic creatures
46 Pairs
48 Gene or Grace
49 Airfoil
50 Display model
55 Concerning
56 American omegas
57 So long!
58 Pink Floyd album,
   "__ Heart Mother"
59 Obtain fruit with
   mouth only?
61 Twining together
63 Trend upward
64 Supergiant star in Cygnus

66 Blooms-to-be
67 Part of IBM
68 Illinois city
70 Open storage
72 Our moon
74 1946-52 N.L.
   home-run leader
76 Protruding parts
78 Becomes faint
80 Couples' furniture?
82 With some apprehension
83 "The Four Seasons" star
84 More nobly
85 Abner's partner
86 Bayer product
87 With ice cream
88 Moveable wing surface
92 Long-time Dolphin
93 Muslim prayer direction
95 Byron of golf
98 Plays a trump card
99 Downing Street address
101 Pelion's partner
103 __ dixit
104 Go-getter
106 Ruckuses
109 Mama in a wool coat?
111 Work unit

CANDY-CODED

by James E. Buell

ACROSS

1 Post-operative prog.
6 Give a grant
11 Pitcher's miscue
15 Pillow cover
19 Olfactory stimulus
20 Western resort lake
21 Mutt of Garfield's jokes
22 Turner of "The Postman Always Rings Twice"
23 100 Grand Bar?
27 Linguistic suffix
28 "Be __ as it may..."
29 Grace enders
30 Denver basketball player
31 Many eBay offerings
33 Eggs on
34 Norm's unseen wife on "Cheers"
35 "Losing My Religion" group
36 Roomy dress?
37 Tokyo ta-ta
41 Significant
44 Pay Day Bar?
46 Joie de vivre
47 Largest satellite in the solar system
48 Walter __ Army Medical Hospital
49 Panic button on a PC
50 Eight-to-ten Cub Scouts
51 Rayburn and Simmons
52 Commented sheepishly
54 Genders
56 __ lettuce
58 Ballroom dance
59 Baden-Baden or Bath
60 Milky Way Bar?
67 Dog tags, briefly
68 Cloverleaf ramps
69 Spot for a hoop
70 Snicker
73 El Greco's birthplace
74 Cut of steak
76 Long, fluffy scarf
77 Tony-winning actress Hagen
78 Litigator
79 Verbal exams
80 For both sexes
81 Butterfinger Bar?
86 Persnickety
87 Hour, e.g.
88 Advancements
89 Rapper Dr. __
90 Part of A.M.
91 Cove
92 Vacillates
96 Come forth from obscurity
99 "The Prince's Birthday" painter
100 Spicy cuisine
101 Chip load
102 Dove Bar?
106 Sundance's girlfriend
107 Study late
108 Linda of "Alice"

109 Big crowd
110 River beneath the Brooklyn Bridge
111 Kitchen finish?
112 Threnody
113 Boss of Tammany Hall

DOWN

1 Pro driver
2 Eradicate
3 Keeps one's fingers crossed
4 "Bel __"
5 Scrapper
6 Map volume
7 Cool one's heels
8 Satisfied sighs
9 Member of a service club
10 "The Naked Ape" author Morris
11 Welcome benefits
12 Hubbubs
13 Smith or Taylor
14 Acutely observant
15 Catchphrases
16 Reagan's secretary of state
17 Archer or Meara
18 Dillon or Damon
24 Attention-getter
25 Moisten with droplets

26 Peer among peers
32 Elvis __ Presley
33 Earnest appeals
34 Like a windmill
36 Comic Johnson
37 Nothing to __ at
38 Tippy-top
39 Ploy
40 Rudiments
41 Current events sources
42 McCowen and Guinness
43 Jackson or Reno
44 Target-spotter's interjection
45 Enraged
47 Sea swallows
51 Crystalline cavity
52 Sew loosely
53 Priest's robes
54 Fiery particle
55 Warren of the Supreme Court
57 Runny cheese
58 Formal document
59 Extends across
61 Least little bit
62 Bring to bear
63 Empire
64 Gray wolves
65 Melancholy woodwinds

66 All set
70 Bunch of hair
71 Ornamental case
72 Soccer star Mia
73 Radioactivity unit
74 Forward section
75 Neighbor of Vietnam
78 Prison term
79 Of the Far East
80 Prompts
82 Old Stutz model
83 Fencing move
84 Resignee of '73
85 Light amber brew
86 Shipping costs
89 Collegiate official
91 Knocker's reply
92 Glistening
93 Think the world of
94 "Salome" playwright
95 Burn up the road
96 Three-sided rapier
97 Physical starter?
98 Diner sign
99 32-card game
100 Branch of math
103 NYC subway line
104 Brink
105 By what means

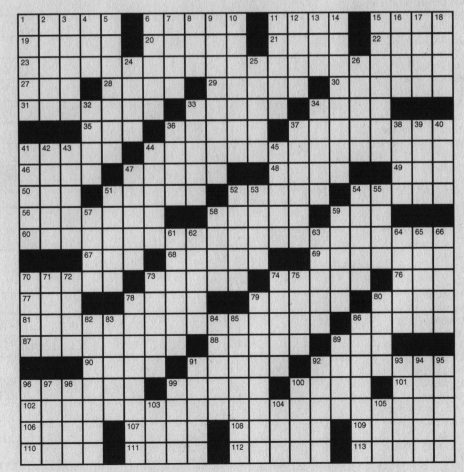

202

TIMELY QUIP

by James E. Buell

ACROSS
1 Rattles
8 Classic Hitchcock film
14 Under optimum conditions
20 Receptacle for preventing waste
21 Island salutations
22 Contemptibly slight
23 Start of a timely quip
25 Better than even chance
26 State south of Bhutan
27 Smooth the way for
28 Witnessed
30 Latest info
31 Prods into action
33 For each
36 "Luck and Pluck" penner
38 Mountaineer's spikes
41 Discharged
43 Getty or Parsons
47 Part 2 of quip
51 Gauge face
52 Contemporary Persia
53 Louver
54 Muslim prayer leaders
55 Made tracks
56 Single copy
59 Turkish monetary unit
61 __ culpa (Sorry 'bout that)
62 Prevail by a small margin
64 Descry
66 Ethel Mertz, e.g.
69 John Lennon's Plastic __ Band
70 Part 3 of quip
72 Middling grade
73 Give some confidence to
77 Carpe __!
78 Convince
82 Margaret Atwood short story, "Bluebeard's __"
83 Cauterize
85 Blacktop
87 After the fashion of
88 Ticked off
91 Boy with a bow
93 Banjo player Scruggs
94 Highlands family
95 Part 4 of quip
100 Hot under the collar
101 Rolls up
102 Cure
103 Nobleman
105 Four qts.
106 Bottomless pit
108 Listen to
111 Truant from the troops
113 "Othello" evildoer
115 University in Medford, MA
119 Optimistic
121 End of quip
125 Car buyer's incentive
126 Frank's comic-strip partner
127 M.L. King's widow
128 Didn't hold water
129 Lumet or Poitier
130 Get on Amtrak

DOWN
1 '30s movie dog
2 Scoffs of contempt
3 St. intersectors
4 Define success
5 Friendly relations
6 "Evil Woman" grp.
7 Swung around
8 Sidekicks
9 Ignore the alarm
10 Shout of pain
11 Greek letter
12 Bowler and boater
13 Milo or Tessie
14 Included within
15 Rocker Nugent
16 Nightmare
17 Mobil rival of old
18 Feed, as hogs
19 Actress Daly
24 Some degs.
29 Sister of Orestes
32 Persevering
34 Energy unit
35 D.C. VIPs
37 Ornamental case
38 San Diego pro
39 Trojan War story
40 Plucked sound
41 Polish off
42 Ho-hum
44 Alpaca kin
45 Smeared with calcium oxide
46 Written test
48 Yank's ally
49 Feed
50 Man's talons
56 Many millennia
57 Opinion page, briefly
58 Water wheel
60 Subordinate
63 Dawn goddess
65 PGA pegs
67 Work for a body shop
68 Zodiac sign
70 Maudlin
71 Thrusts forward
73 Bridle straps
74 White heron
75 Desert plant
76 Extend an income source
78 Soft ending?
79 Market price
80 African antelope
81 Newman or Travis
84 Gambrel or mansard, e.g.
86 Possesses
89 Cricket intermission
90 Ms. Bombeck
92 Close-fitting
94 Rush hour participant
96 Infused with oxygen
97 Slice of history
98 Plane curve
99 Take it again from the top
104 Class writing
106 Birthday secret?
107 Bologna bowling
108 Fling with force
109 Fencer's weapon
110 Palindromic pop group
112 Singer or Petty
114 Pretentious
116 Greek cheese
117 Leatherwood
118 Ballplayer Musial
120 Goddess of folly
122 Moreover
123 Corral
124 Tiriac of tennis

203

by Robert H. Wolfe

ACROSS

1 Antithesis: abbr.
4 Endangered ape, briefly
9 Rite spot
14 Farm work
19 So that's it!
20 Pay tribute to
21 Olympic skier Phil
22 Dear
23 Show about a wise priest?
26 Graff of "Mr. Belvedere"
27 Coral colonies
28 4 on the phone
29 Eternally
30 Prototype
31 Faded to the extreme
32 Trucker's truck
33 Reporter's pay scale
35 Live on
36 Leading ISP
37 Forbid anew
39 Track event
40 Indigo and anil
41 Show about a forgetful actor?
45 Happiness
46 Support for glasses
47 Superlatively frosted
48 Buyer-beware warning
50 Krazy kartoon karacter
51 Recon missions
54 Lee or Getz
55 Caribbean nation
59 Seater
60 Lack of honor
63 Twitch
64 Type of chart
65 Tourist's tote
68 Ups
69 Author Levin
70 Pt. of speech
71 Skim on a wet road
73 Brought to heel
75 Explorers
77 Romances
78 Those who dote
80 Evergreen
81 Sup
82 Yukon tributary
84 Float on the wind
86 Algerian port
88 Show about the life of Bruce Springsteen?
93 Color gradations
94 Ladder step
95 Composer Erik
96 Greek letter
97 Go astray
98 Changes charts
100 Gomez's cousin
101 Nappy leathers
104 View again
106 Language of China's Hmong
107 Actor Ayres
108 Comedienne Georgia
109 Get hitched in a hurry
110 Show about Mars?
114 Forklike
115 Wish granter
116 Muse of poetry
117 Shoe-box letters
118 Desert havens
119 Test composition
120 Evil spirit
121 Abnormal: pref.

DOWN

1 Lummox
2 Pyramid honoree
3 Kneecap
4 Cooks
5 Jazz pianist Jankowski
6 Squid fluid
7 Curs
8 Outlaw
9 Morning hrs.
10 Tag
11 Show set in Monticello?
12 Stocks of weapons
13 Travel backward?
14 Ring of time
15 Gram starter?
16 Show about Doris, then Dennis, then Laraine?
17 Backslider
18 Aldous Huxley novel, "__ in Gaza"
24 "__ Haw"
25 Stiffening fabric
31 Fido's foot
34 Go right!
37 Deli loaves
38 Cool, man
40 College VIP
42 What rolls on a Rolls
43 Very hot day
44 Wire measure
49 Israel natives
50 Wedge-shaped piece
51 Insects in their cocoons
52 Stage comment
53 Spinoff of 11D?
54 Tool attachment
55 Army rcts.
56 Hwy. sign abbr.
57 More fraught with danger
58 Certain schs.
60 Comparative suffix
61 Show about dirt farming?
62 Falsehood
66 River to the Firth of Clyde
67 Drs.
72 Name on many movie theaters
74 Part of U.A.E.
76 Models in parts
78 Pay to play
79 Morse symbol
81 Eternal water-pourers in Hades
82 Reeled
83 So to speak
84 Cabby's query
85 1855 French novel by Gerard de Nerval
86 Comstock output
87 Pick (through)
89 Mr. Selassie
90 Logically arranged
91 Winters of Hollywood
92 Signal for help
98 Orchestra section
99 Bulgaria's capital
101 Struggle
102 Like a game going into overtime
103 Vanity
105 Fencing blade
111 Eccentric
112 '60s war zone, casually
113 Some on the Somme

Y, CHROMOSOMALLY

by Willy A. Wiseman

ACROSS

1 Portuguese saint
4 Start of the 15th century
8 Trouble spot
14 Wealthy one
19 SASE, for example
20 Bellicose deity
21 Take a puff
22 Convex molding
23 Birthday figure
24 Spike or brad
25 Argentine grasslands
26 "More Than I Can Say" singer
27 Empathy
30 Scorpion's stinger
31 Apart
32 Stiller or Affleck
33 Phantom
35 Opposite of "I volunteer!"
36 Possible misogynist
41 Earlier Japanese title
44 Icebound Russian sea
45 Singer Reed
46 Adherent: suff.
49 Oater actor Jack
50 Asian ox
52 Torino three
53 K–O connection
54 __-jongg
55 Nevertheless
56 New Jersey city
58 "Dancing Queen" singers
59 Academy frosh
61 Razed
62 Once again
63 Native-born Israeli
64 Baby food
65 Jazz guitarist Montgomery
66 Dynamite man
68 Ecology pioneer
69 Mitigated
73 Lady of Spain
74 Manufactured
75 "Kyrie" group
76 Sticky stuff
77 Distant
78 Moreover
79 Smash defense
80 Sleuth Charlie
81 Feudal peon
82 Opp. of NNW
83 Frigid
84 "The Stunt Man" star
86 Young pigs
88 Poem for Father's Day?
92 Wit
96 Fluctuating singing
97 Abu Dhabi, Dubai et al.
98 Soprano Patti
100 Singer Shirley
102 Number of priests?
105 John who was Gomez Addams
106 Without delay!
108 Baseball family name

109 Grave engraving
110 Spectacle
111 Brunei's island
112 Noblewoman
113 Yeats offering
114 Clocked
115 Dirty looks
116 Seasons in Burgundy
117 Way cool!

DOWN

1 Type of coral
2 San __, TX
3 Spotted wildcat
4 "Time"-honored tradition?
5 Very slow pace
6 Make a god of
7 Presque __
8 Ancient Jewish rabbi
9 Surfing the Web
10 Word used in comparisons
11 Big theory?
12 "Mr. Blue Sky" rock grp.
13 Some along the Somme
14 Sudden plunge
15 King Arthur's paradise
16 Excuse for roughhousing

17 Butter sub
18 Given life
28 Superman's sweetie
29 Israeli statesman Abba
30 Drinking spot
33 Dolt
34 Lauren and Timothy
36 Silent
37 Supplied with hints
38 Plower's follower
39 Siesta shades
40 Sushi choice
42 Bullring bravos
43 Gangster's rod
46 Gremlins
47 Author of "A Sea Change"
48 Richard Dreyfuss/Susan Sarandon film
50 Needlefish
51 Lunched
56 Frozen treat
57 Neighbor of Nor.
58 Severn tributary
60 Runny cheese
61 Australian isl.
62 Either Madison or de Maupassant?
64 Cook a bit

67 Last name of 28D
70 Show to seats
71 One-time link
72 O.T. book
73 Common rail
74 Disfigure
75 Miscellaneous
76 Earth: pref.
79 Became more clamorous
81 That girl
85 Switch positions
86 Hook's mate
87 Takei's "Star Trek" role
89 Trigonometric function
90 Anabaptist leader Jakob
91 Crude boors
93 Reflect
94 Iroquois tribe
95 Spoke roughly
98 G-sharp
99 Semiconductor
100 Rope fiber
101 Fungi sacs
102 Golfer's cry
103 Frank or Jackson
104 Death rattle
106 "Nova" network
107 Silver or Ely

by Robert H. Wolfe

ACROSS

1 Develop from larvae
7 CXLV × X
11 Malicious burning
16 Day of the NHL Hall of Fame
19 Some poplars
20 Jewish month
21 Smackers
22 Class for U.S. immigrants
23 Sandal ties
24 Information
25 Meat jelly
26 Botanist Gray
27 Contribute a tenth
28 Workaholic's vacation?
31 Pentyl
32 Be mouthy
33 "Frankenstein Unbound" author
34 Berth place
35 Anatomical pouch
36 Atomizers
38 Actor McKellen
39 Loving: suff.
40 Textile lubricant
42 Cut consequence
44 Should that be the case
47 Relief pitcher Robb
48 Apia populace
50 Namely
52 Those who make amends
54 Presumptuous
55 Mlle. from Madrid
56 Misplays
58 Signify
59 Assistant
61 Levantine ketch
62 Classy
66 Scathing review
67 Branch of learning
68 Reek
69 I love, in Latin
70 Hebrides isle
72 Block up
73 Some time soon
74 Cinch
75 Pass gossip
77 Glasgow toppers
78 Word of honor
80 Continue your fantasy
83 Actress Slezak
85 Blotto
86 Corded fabric
87 Major constellation
89 Computer brand
90 Beside
91 So long, senor
93 Like Brahms' piano trio No. 1
95 Non-holy rollers?
97 Dr. Dre forte
100 Composer Bartok
101 Timing-signal light
104 French summers
105 Actress Olin

106 Burly Duke?
109 Fluffy
110 Part of HRE
111 Place for high living?
112 Smile
113 Mexican menu item
114 His: Fr.
115 Alerts
116 "The Mod Squad" character
117 Diamond Duke
118 Endeavor
119 Snoops
120 Border
121 __ out (dwindles)

DOWN

1 Ziti and penne
2 Last syllable of a word
3 Social group?
4 Gian Carlo Menotti opera, "__ and the Night Visitors"
5 Not pass the bar?
6 Capital of Senegal?
7 One of the Gorgons
8 Elegant hassle?
9 Import tax
10 Domesticated South American ruminant
11 Coetzer of tennis
12 "William Tell" composer
13 Last year's frosh
14 Medleys
15 Letters of salt
16 Newspaper screamer
17 Attacker
18 Confinements for tots
28 Milking parlors
29 Legal defense
30 Approximate ending
32 Sharp healer?
36 Ticket datum
37 NHL coach Bowman
39 Impoverished
41 Meat cut
43 Not home
45 Cereal meal
46 Sturdy dock supports?
48 Cesspools
49 Like raised oars
51 Annoying ads?
53 Grp. that advises the Pres.
55 Thread holder
57 Forays
60 Barkin and DeGeneres
63 Accessible weapon?

64 Reflection
65 Got by
68 Moves sinuously
71 Slice of history
73 Fan or lymph ending
74 Observed
76 Big birds Down Under
79 13 popes
80 Most dull
81 Good Shepherd
82 Convulsive condition
84 Religious leader
85 Eucharist plate
88 Flying group
92 One with two left feet
94 Bare minimum
96 Immediately
98 Branched horn
99 Check writers
101 Cuss
102 Country singer Clark
103 "A Wrinkle in Time" author Madeline L'__
105 Boundary
107 Harsh cry
108 Spreadsheet
109 Narrow country road
113 Child's meas.

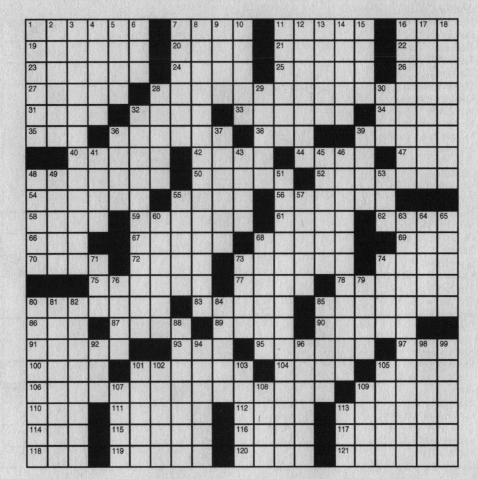

by Josiah Breward

ACROSS

1 Developer of vaccine for anthrax
8 Obstructs
14 PLO leader
20 Wide-open space
21 Use another worm
22 Nabokov novel
23 Cosmopolitan UN member?
25 Contaminates
26 Dweebs
27 Writer a.k.a. Barbara Vine
28 Scand. country
29 Allow
30 Dundee dagger
31 Wag
32 Smashing Monica
34 Bowling alley
35 African rum cake?
39 Gun it in neutral
40 Curves
41 Trail persistently
44 Diamond scores
45 Gore and Smith
47 Completely lacking
49 Draws breath
51 Discoloring stains
53 Carnival city
54 Director Craven
57 Places at intervals
58 Dubai bard?
60 Year in the Yucatan
61 Trousers
62 Elect (to)
63 Sleeve opening
64 Old-time gumshoe
65 Pension $$
66 Melted together
68 Middle Eastern rulers
69 Job benefit
70 Flock leader
71 Apollo's twin
73 __ had it!
74 Suffice
75 Neighbor of Wash.
76 Valletta panorama?
78 St. Lawrence, e.g.
79 Sawbuck
80 Easy dessert?
81 Childhood taboos
82 North of New York City
83 City on the Trinity
86 Sigma follower
87 Privy to
88 Nod of the head
89 Kukla's friend
91 Slovenly person
93 Mashhad melee?
96 Dirty
97 Enliven
99 Cambodian currency
100 Slant
104 Chinese pan
105 Highland boy
106 Smooth musical passages
109 Composer of "The Nubians of Plutonia"
110 Nuclear
112 Toledo runner losing at the Olympics?
114 Eastern shores of the Mediterranean
115 Jazz pianist Hancock
116 Most macabre
117 Heavy curtains
118 Ford flops
119 Frocks

DOWN

1 Unskilled farm workers
2 Choppers
3 Extra
4 One behind the other
5 Slaughter in Cooperstown
6 Tampa sch.
7 Gets back into shape
8 Actress Vaccaro
9 Licentious
10 Hautboy
11 Perkins and Hubbell
12 Assassin
13 Universal meas.
14 Choir section
15 Laugh loudly
16 The Greatest
17 Arm of the Baltic Sea?
18 Be present at
19 Samples
24 Seasonings
28 Last word of "The Raven"
31 Poirot's collection
33 Directed
34 Floral loop
36 City in Provence
37 Hay unit
38 Maui farewell
40 Pat or Daniel
41 Unnerve
42 Marching for inspection
43 African tennis player?
46 Shop
48 Lab containers
50 Deeds
51 Jason or Justine
52 Highest points
55 Devitalize
56 Some salmon
58 Disturbed
59 Mourning period of Judaism
62 Jumped farther
66 Having delicate health
67 Chunk of the fairway
69 Bog product
71 Sufficient to one's needs
72 Biblical mount
74 CNN newsman Frank
77 Go bad, as milk
78 Go bad, as perishables
82 Still tired
84 Be ill
85 Small drink
87 Bulge at the back of the head
89 Dallas gunman
90 Ransacker
92 Swallowed in a hurry
94 Shaw and others
95 Yiddish aggravation
97 Treaties
98 Bosc and Bartlett
101 Prayer's joints
102 Obliterate
103 Bumps on a hog?
105 Subway route
107 Taunting remark
108 Blue dye
109 Very dry
111 Tourist's guide
112 That woman
113 That woman

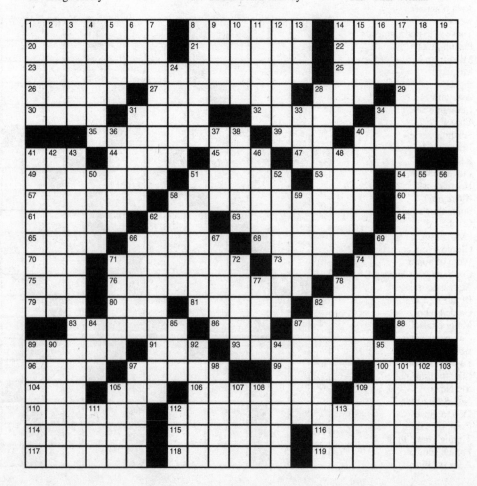

by Ed Voile

ACROSS

1 Author of "The Sound of Waves"
8 Stick with a stick
12 Raggedy doll
15 Huber of tennis
19 Pain pill
20 Davenport's location
21 Mauna __ volcano
22 Teller's partner
23 Maine invasions?
27 PC key
28 Passes into law
29 Levi's "Christ Stopped at __"
30 German article
31 Bird in "Peter and the Wolf"
34 Sounds of uncertainty
35 Angelico and Diavolo
36 "Gianni Schicchi" soprano
38 Weasel's kin
41 Dolt
42 Star of "The French Lieutenant's Woman"
43 Pennsylvania invasions?
48 Swiss river
49 __ longa, vita brevis
50 Comic Johnson
51 Pelvic projections
52 Has one's say
55 Tips
56 Cassino cash, once
57 Johannesburg's nation: abbr.
60 Create a gorge
61 Spiral pin
63 Indigenous people of Japan
64 __ ex machina
65 Alaska invasions?
69 Fortas and Lincoln
70 Telescope part
71 Stumbles
72 Hang in loose folds
73 Sure thing!
74 Wind blast
75 Glaswegian
76 Stationary part
77 Chesterfield
78 "High Hopes" lyricist
79 Ash Shariqah, Dubai et al.
81 Chicago hrs.
82 Wyoming invasions?
89 Dodges
90 Equal
91 Drew close
92 __ Arabia
93 Guns the engine
94 Hyson or pekoe
95 Syrian leader
99 Taste
100 Peter of Herman's Hermits
102 Gives lip
105 Comic/actress DeLaria
106 Florida invasions?
111 Will of "The Waltons"
112 Calendar watch abbr.
113 Leander's love
114 Low-price version
115 Roush and Hall
116 Fast flier's letters
117 Bucket in a car
118 Le Champs __

DOWN

1 Papas' partners
2 Elba or Capri
3 Sees
4 "__ Girl Friday"
5 Choler
6 __ High Stadium
7 In a short time
8 Ewer
9 Origins
10 Possesses
11 River block
12 "Arabian Nights" character
13 Forbidden acts
14 Former sports org.
15 Showery mo.
16 Provoker
17 Prepared to pray
18 Lures into danger
24 Finnish baths
25 Organism requiring oxygen
26 Old photograph
32 TV oldie, "__ Ramsey"
33 Noah's boat
35 Typefaces
37 Important times
39 Business degs.
40 End of cash?
41 Audubon Society member, perhaps
42 Vail feature
43 Standard salary
44 Leg warmer
45 Spaces between leaf veins
46 More reasonable
47 Coarse cotton trousers
53 Rehan and Huxtable
54 Plunk starter?
55 Goes wrong
56 Enunciation problem
57 Chance to get even
58 Guess so
59 Maintains
61 Teeter-totter
62 Is unable
63 Mine entrance
64 __ mater (brain covering)
66 Promontories
67 Presses
68 Banned insecticide
74 Actor Cuba
75 Rescues
76 Char
77 Lose traction
78 Dexterous
79 Constrained state
80 Coach Parseghian
82 Way by
83 Benefited
84 Paired up
85 Form a fan-shaped pattern
86 Single attempt
87 Teachers' grp.
88 Today's LPs
93 Some IRAs
94 Carpathian range
96 Gradient
97 Eagle's abode
98 Goes out with
101 Trigger treats
102 Koko's dagger
103 Behold, to Caesar
104 Satirist Mort
107 April 15 grp.
108 Expressions of surprise
109 "The Bridge of San Luis __"
110 Ballet step

FOLLOWED BY A...

by Willy A. Wiseman

ACROSS

1 Rejects vehemently
7 Pickled
13 Cartilage in meat
20 Soccer keeper
21 Threaten to fall
22 Cattleman
23 Yellowstone coat?
25 One who came in
26 Implement
27 __ Na Na
28 Athlete's deg.
30 White Sea bay
31 Draft letters
32 Pole with a blade
34 Literary snippets
36 Singer DiFranco
38 Gull's cousin
39 Biopic celebrating Judy Garland?
44 Cushion
45 Rubber base
48 Resistance unit
49 Hardened
50 Bigger pic
51 Parasitic pest
53 Guided-projectile defense: abbr.
55 Playground game
56 Mom's sister, informally
58 Yuck!
59 Increase dishes for heavy folk?
63 Air pressure unit
64 Gets more profound
66 Join up
67 July 26th honoree
70 Garfield's buddy
71 Mil. training course
73 Abel to Adam
74 Spanish Mrs.
76 Earth goddess
77 Butterfly catcher
79 Money in Cape Verde
82 Money in Madrid, once
84 Alternatives
85 Lollobrigida cheesecake?
87 Mod ending?
88 North Dakota city
90 Online shorthand in reply to a joke
91 Fa–la link
92 Conventional representation
94 $ from a bank
95 Suppressers
99 Dawn goddess
101 Connery and O'Casey
102 Learning inst.
103 All-you-can-eat pocket bread?
106 Stadium level
108 H. Rider Haggard novel
109 Silly Caesar
110 Down in the dumps
111 Blubber
114 Wasted time
116 Beat or Jazz, e.g.
118 By way of
120 Measure again precisely
123 More heavily fleshed
125 Lansbury's remake of a Dietrich film?
128 As a group
129 Oberon and others
130 Praised
131 Began
132 Preoccupy
133 Knights' chargers

DOWN

1 "__ Dei"
2 Watercraft
3 Despises
4 Lena of "Havana"
5 Spanish rivers
6 Elder
7 Letters on Cardinals' caps
8 Klutz's comment
9 Ogden resident
10 Locks of hair
11 Mouse-spotter's cry
12 Dreary
13 Spirogyra
14 Took off
15 Centerward
16 Bloodhound's trail
17 Nursery rhyme musical?
18 "Shampoo" co-star
19 Off course
24 Texas mission
29 Beauty contests
33 12-step program
35 Qty.
37 Small piece of France?
39 __-de-lance
40 Ferric __ (Fe_2O_3)
41 Saunter
42 Abominable snowmen
43 Conform
45 Applied by spreading
46 Go along with
47 Use a monk as a beast of burden?
52 One who gives his heart?
54 Yiddish man with fortitude
57 Employment
60 UCLA rival
61 Pull
62 Siva worshipers
65 Oil: pref.
67 Charles Camille Saint-__
68 Kevin of "SNL"
69 Art supporters
72 Abalone eater
75 Troy, NY campus
78 Cornerstone abbr.
80 Pope who dealt with Attila
81 Certain reeds
83 Speak biblically
85 Spoke nonsensically
86 Paint finish
88 Picks the wrong moment
89 Occurrence
93 __ culpa
96 Jackson and Derek
97 Rent-sign abbr.
98 Wood fragments
100 Let live
104 Fit for consumption
105 Models of perfection
107 Make roof repairs
111 Blue shoe material?
112 Eyed covetously
113 Necklace units
115 Intervening space: abbr.
117 Start of a sphere?
119 Pub choices
121 Insect pest
122 Fever with chills
124 Language ending
126 Lang. of Israel
127 Ship letters

FIGHTING WEIGHT

by Alan P. Olschwang

ACROSS

1 Landowner of the California gold rush
7 Eight on Mount Vesuvius
11 Cote call
14 Tic
19 Sign up
20 Land on a coast
22 Slatted wooden container
23 Units of wisdom?
24 Start of Bob Thaves quote
26 French cup
27 Earns
28 Matter-of-factly
29 Digits
30 Part 2 of quote
33 Futilely
35 Location for one's first drive
36 Questioning interjections
37 Lulu
40 Always, in a poem
41 Fund provider
44 Of the dawn
47 Moral failings
51 Part 3 of quote
54 Hatcher and Copley
57 Taking it on the __ (fleeing)
58 Nurture
59 Make an effort
60 Gradual impairment
61 Aspersion
63 Winged mammal
64 8th-century empress of Byzantium
66 Eager
68 Part 4 of quote
69 Edged
72 Extremely pale
73 Bounder
74 Skinny
75 Pocket bread
76 Grouped merchandise
78 "Long Day's Journey into Night" playwright
80 Atlantic food fish
81 Fleece
82 Part 5 of quote
87 Cosmetician Lauder
88 Disseminates
89 Responses
93 Indy stop
95 Trigger treats
96 Dam-building grp.
97 Surprising word
98 Mnemonic devices
102 Part 6 of quote
107 Fit of sulking
108 Part of a pansy
111 Tim of "WKRP in Cincinnati"
112 Austrian physicist and philosopher Mach
113 End of quote
116 Plaza Hotel girl of the comics
117 Employ again

118 Most incisive
119 First antiseptic surgeon
120 Gustatory sensation
121 '50s presidential candidate
122 Summertime coolers
123 Ramada chain

DOWN

1 Divided by a membrane
2 Still on the plate
3 Threw away
4 Human trunks
5 Actress Barkin
6 Scottish author's initials
7 Basketry willows
8 Hikers' shelters
9 Italian poet
10 Geisha's sash
11 Max or Buddy
12 Base children
13 Ms. Rogers St. Johns
14 Learning inst.
15 Verb tense expressing the past
16 Burr or Copland
17 Harden
18 Untidy
21 Peculiar
25 Phoenician port
27 Former Indian PM
31 Equal
32 Purple seaweed
34 Adored
38 Milk choice
39 Grain rot
42 Egyptian judge of the dead
43 Barbell lbs.
44 Gelling agent
45 Einstein's birthplace
46 Cosmetic liquid
48 Social circle
49 Continental abbr.
50 Swine pen
52 Sticky stuff
53 Saxophonist Mulligan
54 A couple
55 Bard's contraction
56 Drum beat
61 Secretarial skill
62 Hermits
63 Flower at first
65 Brother's boy
67 Request show
68 Tutu's milieu
69 Portend
70 Greek letter
71 __ es Salaam
73 Bow of film

74 Supervisor
76 Tiger's position
77 Mil. training course
79 False pretenses
80 Dancer Charisse
81 Urban rds.
83 He hires his niece
84 Bind with cord
85 Justice Souter
86 Premed class
90 Vulcanized rubber
91 French composer Albert
92 Data organizers
94 Classify
96 Plot surprises
98 Nautical direction
99 Chick of jazz
100 Choate or Putnam
101 Holy city of Islam
103 Riled
104 Reagan cabinet member
105 Sun: pref.
106 Winter coat?
109 Sacred bull
110 Letters before the World Series
114 Churchill's gesture
115 Group of shrinks
116 Slippery tree

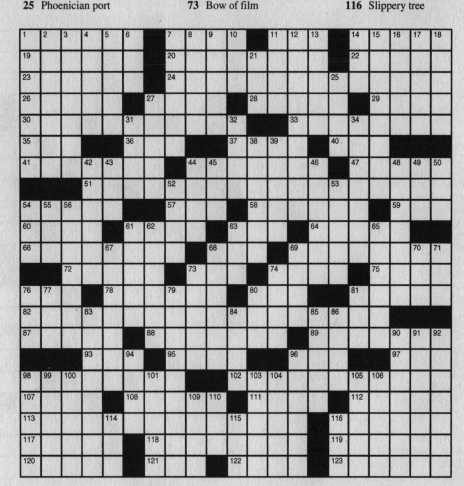

PRESIDENTIAL INAUGURATIONS

by Robert H. Wolfe

ACROSS
1 Chanel of fashion
5 Awry
10 Plucker's instrument
15 Cries of discovery
19 McCarthyism letters
20 Nuisances
21 James and Tommie
22 Leven or Lomond
23 Presidential runner?
25 Rub
26 Focal points
27 Cellmate
28 A Fleming
29 Dock
30 Rod of tennis
31 Phooey!
33 O.T. book
35 Eur. country
37 Wind dir.
38 Graff of "Mr. Belvedere"
39 Presidential salon worker?
43 Has recourse
45 Sets free, as pigs
46 Spanish explorer Juan de __
47 Thais, e.g.
48 Slugger Sammy
49 Tanguay and Gabor
51 Greetings
53 Donation
56 Of birth
58 Gave up
60 To and __
61 Mr. Philbin
64 Reno resident
66 Wildebeest
67 Charged particle
68 Buenos __
69 Little terror
70 Unites
72 Spectacle
74 Actress Arthur
75 Puncture starter?
77 Young hare
79 Topless little pies
80 Open container
81 Plundered
83 Banquet
85 Tiny amount
87 Humiliate
88 Letter opener
89 Before a while?
93 E.T.s
95 Make up (for)
97 Matador
99 Investigated thoroughly
101 Presidential hit man?
103 Smell
104 Actor Kilmer
106 Candler or Gray
107 "Wheel of Fortune" purchase
108 End of a duel?
109 Window elements
110 Sprite in "The Tempest"
112 Frat party staple

114 Horse morsel
116 Nabokov novel
117 Say
118 Presidential fisherman?
122 Itemization
123 Pencil need
124 "Mrs. __ Goes to Paris"
125 Roll-call reply
126 Grub
127 Greek island
128 Zigzag turns
129 Cruising

DOWN
1 All the tea in China
2 Possessive pronoun
3 Tomato sauces
4 Eight in Madrid
5 Tax mo.
6 First family of Florence
7 Madonna hit, "La __ Bonita"
8 British weapons
9 Lat. or Lith., once
10 Baroque master
11 Appalled
12 Approaches
13 Presidential singer?

14 Full of: suff.
15 The whole time
16 Presidential poet?
17 Stress
18 Former English counties
24 Deprive of courage
29 Contorted
30 Actress Bonet
31 A/C figures
32 Pisa's river
34 Map in a map
36 Period
40 Tightwad
41 Anthracite transporter
42 Went up and down
44 ESPN anchor Rich
47 Math course
50 Presidential restorer?
52 Vacation boat
54 Feigned manner
55 Shades
57 State south of Bhutan
58 Like some good bonds
59 Powders
61 Synagogue figure
62 MacDonald's refrain
63 Presidential adversary?
65 Rate

71 One who resists
73 Cadillac model
76 Youngest son
78 Toward the belly
82 Morning hrs.
84 Gomez Addams on TV
86 Sources of nutrition
88 Gym wear
90 Names anew
91 Hit signs
92 Legal wrong
94 Balin and Claire
96 Tie-breaker periods: abbr.
98 Gibson garnish
99 Mottle with spots
100 Muse of astronomy
101 Customer
102 Smith of "California Suite"
105 Bandleader Shaw
111 Art Deco designer
113 Otologist's focus
115 Turkish title
117 Product bars, in brief
118 "Norma __"
119 Horse's relative
120 Before, to Blake
121 Stephen of "The Crying Game"

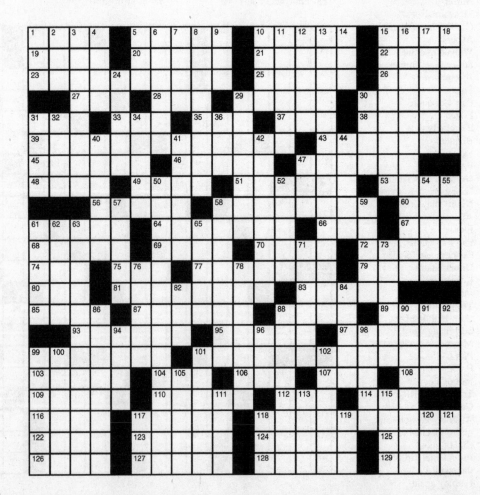

ACROSS

1 Flags down
6 Aberdonian or Glaswegian
10 Valiant
15 Escritoire
19 Start
20 Architect Pei's first name
21 Abominable snowmen
22 Unit cost
23 More likely to cause mutation?
25 Feline of the forest?
27 Solid fat
28 Ornate wardrobe
30 Euripides drama
31 PAU's successor
32 ESA's partner on the ISS
34 City in the Ruhr Valley
35 Guides
37 Very unruly
39 Jetty
40 Surcharge for a sleeper?
43 Cheap gem?
48 Yawning gulf
49 Prevailing condition
51 "Joanie Loves Chachi" star Scott
52 Son of Agrippina
53 Designer Claiborne
56 Raise one's voice
57 Ride to the guillotine
60 Farmer's color?
63 Dove or Rudner
65 Sportscaster Howard
66 With 68A, winning grownup?
68 See 66A
70 Greek ends
74 Knights' titles
76 Fair pictures?
81 Leathernecks
83 Slapstick ammo
85 Blocker of "Bonanza"
86 Margarine
87 Rotation line
88 Accuse (a public official)
91 Venice campanile architect
92 Loaded chum?
95 Diminutive swallow?
99 Pub quaffs
100 Expellers
101 Coetzer and Plummer
105 Heraldic band
106 Part of U.A.R.
107 Nabokov book
110 Flood shield
111 Decomposed hemoglobin
114 Think-tank member
116 Well-tanned constable?
118 Colorado privy?
120 Dismounted
121 In the know
122 Actress Arden, casually
123 "Guitar Town" singer Steve
124 Beatty and Buntline
125 "Lou Grant" star
126 Knocks lightly
127 Frock

DOWN

1 Tell me the reason
2 Hill or Loos
3 __ of Scilly
4 Spartan queen
5 Breastbones
6 Enlists oneself
7 Third grade
8 One Chaplin
9 With heat
10 Proverb
11 Lubricate again
12 Doer: suff.
13 Viz. in full
14 Pre-tee?
15 Like prunes and raisins
16 Bald raptor
17 Man the tiller
18 "Growing Pains" co-star
24 Lariat
26 Twyla of dance
29 More macho
33 Lackland, e.g.
36 Egad!
37 Pitcher Gregg
38 __ jacet
39 Set
40 Twinge
41 Over, in Germany
42 Vega's constellation
43 Cheap property in Monopoly
44 Recedes
45 Rhine tributary
46 Cambodian cash
47 Slump lazily
50 DXXVII doubled
53 Rental agreement
54 NYC subway line
55 Olympian deity
58 Coll. Huskies
59 Additional
61 Crimebuster
62 Sentimental
64 Part of USMA
67 Cleveland's lake
69 Refrain syllable
70 Poetic tentmaker?
71 Long skirt
72 Sevareid or Idle
73 Lillian or Dorothy
75 Marine aquarium additive
77 __ for the asking
78 Plenty
79 "Aurora" fresco painter Guido
80 Roger Rabbit feature
82 Circus additions
84 Romy of "What's New, Pussycat?"
89 Docs
90 Polloi preceder
91 Cut the hair of
93 Half a Black Forest spa
94 Spat ending?
96 __ encryption
97 Flourishes
98 Gettysburg victor
100 Ink roller
101 Composer Berg
102 Oberon of films
103 Steer clear of
104 Salamanders
105 Three-player card game
107 Love Italian-style
108 Arlene and Roald
109 Queen __ lace
112 Abba of Israel
113 St. Petersburg's river
115 Close to closed
117 Lamb's lament
119 Puppy bite

ACROSS

1 Put to sea
9 Graham and Stewart
16 Mehemet and Muhammad
20 Rid of evil spirits
21 Fashionable as pie?
22 Thin coin
23 Fashionable nonsense?
25 Islamic call to prayer
26 Ryan or Tatum
27 Quench
28 Stylish clothes
30 CIA forerunner
31 Myrna of "The Thin Man"
34 Diminishes
37 Syst. of sound syllables
38 Narrow inlet
39 Fashionable Presbyterian?
42 Summer hrs.
43 Early Christian pulpit
46 Some French?
47 Hurry up!
48 Incense spice
50 Hits on the head
52 Of the sun
56 High crag
58 Photo blowup
59 Like cloisonne
61 Type of duck?
62 Popular cookie
64 Lummoxes
67 Abner's size?
68 Fashionable truth?
71 __ of Worms
72 Japanese flower arranging
74 Long of "The Broken Hearts Club"
75 Formula math
77 Dark time in ads
78 Fashionable silk coat?
83 Ex-Bruin Bobby
84 Terminates
85 Illustrator Peter
86 Inelegant denial
87 Dickens novel, "Little __"
89 Voluminous Brit. ref. source
91 Held first place
92 Lucy's best friend
94 __ Carlo
95 Button your lip!
98 "Do Ya?" rock grp.
100 Cambridge sch.
102 Prepared to drive
103 Magic spell
104 Fashionable Chinese tree?
110 Mass gown
111 Way in: abbr.
112 H.S. students
113 Scoffer's comment
114 __ Clemente
117 Vegetable with a knobby root
120 Fixer-upper phrase
122 Sufficient
124 Trunk bulge
125 Fashionable religion?
130 Most recent
131 Got the joke
132 Undercover
133 In __ (existing): Lat.
134 Catch
135 Nonpareil

DOWN

1 I want in!
2 Nerve parts
3 Stadium roofs
4 Writer Bombeck
5 Partner of Charybdis
6 Show on TV
7 Late starter?
8 Permits to
9 Rum cocktail
10 Ginsberg and Drury
11 Brit. flyboys
12 PA nuclear reactor
13 "The Queen's Wake" poet
14 Type of penguin
15 Egyptian god of the lower world
16 Hebrew month
17 Fashionable reptile?
18 Ezra Pound or Amy Lowell, e.g.
19 Able to perceive
24 Actress Goldie
29 Italian poet
32 Long in the tooth
33 __ Saint Laurent
35 Numerical ending
36 T-bar
39 Pop
40 Luigi's island
41 Arrowsmith's first wife
43 Benzene derivative
44 Anatomical model
45 Fashionable love letters?
49 Battery electrode
51 Hindu deity
53 Fond du __, WI
54 __ acids
55 Followers
57 French historian
60 Actress Judi
63 Eyed covetously
65 Ceramiclike compound
66 Began
69 Artist Dufy
70 Pleasure cruiser
73 Plague (with)
76 Grab hold of
79 Angler's basket
80 Less than 100 shares of stock
81 Say what?
82 Throat-clearing sounds
88 Kind of IRA
90 Con man
93 Branch
95 Fetter
96 Bonham Carter and Rubinstein
97 Branched cluster of flowers
99 Be obliged to
101 Acapulco aunt
105 Ogden resident
106 Better arranged
107 Kind of job?
108 Vast landmass
109 "Casey at the Bat" poet
114 Steeple top
115 Laxative drug
116 Slangy refusal
118 Russian-born artist/designer
119 Shank of the leg
121 Clipped-off piece
123 CLXV times X
126 Car's elec. syst.
127 __ Na Na
128 Resembling: suff.
129 Hemi-fly?

WHO SAID WHAT

by Frances Burton

ACROSS

1 Swindle
5 Cappuccino sellers
10 Robbery
15 Jules Verne's captain
19 Byron poem
20 Italian violinmaker
21 God of Islam
22 Israeli airline
23 Present Persia
24 W. Hemisphere protection syst.
25 "Politics is applesauce"
27 "The people like to be humbugged"
29 Film cuts
31 Mandarin or satsuma
32 Cheekier
33 Genetic duplicate
34 Post
35 Speech on Sun.
36 Inventing facts
37 Championship
38 Princely
41 Thomas and Horace
42 Hot Lips in the movie "M*A*S*H"
46 Book after Joel
47 Vast multitude
48 Plumber's aid
49 "__ You Being Served?"
50 Playground game
51 Mecca resident
52 Substandard urban housing
53 __ blanche
55 Concealed shooters
57 Restricts
59 __ out (fell asleep)
60 Accuse
61 Battery electrode
62 Country singer Travis
63 Says howdy
65 Stick-up artist
66 Restoration
69 British peers
70 Ins and outs
71 Death notices, briefly
73 In the past
74 Royal pronoun
75 Short-lived craze
76 Extent
77 Reclines
78 More brutish
81 Black tea
82 Beach tracts
83 Complains
84 Parts of hammers
85 Soak up rays
86 Gnawing mammals
89 Senator Gorton
90 Garment worn over armor
94 Vinegary
95 To any extent
96 "Start every day with a smile and get it over with"
97 "Isn't that special?"

99 Wading bird
101 Peru's capital
102 Lena of "Havana"
103 TV executive Arledge
104 Buff
105 Finished
106 Shuttle grp.
107 Tijuana address
108 Located
109 Sawbucks

DOWN

1 Falls off
2 Magna __
3 Semitic people
4 Bull Run location
5 Food packer
6 Nice love?
7 Cultivate
8 Greek vowel
9 Second job
10 Hemming follow-up?
11 Select group
12 Troubles
13 Actor Mineo
14 Choke
15 Invalidator
16 Gage bestseller
17 The Shadow's girlfriend

18 Mary-Kate or Ashley
26 Pope's fanon
28 Cambodian cash
30 Puts on
33 "Girls just want to have fun"
34 Jockey's garb
36 Animal fat
37 Opposing sides
38 Squeals
39 Arabian sultanate
40 "You can observe a lot just by watching"
41 Cursor mover
42 "When the going gets tough, the tough get going"
43 "It is easier to stay out than get out"
44 Uffizi Palace display
45 Poverty
47 Damages
48 Shift out of place
51 Bleachers, e.g.
52 Smoky, foggy conditions
53 Change
54 Pay to play
56 Begged
58 Actress Stevens
59 El Greco's birthplace
62 Rubbish

63 Soft, thick lump
64 Rake
65 Relocates
67 Venerable
68 Defeat
70 Horse controls
72 Ghostly greetings
75 Some train units
76 Like clementines
77 Guinevere's lover
79 "The Bartered Bride" composer
80 Quinine water
81 Bell sound
82 Bombay wrap
84 Active participant
85 Grown in dense clumps
86 Health hazard gas
87 Central Florida city
88 Potvin or Savard
89 Shorthand, for short
90 Part of an act
91 Yellowish green
92 Madison Ave. pros
93 Winter Palace rulers
95 Severn tributary
96 Court order
98 Lobster eggs
100 4 on the phone

ACROSS

1 Polyester fabric
7 Bushes
13 Ambiguous
20 Surfing the Web
21 Person with a financial burden
22 Ship-strengthening timber
23 POINTER
25 Welsh dish
26 "__ and the Night Visitors"
27 Zoroastrian sacred texts
28 Len of "The Four Seasons"
29 Lion's locks
30 Dessert pastries
31 Soprano Gluck
33 Ornamental tree with pods
36 Resident's suffix
37 Light touches
38 CHOW
40 Brain, spinal cord, etc.
41 Michael of the Monkees
43 Haughtily aloof
44 Mailed
45 Ice Shelf
46 Heirs' inheritance
47 Squeal
48 Framework post
49 French title
50 BEAGLE
53 Plains of Patagonia
54 Burns poem, "__ O' Shanter"
57 Loses one's cool
58 Scottish prefix
59 City on the Loire
60 Ruler fraction
62 Taxing agcy.
63 Shrew
64 Consumed
65 Before
66 Flirts
68 Mongrel
69 Writer Walker
71 Positive RSVP-er
72 Klown on "The Simpsons"
73 PUG
76 Onions' kin
77 Poking blows
78 Chinese Chairman
79 Consumes completely
83 Divorcees
84 Ambiance
85 Peanut product
86 Constituent of DNA
87 First name of a canine star
88 BOXER
90 Engendered
91 Carried out
92 Large Asiatic deer
94 Plane-crash grp.
95 __ of Orleans
96 Ten: pref.
97 Dark Chinese tea
99 M. de Balzac
101 Leslie of "Gigi"
102 Troops on horseback

104 HUSKY
106 Bridal wreath and meadowsweet
107 South Carolina river
108 Wise counselor
109 Sawhorse
110 Medicates
111 Blood conduit

DOWN

1 Essential neurotransmitter
2 Fills with life
3 Most sanitary
4 Nouveau __
5 "The __ lama he's a priest..." (Nash)
6 Prefix with natal or classical
7 Indentured servants
8 Pelts
9 Guns it in neutral
10 Whole
11 Don't panic!
12 Bishopric
13 Gumbo ingredient
14 Lesser panda
15 Story in installments
16 Singer Laine and others
17 GREYHOUND
18 King of France
19 Tolkien's talking tree
24 Belief
28 Drew near
30 Fatherhood
32 Enigmatic
34 Example cited
35 Evaluates
37 Pocket breads
38 Does something
39 Word after tight or split
42 Crackers
43 McKellen and Woosnam
45 Lover with a roving eye
47 Rends
48 Rug type
49 Cool prez
51 Violent conflicts
52 Impertinent
53 Made impossible
54 Dry jests
55 __ nervosa
56 PAPILLON
59 Relating to the ear
61 Corn covers
63 Humble homes
64 Additionally
67 "Star Trek" extras?
68 Blue shade
69 Asian inland sea
70 Allayed
73 Trimming
74 Exude
75 Strong desire
77 Quantity of moonshine
80 Ore of iron
81 Monochromatic
82 Fusspot's trait
84 Of the dawn
85 "Look Back in Anger" dramatist
86 Shakespearean sprite
88 Portable platform
89 Warren and Dustin's cinematic flop
90 Canal boats
93 Wild swine
95 "Water Lilies" painter
96 Dishearten
98 Wall St. group
100 __ bene (pay close attention)
101 "Breaker-breaker" buddy
102 Chicago hrs.
103 Spring mo.
104 Pre-2004 booming jet
105 Singer Sumac

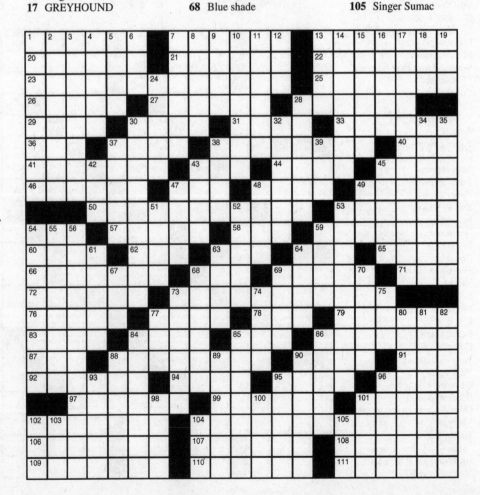

by Robert H. Wolfe

ACROSS

1 Colorful ducks
6 Shortened aliases
10 Rough journey
14 "The Merry Widow" composer
19 Abraham's son
20 Frozen fog
21 Yeats' country
22 Dancing Castle
23 Nicholson film about wrist management?
26 Heads
27 Pliant
28 Wood pattern
29 RPM part
31 E-mail period
32 Way through
34 NASA booster
36 School grp.
37 Against
41 Lifted
42 Ex-Spice Girl Halliwell
43 Paint layer
44 Lawyer Roy
45 Squiggly swimmer
46 Box to train
48 Cancel
50 Half of half-and-half
52 Setback
55 Rounds or clips
57 Fence openings
58 Astronomical shadow
59 Actor Jannings
60 Impudence
61 Photo-__
62 Egyptian dog
64 Track shapes
66 Toss out
68 Health haven
71 Jubilant
72 List
74 Adds protective layers
76 Mil. honor
77 Soft throw
79 Film version
80 Elements
81 Bandleader Winding
83 Nagy of Hungary
85 Sea fliers
87 Old French soldier
88 State of India
90 Dock of the bay
91 Makeover
92 Utter oaths
93 Joel of "Sullivan's Travels"
95 Base meal?
97 Santa's helper
99 Major ending?
100 "Dies __"
101 Little piggies
103 Page size
106 Tinted
107 Fig. list
108 Drunkard
109 Yves Saint __

111 Every last one
112 Elect (to)
113 __ und Drang
114 Water down
119 Unsighted
121 Benigni film about Ponti's view of Loren?
125 Arrowsmith's first wife
126 Persepolis site
127 Geological periods
128 Owl calls
129 Best and O'Brien
130 Acidic
131 Mach+ jets, once
132 Follow afterward

DOWN

1 Muscle twinges
2 Jacob's twin in the Bible
3 Senior citizen's grp.
4 Northern Scandinavian
5 Dandruff source
6 Biblical boat
7 Granger film co-starring Shields and Yarnell?
8 Without guiding principles
9 Disposal problem
10 Ager of parents?
11 Make free (of)

12 Work unit
13 Large enough fish
14 Seventh sign
15 Before, before
16 Williams film about the bard?
17 Supply commentary
18 Says over
24 Tenancy period
25 Legal holdings
30 "The Chalk Garden" dramatist Bagnold
33 Stone marker
34 Old World lizard
35 MacLaine film about mononucleosis?
37 Defendant
38 Control groups
39 Rooney film about a rotten onion?
40 Spinning one's wheels
43 Applaud
47 Time for a seder
49 Self-indulgent sprees
51 Beat the clock?
53 Hindu god
54 Stirs
56 Buckeyes' sch.
63 Chapel vow
65 Zodiac cat

67 Dolt
69 Bishop
70 Guaranteed
73 Order at the front
75 Complained like Sylvester
78 Liquid taste
82 Rhine tributary
84 Actress Witherspoon
86 Figure out
88 Friendly
89 Used an arrow key
94 On the peak of
96 Conductor Sir Georg
98 Like subtle color blending
102 Surpass in cunning
104 Reasons
105 Some sports cars
108 Nehi and Pepsi
110 One-tenth donation
113 Dispatched
115 Literary notable
116 E.T. vehicles
117 Ballet skirt
118 Choice word
120 Charlton Heston's org., once
122 "Rosemary's Baby" writer Levin
123 Distant
124 Palm Sunday transportation

BIRDS IN MIND

by Ed Voile

ACROSS

1 Possible mirages
6 Mother-of-pearl
11 Caspian feeder
15 Fiery gem
19 Drink like a pig
20 Lazybones
21 Call from the crib
22 Medieval weapon
23 Rabble-rousers for the birds?
25 Imaginary eternal flowers
27 Flowering
28 C-in-C's sidekick
30 Like DNA strands
31 Roman deck count
32 Alarm bell
35 Wagner heroine
38 "__ Haw"
39 Hrs. of summer
40 Avian utensils?
42 Half a round trip
44 More like a wallflower
45 Seemingly indifferent people
47 WWII arena
48 Seat for several
51 Chill
53 Agamemnon's father
55 Mahler's "Das Lied von der __"
58 Zoroastrian texts
61 Follow twisters like a bird?
64 Relatives
65 Canine restraints
67 "...have you __ wool?"
68 Spanish province
69 Math-proof letters
70 Buchwald or Garfunkel
71 Not counted among the injured
73 Denali's location
75 GI entertainers
76 __-jongg
77 Stingy
78 Sound sheepish?
79 Jack Russell, e.g.
81 Inhabitant: suff.
82 Dish of nibs?
86 Abilities
87 Croat's neighbor
89 Son-of movie
90 "The Gold Bug" author's inits.
92 Different
93 Mythical bird
95 Oxidized
97 Antigone's uncle
100 Defames
103 Futuristic coif adornment?
105 Begley and Wynn
108 Dickens character
109 Novelist Waugh
111 Creep, as in subservience
112 I.M., the architect
113 Orphan's instant parent
115 Eld

117 Popularity figure
119 State a parallel example
122 Fashionable fake fingernail?
125 Art Deco designer
126 Russian ruler
127 First Ottoman
128 Act the ham
129 X
130 Mind readings?
131 City on the Ruhr
132 Lyricist Carole Bayer __

DOWN

1 Dallas gunman
2 Excuses
3 Naturally illuminated
4 Cogito __ sum
5 Irregularly shaped stain
6 Actress Long
7 Append
8 U-shaped fastener
9 Continues a lease
10 Gaelic tongue
11 Actress Thurman
12 Battering device
13 "__ and the Night Visitors"
14 "Streets of __," McMurtry novel
15 Present starter?
16 Product of a birds' bee?
17 Peloponnesus region
18 Ballerina Collier
24 Atlanta university
26 Coeur d'__, ID
29 Embroidered loops
33 Ethan or Joel of movies
34 Ship's pole
36 Outer edge
37 Seminole chief
41 European peninsula
43 French season
44 Back talk
46 Most certain
48 Deli offerings
49 Pigged out
50 The latest in fowl fashion?
52 Carson's predecessor
54 Fumigates
56 Locomotive engines
57 Sanction
59 Pollex
60 Roman hero
62 Bank payt.
63 Jack London's boat
66 Alternative to a salt cellar
72 Poorly matched
73 Letters on cars

74 Cochineal pigment
78 Amazon city
80 Nice nothing?
83 Timeworn
84 Woundwort
85 Anarchist Nicola
88 Squeeze snake
91 O.T. book
94 Island of the Labyrinth
96 Stray from a topic
98 Fine-grained corundum
99 Catholic community members
100 "Coal Miner's Daughter" star
101 Skater Ito
102 Gracefully slender
104 Clobbers
105 Afterword
106 Mean explicitly
107 Check endorser
110 Delete
114 U.S. leader
116 Reed in the winds
118 Writer Janowitz
120 Chasing game
121 Hesitation sounds
123 Abu Dhabi et al.
124 Former station from Tenn.

HUSTLER'S ADVICE

by Alan P. Olschwang

ACROSS

1 Neck parts
6 Kind of panel or power
11 __ as a billiard ball
15 Peck in "Moby Dick"
19 Barcelata song, "Maria __"
20 Eliminate the superfluous from
21 Alain's friend
22 Cartoon possum
23 Laughing
24 Madison Ave. pro
25 Transmitted
26 Skin hole
27 Start of Paul Newman quote
31 Prickly plant
32 Man from Muscat
33 Eye parts
34 Burns with hot liquid
37 Type of beer
39 Claw
41 Part 2 of quote
43 Clear frost
45 Incline
49 Uno e due
50 Truly
51 Final profit
53 Golden best friend?
55 Rod Stewart hit song, "Da Ya Think I'm __?"
57 Map line abbr.
59 Gershwin and Remsen
61 U.S. diplomat Silas
62 Greek marketplace
65 Southern constellation
66 Deposit
68 Diarist Anais
69 Part 3 of quote
75 Guided-projectile defense: abbr.
76 Sad
77 Olfactory trigger
78 Flooded
79 Watered fabric
81 Carpentry device
82 Pitcher's pride
83 Pronounce indistinctly
87 Audience
90 Erie Canal mule
92 Ques. response
95 Id companion
96 Breathing: abbr.
97 More central of two
99 Part 4 of quote
102 Handlelike parts
104 Voice a thought
106 "The __ Queene"
107 Flinches
110 Motile organic cell
112 Thuds
114 End of quote
120 Dublin's country
121 Newsman Huntley
122 Took into custody

123 Requisites
124 Pot builder
125 Samoan cash
126 Already up
127 Golfer with an army
128 Pekoe and Earl Grey
129 Herring's kin
130 Way in
131 Surgical tool

DOWN

1 Florentine glassmaker Antonio
2 Arabic letter
3 Austin __ State U.
4 Aggrandize
5 Sabbath for some
6 Let live
7 Hospital worker
8 Like it or __ it!
9 Similar thing
10 Give a new title to
11 Washbowl
12 Pleasantries
13 Cod cousin
14 Car-wash worker
15 Presidential pick
16 Tackle-box items
17 Come to terms

18 Dutch colonists in South Africa
28 French river
29 Personal play space
30 Niner or Buc
34 Some NCOs
35 TLC part
36 NYSE alternative
38 Top-notch
40 Play part
42 Lawyer in the Scopes trial
44 Clear a videotape
46 Former Mrs. Trump
47 Stalin's predecessor
48 General direction
52 Moves on sneaky feet
54 Pastoral poems
56 Flap gums
58 Greek cross
60 German river
63 Greek physician
64 Barcelona gold
65 Tacks on
66 Sheriff or constable
67 Arab cloak
69 Harry Truman's birthplace
70 Milton of Uganda
71 Leaves off the list

72 Cacophony
73 Black goo
74 Inarticulate sounds
80 Comebacks
81 Bolivar's homeland
82 NASA's Shepard
84 Lascivious gander
85 Unsightly fruit?
86 Play part
88 Examines in minute detail
89 Alfonso's queen
91 Falling pollution
93 Rule for Jack Sprat
94 Of endurance
98 Corner piece
100 More info-packed
101 Mosaic piece
103 Utmost degree
105 Coyote State's capital
107 Workout wetness
108 Yours, long ago
109 Heart connection
111 Sequence of eight
113 Horse/donkey offspring
115 Persian ruler
116 Part of VMI
117 Cravings
118 Garfield's patsy
119 PC operator

MASTERS GAME

by Robert H. Wolfe

ACROSS

1 Metcalf of "Roseanne"
7 Santa's laundry problem
11 Perched on
15 Type measure
19 Loafers
20 "Paper Lion" star Alan
21 Davis of golf
22 Judah's son
23 Counter of golf supports?
25 Golfer's island?
27 Altercation
28 Speaker's platform
29 Capital on the Missouri River
30 Golly!
31 Impromptu
33 Spotted cavy
34 Pixielike
36 Cow collective
37 Fluorine and chlorine
39 Actress Lena
41 Formerly
44 Traveler's stopover
45 Andirons
46 Puerto __
47 Throngs
49 Pheasant's brood
50 Unit of work
51 Greek letters
52 Lake near Reno
53 Outmoded e-mail
55 Sock with diamonds
56 Movie house
57 Poison ivy and poison oak
58 Kenneth or Belle
60 Funny Foxx
61 Tight spot
62 Soggy
63 New Zealand parrot
64 Fiery stone
68 In the place
70 Writer Lurie
72 Location of the road to Mandalay
73 At large
76 Plath and Pankhurst
77 Concord
78 Afrikaners
79 Sun Devils' sch.
81 British peer
82 Waiting to bat
83 Here again
84 Gifts
86 Jan. honoree
87 E. O'Brien film
88 Major attachment
89 Go faster than
90 Half a tape
92 Gilbert and Teasdale
94 Rozelle of football
95 Main, e.g.
99 Acknowledge
100 Blemishes
102 Artist Chagall
103 Firefighter's carries?
104 Like visionary golfers?
106 Golfers who avoid cart paths?
108 Green shade
109 Try to outrun
110 "Bus Stop" dramatist
111 Arthur C. of sci-fi
112 Singles
113 Storage building
114 Cries of contempt
115 Bowling lanes

DOWN

1 Petrol unit in Eng.
2 Privately for two
3 Full of: suff.
4 Got back to even
5 First female golfer?
6 CPA's approximation
7 Pay
8 Stan's friend
9 Poetic works
10 Feather stickum?
11 Pond scum killers
12 Bullfighter
13 Higher than
14 Noblewoman
15 D.C. old-timer
16 Lack of means
17 Conforming to orthodox rules
18 North of golf
24 Festoon
26 "__ Blu Dipinto Di Blu (Volare)"
29 Faded
32 Brooches
33 Quintessential golf score?
35 Dangerous place on a golf course?
37 Secluded spot
38 Early bird?
40 Winning margin
41 Broadway figure
42 Test score
43 __ and aahed
45 Thin covering
48 Golfer with good club control?
49 Old musical staff notation
51 Yow, it's cold!
53 Peter the Great, e.g.
54 Spend the summer
55 Drivers' org.
58 Norse toast
59 Hamilton bills
61 Clampett patriarch
65 Snooped
66 Sunoco rival
67 Sri __
69 Is down with
71 Gentlemen
72 Elevated sand trap?
73 Singer Lane
74 Ship's petty officer
75 Four-sided figure
76 Hung
79 Indonesian island group
80 Carefully planned and executed performance
82 Ye __ Shoppe
84 Wall hangings
85 Grub
86 Richmond or Miller
90 Platoon pooh-bahs
91 Footless
93 Peer Gynt's mother
95 "Brideshead Revisited" author
96 Val d'__, France
97 Energetic
98 Sibilant letters
99 Wine: pref.
101 Hindu maid
102 "Near Changes" poet Van Duyn
105 "__ Miserables"
106 Tease
107 Indianapolis' __ Dome

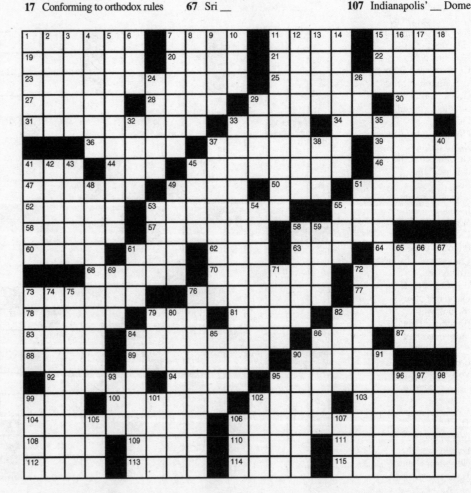

by Josiah Breward

ACROSS

1 Fundamental
6 Revealed oneself
14 Point a finger at
20 University of Maine town
21 Tagalog speaker
22 Sandra Bullock thriller
23 DOWN
25 More affectionate
26 Horse's front two
27 Take a load off
28 Lionel Barrymore film, "__ Lupin"
29 Cleave
30 Sweet syrupy drink
33 Even more adorable
34 Skeleton's whereabouts?
37 LOW
39 Mil. honor
42 "Atlas Shrugged" author Rand
43 Confederated
45 Comic Johnson of "Laugh-In"
46 Cup or pay attachment?
47 Musical cue
50 Leading ISP
51 First-rate
53 "Cosmos" author Carl
55 Lake near Reno
56 DEPRESSED
60 Italian art patron
61 Offer more for
63 Standish's messenger
64 Whittler
66 Timetable abbr.
68 Greek letters
69 Anterior
70 Nordic flyers' letters
71 NASA outpost
72 Prepare for reshipping
74 Ancient Greek physician
75 Having no motion
77 Former Dodger Hershiser
78 GRAVE
81 Feeds the kitty
84 Jagger and Fleetwood
86 Sam or Trevor
87 Patriotic men's org.
88 Shoulder warmer
89 Leverson or Huxtable
90 "Dies __"
92 Dull finishes
95 Canine first name
96 Speech on Sun.
97 SAD
100 Followed orders
103 Clark's role of a lifetime
105 Stir into activity
106 Grain coat
107 Ineffective
109 Abet's partner
110 Superlatively diminutive
114 Major suit
115 BLUE
119 Lodestone

120 Spikes for traction on ice
121 Twisted sideways
122 Nods off
123 Stag's counterpart
124 Olympic figure skater Carol

DOWN

1 Big laugh
2 Younger Guthrie
3 Excessively acid
4 Reasons by deduction
5 Colombian export
6 Rubbed out
7 Artist Mondrian
8 Old-time high note
9 Future louse
10 N.T. book
11 Type of locomotive
12 Still green
13 Emily of etiquette
14 To blame
15 Snorting, joyful laughter
16 Swing a thurible
17 UPSET
18 Spotted
19 Nice to be?
24 Busybody
30 Holding cells

31 Shoshone
32 Inc. in Ipswich
33 Winner of seven batting titles
34 Nav. rank
35 Vega's constellation
36 SULKY
37 Smoke mass
38 Church law
40 Candidate lists
41 Chair craftsmen
44 __ lazuli
48 Five centimes, once
49 Allstate alternative
51 After-market purchases
52 River into the Baltic
54 Ate starter?
57 Writer Ellison
58 Saarinen senior
59 Coll. sports org.
62 Tulip-to-be
65 Namesakes of a wire-haired terrier
66 Odors
67 Second spin?
69 Discomfort
70 Cubic meter
73 Large deer

74 Watery porridge
75 Condition
76 Bank payt.
79 Not likely
80 Plant fiber
82 Writer Wiesel
83 Transmit
85 Evade
91 Examines again
92 Half a Kenyan rebel?
93 6-pack muscles?
94 More teed off
98 Baseball bird
99 Dennis of the NBA
101 Send packing
102 Isolate
104 Mezzo-soprano Marilyn
106 King or Ross
107 Resistance units
108 Greenish blue color
109 Author of "The Nazarene"
110 Floozy
111 Lateral beginning?
112 Instigates litigation
113 Mack and Williams
116 Powerful ruler: abbr.
117 FDR program
118 Possessive pronoun

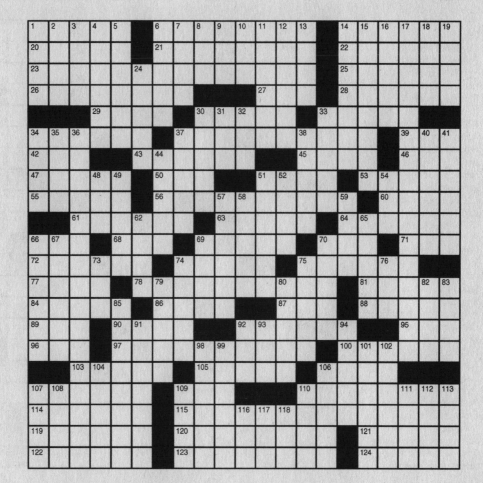

URBAN INTERCHANGES

by Willy A. Wiseman

ACROSS

1 Discard
6 Mother of Calcutta
12 Comic Imogene
16 Plant microphones
19 Motif
20 Unwrapped
21 Grunts
22 K–O connection
23 Minute amounts
24 Actress Ryder
25 Early embryonic form
27 Franco to Issei in California?
29 DDE's rival
30 Great distance
31 Stockpiled
32 Likewise
34 Quiet
36 Cinder ending?
37 Cause of atrophy
42 Explorer da Gama
44 Pigpen
45 __ Plaines, IL
46 Albania's capital
47 Terrier foot
48 Naming names grp.
50 Put a luxury car in a Michigan garage?
52 Companion
55 Largest desert
58 Corp. honchos
59 Displaced person
60 Freshwater fish
61 __-Magnon
63 Land
66 Blue Eagle org.
67 Lunar valleys
68 Waterfront dive in Maine?
70 Aluminum silicates
72 Foreign student's subj.
73 Artillery piece
74 Sleeve card?
75 Privileged few
76 Use of an astringent
79 Red and Galilee
81 On point performance
82 Big deal!
83 Cathedral collapses in Virginia?
87 All-out feast
88 Harass for payment
89 Sun god
90 '60s war zone, briefly
93 Earth: pref.
95 Drive out
97 Process sea water
98 Jupiter
99 Retiree
101 __ juris
103 Performer on the road
105 Statutes
106 Sandhurst sch.
108 Lawn game in Kentucky?
113 Two dots over a vowel
115 "Brigadoon" lyricist
116 Monarch's loyal subject
117 Finnish twins?
118 Horne of music
119 Frozen cliffhanger?
120 Impatient
121 Profit figure
122 Indigo and anil
123 "__ by Starlight"
124 Russian rulers

DOWN

1 Suppressed
2 Harmonized hymn
3 Sells direct
4 Bynes of Nickelodeon
5 "Home Alone" co-star
6 Drags behind
7 Monumental
8 Splitsville?
9 Hall-of-Famer Slaughter
10 Upper house
11 Hersey's bell town
12 Oscar winner Gooding
13 Flirtatious eyers
14 Follow after a Camaro in Maryland?
15 Onager
16 Deceives advisors in Iowa?
17 Two dots over a vowel
18 Twisted
26 Create lace
28 Ms. Gandhi
33 Oblong circle
35 The March King
38 Irritate
39 "My Gal __"
40 Mythical horned beast
41 Rational
43 Arista
46 Floozies
47 Model
49 Coll. sports grp.
50 Cezanne or Gauguin
51 Alternative to a medical examiner
53 Give a new score to
54 Silver server
55 On-the-job malady
56 Noble Brit
57 Mae in California?
59 Tours to be
61 Eliz. II's son
62 Managed
64 Disconcerts
65 French lake
69 Deck-crew leader
70 Dining-out experiences
71 Hardships
73 Souvenir T-shirt in the Garden State?
77 Group of wds.
78 Former home-video show host
80 Suffer stiffness
81 Blind drunk
83 Atlanta-based medical org.
84 Crude shelters
85 St. with keys
86 Feel poorly
90 Panamanian dictator, once
91 Emma Peel, for one
92 Corporate unions
93 Kind of calf or boy
94 Lancelot's lady
96 Royalty fur
97 Straightforward
98 Child and Roberts
100 Ukr. or Lith., once
102 Jamaican citrus fruits
104 Tiny hooter
107 Gray and Candler
109 New York canal
110 Bus. letter abbr.
111 Jodie Foster film
112 La __ Tar Pits
114 Yore

ACROSS

1 Sweetening substance
8 Green Bay team member
14 Numskull
20 Animate
21 Sweet-smelling gas
22 1998 Masters golf champion
23 Cashing in
25 Fireplace shelf
26 Crisis situations
27 Civil libs.
29 Caviar
30 "The Sweetheart of Sigma __"
32 Golfer's starting point
33 Strait of __ de Fuca
34 Swashbuckler Flynn
37 Cues
40 Subcontracting
45 Actress Claire
46 Golf score
49 Oblique: abbr.
50 Years and years
51 Acacia crawlers
52 Leafstalk
53 Currently working
55 This evening
57 Approaching evening
60 Saturated
61 GOP member
64 Beach bird
65 Alaska buyer
67 Arrowsmith's first wife
68 French pronoun
70 Vault
72 Light, granite rock
74 Crawled, in a way
75 Holy hymn
77 Pogo, for one
81 Oklahoma city
83 Compass dir.
84 Door frame element
86 Acting rowdy
89 Scalia of the Supreme Court
91 City on the Erie Canal
92 As a group
96 Nickel or dime
97 Vegas lead-in
99 Inscription on the cross
100 Simultaneous releases of bombs
101 East ender?
102 Intercepting
105 High-pitched barks
106 Fluid transition
108 Lips
109 "The Hundred Secret Senses" writer Tan
112 O.J.'s judge
113 Deli sandwich letters
114 Scottish uncle
115 Advice columnist, in Britain
120 Having dark hair: var.
123 Forcing a way
127 Esteem
128 First female English Channel swimmer
129 Stockpiler
130 Take stock of
131 Hannah and Hall
132 Bonds metals

DOWN

1 Speech on Sun.
2 Nice one?
3 Single-reed woodwind
4 Mature
5 "Ars Amatoria" poet
6 French legislative body
7 Author Madeline L'__
8 Look intently
9 Element fig.
10 Eliz. II's son
11 Plunk starter?
12 Football play
13 Put on a revival
14 __ de plume
15 Turkish inn
16 Choir member
17 Diluting
18 Pique
19 Russian chess master
24 Great Barrier __
28 Honker
30 Pork cut
31 Abuzz abode
33 Picture puzzle
35 In rapid retreat
36 Patronymic
38 Math subj.
39 Wear
41 Tennis situation
42 Wedding tokens
43 Bea Arthur sitcom
44 __ cuantos (a few)
47 Lotion additives
48 Reseal a package
51 Helpers
54 Notable periods
56 Lon __ of Cambodia
58 Guaranteed to get
59 Quarterback Dave
61 Puts back
62 Hamlet's castle
63 Wiretapping
66 Balls
69 Singing John
71 Biblical twin
73 Tropical vine
76 Guys
78 Non-violent demonstrations
79 Employing
80 Chip starter?
82 In the half-light
85 Julie Andrews film, "Darling __"
87 Childlike person
88 Church area
90 Mother-of-pearl
93 Seclusion
94 Alternative to 9
95 Exxon, once
98 Was very thrifty
102 Roberta or Bernadette
103 Widow of Ferdinand Marcos
104 Canine tooth
107 Forearm bones
110 Fables
111 Loudmouth
115 Wrong
116 Four fluid ounces
117 Fifths of a five?
118 Asian mountain range
119 North of Paris?
120 Bikini top
121 Scale notes
122 Gridiron scores, briefly
124 "__ the fields we go..."
125 Eur. country
126 60-minute units

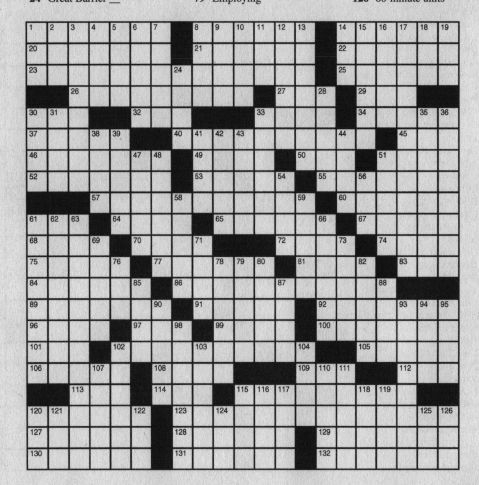

MM IS FOR...

by Arlan and Linda Bushman

ACROSS

1 Spike, as punch
5 Cow
10 Particulars
15 Autobahn autos
19 "Roots" author Haley
20 Publication
21 "Vertigo" actress
22 Diamond Head locale
23 ...her favorite museum display
26 Plug up
27 Cubs rivals
28 Brace (oneself)
29 Dry streambed
31 Bread fragment
34 First word of Kramden's laugh
35 1971 Charlton Heston flick, with "The"
39 ...her favorite art store purchase
43 Infrequent
44 Commotion
45 Anabaptist sect
46 King, to Henri
47 Grinding teeth
49 Cracked
50 Additional
51 Penetrating
53 Guitar part
54 One plague on Egypt
55 Bloom-to-be
56 Speaks freely
58 Schooner contents
59 Come to terms
60 Pool table roller
62 Ill-tempered individual
64 Of a people: pref.
66 Layer
67 Remain floating in air
69 Artful film sequence
73 Cut again
75 Bone-dry
76 Kudrow friend?
77 Mail, for example
80 __ Speedwagon
82 Income
84 Glasgow boy
85 Bank transactions
86 Psychologist Jung
88 1984 Harry Dean Stanton film, "Paris, __"
89 FDR's pooch
90 Poultry output
91 Nose (out)
93 Cosell's coverage?
94 Pesto herb
95 Std.
96 Bologna greeting
97 ...her favorite spot for family photos
100 Testing procedure
102 __ pro nobis
103 Stretch of land
104 Pennsylvania port
105 Govt. bond
107 Can't abide
111 Rotunda feature
113 ...her ritzy New York digs
118 Persian Gulf country
119 Not sotto voce
120 Syrian leader
121 Participating
122 Spanish painter
123 Gunpowder ingredient
124 Afresh
125 Inquires

DOWN

1 Tibetan monk
2 Regrettably
3 Copper coin
4 Work out
5 Chinese dumplings
6 Botanist Gray
7 Naval letters
8 Bonkers
9 Develop a bite?
10 Physically present
11 Drudgery
12 Threshold
13 PC alternative
14 Satay holders
15 __ nova
16 ...her choice of college studies
17 Sci-fi Doctor
18 Dine
24 Type of singer
25 Upgrade guns
30 Long duration
32 ...her favorite French performer
33 Noted journalist Heywood
35 Mythic consultant
36 ...her workaday profession
37 Words from the wise
38 Scandinavian
39 Latino dances in 4/4 time
40 Quantity
41 Bridge support
42 Art in bad taste
48 Comic DeLaria
49 Specialized lingoes
51 Superexcellent
52 Guilder replacements
54 Farmer of cookbooks
56 Horse operas
57 Patio brick
61 Feudal honchos
63 Soft hat
65 Wagner of the Pirates
68 Musical sound effect
70 Finally
71 Net defender
72 Ultimate conclusion
74 Induce irritability
77 On one's toes
78 Two-way radio word
79 ...her favorite pop tune
81 Rink legend Bobby
83 Jump for joy
87 Citrus drink
89 Disney classic
91 Emergency responder
92 Predictable cards?
94 Club component
96 MDX divided by X
98 Wickerwork material
99 Chronic disorder
101 Spectacle spot
105 Weekday abbr.
106 Comfort
108 Metal containers
109 Catchy refrain
110 Austrian river
111 Excavate
112 Spanish gold
114 Will Smith role
115 Ready alternative?
116 Austral. state
117 Bad in Limousin

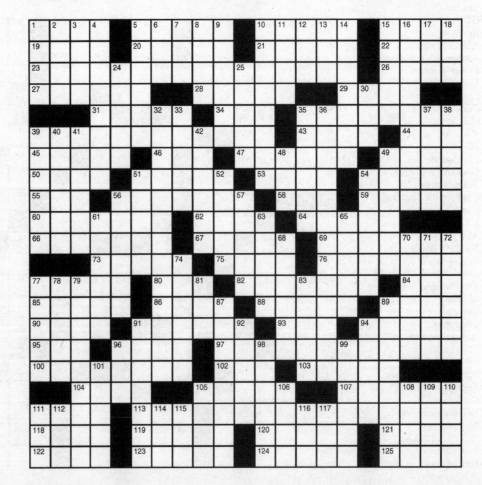

by Josiah Breward

ACROSS

1 Forum figure
8 Stanzas containing irregular lines
16 Host before Carson
20 Country's top bishop
21 Like hard work
22 Not taken in by
23 Start of first quote
25 Bristle
26 Old Italian bread?
27 Beer glasses
28 Set up a setup
30 Wet soil
31 Arrowsmith's wife
33 Reliquary
34 Part 2 of first quote
38 Hosp. area
40 Fantastic!
41 Devour
42 "The Day the Earth Stood Still" star
43 Part 3 of first quote
49 Charles Camille Saint-__
50 "Ben-__"
51 Poetry collection
52 Half and half?
53 PAU's successor
55 Bilko or Snorkel: abbr.
56 Brouhaha
57 Keanu in "The Matrix"
58 D.C. old-timer
60 More down
63 End of first quote
67 Members of rhythm sections
71 White-tailed eagle
72 King, to Henri
73 Pub order
75 Pick out
76 Detection equipment operator
80 Source of this puzzle's quotes
85 Bank employee
87 Tallahassee sch.
88 Tic-tac-toe win
89 Record time?
90 AOL, e.g.
93 By way of
94 Actor McKellen
96 Planted
97 __-disant (so-called)
98 Gettysburg victor
100 Start of second quote
105 Henner of "Taxi"
107 Cash dispenser's letters
108 Mazel __
109 Abbr. on many cameras
110 Part 2 of second quote
112 Sacred bull
114 Gridiron lines
118 Create lace
119 Tap gently
120 Ants
122 Ecological cycle
123 BTU part

125 End of second quote
130 Powerful stink
131 Bayer pills
132 Repair fabric
133 Exxon, formerly
134 Most full of info
135 "Lou Grant" star

DOWN

1 Overflow
2 "Sesame Street" character
3 Explosive stuff
4 Language of Ethiopia
5 NJ inventor's initials
6 Singer Redding
7 Oscar de la __
8 Uncomplaining
9 Circular wind
10 Edges
11 End of pay?
12 Hrs. in Seattle
13 __ polloi
14 Atlanta university
15 Elder
16 Neg.'s opposite
17 Windflowers
18 Bringing into harmony
19 Automotive trial

24 __ wheel
29 Conjectures
32 Sunflower seed
34 Semi-eternity?
35 Looks aghast
36 Afr. nation
37 Recombinant __
39 Higher one
43 "Casey at the Bat" poet
44 Writer Welty
45 Nearby
46 Ungulate's foot
47 Arias for one
48 Skywalker's mentor
54 Circulars
58 PGA member
59 Leave out
61 Shelter a fugitive, e.g.
62 Get to one's feet
64 Bog base
65 Caen's river
66 Stirling toppers
68 Widely scattered
69 Lethargy
70 Flummox
74 Bud's buddy
77 Made merry
78 1051
79 Jai __

81 Former Spanish toehold in Africa
82 Jeering cry
83 Disturbing cries
84 Missing people
86 Rodeo rope
90 Childish
91 Ocean corridors
92 Equalities
95 Military force
96 Part of USSR
99 Fourth of MMXVI
101 Rage
102 Pollen makers
103 Part of a sailing ship
104 Colorful marine fishes
106 Ogden resident
111 Very overweight
113 Long look
115 Actress Ada
116 Took the wheel
117 Waste conduit
120 Actress Arden, casually
121 Luge
124 Ring decision letters
126 Municipal grp.
127 Towel word
128 Onassis, to pals
129 Niger-Congo language

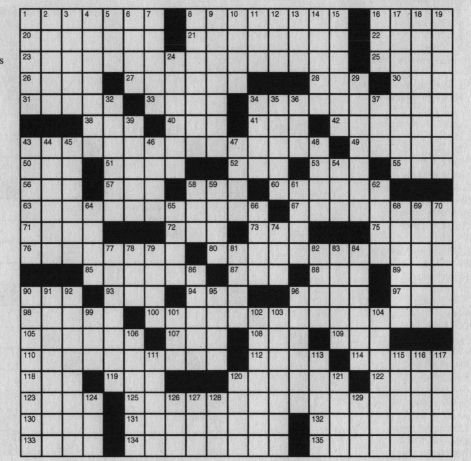

by Robert H. Wolfe

ACROSS

1 Neighborhoods
6 Handle roughly
10 Pitching infraction
14 A course
19 Speed spurt
20 Car shaft
21 Two-time Indy winner Luyendyk
22 Disco dancing
23 Novelist Brookner
24 Touchy
26 Jerry Lee or Jerry
27 Slower method of sending
29 Anoint, of old
30 NASA's ISS partner
31 Performing couples
32 African antelope
33 San Diego players
34 H.S. course
35 Birdhouse nester
36 Poisonous shrub
37 Permanent binder
40 The one there
41 Hen dens
43 Qty.
46 Assumed name
47 Diving bird
48 Trousers
49 Japanese golfer Aoki
50 Baton
51 Gold measure
52 Mine finds
53 Motionless
54 Contemptible behavior
56 Jeremy of "Damage"
58 Remove adhesive
59 Spherical
60 Signal light
61 Lauder of cosmetics
62 Leaning
64 "The X-__"
65 Wormwood
68 Office worker
69 Wedge-shaped cleaver
70 Time-waster
72 Residents of: suff.
73 "__ to Zanzibar"
74 Wild swine
75 __ Bien Phu, Vietnam
76 Poe pieces
77 Med. printout
78 Haughty
79 Average marks
80 Route
81 Ordinary
83 __ En-lai
84 Golf scores
85 Spicy cuisine
87 Flourish on a letter
89 Gone by
90 Simile center
93 Abate
94 Kept on a leash by
97 Cheri of "SNL"
98 Pen choice
99 Big name in wine
100 Propaganda pamphlet
101 Milky stone
102 "King Kong" actress
103 Close, to Blake
104 Great Lakes acronym
105 Meeting: abbr.
106 "I Remember Mama" character
107 Cairo in "The Maltese Falcon"

DOWN

1 Degrade
2 Ancient symbolic letters
3 "Fear of Flying" writer Jong
4 Concerning
5 Replacements
6 Army's mule or Navy's goat
7 Edmund Wilson's "__ Castle"
8 Arm bone
9 Curacao to the Virgin Islands
10 Robin's partner
11 Parliament's attachment?
12 Fuming
13 Boat part
14 Deep bows
15 Meeting outline
16 Small E or G, e.g.
17 Limber
18 Prescribed amounts
25 A little land
28 Gold powder
33 Litter
34 Bed part
35 Hold your horses!
36 Boozers
37 Crow calls
38 Vivacity
39 Baseball group
40 British Conservative
41 Chili con __
42 Change for a fin
44 Japanese ship name
45 Handy bag
47 Cooking fat
48 1966 Johnny Rivers hit
49 Clever
51 Superman's pen name?
53 Former Peruvian currency
55 Shipboard bed
57 Sally Field movie, "Norma __"
58 CCCP, to us
60 Long, deep, narrow inlet: var.
61 Scrooge, to friends
62 Land measurement
63 __ gin fizz
64 German wife
65 Beer choices
66 Raises skirts?
67 Caesar's existence
69 Hoodwink
71 God of France
74 Highland hillside
76 Iberian Peninsula country
78 Parsons' platforms
79 Sound like a bird
80 Money
82 Root
83 Fishermans' baskets
84 Duke and Sheehan
85 Textile
86 Active lead-in
87 Shoot from hiding
88 Best and O'Brien
89 Of punishment
90 More fit
91 Kind of panel
92 Before, before
94 E.T. vehicles
95 Add to staff
96 Spanish hand

BASEBALL BY THE NUMBERS

by Randall J. Hartman

ACROSS

1 Sidewalk eatery
5 Youngsters of the flock
10 Qatar resident
14 Indian state separated from others by Bangladesh
19 Eager
20 System of principles
21 Lead singer of U2
22 Main Street structure
23 #5 of baseball
27 Used chairs
28 Egyptian goddess of fertility
29 Thumbs up for John Glenn
30 Poplar trees
31 Apples, pears, etc.
33 "M*A*S*H" co-star Jamie
35 Roman gods
37 Has permission
38 #3 of baseball
44 Sigourney Weaver thriller
45 Wilander of tennis
46 Of vinegar
47 One of the Fab Four
48 Capital of Western Samoa
49 A skunk has one
50 Tenant's contract
54 Kett of an old comic strip
55 #24 of baseball
58 Indiana city on Lake Michigan
59 Korvald or Onsager
60 Zone
61 Compactly
65 Diagrams made to scale
67 Light, dry, white wine
68 Huge numbers
69 "Tonight Show" host before Carson
70 Nitty-gritty
71 #4 of baseball
75 Old World duck
79 Key PC key
80 __ cuantos (a few)
81 "A Room of __ Own"
82 Clear the stubble
83 Benchmark test
85 Black, to Byron
86 Dripped
87 #39 of baseball
91 Nov. and Dec.
92 Herndon and Cobb
93 City on the Oka River
94 Sloshing
95 One who is a tolerator
98 Israeli gun
99 Editor's notation
100 __ you kidding me?
103 #8 of baseball
109 Martini garnish
110 Saltwater lake of Asia
111 Serious
112 Sicilian volcano
113 Military negative
114 Old-time journalist Ernie
115 Partnered
116 Smile expansively

DOWN

1 Taxis
2 Taj Mahal site
3 Clue for Sherlock
4 Freudian topic
5 Reduces
6 In danger
7 Conductance units
8 Dribble catcher
9 __-fi
10 Soak up
11 Straight mover, in chess
12 Massachusetts cape
13 Halloween cry
14 Yard-sale caveat
15 Cease
16 Invoking the force of religion
17 Showplaces
18 Cluttered
24 Geisha garb
25 Nostrils
26 Singer Bonnie
32 Last of all
33 Thrash
34 Mongolian range
35 Misleading attractions
36 Still-life picture pitchers
38 Fabled loser
39 Dismounted
40 Hint at
41 Detection devices
42 Most cunning
43 Long, cold period
48 Lofty
49 Eastern sultanate
51 Indigo plant
52 Carrier plane feature: abbr.
53 Slave of the past
55 Guitarist Joe
56 Satellite of Jupiter
57 Flagrant
58 Prescription option
61 Pineapple brand
62 MBA class
63 Not masc. or fem.
64 With wisdom
65 __ Springs, Colorado
66 Minstrel's ballads
67 __ van der Rohe
69 Playboy centerfolds
70 Davis of "Thelma & Louise"
72 Boozer
73 Regal
74 Hillock
75 Catches fungoes
76 Hurry up
77 Of all time
78 Ties the knot
82 Put to sleep
84 Part of the Carpathians
85 Weird
86 Degraded
87 Snook
88 Egyptian god
89 Garden sprayer
90 Grammatical case
91 Georgia city
96 556, to Cato
97 Peeping Tom
98 Caspian feeder
99 Card game for three
101 Author Jaffe
102 Midterm or final
104 Dupe
105 The old college __
106 Hollywood studio's letters
107 Spanish Mrs.
108 Winger, casually

UN-FUL-FILLED

by Willy A. Wiseman

ACROSS

1 Maria of La Scala
7 Unskilled laborers
12 Taxation without representation issue
20 One-celled organism
21 1986 Indy winner
22 French stewlike dish
23 Jurisprudence expert?
25 One of Seven Hills
26 Disinclination to act
27 Sacred
29 Mothballed Mach+ jets
30 Mus. collection
31 Golfer Ballesteros
33 Sicilian city
37 Small boy
38 Swearword
40 Earthenware crocks
44 Of an arm bone
45 Latin eggs
46 With 70A, source of magician's magic?
50 Legendary vaudevillian
52 Composer Villa-Lobos
55 Cornerstone tablets
57 Plus
58 Belgian port, locally
60 One who writes wryly
64 National syst.
67 Boom times
68 Conspiracy unit
70 See 46A
72 Actress Lucy
73 Actress Long
74 Rutger of "Blade Runner"
76 Lyon's river
77 Wt. increments
78 Eurasian crow
79 Ancient religion?
83 Swan lady
84 Bowlike object
85 Coin channel
87 Pay the tab
89 Solzhenitsyn setting
91 Pen point
93 From the stars
95 "Schindler's List" star
96 Holstered guns
101 Forgery painter?
103 Vein of iron
104 Law of the French succession
106 Brazilian beverage
107 Assns.
111 Sea of France
112 Is sparing with
114 Periods
117 Altar of stars
118 __ breve
120 Charles de __
124 Century subdivisions
126 Exposed
130 Features of phantom limbs?
132 One who draws conclusions
133 Actress Verdugo
134 Pulpy refuse
135 Upper-throat lymphoid tissue
136 Bonheur and Parks
137 Distinctive mannerisms

DOWN

1 Spotted cat
2 Mother in "The Glass Menagerie"
3 Bottommost
4 Goneril's father
5 Borders on
6 Composer Erik
7 PGA member
8 Listening devices
9 Miami or Lima location
10 Part of NLCS
11 Slicker
12 Tiny, shiny disk
13 Mazel __!
14 Consumed
15 British isle
16 Places
17 Big-stick economic policy?
18 Peso percentage
19 Jagger's "Ruby"
24 Widespread confusion
28 Half a Kenyan rebel?
32 Part of BPOE
34 Sturm __ Drang
35 Forlorn
36 "Norma" melody
39 Dislike intensely
41 Why don't we?
42 Mr. T's group
43 Conductor Sir Georg
47 Blanketlike cloak
48 Crucibles
49 Mediocre
51 High school subj.
52 Nags
53 Discovery
54 Little Stevie's sitcom?
56 Notable times
59 Get away from
61 Myth ending?
62 Blackthorns
63 Watching over
65 Genus of cholera bacteria
66 Standard Italian literary language
69 Louie in a car
71 Navy builder
75 Pro __ (in proportion)
80 Ingrid in "Casablanca"
81 Aquarium fish
82 Offends
86 Draw
88 Paper tablets
90 Younger Saarinen
92 Low voice
94 Cargo
96 Neighbor of Ethiopia
97 Politically divided island
98 Squealer
99 Letters for 1051
100 Backup group
102 Electron tube
105 El regulators
108 Tire type
109 Homer's home
110 Mouths off
113 Natural starter?
115 Here-today employees
116 Get a move on!
119 Yemen's capital
121 Composer Schifrin
122 Whoppers
123 Sicilian resort
125 Soldiers as one
127 Male sib
128 Onassis nickname
129 Blushing
131 Bell and Barker

by Arlan and Linda Bushman

ACROSS

1 Urban cruisers
5 Composer Jerome
9 Opulent
13 Divvies up
19 Confederate
20 Director Kazan
21 Ancient Middle East city
22 Get a close-up
23 Dad's favorite loungewear
26 Actress Lansbury
27 First-rate
28 EPA concern
29 Rural steps
31 Pol. neighbor
32 Writer Bagnold
34 Dad's favorite amusement center
37 Wood-eating pests
41 Khartoum's river
42 Held up
43 High dudgeon
44 Saucers
46 "Cabaret" director
48 Metal-shaping stand
52 Dad's favorite backyard gatherings
56 Hyperbolic time spent waiting
58 Philatelist's find
59 Small duck
60 Kind of pool or wave
62 WWI battle site
63 Curdled milk product
65 Sharp point
67 Informs
69 Group of docs
70 Dad's favorite driving maneuver
75 Guitarist Paul
78 Skater Sonja
79 __ Aviv-Jaffa
80 Lathered
84 Potent beginning?
86 Guy wires
88 Enunciation problem
91 Ultraviolet filter
92 First to the South Pole
94 Dad's favorite puttering-around clothes
97 Aesop specialty
98 Of birth
100 Store lure
101 Shatner novel "__ War"
102 Noted Israeli diplomat
104 __ be fun!
106 Some cipher handlers
109 Dad's favorite Italian dish
114 Agatha contemporary
115 Rationers of WWII
116 Nest sound
117 Nov. election day
119 Holiday drink
123 City southeast of Roma
125 Dad's favorite New Year's spectacle

128 Ran on and on
129 Nat. sci. branch
130 Mustachioed Spanish artist
131 Uniform
132 Underscore
133 Cry of surprise
134 Squabble
135 Bronte heroine

DOWN

1 Cook's title, for short
2 Jai __
3 Radar signal
4 Network
5 Go on and on
6 English cathedral city
7 Full-blown
8 Rights grp.
9 Drawn from actual events
10 Big Blue
11 Ranks
12 "__ la vista, baby!"
13 Flowering shrub
14 Sayles movie
15 Mill input
16 Greek letter
17 Floor specialist

18 Jack London's boat
24 Burt's ex
25 A Cusack
30 Rumor fodder
33 Trim meat
35 Silver medalist's lament
36 Thoughtful money?
37 Slightly drunk
38 Frost's Muse
39 Mark sale items
40 Tender
45 Cup of the NHL
47 Passover feast
49 Rival of AmEx
50 Tidbit
51 Vega's constellation
53 Lay-abed's refrain?
54 Woman with a talk show
55 Nastase of tennis
57 New York Bay island
61 Type of type
64 Ringlet
66 Three-letter sandwich
68 Nose around
71 Insect sensors
72 Woody vine
73 Bombard
74 Middle East strip
75 Bread purchase

76 Thompson of "Wit"
77 Social slight
81 Florence's __ Vecchio
82 Set down
83 Items in cubicles
85 Coastal recess
87 Outpouring
89 Roe source
90 Martinique peak
93 Complete failures
95 Insurance giant
96 Broken down
99 Orchestral kettledrums
103 Garden parasites
105 Praise
107 Gymnast Korbut
108 Al Roker measure
109 Wannabe lakes
110 Isolated
111 Flavor
112 Give back
113 Exigencies
118 Give way suddenly
120 Dark blue
121 Baltic feeder
122 Sarazen of golf
124 Individual
126 Gullible person
127 In the manner of

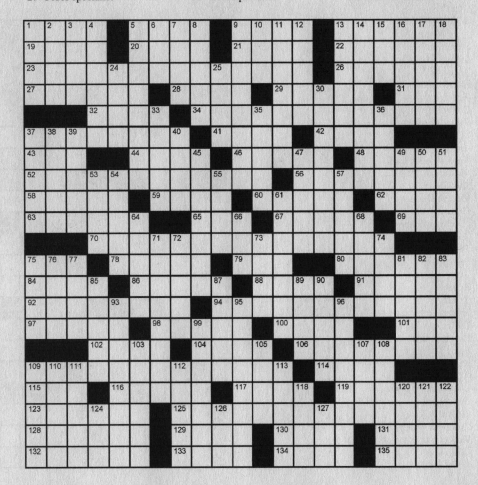

DOUBLE YOU

by Bill Swain

ACROSS

1 Little devil
4 Port __ cheese
9 Charterhouse city
14 Also-ran
19 Galley propeller
20 Amherst sch.
21 Perfect example
22 Showplace
23 Sends postcards from a cruise?
26 Went spelunking
27 Ball's partner
28 Command to Fido
29 Jean-__ Godard
30 Oily resin
31 Night: pref.
32 Platter spinners
35 Travel charges
37 Promoting peace
38 Obtain an arrest warrant
40 Jazz singer Laine
41 Harem room
42 Vote for
43 Bread for a Cuban sandwich?
45 Witty remark
46 Class for U.S. immigrants
47 Plant louse
50 Corral
51 Solidarity leader
53 __ of Marmara
54 Stranglers?
60 Stomped (on)
63 Approval
65 Embellishes
66 Not as many
67 Commands
68 Panels of jurors
70 "The Deer Hunter" director
71 Amphitheater levels
72 William of "Murder, She Wrote"
73 Mojave Desert city
74 Persian poet
75 Handball championship?
78 Spinal cord, etc.
79 "Broken Arrow" actor
81 Sturdy tree
82 Actor Jeff
84 Retriever, for short
86 Smack
87 Jacked-up pickup?
92 Collector's French coin
93 Pacino and Hirt
94 Switch tail?
95 Rapacious insect clan
99 Adds protective layers
101 Long-time pal
102 OK school
103 Gather in
104 Complete successfully
105 Perfect-game box score
106 "Do Ya" rock grp.
108 Roman senate

109 "The Lost Galleon" poet
110 Concern for an aging Zorro?
115 Euphemistic oath
116 Veranda in Hawaii
117 Sun: pref.
118 Inhabitant of: suff.
119 Bus terminal
120 New Zealand Olympic runner
121 Jots
122 Draft letters

DOWN

1 Hawkeyes
2 Pith
3 Charming man?
4 Egyptian port
5 Morning hrs.
6 Tai language
7 Tampa sch.
8 Recipe meas.
9 Former Spanish coin
10 Classified __
11 Change the distribution
12 Fowles novel, with "The"
13 Guinness or Waugh
14 Cut
15 Pope's fanon
16 Certain young trick-or-treater
17 Foes
18 Extreme
24 Japanese floor mat
25 Rump-bone's shape
32 Letters from the morgue
33 Pursue with gusto
34 Confined in a pigpen
36 Poetic pasture
37 Images of gods
39 Eliminators
41 Bradley and Sharif
44 Wind dir.
47 Tie types
48 City on the Illinois
49 Given the wrong coat?
51 Harmless cysts
52 Parts of pipes
55 Finnish twins?
56 Ayn and Sally
57 Half-wit
58 Bellini opera
59 Coll. seniors' test
61 Wife of Paris
62 Heavy-lidded
64 Green finch
66 Lightning bug
68 Bob the TV handyman

69 Blowup of a pic
70 Wheel on a rotating shaft
72 Viral lumps
73 Guys with bread?
75 Mournful cries
76 Drive a dinghy
77 Cartoonist Wilson
80 Clearest in detail
83 Ginger root
84 Under control, as a dog
85 Property holding
87 Female lead
88 Worldwide help grp.
89 One of Regan's sisters
90 Games authority
91 Rhea's relative
96 Carnivorous marine worms
97 Contaminates
98 Sudden flows
100 Top
101 "Over There" composer
105 Wide-eyed predators
107 Snake: pref.
108 Business VIPs
111 Sidekick
112 Zodiac sign
113 PC key
114 OSS, now

OENOPHILES

by Robert H. Wolfe

ACROSS

1 Detailed design, for short
5 Bursts of energy
11 Barbecue rod
15 NASA destination
19 Story
20 Croquet arch
21 Other
22 Eye layer
23 Jacket type
24 Whole
25 Vincent Lopez theme song
26 Fuzz
27 Spirited president?
30 Clinton's Guinier
31 Park and Lex.
32 Horace work, "__ Poetica"
33 Subsequently
34 Debate
37 Treading the boards
42 Gorged
44 Spirited puppeteer?
46 Everest guide
48 Tends after
49 Forrest's family
51 Estrange
55 Smidgen
56 Smacking sounds
58 Cool one
60 "The Ballad of the Green Berets" singer
61 Fill an empty flat
63 Bud
64 Majority of infielders
65 Writer Sinclair
68 Spirited "GWTW" character?
72 Wipe out
73 Vacillates
75 Unit of work
76 Planted items
78 Oral delivery
79 Floral loop
80 "It Happened One Night" director
82 Bachelor's last words
85 Inform again
87 Home of the Heat
89 Concentrating viewer
92 Flat-bottomed fishing boats
94 Spirited Rosalind Russell role?
96 Moral anguish
99 Rollaway bed
101 Braxton and Morrison
102 Arkin and King
103 Parseghian of football
104 Distant
106 Horace or Thomas
107 Spirited film producer?
116 Religious ceremony
117 French composer Satie
118 Bit of food
119 "__ la Douce"
120 Like Nash's lama
121 Face the day

122 Superlatively slippery
123 Enthusiasm
124 Wooded valley
125 Teacher's deg.
126 Cooks with dry heat
127 Salinger girl

DOWN

1 Fret
2 Way to go
3 "The Time Machine" people
4 Man/horse beasts
5 Sorenstam, e.g.
6 Mr. Clean rival
7 Start of "Hamlet"
8 Downhill wear
9 Mother of France
10 Anna of "Nana"
11 Spanish men
12 Deere output
13 Isolated land
14 Rent
15 Spirited Defoe character?
16 Fly
17 Curdling substance
18 Swift forte
28 Turn inside out
29 Old crone

33 Soothed
34 Off. underling
35 Flightless bird
36 Went right
38 Nullify
39 Crawled, in a way
40 Robbins and Roth
41 Small viper
42 Subj. for Billy Graham
43 U.S. pension act
45 Mournful cry
47 Topper
50 Get lost!
52 Soprano Gluck
53 PGA pegs
54 Coastal bird
57 Towel word
59 Everyone
61 Spirited funny lady?
62 Congressmen, often
63 Small, thickset dog
64 Fox's title
65 Cold War letters
66 Le Pew of cartoons
67 Ager of parents
69 Poor mark
70 Projecting edge
71 Observation
74 Buzzing sounds

77 Bridge position
79 Caustic substance
80 Lyricist Sammy
81 In the middle of
82 Land of Lake Urmia
83 Actress Moore
84 Mine products
86 Disapproving interjection
88 Hosp. area
90 Greek giant
91 Liquidate into a sinking fund
93 Caressed
95 Proximal
96 Exemplar of stiffness
97 "Seinfeld" character
98 Fireplace shelf
100 Way cool!
103 Liqueur flavor
105 Soft fabrics
107 Part of speech
108 Part of the eye
109 Arabian leader
110 Daft
111 Opera song
112 Manipulates
113 Angry states
114 Prayer leader of Islam
115 Mall event

SPORTS DREAMS

by Josiah Breward

ACROSS

1 Progeny
6 Advanced deg.
9 Refinement
14 Long cuts
19 "Gymnopedies" composer
20 Tic-tac-toe outcome
21 Earthenware crocks
22 Martinique volcano
23 Gridiron dream
25 Track dream
27 __ prosequi
28 Inner Hebrides isle
29 Tomei of "My Cousin Vinny"
30 Trinket
33 Promissory notes
34 Apple seed
36 Thanks __!
37 Nautical dream
39 Links dream
41 Smack
42 Pugilist Max
43 Northern European location
44 Way in: abbr.
45 Plummets
47 "Magnum, P.I." star
48 Bikini part
51 Killing of gods
53 Petulant or pouty
54 Grab hold of
55 Ninth day before the ides
56 Small, temporary shelter
57 Identical: pref.
58 Hoffman of "All the President's Men"
60 Cool or groovy
61 Tax letters
62 Miserable dwellings
63 Fireplace remnants
64 Items of men's jewelry
66 Challenger
67 Spanish rivers
68 Talking idly
69 __ maneuver
72 Slangy negative
73 Scottish aldermen
74 "Philadelphia" director
75 Sis' sib
76 Without any family ties
77 Cordon __ (master chef)
78 Slope apparatus
79 Ballpark dream
82 Racetrack dream
85 Appoint
86 Suffix for approximations
87 French games
88 Sanitize
89 __ Coast (French Antarctica)
91 Policeman's route
92 Louis Prima's singer Smith
93 Ballpark dream
96 Court dream
100 Awards honcho
101 Spanish priest
102 Ex-Giant Mel
103 Expels
104 Orchestra section
105 That is (to say): Lat.
106 Two before U
107 Falling ice

DOWN

1 Former draft org.
2 City near Lourdes
3 Org. of Sampras
4 Frankfurters
5 Orange oil
6 Eight-ball settings
7 Inventor Elias
8 $
9 Adopted
10 McBeal and others
11 Roy Rogers at birth
12 "__ O' Shanter"
13 Psychic's ability
14 Source for the family pet
15 "The Thomas Crown Affair" composer
16 Philippines port
17 Scorpion's segment
18 Staid
24 United group
26 Accuse (a public official)
28 Go bad, as milk
30 __ beans
31 Ammonia derivative
32 Kennel dream
33 Clinches
34 Upholstery fabrics
35 Most sick
38 Mineo and Maglie
39 Horse leaders
40 Squid's defense
43 Allowing to
45 The end
46 Middle East gulf
47 Watch abbr.
48 Culinary dream
49 Muslim weight
50 Cookie man
52 Pigeon shelters
53 Kennel collection
54 Chairman's mallet
56 Sanctimony
57 Crooner Mel
58 Euphemistic oath
59 VOA group
60 Miami racetrack
62 Actor Corey
64 Warbling sounds
65 Those elected
66 Soothing substances
68 Violas
69 Villainous Uriah
70 Birds' crops
71 Mezzo-soprano Marilyn
73 Open an auction
74 559 in old Rome
76 Tolled solemnly
77 Very dry, as champagne
78 Waitress' load
79 Beaver or dog, at times
80 Detection antenna housing
81 Set an arbitrary punishment
82 Silver server
83 Zeno of __
84 Stringed instruments
87 Mocks
90 Mid-month
91 Wait
92 Models in parts
94 Cure starter?
95 Far out!
96 Opponent
97 Full of: suff.
98 Shoshone tribesman
99 Queue after Q

by Sheryl Scott

ACROSS

1 Rental agreement
6 Be identical
14 Seasoned
20 Cancel
21 Matchless?
22 Flammable solvent
23 Wood-burning cookers
25 Holdups
26 "Xanadu" grp.
27 Crumbly mineral residues
28 Tent stake
30 Assessed
31 1961 Antonioni film
33 Diverse assemblage
36 Dander
37 Weakness of humanity
41 "Kidnapped" author's initials
42 Periphery
43 Typewriter roller
46 Pull
47 Schedule figs.
48 Of the ear
49 Prevalent
50 Energy form
52 Actor Montand
53 Nabokov novel
54 Large antelope
56 Indoor TV antenna
59 Peak in Greece
60 Camera abbr.
61 Greek contest
63 Provides the crew for
64 Leave at the altar
66 In a shabby way
68 Colorful mounts
70 Automobile displays
73 1970 Paul Newman movie
74 Reagan's secretary of state
75 Skunk River's state
76 Demure: colloq.
77 When the French fry?
79 Countermarch
83 Chalkboard
85 Shed
86 18th-century Scottish philosopher
87 Basketry willow
89 Bruins' sch.
90 Resembling: suff.
91 Diner food
92 Gander's mate
94 Graphic artist M.C. __
96 Tenth mo.
97 Economic stat.
98 Look like a tourist?
100 Greek letter
101 Praise too highly
103 Nodding approval
107 Madame de __
109 Herndon and Cobb
110 Dodger
113 Letters from the morgue
114 Intensely hot
116 Bedroom piece

120 Deep-seated mutual hatred
121 Relaxation treatment
122 Rays
123 Views again
124 Evaluator
125 Spacek of "Carrie"

DOWN

1 Jacket flap
2 "__ Gay"
3 Writer Chekhov
4 Hero, for short
5 One voted in
6 Waste glass gathered for remelting
7 Cameo gem
8 __ dixit
9 Cole and Hentoff
10 AFL-__
11 Sportscaster Cross
12 Profoundly
13 Ford lemon
14 Keep it quiet!
15 Noblewoman
16 Corn lily
17 Glutton's pride
18 Intestinal inflammation
19 Othello's love
24 Moves from dusk to dark
29 Elasticized band
32 Frequently
33 Actor Gulager
34 Morsel for Dobbin
35 Boxer's Achilles' heel
38 Briny deep
39 Loose fat
40 Rooster's pride
43 News media
44 French textile center
45 1932 Gary Cooper film
47 Tanguay and Gabor
51 Helen of __
52 Cravings
53 Survey
55 Speaker's platform
57 Public persona
58 Summer color
62 Hearty, but insincere, greeting
65 Gershwin and Levin
67 Fine, dry particles
68 "Hurlyburly" playwright
69 OPEC product
70 Clean coal
71 Book datum
72 Sling mud
74 Buzzes

75 Slicker in winter
77 Auth. of "A Room With a View"
78 Type of phone
80 Production
81 Ninnyhammer
82 African fox
84 Fortuitous
88 Real stinker
91 Middle word of a French motto
92 Remove innards
93 Eng. honor
95 Egyptian beetles
98 Skin eruptions
99 Silent assenter
102 Spandex brand
104 Notions
105 Typical patterns
106 Boastful
108 View from Cleveland
110 Customary extras, briefly
111 French you
112 '60s hairstyle
115 Abnormal: pref.
117 Two before U
118 Sault __ Marie, MI
119 Chinese dynasty

by Robert H. Wolfe

ACROSS

1 Make a new part
7 Foreigner
12 Guitarist's gadget
16 88D forerunner
19 Expiator
20 Big spoon
21 Verbal
22 Highland negative
23 Make money trading bicycles?
25 Folk wisdom
26 Refrain syllable
27 Wash. neighbor
28 Seoul resident
29 Stance
30 Melville's captain
31 Seethe
32 __ go bragh!
33 Rational
34 Lake __ Vista, FL
35 Rental units: abbr.
36 __ Quentin
37 Machine with a movable boom
39 Turkish titles
40 Carnival city
41 Advanced deg.
42 Like a lazy man's bicycle?
44 Mil. training course
45 Spanish district
47 Thaws
48 Contaminate
50 Feature of an obsessive mind
52 Colorful houseplants
55 Thicket
58 Corridor
59 Theatrical backdrop
61 Garr of "Tootsie"
62 James and Tommie
63 Fencing tool
64 Ancient Chinese money
65 Use boiling water
66 Queen of Sparta
67 Live wires
68 Back of a major?
69 Spouses
70 Plumage
72 A.k.a. Bull Run
74 Sierra __
75 Swabby
77 Adjust in advance
81 Calendar-watch abbr.
83 Training on a bicycle?
85 Wee one
86 Beer choice
87 Armistices
89 Disunite a fly?
90 Thumbs up
91 Let it stand!
92 Desert stopover
93 Therefore
94 Ice mass
95 Abode of buzzers
96 Workplace watchdog org.

97 Hilo garlands
98 Wet smacks
100 __ we there yet?
101 Harper or Spike
102 Golf scores
103 Puffing and puffing on a bicycle?
106 Sale-tag abbr.
107 Send forth
108 "__ Longstocking"
109 Zoroastrian texts
110 Curvy letter
111 Links pegs
112 Build up
113 Oliver and Jay

DOWN

1 Uncooked
2 Present-day Abyssinia
3 Publishing house staffer
4 Ryan and Shaquille
5 Tillis or Torme
6 Footwear on a bicycle?
7 Armstrong, __ and Collins
8 Burdened
9 Notion
10 Distinctive flair
11 "__ Blu Dipinto Di Blu (Volare)"

12 Commissioned rank
13 Came up
14 Prune
15 Catalonian cheer
16 Being grilled on a bicycle?
17 New York resort lake
18 Marine catch
24 Defense grp.
29 Trousers
30 Group of GIs
31 One end of a fishhook
33 Ump's call
34 Count of jazz
37 Gum ingredients
38 Moranis or Springfield
39 One of David's songs
41 Evergreens
42 Envelope closer
43 French stars
46 Optimistic
47 Window dressing
49 Crackpot
51 Math proposition
52 Iraklion resident
53 Perry's creator
54 Caesar and Vicious
55 Young whale
56 Pointed arch
57 Short pants on a bicycle?

59 Get ticked
60 Snooze
65 Sting
67 Taxonomic group
71 Aspirations
72 Christmas trio
73 Mouthpiece on a bicycle?
75 Carries a tune
76 Automaker Ferrari
78 One who writes wryly
79 Last-minute hour?
80 Henri's head
81 Candidate for cement boots
82 Pencil ends
84 Strict grammarians
85 Babe
88 Spook agcy.
90 Singer Morissette
91 Mover's partner
93 Strange
94 Coin tosses
97 Weak, as an excuse
98 Wedge-shaped piece of wood
99 Dad
102 Preferred one
103 Figs. expert
104 Egg: pref.
105 Dodge fuel

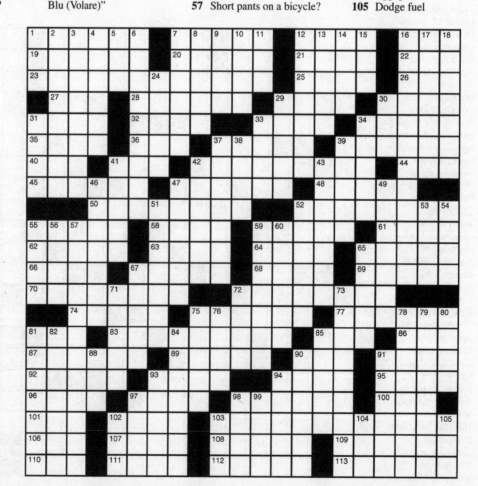

by Willy A. Wiseman

ACROSS

1 Trace
8 Cardinal flowers
16 Ionian Sea gulf
20 __ Culture Society
21 Angel Gabriel's salutation
22 Be inclined?
23 Play about a pleasant grove?
25 Chow __
26 Russian chess master
27 Namesakes of a Russian saint
28 Sun. homily
29 University in Philadelphia
31 $ from a bank
32 Journalist Jacob
33 Actor Marvin
34 Lug
35 Gain a lap?
36 Roulette bet in Monte Carlo
38 Pollux's twin
40 Medico
41 Walker or Black
43 Joys
45 Novel about a toy farm?
48 Piccadilly pea soup
50 Wapiti
51 Rent-sign abbr.
52 Original
53 Of a parent-child Freudian relationship
57 The king of France
59 Place
60 Signal
63 Baroque English palace
65 Boredom
67 Seek prey
68 Roald Dahl's fish story?
73 Slaughter in Cooperstown
74 Imperial Russian Ballet, today
75 Like clothing
76 6-pointers
77 Part of TGIF
79 Full of: suff.
82 More meager
83 6 on the phone
84 Once existed
85 W. Hemisphere grp.
87 Greenstreet, casually
88 Play about a Cote d'Azur house?
94 Chesterfields
98 Portuguese enclave in China
99 Canad. province
100 Pull the plug
102 Stronghold
103 Mandela's org.
104 Until
106 Psychedelic drug
107 Chilean tennis star
109 Pt. of speech
110 Defeat decisively
112 Group of GIs
113 "__ la vista, baby!"
114 Yucatan uncle
115 Soft drink
116 Book about degrees of anger?
120 Grade sch.
121 Fixed
122 Agent causing genetic change
123 Breathing: abbr.
124 So it would seem
125 Runaway lovers

DOWN

1 Evaluating thoroughly
2 Alternative fuel
3 Breed of sheep dog
4 Muscle spasm
5 God's blood
6 Of Scottish Highlanders
7 Mournful
8 Sets down
9 Egg: pref.
10 Amok
11 Host
12 Actor Bert
13 One Gershwin
14 Spacecraft antechamber
15 Assassinated Egyptian leader
16 __ mater
17 Tries to land a sucker
18 Shadowing
19 Actress Bening
24 Fight, in Dogpatch
30 Clandestine
33 Empirical philosopher
34 Rocky crags
37 Purifies
39 Chime
40 Part of A.D.
42 Jurisprudence
44 Former frosh
46 Inaccurate
47 Wildebeest
49 Earth goddess
53 __ d'art
54 Large antelope
55 Showroom models
56 Connections
58 "Superman" star Christopher
59 Conifers
60 Restrains
61 I give up!
62 Former anesthetic
64 1501
66 Walter Reuther's org.
67 Knew about
69 AWOL student
70 "The Planets" composer
71 Spigots
72 Addresses a god
77 Endow with a spirit
78 As well
80 Extremely
81 Soviet news agcy.
83 POW possibly
84 Drunkard
86 Hindu maxims
88 Hoarder
89 Sewer entrance
90 Gives one's consent
91 Cut a V into
92 Hungarian horsemen
93 Foul
95 Film clips
96 Judge
97 __ wort
101 Unspecified large amount
105 "Gloria __"
106 "Foreign Affairs" author
108 Handled
111 End-table item
112 Lab medium
113 Actress Lamarr
117 Pollution patrol grp.
118 Narcs' grp.
119 Knock sharply

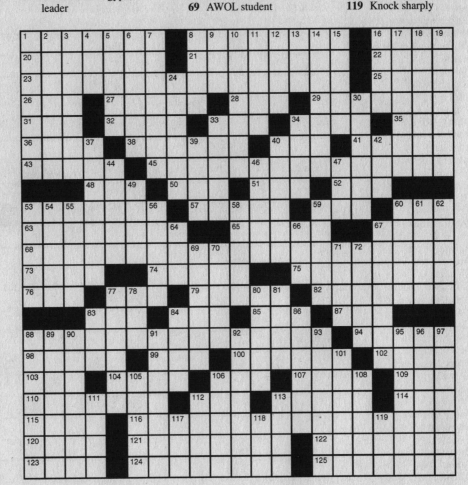

by Stanley B. Whitten

ACROSS

1 Cicatrix
5 Camera setting
10 Sportscaster Rashad
15 Hairdo
19 Writer Wiesel
20 Arrive at
21 Because of
22 Mahler's "Das Lied von der __"
23 Animal from Texas?
25 Animal from Georgia?
27 Chief constituent of wood
28 Building additions
30 Brazilian dance
31 90 degrees from vert.
32 Well-read
34 Hawaiian island
36 Disgust
38 Vegas competition
39 WWII landing craft
41 Donny or Marie
43 Part of VMI
44 Part of NOW
47 "My Friend __"
48 Luger, e.g.
50 Interjections of delight
53 Animal from Ohio?
57 Atlas page
60 Continental hours: abbr.
61 Ribbed cloth
62 "Foucault's Pendulum" writer
63 Tolerate
65 Roman salad?
67 Low dam
70 Boarded a jet
72 The __ Office
73 Animal from New York?
77 Nine: pref.
78 Almost a desert
80 Frog cousin
81 Unit of gene activity
83 Pollex
84 Eccentric wheel
86 Mexican shawl
89 Op. __ (footnote abbr.)
90 Saturate
91 Animal from Washington?
95 TV spots
96 Small, low island
97 Small, mountain lake
98 One of Moses' scouts
100 Goad
103 Overly refined
106 Jewel
107 Poetic meadows
111 Glottal
113 Facility
115 Attack
118 Santa __ winds
119 Mountain nymph
121 Skin: pref.
123 Brawniness
124 Animal from Washington?
127 Animal from Florida?
129 Arabian prince

130 Tuscany city
131 Assumed name
132 Perry's creator
133 NaCl
134 Grasslike plant
135 Head of costume design
136 Poor grades

DOWN

1 Vendor
2 Bloom of filmdom
3 BB shooter
4 Bequeath again
5 Forward section
6 D.C. VIP
7 Seize
8 Spotted wildcat
9 Animal divisions
10 Vladimir Nabokov novel
11 Crude shelters
12 Very dark: pref.
13 Cossack chief
14 First tennis Grand Slam champion
15 Govt. financial grp.
16 "Little __ Annie"
17 Fools
18 Weasel's cousin
24 502 to Cato

26 Sch. helpers
29 De-fleeced?
33 1985 John Malkovich film
35 West Point sch.
37 German article
40 Civil rights org.
42 Buddy Down Under
45 Eight: pref.
46 Looking glass
47 Purpose
49 River to the Caspian Sea
50 Makes overtures
51 Bum's rush
52 Get ticked
54 Corn-Belt state
55 "New Jack City" co-star
56 No longer here
57 Spanish island
58 Lymphoid tissue
59 Formalists
64 Scourge
66 Willowy
68 O.J. trial judge
69 Purpose
71 Move forward
74 Parasites on people
75 Dutch cheese covered with red wax
76 Arabian port

79 "Dancing Queen" singers
82 Pierre's pop
85 Deal (out)
87 Speed contest
88 Long-tailed lizard
92 Darnel
93 Merit
94 Tire feature
96 Bellow
99 Exploded
100 Candidate lists
101 Kind of hat
102 RNA constituent
104 Edmund Spenser's "The __ Queene"
105 Burned
106 Ford or McRaney
108 Game played with 32 cards
109 One of a pair of genes
110 Cubic meters
112 __ de plume
114 Bristles
116 Big hit
117 Daystar
120 Bell sound
122 1500 more than 24D
125 Food scrap
126 Menlo Park initials
128 Tap gently

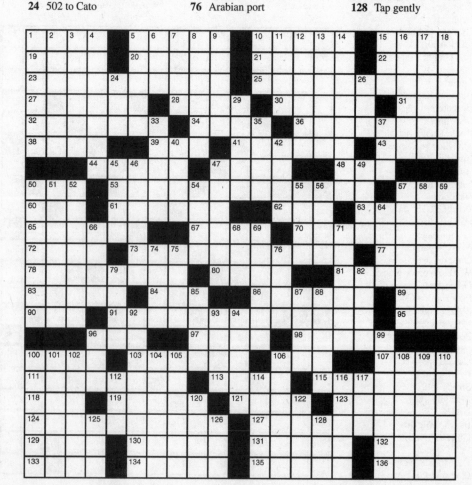

LACK OF OXYGEN?

by Randall J. Hartman

ACROSS

1 Pine Tree State
6 Fair to partly cloudy, e.g.
14 Banjul location
20 Up and about
21 Worthy of penance
22 Water, water everywhere
23 Unambiguous roll of the dice?
25 Old-time roofing material
26 Controversial doctrine
27 Spanker or spinnaker
28 Young wolf
29 "Runaway" singer Shannon
30 Biblical ark-itect
33 That guy's
34 "The Island of the Day Before" author
37 Tablelands
40 Calico?
45 "For Your Eyes __"
46 "Doctor Zhivago" heroine
47 Pebble Beach shout
48 Roman historian Cornelius
49 Tiger's org.
50 Use scissors incorrectly
52 Disunite
55 Jai __
56 Esteemed beer?
59 Sordino
60 Rose or Fountain
61 Whole
62 Fall event?
64 Support personnel
66 Having a legally valid will
68 Violent outburst
70 Tipped off
74 Making knots
76 Greek portico
77 Road company
78 Father
81 Lamentation
83 Senator doing laps?
86 Alexander or Nicholas, e.g.
87 Organic compound
89 Fumes
90 Pollution patrol grp.
91 Wood for bridge pilings
93 Quiz
95 Pierre's girlfriend
96 Narrow valley
97 Shakespeare teaching Shakespeare?
101 Sticky and viscous
102 Dallas sch.
103 Meadow bellow
104 Adam's youngest son
105 On behalf of
106 Draws closer
108 Indy winner Luyendyk
111 City near Leipzig
115 In possession of
117 Dads with kids in college?
121 Puncture
122 Reclusive
123 Pointers
124 Thoroughfare
125 Craven
126 Come in!

DOWN

1 SAT test section
2 1975 Wimbledon champ
3 Roman way
4 Climatic comment
5 Obliterates
6 Blubber
7 Singer Redding
8 Ponselle or Parks
9 Brendan Fraser movie, "__ Man"
10 Cancel
11 Jurist Fortas
12 P. Hearst's kidnappers
13 Dutch painter Gerard __ Borch
14 Medieval
15 Truman's secretary of state
16 Ground grain
17 Louisville Slugger employees?
18 Corp. abbr.
19 Fire residue
24 Part of a wd.
28 With what motive?
31 Book after Joel
32 Seraglio
35 Zagreb resident
36 Actor Davis
37 Tot
38 Locomotive
39 Biases
40 Payment option
41 Sacramento Kings' arena
42 Ridicules
43 Birthmark
44 Playground game
46 Period of existence
50 Marine eel
51 Wrongful acts
53 Kett of the comics
54 Analytical measure
57 Giggled
58 Mob melees
63 Ship fronts
65 Simple plants
67 Adam's grandson
69 Rum drink
71 Elvis' Mississippi hometown
72 Epic poetry
73 Dana of "China Beach"
75 Like most fences
78 Piercing pains
79 Imam's religion
80 Groovy sprinter?
82 Link
84 Short note
85 Principal
88 Speed event
92 Love affair
94 Bullfighter
96 The Riddler on "Batman"
98 Fail to remember
99 Dawn goddess
100 Three times
101 "Faust" poet
105 Drug-testing grp.
107 Cork's country
109 Amazon dolphin
110 First governor of Alaska
112 E-mailed
113 Comic Johnson
114 Cold War letters
115 Wife of Saturn
116 Intelligence
117 Hair of the dog
118 Nice one?
119 Presidential advisory grp.
120 Plane ride: abbr.

WHAT'S MY LINE?

by Frances Burton

ACROSS

1 Bruins' sch.
5 Miami-__ county
9 Lots of land
14 John Jacob or Mary
19 Lion sound
20 Writer/director Kazan
21 Dotty
22 Motilal or Jawaharlal
23 Wine steward
25 Doc in the army
26 Clutches
27 Obvious
28 Poison specialist
30 Henri's head
31 Pine sap product
32 Peel
33 Act alluring
36 Slacks
37 Flails
41 On the qui vive
42 Spelunking location
43 Fine-tune
45 Gardner of "The Barefoot Contessa"
46 Calcium oxide
47 Call a chicken?
48 Fled
49 Choir attire
51 "Much __ About Nothing"
52 Coin collector
56 Utopias
57 Humiliates
59 Join together
60 Flashy or jaunty
61 Lothario's cousin?
62 Beds for babies
63 Grassy patch
64 Black suit
66 Chalkboard
67 Gliding step
70 Come to a point
71 Stamp collector
73 Luckman or Caesar
74 Fundamental values of a culture
75 Charged atom
76 French wines
77 Rug with a thick, rough pile
78 Lunched
79 Velocity
81 Aaron or Greenberg
82 Setting
83 Smokey Robinson and the __
86 Emissary
88 Stock units
89 Blockhead
90 Garbles
91 Carson's predecessor
92 Mapmaker
96 Lucky clover type
100 Bread spreads
101 Walt Disney's middle name
102 Member of a hotel staff
103 Lustrous finish for velvet
104 Keep from happening
105 Try to outrun
106 Stadium level
107 Web locations
108 Marina skyline elements
109 Cheers for toreadors
110 One twixt 12 and 20

DOWN

1 Bear constellation
2 Henhouse
3 Light source
4 Rotating part of a dynamo
5 Take out
6 Skirt style
7 Menu plan
8 Auditory organ
9 Nearly
10 Live in peace with others
11 "The Thinker" sculptor
12 Historic tale
13 Servile, self-seeking person
14 Goat with long, silky hair
15 Worsted twilled fabrics
16 Siamese
17 Globes
18 Oxidation
24 Build
28 Sound property
29 Merry spree
31 Great reviews
33 Caesar or Waldorf, e.g.
34 Slur over
35 Human population specialist
36 Helen of Troy's abductor
37 Tantalize
38 Dealer in men's clothing and accessories
39 Decathlon tenth
40 Impudent
42 Walk-on appearance
44 Court orders
47 Weekend cowboys
49 Feast
50 Smells
52 Dubbers
53 Wall painting
54 Singer Baker
55 Country occupied by China
58 Calgary Stampede, e.g.
60 Cheese choice
62 Singer Patsy
63 Move furtively
64 Energy form
65 Singer Smith
66 Footlong containers
67 Flash of light
68 Sawyer or Lane
69 Outer limits
71 Vain hope
72 Cowgirl Dale
77 Rhett's love
79 Trudge along
80 Old-time country singer Vernon
81 Bonn mister
82 Puppeteer Lewis
84 Moss Hart's autobiography
85 Shuts
87 Invitees
88 Tasty toppings
90 Infiltrators
91 __ de Leon
92 Fuzz
93 Jai __
94 Tenant's expense
95 Thomas __ Edison
96 Equine kid
97 One of HOMES
98 1958 Pulitzer novelist
99 Simple plant
102 __-Magnon

ACROSS

1 Touched down
5 Drug cops
10 Hook's right-hand man
14 Pamphlet
19 Satellite
20 George or T.S.
21 Crow's-nest site
22 Camera-ready proof
23 Improperly situated
25 Properly situated
27 Monument figure
28 Missing people
30 Greeley or Mann
31 Medieval slave
33 Lot of land
34 Flavored
36 Possesses
39 Kitchen ending?
41 Footstool
43 Owing
46 Not owing
52 Actress Ione
53 Inner embryonic layer
57 Hang glider
58 Outcropping
60 Giant cactus
63 Accra location
64 Woody vine
68 __ oblige (honorable generosity)
70 Muscle spasm
71 Incompatible
75 Compatible
77 Definite article
78 Personification of death
82 So much, in music
83 Songwriter Greenwich
85 Party planner
87 Desert plant
91 Brings up
93 Superlatively shabby
97 Bangkok native
98 Orderly
101 Disorderly
103 Studies again
107 Crowd sound
108 Sch. org.
109 Be inactive
114 Cad's come-on
116 Black cuckoos
118 Multitude
119 After-market purchases
121 Wipe from memory
125 Noticeable
128 Not noticeable
130 Rods' partners
131 Lascivious gander
132 Dismal, in poetry
133 Primary
134 Door
135 Rx items
136 Brawl
137 Writer Ferber

DOWN

1 Andy's pal
2 Cad
3 Bit
4 Govt. bond
5 Remedy for grief in the "Odyssey"
6 Rival of Tide
7 Coin of Iran
8 Powdered chocolate
9 Foul odor
10 Looks for cameras
11 Numerous
12 Psychic's ability
13 Ike's arena
14 Small groups
15 Grade starter?
16 Of bees
17 "Operator" singer
18 Added shading
24 Red signal flare
26 Plumed military hats
29 Notable time
32 School near Windsor
34 Five centimes, once
35 Letters for shock treatment
36 Sibilant sound
37 Cross with a loop at the top
38 Eyelid infection
40 Olden times, in olden times
42 Mogadishu man
44 Telephone call?
45 Dawn goddess
47 John of Creedence Clearwater Revival
48 Morse symbol
49 Muse of lyric poetry
50 Bight of __
51 Austin of tennis
54 Tribe of Israel
55 Pride in oneself
56 Massage
59 Rachmaninoff's "__ Songs"
61 Tenant's payment
62 Workplace safety grp.
65 Hardwood tree
66 Central Park S. landmark
67 "Thinking Out Loud" author Quindlen
69 __ Luis Obispo, CA
71 Cheri of "SNL"
72 Polish cavalryman
73 Purposeful
74 Cows and bulls
76 Orifice
79 Pekoe or Assam
80 Scrap of food
81 Sun's fall
84 Late starter?
86 __ Grande
88 Fellow
89 Platitudinous talk
90 Radames' beloved
92 Hair piece?
94 Continental abbr.
95 Ancient Greek portico
96 Pacer's path
99 Veteran's abbr.
100 Mineral vein
102 Fast food order
104 Birch relatives
105 Performed
106 Netlike caps
109 Pie piece
110 Mortise insert
111 Representative
112 Donor
113 Cacophonous
115 Habituate: var.
117 Slug trail
119 Served perfectly
120 Leave text as is!
122 Oh my gosh!
123 Like a wafer
124 Sicilian spouter
126 Slippery __
127 Born
129 Morsel in a feedbag

by Alan P. Olschwang

ACROSS

1 Pauper's plea
5 Cloth connections
10 Concluding passage
14 Spacek of "Coal Miner's Daughter"
19 Wyle or Webster
20 Endurance test
21 Simians
22 Nonsense
23 Start of Dick Vermeil quote
26 Viscounts' superiors
27 Arose
28 REM singer
29 Daughter of Tantalus
31 Periphery
32 Annan of the United Nations
34 Stellar blasts
36 Strasbourg's region
38 Vegas opening?
41 Trudge
43 Part 2 of quote
46 Scrapes (by)
48 Puerile
50 Harriet __ Stowe
51 Sword or missile
53 Doughnut-shaped
55 Music rights grp.
59 Part 3 of quote
61 Stock sellers group: abbr.
63 __ de la Plata
64 Reindeer rack
65 Calendar abbr.
67 Wedding party members
69 Aching
71 Or else, in music
73 Fast-moving snake
76 River under the Brooklyn Bridge
77 French politician Jacques
79 Lorne Michaels' show: abbr.
81 Rife
83 __ Arbor, MI
84 Theatrical sketch
87 Part 4 of quote
91 Forum wear
93 Short negligee
95 Doing the same old same old
96 Santee Sioux
98 Hebrew months
100 Brooding place
101 Part 5 of quote
105 Abound
107 Tree juice
108 Esprit de corps
109 "Divine Comedy" poet
111 June 6, 1944
113 Gold in Guadalajara
114 Stiller's partner
117 Like nostalgic fashions
119 Female vampire
123 French writer Zola
125 End of quote

128 Half a Black Forest spa
129 Fencer's foil
130 Eurasian wheat
131 Sea eagle
132 Plus feature
133 "The Day of the Locust" author Nathanael
134 Oxeye __
135 Insolent rejoinder

DOWN

1 Black cuckoos
2 Urban studio
3 BLT addition
4 Quivered
5 Meas. base
6 Wearing away
7 __ it the truth?
8 Morning in Metz
9 Turtlenecks and ponchos
10 Cleveland pro
11 Vigilant
12 Lucy's love
13 Concerning
14 Anadromous trout
15 One Gershwin
16 Contemptuous address, once
17 Dovetail
18 Sycophants

24 Japanese veggies
25 Actress Campbell
30 "Mass in B Minor" composer
33 Old-time firearm
35 Referee
37 Watery passages: abbr.
38 Licentious
39 Tropical evergreen
40 Like mariners
42 Crocs' cousins
44 Malicious
45 Bruins sch.
47 Lutheran theologian
49 Cognition
52 Type of bran
54 Switch positions
56 Living things
57 Affectations
58 Work station
60 __ Plaines, IL
62 Startled
66 To some extent
68 Tim of tennis
69 Ella's forte
70 Cry of distress
72 Snakebird
74 __ emptor
75 Scottish uncle

78 Attack
80 Man San and Ed
82 Writer Rand
85 PC symbol
86 Actor Jacques
88 Caroused
89 Philosopher Nicholas de __
90 Letters before www
92 Ethiopian town
94 Authoritative commands
97 Patella's place
99 Certain chemical reactions
101 Single-celled organism
102 Shearer and Zimmer
103 "Star Wars" characters
104 Concerning
106 Bamako's land
110 Earlier word forms
112 "The Dresser" director Peter
115 All over again
116 Lariat
118 Birthplace of Nostradamus, Saint __
120 Actress Sorvino
121 Hostelries
122 Drawn-out periods
124 Trevino of golf
126 Fido's doc
127 Weep

MISSTATED SONGS

by Willy A. Wiseman

ACROSS

1 Make holes
4 That guy's
7 Fast, for example
14 Peruvian grazer
19 Subterfuge
21 Gets by with less
22 Felt ill
23 Misstated Ray Charles hit?
26 Jason's galley
27 Golf standard
28 Seattle summer hrs.
29 13th-century Florentine painter
30 Gothic rib
33 Calf-length skirt
35 Zilch
36 Neighbor of Syr.
37 Misstated Billy Joel hit?
42 Precursor of the CIA
43 Room divider
44 World Series semis
45 List element
49 Plant pets
50 Balin or Claire
51 __ del Fuego
53 Nancy of "The Facts of Life"
56 Misstated Mountain hit?
60 Misstated R. Dean Taylor hit?
63 Birds' display areas
64 Twice DLXXV
65 Barbecue fare
66 Acorns, later on
67 Stimulus
69 Memorization method
70 Mass gown
71 Does wrong
73 Misstated Beach Boys hit?
76 Misstated Neil Diamond hit?
80 Computer services corp.
81 Lacked
82 "Rosemary's Baby" author Levin
83 Utah lilies
85 Old Gaelic
86 Ferrer of "Cyrano de Bergerac"
88 Respect
90 Letters on candies?
93 Misstated Lynyrd Skynyrd hit?
98 Subscription form: abbr.
101 Data, casually
102 Hungarian river
103 Sleeping sickness carrier
104 Before
106 Ocean off NC
108 Always, to Shelley
110 Too much in France
111 Misstated Mitch Miller hit?
116 Susan Dey TV series
117 One voted in
118 Festive dance party
119 Snaking curves
120 Fermented
121 Letters for psychics
122 "__ Ventura: Pet Detective"

DOWN

1 Anne of "My Favorite Year"
2 Creamy whites
3 British revenuers
4 Royal letters
5 Quadrennially prominent grp.
6 Take a picture
7 Ancient Canaanite
8 Dance in France
9 Never mind
10 Take care of
11 Def. weapon
12 Chapel vow
13 Lower ranks
14 Nonclerics
15 Peru's capital
16 Acceptable excuse
17 Diner handouts
18 Viper
20 "The Perfect __"
24 Egyptian pharaoh
25 Short skirt
31 Empty seat
32 Live oak
34 Blocker or Rather
35 Gridiron division
38 Refrain syllable
39 Sicilian town
40 "The Good Earth" heroine
41 God of France
46 Nervous quivers
47 Ramrod straight
48 Like a hen party
49 Business VIPs
50 Candidate to like?
51 Tongue-clucking sound
52 Smartness meas.
53 Glacial deposit
54 Spine-tingler
55 Mine buckets
56 Make a request
57 Rent-sign abbr.
58 Strike heavily
59 Dynamic opening?
61 Purple seaweed
62 Sov. news agcy.
67 Mexicali Mrs.
68 Confine
69 Journalist Jacob
71 Helm dir.
72 Laver of tennis
73 Tumor: suff.
74 "Cat Scratch Fever" singer
75 Dwarflike creatures
77 __ of March
78 Kind of list
79 Cookie choice
83 Music player
84 Post-dusk
86 1995 Steven Weber movie
87 Ear: pref.
88 Med. printout
89 Hardened
90 Erik of "CHiPs"
91 Of certain subatomic particles
92 Amount of ooze
94 Surviving spouses
95 Enough, old-style
96 Legendary Giant
97 Begin to prevail
98 Philosopher Pierre
99 Ostrich kin
100 Prison quarters
105 Winglike parts
106 On the waves
107 Fict. sleuths
109 Stratagem
112 Bullring cheer
113 Service charge
114 Christian letters
115 Nurse a drink

by Randall J. Hartman

ACROSS

1 WWII ration-book group
4 Javelin's path
7 Inessential facts
13 Wall bracket
19 Racecar safety device
21 Grieve audibly
22 Light beams
23 Clark Kent's Visa?
25 Surpass in cunning
26 Judah's son
27 Hail to Caesar
28 Hook's mate
29 Puckered fabric finish
30 601
31 Cartoon deputy
33 Per person
36 Part of USA
37 Luau dish
38 Makeup comments by Bruce Wayne?
43 Nincompoop
44 Inclined to flow
46 More rational
47 Hot sandwich on rye
49 Star of "The Ruling Class"
51 Use piercing wit?
54 New England milkshake
57 Old sailors
59 Actor Morgan's fan-club motto?
62 Poisonous snake
65 Dry by rubbing
67 Stallone in "First Blood"
68 Tiff
69 #6 on the dial
70 Climbed
73 "Spartacus" screenwriter Trumbo
76 Author Umberto
77 Baja buck?
79 Fathered
81 One of HOMES
82 Stimpy's pal
83 David's monologue gone bad?
88 Gusto
90 Weasel cousin
91 Magellan, for one
93 Wall covering
97 Indians, e.g.
100 Point of contention
102 Vermont's Allen
103 Possess
105 Fire Brokaw?
109 Before, to Burns
110 Okinawa port
112 Festive event
113 Points of pens
114 Peer Gynt's mother
115 Former Spanish dictator
118 Dalmatian feature
121 Scrap of food
122 1987 Best Actress winner
124 Shoe part
125 Blockbuster decision?
128 Intensify color
129 Arctic cover
130 __ down (diluted)
131 Builds
132 Manager
133 Comic Louis
134 Byrnes of "77 Sunset Strip"

DOWN

1 Roughly
2 Remove, as dents
3 "Dog Day Afternoon" star
4 Shortened bk.
5 Chain of inns
6 Scarflike ties
7 RN treatment
8 Cheerleader cries
9 Prayer leader of Islam
10 Dancer Ben
11 Moving along
12 Got a bite
13 Swill
14 Greater omentum
15 Port of Rome
16 Report by Edward R. Murrow?
17 Turning points
18 Chemical compounds
20 Filmmaker Riefenstahl
24 Composer Randy
32 Yiddish thief
34 Horn: Fr.
35 Color property
37 Niner or Buc
38 Rules of an organization
39 __-do-well
40 Fast-food request
41 Foolish talk
42 Spanish river
45 "__ as a Stranger"
48 Dumbo's "wings"
50 Guitarist Clapton
52 Be first
53 Jane Austen novel
55 "Peyton __"
56 John of rock
58 Charley horse, e.g.
60 Ready and willing companion
61 __ Dame
62 More than enough
63 Look of contempt
64 Express mail?
66 Charles Lamb
71 Sea fliers
72 Liability
74 Monet's medium
75 Straighten up
78 Singer Redding
80 Style of Greek architecture
84 Geraint's loyal wife
85 Back part
86 Meal mixture
87 Buffalo
89 Wacko
92 Thick, fleshy, young shoot
94 Carroll cat
95 Bounced around
96 Ace, when not eleven
98 Egg concoction
99 Fat farm
101 Darken
103 Burning
104 Brothers of Hollywood
106 __-Lorraine
107 Inventor of logarithms
108 Off target
111 Playful prank
114 Continuous pain
116 Penny
117 Makes a choice
119 At some prior time
120 Govt. agent
123 Comic Foxx
125 Oil-well device
126 Likely
127 Sault __ Marie

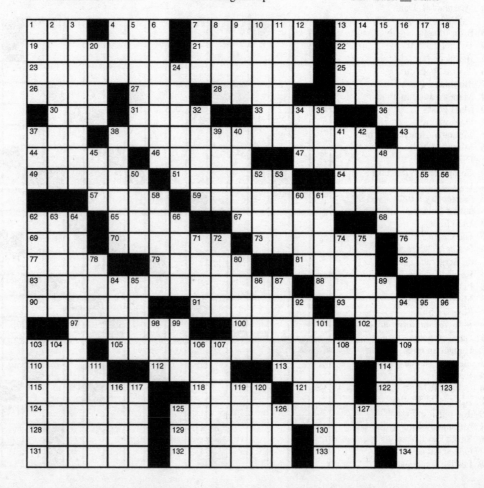

by Edgar Fontaine

ACROSS

1 Broad comedy
6 "The Godfather" subject
11 Leak slowly
15 Riches, formerly?
19 For all to hear
20 Dark shades, in poetry
21 Commiseration
22 Continental dollar
23 Ski-slope devices
24 Travels the Web
25 Sixth Hebrew month
26 Shootout signal
27 Persian poet of "Garden of Roses"
28 Diluted
29 Track-and-field event
31 Bonheur and Parks
33 Logger, at times
35 Posted
36 Entertainer
38 Fourth-year student
39 Kind of ICBM
40 40th president
42 Fed the livestock
46 2000 lbs.
47 One of Bolivia's capitals
48 "O Sole __"
49 Memorizing process
50 Of the intestines
53 Part of TGIF
54 Iditarod competitor
58 Vein pursuit
59 Made of baked clay
61 Rock
62 Manacled
64 Reckless revolver bravado
68 Capital of Turkey
71 Ashcan School painter John
72 Ripens
76 Fifth of MV
77 Baby pacifier
79 Eq. rights movement
81 Maxim
82 Gideon Fell's creator
84 Eterne
85 Assisted
87 Tail wiggle
88 Runway departures
91 Desi Arnaz role
95 Tab's target
96 Call off
97 Bare minimum
98 Northern Ireland
101 Six feet of water
102 Field doc
103 King of the Cowboys
105 Gleeful
107 Spawned
110 Cappelletti or Marchetti
111 Leave out
112 Hindu tunes
113 Tastelessly showy
114 Therefore: Lat.
115 Lake Victoria outlet
116 Makes a long story short?

117 Tolerate
118 See fit
119 Building add-ons
120 Decompose
121 Butterfly with eyespots

DOWN

1 Minnesota __
2 Provencal love song
3 Wile E. Coyote's prey
4 Books dealing with unusual topics
5 Meese and Wynn
6 Flat-top hills
7 Be adjacent to
8 Ancestors
9 Encroach
10 Ancient empire on the Tigris
11 More meager
12 Duck down
13 List-shortening abbr.
14 Pharaoh's tomb
15 1948 Howard Hawks movie
16 Of the ear
17 Meal prayer
18 Scattered (seeds)

28 Electoral districts
30 Unit of length
32 Choice: abbr.
34 Chaney of film
36 Jazz clarinetist Shaw
37 Dough
38 Splinter group
39 Frame of mind
41 Spoils
42 Castro
43 Skyline component
44 To be in Toulon
45 Land title
48 Carte before the course
51 Gillette razor
52 Peasant
54 Wander away
55 Daffy bird?
56 Eight: pref.
57 __-percha
60 Jacob's brother
61 Stuffed shirt
63 Internecine conflict
65 Man and Capri
66 Winglike
67 Burning coal
68 $ in the bank
69 College sports org.

70 Scottish church
73 Boot camp trainee
74 Yikes!
75 Utah lilies
78 Remaining
79 Miraculously
80 Pastoral poem: var.
83 Public lavatory
85 Special praise
86 Supped
89 Butter alternative
90 Kind of conclusion
91 Double-crosser
92 Was intrinsic
93 Massachusetts cape
94 "Open sesame!" man
96 Hindu groupings
98 Exhorted
99 Roanne's river
100 Irish playwright J.M. __
101 Ruffle
102 Sloppy
104 Olympic runner Zatopek
106 Cheerio!
108 Jacuzzi effect
109 Color alterer
113 Heating fuel

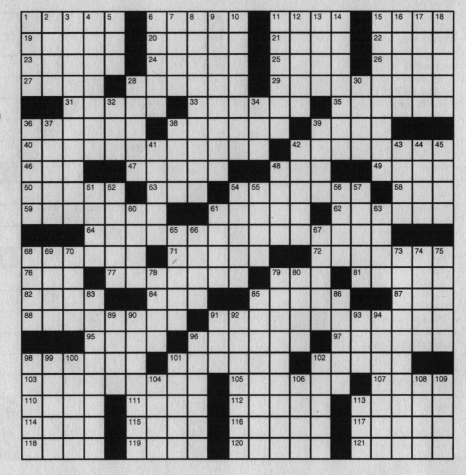

SYSTEM TWOSOMES

by Ed Voile

ACROSS

1 __, Porthos and Aramis
6 Optional
14 Greek letters
20 Colette novel
21 Nourished and cared for
22 Witty reply
23 __ Haute, IN
24 Two elements
26 Tax agcy.
27 "Dracula" author
29 Indigo and anil
30 Sting
31 O.T. book
32 Over distance: pref.
33 End of a racket?
36 Mach-2 breakers, once
38 Colonial cuckoo
39 Two ancient Greek gods
43 Irish toast
45 Eyelid inflammation
46 Pierre's noggin
47 Noted Israeli diplomat
49 '02 British Open winner
50 "Over the Rainbow" composer
52 Of a Judaic mysticism movement
55 Type of pear
59 Disavowed
61 Two cars
63 Senior
64 Positive attitude
65 Hit head-on
66 Dundee denial
67 Dodgers, once
68 Uneven haircuts
69 October 4th saint
72 Zany Imogene
73 Nabokov novel
74 Manipulate
75 Event before a golf tournament
76 Makes airtight
77 Two tennis stars
82 Stretcher on wheels
83 One of the Fords
84 Cardin and Cartier
85 Ran at an easy pace
86 Xenon or neon
88 In due time
89 Israeli carrier
91 Close to closed
94 Beet soup
98 Two Disney characters
101 Gray or Candler
102 Western lawman Wyatt
104 Twice DCCLXXV
105 Twice CCI
106 Lily or launch follower
107 Mark __-Baker
109 Wry face
111 Lucky charm
113 "__ Gotta Be Me"
114 Two gods of the sea
118 Morning in Metz
120 Rock-boring tool
121 Sigourney Weaver film, "__ in the Mist"
122 Excrete
123 Analyzes chemically
124 Triers
125 Standards

DOWN

1 Pretenses
2 At that place
3 Two candy bars
4 Bobby of the NHL
5 Sonora snooze
6 Encourage
7 Take care
8 Nice to be?
9 Nervous system disorder
10 Decade count
11 Levin or Gershwin
12 Sell
13 Mary Baker and Nelson
14 Bridge framework
15 "I Saw __ Again Last Night"
16 Customary extras, briefly
17 Bird with a big beak
18 Thoroughgoing
19 Flummox
25 Disorder
28 Like three-ring circuses
34 "Oedipus" composer Georges
35 Toy-cube inventor
37 Dar es __
40 Eagle quarters
41 Suspended anew
42 Thompson of "Family"
44 Money __ everything!
48 Diarist Anaïs
51 Celtic sea god
53 Helps out
54 Type of portable memory
56 Two Roman gods
57 Deity's spokesperson?
58 Anxious
59 Vulgarize
60 Sidestepped
61 Call for ewe
62 __ Rafael, CA
64 Cut-price
68 987-65-4321 grp.
69 English composer
70 Timid: var.
71 Pas' mates
72 Brunch choice
74 Open ties
75 Bar selection
76 Dine
78 Mind readings?
79 Long or Peeples
80 __ Xiaoping
81 Toy-truck sound effect
82 Actress Hawn
85 Lacking property
87 Tribal healers
90 Ceiling with recessed panels
92 Throwback
93 Rats and squirrels
94 Golf-ball material
95 Basketry willows
96 Open grasslands
97 Disney sci-fi film
99 Without qualification
100 Coal miners
103 Nickname of Carlton Fisk or Ivan Rodriguez
108 Palm thatch
110 Genesis character
112 Stubborn beast
115 Shaft of light
116 Hosp. intake areas
117 Ms. Zadora
119 In the past

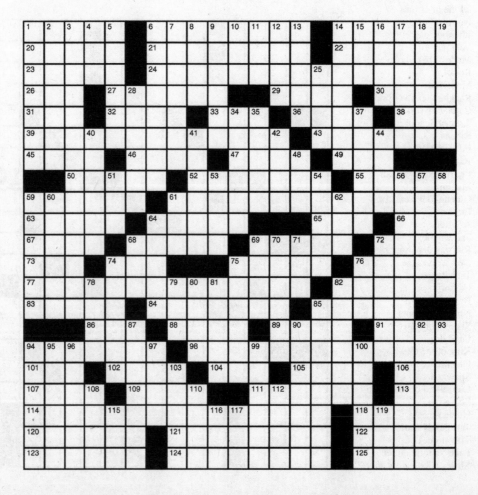

MOVIE TIMES

by Robert H. Wolfe

ACROSS

1 Wooden shoe
6 Peace symbol
10 "The __ on the Floss"
14 Of birth
19 Muezzin's God
20 Yemen's gulf
21 Largest continent
22 Milo of "The Verdict"
23 French river
24 Relating to both eyes
26 Cheri of "SNL"
27 1950 Swanson film
29 The Saint's first name
30 Tack on
31 Hold dear
32 Zzzz letters
33 Younger Saarinen
34 Former Israeli P.M.
35 Towel word
36 No votes
38 Meat cut
41 Hispanics
44 __ de deux
45 Biblical weed
46 __ of Cleves
47 Area under a grate
48 Make sharp
49 Olympic sport
51 "The West Wing" star
52 State of mind
53 Mythical bird
54 Many a high schooler
55 Sweetie
56 Plumbago
59 Neighbor of Iran
61 Guy's honey
64 Swiss canton
65 Dried up
66 Cool one
67 Enterprise crew member
68 After the style of
69 Cribbage item
70 French chalk
71 Post-slalom?
73 Respiratory ailment
74 Make better
76 Cadence count word
78 Fever and shivers
79 See ya __!
81 Provides with cars
84 Farrow and Sara
85 Equestrian school
86 Guns it in neutral
87 Elan
88 Finish
89 Good-for-nothing
90 Hindu title
91 Red root
92 Freudian concepts
93 Story-telling uncle
94 Burpee kernel
96 Black cuckoo
97 Peaceful protest
98 Wildebeest
101 Seasoning perennial

103 1975 Pacino film
107 Bandleader's command
108 Not attached
109 Metrical units
110 Coral isle
111 Philbin's co-host
112 Fermentation sediment
113 Ream component
114 As such
115 "East of __"
116 Formerly, formerly
117 __ bird special

DOWN

1 Spicy Mexican sauce
2 Audibly
3 Hunter's hideaway
4 Boat movers
5 1996 MacLaine film
6 Plays at
7 Detestable
8 Scene of the action
9 Organic compound
10 Grayish violet shades
11 Major religion
12 1999 Robin Williams
   movie, "Jakob the __"
13 Clarified fat
14 Gallows ties
15 Up and about
16 1986 Fonda film
17 Dynamic leader?
18 Put in a reclining position
25 Cherry red
28 Fortuneteller's card
33 Support for a lobster's
   vision
34 Hollow tube
35 Golf equalizer
36 Self-admirer of Greek
   mythology
37 Exist
39 Hostelry
40 Beseech
41 Tie with ropes
42 On land
43 1970 Von Sydow film
44 "The House at
   __ Corner"
45 Gemini count
46 Pub potable
48 Trousseau holder
50 1988 Gibson film
52 Loamy fertilizer
53 Preps for another fight
57 Fulfilled
58 Gentle blow
60 Deceptive maneuver

62 Maintain
63 Bay tree
72 My goodness!
75 Dawn goddess
77 Winter hrs. in NY
80 Social insects
81 "__ Winterbourne"
82 "__ the ramparts..."
83 26th letter
84 Average
85 Dwight's wife
89 Superlatively soggy
91 Common insect
92 Cleveland player
93 Ransacks
95 Pandora's box contents
96 With jaw hanging
97 Scimitar's cousin
98 "__ Pyle, USMC"
99 International prize
100 Oneness
101 Fellow
102 "The __ Report: A
    Nationwide Study of
    Female Sexuality"
103 Truth's partner
104 Roman poet
105 New Haven campus
106 Okinawa port

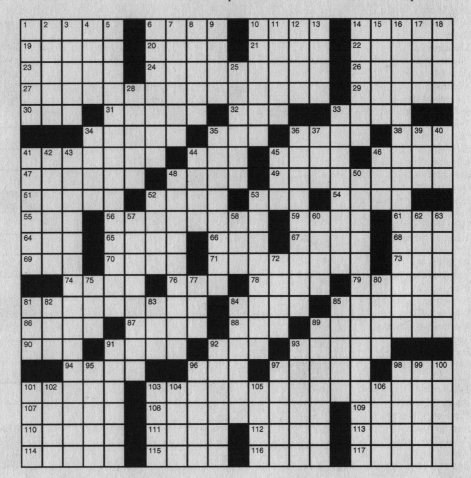

by Alan P. Olschwang

ACROSS

1 Scatterbrained
6 Busboy's tote
10 __ Valley, CA
14 Located
19 Tropical lizard
20 Aperture
21 Oklahoma city
22 __ myrtle
23 Start of David Lloyd George quote
26 Proprietor
27 Fit of pique
28 Sea eagle
29 "The Discreet Charm of the Bourgeoisie" director
30 One cubic decimeter
31 Long sandwich
33 Fundamental
34 Bristol-Myers toothpaste
36 Type of music
40 Cold sufferer, perhaps
42 Greek letters
45 Strike
46 Part 2 of quote
49 Come to terms
51 To laugh in Toulouse
52 Keatsian work
53 Spoil
54 John Glenn's state
55 "Chico and the Man" co-star
57 Marshland
59 Literary anthology
60 Be conspicuous
62 Matured
64 Splash and spot
66 Part 3 of quote
69 Twenty Questions classification
73 Side in a contest
74 Hiroshima bomber
79 Sun-dried brick
80 Double bend
81 Ethical Culture movement's founder
83 "The Joy of Cooking" author Rombauer
84 City on the Truckee
85 Hood's heater
87 Lone Star State sch.
88 Bread spreads
89 Part 4 of quote
95 Lilly or Wallach
96 Monthly payment org.
97 Social circle
98 Fuel transporter
100 Rwanda's Hutu rivals
102 Curiously
104 Jokester Jay
105 Buddhist shrine
107 Right-angle degrees
109 Average grade
110 Apothecary measure
114 Actress Sophia
115 End of quote

118 Puerile
119 District
120 Nastase of tennis
121 Lotion additives
122 Card-game displays
123 Mr. Parker?
124 Transgressions
125 Crystal-lined rock

DOWN

1 June honorees
2 Privy to
3 Singer Tennille
4 Lazy folk
5 Thus far
6 Alcatraz
7 Horse color
8 TV alien
9 __ buena
10 Fishing with nets
11 Persuades
12 Parasitic arachnid
13 Worshipped
14 Peter of "Bosom Buddies"
15 Golfer Hale
16 Equivalent in effect
17 Fencing sword
18 Earl __ Biggers

24 Soviet minister assassinated 12/23/53
25 Man from Sydney
32 Italian noble family
33 George Orwell's surname
35 Le Pew of cartoons
36 Bedlam
37 Scanty
38 Courtyards
39 Add the bubbles
41 School founded in 1440
43 Make one
44 Mexicali mister
47 Heavy shoes
48 Worry
50 Long, long time
55 __ Nostra
56 Fling
57 Prolongation of a chord
58 Flock female
59 Greater omentum
61 Calamitous
63 Estuary
64 "Auld Lang __"
65 Substandard
67 Gal. parts
68 Oracle site
69 Chagall and Connelly
70 Conceptions

71 Artificial
72 Black, in poetry
75 Be sick
76 Frat member
77 Soap plant
78 Mr. Arafat
80 To be in Tours
82 Trap bait
85 Classic Pontiac models
86 Sea anemone
87 Comfortable with
88 Muscat sultanate
90 Gasoline hydrocarbons
91 Middle Eastern river
92 Alley entrance, perhaps
93 Pairs of genes
94 Harden
99 Protuberance
101 Overturn
103 Gradual recovery
105 Willowy
106 Sound quality
108 Japanese ornamented box
109 First felon
111 "Typee" sequel
112 Went fast
113 Latin being
116 Letters for 1051
117 Spree

NOISY NEIGHBORS

by Sheryl Scott

ACROSS

1 '56 and '70 U.S. Open tennis champion
9 Molded ground pork and cornmeal
17 Hasty escape
20 Money-grubbing states
21 Wake of an aircraft
22 Gardner of films
23 1973 Michael Moriarty movie
25 Pen maker
26 Sanctifier
27 Embassy leader: abbr.
28 Last letter of words?
29 Sling mud
31 Neighbor of Leb.
32 Arista
34 Greek letter
36 Venetian bridge
37 Roofer's stone
40 Quick studies?
43 Actor Hugh
46 Cigar dropping
48 Alexandrian astronomer
49 "I Don't Like Mondays" group
52 Linz loc.
53 In case
57 Start-up buttons
58 Prefix with angle or lateral
59 Tic-tac-toe win
60 Otto I's realm
61 Buckwheat dish
62 Dutch commune
63 Holm and McKellen
65 Lukewarm
67 Slow musical passages
68 Bull's-eye location
72 Hams it up
73 Port west of Hong Kong
74 Manure
75 Jeff Lynne's grp.
77 Landlord's income
78 Mata Hari or 007
79 Minor devil
81 Cost to participate
82 Animal gullet
83 First of the pot
84 Health haven
85 Supercharged forge
88 Virginia of "A Town Like Alice"
91 O.J.'s judge
92 Struck with a ball-shaped hammerhead
93 Catch sight of
97 Beginning
99 Noisemaker
100 Booze, butts and bullets bureau
101 The Greatest
102 Pops
105 Irregularly notched
106 Vietnam Memorial artist
108 Jean-__ Godard
110 Shift
114 Sebaceous cyst
115 Rice Krispies trio
119 Writer LeShan
120 Divides into three
121 Uncorrupted
122 Chat-room chuckle letters
123 Approached aggressively
124 Coasts

DOWN

1 Synagogue figure
2 Track shapes
3 More rational
4 Work units
5 Ingenuity
6 Painful throb
7 Ogle
8 Psychedelic drug
9 Layer of impurities
10 Beach breaker
11 E.R. staffers
12 By my lowest estimation
13 A-one workers
14 Fido's feet
15 __ Abner
16 Place of ideal happiness
17 Designers' IDs
18 Fly an aircraft
19 Keystroke mini-programs
24 Managed
30 Neighbor of D.C.
33 Break from a habit
35 Spigots
36 Eurasian deer
37 Actor Alastair
38 Open frameworks
39 Parkas
40 Muddled
41 Saved up
42 Investigator's lead
43 Shawm's offspring
44 Male slaves
45 Pennsylvania college
47 Overflow letters
50 Zephyr
51 Pedicurist's target
54 Crime novelist Loren D. __
55 Oxford fastener
56 Isl. of Australia
60 Royal address letters
61 Fish dish
64 Oriental skiffs
66 Product of bacterial putrefaction of protein: var.
67 Teams' starters
69 Tries
70 Hound sound
71 Botch
72 Stretch of time
76 Was obligated
78 "Pursuit of the Graf __"
80 Hrs. in Seattle
84 Terrier type
85 Prot. sect
86 Cat's-paw
87 Court divider
89 Bell-like keyboard instrument
90 Fine distinctions
93 Loosely twisted worsted yarn
94 "Streets of __"
95 Unmelodic
96 Recently
98 __ Creed
101 Half an anti-aircraft gun
102 __ up (spoke)
103 In unison
104 Clan divisions
106 Non-cleric
107 __ facto
109 Tritons' sch.
111 Mandlikova of tennis
112 Son of Seth
113 1601
116 AEC replacement
117 New GI
118 Fleur-de-__

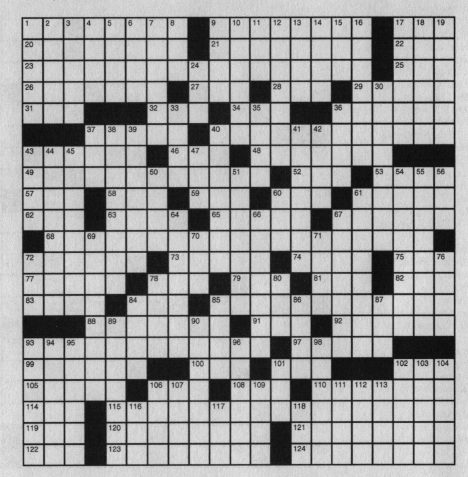

2000 ELECTION OLDIES

by Josiah Breward

ACROSS

1 Music rights grp.
6 Former Turkish titles
12 Whitney and Wallach
16 Roulette bet
19 Italian writer Calvino
20 Range
21 __ Hari
22 Individual
23 Van Morrison song from "Astral Weeks"?
26 Recipe abbr.
27 Swirls
28 __ gin fizz
29 Corn unit
30 Argentine grassland
32 Eisenhower's WWII arena
33 __ Palmas
35 Lubricate
36 Nastase of tennis
38 Schedule figs.
39 Paul Simon song from "Graceland"?
43 Japanese soup
46 Archaic: abbr.
47 They: Fr.
48 Bellowed
49 Develop and hatch
52 Emigrant's subj.
54 Narrow opening
55 With 70A, Joni Mitchell song from "Blue"?
59 Ear-related
63 Tamper-resistant pill
64 Soft metal
65 Taken __ (surprised)
68 4th of July, e.g.
69 FDR follower
70 See 55A
74 112.5 degrees from S
75 Shoshone
76 Slow mover
77 Antagonist
78 Peninsula of Croatia
80 Nothing but
82 Hendrix song from "Are You Experienced?"
86 12 o'clock high
89 California fort
90 Medieval trumpets
91 Dar es __, Tanzania
94 Mayday!
96 Convened
97 Latin being
98 What 23A, 39A, 55A and 82A are?
104 Itemize
105 Jogger's gait
106 Journalist Hentoff
107 Teachers' org.
108 Part of UF
111 African fever
113 Wool producer
114 Pot sweetener
116 Parts of eyes
118 Linguistic suffix
119 Outgoing Jim Stafford song?
123 Agt.
124 Long period of time
125 Most sick
126 Rock
127 Former draft org.
128 Dangle
129 Mocks in fun
130 Optimist

DOWN

1 Evangelist McPherson
2 German city
3 Louisiana tribe
4 Jai follower
5 Shaddock fruit
6 Tent stake
7 Chopping tools
8 Ground-hugging stems
9 Valiant
10 Actress Lansbury
11 Sault __ Marie
12 Preserves to prevent decay
13 Actress Metcalf
14 Part of TGIF
15 Comic Mort
16 Turning muscle
17 Catch
18 Overthrew
24 Jacob's brother
25 "The Threepenny Opera" composer
31 Smooth, in music
34 Glenn or Turow
37 British nobleman
39 "__ Never Walk Alone"
40 Aid a crook
41 Leslie Caron film
42 Old card game
43 Robert of "Cape Fear"
44 Too quickly
45 Symbol of sovereignty
50 Max and Buddy
51 Gomez Addams on TV
52 Kuwait's ruler
53 Summon
54 Graceful bird
56 European nation
57 Sub-Saharan region
58 Pres. Lincoln
60 Vacuum bottle trademark
61 Greek settlers of Asia Minor
62 Sanitize
66 Silk-cotton tree
67 Bandleader Kay
71 "High Hopes" lyricist
72 Hurry along!
73 For both sexes
79 Strives
81 Passes into law
83 Banter teasingly
84 Frosts
85 "Rocket Man" rocker John
87 Feed-bag morsel
88 Bypass
91 Vendors
92 Assumed names
93 Panama Canal engineer Ferdinand de __
94 Overwhelming with flattery
95 Aquatic mammal
96 Courageous spirits
99 Salem's state
100 Make possible
101 Asian metropolis
102 Singer Diamond
103 Loud and flashy
108 Lens setting
109 Sierra __
110 "Lou Grant" star
112 Indian nursemaid
115 Choice word
117 Centerward
120 Affirmative vote
121 Lang. course
122 $ percentages

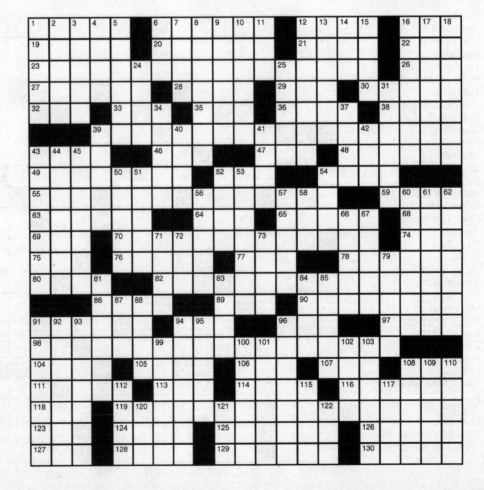

ANIMAL ANTICS

by Frances Burton

ACROSS

1 Pravda's news agcy.
5 Singe
9 Stage whisper
14 Karpov's game
19 Qualified
20 Queen of Olympus
21 German noble
22 Kindled again
23 Big name in faucets
24 Mare's morsels
25 Regretting
26 Very angry
27 Dessert after hot dogs?
29 Inept stargazer?
31 Certify
32 Mother of Clytemnestra
34 One of the Channel Islands
35 Schooling marine fishes
39 Stench
44 Ladder part
48 Combat
49 Roman games official
51 Poe's lady
52 Saintly circles
54 Void's partner?
56 Spelling or Amos
58 Fine porcelain
59 Apportion
60 Eat crow like a monkey?
63 Like Nash's lama
64 Equipped
66 Bancroft or Hathaway
67 Party workers
69 Close attention
71 Henry __ Wallace
74 Abrasive tool
75 "Liederkreis" composer
79 Wet expanses
81 Tramples
85 Circle
86 Bullwinkle's whiskers?
90 Old MacDonald's refrain
91 Sen. Hatch of Utah
93 Planted
94 Banana wrapper?
95 Zigzag turns
96 Prohibited
98 Mother-of-pearl
100 6-pack muscles?
102 Standard Oil brand
103 Jacket arms
105 Not even second best
108 In the center of
110 Latin handle
111 Treat badly
116 Avian versions?
121 Damage religious figurines?
124 First book of the Minor Prophets
125 Declare
126 Memorization by repetition
127 Mindset
128 Colorado ski resort
129 King Arthur's father
130 Unpack
131 Back of kitchen?
132 Looks after
133 Decants
134 Geek
135 Spotted

DOWN

1 Florida city
2 In the vicinity
3 Caught some Zs
4 Feel
5 Mississippi people
6 Make sound
7 Johnson of "Laugh-In"
8 Fight, Dogpatch-style
9 Chafed
10 City on San Francisco Bay
11 Garden bloom
12 Things to avoid
13 Persistence of memory
14 Makes a rustling sound
15 Leander's love
16 Biblical land
17 Web location
18 Tail of a spin?
28 Belief system
30 Preacher Roberts
33 Soon, poetically
36 Water-to-wine city
37 Drummer Gene
38 Work hard
40 How sea hogs act deliberately?
41 "Lorna __"
42 Command
43 Film holders
44 Rug type
45 Fable
46 Jazz great Fitzgerald
47 Broke hedgehog?
50 Idle or Stoltz
53 Fulton's power
55 Al Capp's hyena
57 Muslim garment
61 Minimum
62 Info from schedules
65 Whiskey shot
68 First name in cosmetics
70 Slaughter in Cooperstown
72 Harvesters
73 Carp cousin
75 Messy people
76 Reef-maker
77 Mezzo-soprano Marilyn
78 Showdown time
80 Shave off
82 Muddle
83 Pastry items
84 Mediocre
87 Swing at
88 Sorcerer
89 Isle near Corsica
92 Reno populace
97 Moore of movies
99 Dishwasher's assistants?
101 Allowance
104 Puts off going to bed
106 Polyester fabric
107 Shade tree
109 Me too
112 Locations for earrings
113 Bring together
114 Do figure eights
115 City on the Ruhr
116 Eh?
117 Pastel shade
118 TV letters for games
119 Requirement
120 Honolulu's island
122 Have aspirations
123 Cato's way

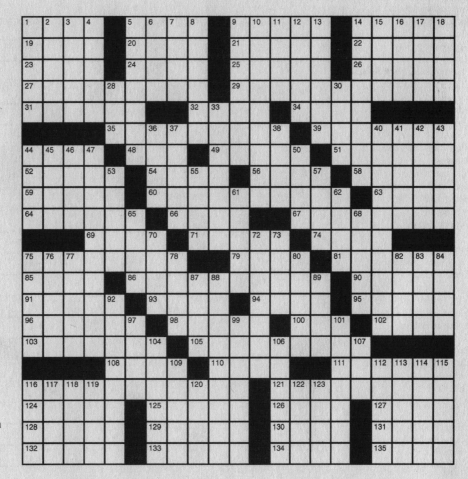

by Ed Voile

ACROSS

1 Ptolemy's treatise
9 Clumps of earth
14 Maria of La Scala
20 Island in the Baltic Sea
21 Satellite of Jupiter
22 Consecrate
23 Move hurriedly on hands and knees
24 1998 Olympic figure skater
26 $ dispenser
27 __ culpa (Sorry 'bout that)
28 Shakespearean contraction
29 Programmer's instruction
30 Foamy brew
31 Man on the moon
35 Adorns with a mantle
38 See ya!
39 Region
40 Resembling: suff.
42 Fly alone
43 Pachyderms
46 Part of DJIA
48 Foch and Simone
51 Killer whale
52 One-base hit
53 Young kangaroos
54 Spanish island
58 Lamenter's words
59 Provencal love song
61 Asian holiday
62 Awn
63 Negligible amount
64 Kin by marriage
66 Fitted replacement footwear
67 "The Memphis Blues" composer
69 Sunflower State capital
73 Loos and Louise
75 Pool sticks
76 More salt than pepper, hairwise
77 National rep.
80 "M*A*S*H" co-star
81 Actor Tamiroff
82 Sss-sayers
83 Soprano Anna
85 Scrap piece
87 Job to do
88 Procession of matadors
89 French fathers
90 Makes seem less serious
95 Smith or Mulgrew
97 Morse unit
98 Spanish healthy
99 Gateway competitor
100 Boot adjuncts
103 "Mambo Mouth" comic
107 Religious woman
108 Greek drink
110 Attention-getting calls
111 Hosp. workers
112 Five centimes, once
113 Four-time Masters champion
117 Gem cutting
119 Color fabric, '60s-style
120 Intended
121 Dark red dye
122 Tiresome speech
123 Namesakes of a wire-haired terrier
124 A sprinkling with holy water

DOWN

1 Actor Armand
2 Of milk
3 French casserole
4 Coach Parseghian
5 Asexual budlike propagule
6 Burning coal
7 Author of "Lilith"
8 Inventor's initials
9 Et __
10 Argentine plain
11 Galley propeller
12 Lugging
13 Pasolini picture
14 Fowl choices
15 Black cuckoo
16 Actor Chaney
17 TV's Denise Huxtable
18 Twistable joint
19 Porkers' pads
25 Resident's suffix
28 Tours summers
32 Racetrack circuit
33 Mlle. from Madrid
34 Nary a soul
36 Former Eagles QB
37 Spicy stew
41 Dana and Ron
44 "The Trip to Bountiful" playwright
45 Pastoral paradise
46 Mr. Magoo's voice
47 Peddle
49 Assent asea
50 Retired jet
52 __ Tzu
54 Besmirch
55 High dudgeon
56 Constantine's birthplace
57 Workplace safety grp.
58 Circle segments
60 Cohort of a ball boy?
63 Appeared smaller by comparison
64 As previously said: Lat.
65 Hot tubs
68 Nevers night
70 Hole in a needle
71 Plunk starter?
72 MGM motto starter
74 Too much French?
77 Unit of elec.
78 Large, extinct bird
79 Foremost behaviorist
81 Vinegary: pref.
82 3-D images
84 Achievement
86 Southwestern beans
87 Diminish gradually
90 Chums
91 Carpentry tool
92 Mocking playfully
93 City east of L.A.
94 Sheds
96 Became worn away
98 Quick drinks
100 Pesky insects
101 Of gold
102 Dine
104 African carnivore
105 Remove a cover
106 Val d'__, France
109 Site of Hannibal's defeat
114 Keats opus
115 Caustic solution
116 Tangled mass
117 Air-travel watchdog grp.
118 Old sailor

by A.J. Santora

ACROSS

1 Neighbor of Vietnam
5 __ Khan IV
8 Culture media
13 Ancient people of Campania
19 Long-tongued predator
21 "Bad, Bad __ Brown"
22 Like rhymes and verses
23 "Macbeth" prop
25 Dahl or Golonka
26 Bar legally
27 Clear the windshield
29 Universal soul
30 Appease
34 HST or DDE
36 Teacher's favorite
38 __ dixit
39 Makes another offer
40 Crow
41 Three-card straight flush
43 Icy abode
44 __ go bragh!
45 Strays from the topic
48 Half a Kenyan rebel?
49 Visitors' vehicles?
53 Recipe abbr.
54 Grade sch.
56 __ it the truth?
57 __ jacet
58 1929 Bebe Daniels movie
60 Plumber's concern
62 "__ Bulba"
64 Talk and talk and talk
65 Pot's accusation?
70 Singer Davis
71 Having paddles
72 Winter apple
73 Examines again
76 To and __
77 Tropical rodent
78 New or raw follower
81 Helm dir.
82 Hockey goal?
86 Clare of "Bleak House"
87 Old Roman coins
89 Draft classification
90 Had aspirations
92 Matched set of jewelry
93 "Pomp and Circumstance" composer
95 Spicy cuisine
96 At what time?
98 Part of MD
99 Pride member
100 Embolden
101 Magazine display stands
103 Immune system member
105 Chills
107 "Star Trek" extras
109 What an heir's life is served on?
115 Wine choice
116 Marcus Aurelius or Cicero, e.g.
117 Harding's successor
118 Grammer of "Frasier"
119 Organic compound
120 Response: abbr.
121 From

DOWN

1 Statute
2 Tropical cuckoo
3 Ex-Giant Mel
4 NYSE watchdog
5 Words in Alamogordo, NM headlines
6 "The Last Remake of Beau __"
7 Shell rival
8 Every bit
9 Barbara Bel __
10 Take into custody
11 Housetop
12 Like three Gospels
13 Ration-book group
14 Common rail
15 Boston five
16 Much ado about nothing?
17 Foch and Simone
18 Act part
20 Before
24 Designate
28 __ counter
30 First in quality
31 On the up and up
32 One colorful dish of the day?
33 AFL-__
35 Called up
37 Country singer Clark
40 Revive
42 Dissolves and assimilates
44 Watching
45 Admission ticket
46 Old-time thrusting sword
47 Paddle
50 Recumbent
51 Seal, as a deal
52 Exposed to the public
55 Pooh's creator
59 Governed
61 Egyptian coin
62 __ cotta
63 Off-course wanderer
65 Concerns
66 Coeur d'__, ID
67 Weapon handles
68 City near Pisa
69 Biblical twin
74 Drum with fingers
75 Hush-hush
77 Catholic sacrament
79 Fred's first dancing partner
80 Burdened
83 Aril
84 Business image
85 Of word sequences
88 Oil vessels
91 Neath's opposite
93 '00 film, "Billy __"
94 Old-time actress Langtry
95 Stringed instruments
96 Destruction
97 City near Leipzig
100 Climb aboard
102 Macbeth's dagger
104 Superlative endings
106 Puget Sound whale
108 Hog home
110 TV adjunct
111 Aunt in Alicante
112 6-pointers
113 Self
114 Ring off.

by Alan P. Olschwang

ACROSS

1 Body of water
5 Fat avoider
10 Movie pig
14 Spacek of "Carrie"
19 USA part
20 Ms. Massey
21 Premed course
22 Related on the mother's side
23 Actress Theda
24 "Flirting with Disaster" co-star Tea
25 Make reference to
26 Some Egyptian clerics
27 Start of Jim Murray quote
30 Civil War historian Shelby
31 Closest to the ceiling?
32 Adolescents
33 Annoys persistently
34 A mean Amin
35 Odor
37 Quartet voice
39 Distinctive flair
42 Part 2 of quote
48 Deep tolls
50 Little Jack Horner's last words
51 Mexicali Mrs.
52 Addams Family cousin
53 A Stooge
54 Pal
55 Richardson novel
58 AAA advice
60 Catch sight of
61 Decorative ribbon
63 Dull finishes
66 Sword parts
67 Killer whale
68 Part 3 of quote
70 Isao of golf
71 Mrs. Eisenhower
73 Coming attraction
74 Urban porches
78 Lyric poems
79 Thin strip of wood
80 Hams it up
82 Mate's reply
83 Frenzied
84 Can opener
85 King of Judea
88 Year in Acapulco
89 Organic compound
91 Part 4 of quote
96 Sign over
97 Jackson's secretary of war
98 Derived from oil
99 Conclusion of an auction?
101 Donna of the LPGA
104 Animal track
106 Ethiopia neighbor
110 In debt
111 End of quote
114 Hawaiian porch
115 Toward shelter
116 Leading

117 Automatic tournament advances
118 Sharp mountain ridge
119 Goneril's father
120 Insect stage
121 Byron poem
122 Passover meal
123 Gathered grp.
124 Harden
125 Grade sch.

DOWN

1 "The Threepenny Opera" director
2 Cornhusker city
3 Orange blossoms derivative
4 Speaking with lengthened vowels
5 Oder region
6 Fabric fold
7 Chamber
8 Writer Quindlen
9 Contaminated
10 Single guy
11 Charged particle
12 Plain-woven fabric
13 Somme summers
14 Beach property
15 One type of boat motor
16 Wooden shoe
17 Assert
18 Some votes
28 Neither sm. nor lge.
29 Shafts sunk into the earth
33 Tiny pests
35 W. __ Maugham
36 Work hard
38 People conquered by the Iroquois
39 Wanes
40 Clumsy clod
41 Wife of Perseus
43 Ready for the challenge
44 Andrea del __
45 Involve incriminatingly
46 Plunder
47 Allows to
49 Parking spot
56 Docs' group
57 Follower of Joel
59 Germanic
60 Japanese deer
62 Goddess of strife
64 Reverence
65 Phoenician seaport
66 Basketball game
69 Out-of-sight fences
70 Exist

71 NYC cultural attraction
72 Eliot's Bede
73 Prohibition
75 Famed British school
76 Scrutinized
77 Very dry
79 Actress Christine
81 Will you allow me to?
84 Even more nasal
86 Hoaxing
87 Permit
90 Word-lover's board game
92 Newborn
93 Shoe parts
94 Antennas
95 Of a hypothetical surface of the Earth
100 Eminem's twins?
101 Soft drinks
102 Cognizant
103 Yearned
105 Guilty and not guilty
106 Mow closely
107 Devoted
108 Grenoble's river
109 State south of Bhutan
111 Festive
112 The one there
113 __ and now

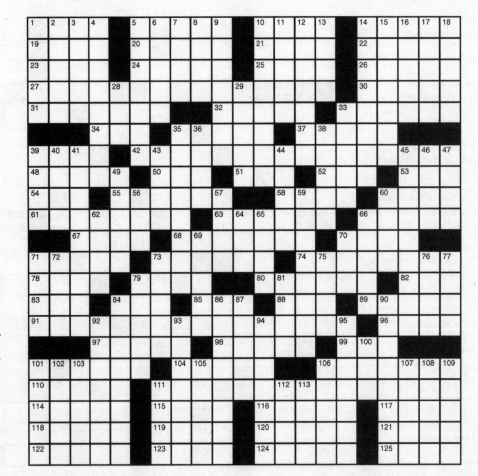

ANSWERS

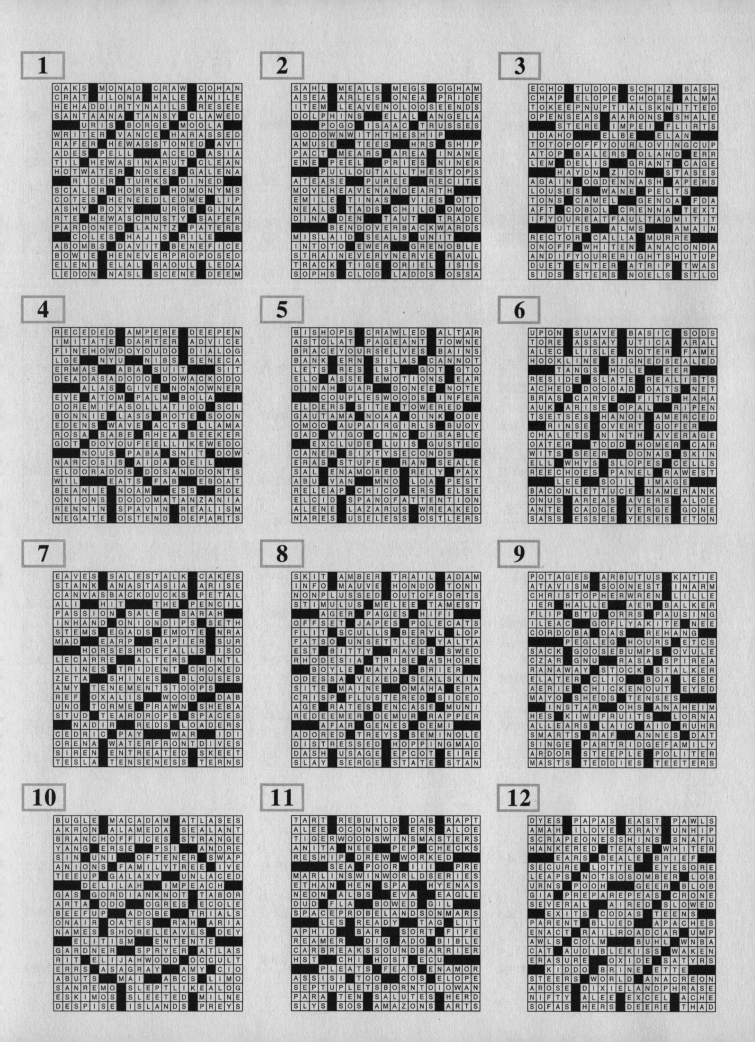

13

```
PELE  SPOOF  HATED  ANEW
ALEX  TIDAL  UTILE  SOME
PIGINAPOKE  MONKEYSUIT
PASSOVER  MAIMS  PAINTS
  TOED  HINDS  FENS
REBIND  SANTO  MANGIEST
IRENE  TIGERSEYE  LEO
DRAG  BOAT  USED  PENN
GOV  RABBITEARS  LAPSE
ELEVATES  RANGY  BOTHER
  RATTY  SUSIE  GRATA
SABLES  WHEEL  PLATINGS
CHOIR  HORSELAUGH  TAI
HEAD  EMIR  ARTS  SMUT
MAR  MARESNEST  STAGE
ODDITIES  POSTS  LEANED
  NESS  TROTS  BOAR
ARGUES  SHINE  TOOLSHED
BEARMARKET  LIONSSHARE
BETE  RAISE  LARGE  IVAN
EKED  YESES  ENSOR  PEST
```

14

```
MOSS  GRACE  RULER  ANIL
ASTA  LEDON  ECOLE  NINE
WHATSUPDOC  HOWSTRICKS
RANCHERS  ALENE  RETEST
  HERO  ASIANS  AAR
UNWED  SLEET  SCRAWLS
POHL  ANAIS  SPRATS  HOW
PROS  TOYS  HUNS  MADE
ESS  WHOSTHEBOSS  SATED
REORIENT  EVENT  SHRINE
  NAPES  DAILY  ACADS
EIFFEL  PERLE  CREDITOR
DRIER  WHATSMYLINE  RUE
GARR  GAIN  OISE  PUTT
ENS  DARLAS  RUNES  ATRA
SITTERS  IRENE  OTHER
  OLD  WAXING  MARC
ASTUTE  ALICE  WIREHAIR
YOURANGSIR  WHATLLITBE
ELBE  ETHNO  EMCEE  ENID
SEED  DOYEN  DOORS  RODS
```

15

```
IOUS  ZAG  OHBOY  AURORA
PENH  EDO  PUPAE  LLAMAS
SIDE  BOTTOMOFTHENINTH
ELEA  UNHORSE  IRANI
RTS  AINT  DARTS  VIC
INTHENICKOFTIME  TODO
COHERE  RENO  NEURAL
INE  ALS  CAESAR  ERNEST
NSW  CLOSETOTHEEDGE
ETI  SASSOON  ISSUERS
SORE  USSR  DOCS  PLOT
SPEARER  SARANAC  ESE
SAVEDBYTHEBELL  VAL
RELIVE  YOUALL  REA  ENL
ATONES  EGAN  CRENNA
SUNG  BRINKOFDISASTER
PIG  AROSE  ZION  SCH
HOMER  STANZAS  OHMS
TWOMINUTEWARNING  ROOK
AERATE  STACK  LET  TUTU
BENNYS  PANTS  YRS  SRTA
```

16

```
LAPSE  LAST  SCAT  ABBES
ORIEL  ALOE  GAMY  LEAST
YOKEL  RADARTRAP  FARCE
AMER  PANAMA  THELOUDER
LASSIE  LPS  WON  INN
SCREWUPS  TRISECTS
HETALKEDOFHISHONOR
ELATE  AGLOW  WITS  ASIA
ASHE  CLEF  ADORE  USERS
PEI  REM  SLURS  SNEAKS
TRANSCENDENTALISM
ORIENT  ARIOT  DOT  OUT
ROAST  SNIPE  SAVE  PURE
RENE  LOVE  MIAMI  RANGE
THEFASTERWECOUNTED
DISSENTS  DRESSERS
ONT  LTC  OSS  ITALIC
OURSPOONS  OUTING  MIRA
DRAPE  VALENTINE  SONAR
LEPER  EMIL  ARCS  ARETE
ESSES  RENO  HEAT  CEDED
```

17

```
EDINA  KEGS  MAAM  PAILS
VENOM  DRAT  OHIO  INDIA
AVIAN  LEIA  MANO  STEEL
NOTHEYACTRAMBUNCTIOUS
  SENT  LII  BLOC
ARISING  MIME  CEIL  POP
TANKA  AONE  SIAM  AIDE
THEYCOULDGETLAMBASTED
ERS  RHEAS  WARS  ATARI
SAS  TAU  WIND  BRR
THEIRTHINKINGISWOOLLY
  ROE  SOIL  WAN  AAA
TRIAL  WHIT  BRIAN  CST
MOSTLYITSSHEARMADNESS
AXLE  OSAY  ANTE  EERIE
NYE  RUHR  GIGS  DINESEN
  PARE  UFA  MONA
IMTIREDOFTALKINGTOEWE
CARTE  FIAT  ENNA  URIEL
EXITS  OSTE  SUET  RENAL
DIGIT  REAR  ERSE  ELENA
```

18

```
EDIFY  SLAM  REBEL  RCMP
RENEE  HOLY  OSAGE  ELEA
MAKEAPERFORATION  BURN
ALLTHERE  BERETS  TESLA
SSE  NILE  DEE  ARCTIC
CONFERFORMALLY  ENE
LILAC  FILE  SMITS  RSA
INARUT  ETAS  BLOTTO
ASK  LUNG  ETHER  SIFTS
ITE  ALOUS  TOROSE  ASHE
SAN  RIVERCROSSING  HIT
ELEC  PORTIA  TILDE  RST
SLAPS  NAACP  ATOM  UTE
RAPIDS  OTIS  NIMBLE
EMS  ASSET  TART  NOSES
SEE  CITYONLAKEERIE
TRACES  NEA  SLUE  SAG
RITAS  LEGACY  ATALANTA
ATTN  LUXURYAUTOMOBILE
DELE  ARIEL  WREN  NEPAL
ADES  BETSY  LIDS  GLESS
```

19

```
STLEO  OPPOSITE  STPAUL
AROID  SOFTENER  CRADLE
MANDARINCOLLAR  RELINE
EDGELESS  LEAK  RESMEAR
TIM  SONY  BEE  OURS
MARIS  STAGE  PASCAL
CHUCKBERRY  MEG  HAINES
CAB  SYRIA  CANNA  AVAST
CBER  LAP  COMPOSE  ELSA
TAI  FORMALIST  DEL
INTERNATIONALDATELINE
OER  CEMENTERS  EAT
TRIO  SEEDILY  SOL  DADA
AVERT  STEEL  BOWLS  YUL
SEDAKA  HRS  PRUNETREES
NOSHES  SHIN  FOILS  RUSSO
PRIG  SIS  SIRE  ION
RENEGED  GUST  ROLLTOPS
OLDMAN  INTHELIMELIGHT
WERENT  RARENESS  EERIE
STINGS  STARTREK  DRESS
```

20

```
CLOD  AGAIN  ORGS  RYANS
RICE  GALBA  RARE  EERIE
OMAR  ATEAM  AMEN  SLANT
SILVERSCREEN  ESTELLES
STAIR  STAG  NEATO
SNEAD  ADEPTLY  WERE
REDHERRINGS  SHE  ASTER
ALI  SERVES  TAUS  STUNS
BLEW  CAEN  HELMS  TRITE
BETH  TYRE  IAMB  FOE
INSIDES  ARK  BORATES
TAD  BASE  TSAR  KHAN
FRIED  ELLIS  EAST  SEGO
LIVED  NUTS  CALAIS  TER
ITALY  GEO  PURPLEHEART
PANE  TIPSTER  ATSEA
PAINE  AERO  ERODE
KATHLEEN  BLACKPANTHER
ILIAD  ECOL  NEILL  HANA
DONNA  RIDE  TAROT  ERIS
SEATS  SLED  SNIPS  NAME
```

21

```
GLOM  STALIN  AWARENESS
RIME  CASINO  DECORATOR
AMANWHOHASNEVERGONETO
SORTIE  REFS  DIET
INLAW  TASK  DRIVELS
SCHOOLMAYSTEAL  CILIA
TEEN  BRO  SEEPS  BING
ASA  SAL  NRA  LOUT  RODE
FAD  CLEM  ASS  RATATAT
FROMAFREIGHTCARBUT
SENOR  SLURRED  ROSAS
IFHEHASAUNIVERSITY
AMASSED  AMT  NICE  KHZ
DART  RIPE  SSA  COT  KEY
ELIE  BEING  PAT  DING
PLASM  EDUCATIONHEMAY
TESTATE  SLAM  DROOP
PITT  CREW  SWATHE
STEALTHEWHOLERAILROAD
CORRELATE  LIAISE  TUNE
HOARSENED  SANDER  STAN
```

22

```
HAHA  AROMA  ABASH  ADAM
ACED  CAFES  RODEO  SERE
THROWOFFTHESCENT  SPEW
SEAPORTS  ALECS  SPIRAL
TONS  MANE  THOSE
IMBEDS  ARENA  SHOOTSAT
ROLES  MEDDLEWITH  STY
EROS  SHIN  MAES  STIR
NOW  GLUTONESELF  WAHOO
ENTIRETY  OVINE  COVENS
HOODS  STAND  SALEM
GRETAS  LEONE  AIRFRAME
ROWAN  HORNSWOGGLE  RAP
AAHS  MONA  GUNS  SKYE
TRI  CARICATURE  BEEBE
ASSOONAS  LINES  CRATES
TORAH  DADS  GLOB
BELLES  BASAL  PLATOONS
IDEO  STICKLIKEASHADOW
ANON  ARECA  NAACP  ROSA
SANG  SARAN  GYRES  DREG
```

23

```
MAGNA  LAMP  PLAN  SMART
ENROL  ELIE  LIRE  TUBER
ATALL  VICE  ABIE  AROSE
DOYOURECALLNEARSTIVES
ENS  VALE  EELS  TENETS
AIMS  SWAT  CEDE
STAYUP  AHAS  LORE  AMA
WASAMANWITHSEVENWIVES
ALIT  GIANT  ANEW  AGANA
PESO  ETRE  SPAR  PINSUP
LURED  OHS  ROLLO
IDYLLS  ABLY  NOAA  RAVI
LEMAN  OBOE  YEAST  AMID
SUCHAPOLYGAMISTICMALE
ASA  APES  LILT  NAUSEA
TARS  BARS  SIRS
ASHORE  SPAN  RAZE  SAG
SHOULDBEINASTIVESJAIL
HARTE  RANG  LOGO  SABLE
EMDEN  ALEE  AMOR  EDIES
SEEDS  NERD  VERY  SENDS
```

24

```
APART  SHEB  PEALE  SSGT
DONEE  HANA  IRVIN  TORO
ALTAR  ENOS  NAOMI  RUIN
RAILROADCROSSING  ISNT
TAR  CHARTED  MIKADO
ASTO  AGA  ERR  PARE
SPARETIRES  ISEE  ABODE
HOP  LEG  REAP  PAPERBOY
EDITED  GRAPEVINE  EINE
RERUN  SIAMESE  UPDATES
RATTAN  RETOOK
LOOKSEE  DOLLARS  MEARA
ABLE  TEASPOONS  DARREN
POLYMERS  EXOD  ARI  LAG
SLAVE  ESPN  TAPDANCERS
USED  ELI  UAW  ASST
MEDLAR  CLIMPSON  ITT
ALIT  SPLITPERSONALITY
JUJU  ALIST  ALTI  NICHE
ODOR  TENSE  NOEL  SKOAL
RENE  ZAGER  SPRY  YENTL
```

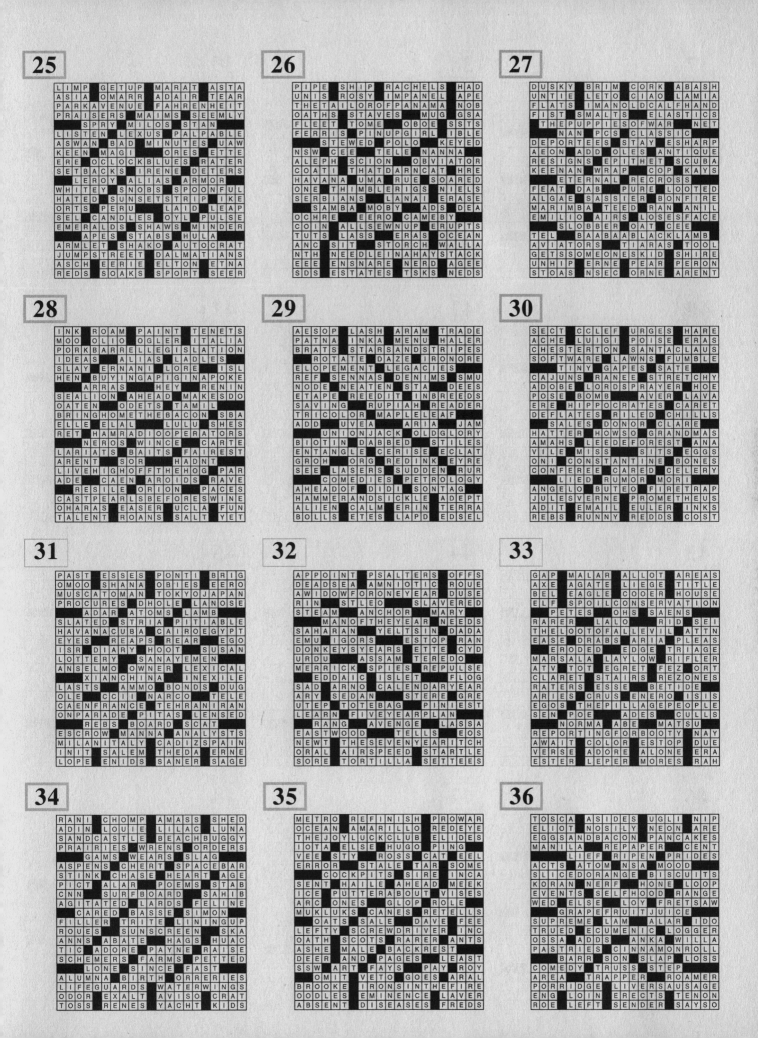

25

```
LIMP  GETUP  MARAT  ASTA
ASIA  OMARR  ADAIR  TEAR
PARKAVENUE  FAHRENHEIT
PRAISERS  MAIMS  SEEMLY
      SPRY  MILOS  STAN
LISTEN  LEXUS  PALPABLE
ASWAN  BAD  MINUTES  UAW
KEEN  MAGI  ORES  ETTE
ERE  OCLOCKBLUES  RATER
SETBACKS  IRENE  DETERS
  LEROY  ALIAS  ARMOR
WHITEY  SNOBS  SPOONFUL
HATED  SUNSETSTRIP  IKE
ORTS  PERU  LAID  LEAP
SEL  CANDLES  OYL  PULSE
EMERALDS  SHAWS  MINDER
   APES  STABS  HULA
ARMLET  SHAKO  AUTOCRAT
JUMPSTREET  DALMATIANS
ASCH  EERIE  ELTON  ETNA
REDS  SOAKS  SPORT  SEER
```

26

```
PIPE  SHIP  RACHELS  HAD
UNIS  ROSY  IMPANEL  APE
THETAILOROFPANAMA  NOB
OATHS  STAVES  MUG  GSA
FLEET  TOME  OBOE  SSTS
FERRIS  PINUPGIRL  IBLE
   STEWED  POLO  KEYED
NSW  CEE  TELE  NANNA
ALEPH  SCION  OBVIATOR
COATI  THATDARNCAT  HRE
HAVANA  UMA  RUE  SOARED
ONE  THIMBLERIGS  NIELS
SERBIANS  LANAI  ERASE
  SAMBA  MOBY  ADS  DEA
OCHRE  EERO  CAMEBY
COIN  ALLSEWNUP  ERUPTS
TUTS  LASS  ERAS  OCEAN
ANC  SIT  STORCH  WALLA
NTH  NEEDLEINAHAYSTACK
EEE  ENSNARE  NERD  AGEE
SDS  ESTATES  TSKS  NEDS
```

27

```
DUSKY  BRIM  CORK  ABASH
UNTIE  LETO  CIAO  LAMIA
FLATS  IMANOLDCALFHAND
FIST  SMALTS  ELASTICS
THEPUPPIESOFWAR  NET
   NAN  PCS  CLASSIC
DEPORTEES  STAY  ESHARP
AEON  ADD  OLES  ANTIQUE
RESIGNS  EPITHET  SCUBA
KEENAN  WRAP  COP  KAYS
    ETERNAL  RECROSS
FEAT  DAB  PURE  LOOTED
ALGAE  SASSIER  BONFIRE
MARIMBA  TEED  RAN  ANIL
EMILIO  AIRS  LOSESFACE
   SLOBBER  OAT  CEE
TEL  BAABAABLACKLAMB
AVIATORS  TIARAS  TOOL
GETSSOMEONESKID  SHIRE
UNHIP  ERNE  PEAR  PERON
STOAS  NSEC  ORNE  ARENT
```

28

```
INK  ROAM  PAINT  TENETS
MOO  OLIO  OGLER  ITALIA
PORKBARRELLEGISLATION
IDEAS  ALIAS  LADLES
SLAY  ERNANI  LORE  ISL
HEN  BUYINGAPIGINAPOKE
  ARRAS  HEY  RENIN
SEALION  AHEAD  MAKESDO
OATEN  ODETS  TAMIL
BRINGHOMETHEBACON  SBA
ELLE  ELAL  LULU  SHES
RET  HAMRADIOOPERATORS
  NEROS  WINCE  CARTE
LARIATS  BAITS  FAIREST
ARENT  SOR  HADNT
LIVEHIGHOFFTHEHOG  PAR
ADE  CAEN  AROIDS  RAVE
   RESILE  ORION  PACES
CASTPEARLSBEFORESWINE
OHARAS  EASER  UCLA  FUN
TALENT  ROANS  SALT  YET
```

29

```
AESOP  LASH  ARAM  TRADE
PATNA  INKA  MENU  HALER
BRATS  STARSANDSTRIPES
   ROTATE  DAZE  IRONORE
ELOPEMENT  LEGACIES
REF  SENNAS  DENIMS  SMU
NODE  NEATEN  STA  DEES
ETAPE  REEDIT  INBREEDS
SAVING  RUPIAH  READER
TRICOLOR  MAPLELEAF
ADD  UVEA  ARIA  JAM
UNIONJACK  OLDGLORY
BIOTIN  DABBED  STILES
ENTANGLE  CERISE  ECLAT
GROH  ORG  REDINK  EYRE
SEE  LASERS  SUDDEN  RUR
COMEDIES  PETROLOGY
AHEADOF  DIDI  SONTAG
HAMMERANDSICKLE  ADEPT
ALIEN  CALM  ERIN  TERRA
BOLLS  ETES  LAPD  EDSEL
```

30

```
SECT  CCLEF  URGES  HARE
ACHE  LUIGI  POISE  ERAS
CHESTERTON  SANTACLAUS
SOFTWARE  LAWNS  FUMBLE
   TINY  GAPES  SATE
CAJUNS  RANEE  STRETCHY
ADOBE  LORDSPRAYER  HOE
POSE  BOMB  AVER  LAVA
ERE  HIPPOCRATES  CARET
DEFLATES  RILED  CHILLS
  SALES  DONOR  CLARE
HATTER  HOWSO  GRANDMAS
AMAHS  LEEDEFOREST  ANA
VILE  MISS  SITS  EGGS
ONI  CONSTANTINE  BONES
CONFEREE  CARED  CELERY
   LIED  RUMOR  MORI
ANGELO  BUTEO  FIRETRAP
JULESVERNE  PROMETHEUS
ADIT  EMAIL  EULER  INKS
REBS  RUNNY  REDDS  COST
```

31

```
PAST  ESSES  PONTI  BRIG
OMOO  SHANA  OBIES  EERO
MUSCATOMAN  TOKYOJAPAN
PROCURES  DHOLE  LANOSE
   ADAR  ATOMS  LAMB
SLATED  STRIA  PITIABLE
HAVANACUBA  CAIROEGYPT
EYES  REAPS  REAR  EGO
ISR  DIARY  HOOT  SUSAN
LOTTERY  SANAYEMEN
ANSELMO  OWNER  LEXICAL
XIANCHINA  INEXILE
LASTS  AMMO  BONDS  DUG
OLE  CCII  NARCO  TELE
CAENFRANCE  TEHRANIRAN
ONPARADE  PITAS  LENSED
   REBS  BOARD  SCAT
ESCROW  MANNA  ANALYSTS
MILANITALY  CADIZSPAIN
INIT  SALEM  THEDA  ERNE
LOPE  ENIDS  SANER  SAGE
```

32

```
APPOINT  PSALTERS  OFFS
DEADSEA  AMNIOTIC  ROUE
AWIDOWFORONEYEAR  DUSE
RIN  STLEO  SLAVERED
STEAM  ANCHOR  MARY
  MANOFTHEYEAR  NEEDS
SAHARAN  YELTSIN  DADA
EMU  IGORS  ESTOP  RAN
DONKEYSYEARS  ETTE  CYD
URDU  ASSAM  TEREDO
MERRICK  SPIES  REPULSE
EDDAIC  ISLET  FLOG
SAD  ARNO  CALENDARYEAR
ARY  SEDAN  STERE  GRE
UTEP  TOTEBAG  PINIEST
LEARN  FIVEYEARPLAN
RANG  AVENGE  LASSA
EASTWOOD  TELLS  EOS
NEWT  THESEVENYEARITCH
ORAL  AIRSPEED  STARTLE
SORE  TORTILLA  SETTEES
```

33

```
GAP  MALAR  ALLOT  AREAS
AXE  AGATE  LIEGE  TITLE
BEL  EAGLE  COOER  HOUSE
ELF  SPOILCONSERVATION
PETES  OHS  SAENS
RARER  LALO  RID  SEI
THELOOTOFALLEVIL  ATTN
EASE  DRABS  ARIA  PLEAS
   ERODED  EDGE  TRIAGE
MARSALA  LAYLOW  RIFLER
ATV  TOT  EGRET  FEZ  ORT
CLARET  STAIRS  REZONES
RATERS  ESSE  BETIDE
ARIES  CRUS  ENERO  ISIS
EGOS  THEPILLAGEPEOPLE
SEN  POE  ADES  CULLS
   NORMA  ABE  MATSU
REPORTINGFORBOOTY  NAY
AWAIT  COLOR  ESTOP  DUE
VERSE  ADORE  ALONE  ERA
ESTER  LEPER  MORES  RAH
```

34

```
RANI  CHOMP  AMASS  SHED
ADIN  LOUIE  LILAC  LUNA
SANDCASTLE  BEACHBUGGY
PRAIRIES  WRENS  ORDERS
   GAMS  WEARS  SLAG
ASPENS  CHERT  SPACEBAR
STINK  CHASE  HEART  AGE
PICT  ALAR  POEMS  STAB
CNN  SURFBOARD  SAHIB
AGITATED  LARDS  FELINE
  CARED  BASSE  SIMON
FILLER  TRITE  LININGUP
ROUES  SUNSCREEN  SKA
ANNS  ABATE  HAGS  HUAC
TIC  ADORE  PAYNE  RAISE
SCHEMERS  FARMS  PETTED
   LONE  SINCE  FAST
ALUMNA  BIRTH  ORRERIES
LIFEGUARDS  WATERWINGS
ODOR  EXALT  AVISO  CRAT
TOSS  RENES  YACHT  KIDS
```

35

```
METRO  REFINISH  PROWAR
OCEAN  AMARILLO  REDEYE
THEJOYLUCKCLUB  ELIDES
IOTA  ELSE  HUGO  PING
VEE  STY  ROSS  CAT  EEL
ERROR  STALE  TAR  SOME
  COCKPITS  SIRE  INCA
SENT  HAILE  AHEAD  MEEK
ICE  PUTTERABOUT  VISES
ARC  ONES  GLOP  ROLE
MUKLUKS  CANES  RETELLS
OATS  SALE  DAVE  FEE
LEFTY  SCREWDRIVER  INC
OATH  SCOTS  RARER  ANTS
ASHE  MALE  BACKREST
DEER  AND  PAGES  LEAST
SSW  ART  FAYS  PAY  ROY
OMIT  VETO  GOES  ARAL
BROOKE  IRONSINTHEFIRE
OODLES  EMINENCE  LAVER
ABSENT  DISEASES  FREDS
```

36

```
TOSCA  ASIDES  UGLI  NIP
ELIOT  NOSILY  NEON  ARE
EGGSANDBACON  PANCAKES
MANILA  REPAPER  CENT
   LIEF  RIPEN  PRIDES
ACTS  ATOM  NSA  MOOD
SLICEDORANGE  BISCUITS
KORAN  NERF  HONE  LOOP
EVENTS  SELFHOOD  RANGE
WED  ELSE  LOY  FRETSAW
  GRAPEFRUITJUICE
SUPREME  LAM  ALAR  IDO
TRUED  ECUMENIC  LOGGER
OSSA  ADDS  ANKA  WILLA
PASTRIES  CINNAMONROLL
   BARR  SON  SLAP  LOSS
COMEDY  TRUSS  STEP
AREA  TRAPPER  ROAMER
PORRIDGE  LIVERSAUSAGE
ENG  LOIN  ERECTS  TENON
ROE  LEFT  SENDER  SAYSO
```

37

```
A L I S T   T S A R   B A R A   S C R E W
W I S E R   A C M E   E L O N   T H E D A
L L A M A   R O O M   N A U T   G I V I N G I N
        Q U I T   T E A C H   M A G N E T
A C C R U E   S E T T L E R   I T E
Z I O N I S T   P A S S I O N   E C L A T
T R I A L T R I A L   B U N T   H A L O
E R N   E T C   S T A G E R   A R I L
C I S S Y   A S T O N I S H   I N N A T E
    P O E T   G I T   A G O G
G A L E N A   G A L T I E R I   D E P T H
O B O L   S E R V E S   D O M   E R A
B E L L   E L E A   F I N A L F I N A L
S L A S H   M E T O P I C   T E R R A C E
    S E A   N A N E T T E   F E E L E R
G A S P A R   G R E A T   T A T E
A L O E R T E R   S L I G H T S L I G H T
M A L L S   B E E T   N O N E   O N A I R
E N O L A   B E N E   G R I S   A F I R E
S A S S Y   S N A P   S E C T   D O N E E
```

38

```
C A B S   F O N T S   G R A M S   S A V E
A L E C   E L I O T   R E F I T   E R A T
P I E R   M I N E O   I N T R O   P A S T
P A P A L O V E D M A M A   A U N T B E E
      B O R E   A C I N G   T I E
Z A M B I A   F I C H E   E R E C T O R S
O B O L S   M O T H E R G O O S E   L A P
R E T E   M A R C   A D I T   E D D A
R A H   D U T C H U N C L E   L E G I T
O M E L E T T E   P A N E S   C A R R I E
    R A C E S   A S T O N   S Y R I A
S H I R K S   E L E C T   W E A K E N E D
H A N G S   M O T H E R H E N S   D A R
I S L E   R U B E   A I D S   E D G E
S T A   M A M A S F A M I L Y   K O A L A
H A W A I I A N   A S I D E   B A L D E R
    M C L   K A R T S   B A L I
S I S T E R S   M A A N D P A K E T T L E
P O O R   O A R E D   A R I S E   H O E R
A N N A   A R E N A   M A K E R   I N N S
T A S K   D A D D Y   E M E R Y   C E D E
```

39

```
G A B   R E T R A P   J E S T   S C O N E
E R A   E T O I L E   E R O S   A L L O Y
O T T O V O N B I S M A R C K   L E Y T E
D U M P S   C O E N   C O M M I T
I R A E   J A M E S M A D I S O N   P O E
C O N C R E T E   O R E S T E S   I N S
E N T A I L   P A L E D   B A S T
T R A C Y A U S T I N   N E T   O L D
R E B U S   L E N I E N T   C L O U D S
I N R E   O P E R E T T A   T H I C K E T
B A A   A R E S   A P O   A R A N   A N A
A M H E R S T   S T I N G I E R   A K I M
L E A N T O   S P E C I A L   M O I R E
    M O E   M I R   K A T E J A C K S O N
I T L L   M A G I C   N E R O L I
M R I   C O R N E A S   O N E I R O N S
B E N   R I V E R P H O E N I X   I N O N
R A C I A L   S A B A   A E T N A
U C O N N   M O N T G O M E R Y C L I F T
E L L I E   A R E A   L O T I O N   M A C
D E N T S   T E E N   I N C A S E   E T H
```

40

```
A B A S H   E B B S   A L A R M   U S E D
L O G I A   G A L E   B I L B O   N O V A
F E E L I N G L O W   E A T I N G C R O W
A R E O L A   M A E S T R O   G O T T E N
    I S R   T R O T S   M O R I
A B S E N C E S   A P E   C O O K O U T S
G O I N G A L O N G   D R E S S I N G U P
E R G S   R E A R E R   A L E E   G R E
R E N E W   A V A   O B I T S   S T A R E
    M O O R E   P U R L S   B L A M E D
O A T B R A N   T A L E S   T A O I S T S
T R O L L S   C U B A N   A R T E L
T A M E D   N O R A D   U N A   S W O R E
A R T   I A M B   E S S A Y S   I R O N
W A I T I N G F O R   P O I N T I N G T O
A T T O R N E Y   O W L   S O A N D S O S
    R A U L   A T E A M   R M S
E S S E N E   C L I N T O N   E I S N E R
P A I R I N G O F F   T O Y I N G W I T H
I S T O   D E E R E   E L E C   H E N C E
C H E S   O R D E R   R A T E   T E A S E
```

41

```
A P H I D   S E R B I A   C C V I   D E B
M O O L A   C R I E R S   E L E A   E M E
E S S E N C E O F L E A R N I N G   T I S
B E T   S U N S E T   E S P I O N A G E
A R I   O R E   D I D O   A C R E
L I N E S I S T O F O R G E T T H E M
A C E D   R O O T S   O D I U M
D E L I B E R A T E   B I T T E R E S T
S O Y O U C A N   H A R S H   E N C E
    T R O T   A R A B I A   G A S T O N
A F R   G L E N D A J A C K S O N   S T N
P L E A S E   A D V I S E   E R N S
S E A M   M U L E S   M A K E T H E M
E X C O R I A T E   C H I L I S A U C E
    Q U I L L   C O L I C   S N U G
S O U N D L I K E Y O U T H O U G H T
A N A T   O R S O   B L U   Z I G
P R I S S I E S T   S T E L A E   H O E
P U N   O F T H E M T H A T I N S T A N T
H S T   A N T E   I C E B A G   T A L I A
O H S   P I E R   T U S S L E   S P L A T
```

42

```
T O S C A   A T B A T   I T S Y   T S A R
O R E A D   L O R R E   L O W E   A I D A
F R E N C H T O A S T   I R I S H S T E W
U S D A   M I T Z I   M A Y S   U T I L E
    D U O   S I N G E D   S E M I N A R
A G A I N   M I L E R S   C L A N
R E P A I R M E N   I S A   H A N G A R S
T A I N T E D   U S N   S C E N E   L E T
A R A B I C   S T P   P A L E D   G I N A
    A V A   I S O T O P E S   E B E N
M I N C E P I E   N O M   V E S T R I E S
O L E O   D R A G R A C E   C A M
D O W N   C A R N E   D O R   A C A R I D
E N E   B A H A I   T E L   T R I N A R Y
M A R T I N O   L E A   D R A F T S M A N
    H O O P   S O R T E D   L A P S E
G A L I L E O   E N S O U L   N Y U
O R E N A   T I L E   B R I A R   S A I L
L I M A B E A N S   B A K E D A L A S K A
D E M I   S T O A   E L E V E   O G E E S
A L A R   E O N S   D O Y E N   Y E A S T
```

43

```
N I N A   C A P E K   A G A R   T I R E D
I D O S   A S O N E   N O N O   A B U S E
N I T S   S A L V E   I N C A   B I T T Y
J O S E P H P O O L I T Z E R   A S H E S
A T O N I C   N I E K R O   C R E W
    T A R D E   R E A   W A R D S H I P
A B C   F O R G E   P E P Y S   I R A
L A H R   P U R R S   S A T E S   T S A R
A T E U P   S I R E   A R T   T R I T E R
R E S T A T E   O V E N   I S A I A H
M D S   C H A R L E S D E G O L F   E A R
P A T I N A   R E A R   A S T R I D E
S P A R S E   M I A   L A M P   S I M O N
P U L E   V I R A L   S T O I C   B E R T
A R M   D E L O N   O N E R S   R E S
S L I V E R E D   I S M   T R E A S
    N O S Y   U N C A S E   A G O R A S
P A T T I   T E N N I S T H E M E N A C E
S N E E R   A B B A   S L A V E   A B U T
A E R I E   B R A T   E E L E R   T I T O
T W I N E   S O R E   D O L L S   A D E N
```

44

```
S A M S   P A I L S   T H E F T   E R M A
E M M A   L U M E T   A I M E E   D O O M
P U M P K I N P I E   B R O W N B E T T Y
T R I P L E T S   A B L E R   S A R A H S
    H E S S   G R E E D Y   I L L
B O G I E   P O I N T   R O S E B U D
E M I R   S W O R N   S E L E N A   A T E
B A N E   M I L E   L O G S   S K I N
O R G   B A N A N A S P L I T   S P E L T
P R E P A R E R   S T O A S   E P O D E S
    R E S T S   D O R I S   A T R I A
S A B L E S   F I N A L   A C H I L L E S
C U R T S   R I C E P U D D I N G   A M A
A D E S   G E N E   A L D O   P S A T
R I A   B R E E D S   P R E S S   O K I E
F E D E R A L   P U R E R   S E A L S
    M E N   A R E N A S   C H A T
S I N B A D   L I N E N   P R O V I S O S
C R E A M P U F F S   C H E E S E C A K E
O M A R   A G I L E   E S T E E   A G R A
T A L K   S H E E R   S T E P S   L E A N
```

45

```
C A L D E R A   H A J J   P A P   M E A L
A V I A T O R   A L O U   O B I   A R T E
N O R T H W E S T E R N R I C E U N I O N
S N E E   T L C   Y E A   S T L U C I A
    H A H A H A   A T V   I E R
T H E C I T A D E L Q U E E N S M E R C Y
O A X A C A   E S A U   L E M A   A H A
D O U R   M A N T U A   A G A R
O L D D O M I N I O N T E M P L E B A R D
S E E   R E T R O   T W A   E X I S T S
    S A N T A N A   T R U S T E E
S T E A L S   I T A   E N S O R   A S U
K I N G S A U B U R N B R O W N T U F T S
I D L E   B E M A T A   S O O T
M A A   A G E R   I N T L   A H E R N E
S L I P P E R Y R O C K R I V E R R E E D
    A R O   L O U   S A L I S H
E X P L O I T   S S T   I L S   A C H E
F R I E N D S C A T H O L I C B U T L E R
F A N S   A K A   E A S E   I L L W I L L
S Y S T   L S D   D I E D   D U E T I M E
```

46

```
L A B S   A S S A M   M E C C A   E T E S
O M O O   N I E C E   A P A R T   S A R A
D O U B L E R E E D   R E V O L U T I O N
E S T E E M E D   I V I E S   A N A L O G
    R O I S   I C O N S   S N I T
P A T I N A   A L A T E   B U T T E D I N
O P I N E   M I L E S D A V I S   O L A
R I N G   A N O A   E R A S   A N I S
T A P   N O N C R E D I T   D I N A H
S N A R L I N G   E X E C S   P O M A D E
    N O O S E   S C A L E   M A T E S
C H A I S E   A T O L L   D A N S E U R S
H E L L S   M A N T A R A Y S   M O W
E L L S   L O A N   O D A Y   A M M O
A G E   F A T S D O M I N O   S N E E R
P A Y M E N T S   N A N A S   H O T R O D
    O R D O   S E R F S   B A L I
P S A L M S   A N E M O   B A R I T O N E
S O L D I E R B O Y   L A Y L A D Y L A Y
S A T E   N A C R E   D O T E S   P I T A
T R O D   D O S E D   S L E D S   E N O S
```

47

```
A N A   D I C E R   L I S P   A T T I L A
P A L   A W A R E   A N T I   T H A W E R
H U T   L I M A S   P S A T   H E N R Y I
I S A Y A L I T T L E P R A Y E R   I D A
D E R A I L S   E L I   U N E A T E N
S A S K   F O L I O   R I C K S   P E N S
    S H O L E M   S I G H S   S O T
S R I   E L E N A   O T O E   I T C H E D
C A H I L L   B I D   T R I B E   E V A
A D E S   O N S E T S   Y U L E S   S I R
L I A M   W A I L S   S O B I G   T O N K
P A R   C H I L I   M O U S E Y   O N C E
E T A   L I L L E   A P B   O X Y G E N
R E S L A M   I V A N   A M P U L   S S S
    Y U M   S E E M S   B A R R I E
M A M A   D U R R A   B E B O P   S P C A
I M P U T E R   T R I   C A P P E R S
N E H   I C A N S E E C L E A R L Y N O W
I L O I L O   A O U T   I R I D O   C S A
M I N C E R   S A R I   M I N O T   L S T
S A Y E R S   A P S E   P E E N S   L E M
```

48

```
D E C A N T S   U R S U L A S   S H A R P
E A R H A R T   C O N N E R Y   I O N I A
C R U S H E R   S M A C K O N E S L I P S
A L I   U N I   C A P O   S T E L E S
Y O S   M C V I   O P I A T E   I N A
E B E N   H E D G E C L I P P E R   N E G
D E R E K   N E U R O   G A I L   P E R E
W E E K   S A L A M I   A L A R
A T E   P U N T R E T U R N   E N O S I S
G R I S T L E   S T O A S   Y U C C A
R E G T   P R O E M   E N T I A   S H E L
E T H E R   F I D E L   F L A T O U T
E S T A T E   L I N E R N O T E S   O P S
    M E S H   B U R I E R   S T A N
H O G S   C A U L   O N T A P   A L E C S
A V A   B A R G E R I G H T I N   A R O O
R E L   O P P O S E   E T A S   G L I
O R A N G E   G A L A   A D A   L E R
L E T T E R C A R R I E R   P I N N A T E
D A I S Y   F R E E D O M   A R T I S T E
S T A B S   L I S T E N S   T S E T S E S
```

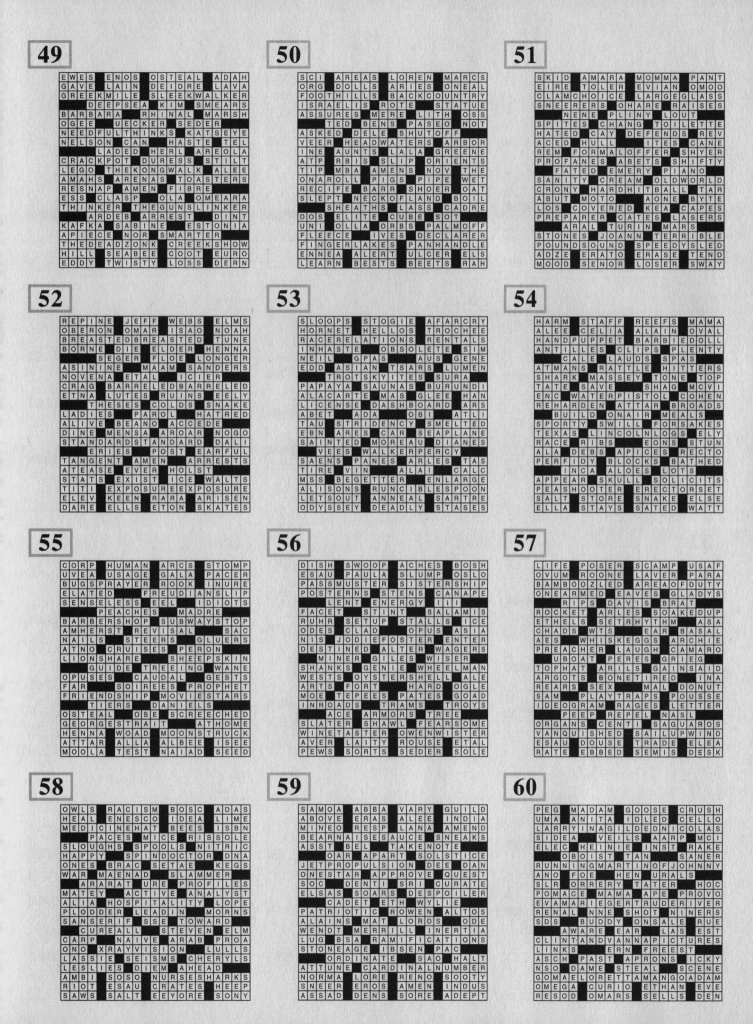

49 50 51
52 53 54
55 56 57
58 59 60

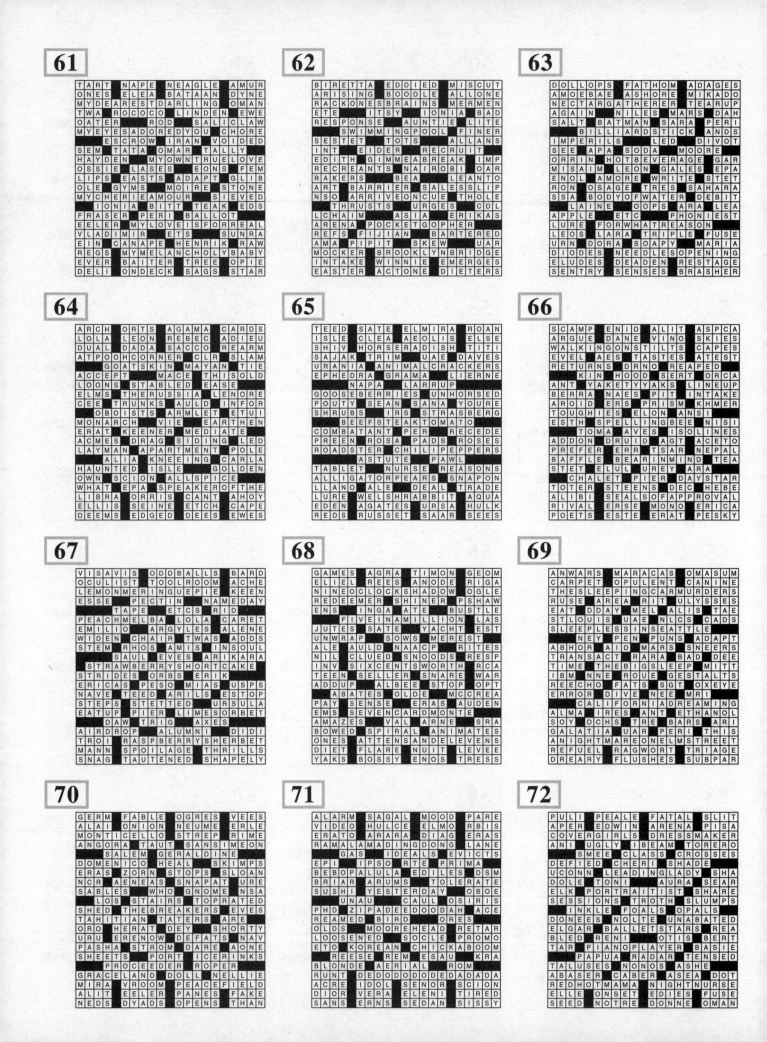

61

```
TART  NAPE  NEAGLE  AMUR
ONES  ELEA  BATAAN  DYNE
MYDEARESTDARLING  OMAN
TWA ROCOCO LINDEN  EWE
OATER   ROD  SALICLAW
MYEYESADOREDYOU  CHORE
ESCROW IRAN  VOIDED
SEM TATA OMAR  TALLY
HAYDEN  MYOWNTRUELOVE
OSSIE LASES  EONS  FEM
LIPS EASTS ADAPT  GLIB
OLE GYMS MOIRE  STONE
MYCHERIEAMOUR  SIEVED
IONIA BITT  TEAK  EDS
FRASER PERI  BALLOT
EELER MYLOVEISFORREAL
VLADIMIR  ETS  SUNRA
EIN CANAPE HENRIK  RAW
REGS MYMELANCHOLYBABY
EVER BAITER TREE  OPIE
DELI ONDECK SAGS  STAR
```

62

```
BIRETTA EDDIED MISCUT
ARISING BOODLE ALLONE
RACKONESBRAINS MERMEN
ETE  ITSY IONIA  BAD
RESPONSE AUNTIE LITE
SWIMMINGPOOL  FINER
SESTET TOTS  ALLANS
INT EIDER  RECRUIT
EDITH GIMMEABREAK IMP
RECREANTS NAIROBI OAR
RAKERS  BEA  LEANTO
ART BARRIER SALESSLIP
NSO ARRIVEONCUE THOLE
THRUSTS URGES  CDL
LCHAIM ASIA  ERIKAS
ARENA POCKETGOPHER
REFS FIJIAN BARTERED
AMA PIPIT SKEW  UAR
MOCKER BROOKLYNBRIDGE
INTAKE WINNIE EMERGES
EASTER ACTONE DIETERS
```

63

```
DOLLOPS FATHOM ADAGES
AMOEBAE ASHORE MIKADO
NECTARGATHERER TEARUP
AGAIN NILES MARS  DAH
SALT BATMAN SARA  PERI
BILLIARDSTICK  ANDS
IMPERILS  LED  DIVOT
SEE APA SODA  MOORE
ORRIN HOTBEVERAGE GAR
MISAIM LEON GALES  EPA
ENOL AMORE WRITE STET
RON OSAGE TRES  SAHARA
SSA BODYOFWATER DEBIT
LAINE OOPS  ARA  LEA
APPLE ETC  PHONIEST
LURE FORWHATREASON
LEOS LARA TRIPLE FUSE
URN DORA SOAPY  MARIA
DIODES NEEDLESOPENING
ELUDES DEADEN RESTAGE
SENTRY SENSES BRASHER
```

64

```
ARCH ORTS AGAMA  CARDS
LOLA LEON REBEC  ADIEU
DUAL DADA SACCO  REARM
ATPOOHCORNER CLR SLAM
GOATSKIN MAYAN  TIE
ACCEPT MACE THISOLD
LOONS STABLED  EASE
ELMS THERUSSIA LENORE
CEE TRUNKS AULD INFOR
OBOISTS ARMLET ETUI
MONARCH VIE  EARTHEN
ERAT KEENER MEDIATE
ACMES DRAG SIDING LED
LAYMAN APARTMENT POLE
ALIA KNEEING  CARLA
HAUNTED ISLE  GOLDEN
OWN SCION ALLSPICE
WHAT EPA SPEAKEROFTHE
LIBRA ORRIS CANT  AHOY
ELLIS SEINE ETCH  CAPE
DEEMS EDGED DEES  EWES
```

65

```
TEED SATE ELMIRA  ROAN
ISLE CLEA AEOLIS  ELSE
SHIV HORSERADISH TITI
SAJAK TRIM UAE  DAVES
URANIA ANIMALCRACKERS
EPHEDRA GRAMA  LIERNE
NAPA   LARRUP
GOOSEBERRIES UNHORSED
POUTY SEAN SANA YOURE
SHRUBS IRS  STRASBERG
BEEFSTEAKTOMATO
COMBATANT PER  RECEDE
PREEN ROSA PADS ROSES
ROADSTER CHILIPEPPERS
ASTUTE  PAWL
TABLET NURSE  REASONS
ALLIGATORPEARS SNAPON
LLANO ALE DEAL  TRADE
LURE WELSHRABBIT AQUA
EDEN AGATES URSA  HULK
REDS RUSSET SAAR  SEES
```

66

```
SCAMP ENID ALIT  ASPCA
ARGUE DANE VINO  SKIES
WALKINGONSTILTS CAPES
EVEL AES TASTES ATEST
RETURNS DRNO  REAPED
KIN HOOD SERT  ORCA
ANT YAKETYYAKS LINEUP
BERRA NAES PIT INTAKE
AROID ERS PRISM KHMER
TOUGHIES ELON  ANSI
ESTH SPELLINGBEE NISI
TOMA AVES ISOLINES
ADDON DRUID AGT ACETO
PREFER ERR TSAR NEPAL
BAFFLE BEARINMIND TEA
STET ELUL UREY  ARA
CHALET PIER DAYSTAR
TOTER STEENS DEC HEBE
ALIBI SEALSOFAPPROVAL
RIVAL ERSE MONO ERICA
POETS ESTE ERAT PESKY
```

67

```
VISAVIS ODDBALLS BARD
OCULIST TOOLROOM ACHE
LEMONMERINGUEPIE KEEN
ESSE PECTIN  NAMEDAY
TAPE ETCS  RID
PEACHMELBA LOLA CARET
EMILIO ARGYLES ALENE
WIDEN CHAIR TWAS ADDS
STEM RHOS AMIS INSOUL
SAUL EVES  ARIKARA
STRAWBERRYSHORTCAKE
STRIDES ORBS  ERIK
ERICAS PESO MIAS USPS
NAVE TEED ARILS ESTOP
STEPS STETTED URSULA
EATUP PIER LIMESORBET
DAW TRIG  AXES
AIRDROP ALUMNI  DIDI
TROI RASPBERRYSHERBET
MANN SPOILAGE THRILLS
SNAG TAUTENED SHAPELY
```

68

```
GAMES AGRA TIMON  GEOM
ELIEL REES ANODE  RIGA
NINEOCLOCKSHADOW OGLE
REDEEMER SHINER PSHAW
ENS INGA ATE  BUSTLE
FIVEINAMILLION LAS
JUTES SATE YACHT EST
UNWRAP SOWS  MEREST
ALE AULD NAACP RITES
NIL CLUED SNOODS RESP
INV SIXCENTSWORTH RCA
TEEN SELLER SNARE WAR
ADDUP ALBEE STOP  OPT
ABATES OLDE  MCCREA
PAY SENSE ERAS AUDEN
EMS SEVENCARDMONTE
AMAZES VAL ARNE  SRA
BOWED SPIRAL ANIMATES
ONES ATTENSANDELEVENS
DIET FLARE NUIT LEVEE
YAKS BOSSY ENOS TRESS
```

69

```
ANWARS MARACAS OMASUM
CARPET OPULENT CANINE
THESLEEPINGCARMURDERS
RUSE AREA RIT ULYSSES
EAT DDAY MEL ALIS TAE
STLOUIS UAE NLCS CADS
SLEEPLESSINSEATTLE
NEY PEN PUNS  ADAPT
ABHOR AID MARS SNEERS
TRANSACT RARA BAD DEE
TIME THEBIGSLEEP MITT
IBM NNE ROUE GESTALTS
REECHO FATS SGT OXEYE
ERROR DIVE NEE  MRI
CALIFORNIADREAMING
ALMA IRES ANT ETHANOL
SOY OCHS TRE BARS ARI
GALATIA UAR PERI THIS
ANIGHTMAREONELMSTREET
REFUEL RAGWORT TRIAGE
DREARY FLUSHES SUBPAR
```

70

```
GERM FABLE OGRES  VEES
ALAI ONION NEUME  ERLE
MONTICELLO STREP RIME
ANGORA TAUT SANSIMEON
SALEM GERALDINE
DOMENICO HEAL  SKIMPS
ERAS ZORN STOPS SLOAN
NCR AENEAS SNAPAT URE
SABLES WHO GNOME  NSA
LOS STAIRS TOPRATED
SHED THEBREAKERS EVES
TAHITIAN TATERS  ARE
ORO HERAT DEY  SHORTY
URU ERENOW DEFATS NAV
PASHA STROM DARE  AONE
SHEETS PORT ICERINKS
PROCEEDER  ROPER
GRACELAND DOLL NELLIE
MIRA VROOM PEACEFIELD
ALIT EELER PANES  FAKE
NEDS DYADS OPENS  THAN
```

71

```
ALARM SAGAL MOOD  PARE
VIDEO HULCE ELMO  RBIS
ERATO ARARA DIAG  ERAS
RAMALAMADINGDONG LANE
GAS IDEALS  EVICTS
EPI IPSO RTE  PRIMA
BEBOPALULA EDILES DSM
BRIAR ARUMS  TOLERATE
SUSHI YESTERDAY OBOE
UNAU CAUL  OSIRIS
PHD ZIPADEEDOODAH ACE
REAMED BIRD  ORES
OLDS MOOREHEAD RETAR
LOOSENED SOCLE PROMO
ETO KOREAN CHICKABOOM
REESE REM ESAU  KRA
BLONDE AERIAL  ROM
RUNT DEDODODODEDADADA
ACRE IDOL SENOR SCION
DIOR VERA ELENI TIRED
SANS ERNS SEDAN SISSY
```

72

```
PULI PEALE FATAL  SLIT
APER EDWIN ARENA  PISA
COVERGIRLS DRESSMAKER
ANI UGLY IBEAM TORERO
SMEE CLASS  CROSSES
DEFIED CHERI  SHADE
UCONN LEADINGLADY SHA
DOLE TONI AURA  SEAR
ELK PORTRAITIST SHARE
SESSIONS TROTH SLUMPS
INKLE FOALS  OPALS
DONEES NOLTE UNABATED
ELGAR BALLETSTARS REA
BLED RENI OTIS  BERT
TAR PIANOPLAYER BASIE
PAPUA RADAR  TENSED
TALUSES NONOS  ASHE
ABASER CABER ASEA DOT
REDHOTMAMA NIGHTNURSE
ELLE ONSET EDIES  FUSE
SEED NOTRE DONNE  OMAN
```

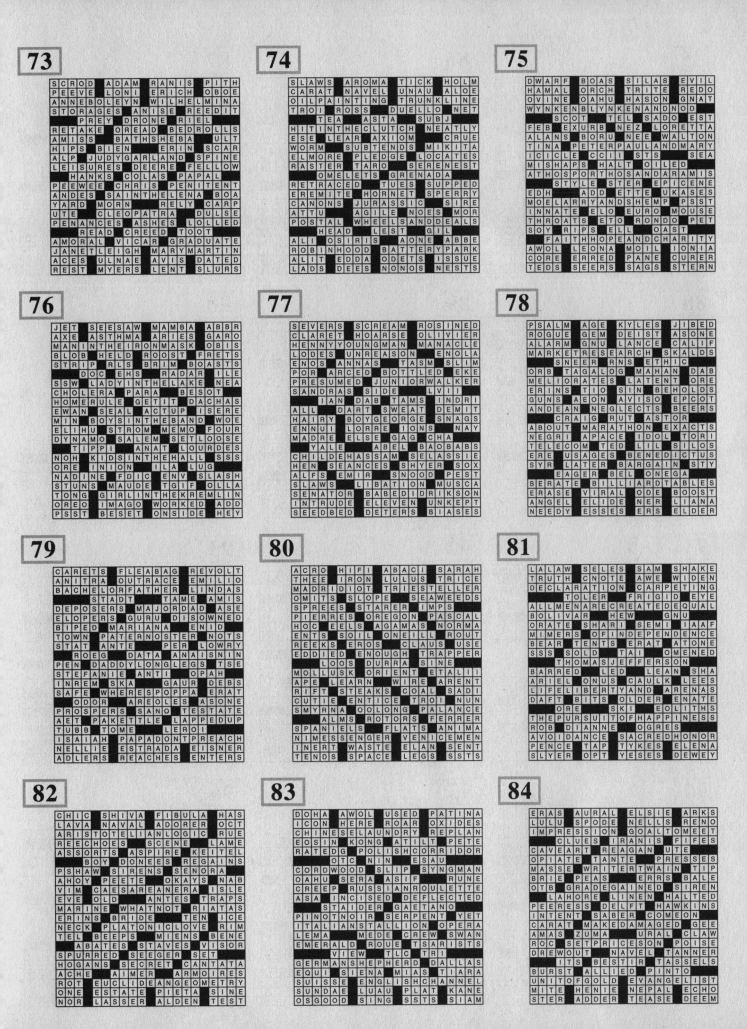

85

```
ASSAM HABIT STAT ABAS
INIGO AGATE CARA LILA
MALEORDERCATALOG EGAD
SPONGE NEH ATLAS USIA
   TOILED CHER STINT
MCM ONOS DOTER FAIR
ARA GENE ELIS PALACES
ROI URIS WIL SERENADE
TODAYS WOVE ETC SLEW
SKIMP SHARI OGEES INS
   MIA PAYMASTER OFF
REP NAILS HAIRS LOOKS
OARS RCA PUNS EDERLE
TROPHIES RST RAMI NIA
ENVIOUS ROSA EPEE INN
   ENOS PEPYS DERR AES
HOMED COCA CURIAE
EVEL ALLAN MAC TURBOS
LINE BELLESARERINGING
ENTS BREL ASTRO TOLET
NESS EKES THESE STERS
```

86

```
MAWR IRS LASSER BOZOS
ANYA SUE ALTONA ERASE
MIAMIBEACHBEACH LINTS
ALTMAN WORSEN SNEEZES
   TEN LAO DDE OMNI
USERS ELGAR SLID TBAR
CEA KALAMAZOOZOO ACE
STRATA SNIDE EUDORAS
DIPLOMA CASAS BARBRA
   FRANKFORTFORT NAIL
SABRE NAE ARI FERDE
CRUE DAVENPORTPORT
HERDER ALOUS SMITING
LOBSTER TRASS STEREO
ELA HYDEPARKPARK ORB
PANT FALL SAILS BANDS
   KUDU FAA CIA EMS
RIBLESS STATEN AERIAL
ISAAC CAMBRIDGEBRIDGE
CANNA AVIATE ETE TERN
HOKEY NECTAR RST ASAS
```

87

```
MANILA ORELSE ASA DRE
AMATOL AERIAL REM RUR
JANETMARGOLIN FEBRILE
ATOMISM MOLLIE SLAVIC
   OMAHA IONIA EVENT
MARINATE APRONSTRINGS
MRED NITROUS SOS
CILIA TILT BRAM ORTS
MAYORSHIP JUNIORMISS
   SPEE SOUSA GOESAT
RETAILS TANGS PRUNERS
ALUMNI EASTS PEAT
JULIETCAPS AUGMENTER
ALEE PLUS MIES SERRA
   GEO RANCHOS WEST
SEPARATENESS OCTETTES
LURIE HEEDS SNARL
ABODES REDACT LIMITED
NOVELLA DECLARATIVELY
TEE EUR NEREID CRANIA
SAD YES TREADS HANSEN
```

88

```
SCHMO SERGE AIMED CNN
ARIES UTHER PRADO REE
FOSTERSHOME PORTRAYAL
ANSA OPENS RANI MISTS
RYE ADELE MORONS STLO
INSULIN BASERATE AYN
   SANDSCASTLE AXIL
ABCDE ARDORS IMPOSTS
MALA BOLOGNA FOP SPAT
ETI CANINES MIDST ABA
REF ELEVES CANAPE LUG
IMF ELIAS RARITAN ALE
CAST SDS MENACED SCAR
ANDORRA CUSACK PIERS
   WINO HOLIDAYSINN
ODE SONATINA TRIGGER
YELL MATTES YUKON HRE
SALON OLOR RONIN ROAD
TRIBESMEN COURTSHOUSE
EIN WRIST UNLIT ALLEY
REG TASSO PALPS HESSE
```

89

```
TEEM SATES CERES SHOP
ALTI OCHRE AMUSE TAGS
BACKFUTURE LASTSHEILA
UNSHARED POLIS TARGET
   AXED RAVEL NINE
DENIED TIGER SUNDOWNS
ARILS NEVERSUNDAY ROI
RAGS TONE TIES MORT
ETH DAYTRIFFIDS RANGE
ROTARIES ORALE HINGES
   IRONS STOKE LOGIA
AUGUST TEASE AUTOCRAT
PLUMS NOTSTRANGER MNO
INAS SODA NOEL CLIP
NAN RIDDLESANDS COATS
GRANOLAS ROXIE GALWAY
   OPEL MERLE PARD
STOLEN PACER SALESREP
TALESCRYPT OUTTOWNERS
UKES EARLE STARR ANIS
BEGS STEED EERIE POST
```

90

```
UPROARS FAILS STRATUS
PAINFUL OSTIA ARACHNE
ENTERLAUGHING LANTERN
NOTS EDGY STELE DOJOS
DUETS ELIA STASH ROBO
STREEP ISMS DIEU YER
   PREF HAPPYDAYS LDS
ARP ONUS TYRO NEHRU
DEE WASABI OKS REECHO
ATOR NILE SWOOP RAKER
POPE GLADALLOVER DCCI
TOLLS SAPOR NINE SLAG
SLEETS MOD POETIC UTE
ATALL SAAR TUNA BEN
   CUR GOODTIMES PERK
ENE EMMY ASIS RELIEF
LEFT OBEYS SETI DUNCE
EQUIP AREAS SODA GLOW
SUNNIER ACERTAINSMILE
TANGLED SCAPA OCTANES
ELYSEES TONIS MEANEST
```

91

```
ASSET CSPAN NIPA KNAR
STALE UTILE IRAS AERO
LENIN BYEBYELOVE THOU
EVA SPILT GENL CHRIS
EIN PETEROSE OCCLUDE
PEDROS ROOMSERVICE
   RETAG OUTDO IPECAC
SPED CAMP ANE NOLO
TEA THREEONAMATCH NIL
ATSEA BANGOR CHEATED
REFERS THEBLOB ELLENS
GRANTOR ELEVES OSMAN
ASU SUNRISESUNSET PTA
TOLD DAN METS STEP
ENTERS GRETA STLEO
   MOSQUITONET REEFER
SHIATSU HONDURAS CLU
WARNS EIRE GRAYS OAS
AGED BEFOREHAND ERUPT
TUNE INNS TORII PERSE
SEED OSIS SESNO SATED
```

92

```
SOMA ERIS SNEE CHAISE
CRIB LOLL HORN HACKER
ALAN ELIA ANAT EMCEES
NOMENCLATURE IDEAL
SPIGOTS SNOW CORNICES
   AVOID ANSWERS MINT
BUTTERNUTS IDI SALSA
ASHEN BAKERS CAPTION
RUE ANO BETIDE FRIARS
BRIT ABA DECOY LIZ
SPREADING MENAGERIE
   MRI ALARM SUM DONS
SUPPER SERIAL NED ADS
ABREAST ANDREA EDDIE
NOIRS ERN COMPARISON
DAMA PRESIDE PETAL
STAMPACT GRAS ALIENOR
   EAGER NAUTICALMILE
PRONTO ATOM RAHS MEDE
RANTED CARA OGEE ACES
ODESSA TRES MOSS SERE
```

93

```
BORN FATAL STAR INCAS
EROO IMAMS LENO PAIGE
ABUT JUSTUNINTERESTED
RIGHTISTS APES ACHENE
STEARATE POUTY CAESAR
   PIN SCAMP SIC
ADIPOSE ALI ALAE PANG
DENY MAR IDOLS ELIE
AFRAIDILLFINDOUT RICE
STIBNITE INDENT AFTER
   ONT AROID ONE
BOLUS SELENA HARDCORE
EXIT CONFOUNDEDBYTHAT
DELI ADORN ERE LOBO
SNIT LOSE BRA STAYSIN
   RIM PIANO ALA
SCOPES SCANT PALOMINO
ARRANT TANG TIDEWATER
VERYEAGERTOLEARN ZAMA
OPINE ALTE OCTET ELAL
YESES REED AHEMS DOTS
```

94

```
TOGA SOUPS STEAD TROD
ELON ANGIE TERRE RACE
MEAT VILLA ERICS ANTE
POLITICIANSARE EDDIED
SST ROE SCALA ARRESTS
   EDER STEN CASTES
ANNES THESAMETHEWORLD
LODI CHAR ASTOR NEAR
OVERTHEY PAR URSA ACE
EARDRUM TRITONE RILED
   REB PROMISE ORG
CODES TAUTENS TRANSIT
ODE SPAR EDS TOBUILDA
MEMO ELEMI VATS TEAK
BRIDGEEVENWHERE GEESE
   DARNER HORA WASP
GROMMET CLIMB IOU OLD
LEVEES THEREISNORIVER
AMIN SARAN RAISE NERO
DINT EDINA EGGER CROP
ETES SEPTS DENTS ASIS
```

95

```
SACRE MANETS MORI GAR
APRIL ELEGIT EVEN UDE
DOUBLEDAGGER LISTENER
SSS LES PEAT HURTLE
ATTACKS OMITS GORSHIN
CLINTS DYANCANNON ENT
KEENS MULISH OAT TEAS
SSR AOK DOT JAN
   BULLETTRAIN MANGLE
CARAMIA ROONE RISKIER
CRITTER INUIT ESPANOL
CAFTANS GESTE THERESE
INLETS MORTARBOARD
   ERA BEN LOP SAM
DUTY PAM OSTEAL ELENI
ETH ARROWSMITH STINTS
ARROYOS AMASS SKEETER
DIODES ASOR TRA ICU
PLUSSIGN STILETTOHEEL
ALG HEAD EIDOLA MONDE
NOH ARMY SEINES ANTES
```

96

```
MEN GARBO OATER JADED
ANO REOIL SCONE OBOLI
RRS AGANA TENON EYDIE
CATCHINGFORTYWINKS
UPROARS MIAS AIMSTO
STORM EDICT SAID AER
DEADTOTHEWORLD WHO
UPTO TINES ALAS RIEN
SLAB RDA SCRIM MINEO
DUKAKIS PUTRID SING
AMI OUTLIKEALIGHT LAS
   NOAM ENERGY CUTSOUT
SAGAN RINSE ALT OGRE
WEAK SAGA IMPEI LSAT
EIN INTHELANDOFNOD
LOA GOES OPTIC BOAST
LUPINO IGOR AUTUMNS
   GETTINGSOMESHUTEYE
PAOLO UNFIT ORCUS CDT
ANJOU STEAL ADORE HES
PESOS HORSE TATAR ERE
```

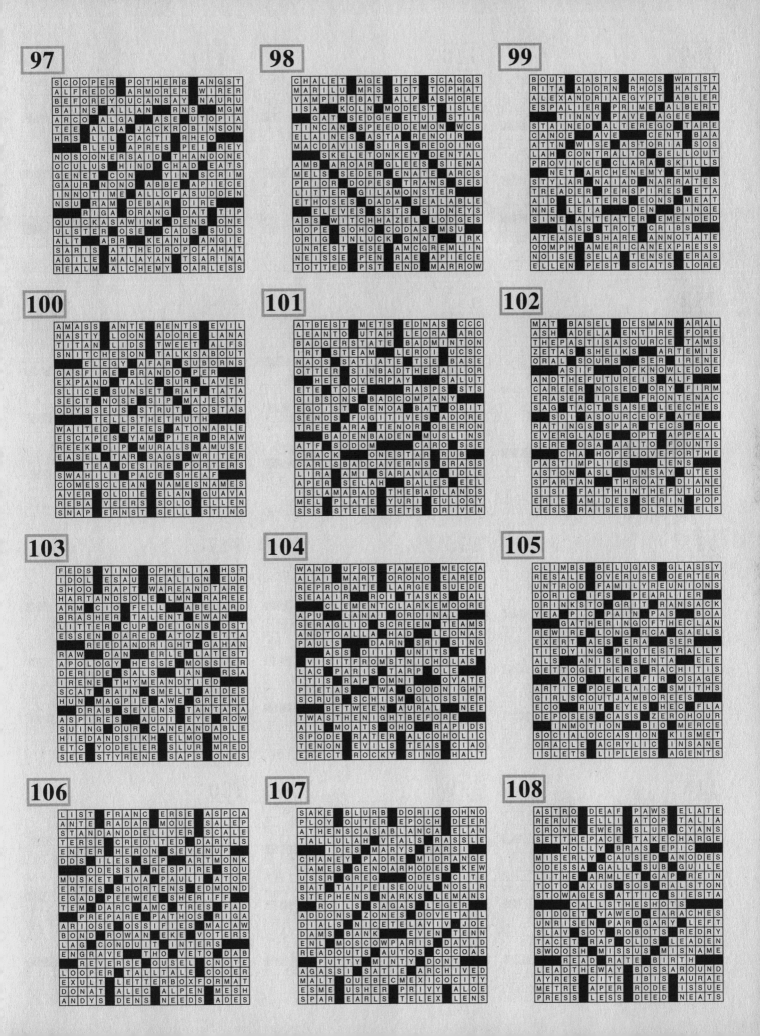

97

```
SCOOPER POTHERB ANGST
ALFREDO ARMORER WIRER
BEFOREYOUCANSAY NAURU
BAINS ALLAN RNS MGM
ARCO ALGA ASE UTOPIA
TEE ALBA JACKROBINSON
HRS LIL CACTI RHEO
BLEU APRES PEI REY
NOSOONERSAID THANDONE
OCULUS HIND CHAD EATS
GENET CON YIN SCRIM
GAUR NONO ABBE APIECE
INNOTIME ALLOFASUDDEN
NSU RAM DEBAR DIRE
RIGA ORANG DAT TIP
QUICKASAWINK DENS ONE
ULSTER OSE CADS SUDS
ALT ABR KEANU ANGIE
SARIS ATTHEDROPOFAHAT
AGILE MALAYAN TSARINA
REALM ALCHEMY OARLESS
```

98

```
CHALET AGE IFS SCAGGS
MARILU MRS SOT TOPHAT
VAMPIREBAT ALP ASHORE
ISA KOLN MODEST ISLE
GAT SEDGE ETUI STIR
TINCAN SPEEDDEMON WCS
ELAINES ASTA RENOIR
MACDAVIS SIRS REDOING
SKELETONKEY DENTAL
AMB AROAR GLEES SIENA
MELS SEDER ENATE ARCS
PRIOR DOPES TRANS SES
LITTER GILAMONSTER
ETHOSES DADA SEALABLE
ELEVES SSTS SIDNEYS
ABS WITCHHAZEL LODGES
MOPE SOHO CODAS MSU
ORIG INLUCK GNAT IRK
UNREST ESE AMCGREMLIN
NEISSE PEN RAE APIECE
TOTTED PST END MARROW
```

99

```
BOUT CASTS ARCS WRIST
RITA ADORN RHOS HASTA
ALEXANDRIAEGYPT ABLER
ESPALIER PRIME ALBERT
TINNY PAVE AGEE
STAINED ALTEREGO TARE
CANOE AVE CENT BAA
ATTN WISE ASTORIA SOS
LAH CONTRALTO SELLOUT
PROVINCE CLARA SKILLS
NET ARCHENEMY EMU
STYLAR NAIAD NARRATES
TREADER PERSPIRES ETA
AID ELATERS EONS MEAT
NNE LEIA DEN BINGE
SINE ANTEATER EMENDED
LASS TROT CRIBS
ATEASE SHARE ANNOTATE
OOMPH AMERICANEXPRESS
NOISE SELA TENSE ERAS
ELLEN PEST SCATS LORE
```

100

```
AMASS ANTE RENTS EVIL
NASTY LOON ADORE LANA
TITAN LIDS TWEET ALFS
SNITCHESON TALKSABOUT
ELEGY AFAR SUBORNS
GASFIRE BRANDO PER
EXPAND TALC SUR LAVER
SLICE SUNSET RAF TATA
SECT NOSE SIP MAJESTY
ODYSSEUS STRUT COSTAS
TELLSTHETRUTH
WAITED EPEES ATONABLE
ESCAPES YAM PIER DRAW
REEK DIP MURALS AMUSE
EASEL TAR SAGS WRITER
TEA DESIRE PORTERS
SWAHILI PACE SHEAF
COMESCLEAN NAMESNAMES
AVER OLDIE ELAN GUAVA
REBA VEERS SOLO ELLEN
SNAP ERNST SELL STING
```

101

```
ATBEST METS EDNAS CCC
LEANTO UTAH LEORA ARO
BADGERSTATE BADMINTON
IRT STEAM LEROI UCSC
NAOS SATIATE TSE BASE
OTTER SINBADTHESAILOR
HEE OVERPAY SALUT
ETE TONE RASPS STS
GIBSONS BADCOMPANY
EGOIST GENOA BAT OBIT
SENDS FUGITIVES ADORE
TREE ARA TENOR OBERON
BADENBADEN MUSLINS
ATF SODOM CARO SSE
CRACK ONESTAR RUB
CARLSBADCAVERNS BRASS
LIRA AMI SARANAC IDLE
APER SELAH BALES EEL
ISLAMABAD THEBADLANDS
MEL PLATE YURI EULOGY
SSS STEEN SETS DRIVEN
```

102

```
MAT BASEL DESMAN ARAL
ASH ADELA ENTIRE FORE
THEPASTISASOURCE TAMS
ZETAS SHEIKS ARTEMIS
ORAL SOURS SER IRENE
ASIF OFKNOWLEDGE
ANDTHEFUTUREIS ALF
CAREER NOSED ORY FIRM
ERASER IRE FRONTENAC
SAG TACT SASE LEECHES
SDI ASOURCEOF ATE
RATINGS SPAR TECS ROE
EVERGLADE OPT APPEAL
SERE OSA AALTO FOUNTS
CHA HOPELOVEFORTHE
PASTIMPLIES LENS
ASTON ASL UNSAY UTES
SPARTAN THROAT DIANE
SISI FAITHINTHEFUTURE
ERIE AMIDES SERIN POP
LESS RAISES OLSEN ELS
```

103

```
FEDS VINO OPHELIA HST
IDOL ESAU REALIGN EUR
SHOO RAPT WAREANDTARE
HARTANDSOLE LMN RAREE
ARM CIO FELL ABELARD
BRASHER TALENT EWAN
LITTER CUP DEIGNS DST
ESSEN DARED ATOZ ETTA
REEDANDRIGHT GAHAN
RAW DAN ERLE LATEST
APOLOGY HESSE MOSSIER
DERIDE SALS IAN RSA
IRENE THYMEANDTIED
SCAT BAIN SMELT AIDES
HUN MAGPIE AWE GREENE
DRAB SEVENS TANTARA
ASPIRES AUDI EYE ROW
SUING OUR CANEANDABLE
HIEDANDSIKH ELMO MOLE
ETC YODELER SLUR MRED
SEE STYRENE SAPS ONES
```

104

```
WAND UFOS FAMED MECCA
ALAI MART ORONO EARED
REPROBATE LARGE SUEDE
SEAAIR ROI TASKS DAL
CLEMENTCLARKEMOORE
APU LANAI ORDINAL
SERAGLIO SCREEN TEAMS
ANDTOALLA HAD LEONAS
PAULS DARN SRISING
ASS DIII UNITS TET
VISITFROMSTNICHOLAS
LAC PARIS TARP OLE
ITIS RAP OMNI OVATE
PIETAS TWA GOODNIGHT
SCRUB SCHISM GLOSSIER
BETWEEN AURAL NEE
TWASTHENIGHTBEFORE
AIL MOATS OHO RAPIDS
SPODE RATER ALCOHOLIC
TENON EVILS TEAS CIAO
ERECT ROCKY SINO HALT
```

105

```
CLIMBS BELUGAS GLASSY
RESALE OVERUSE OERTER
UNTROD FAMILYREUNIONS
DORIC IFS PEARLIER
DRINKSTO GRIT RANSACK
YEA PIC PAIN PAS BOA
GATHERINGOFTHECLAN
REWIRE LONG RCA GAELS
EXERT AES ERA SER
TIEDYING PROTESTRALLY
ALS ANISE SENTA EEE
GETTOGETHERS RACHITIS
ADO EKE FIR OSAGE
ARTIE POE LAIC SMITHS
GIRLSCOUTJAMBOREES
ECO RUT EYES HEC FLA
DEPOSES CASS ZEROHOUR
INMOTION BIO MERCE
SOCIALOCCASION KISMET
ORACLE ACRYLIC INSANE
ISLETS LIPLESS AGENTS
```

106

```
LIST FRANC ERSE ASPCA
ANTE RADAR MOUE SALEP
STANDANDDELIVER SCALE
TERSE CREDITED DARYLS
ENTER HERON SEVENUP
DDS ILES SEP ARTMONK
ODESSA RESPIRE SOU
MUSKET TVA PAULI ATOR
ERTES SHORTENS EDMOND
EGAD PEEWEE SHERIFF
TEM DARC AMC TRES FAD
PREPARE PATHOS RIGA
ARIOSE OSSIFIES MACAW
BOND ROWAN EKE VOTERS
LAG CONDUIT INTERS
ENGRAVE THO VETO DAB
REVERSE OUSEL CNOTE
LOOPER TALLTALE COOER
EXULT LETTERBOXFORMAT
DONAT ALEC ALPEN MESH
ANDYS DENS NEEDS ADES
```

107

```
SAKE BLURB DORIC OHNO
PLOY OUTER EPOCH DEER
ATHENSCASABLANCA ELAN
TALLULAH VEALS RASSLE
IDES MARYS FARSI
CHANEY PADRE MIDRANGE
LAMES GENOARHODES KEW
USSR GREG ODES CITE
BAT TAIPEISEOUL NOSIR
STEPHENS NARKS LEMANS
ROILS SAGAS LEGER
ADDONS ZONES DOVETAIL
DIALS NICETELAVIV JOE
DAMS BANK EVEN TENN
ENL MOSCOWPARIS DAVID
READOUTS AUTOS COCOAS
PUTTY MINTY
AGASSI SATIE ARCHIVED
MALT QUEBECMEXICOCITY
ESME USHER PRIVY ALOE
SPAR EARLS TELEX LENS
```

108

```
ASTRO DEAF PAWS ELATE
RERUN ELLI ATOP TALIA
CRONE EWER SLUR CYANS
SETTHEPACE TAKECHARGE
HOLLY BRAS EPIC
MISERLY CAUSED ANODES
ODESSA GALL SUB GUILE
LITHE ARMLET GAP REIN
TOTO AXIS SOS RALSTON
STOWAGES ATTIC SIESTA
CALLSTHESHOTS
GIDGET YAWED EARACHES
UNRISEN PAR GARY LEFT
SLAV SOY ROBOTS REDRY
TACET RAP OLDS LEADEN
SWOOSH MISSUS MISNAME
READ RATE BIRTH
LEADTHEWAY BOSSAROUND
AYRES CITE IBIS AURAE
METRE APER RODE ISSUE
PRESS LESS DEED NEATS
```

109

```
LAHR  RATES  SERA   MASTS
OGEE  UBOAT  PAIR   OCTET
ORAD  BERRA  ERST   STORE
TERRIBLYPLEASED     SNARE
SESAMES    ERR  RELEASED
      FIR  AFLAME  CAST
PRETTYUGLY  ALSOP   UCLA
LHASA  NEE  GNAW   SERIAL
YOU  TESSERA  NAP   SALVE
     FETE  COLA  MEASLIER
OLIO  RACEWALKING   LAST
DEMURELY  STAR    GARY
OVINE  SRO  ERASURE  WHY
REDDEN  URSA  ICI   TAHOE
SEEM  ESSEN  STANDSDOWN
      INIT  LATEST  RID
TASSELED  CON   MANIPLE
ANISE  WORKINGVACATION
TONIS  ARAB  ELIHU  INGA
ADANO  RITA  TONAL  OTIC
REIGN  TSAR  TWYLA  NOCT
```

110

```
TSPS  MAMAS  SWIRL  PTAS
SHUE  IDEST  AODAI  AWOL
KAZANTZAKISGREEK   MANY
SHOWERED  COEDS  ESPIES
      SELES  SKITS  UNPEN
CAMELS  BIBLE  SNEERSAT
HEADY  CARYSARTIST  WRY
ARFS  ERIE  OUTS  PAIL
III  WILDESLADY  BOISE
REALNESS  VEERS  CONFER
      AARP  PINTS  SEAT
BOOTHS  ROAST  TERRIBLE
ATRIA  MILNESBEAR  YEA
SAWN  VIVA  AMMO  CRAG
IRE  LECARRESSPY  MOOSE
CULTURAL  ESTEE  TANNER
      LUCAS  BASAL  BANNS
LISTEN  ALDER  MEMOIRES
USPO  DEFOESMANSERVANT
MEIR  ATTAR  ALGER  EKCO
PEGS  SCATS  PARTS  DEEP
```

111

```
DRAB  SPEND  AWAIT  JOTS
OAHU  HANOI  SHINE  ALOE
ENOL  ARGON  HORDE  YELL
SKYLARKING  CRYINGWOLF
      DEPEND  HAL  ASIA
SAVOR  REASONER  GLASS
PLAZAS  DYER  DUAL  KIWI
IGNITED  SASS  BRA  IDOL
TONNEAUS  MITT  ENSNARL
SLAG  FLAT  NERO  CAGNEY
      TALKINGTURKEY
APPEAR  IDEA  EARL  HUMP
CARAMEL  YARN  LIESOVER
INIT  RID  ROOM  STATUTE
DEMI  SPEC  USAF  SIDLES
SLANT  CORNERED  GOADS
      GIBE  ROD  ANALOG
CATCALLING  DUCKINGOUT
ODOR  OSSIE  IDIOT  IDLE
RENO  OILER  RENTE  NINA
KNEW  PEERS  EDGAR  GEAR
```

112

```
AHAB  BAMBI  DORA  ASHER
DEDE  UNCENTERED  STELE
DROVERCLEVELAND  KOANS
ABRIDGE   ALECTO  SODOM
MINES  ODDS  HANS  GYRE
SESS  SECRETS   OMERTA
   JESTERAARTHUR   OER
SAWHORSES  RUCHE   ETO
PLAIN  TSP  TARN  DISCH
OGREISH  EASE  UNO  EERO
NOR  HAIRYTRUMAN   VIN
GRIP  ERN  LYNN  SANREMO
YENTA  AFTA  ELS  EELER
GAS  ROUTS   OPERETTAS
ASH  SHERBETHOOVER
CHASTE  ROOSTED  ORBS
CART  BALD  MAES  SCARY
ORDER  SURTAX  TOUCHED
SPIRO  SMARTENVANBUREN
TINED  APPEARANCE  LAZE
SEGOS  DYES  STATS  THEY
```

113

```
MOMS  AMES  ARABS  REEDS
AMAH  ROAM  RENAL  EMAIL
SANA  INRE  SINAI  HERVE
THERESONLYONE  GNARLED
SATIRES  TEND   THING
   ANOLES  ERATO  EACH
THATS  MAR  TEETERS  ROO
REDEEMER  HARDERTOFIND
ARMADA  CROSSE   LADES
COIL  CHEERS   FAVOR
ENT  THANANEEDLEIN  NAT
   PEONY  LYRICS  HOWE
ROMAN  SHIEST  TIARAS
AHAYSTACKAND  TRANSMIT
SIR  EARRING  CEO  THATS
POTS  BRAND   ARROYO
   ACLAM  ISLE  TATTING
BRADLEY  INCLAMCHOWDER
LINDA  ADAGE  TARO  ILIA
ALTER  LOGON  OMOO  CELT
BLINK  SCONE  REPS  ESSE
```

114

```
ELMS  ACRE  ABHOR  COSTA
COOT  CREW  ROUTE  OATES
HOROSCOPE  COMICSTRIPS
ONTOP  SALE  HECATE  LEA
   LEGISLATOR  PAROLED
SATIATES  GROUP   LID
ADHERER  CLASSIFIEDADS
CRY  SLUED  URN   ROT
REMOVE  ETS  APSE  APNEA
AMERICANA  IDA  EERIEST
   CROSSWORDPUZZLE
IMPUGNS  AWE  OPERETTAS
SOUSA  IDYL  DOT  ANYHOW
LOL  ESE  RESOD   UDE
EDITORIALPAGE  ROADMAP
   OPA  LARGE  DECREPIT
CALYPSO  NEARMISSES
ARE  REMEDY  MORS  AKRON
MOVIEREVIEW  LEADSTORY
USERS  GENRE  ALGA  OISE
SEEKS  ANGST  RYES  PLOT
```

115

```
ABELS  SPOT  ASHE  OMBRE
COROT  ELLA  STAN  PARES
CLIVE  WAIL  SUIT  ARIES
TAKEAREINCHECK  PLEASE
   BLURTS  INCUBI  ORES
ALEUTS  ASTO   LEAF
NEIGHSAYERS   MARICHAL
TAN  EVERT  ODES  RHONE
SKEW  TATA  CARAT  MILAN
   HTS  SEASIDE  ACTIN
ARNIE  ROANRIVER  SASSY
COENS  AMBROSE   MSG
OMENS  MELON  SAGA  ORDO
REDYE  BREL  SITAR  HOP
NOSTRILS  MANESQUEEZE
   HARE  ETON  UNSEEN
BITE  ARETHA  RESEAT
ADOPTS  THEBRIDLESUITE
CANOE  WYNN  OLGA  KAREN
OHGOD  AMIE  BEET  ERATO
NOAHS  FACT  EYRE  DYNES
```

116

```
PLATS  AFT  PSEUD  SHONE
RELET  MOO  ACCRA  WANED
EVOLUTION  POLAR  ANTON
PEEL  ISLIKEWALKINGONA
SESTETS  ERST   SEA
   ALA  ACRE  SNEERING
ROLLINGBARRELTHE  NOR
OKIE  LADY  VIAL  CAPRA
ORE  GRITS  PECK  FORUMS
FASTLANE  WALKERISNTAS
   HALT  MARYS  ANTI
INTERESTEDIN  SMILESON
NOOSES  RIDS  GOOSY  AMA
SONES  REEL  TERN  ZING
ENA  WHERETHEBARRELIS
TELETHON  ERRS   IER
   RIO  ISLE  ENDORSE
GOINGASINKEEPING  HIPS
ABLER  ADDAX  ONTOPOFIT
ROSSI  PEETE  ETE  DULCE
SEATS  SEXES  TOR  TREYS
```

117

```
SCRIP  OHARE  BARI  BAAS
AROMA  RATES  ARON  EXIT
HEAPTHRILLS  TASS  AIDE
LENORE  RAE  LOBSTERLAW
   LONE  NAMER  WAND
PALIN  MATRIX  HOLISTIC
EDIT  SPLINT  WORLD  ASH
PAPERLIPS  MENDS  SILO
OPP  OARS  GEODES  RAGES
STIMULI  SLANGS  HECATE
   STOCKMARKETRASH
ANADEM  LADLED  EROSIVE
PECOS  HURLEY  SPAR  NIP
SHES  GETTY  FIRSTLASS
ERR  CRAZY  TWINES  INTO
SUBTLETY  BEINGS  ABEAM
   EONS  OUNCE  SOME
POTATOHIPS  HAG  VELCRO
EARP  BEBE  FIRESIDEHAT
THEO  LEER  OTTER  ERECT
SUET  ETTA  BASSI  OSTEO
```

118

```
MAST  ORCH  IDAS  POMONA
ALTA  BRAE  NIPA  INOUYE
DOUBLESTANDARD  GETTER
DUDLEY  TRAIL  EMILIO
   EDAM  STAEL  GRIFFIN
SONS  BOSTONCOMMON  TCU
QUI  ELUL  ATTU  NETHER
UNGENEROUS  TMI  RHEAS
ACHED  NOTUPTOPAR  DOGE
DETROP  PETRO  SNEE  RES
   COWLS  STOWE  SALAD
ESL  SONG  OMARS  MERIDA
REUP  PARANORMAL  VINES
ALBEN  GAR  DANADELANY
SERIES  PITA  TRIS  RTE
ECO  ONTHEAVERAGE  SYST
   STUMPED  STALE  ORCA
   TERESA  TILES  EUROPE
ABIDER  WELLACCUSTOMED
BANANA  OGEE  HOSE  NOSE
EYELET  LORD  OWES  GOON
```

119

```
OJIBWAS  HOARSE  RESNAP
DONAHUE  INCITE  EROICA
EVIDENT  PURDUECHICKEN
RET  ATTS  SEED  HANKERS
   STYLAR   ICONS
PLATO  EMORYBOARD  LOOM
RENAN  SPREES  SEL  ARNA
INVITE  REMNANT  ETUDES
MAINEFRAME  ALA  ARENT
ESL  RTES  LARDED  YARDS
   URSA  STRIA  MILS
LIPPI  PHASIC  FIDO  TSE
ANISE  SAT  KNOXAROUND
STAIRS  COARSEN  SMILED
SEND  AUK  REHIDE  ALLAY
ALOE  PRATTFALLS  DEEDS
   SPITE   SETTER
PASSAIC  ROSS  SHES  MVP
TULANEHIGHWAY  ECUADOR
ATONES  LUNATE  THINICE
HOBART  EMOTES  ESTEVEZ
```

120

```
EDIT  TENT  LAGERS  SPAT
BONA  IRAE  AGARIC  TILE
BUCKINGHAMPALACE  ACID
SPHERES  POD   SEPTIC
   TIS  CORONA  TORAHS
HAWES  TATEGALLERY  DOE
OPENEDUP  SEDATE  PISA
OPS  SENECA  ETCS  ELEM
PETR  MARBLEARCH  HALAS
LAMAZE  SEPAL  HERESY
ALICIAS  RITES  SIROCCO
   NOONES  NEROS  BRUINS
JASON  ALBERTHALL  PROM
ATTN  ICAL  SOVIET  CTO
MIES  ROTUND  ANTIQUES
BOR  TOWERBRIDGE  RUSSE
   SNAPON  BAILIE  MAO
BURIES  LES   SADNESS
LOBS  STPAULSCATHEDRAL
AREA  TRUDGE  OMAR  AMMO
BRYN  SENSOR  SAGE  MAST
```

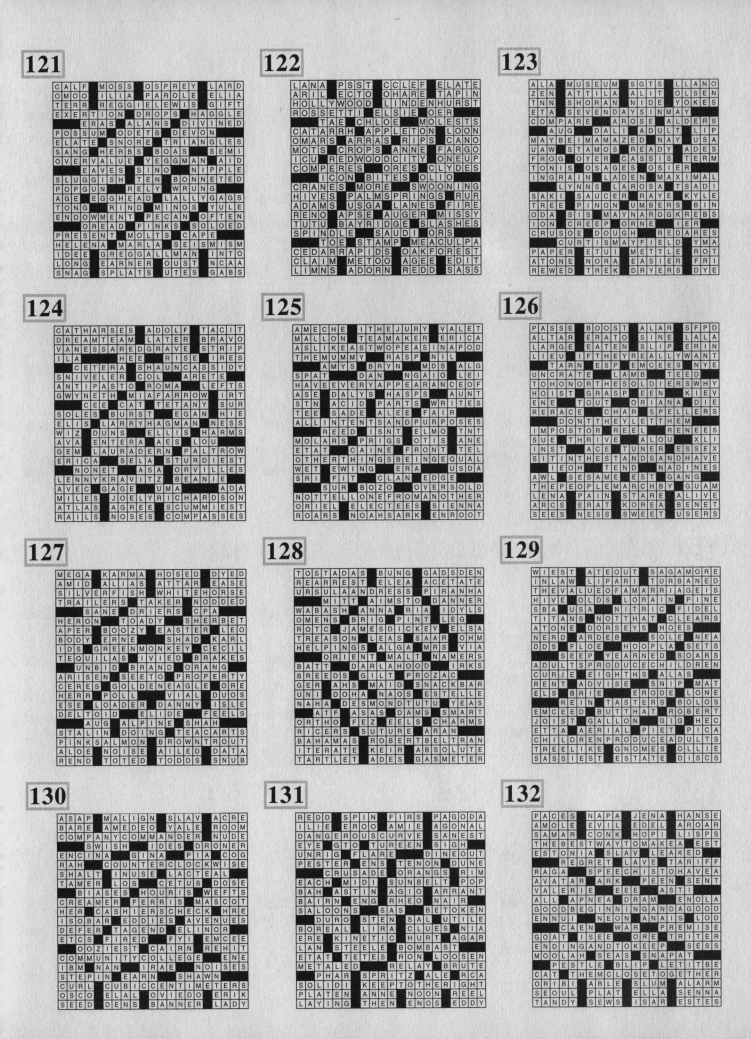

121 122 123
124 125 126
127 128 129
130 131 132

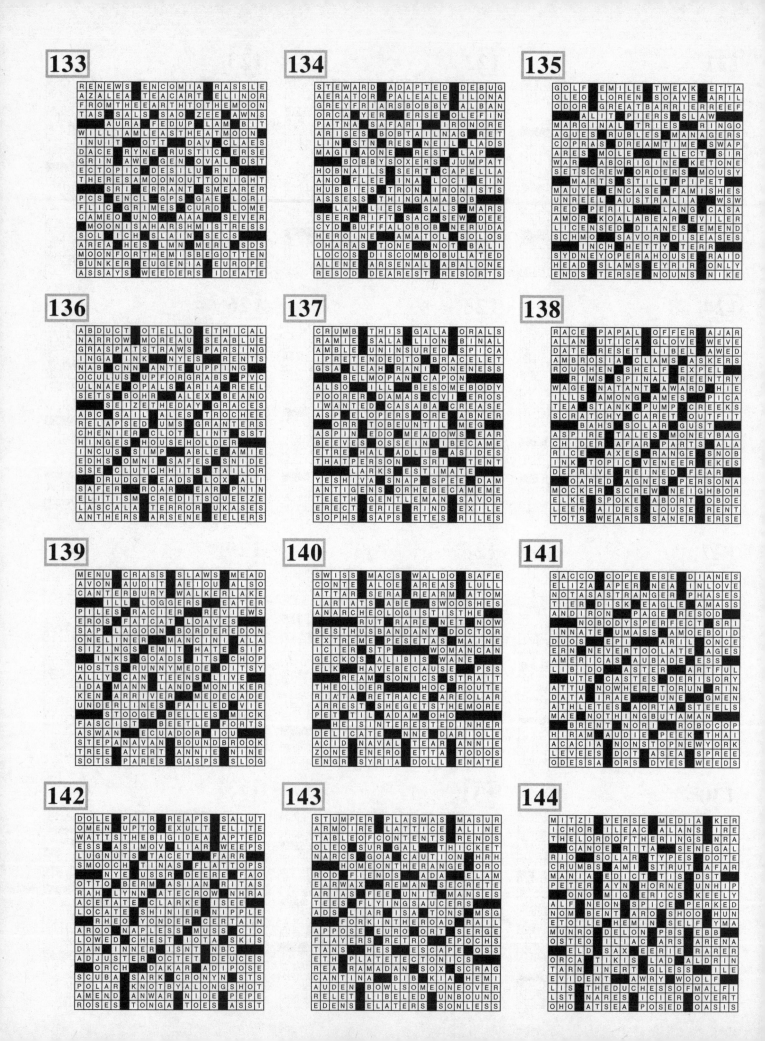

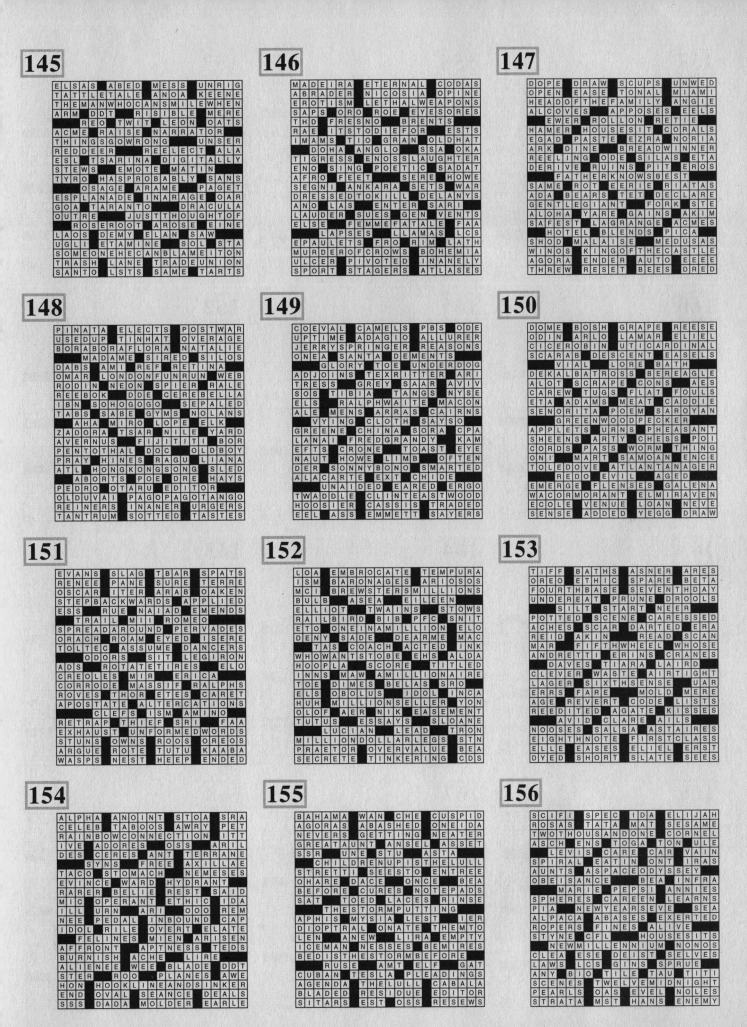

145

```
ELSAS  ABED  MESS  UNRIG
TATTLETALE  ANOA  KEENE
THEMANWHOCANSMILEWHEN
ARM  DDT  RISIBLE  MERE
REO  TWIT  LEON  OATS
ACME  RAISE  NARRATOR
THINGSGOWRONG  UNSER
REDDEER  REELECT  ALA
ESL  TSARINA  DIGITALLY
STEWS  EMOTE  MATIN
TYRO  HASPROBABLY  SANS
OSAGE  ARAME  PAGET
ESPLANADE  INARAGE  OAR
GOA  TARANTO  DRACULA
OUTRE  JUSTTHOUGHTOF
ROSEROOT  AROSE  EINE
LAOS  DEMY  ELAN  SAW
UGLI  ETAMINE  SOL
SOMEONEHECANBLAMEITON
TRASH  LANE  TRADEUNION
SANTO  LSTS  SAME  TARTS
```

146

```
MADEIRA  ETERNAL  CODAS
ABRADER  NICOSIA  OPINE
EROTISM  LETHALWEAPONS
SAPS  ORO  ROE  EYESORES
THD  FRESNO  BRENTS
RAE  ITSTODIEFOR  ESTS
IMAMS  TIO  GRAN  OLDHAT
DOHA  ANGLO  SSA  OKA
TIGRESS  ENOSSLAUGHTER
ENO  SING  POETIC  SADAT
AFRO  FEET  SERE  HOWE
SEGNI  ANKARA  SETS  WAR
DRESSEDTOKILL  DELANYS
ANO  LAS  ENTER  SARI
LAUDER  SUES  GEN  VENTS
ELSE  FEMMEFATALE  FAA
LAPSES  LLAMAS  LCS
EPAULETS  FRO  RIM  LATH
MURDEROFCROWS  BOHEMIA
ULCER  PIVOTED  INANELY
SPORT  STAGERS  ATLASES
```

147

```
DOPE  DRAW  SCUPS  UNWED
OPEN  EASE  TONAL  MIAMI
HEADOFTHEFAMILY  ANGIE
ALCOVES  APPOSES  EELS
EWER  ROLLON  RETIE
HAMER  HOUSESIT  CORALS
EGAD  PASTE  EZRA  NORIA
ARK  DINE  BREADWINNER
REELING  ODE  SILAS  ETA
DERIVE  RUINS  PIT  EROS
FATHERKNOWSBEST
SAME  ROT  EERIE  RIATAS
ADA  BEARS  TET  DECLARE
GENTLEGIANT  FORK  STE
ALOHA  YARE  GAINS  AKIM
SAFEST  LAGRANGE  ACMES
HOTEL  BLENDS  PICA
SHOD  MALAISE  MEDUSAS
WINOS  KINGOFTHECASTLE
AGORA  ENDER  AUTO  EEEE
THREW  RESET  BEES  DRED
```

148

```
PINATA  ELECTS  POSTWAR
USEDUP  TINHAT  OVERAGE
BORABORAFLORA  NATALIE
MADAME  SIRED  SILOS
DABS  AMI  REF  RETINA
OMAR  LONDONFUNRUN  WEB
RODIN  NEON  SPIER  RALE
REEBOK  DDE  CEREBELLA
IBN  SOHOGOGO  SEPALED
TABS  SABE  GYMS  NOLANS
AHA  MIRO  LOPE  ELK
ZADORA  TSAR  NILE  YARD
AVERNUS  FIJITITI  BOR
PENTOTHAL  DOC  OLDBOY
PRAY  HINES  RAGU  LIANA
ATL  HONGKONGSONG  SLED
ABORTS  POE  DRE  HAYS
PEDRO  OTARU  EDITOR
OLDUVAI  PAGOPAGOTANGO
REINERS  INANER  URGERS
TANTRUM  SOTTED  TASTES
```

149

```
COEVAL  CAMELS  PBS  ODE
UPTIME  ADAGIO  ALLURER
JERRYSPRINGER  REASONS
ONEA  SANTA  DEMENTS
GLORY  TOE  UNDERDOG
ADJOINS  TEXRITTER  ARI
TRESS  GREY  SAAR  AVIV
SOS  TIBIA  TANGS  NYSE
ELS  RALPHWAITE  MACON
ALE  MENS  ARRAS  CAIRNS
VYING  CLOTH  SAYSO
GREENE  CHINA  SORA  CPA
LANAI  FREDGRANDY  KAM
EFTS  CRONE  TOAST  EYE
NAUT  HOWE  LIMB  OFTEN
DER  SONNYBONO  SMARTED
ALACARTE  EXT  CHIDE
UNAIDED  EARED  ERGO
TWADDLE  CLINTEASTWOOD
HOOSIER  CASSIS  TRADED
EEL  ASS  EMMETT  SAYERS
```

150

```
DOME  BOSH  GRAPE  REESE
ODIN  ARLO  LAMAR  ELIEL
CICEROBIN  UTICARDINAL
SCARAB  DESCENT  EASELS
VIAL  LORE  BATH
DEKALBATROSS  BEREAGLE
ALOT  SCRAPE  CONS  AES
CAREW  TUGS  FLAT  FOULS
ETA  ADAMS  MEAT  CADDIE
SENORITA  POEM  SAROYAN
GREENWOODPECKER
APPLETS  URNS  PHEASANT
SHEENS  ARTY  CHESS  POI
CORDS  PASS  WORM  THING
ONI  MART  SAMOAN  ENCE
TOLEDOVE  ATLANTANAGER
REDO  EVIL  AGED
EMERGE  FLENSES  GALENA
WACORMORANT  ELMIRAVEN
ECOLE  VENUE  LOAN  NEVE
SENSE  ADDED  YEGG  DRAW
```

151

```
EVANS  SLAG  TBAR  SPATS
RENEE  PANE  SURE  TERRE
OSCAR  ITER  ARAB  OAKEN
STEPBACKWARDS  APPLIED
ESS  RUE  NAIAD  EMENDS
TRAIL  MII  ROMEO
SPREADAROUND  PERVADES
ORACH  ROAM  EYED  ISERE
TOLTEC  ASSUME  DANCERS
ODORS  SIT  LEGIRON
ADS  ROTATETIRES  ELO
CREOLES  MIR  ERICA
CORRODE  MASSIF  RALPHS
ROVES  THOR  ETES  CARET
APOSTATE  ALTERCATIONS
CLEFS  ISM  AMINO
RETRAP  THIEF  SRI  FAA
EXHAUST  UNFORMEDWORDS
STUNS  OWNS  ROOS  OREOS
ARGUE  ROTE  TUTU  KAABA
WASPS  NEST  HEEP  ENDED
```

152

```
LOA  EMBROCATE  TEMPURA
ISM  BARONAGES  ARIOSOS
MCI  BREWSTERSMILLIONS
BULB  ASEA  EILEEN
ELLIOT  TWAINS  STOWS
RAILBIRD  BIB  PFC  SNIT
ETO  ONEINAMILLION  ELO
DENY  SADE  DEARME  MAC
TAS  COACH  ACTED  INK
WHOWANTSTOBE  EHS  ALDA
HOOPLA  SCORE  TITLED
INNS  MAW  AMILLIONAIRE
TOE  DIMES  BELAS  SRO
ELS  OBOLUS  IDOL  INCA
HUH  MILLIONSELLER  YON
OLOF  AER  NIK  EASEMENT
TUTUS  ESSAYS  SLOANE
LUCIAN  LEAD  TRON
MILLIONDOLLARLEGS  STN
PRAETOR  OVERVALUE  BEA
SECRETE  TINKERING  CDS
```

153

```
TIFF  BATHS  ASNER  ARES
OREO  ETHIC  SPARE  BETA
FOURTHBASE  SEVENTHDAY
UNDEREAT  PRUNE  DROOLS
SILT  START  NEER
POTTED  SCENE  CARESSED
ACHES  SCAR  DARTED  ERA
REID  AKIN  READ  SCAN
MAR  FIFTHWHEEL  WHOSE
ANDRETTI  ERINS  CRANES
DAVES  TIARA  LAIRD
CLEVER  WASTE  AIRTIGHT
LAGER  SIXTHSENSE  UAR
ERRS  FARE  MOLD  MERE
AGE  REVERT  CODE  LISTS
REEDITED  AGATE  KISSES
AVID  CLARE  AILS
NOOSES  SALSA  ASTAIRES
EIGHTHNOTE  FIRSTCLASS
ELLE  EASES  ELIEL  ERST
DYED  SHORT  SLATE  SEES
```

154

```
ALPHA  ANOINT  STOA  SRA
CELEB  TABOOS  AWRY  PET
RAINBOWCONNECTION  ITT
IVE  ADORES  OSS  ARIL
DES  CERES  ANT  TERRANE
SYNS  FREE  AXILLAE
TACO  STOMACH  NEMESES
EVINCE  WARD  HYDRANT
RARER  BELIE  REST  SAID
MIC  OPERANT  ETHIC  IDA
ILL  URN  ARI  OOO  REM
NEE  PEDAL  INBOUND  CAP
IDOL  RILE  OVERT  ELATE
FELINES  MIEN  ARISEN
AFFRONT  APTNESS  TEDS
BURNISH  ACHE  LIRE
ALIENEE  WEE  BLADE  DDT
STER  ROO  PLANES  AWE
HON  HOOKLINEANDSINKER
END  OVAL  SEANCE  DEALS
SSS  DADA  MOLDER  EARLE
```

155

```
BAHAMA  WAN  CHE  CUSPID
AGORAS  ABASHED  ONEIDA
NEVERS  GETTING  NEATER
GREATAUNT  ANSEL  ASSET
SSR  UNE  STU  ASTA
CHILDRENUPISTHELULL
STRETTI  SEESTO  ENTREE
OHARE  DACE  ONCE  BEA
BEFORE  CURES  NOTEPADS
SAT  TOED  LACES  RINSE
THESTORMPUTTING
APHIS  MYSIA  LEST  IER
DIOPTRAL  ONATE  THEMTO
LEN  ANEW  LIRA  EMPTY
ICEMAN  NESSES  BEMIRES
BEDISTHESTORMBEFORE
RUSE  AMT  ELF  GAT
CUBAN  TESLA  PLEADINGS
AGENDA  THELULL  CABALA
BLADED  RESIDUE  EDITOR
SITARS  EST  OSS  RESEWS
```

156

```
SCIFI  SPEC  IDA  ELIJAH
ROSAS  TATA  MAT  SESAME
TWOTHOUSANDONE  CORNEL
ASCH  ENS  TOGA  TON  ULE
LEVIS  CARE  CAR  VAIN
SPIRAL  EATIN  ONT  IRAS
AUNTS  ASPACEODYSSEY
OBEISANCE  BEA  INFRA
MARIE  PEPSI  ANNIES
SPHERES  CAREEN  LEARNS
PIA  NEWYEARSEVE  SEA
ALPACA  ABASES  EXERTED
ROPERS  FINES  ALIVE
STYNE  CFL  HOUSESITS
NEWMILLENNIUM  NONOS
CLEA  ESE  DEIST  SELVES
LAWS  LCS  GINS  SPRUE
ANY  BIO  TILE  TAU  TITI
SCENES  TWELVEMIDNIGHT
PEARLS  OAS  EVEL  NOLES
STRATA  MST  HANS  ENEMY
```

157

```
RESCALED PROCLAIM SAR
OTTORINO LAURENCE INE
DROWSETHEINTERNET ENC
SEW GRAMA SOO TARSAL
FLEA BBC NIA ETTA
ASSAM PAELLA PTBOATS
RULING DREAMOFTHECROP
BRER ORE PARR ONCE
OGEE SENTA NAOS USER
RIPRAPS ARID WARCRIME
ECU GENERATIONNAP SBA
TANTALIC BOND GNOSTIC
ALDO KOFI EASES CATT
ELIS NEAT ORO ONTO
GORESTYOUNGMAN MERCER
OUTDONE SIEVED PEERS
OTHO ARE FRI ISAR
DRESSY ELK ISAAC TDS
MAR NOTHINGTOSNOOZEAT
ACU IRRITATE SAUTERNE
NEG TEETERED ESTONIAN
```

158

```
FINAL CAMPUSES SISTER
AGANA ALIENATE PRAISE
CONTRITEKNIGHT RAMMED
ERA DAH ESSO SITU
UNMET SHIITERITE
QUITEBRIGHT ABLE ANIL
ADLERS DERALTE DMITRI
TIES PIRATE AREA EAT
ANA EFREM REMELT NNE
RECOPIES TANS CICADAS
MIGHTMAKESRIGHT
PANACHE OMAR EPHEMERA
ILE ETALII CHETS WAS
TIP NOTA NADIAS DINS
SOAPER INGRAIN SEANCE
ATLI FONT FRIGHTNIGHT
WHITELIGHT SOOTS
SLID RATE OLE PIN
RAGTAG SLIGHTOVERBITE
SMOOTH HENHOUSE EASES
TAPPET AVIARIES DRAMS
```

159

```
ERNST MALT BOLE CODED
LEACH DRAY OPEN ANILE
IFYOURSUCCESSIS PETIT
ASSURE MUONS GOETHE
RIPS NOD NOTONYOUR
CHI BATMAN RELAPSE
LONELIER HALER DREW
OWNTERMSIFITLOOKS ARI
PESOS PLEAS APODAL
ROUSER CABALIST
GOODTOTHEWORLDBUTDOES
AILMENTS DIESEL
SLAVED BRUNT IDIOT
PEN NOTFEELGOODINYOUR
EDDS ROLLE SENTENCE
ASPECTS WRASSE SHE
HEARTITIS PIE KEGS
ARAGON PATSY TRADES
MOREL NOTSUCCESSATALL
ASONE IBIS HULA TENSE
LENTS PINT YELP EDGED
```

160

```
BOER HADES PEEKS JOUR
LUNE AGORA EGRET URSA
OTTO HONUSWAGNER LIIII
ODE PANACHE RELATIONS
MORAL ITT AGO STRANGE
MAIZES PALM AYN
FRESCOES COLLAR ABET
LISTENS JANE TESS ETE
ACCESS TONES ASPIRATE
BEER AHEAD HEINEKEN
DARRELL PHANTOM
NINAFOCH ALERT BLAB
EGOMANIA STYLI MOROSE
WON RANG ITEM CABANAS
TREE GUTTER PARSNIPS
RES ERAS BELTED
DESALTS ART UNE STAMP
ICESKATES OCTANES WAR
NORM NETHERLANDS MALI
ALOU DARES UNCAP ORTS
HEWS SLEDS BEERY EDAM
```

161

```
FROME CROWD GREG BLOC
AESOP HONER AUTO REPO
CUTTHROATTACTICS ETHN
INRE ELMO GLEN HITHER
NIAS TEE TSE MARSALA
GOV MURDEROFCROWS LID
SNAPON NON LOOK TWAS
AVERTED NAOS HUE
MADRE HER FEMMEFATALE
AGRA BENGALI USOPEN
OLES LADYKILLERS ROYS
RESIDE RELIVES INTO
ITSTODIEFOR KEN BASER
EEE NOON WISTFUL
GODS KING SON URSULA
ACT ENOSSLAUGHTER PET
STOLLEN INK AOL ARIL
BAKULA BAER OGRE ROSA
AVIS DROPDEADGORGEOUS
GILT EELS MIDAS ENTRE
SALS DATE OSSIE EASES
```

162

```
SHUN SCALE SAMBA PAST
TOLA ALGIN ARIES ISLE
OMNI LOOKDAGGERS CHAN
MEAL AGREED ONEA KENT
POSEUR ADAMS STUDENTS
DRIES RAHS SLID
POODLES NEAT TROPES
OSLO STAFF EIRE EVADE
SHAWL SWORDPLANT ETNA
TANNED AREAS ICECREAM
ERIK ELK PESO
BATHROBE LAIRS HARLAN
AGRA PINPOINTED LAINE
RAITT SELA SEDER ZANE
BROCKS DADO MINORED
HOUR NERD RIPER
ACCESSES RAISE ORBITS
ROUT ANTI LAPSES ANAT
SUBJ NEEDLEPOINT CARA
OREO NEWLY EDDIE KNOT
NTSB ESSES REEDS SETS
```

163

```
THRONE FORTS LIGATURE
REOPEN INERT ISOLATED
ARTIST LABIA CALAMINE
MOUNTRAINIER KOD PLAN
MINI YIP DREGS WHEELS
ENDON MIT SRO PAAR
LEANED NET AMITY TAM
VERONICALAKE SOSO
BAGGAGE COX GARNERED
AUER UPON REAP TIPPI
STREAMOFCONSCIOUSNESS
HOMER FORE TELL EDIT
ECOTYPES ARP ACEROSE
RUNS OCEANSELEVEN
SED SOUTH TIE ROCHES
COLA AFL PRO SHANE
ALCOTT ABOUT IRS ERTE
LIAR APT SPRINGPEEPER
BARNABAS SOUSE ARSINE
UNDERLIE INCAS SLEETS
MASEKELA LEERS MESSES
```

164

```
TIFF DANAS AGLET ARAB
AGUA ORONO BROMO LAVE
COMICSTRIP BUGSPRAYER
TRELLIS PEABO SIMONE
ODYSSEYS COCONUT
CALICO PEDE STOIC SES
BRISK FREUDIANSLIP
ENOL BLIMP GLUT ATRA
RONI RUES KNOT TAURUS
SPOORS INON MOLLUSK
PAH MORTIMERSNERD CTS
ACADEMY SPEE ATTACK
SIRENS GAUL FIRE OSLO
ODEA TRIG SAVES ATOM
RUSSIANSPIES CLOVE
ABS NEATH WATT CASPER
CLAVIER BACHELOR
AUDIOS ALONE ARRESTS
REDSNAPPER BEAUTYSPOT
ISLE WASTE ADORE TUNA
DYES STOOD RELAX EDGY
```

165

```
EPISODES DEFINES PADS
DATABASE EDUCATE ABEL
THEFIRSTANGRYMAN WIPE
ISR TIE TINGLE
WPA PETULA WITHIN TOT
ALB ONEFALSETHING ORE
TAIL NON ASSUMER WED
ENROBE STINT LEON
RETOOLS ANTOINE SKILL
FTH BANS HEFTED SINAI
ARIA NITRO ETAGE EGGS
LENAS PENTAD LALO ENT
LETAT ENABLED REVERIE
HAIM LINER AIKMAN
RAE LADADOG IOS GAPE
ELF THEWRONGSTUFF NPR
AMA EAGLED OTHERS YES
REMEDY FBI ATA
ERIK ANAMERICANCOMEDY
NILE NOMINEE SEAPOWER
DAYS ABYSSES PASSKEYS
```

166

```
BORN EDNA SCALE PERIL
ALOE TRIM TONAL SWEDE
LETSTHECATOUTOFTHEBAG
DOCTRINE ROSS HARASS
ICC SOLI CREWS
CATONAHOTTINROOF ABA
DRIVEL ROSE OUST SMUG
ROLES FEN HUGE ACORN
OMEN PLAYSCATANDMOUSE
MAD RUED PARER ABORTS
JINX RIGOR QUIP
ASSISI SOREL PUNT WHO
INTHECATBIRDSEAT CRIB
TARAS DOIT CRY ALONE
CRUD TMAN SLID STANDS
HEM CATGOTYOURTONGUE
TEENS PENN ION
AERIAL ZINC EGRESSES
GRINSLIKEACHESHIRECAT
HINGE PATTI ANTE NASA
ANGEL STAEL TESS TREY
```

167

```
POMP ROTATE MELS ARES
ICAL CORDON ALAI NEVE
PUTONTHEDOG DOGEATDOG
ELENI SALT LEPERS ELM
TOOKTO DELIA ERRS EVE
ERMA DENTS SANDMEN
GLADIOLA THAT ASST
ROM DOGINTHEMANGER
ASONE MARE OMARR AFL
NENE GRENADES FAILURE
DOGTIRED LOA LUCKYDOG
PUSHPIN RAGTRADE RILE
ATT SETAE HOES SABIN
DOGANDPONYSHOW LCD
VASE DIEU ARTINESS
AMISTAD PESOS ARNE
LEG AVER RENTS ADVERB
INN BASILS LAWS LABIA
ADOGSLIFE GOTOTHEDOGS
NERO ORTS LAURIE ALEE
TRAP NESS INSERT NILS
```

168

```
RENT PABLO FAILS AIDS
IGOR INLET ORLOP GNAW
POTIONNUMBERNINE ODIE
TUTOR LEIA CRUISE
IDLER DEEMED IOTA
NEAR ARGONNE DAVINCI
TAS AMERICANSTYLE CAD
OCS REBILL THAT PARE
TOI EBONY STURDY OLGA
ONESTAR COOKE SILOS
WHENAMANSAWOMAN
TAFIA WEANS NARTHEX
ALAS GRANNY STINT ALE
ELLS RAIL ECHOER TAR
GEL DOCTORSTRANGE FIX
UNITIVE UPRAISE TUNE
NILE REDEEM VALES
LOWELL USDA ASSES
ENID LETTERSINTHESAND
DUTY ETHER ARTIE ETUI
ASHE ROSES WEIRD LEND
```

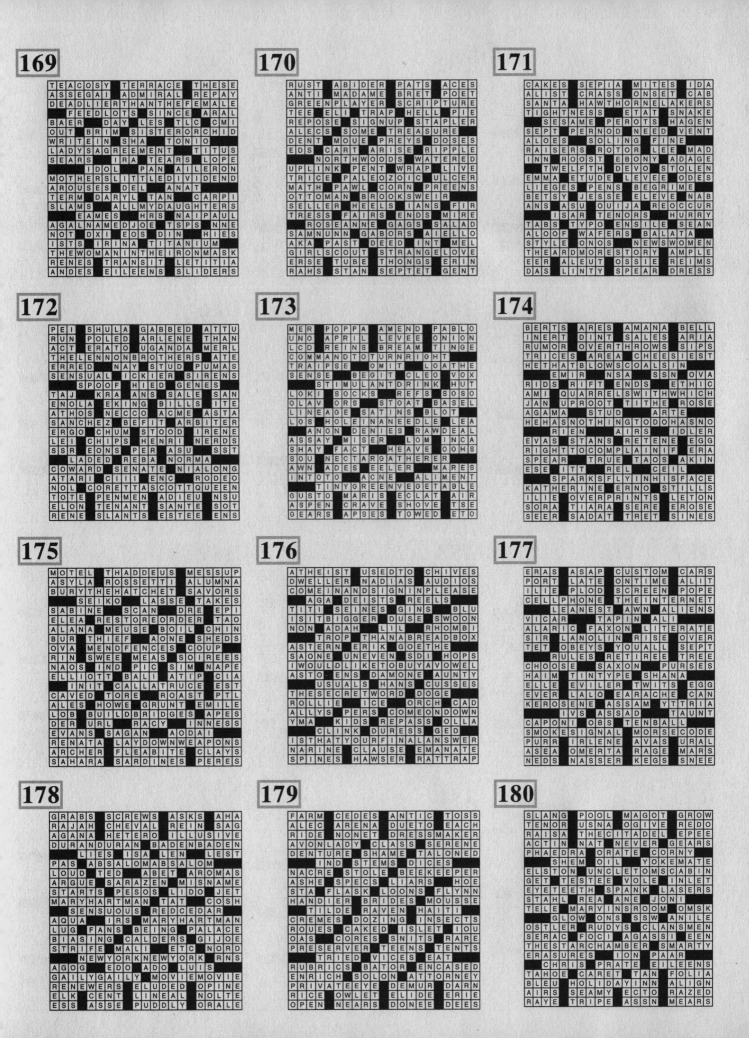

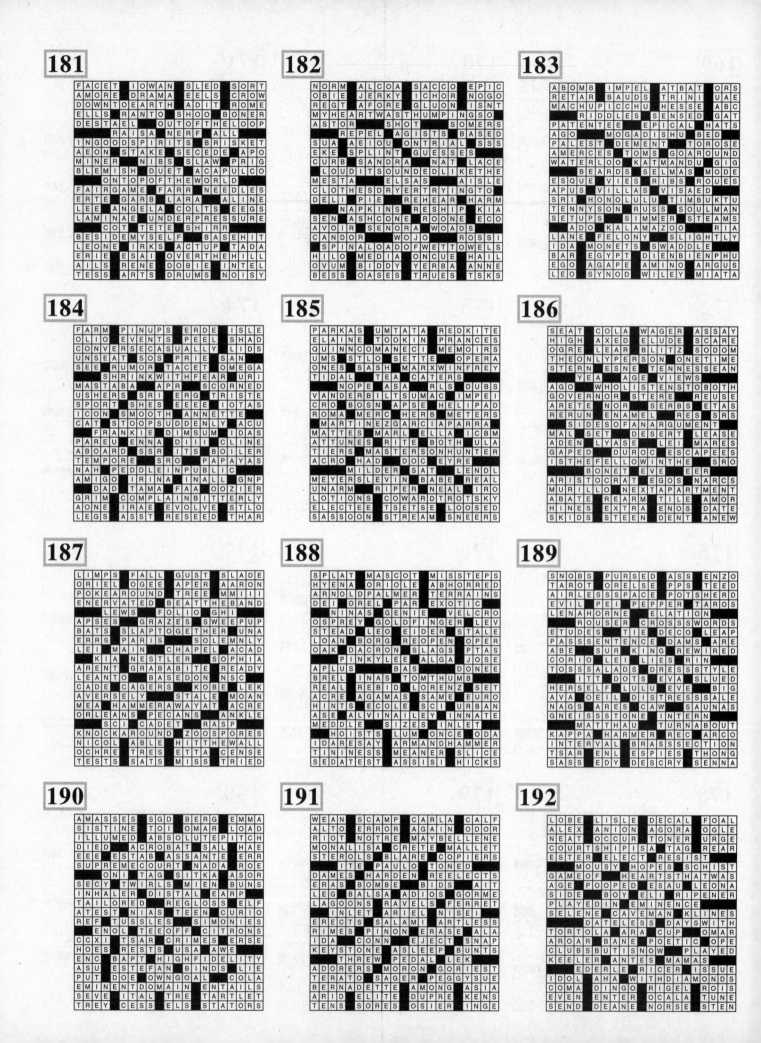

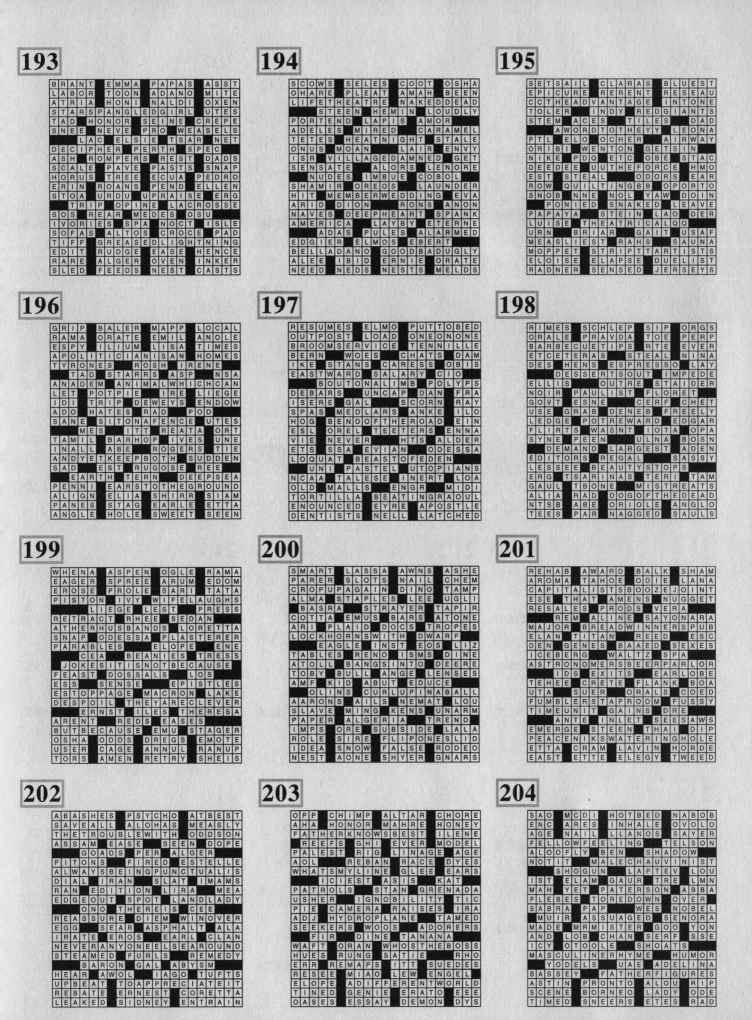

205

```
PUPATE MCDL ARSON HAP
ALAMOS ELUL MOOLA ESL
STRAPS DATA ASPIC ASA
TITHE BUSYMANSHOLIDAY
AMYL SASS ALDISS SLIP
SAC SPRAYS IAN PHILE
OLEIN SCAB IFSO NEN
SAMOANS TOWIT ATONERS
UPPITY SRTA ERRORS
MEAN DEPUTY SAIC CHIC
PAN OLOGY STINK AMO
SKYE CLOG ANYDAY SNAP
RETELL TAMS PLEDGE
DREAMON ERIKA PIEEYED
REP URSA ACER ALONG
ADIOS INB SKATES RAP
BELA STROBE ETES LENA
BEEFYWELLINGTON LINTY
EMP AERIE GRIN TAMALE
SES WARNS LINC SNIDER
TRY PRIES EDGE PETERS
```

206

```
PASTEUR BLOCKS ARAFAT
EXPANSE REBAIT LOLITA
OMANOFTHEWORLD TAINTS
NERDS RENDELL NOR LET
SNEE CARD SELES LANE
MALIBABA REV BENDS
DOG RUNS ALS DEVOID
INHALES BLOTS RIO WES
SPACES UAEHOUSMAN ANO
PANTS OPT ARMHOLE TEC
IRAS FUSED EMIRS PERK
RAM ARTEMIS IVE SERVE
IDA MALTAVISTA SEAWAY
TEN PIE NONOS UPSTATE
DALLAS TAU INON YES
OLLIE PIG IRANRIOT
SOIL PEPUP RIEL SKEW
WOK LAD LEGATOS SUNRA
ATOMIC SPAININTHEREAR
LEVANT HERBIE EERIEST
DRAPES EDSELS DRESSES
```

207

```
MISHIMA PROD ANN ANKE
ASPIRIN IOWA LOA PENN
MOOSELOSTONMAINSTREET
ALT ENACTS EBOLI DER
SASHA UHS FRAS NELLA
ERMINE BOOB STREEP
BLACKBEARSINBACKYARDS
AAR ARS ARTE HIPS
SPEAKS ENDS LIRE RSA
ERODE SCREW AINU DEUS
POLARBEARRAIDSONDUMPS
ABES LENS TRIPS DRAPE
YES GUST SCOT STATOR
SOFA CAHN UAE CST
PACKOFWOLVESONRANCHES
AVOIDS PEER NEARED
SAUDI REVS TEA ASSAD
SIP NOONE SASSES LEA
ALLIGATORONTHECARPORT
GEER THU HERO CHEAPIE
EDDS SST SEAT ELYSEES
```

208

```
ABHORS SOUSED GRISTLE
GOALIE TOTTER RANCHER
NATIONALPARKA ENTERER
UTENSIL SHA BPE ONEGA
SSS OAR ANA ANI TERN
FORMEANDMYGALA MAT
LATEX OHM STEELED ENL
ACARID ABM TAG AUNTY
ICK DOUBLECHINA PSI
DEEPENS ENLIST STANNE
ODIE OCS SON SRA GAEA
NETTER ESCUDO PESETAS
ORS BATHTUBGINA ULE
MINOT LOL SOL SYMBOL
INT ABATERS EOS SEANS
SCH BOTTOMLESSPITA
TIER SHE SID SAD SOB
IDLED ERA VIA REGAUGE
MEATIER THEBLUEANGELA
ENMASSE MERLES LAUDED
STARTED OBSESS STEEDS
```

209

```
SUTTER OTTO BAA SPASM
ENROLL SEABOARD CRATE
PEARLS INSIDEMETHERES
TASSE NETS DRYLY TOES
ATHINPERSON BARRENLY
TEE EHS ONER EER
ENDOWER AURORAL VICES
STRUGGLINGTOGETOUT
TERIS LAM FOSTER TRY
WEAR SLUR BAT IRENE
ONTIPTOE BUT BORDERED
ASHEN CAD BONY PITA
LOT ONEILL COD SHEAR
ICANNORMALLYSEDATE
ESTEE SPREADS ANSWERS
PIT OATS TVA BOO
ACRONYMS HIMWITHFOUR
POUT PETAL REID ERNST
ORFIVECUPCAKES ELOISE
REUSE CRISPEST LISTER
TASTE AES ADES MOTELS
```

210

```
COCO AMISS BANJO AHAS
HUAC PESTS AGEES LOCH
ARTHURDLER CHAFE LAVER
CON IAN WHARF
BAH MIC GER SSE ILENE
TRUMANICURIST RESORTS
UNPENS ONATE ASIANS
SOSA EVAS HELLOS GIFT
NATAL RESIGNED FRO
REGIS NEVADA GNU ION
AIRES BRAT WEDS SCENE
BEA ACU LEVERET TARTS
BIN MARAUDED FEAST
IOTA DEMEAN SIRS ERST
ALIENS ATONE TORERO
DUGINTO CARTERMINATOR
AROMA VAL ASA ANI IST
PANES ARIEL KEG OAT
PNIN UTTER REAGANGLER
LIST POINT ARRIS HERE
EATS CRETE ESSES ASEA
```

211

```
HAILS SCOT BRAVE DESK
ONSET IEOH YETIS RATE
WILDERGENE WOODSTIGER
STEARIN ARMOIRE HELEN
OAS NASA MARL LEADERS
OUTOFHAND PIER
PULLMANBILL BUCKPEARL
ABYSS CLIMATE BAIO
NERO LIZ YELL TUMBREL
GRANGERED RITA COSELL
MATURE VICTOR
OMEGAS SIRS CARNEYART
MARINES PIES DAN OLEO
AXIS IMPEACH BUONO
RICHBUDDY SHORTMARTIN
ALES BANISHERS
AMANDAS ORLE ARAB ADA
LEVEE HEMATIN IDEAMAN
BROWNBOBBY DENVERJOHN
ALIT AWARE EVIE EARLE
NEDS ASNER RAPS DRESS
```

212

```
MADESAIL MARTHAS ALIS
EXORCISE ALAMODE DIME
TOMMYROTHILFIGER AZAN
ONEAL SATE GLADRAGS
OSS LOY WANES IPA RIA
CALVINISTKLEIN DST
AMBO DES HIE STACTE
NAILS SOLAR TOR ENL
INLAID LAME OREO OAFS
LIL VERACITYWANG DIET
IKEBANA NIA ALGEBRA
NITE COCOONCHANEL ORR
ENDS HURD UHUH DORRIT
OED LED ETHEL MONTE
SHUTUP ELO MIT TEED
HEX PAULOWNIASMITH
ALB ENT TEENS BAH SAN
CELERIAC ASIS AMPLE
KNAR CHRISTIANITYDIOR
LAST LAUGHED INSECRET
ESSE ENSNARE PEERLESS
```

213

```
SCAM CAFES HEIST NEMO
LARA AMATI ALLAH ELAL
IRAN NORAD WILLROGERS
PTBARNUM EDITS ORANGE
SASSIER CLONE STATION
SER LYING TITLE
ROYAL MANNS KELLERMAN
AMOS HORDE SNAKE ARE
TAG SAUDI SLUMS CARTE
SNIPERS LIMITS CONKED
BLAME ANODE TRITT
GREETS MUGGER RENEWAL
LORDS ROPES OBITS AGO
OUR FEVER SCOPE LIES
BEASTLIER PEKOE SANDS
MOANS PEENS TAN
RODENTS SLADE SURCOAT
ACETIC ATALL WCFIELDS
DANACARVEY EGRET LIMA
OLIN ROONE SHINE OVER
NASA SENOR SITED TENS
```

214

```
DACRON SHRUBS OBSCURE
ONLINE LIENEE KEELSON
PIECEOFADVICE RAREBIT
AMAHL AVESTA CARIOU
MANE PIES ALMA CASSIA
ITE PATS ARMYMEAL CNS
NESMITH ICY SENT ROSS
ESTATE RAT STUD COMTE
DARWINSSHIP PAMPAS
TAM SNAPS MAC ORLEANS
INCH IRS HAG ATE ONCE
COQUETS CUR ALICE YES
KRUSTY POTTERSCLAY
LEEKS JABS MAO USEUP
EXES AURA OIL ADENINE
RIN PUGILIST BRED DID
SAMBAR NTSB MAID DECA
OOLONG HONORE CARON
CAVALRY STRONGLYBUILT
SPIREAS SANTEE MENTOR
TRESTLE TREATS ARTERY
```

215

```
TEALS AKAS TREK LEHAR
ISAAC RIME EIRE IRENE
CARPALKNOWLEDGE BEANS
SUPPLE GRAIN PER DOT
PASSAGE AGENA PTA
ANTI STOLEN GERI COAT
COHN EEL SPAR DELETE
CREAM LOSS AMMO GATES
UMBRA EMIL SASS OPS
SALUKI OVALS OUST SPA
ELATED NAMEOFF ARMORS
DSC TOSS MOVIE PIECES
KAI IMRE ERNS POILU
ASSAM PIER REDO SWEAR
MCCREA MESS ELF ETTE
IRAE TOES OCTAVO DYED
COL SOUSE LAURENT
ALL OPT STURM DILUTE
BLIND WIFEISBEAUTIFUL
LEORA IRAN EONS HOOTS
EDNAS TART SSTS ENSUE
```

216

```
OASES NACRE URAL OPAL
SLURP IDLER MAMA MACE
WINGLEADERS AMARANTHS
ABLOOM VEEP HELICAL
LII TOCSIN ISOLDE HEE
DST CROPSTICKS ONEWAY
SHYER STOICS ETO
SOFA NIP ATREUS ERDE
AVESTA TAILSTORMS KIN
LEASHES ANY LEON QED
ART UNHURT ALASKA USO
MAH MEAN BAA TERRIER
ITE BAKEDBEAKS SKILLS
SERB SEQUEL EAP ELSE
ROC RUSTED CREON
SMEARS ATOMICCOMB EDS
PIP EVELYN GROVEL PEI
ADOPTER YORE RATING
CORRELATE BEAUTYTALON
ERTE TSAR OSMAN EMOTE
KISS EEGS ESSEN SAGER
```

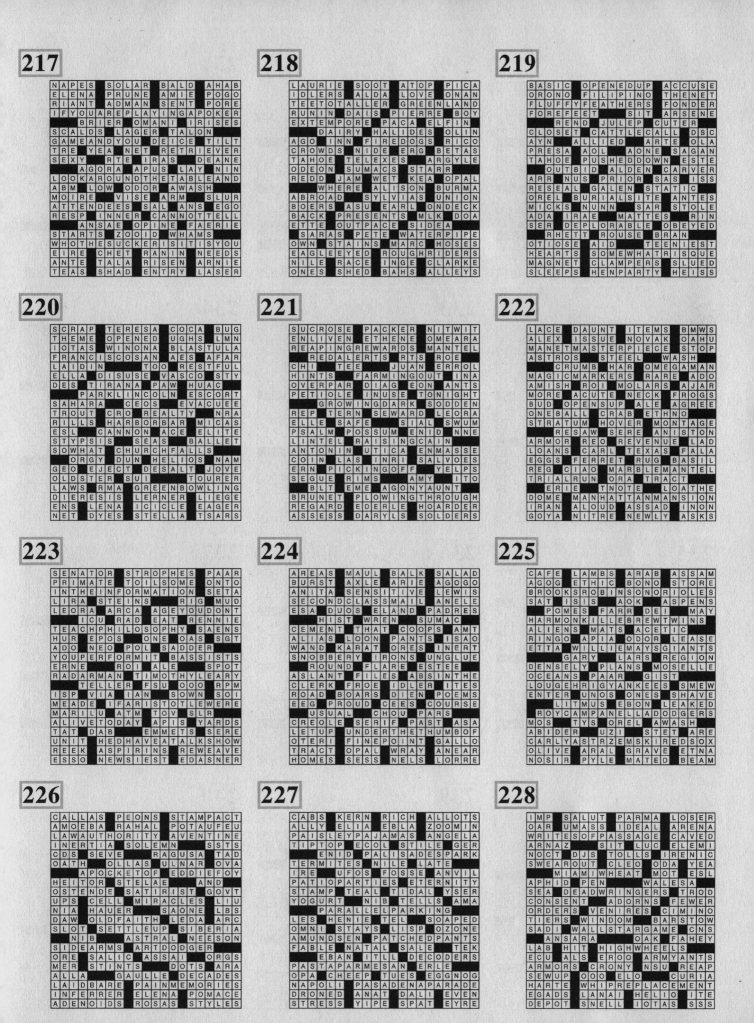

217

```
NAPES SOLAR BALD AHAB
ELENA PRUNE AMIE POGO
RIANT ADMAN SENT PORE
IFYOUAREPLAYINGAPOKER
   BRIER OMANI IRISES
SCALDS LAGER TALON
GAMEANDYOU DEICE TILT
TRE YEA NET RETRIEVER
SEXY RTE IRAS DEANE
AGORA APUS LAY NIN
LOOKAROUNDTHETABLEAND
ABM LOW ODOR AWASH
MOIRE VISE ARM SLUR
ATTENDEES SAL ANS EGO
RESP INNER CANNOTTELL
ANSAE OPINE FAERIE
STARTS ZOOID WHAMS
WHOTHESUCKERISITISYOU
EIRE CHET RANIN NEEDS
ANTE TALA RISEN ARNIE
TEAS SHAD ENTRY LASER
```

218

```
LAURIE SOOT ATOP PICA
IDLERS ALDA LOVE ONAN
TEETOTALLER GREENLAND
RUNIN DAIS PIERRE BOY
EXTEMPORE PACA ELFIN
DAIRY HALIDES OLIN
AGO INN FIREDOGS RICO
CROWDS NIDE ERG BETAS
TAHOE TELEXES ARGYLE
ODEON SUMACS STARR
REDD JAM WET KEA OPAL
WHERE ALISON BURMA
ABROAD SYLVIAS UNION
BOERS ASU EARL ONDECK
BACK PRESENTS MLK DOA
ETTE OUTPACE SIDEA
SARAS PETE WATERPIPE
OWN STAINS MARC HOSES
EAGLEEYED ROUGHRIDERS
NILE RACE INGE CLARKE
ONES SHED BAHS ALLEYS
```

219

```
BASIC OPENEDUP ACCUSE
ORONO FILIPINO THENET
FLUFFYFEATHERS FONDER
FOREFEET SIT ARSENE
REND JULEP CUTER
CLOSET CATTLECALL DSC
AYN ALLIED ARTE OLA
PRESA AOL AONE SAGAN
TAHOE PUSHEDDOWN ESTE
OUTBID ALDEN CARVER
ARR NUS PRIOR SAS ISS
RESEAL GALEN STATIC
OREL BURIALSITE ANTES
MICKS NUNN SAR STOLE
ADA IRAE MATTES RIN
SER DEPLORABLE OBEYED
RHETT ROUSE BRAN
OTIOSE AID TEENIEST
HEARTS SOMEWHATRISQUE
MAGNET CLAMPERS SLUED
SLEEPS HENPARTY HEISS
```

220

```
SCRAP TERESA COCA BUG
THEME OPENED UGHS LMN
IOTAS WINONA BLASTULA
FRANCISCOSAN AES AFAR
LAIDIN TOO RESTFUL
ELLA DISUSE VASCO STY
DES TIRANA PAW HUAC
PARKLINCOLN ESCORT
SAHARA CEOS EVACUEE
TROUT CRO REALTY NRA
RILLS HARBORBAR MICAS
ESL CANNON ACE ELITE
STYPSIS SEAS BALLET
SOWHAT CHURCHFALLS
ORGY DUN HELIOS NAM
GEO EJECT DESALT JOVE
OLDSTER SUI TOURER
LAWS RMA GREENBOWLING
DIERESIS LERNER LIEGE
ENS LENA ICICLE EAGER
NET DYES STELLA TSARS
```

221

```
SUCROSE PACKER NITWIT
ENLIVEN ETHENE OMEARA
REAPINGREWARDS MANTEL
REDALERTS RTS ROE
CHI TEE JUAN ERROL
HINTS FARMINGOUT INA
OVERPAR DIAG EON ANTS
PETIOLE INUSE TONIGHT
GROWINGDARK SODDEN
REP TERN SEWARD LEORA
ELLE SAFE SIAL SWUM
PSALM POSSUM ENID NNE
LINTEL RAISINGCAIN
ANTONIN UTICA ENMASSE
COIN LAS INRI SALVOES
ERN PICKINGOFF YELPS
SEGUE RIMS AMY ITO
BLT EME AGONYAUNT
BRUNET PLOWINGTHROUGH
REGARD EDERLE HOARDER
ASSESS DARYLS SOLDERS
```

222

```
LACE DAUNT ITEMS BMWS
ALEX ISSUE NOVAK OAHU
MANETMASTERPIECE STOP
ASTROS STEEL WASH
CRUMB HAR OMEGAMAN
MAGICMARKERS RARE ADO
AMISH ROI MOLARS AJAR
MORE ACUTE NECK FROGS
BUD OPENSUP ALE AGREE
ONEBALL CRAB ETHNO
STRATUM HOVER MONTAGE
RESAW SERE ANISTON
ARMOR REO REVENUE LAD
LOANS CARL TEXAS FALA
EGGS FERRET RUG BASIL
REG CIAO MARBLEMANTEL
TRIALRUN ORA TRACT
ERIE TNOTE LOATHE
DOME MANHATTANMANSION
IRAN ALOUD ASSAD INON
GOYA NITRE NEWLY ASKS
```

223

```
SENATOR STROPHES PAAR
PRIMATE TOILSOME ONTO
INTHEINFORMATION SETA
LIRA STEINS RIG MUD
LEORA ARCA AGEYOUDONT
ICU RAD EAT RENNIE
TEACHPHILOSOPHY SAENS
HUR EPOS ONE OAS SGT
ADO NEO POL SADDER
YOUPERFORMIT BASSISTS
ERNE ROI ALE SPOT
RADARMAN TIMOTHYLEARY
TELLER FSU OOO RPM
ISP VIA IAN SOWN SOI
MEADE IFARISTOTLEWERE
MARILU ATM TOV SLR
ALIVETODAY APIS YARDS
TAT DAB EMMETS SERE
UNIT HEDHAVEATALKSHOW
REEK ASPIRINS REWEAVE
ESSO NEWSIEST EDASNER
```

224

```
AREAS MAUL BALK SALAD
BURST AXLE ARIE AGOGO
ANITA SENSITIVE LEWIS
SECONDCLASSMAIL ANELE
ESA DUOS ELAND PADRES
HIST WREN SUMAC
CEMENT THAT COOPS AMT
ALIAS LOON PANTS ISAO
WAND KARAT ORES INERT
SNOBBERY IRONS UNGLUE
ROUND FLARE ESTEE
ASLANT FILES ABSINTHE
CLERK FROE IDLER ITES
ROAD BOARS DIEN POEMS
EEG PROUD CEES COURSE
USUAL CHOU PARS
CREOLE SERIF PAST ASA
LETUP UNDERTHETHUMBOF
OTERI FINEPOINT GALLO
TRACT OPAL WRAY ANEAR
HOMES SESS NELS LORRE
```

225

```
CAFE LAMBS ARAB ASSAM
AGOG ETHIC BONO STORE
BROOKSROBINSONORIOLES
SAT ISIS AOK ASPENS
POMES FARR DEI MAY
HARMONKILLEBREWTWINS
ALIENS MATS ACETIC
RINGO APIA ODOR LEASE
ETTA WILLIEMAYSGIANTS
GARY LARS REGION
DENSELY PLANS MOSELLE
OCEANS PAAR GIST
LOUGEHRIGYANKEES SMEW
ENTER UNOS ONES SHAVE
LITMUS EBON LEAKED
ROYCAMPANELLADODGERS
MOS TYS OREL AWASH
ABIDER UZI STET ARE
CARLYASTRZEMSKIREDSOX
OLIVE ARAL GRAVE ETNA
NOSIR PYLE MATED BEAM
```

226

```
CALLAS PEONS STAMPACT
AMOEBA RAHAL POTAUFEU
LAWAUTHORITY AVENTINE
INERTIA SOLEMN SSTS
CDS SEVE RAGUSA TAD
OATH OLLAS ULNAR OVA
APOCKETOF EDDIEFOY
HEITOR STELAE AND
OSTENDE SATIRIST GOVT
UPS CELL MIRACLES LIU
NIA HAUER SAONE LBS
DAW OLDFAITH LEDA ARC
SLOT SETTLEUP SIBERIA
NIB ASTRAL NEESON
SIDEARMS ARTDODGER
ORE SALIC ASSAI ORGS
MER STINTS DOTS ARA
ALLA GAULLE DECADES
LAIDBARE PAINMEMORIES
INFERRER ELENA POMACE
ADENOIDS ROSAS STYLES
```

227

```
CABS KERN RICH ALLOTS
ALLY ELIA EBLA ZOOMIN
PAISLEYPAJAMAS ANGELA
TIPTOP ECOL STILE GER
ENID PALISADESPARK
TERMITES NILE LATE
IRE UFOS FOSSE ANVIL
PATIOPARTIES ETERNITY
STAMP TEAL TIDAL YSER
YOGURT NIB TELLS AMA
PARALLELPARKING
LES HENIE TEL SOAPED
OMNI STAYS LISP OZONE
AMUNDSEN PATCHEDPANTS
FABLE NATAL SALE TEK
EBAN ITLL DECODERS
PASTAPARMESAN ERLE
OPA CHEEP TUES EGGNOG
NAPOLI PASADENAPARADE
DRONED ANAT DALI EVEN
STRESS YIPE SPAT EYRE
```

228

```
IMP SALUT PARMA LOSER
OAR UMASS IDEAL ARENA
WRITESOFPASSAGE CAVED
ARNAZ SIT LUC ELEMI
NOCT DJS TOLLS IRENIC
SWEAROUT CLEO ODA YEA
MIAMIWHEAT MOT ESL
APHID PEN WALESA
SEA DEADWRINGERS TROD
CONSENT ADORNS FEWER
ORDERS VENIRES CIMINO
TIERS WINDOM BARSTOW
SADI WALLSTARGAME CNS
ANSARA OAK FAHEY
LAB HIT HIGHWHEELS
ECU ALS EROO ARMYANTS
ARMORS CRONY NSU REAP
SEWUP OOO ELO CURIA
HARTE WHIPREPLACEMENT
EGADS LANAI HELIO ITE
DEPOT SNELL IOTAS SSS
```

229

```
SPEC SPASMS SPIT MARS
TALE WICKET ELSE UVEA
ETON ENTIRE NOLA LINT
WHITEDEISENHOWER LANI
    AVES   ARS   AFTER
ARGUE ONSTAGE REPLETE
SHERRYLEWIS   SHERPA
SEESTO GUMPS ALIENATE
TAD WHAMS CAT SADLER
  RELET PAL BASEMEN
UPTON REDBUTLER ERASE
SEESAWS ERG   SEEDS
SPEECH LEI CAPRA IDO
RENOTIFY MIAMI STARER
  DORIES CHIANTIMAME
REMORSE TRUNDLE TONIS
ALANS   ARA   AFAR
MANN VINODELAURENTIIS
RITE ERIK MORSEL IRMA
ONEL RISE ICIEST ZEAL
DELL BSED ROASTS ESME
```

230

```
SPAWN PHD TASTE SLITS
SATIE OOO OLLAS PELEE
SUPERBOWL OLYMPICGOLD
NOLLE   SKYE   MARISA
BIBELOT IOUS PIP ALOT
AMERICASCUP HOLEINONE
KISS BAER   LAPLAND
ENT FALLS SELLECK BRA
DEICIDES PETTISH GLOM
NONES PUPTENT TAUTO
DUSTIN HIP IRS HOVELS
ASHES TIEPINS DARER
RIOS PRATING HEIMLICH
NAW BAILIES DEMME BRO
KINLESS BLEU   TBAR
GRANDSLAM TRIPLECROWN
NAME ISH JEUX CLEANSE
ADELIE   BEAT   KEELY
WORLDSERIES FINALFOUR
EMCEE PADRE OTT OUSTS
REEDS IDEST ESS SLEET
```

231

```
LEASE COINCIDE SPICED
ANNUL UNPAIRED HEXANE
POTBELLYSTOVES HEISTS
ELO CALXES PEG RATED
LANOTTE   COLLAGE IRE
  FEETOFCLAY RLS RIM
PLATEN CLOUT ETAS OTO
RIFE STEAM YVES PNIN
ELAND RABBITEARS OSSA
SLR AGON MANS JILT
SEEDILY ROANS CARLOTS
  WUSA HAIG IOWA MIM
ETES DOUBLEBACK SLATE
MOLT HUME OSIER UCLA
FUL EATS GOOSE ESCHER
OCT GNP RUBBERNECK
RHO ADULATE OKAYING
STAEL TYS EVADER DOA
TORRID CHESTOFDRAWERS
ENMITY RESTCURE BEAMS
RESEES ASSESSOR SISSY
```

232

```
RECOMB ALIEN CAPO OSS
ATONER LADLE ORAL NAE
WHEELANDDEAL LORE TRA
IDA KOREAN POSE AHAB
BOIL ERIN SANE BUENA
APTS SAN CRANE PASHAS
RIO PHD SHIFTLESS OCS
BARRIO DEICES TAINT
  ONETRACK COLEUSES
COPSE HALL SCRIM TERI
AGEES EPEE TAEL SCALD
LEDA GOERS ETTE MATES
FEATHERS   MANASSAS
LEONE SEAMAN PRESET
SEP PUMPINGUP TOT ALE
TRUCES UNZIP AOK STET
OASIS ERGO FLOE HIVE
OSHA LEIS SPLATS ARE
LEE PARS CHAINSMOKING
IRR EMIT PIPPI AVESTA
ESS TEES AMASS NORTHS
```

233

```
VESTIGE LOBELIAS ARTA
ETHICAL AVEMARIA LEAN
THECHEERYORCHARD MEIN
TAL OLGAS SER LASALLE
INT RIIS LEE TOTE SIT
NOIR CASTOR DOC CLINT
GLEES CLOCKWORKGRANGE
  FOG ELK RMS NEW
OEDIPAL LEROI PUT CUE
BLENHEIM ENNUI HUNT
JAMESANDTHEGIANTPERCH
ENOS KIROV WEARABLE
TDS ITS ULENT SPARSER
MNO WAS OAS SYD
AMAISONINTHESUN SOFAS
MACAO ONT UNSTOP FORT
ANC UPTO LSD RIOS OBJ
SHELLAC AUS HASTA TIO
SODA THEGRADESOFWRATH
ELEM REPAIRED MUTAGEN
RESP IDARESAY ELOPERS
```

234

```
SCAR FSTOP AHMAD COIF
ELLIE REACH DUETO ERDE
LAREDONKEY ATLANTAPIR
LIGNIN ELLS SAMBA HOR
ERUDITE OAHU NAUSEATE
RENO LST OSMOND INST
  WOMEN IRMA GUN
AHS CINCINNATIGER MAP
CET TRICOT ECO ABIDE
CAESAR WEIR ENPLANED
OVAL OLEANTEATER NONA
SEMIARID TOAD OPERON
THUMB CAM SERAPE CIT
SOP BREMERTONAGER ADS
  CAY TARN CALEB
SPUR EFFETE GEM LEAS
LARYNGAL EASE ASSAULT
ANA OREAD DERM MUSCLE
TACOMARMOT TAMPANTHER
EMIR SIENA ALIAS ERLE
SALT SEDGE EDITH DEES
```

235

```
MAINE FORECAST GAMBIA
ASTIR ATONABLE OCEANS
THECASTISCLEAR THATCH
HERESY SAIL   WHELP
  DEL NOAH HIS ECO
MESAS CATOFMANYCOLORS
ONLY LARA FORE NEPOS
PGA MISCUT SEVER ALAI
PINTOFHONOR MUTE PETE
ENTIRE TRIP STAFF
TESTATE STORM ALERTED
TYING STOA   TROUPE
SIRE MOAN SWIMMINGPOL
TSAR ESTER STEAMS EPA
ALDER EXAM AMIE GLEN
BARDOFEDUCATION GOOEY
SMU MOO SETH   FOR
  NEARS ARIE DESSAU
OWNING FUNDINGFATHERS
PIERCE UNSOCIAL HINTS
STREET RECREANT ENTER
```

236

```
UCLA DADE ACRES ASTOR
ROAR ELIA LOOPY NEHRU
SOMMELIER MEDIC GRABS
APPARENT TOXICOLOGIST
  TETE ROSIN PARE
SEDUCE PANTS THRASHES
ALERT CAVE TWEAK AVA
LIME DARE RAN ROBES
ADO NUMISMATIST EDENS
DEGRADES UNITE SPORTY
ROMEO CRIBS SWARD
SPADES SLATE GLISSADE
TAPER PHILATELIST SID
ETHOS ION VINS SHAG
ATE SPEED HANK SCENE
MIRACLES AGENT SHARES
  CLOD SLURS PAAR
CARTOGRAPHER FOURLEAF
OLEOS ELIAS CONCIERGE
PANNE AVERT RACE TIER
SITES MASTS OLES TEEN
```

237

```
ALIT NARCS SMEE TRACT
MOON ELIOT MAST REPRO
OUTOFPLACE INPOSITION
STATUE LONELY HORACE
  ESNE ACRE SEASONED
HAS ETTE   HASSOCK
INTHEHOLE OUTOFDEBT
SKYE ENDODERM SOARER
SHELF SAGUARO GHANA
  LIANA NOBLESSE TIC
OUTOFSYNC INHARMONY
THE THANATOS TANTO
ELLIE CATERER YUCCA
RAISES TATTIEST THAI
INCONTROL OUTOFHAND
REREADS ROAR PTA
STAGNATE LINE ANIS
LEGION ADDONS DELETE
INEVIDENCE OUTOFSIGHT
CONES LEER DREAR MAIN
ENTRY MEDS SETTO EDNA
```

238

```
ALMS SEAMS CODA SISSY
NOAH TRIAL APES TRIPE
IFYOUDONTINVEST EARLS
STOOD STIPE NIOBE RIM
  KOFI NOVAE ALSACE
LAS SLOG VERYMUCHTHEN
EKES INANE BEECHER
WEAPON TOROIDAL ASCAP
DEFEATDOESNT NASD RIO
  ANTLERS SEP USHERS
SORE OSSIA RACER EAST
CHIRAC SNL RAMPANT
ANN SKIT HURTVERYMUCH
TOGAS CAMISOLE INARUT
  DAKOTAN IYARS NEST
ANDWINNINGIS TEEM SAP
MORALE DANTE DDAY
ORO MEARA RETRO LAMIA
EMILE NOTVERYEXCITING
BADEN EPEE EMMER ERNE
ASSET WEST DAISY SASS
```

239

```
DIG HIS ABSTAIN LLAMA
EVASION MAKESDO AILED
SOUTHCAROLINAONMYMIND
ARGO PAR PDT CIMABUE
LIERNE MIDI NONE ISR
VERMONTSTATEOFMIND
OSS SCREEN NLCS ITEM
  CHIAS INA TIERRA
MCKEON ARKANSASQUEEN
OHIOWANTSME LEKS MCL
RIBS OAKS SPUR ROTE
ALB ERRS OREGONGIRLS
ILLINOISWOMAN UNISYS
NEEDED IRA SEGOS
ERSE JOSE ESTEEM EMS
  SWEETHOMETENNESSEE
BRC INFO EGER TSETSE
AHEADOF ATL EER TROP
YELLOWROSEOFLOUISIANA
LALAW ELECTEE SHINDIG
ESSES YEASTED ESP ACE
```

240

```
OPA ARC TRIVIA SCONCE
ROLLBAR LAMENT LASERS
SUPERMANCHARGE OUTWIT
ONAN AVE SMEE PLISSE
DCI DAWG EACH AMER
POI BATMANONROUGE ASS
RUNNY SANER   REUBEN
OTOOLE NEEDLE FRAPPE
  TARS FREEMANFORALL
ASP WIPE RAMBO SPAT
MNO SCALED DALTON ECO
PESO SIRED ERIE REN
LETTERMANBOMB ELAN
ERMINE STRAIT STUCCO
  ASIANS ISSUE ETHAN
OWN DROPANCHORMAN ERE
NAHA GALA NIBS ASE
FRANCO SPOT ORT CHER
INSTEP RAINMANORSHINE
RETINT ICECAP WATERED
ERECTS GERENT NYE EDD
```

241

```
FARCE MAFIA SEEP RAGS
ALOUD EBONS PITY EURO
TBARS SURFS ADAR DRAW
SADI WATERY RELAYRACE
ROSAS BIRLER MAILED
AMUSER SENIOR MIRV
RONALDREAGAN FODDERED
TON SUCRE MIO ROTE
ILEAC ITS SLEDDOG ORE
EARTHEN STONE CUFFED
RUSSIANROULETTE
ANKARA SLOAN MATURES
CCI LULLABY LIB ADAGE
CARR EER AIDED WAG
TAKEOFFS RICKYRICARDO
SLOT CANCEL NOLESS
ULSTER FATHOM MEDIC
ROYROGERS ELATED BRED
GINO OMIT RAGAS GAUDY
ERGO NILE EDITS ABIDE
DEEM ELLS DECAY SATYR
```

242

```
ATHOS ELECTIVE THETAS
CHERI MOTHERED RETORT
TERRE BORONANDMERCURY
IRS STOKER DYES SCAM
NEH TELO EER SSTS ANI
GAEAANDURANUS SLAINTE
STYE TETE EBAN ELS
ARLEN HASIDIC ANJOU
DENIED BUICKANDSATURN
ELDER CANDO RAM NAE
BUMS SHAGS AMMON COCA
ADA USE PROAM SEALS
SERENAANDVENUS GURNEY
EDSEL PIERRES LOPED
GAS ANON ELAL AJAR
BORSCHT GOOFYANDPLUTO
ASA EARP MDL CDII PAD
LINN MOUE AMULET IVE
AEGIRANDNEPTUNE MATIN
TREPAN GORILLAS EGEST
ASSAYS ESSAYERS NORMS
```

243

```
SABOT DOVE MILL NATAL
ALLAH ADEN ASIA OSHEA
LOIRE BINOCULAR OTERI
SUNSETBOULEVARD SIMON
ADD VALUE REM EERO
PERES HIS NAYS RIB
LATINOS PAS TARE ANNE
ASHPIT HONE WRESTLING
SHEEN MOOD ROC TEEN
HON GRAPHITE IRAQ GAL
URI SERE CAT SULU ALA
PEG TALC APRESSKI FLU
HEAL HEP AGUE LATER
MOTORIZES MIAS MANEGE
REVS ZEST END WASTREL
SRI BEET IDS REMUS
SEED ANI SITIN GNU
CHIVE DOGDAYAFTERNOON
HITIT AVAILABLE IAMBI
ATOLL RIPA LEES SHEET
PERSE EDEN ERST EARLY
```

244

```
DITSY TRAY SIMI SITED
ANOLE HOLE ENID CRAPE
DONOTBEAFRAIDTO OWNER
SNIT ERN BUNUEL LITER
HERO BASIC IPANA
CLASSICAL SNEEZER MUS
HIT TAKEABIGSTEPIFONE
AGREE RIRE ODE RUIN
OHIO CHARO FEN CENTO
STANDOUT GREW SPATTER
ISREQUIREDYOU
MINERAL TEAM ENOLAGAY
ADOBE ESS ADLER IRMA
RENO GAT UTEP OLEOS
CANNOTCROSSACHASM ELI
SSA COTERIE OILTANKER
TUTSI ODDLY LENO
STUPA NINETY CEE DOSE
LOREN INTWOSMALLJUMPS
INANE AREA ILIE ALOES
MELDS NOSY SINS GEODE
```

245

```
ROSEWALL SCRAPPLE LAM
AVARICES CONTRAIL AVA
BANGTHEDRUMSLOWLY BIC
BLESSER AMB ESS SMEAR
ISR AWN ETA RIALTO
SLATE CRASHCOURSES
OBRIAN ASH PTOLEMY
BOOMTOWNRATS AUS LEST
ONS TRI OOO HRE KASHA
EDE IANS TEPID LENTOS
SMACKDABINTHEMIDDLE
EMOTES MACAO DUNG ELO
RENTS SPY IMP FEE MAW
ANTE SPA BLASTFURNACE
MCKENNA ITO PEENED
CLAPEYESUPON ONSET
RATTLE ATF ALI PAS
EROSE LIN LUC CHEMISE
WEN SNAPCRACKLEANDPOP
EDA TRISECTS INNOCENT
LOL ACCOSTED SEASIDES
```

246

```
ASCAP PASHAS ELIS RED
ITALO EXTENT MATA ONE
MADAMEGEORGEWBUSH TSP
EDDIES SLOE EAR LLANO
ETO LAS OIL ILIE ETAS
YOUCANCALLMEALGORE
MISO OBS ILS ROARED
INCUBATE ESL SLOT
THELASTTIMEISAW OTIC
CAPLET TIN ABACK HOL
HST RICHARDCHENEY ENE
UTE SNAIL FOE ISTRIA
MERE HEYJOELIEBERMAN
NOON ORD CLARIONS
SALAAM SOS MET ESSE
ELECTIONTHEMESONGS
LIST TROT NAT NEA FLA
LASSA EWE ANTE IRISES
ESE MYGIRLBILLCLINTON
REP AEON ILLEST STONE
SSS HANG TEASES HOPER
```

247

```
TASS CHAR ASIDE CHESS
ABLE HERA BARON RELIT
MOEN OATS RUING IRATE
PUPSICLES ASSTRONOMER
ATTEST LEDA SARK
MACKERELS MALODOR
STEP WAR EDILE LENORE
HALOS NULL TORI SPODE
ALLOT APEOLOGIZE ONEL
GEARED ANNE CATERERS
CARE AGARD RASP
SCHUMANN SEAS STOMPS
LOOP MOOSETACHE EIEIO
ORRIN SOWN PEEL ESSES
BANNED NACRE ABS ESSO
SLEEVES THIRDRATE
AMID ANSA ILLUSE
WRENDITIONS CHIPMONKS
HOSEA STATE ROTE BIAS
ASPEN UTHER OPEN ETTE
TENDS POURS NERD SEEN
```

248

```
ALMAGEST CLODS CALLAS
SAAREMAA ELARA ANOINT
SCRAMBLE TARALIPINSKI
ATM MEA EEN GOTO ALE
NEILARMSTRONG ENROBES
TATA AREA OID SOLO
ELEPHANTS JONES NINAS
ORCA SINGLE JOEYS
MINORCA AHME ALBA TET
ARISTA DRIB INLAWS
RESHOD WCHANDY TOPEKA
ANITAS CUES GRAYER
AMB FARR AKIM HISSERS
MOFFO OFFCUT WORK
PASEO PERES PALLIATES
KATE DIT SANO DELL
GAITERS JOHNLEGUIZAMO
NUN OUZO YOS RNS SOU
ARNOLDPALMER FACETING
TIEDYE MEANT AMARANTH
SCREED ASTAS ASPERGES
```

249

```
LAOS AGA AGARS OSCANS
ANTEATER LEROY POETIC
WITCHESCALDRON ARLENE
ESTOP DEFOG ATMAN
PLACATE PRES PET IPSE
REBIDS BOAST TIERCE
IGLOO ERIN DIGRESSES
MAU FLYINGSAUCERS TSP
ELEM AINT HIC RIORITA
PIPING TARAS RUNON
CALLINGTHEKETTLEBLACK
ALANA OARED RUSSET
RETESTS FRO PACA DEAL
ENE THESTANLEYCUP ADA
SESTERCES ONEA HOPED
PARURE ELGAR CREOLE
WHEN MED LION HEARTEN
RACKS TCELL COOLS
ALIENS ASILVERPLATTER
CLARET STOIC COOLIDGE
KELSEY ESTER ANS ASOF
```

250

```
POND SPRAT BABE SISSY
AMER ILONA ANAT ENATE
BARA LEONI CITE ABBAS
SHOWMEAMANWHOIS FOOTE
TALLEST TEENS GRATES
IDI SMELL TENOR
ELAN AGOODLOSERANDILL
BONGS AMI SRA ITT MOE
BUD PAMELA RTES SPOT
STREAMER MATTES HILTS
ORCA SHOWYOU AOKI
MAMIE TEASER TERRACES
ODES LATH EMOTES AYE
MAD TAB ASA ANO ESTER
AMANWHOISPLAYING CEDE
EATON OLEIC EER
CAPONI SPOOR SOMALIA
OWING GOLFWITHHISBOSS
LANAI ALEE AHEAD BYES
ARETE LEAR LARVA LARA
SEDER ASSY STEEL ELEM
```

RANDOM HOUSE CROSSWORD ORDER FORM

VOL.	ISBN	QUANT.	PRICE	TOTAL

New York Times Sunday Crosswords

New York Times Sunday Crossword Puzzles
Volume 24 • 978-0-8129-3647-6 ___ $8.95 ___

New York Times Sunday Crossword Puzzles
Volume 25 • 978-0-8129-3648-3 ___ $8.95 ___

New York Times Sunday Crossword Puzzles
Volume 26 • 978-0-8129-3649-0 ___ $8.95 ___

New York Times Toughest Crossword Puzzles
Volume 7 • 978-0-8129-3650-6 ___ $8.95 ___

New York Times Crossword Tribute to Eugene T. Maleska • 978-0-8129-3384-0 ___ $13.99 ___

Los Angeles Times Sunday Crosswords

Los Angeles Times Sunday Crossword Omnibus
Volume 5 • 978-0-8129-3683-4 ___ $12.95 ___

Los Angeles Times Sunday Crossword Omnibus
Volume 6 • 978-0-375-72248-6 ___ $12.95 ___

Los Angeles Times Sunday Crossword Puzzles
Volume 25 • 978-0-375-72156-4 ___ $9.95 ___

Los Angeles Times Sunday Crossword Puzzles
Volume 26 • 978-0-375-72174-8 ___ $9.95 ___

Los Angeles Times Sunday Crossword Puzzles
Volume 27 • 978-0-375-72175-5 ___ $9.95 ___

Los Angeles Times Sunday Crossword Puzzles
Volume 28 • 978-0-375-72176-2 ___ $9.99 ___

Los Angeles Times Sunday Crossword Puzzles
Volume 29 • 978-0-375-72177-9 ___ $9.99 ___

Washington Post Sunday Crosswords

Washington Post Sunday Crossword Omnibus
Volume 3 • 978-0-375-72187-8 ___ $12.95 ___

Washington Post Sunday Crossword Puzzles
Volume 15 • 978-0-8129-3492-2 ___ $9.95 ___

Boston Globe Sunday Crosswords

Boston Globe Sunday Crossword Omnibus
Volume 3 • 978-0-375-72186-1 ___ $12.95 ___

Boston Globe Sunday Crossword Puzzles
Volume 14 • 978-0-8129-3487-8 ___ $9.95 ___

Boston Globe Sunday Crossword Puzzles
Volume 15 • 978-0-8129-3488-5 ___ $9.95 ___

New York Magazine Crosswords

New York Magazine Crossword Puzzles
Volume 6 • 978-0-8129-3526-4 ___ $9.95 ___

New York Magazine Crossword Puzzles
Volume 7 • 978-0-8129-3684-1 ___ $9.95 ___

New York Magazine Crossword Omnibus
Volume 1 • 978-0-375-72153-3 ___ $12.99 ___

Chicago Tribune Crosswords

Chicago Tribune Daily Crossword Omnibus
978-0-375-72219-6 ___ $12.95 ___

Chicago Tribune Daily Crossword Puzzles
Volume 5 • 978-0-8129-3560-8 ___ $9.95 ___

Chicago Tribune Daily Crossword Puzzles
Volume 6 • 978-0-8129-3561-5 ___ $9.95 ___

Chicago Tribune Sunday Crossword Omnibus
978-0-375-72209-7 ___ $12.99 ___

Chicago Tribune Sunday Crossword Puzzles
Volume 5 • 978-0-8129-3563-9 ___ $9.95 ___

Random House Vacation Crosswords

Random House All Weather Crossword Omnibus
978-0-375-72200-4 ___ $12.95 ___

Random House Harvest Moon Crosswords
978-0-8129-3628-5 ___ $6.95 ___

Random House Springtime Crosswords
978-0-8129-3626-1 ___ $6.95 ___

Random House Summer Nights Crosswords
978-0-8129-3627-8 ___ $6.95 ___

Random House Winter Treat Crosswords
978-0-8129-3623-0 ___ $6.95 ___

Random House Year Round Crossword Omnibus
978-0-375-72201-1 ___ $12.95 ___

Random House Crosswords

Random House Casual Crossword Omnibus
978-0-375-72244-8 ___ $12.95 ___

Random House Casual Crosswords
Volume 3 • 978-0-8129-3666-7 ___ $9.95 ___

Random House Casual Crosswords
Volume 4 • 978-0-8129-3673-5 ___ $9.95 ___

Random House Casual Crosswords
Volume 5 • 978-0-8129-3674-2 ___ $9.95 ___

Random House Crosswords
Volume 5 • 978-0-8129-3501-1 ___ $9.95 ___

Random House Casual Crosswords
Volume 6 • 978-0-8129-3675-9 ___ $9.95 ___

Random House Casual Crosswords
Volume 7 • 978-0-375-72331-5 ___ $9.99 ___

Random House Casual Crosswords
Volume 8 • 978-0-375-72332-2 ___ $9.99 ___

Wall Street Journal Crosswords

Wall Street Journal Crossword Puzzle Omnibus
978-0-375-72210-3 ___ $12.95 ___

Wall Street Journal Crossword Puzzles
Volume 4 • 978-0-8129-3640-7 ___ $9.95 ___

Wall Street Journal Crossword Puzzles
Volume 5 • 978-0-375-72154-0 ___ $9.95 ___

Specialty Crosswords and Puzzle Reference

Mel's Weekend Crosswords
Volume 1 • 978-0-8129-3502-8 ___ $9.95 ___

Mel's Weekend Crosswords
Volume 2 • 978-0-8129-3503-5 ___ $9.95 ___

Random House Webster's Crossword Puzzle Dictionary
4th Edition • 978-0-375-72131-1 ___ $19.99 ___

Random House Webster's Large Print Crossword Puzzle Dictionary
978-0-375-72220-2 ___ $24.95 ___

Stanley Newman's Crosswords Shortcuts
978-0-375-72306-3 ___ $12.95 ___

Stanley Newman's Movie Mania Crosswords
978-0-8129-3468-7 ___ $7.95 ___

The Puzzlemaster Presents: Will Shortz's Best Puzzles from NPR
978-0-8129-3515-8 ___ $13.95 ___

15,003 Answers: The Ultimate Trivia Encyclopedia
2nd Edition • 978-0-375-72237-0 ___ $24.95 ___

To place your order, fill out this coupon and return to:
RANDOM HOUSE, INC., 400 HAHN ROAD, WESTMINSTER, MD 21157
ATTENTION: ORDER PROCESSING

☐ Enclosed is my check or money order payable to Random House
☐ Charge my credit card (circle type):   AMEX   Visa   Mastercard

Credit Card Number

NAME   SIGNATURE

ADDRESS   CITY   STATE   ZIP

To order, call toll-free 1-800-733-3000

Handling	
CARRIER	ADD
USPS	$5.50
UPS	$7.50

Total Books ___
Total Dollars $ ___
Sales Tax * $ ___
Postage & Handling $ ___
Total Enclosed $ ___

* Please calculate according to your state sales tax rate